Propery of
Merrill Gardens

CONTENTS

THE NEW TESTAMENT
PSALMS

HOW TO KNOW JESUS PERSONALLY

God wants each of us to experience an abundant life filled with meaning, direction, love, and peace. God makes this kind of life possible through a personal relationship with his Son, Jesus Christ. You can start this relationship by accepting Jesus as your Savior and inviting him into your life. But before doing that, here are five truths that will help you understand God's desire for you:

1. *God has a plan for your life.* "No one can receive anything unless God gives it from heaven" (John 3:27). God created you and has good plans for your life. To know those plans, you must know God personally.

2. *God's plan gives meaning.* Jesus replied, "I am the bread of life. Whoever comes to me will never be hungry again. Whoever believes in me will never be thirsty" (John 6:35). Many people seek meaning and purpose for their life. But they never find it because they look for meaning in the wrong things and the wrong people. When you follow God's plans for your life, the most important of which is to know Jesus as your Lord and Savior, you will find meaning and purpose in all that you do.

3. *God's plan gives direction.* Jesus spoke to the people once more and said, "I am the light of the world. If you follow me, you won't have to walk in darkness, because you will have the light that

leads to life'" (John 8:12). Without God's direction, you may not know what to do with your life. You may try a lot of things, hoping to find meaning in each one. But if you have God in your life, he will lead you and show you how to make your life count for him and his Kingdom.

4. *God's plan brings peace.* "I am leaving you with a gift—peace of mind and heart. And the peace I give is a gift the world cannot give. So don't be troubled or afraid" (John 14:27). When you follow Jesus as your Lord and Savior, you will be at peace with God. You will also be filled with God's peace. So when troubles come, you will be able to have peace as you endure hardships.

5. *God's plan is for you to live with him in heaven.* "For this is how God loved the world: He gave his one and only Son, so that everyone who believes in him will not perish but have eternal life" (John 3:16). Before Adam and Eve sinned (Genesis 3), they had a good relationship with God. Therefore, they were not ashamed to come into God's presence. But after they sinned, their relationship with God changed, and they were ashamed to come into God's physical presence. Sin had separated them and the entire human race—including you—from God. But God did not want sin to keep people from having a relationship with him. So he provided a way in which people could be cleansed of their sins and live with him in heaven forever. He gave his only Son, Jesus, as the perfect payment for everyone's sins.

Here are three things you must do in order to know Jesus personally as your Lord and Savior:

1. *Recognize that you are a sinner.* "For everyone has sinned; we all fall short of God's glorious standard" (Romans 3:23). "As the Scriptures say, 'No one is righteous—not even one'" (Romans 3:10). Because everyone is a sinner, no one deserves eternal life with God in heaven. In addition, no one can work hard enough to earn this life. Instead, God gives eternal life to everyone who believes that Jesus Christ is his Son. Before you can appreciate what Jesus has done for you, you need to recognize that you are a sinner in need of God's forgiveness. If you never acknowledge this, you will never receive God's forgiveness for your sins. And you will never enter into heaven.

2. Ask Jesus to forgive you. "Yet now he has reconciled you to himself through the death of Christ in his physical body. As a result, he has brought you into his own presence, and you are holy and blameless as you stand before him without a single fault" (Colossians 1:22). If you recognize that you are a sinner, then you may be ready to ask Jesus to forgive you. Do you believe that Jesus is the eternal Son of God, who died to pay for your sins? If you do and you have never thanked Christ for dying for you, thank him right now in a simple prayer. Pray, "Lord, I thank you for paying for the sins I have committed. I give my life to you. Teach me the right way to live. Amen."

If you have believed in Christ now for the first time, write your name and today's date on the blank lines as a record of the time of your salvation.

Name: _____

Date: _____

Time: _____

3. Turn away from your sins. "Those who have been born into God's family do not make a practice of sinning, because God's life is in them. So they can't keep on sinning, because they are children of God" (1 John 3:9). As a Christian, you may sin from time to time. But you should not continue to live a sinful lifestyle. Putting your faith in Jesus means that you are willingly turning away from your old sinful nature. It also means that you are living to please God. You can live to please God by obeying the commands he has given everyone in the Bible. If you obey God, you can be sure that you are a Christian and will one day have eternal life in heaven.

INDEX

THE LIFE YOU'VE ALWAYS WANTED

WHAT IS THE ABUNDANT LIFE?

The dictionary defines the word *abundant* as meaning *more than adequate, richly supplied, plentiful.* Jesus said, "My purpose is to give them a rich and satisfying life" (John 10:10). So the abundant life is one that is richly supplied with what we need, a life that is available because Jesus came to provide it.

But perhaps we should talk about what the abundant life is *not.* It isn't necessarily a life of wealth, comfort, leisure, or freedom from pain.

But it is a life of access to untold divine resources, the provision God has made for us to live whole, healthy, and hopeful lives. We have everything we need to live the abundant life, the life we were created by God to enjoy. The secret to the abundant life is a close relationship with God as we follow the truths of Scripture.

But unless we know and understand how God means for us to live, unless we dig deeply into his Word, we could wind up starving while the untouched banquet God has laid out for us goes to waste.

HOW DO YOU LIVE THE ABUNDANT LIFE?

Life requires certain elements to sustain it and provide for growth—nourishment, air, and water. If any of these ingredients is in short supply, the living organism will shrivel, weaken, and even die.

The Bible is the nourishment you need to live the abundant life. Jesus is the Bread of Life and Living Water necessary for living as a Christian, and he is made known to you through this book. Although the Bible was written hundreds of years ago, its message is timeless, personal, and practical because it is from God. As the number one best seller of all time, the Bible is the most read book in history! Millions of people have discovered in it answers for their deepest needs—and words of comfort, encouragement, hope, inspiration, and guidance.

The Bible contains the recipe for that which leads to the abundant life: a firm and fulfilling connection to Christ. In 2 Timothy 3:16-17, the apostle Paul reminds Timothy, "All Scripture is inspired by God and is useful to teach us what is true and to make us realize what is wrong in our lives. . . . God uses it to prepare and equip his people to do every good work."

But the Bible is more than an answer book. It is really a library of books filled with inspiring stories, majestic poetry and songs, direct messages and prophecies, and most important of all, the account of God visiting our earth in the person of Jesus Christ.

WHERE DO YOU BEGIN?

If the Bible is fairly new to you, start your reading in the New Testament with the book of Mark (page 59). This book will give you a dramatic introduction to the events that changed the world and can open the door to the abundant life. It is a short, fast-moving biography of Jesus Christ, written by a young man who probably witnessed most of Jesus' three-year ministry. In addition, Mark probably knew Jesus' disciples well and drew on their memories to help write this book.

Then follow the growth of Christianity by reading the book of Acts (page 199). This picks up where Mark ends and continues the dynamic story of the first Christians and how they spread the Good News of Jesus Christ all over the world.

Next read the book of Romans (page 255). This is one of the many letters written by the apostle Paul. It was sent to a group of first-century Christians in Rome. In it Paul clearly tells how selfish, arrogant, sinful humans can find acceptance with God. After you finish Romans, read some of the shorter books in the New Testament before turning to the Old Testament.

In the Old Testament, read the people stories in the book of Genesis. Then continue with some of the other books named after the main characters—Joshua, Ruth, Ezra, Job, Jonah, and others. Be sure to read complete stories instead of stopping at the end of a chapter. For instance, the story of Gideon is covered in Judges 6–8. The story of Jonah is covered throughout the whole book, but it is only four chapters long and can easily be read in one sitting. Then turn to the Psalms (page 455) and read enough of them to get a sense of what it means to worship God and pour out your feelings to him. Save the longer prophetic books (Isaiah, Jeremiah, and Ezekiel) and the books of God's law (Leviticus, Numbers, and Deuteronomy) until last. You may want to set up a pattern of daily reading that includes several Psalms along with a section from either the Old or New Testament.

HOW TO UNDERSTAND WHAT YOU READ

Three important steps will help you understand your Bible as you read.

Observation. The first step is to observe carefully what the author actually wrote. What is he saying? What is the obvious point? It might help if you stop and restate what the passage says in your own words. Or you can underline the key phrase that sums up what the author is saying. You can then try to understand what he means.

Interpretation. The second step is to try to interpret what the author meant when he wrote the passage. Why did he write what he did? What did it mean to him when he wrote it? For instance, in the book of John, the author says there were a lot of other things he could have written, "But these are written so that you may continue to believe that Jesus is the Messiah, the Son of God, and that by believing in him you will have life by the power of his name" (John 20:31). As you read John 5, you might wonder why John included the story of the healing of the man at the pool of Bethesda. This requires the use of your imagination. A Bible commentary and Bible dictionary will also be helpful as you try to imagine what was going through the author's mind as he wrote the passage. You will find a short summary for each Bible book starting on page A40. These book summaries will provide helpful perspective about the author and context for each book. As you read, keep the context in mind. It will help you understand what the author intended. If this step of interpretation is difficult for you, be patient. Take your time and reread the passage until its meaning becomes clear.

Application. The third step involves applying the meaning of the passage to your life. Ask the questions, *So what?* and *What difference does this passage make in my life?* When you apply the meaning of the Bible to your life, you will find that the Bible's purpose is to "teach us what is true and to make us realize what is wrong in our lives. It corrects us when we are wrong and teaches us to do what is right" (2 Timothy 3:16).

Don't be afraid to underline key statements in your Bible or to make notes. This will help you locate passages that hold special meaning for you. To further your understanding, join a Bible study and share with others interested in knowing more about the Bible.

On page A5 of this Bible, you'll find a step-by-step plan to begin a personal relationship with Jesus Christ. On page A34 you will find *Great Verses of the Bible to Memorize.* One of the best ways to grow in your faith is to learn God's word by heart: "I have hidden your word in my heart, that I might not sin against you." (Psalm 119:11). It's not that hard to do. Choose a verse from this list, and then work on learning that verse every day. It won't be long until you know it!

FROM RELIGION TO RELATIONSHIP

The word *religion* can sound cold and stifling, like a bunch of rules that stop us from enjoying life. But God wants much more with you than stiff adherence to a long list of laws and regulations. He wants you to have an abundant life found not in *religion*, but in a *relation-ship* with him through his son Jesus Christ and the power of his Spirit. Here are some Bible verses that will show you how much God wants to know and be known by you.

GOD'S LOVE FOR YOU

When I look at the night sky and see the work of your fingers—the moon and the stars you set in place—what are mere mortals that you should think about them, human beings that you should care for them? Yet you made them only a little lower than God and crowned them with glory and honor. Psalm 8:3-5

You made all the delicate, inner parts of my body and knit me together in my mother's womb. Thank you for making me so wonderfully complex! Your workmanship is marvelous—how well I know it. Psalm 139:13-14

How precious are your thoughts about me, O God. They cannot be numbered! I can't even count them; they outnumber the grains of sand! And when I wake up, you are still with me! Psalm 139:17-18

For I hold you by your right hand—I, the LORD your God. And I say to you, "Don't be afraid. I am here to help you." Isaiah 41:13

The LORD gave me this message: "I knew you before I formed you in your mother's womb. Before you were born I set you apart." Jeremiah 1:4-5

What is the price of five sparrows—two copper coins? Yet God does not forget a single one of them. And the very hairs on your head are all numbered. So don't be afraid; you are more valuable to God than a whole flock of sparrows. Luke 12:6-7

For this is how God loved the world: He gave his one and only Son, so that everyone who believes in him will not perish but have eternal life. John 3:16

Now you are no longer a slave but God's own child. And since you are his child, God has made you his heir. Galatians 4:7

This is real love—not that we loved God, but that he loved us and sent his Son as a sacrifice to take away our sins. Dear friends, since God loved us that much, we surely ought to love each other. 1 John 4:10-11

GOD'S FORGIVENESS

If my people who are called by my name will humble themselves and pray and seek my face and turn from their wicked ways, I will hear from heaven and will forgive their sins and restore their land. 2 Chronicles 7:14

Don't keep looking at my sins. Remove the stain of my guilt. Create in me a clean heart, O God. Renew a loyal spirit within me. Psalm 51:9-10

People who conceal their sins will not prosper, but if they confess and turn from them, they will receive mercy.   Proverbs 28:13

I have swept away your sins like a cloud. I have scattered your offenses like the morning mist. Oh, return to me, for I have paid the price to set you free.   Isaiah 44:22

Listen! We are here to proclaim that through this man Jesus there is forgiveness for your sins. Everyone who believes in him is made right in God's sight.   Acts 13:38-39

Therefore, since we have been made right in God's sight by faith, we have peace with God because of what Jesus Christ our Lord has done for us. . . . And since we have been made right in God's sight by the blood of Christ, he will certainly save us from God's condemnation.   Romans 5:1, 9

Because of his grace he made us right in his sight and gave us confidence that we will inherit eternal life.   Titus 3:7

But if we confess our sins to him, he is faithful and just to forgive us our sins and to cleanse us from all wickedness.   1 John 1:9

Now all glory to God, who is able to keep you from stumbling and will bring you with great joy into his glorious presence without a single fault.   Jude 1:24

GOD'S DIRECTION

He leads the humble in doing right, teaching them his way. The LORD leads with unfailing love and faithfulness all who keep his covenant and obey his demands.   Psalm 25:9-10

Trust in the LORD with all your heart; do not depend on your own understanding. Seek his will in all you do, and he will show you which path to take.   Proverbs 3:5-6

"For I know the plans I have for you," says the LORD. "They are plans for good and not for disaster, to give you a future and a hope. In those days when you pray, I will listen. If you look for me wholeheartedly, you will find me. I will be found by you," says the LORD.   Jeremiah 29:11-14

When the Spirit of truth comes, he will guide you into all truth. He will not speak on his own but will tell you what he has heard. He will tell you about the future. He will bring me glory by telling you whatever he receives from me.   John 16:13-14

I pray that your hearts will be flooded with light so that you can understand the confident hope he has given to those he called—his holy people who are his rich and glorious inheritance. Ephesians 1:18

But don't just listen to God's word. You must do what it says. Otherwise, you are only fooling yourselves. For if you listen to the word and don't obey, it is like glancing at your face in a mirror. You see yourself, walk away, and forget what you look like. But if you look carefully into the perfect law that sets you free, and if you do what it says and don't forget what you heard, then God will bless you for doing it. James 1:22-25

GOD'S STRENGTH AND POWER

Your throne, O God, endures forever and ever. You rule with a scepter of justice. Psalm 45:6

The LORD says, "I will rescue those who love me. I will protect those who trust in my name. When they call on me, I will answer; I will be with them in trouble. I will rescue and honor them. I will reward them with a long life and give them my salvation." Psalm 91:14-16

"To whom will you compare me? Who is my equal?" asks the Holy One. Look up into the heavens. Who created all the stars? He brings them out like an army, one after another, calling each by its name. Because of his great power and incomparable strength, not a single one is missing. Isaiah 40:25-26

LORD, you are my strength and fortress, my refuge in the day of trouble! Nations from around the world will come to you and say, "Our ancestors left us a foolish heritage, for they worshiped worthless idols. Can people make their own gods? These are not real gods at all!" The LORD says, "Now I will show them my power; now I will show them my might. At last they will know and understand that I am the LORD." Jeremiah 16:19-21

The LORD your God is living among you. He is a mighty savior. He will take delight in you with gladness. With his love, he will calm all your fears. He will rejoice over you with joyful songs. . . . I will deal severely with all who have oppressed you. I will save the weak and helpless ones. Zephaniah 3:17, 19

GOD'S SON, JESUS CHRIST

In the beginning the Word already existed. The Word was with God, and the Word was God. He existed in the beginning with God. God created everything through him, and nothing was created except through him. The Word gave life to everything that was created, and his life brought light to everyone. The light shines in the darkness, and the darkness can never extinguish it. John 1:1-5

He came into the very world he created, but the world didn't recognize him. He came to his own people, and even they rejected him. But to all who believed him and accepted him, he gave the right to become children of God. They are reborn—not with a physical birth resulting from human passion or plan, but a birth that comes from God. So the Word became human and made his home among us. He was full of unfailing love and faithfulness. And we have seen his glory, the glory of the Father's one and only Son. John 1:10-14

Christ is the visible image of the invisible God. He existed before anything was created and is supreme over all creation, for through him God created everything in the heavenly realms and on earth. He made the things we can see and the things we can't see— such as thrones, kingdoms, rulers, and authorities in the unseen world. Everything was created through him and for him. He existed before anything else, and he holds all creation together. Colossians 1:15-17

You were dead because of your sins and because your sinful nature was not yet cut away. Then God made you alive with Christ, for he forgave all our sins. He canceled the record of the charges against us and took it away by nailing it to the cross. Colossians 2:13-14

The Son radiates God's own glory and expresses the very character of God, and he sustains everything by the mighty power of his command. When he had cleansed us from our sins, he sat down in the place of honor at the right hand of the majestic God in heaven. Hebrews 1:3

Jesus Christ is the same yesterday, today, and forever. Hebrews 13:8

GOD'S HOLY SPIRIT

If you love me, obey my commandments. And I will ask the Father, and he will give you another Advocate, who will never leave you. He is the Holy Spirit, who leads into all truth. The world cannot receive him, because it isn't looking for him and doesn't recognize him. But you know him, because he lives with you now and later will be in you. John 14:15-17

But when the Father sends the Advocate as my representative—that is, the Holy Spirit—he will teach you everything and will remind you of everything I have told you. John 14:26

But you are not controlled by your sinful nature. You are controlled by the Spirit if you have the Spirit of God living in you. (And remember that those who do not have the Spirit of Christ living in them do not belong to him at all.) And Christ lives within you, so even though your body will die because of sin, the Spirit gives you life because you have been made right with God. The Spirit of God, who raised Jesus from the dead, lives in you. And just as God raised Christ Jesus from the dead, he will give life to your mortal bodies by this same Spirit living within you. Romans 8:9-11

The Spirit is God's guarantee that he will give us the inheritance he promised and that he has purchased us to be his own people. He did this so we would praise and glorify him. Ephesians 1:14

prayer—the great conversation

A conversation is a two-way event. You speak and you listen. That's how prayer works as well. We tell God our thoughts, our needs, our hopes, and then we listen to him speak to us through his Word and his Spirit. One way to pray is to say Scripture to God, inserting your name in the verse. For example, you might say, "For this is how God loved Julie: He gave his one and only son, so that if Julie believes in him she will not perish but have eternal life" (John 3:16, personalized). The following verses will help you understand something of what it means to communicate with God, along with some of the benefits.

RESPONDING TO GOD

The LORD has told you what is good, and this is what he requires of you: to do what is right, to love mercy, and to walk humbly with your God. Micah 6:8

It is by believing in your heart that you are made right with God, and it is by openly declaring your faith that you are saved. Romans 10:10

Look! I stand at the door and knock. If you hear my voice and open the door, I will come in, and we will share a meal together as friends. Revelation 3:20

TALKING WITH GOD

The LORD is close to all who call on him, yes, to all who call on him in truth. He grants the desires of those who fear him; he hears their cries for help and rescues them. Psalm 145:18-19

I will answer them before they even call to me. While they are still talking about their needs, I will go ahead and answer their prayers! Isaiah 65:24

In those days when you pray, I will listen. If you look for me whole-heartedly, you will find me. Jeremiah 29:12-13

Ask me and I will tell you remarkable secrets you do not know about things to come. Jeremiah 33:3

But when you pray, go away by yourself, shut the door behind you, and pray to your Father in private. Then your Father, who sees everything, will reward you. When you pray, don't babble on and on as the Gentiles do. They think their prayers are answered merely by repeating their words again and again. Don't be like them, for your Father knows exactly what you need even before you ask him! Matthew 6:6-8

Keep on asking, and you will receive what you ask for. Keep on seeking, and you will find. Keep on knocking, and the door will be opened to you. For everyone who asks, receives. Everyone who seeks, finds. And to everyone who knocks, the door will be opened. Matthew 7:7-8

Then Jesus said to the disciples, "Have faith in God. I tell you the truth, you can say to this mountain, 'May you be lifted up and thrown into the sea,' and it will happen. But you must really believe it will happen and have no doubt in your heart. I tell you, you can pray for anything, and if you believe that you've received it, it will be yours." Mark 11:22-24

Bless those who curse you. Pray for those who hurt you. Luke 6:28

But if you remain in me and my words remain in you, you may ask for anything you want, and it will be granted! John 15:7

I urge you, first of all, to pray for all people. Ask God to help them; intercede on their behalf, and give thanks for them. 1 Timothy 2:1

Let us come boldly to the throne of our gracious God. There we will receive his mercy, and we will find grace to help us when we need it most. Hebrews 4:16

Confess your sins to each other, and pray for each other so that you may be healed. The earnest prayer of a righteous person has great power and produces wonderful results. James 5:16

The eyes of the LORD watch over those who do right, and his ears are open to their prayers. But the Lord turns his face against those who do evil. 1 Peter 3:12

THANKING GOD

Sing praises to God and to his name! Sing loud praises to him who rides the clouds. His name is the LORD—rejoice in his presence! Father to the fatherless, defender of widows—this is God, whose dwelling is holy. God places the lonely in families; he sets the prisoners free and gives them joy. But he makes the rebellious live in a sun-scorched land. Psalm 68:4-6

It is good to give thanks to the LORD, to sing praises to the Most High. It is good to proclaim your unfailing love in the morning, your faithfulness in the evening. Psalm 92:1-2

Let everything that breathes sing praises to the LORD! Psalm 150:6

All praise to God, the Father of our Lord Jesus Christ. God is our merciful Father and the source of all comfort. He comforts us in all our troubles so that we can comfort others. When they are troubled, we will be able to give them the same comfort God has given us. 2 Corinthians 1:3-4

And give thanks for everything to God the Father in the name of our Lord Jesus Christ. Ephesians 5:20

Always be full of joy in the Lord. I say it again—rejoice! Philippians 4:4

LISTENING TO GOD

"Be still, and know that I am God! I will be honored by every nation. I will be honored throughout the world." The LORD of Heaven's Armies is here among us; the God of Israel is our fortress. Psalm 46:10-11

I have hidden your word in my heart, that I might not sin against you. Psalm 119:11

Your commands make me wiser than my enemies, for they are my constant guide. Yes, I have more insight than my teachers, for I am always thinking of your laws. Psalm 119:98-99

Your word is a lamp to guide my feet and a light for my path. Psalm 119:105

Trust in the LORD with all your heart; do not depend on your own understanding. Seek his will in all you do, and he will show you which path to take. Proverbs 3:5-6

Anyone who listens to my teaching and follows it is wise, like a person who builds a house on solid rock. Matthew 7:24

Anyone with ears to hear should listen and understand. Mark 4:9

And we have received God's Spirit (not the world's spirit), so we can know the wonderful things God has freely given us. When we tell you these things, we do not use words that come from human wisdom. Instead, we speak words given to us by the Spirit, using the Spirit's words to explain spiritual truths. But people who aren't spiritual can't receive these truths from God's Spirit. It all sounds foolish to them and they can't understand it, for only those who are spiritual can understand what the Spirit means. 1 Corinthians 2:12-14

Let the message about Christ, in all its richness, fill your lives. Teach and counsel each other with all the wisdom he gives. Sing psalms and hymns and spiritual songs to God with thankful hearts. Colossians 3:16

If you need wisdom, ask our generous God, and he will give it to you. He will not rebuke you for asking. James 1:5

By his divine power, God has given us everything we need for living a godly life. We have received all of this by coming to know him, the one who called us to himself by means of his marvelous glory and excellence. And because of his glory and excellence, he has given us great and precious promises. These are the promises that enable you to share his divine nature and escape the world's corruption caused by human desires. In view of all this, make every effort to respond to God's promises. Supplement your faith with a generous provision of moral excellence, and moral excellence with knowledge. 2 Peter 1:3-5

TELLING OTHERS

I will tell everyone about your righteousness. All day long I will proclaim your saving power, though I am not skilled with words. I will praise your mighty deeds, O Sovereign LORD. I will tell everyone that you alone are just. Psalm 71:15-16

Therefore, go and make disciples of all the nations, baptizing them in the name of the Father and the Son and the Holy Spirit. Teach these new disciples to obey all the commands I have given you. And be sure of this: I am with you always, even to the end of the age. Matthew 28:19-20

Then he told them, "Go into all the world and preach the Good News to everyone. Anyone who believes and is baptized will be saved. But anyone who refuses to believe will be condemned." Mark 16:15-16

So never be ashamed to tell others about our Lord. And don't be ashamed of me, either, even though I'm in prison for him. With the strength God gives you, be ready to suffer with me for the sake of the Good News. 2 Timothy 1:8

Your godly lives will speak to them without any words. They will be won over by observing your pure and reverent lives. 1 Peter 3:1-2

If someone asks about your hope as a believer, always be ready to explain it. But do this in a gentle and respectful way. Keep your conscience clear. Then if people speak against you, they will be ashamed when they see what a good life you live because you belong to Christ. 1 Peter 3:15-16

CHOOSING JOY AND FINDING PEACE

The abundant life is a life of joy and peace, no matter what your circumstances. It's not a life that's problem-free, but even in the midst of trouble, God is still there for us. He makes joy and peace available, but we must access them through right thinking, right attitudes, and right actions. These Bible verses will help you find the pathway to joy and peace.

REMEMBERING GOD'S PROMISES

I will bless the LORD who guides me; even at night my heart instructs me. I know the LORD is always with me. I will not be shaken, for he is right beside me. Psalm 16:7-8

The eyes of the LORD watch over those who do right; his ears are open to their cries for help. . . . The LORD hears his people when they call to him for help. He rescues them from all their troubles. Psalm 34:15, 17

I waited patiently for the LORD to help me, and he turned to me and heard my cry. He lifted me out of the pit of despair, out of the mud and the mire. He set my feet on solid ground and steadied me as I walked along. He has given me a new song to sing, a hymn of praise to our God. Many will see what he has done and be amazed. They will put their trust in the LORD. Psalm 40:1-3

God is our refuge and strength, always ready to help in times of trouble. So we will not fear when earthquakes come and the mountains crumble into the sea. Psalm 46:1-2

The LORD is good, a strong refuge when trouble comes. He is close to those who trust in him. Nahum 1:7

And now, dear brothers and sisters, we want you to know what will happen to the believers who have died so you will not grieve like people who have no hope. For since we believe that Jesus died and was raised to life again, we also believe that when Jesus

returns, God will bring back with him the believers who have died.
1 Thessalonians 4:13-14

RIGHT ATTITUDES

Be still in the presence of the LORD, and wait patiently for him to act. Don't worry about evil people who prosper or fret about their wicked schemes.   Psalm 37:7

God blesses those who are humble, for they will inherit the whole earth. . . . God blesses those who are merciful, for they will be shown mercy. God blesses those whose hearts are pure, for they will see God.   Matthew 5:5, 7-8

We are pressed on every side by troubles, but we are not crushed. We are perplexed, but not driven to despair.   2 Corinthians 4:8

Get rid of all bitterness, rage, anger, harsh words, and slander, as well as all types of evil behavior. Instead, be kind to each other, tenderhearted, forgiving one another, just as God through Christ has forgiven you.   Ephesians 4:31-32

Dear brothers and sisters, be patient as you wait for the Lord's return. Consider the farmers who patiently wait for the rains in the fall and in the spring. They eagerly look for the valuable harvest to ripen. You, too, must be patient. Take courage, for the coming of the Lord is near.   James 5:7-8

HEALTHY THINKING

So be strong and courageous! Do not be afraid and do not panic before them. For the LORD your God will personally go ahead of you. He will neither fail you nor abandon you.   Deuteronomy 31:6

For you are my hiding place; you protect me from trouble. You surround me with songs of victory.   Psalm 32:7

You will keep in perfect peace all who trust in you, all whose thoughts are fixed on you!   Isaiah 26:3

Don't be afraid, for I am with you. Don't be discouraged, for I am your God. I will strengthen you and help you. I will hold you up with my victorious right hand.   Isaiah 41:10

"But there is no peace for the wicked," says the LORD.   Isaiah 48:22

God blesses those who work for peace, for they will be called the children of God.   Matthew 5:9

It is what comes from inside that defiles you. For from within, out of a person's heart, come evil thoughts, sexual immorality, theft, murder, adultery, greed, wickedness, deceit, lustful desires, envy, slander, pride, and foolishness. All these vile things come from within; they are what defile you.   Mark 7:20-23

Then, turning to his disciples, Jesus said, "That is why I tell you not to worry about everyday life—whether you have enough food to eat or enough clothes to wear. For life is more than food, and your body more than clothing. Look at the ravens. They don't plant or harvest or store food in barns, for God feeds them. And you are far more valuable to him than any birds! Can all your worries add a single moment to your life? And if worry can't accomplish a little thing like that, what's the use of worrying over bigger things?
Luke 12:22-26

Don't let your hearts be troubled. Trust in God, and trust also in me. There is more than enough room in my Father's home. If this were not so, would I have told you that I am going to prepare a place for you? When everything is ready, I will come and get you, so that you will always be with me where I am.   John 14:1-3

I am leaving you with a gift—peace of mind and heart. And the peace I give is a gift the world cannot give. So don't be troubled or afraid.
John 14:27

I pray that God, the source of hope, will fill you completely with joy and peace because you trust in him. Then you will overflow with confident hope through the power of the Holy Spirit.   Romans 15:13

The God of peace will soon crush Satan under your feet. May the grace of our Lord Jesus be with you.   Romans 16:20

Don't worry about anything; instead, pray about everything. Tell God what you need, and thank him for all he has done. Then you will experience God's peace, which exceeds anything we can understand. His peace will guard your hearts and minds as you live in Christ Jesus.   Philippians 4:6-7

Patient endurance is what you need now, so that you will continue to do God's will. Then you will receive all that he has promised.
Hebrews 10:36

You must all be quick to listen, slow to speak, and slow to get angry. Human anger does not produce the righteousness God desires.
James 1:19-20

Give all your worries and cares to God, for he cares about you.   1 Peter 5:7

TACKLING TOUGH ISSUES

Sometimes real life isn't pretty, whether you're a Christian or not. The Bible has help for even the hard questions and the worst of life's circumstances, help that will allow you to live the abundant life even in the midst of difficulty. Here are some verses that give guidance for those challenging times and situations.

INJUSTICE

You must not mistreat or oppress foreigners in any way. Remember, you yourselves were once foreigners in the land of Egypt. You must not exploit a widow or an orphan. If you exploit them in any way and they cry out to me, then I will certainly hear their cry. Exodus 22:21-23

Never take advantage of poor and destitute laborers, whether they are fellow Israelites or foreigners living in your towns. You must pay them their wages each day before sunset because they are poor and are counting on it. If you don't, they might cry out to the LORD against you, and it would be counted against you as sin. Deuteronomy 24:14-15

The LORD is a shelter for the oppressed, a refuge in times of trouble. Psalm 9:9

LORD, you know the hopes of the helpless. Surely you will hear their cries and comfort them. You will bring justice to the orphans and the oppressed, so mere people can no longer terrify them. Psalm 10:17-18

The LORD replies, "I have seen violence done to the helpless, and I have heard the groans of the poor. Now I will rise up to rescue them, as they have longed for me to do." Psalm 12:5

A person who gets ahead by oppressing the poor or by showering gifts on the rich will end in poverty. Proverbs 22:16

Those who are honest and fair, who refuse to profit by fraud, who stay far away from bribes, who refuse to listen to those who plot murder, who shut their eyes to all enticement to do wrong—these are the ones who will dwell on high. The rocks of the mountains will be their fortress. Food will be supplied to them, and they will have water in abundance. Isaiah 33:15-16

What sorrow awaits you who build big houses with money gained dishonestly! You believe your wealth will buy security, putting your family's nest beyond the reach of danger. . . . What sorrow awaits you who build cities with money gained through murder and corruption! Has not the LORD of Heaven's Armies promised that the wealth of nations will turn to ashes? Habakkuk 2:9, 12-13

"At that time I will put you on trial. I am eager to witness against all sorcerers and adulterers and liars. I will speak against those who cheat employees of their wages, who oppress widows and orphans, or who deprive the foreigners living among you of justice, for these people do not fear me," says the LORD of Heaven's Armies. "I am the LORD, and I do not change. That is why you descendants of Jacob are not already destroyed. Ever since the days of your ancestors, you have scorned my decrees and failed to obey them. Now return to me, and I will return to you," says the LORD of Heaven's Armies. Malachi 3:5-7

And I saw a great white throne and the one sitting on it. The earth and sky fled from his presence, but they found no place to hide. I saw the dead, both great and small, standing before God's throne. And the books were opened, including the Book of Life. And the dead were judged according to what they had done, as recorded in the books. Revelation 20:11-12

LONELINESS

Even if my father and mother abandon me, the LORD will hold me close. Psalm 27:10

But you are a tower of refuge to the poor, O LORD, a tower of refuge to the needy in distress. You are a refuge from the storm and a shelter from the heat. Isaiah 25:4

Don't be afraid, for I am with you. Don't be discouraged, for I am your God. I will strengthen you and help you. I will hold you up with my victorious right hand. Isaiah 41:10

"For the mountains may move and the hills disappear, but even then my faithful love for you will remain. My covenant of blessing will never be broken," says the LORD, who has mercy on you. Isaiah 54:10

No, I will not abandon you as orphans—I will come to you. John 14:18

The first time I was brought before the judge, no one came with me. Everyone abandoned me. May it not be counted against them. But the Lord stood with me and gave me strength so that I might preach the Good News in its entirety for all the Gentiles to hear. And he rescued me from certain death. 2 Timothy 4:16-17

PREJUDICE

Be perfectly fair in your decisions and impartial in your judgments. Hear the cases of those who are poor as well as those who are rich.
Deuteronomy 1:16-17

Then Peter replied, "I see very clearly that God shows no favoritism. In every nation he accepts those who fear him and do what is right."
Acts 10:34-35

There is no longer Jew or Gentile, slave or free, male and female. For you are all one in Christ Jesus. Galatians 3:28

My dear brothers and sisters, how can you claim to have faith in our glorious Lord Jesus Christ if you favor some people over others? For example, suppose someone comes into your meeting dressed in fancy clothes and gold jewelry, and another comes in who is poor and dressed in dirty clothes. If you give special attention and a good seat to the rich person, but you say to the poor one, "You can stand over there, or else sit there on the floor"—well, doesn't this discrimination show that your judgments are guided by evil motives? James 2:1-4

SICKNESS

The LORD nurses them when they are sick and restores them to health.
Psalm 41:3

Remember your promise to me; it is my only hope. Your promise revives me; it comforts me in all my troubles. Psalm 119:49-50

O LORD, if you heal me, I will be truly healed; if you save me, I will be truly saved. My praises are for you alone! Jeremiah 17:14

Jesus called his twelve disciples together and gave them authority to cast out evil spirits and to heal every kind of disease and illness.
Matthew 10:1

We know that when this earthly tent we live in is taken down (that is, when we die and leave this earthly body), we will have a house in heaven, an eternal body made for us by God himself and not by human hands. We grow weary in our present bodies, and we long to put on our heavenly bodies like new clothing. For we will put on heavenly bodies; we will not be spirits without bodies. While we live in these earthly bodies, we groan and sigh, but it's not that we want to die and get rid of these bodies that clothe us. Rather, we want to put on our new bodies so that these dying bodies will be swallowed up by life. 2 Corinthians 5:1-4

I have received such wonderful revelations from God. So to keep me from becoming proud, I was given a thorn in my flesh, a messenger

from Satan to torment me and keep me from becoming proud. Three different times I begged the Lord to take it away. Each time he said, "My grace is all you need. My power works best in weakness." So now I am glad to boast about my weaknesses, so that the power of Christ can work through me. That's why I take pleasure in my weaknesses, and in the insults, hardships, persecutions, and troubles that I suffer for Christ. For when I am weak, then I am strong.
2 Corinthians 12:7-10

Are any of you suffering hardships? You should pray. Are any of you happy? You should sing praises. Are any of you sick? You should call for the elders of the church to come and pray over you, anointing you with oil in the name of the Lord. Such a prayer offered in faith will heal the sick, and the Lord will make you well. And if you have committed any sins, you will be forgiven. Confess your sins to each other, and pray for each other so that you may be healed. The earnest prayer of a righteous person has great power and produces wonderful results. Elijah was as human as we are, and yet when he prayed earnestly that no rain would fall, none fell for three and a half years! Then, when he prayed again, the sky sent down rain and the earth began to yield its crops. James 5:13-18

SUFFERING AND DEATH

I have cried until the tears no longer come; my heart is broken. My spirit is poured out in agony as I see the desperate plight of my people. Little children and tiny babies are fainting and dying in the streets. . . . The faithful love of the LORD never ends! His mercies never cease. Great is his faithfulness; his mercies begin afresh each morning. I say to myself, "The LORD is my inheritance; therefore, I will hope in him!" The LORD is good to those who depend on him, to those who search for him. So it is good to wait quietly for salvation from the LORD. Lamentations 2:11; 3:22-26

"God blesses those who are persecuted for doing right, for the Kingdom of Heaven is theirs. God blesses you when people mock you and persecute you and lie about you and say all sorts of evil things against you because you are my followers. Be happy about it! Be very glad! For a great reward awaits you in heaven. And remember, the ancient prophets were persecuted in the same way. . . . But I say, love your enemies! Pray for those who persecute you! In that way, you will be acting as true children of your Father in heaven. For he

gives his sunlight to both the evil and the good, and he sends rain on the just and the unjust alike." Matthew 5:10-12, 44-45

Then Jesus said to his disciples, "If any of you wants to be my follower, you must turn from your selfish ways, take up your cross, and follow me. If you try to hang on to your life, you will lose it. But if you give up your life for my sake, you will save it. And what do you benefit if you gain the whole world but lose your own soul? Is anything worth more than your soul?" Matthew 16:24-26

Jesus told her, "I am the resurrection and the life. Anyone who believes in me will live, even after dying. Everyone who lives in me and believes in me will never ever die." John 11:25-26

What we suffer now is nothing compared to the glory he will reveal to us later. Romans 8:18

All praise to God, the Father of our Lord Jesus Christ. God is our merciful Father and the source of all comfort. He comforts us in all our troubles so that we can comfort others. When they are troubled, we will be able to give them the same comfort God has given us. For the more we suffer for Christ, the more God will shower us with his comfort through Christ. Even when we are weighed down with troubles, it is for your comfort and salvation! For when we ourselves are comforted, we will certainly comfort you. Then you can patiently endure the same things we suffer. We are confident that as you share in our sufferings, you will also share in the comfort God gives us. 2 Corinthians 1:3-7

We are pressed on every side by troubles, but we are not crushed. We are perplexed, but not driven to despair. We are hunted down, but never abandoned by God. We get knocked down, but we are not destroyed. Through suffering, our bodies continue to share in the death of Jesus so that the life of Jesus may also be seen in our bodies. Yes, we live under constant danger of death because we serve Jesus, so that the life of Jesus will be evident in our dying bodies. So we live in the face of death, but this has resulted in eternal life for you. 2 Corinthians 4:8-12

These trials will show that your faith is genuine. It is being tested as fire tests and purifies gold—though your faith is far more precious than mere gold. 1 Peter 1:7

TEMPTATION

But those who trust in the LORD will find new strength. They will soar high on wings like eagles. They will run and not grow weary. They will walk and not faint. Isaiah 40:31

Then Jesus said, "Come to me, all of you who are weary and carry heavy burdens, and I will give you rest. Take my yoke upon you. Let me teach you, because I am humble and gentle at heart, and you will find rest for your souls. For my yoke is easy to bear, and the burden I give you is light." Matthew 11:28-30

The temptations in your life are no different from what others experience. And God is faithful. He will not allow the temptation to be more than you can stand. When you are tempted, he will show you a way out so that you can endure. 1 Corinthians 10:13

Since he himself has gone through suffering and testing, he is able to help us when we are being tested. Hebrews 2:18

God blesses those who patiently endure testing and temptation. Afterward they will receive the crown of life that God has promised to those who love him. And remember, when you are being tempted, do not say, "God is tempting me." God is never tempted to do wrong, and he never tempts anyone else. . . . So humble yourselves before God. Resist the devil, and he will flee from you. James 1:12-13; 4:7

ABUNDANT LIVING

The abundant life is life as God meant it to be. Of course, this side of heaven, we won't experience perfection or an end to difficulty. But by drawing on the endless supply of God's resources made available to us in Christ, we can have what we need for any and every situation. We can live life to its fullest by living it with God. These verses will guide you in accessing God's plentiful resources.

A LIFE OF PURPOSE

"I will bless you . . . and you will be a blessing to others." Genesis 12:2

"Who knows if perhaps you were made queen for just such a time as this?" Esther 4:14

Seek the Kingdom of God above all else, and he will give you everything you need. Luke 12:31

And so, dear brothers and sisters, I plead with you to give your bodies to God because of all he has done for you. Let them be a living and holy sacrifice—the kind he will find acceptable. This is truly the way to worship him. Don't copy the behavior and customs of this world, but let God transform you into a new person by changing the way you think. Then you will learn to know God's will for you, which is good and pleasing and perfect. Romans 12:1-2

In his grace, God has given us different gifts for doing certain things well. So if God has given you the ability to prophesy, speak out with as much faith as God has given you. If your gift is serving others, serve them well. If you are a teacher, teach well. If your gift is to encourage others, be encouraging. If it is giving, give generously. If God has given you leadership ability, take the responsibility seriously. And if you have a gift for showing kindness to others, do it gladly. Don't just pretend to love others. Really love them. Hate what is wrong. Hold tightly to what is good. Love each other with genuine affection, and take delight in honoring each other.
Romans 12:6-10

Work with enthusiasm, as though you were working for the Lord rather than for people. Remember that the Lord will reward each one of us for the good we do, whether we are slaves or free. Ephesians 6:7-8

Work willingly at whatever you do, as though you were working for the Lord rather than for people. Remember that the Lord will give you an inheritance as your reward, and that the Master you are serving is Christ. Colossians 3:23-24

Dear friend, you are being faithful to God when you care for the traveling teachers who pass through, even though they are strangers to you. They have told the church here of your loving friendship. Please continue providing for such teachers in a manner that pleases God. 3 John 1:5-6

A LIFE OF FAITH AND WISDOM

Your commands make me wiser than my enemies, for they are my constant guide. Yes, I have more insight than my teachers, for I am always thinking of your laws. Psalm 119:98-99

Don't turn your back on wisdom, for she will protect you. Love her, and she will guard you. Getting wisdom is the wisest thing you can do! And whatever else you do, develop good judgment. If you prize wisdom, she will make you great. Embrace her, and she will honor you. She will place a lovely wreath on your head; she will present you with a beautiful crown. Proverbs 4:6-9

God saved you by his grace when you believed. And you can't take credit for this; it is a gift from God. Salvation is not a reward for the good things we have done, so none of us can boast about it. For we are God's masterpiece. He has created us anew in Christ Jesus, so we can do the good things he planned for us long ago.
Ephesians 2:8-10

So be careful how you live. Don't live like fools, but like those who are wise. Make the most of every opportunity in these evil days. Ephesians 5:15-16

Let your roots grow down into him, and let your lives be built on him. Then your faith will grow strong in the truth you were taught, and you will overflow with thankfulness. Colossians 2:7

So do not throw away this confident trust in the Lord. Remember the great reward it brings you! Patient endurance is what you need now, so that you will continue to do God's will. Then you will receive all that he has promised. "For in just a little while, the Coming One will come and not delay. And my righteous ones will live by faith. But I will take no pleasure in anyone who turns away." Hebrews 10:35-38

If you need wisdom, ask our generous God, and he will give it to you. He will not rebuke you for asking. But when you ask him, be sure that your faith is in God alone. Do not waver, for a person with divided loyalty is as unsettled as a wave of the sea that is blown and tossed by the wind. Such people should not expect to receive anything from the Lord. James 1:5-7

If you are wise and understand God's ways, prove it by living an honorable life, doing good works with the humility that comes from wisdom. But if you are bitterly jealous and there is selfish ambition in your heart, don't cover up the truth with boasting and lying. For jealousy and selfishness are not God's kind of wisdom. Such things are earthly, unspiritual, and demonic. For wherever there is jealousy and selfish ambition, there you will find disorder and evil of every kind. But the wisdom from above is first of all pure. It is also peace loving, gentle at all times, and willing to yield to others. It is full of mercy and the fruit of good deeds. It shows no favoritism and is always sincere. James 3:13-17

LIFE WITH FAMILY AND FRIENDS

Walk with the wise and become wise; associate with fools and get in trouble. Proverbs 13:20

A friend is always loyal, and a brother is born to help in time of need. Proverbs 17:17

There are "friends" who destroy each other, but a real friend sticks closer than a brother. Proverbs 18:24

Always be humble and gentle. Be patient with each other, making allowance for each other's faults because of your love. Make every effort to keep yourselves united in the Spirit, binding yourselves together with peace. For there is one body and one Spirit, just as you have been called to one glorious hope for the future. Ephesians 4:2-4

Don't be selfish; don't try to impress others. Be humble, thinking of others as better than yourselves. Don't look out only for your own interests, but take an interest in others, too. You must have the same attitude that Christ Jesus had. Philippians 2:3-5

But those who won't care for their relatives, especially those in their own household, have denied the true faith. Such people are worse than unbelievers. 1 Timothy 5:8

Keep on loving each other as brothers and sisters. Don't forget to show hospitality to strangers, for some who have done this have entertained angels without realizing it! Remember those in prison, as if you were there yourself. Remember also those being mistreated, as if you felt their pain in your own bodies. Hebrews 13:1-3

In the same way, the tongue is a small thing that makes grand speeches. But a tiny spark can set a great forest on fire. James 3:5

In the same way, you wives must accept the authority of your husbands. Then, even if some refuse to obey the Good News, your godly lives will speak to them without any words. They will be won over by observing your pure and reverent lives. . . . In the same way, you husbands must give honor to your wives. Treat your wife with understanding as you live together. She may be weaker than you are, but she is your equal partner in God's gift of new life. Treat her as you should so your prayers will not be hindered. 1 Peter 3:1-2, 7

If someone says, "I love God," but hates a fellow believer, that person is a liar; for if we don't love people we can see, how can we love God, whom we cannot see? And he has given us this command: Those who love God must also love their fellow believers. 1 John 4:20-21

A LIFE WITH RIGHT PRIORITIES

Take delight in the LORD, and he will give you your heart's desires. Psalm 37:4

Teach us to realize the brevity of life, so that we may grow in wisdom. Psalm 90:12

Teach me your decrees, O LORD; I will keep them to the end. Give me understanding and I will obey your instructions; I will put them into practice with all my heart. Make me walk along the path of your commands, for that is where my happiness is found. Psalm 119:33-35

Take a lesson from the ants, you lazybones. Learn from their ways and become wise! . . . But you, lazybones, how long will you sleep?

When will you wake up? A little extra sleep, a little more slumber, a little folding of the hands to rest—then poverty will pounce on you like a bandit; scarcity will attack you like an armed robber. Proverbs 6:6, 9-11

Lazy people don't even cook the game they catch, but the diligent make use of everything they find. Proverbs 12:27

For everything there is a season, a time for every activity under heaven. Ecclesiastes 3:1

Seek the Kingdom of God above all else, and live righteously, and he will give you everything you need. Matthew 6:33

Make the most of every opportunity in these evil days. Don't act thoughtlessly, but understand what the Lord wants you to do. Ephesians 5:16-17

Make it your goal to live a quiet life, minding your own business and working with your hands, just as we instructed you before. Then people who are not believers will respect the way you live, and you will not need to depend on others. 1 Thessalonians 4:11-12

Await the mercy of our Lord Jesus Christ, who will bring you eternal life. In this way, you will keep yourselves safe in God's love. Jude 1:21

A LIFE OF SERVING OTHERS

Give to those who ask, and don't turn away from those who want to borrow. Matthew 5:42

Then the King will say to those on his right, "Come, you who are blessed by my Father, inherit the Kingdom prepared for you from the creation of the world. For I was hungry, and you fed me. I was thirsty, and you gave me a drink. I was a stranger, and you invited me into your home. I was naked, and you gave me clothing. I was sick, and you cared for me. I was in prison, and you visited me." Matthew 25:34-36

Do to others as you would like them to do to you. If you love only those who love you, why should you get credit for that? Even sinners love those who love them! And if you do good only to those who do good to you, why should you get credit? Even sinners do that much! And if you lend money only to those who can repay you, why should you get credit? Even sinners will lend to other sinners for a full return. Love your enemies! Do good to them. Lend to them without expecting to be repaid. Then your reward from heaven will be very great, and you will truly be acting as children of the Most High, for he is kind to those who are unthankful and wicked. You must be compassionate, just as your Father is compassionate.   Luke 6:31-36

Invite the poor, the crippled, the lame, and the blind. Then at the resurrection of the righteous, God will reward you for inviting those who could not repay you.   Luke 14:13-14

If your gift is to encourage others, be encouraging. If it is giving, give generously. If God has given you leadership ability, take the responsibility seriously. And if you have a gift for showing kindness to others, do it gladly. Don't just pretend to love others. Really love them. Hate what is wrong. Hold tightly to what is good. Love each other with genuine affection, and take delight in honoring each other.   Romans 12:8-10

So let's not get tired of doing what is good. At just the right time we will reap a harvest of blessing if we don't give up. Therefore, whenever we have the opportunity, we should do good to everyone—especially to those in the family of faith.   Galatians 6:9-10

Don't look out only for your own interests, but take an interest in others, too.   Philippians 2:4

Since God chose you to be the holy people he loves, you must clothe yourselves with tenderhearted mercy, kindness, humility, gentleness, and patience. Make allowance for each other's faults, and forgive anyone who offends you. Remember, the Lord forgave you, so you must forgive others. Above all, clothe yourselves with love, which binds us all together in perfect harmony. And let the peace that comes from Christ rule in your hearts. For as members of one body you are called to live in peace. And always be thankful.   Colossians 3:12-15

I am praying that you will put into action the generosity that comes from your faith as you understand and experience all the good things we have in Christ. Your love has given me much joy and comfort, my brother, for your kindness has often refreshed the hearts of God's people.   Philemon 1:6-7

And don't forget to do good and to share with those in need. These are the sacrifices that please God.   Hebrews 13:16

If someone has enough money to live well and sees a brother or sister in need but shows no compassion—how can God's love be in that person?   1 John 3:17

GREAT VERSES TO MEMORIZE

page A39 · GREAT VERSES TO MEMORIZE

Psalm 139:1-12 .... God Is All-Knowing .... page 581
Psalm 139:13-16 .... God the Creator .... page 581
Psalm 139:23-24 .... Yielding to God's Searching .... page 582

OVERVIEW OF THE BIBLE BOOKS

NEW TESTAMENT & PSALMS

MATTHEW

Author: Matthew (Levi); *Date:* A.D. 60–65; *Genre:* Gospel narrative.
Summary: This Gospel was written with Jewish people in mind and therefore has many references to Old Testament prophecies that Jesus fulfilled. It contains at least 129 quotations or allusions to the Old Testament. Matthew's objective was to show the Jewish people that Jesus was indeed their long-awaited Messiah.

MARK

Author: John Mark; *Date:* A.D. 55–65; *Genre:* Gospel narrative.
Summary: The Gospel of Mark is the account of the life, ministry, miracles, and words of Jesus Christ. In contrast to Matthew, who primarily presented Jesus as the "Messiah," Mark emphasizes the servanthood of the Lord.

LUKE

Author: Luke; *Date:* Around A.D. 60; *Genre:* Gospel narrative.
Summary: Luke was a Gentile who put his faith in Jesus Christ. His purpose for writing an account of Jesus Christ's life, death, and resurrection was to make the message of salvation understandable to those outside of the Jewish faith and culture.

JOHN

Author: John; *Date:* Around A.D. 90; *Genre:* Gospel narrative.
Summary: While the emphasis in the other three Gospels centers around the description of the events in Jesus' life, John focuses on the meaning of those events. For instance, while all four Gospels record the miracle of feeding the five thousand, only John gives us Jesus' message on the "bread of life" that followed that miracle.

ACTS

Author: Luke; *Date:* A.D. 63–70; *Genre:* Historical narrative.
Summary: This book shows the church's early development and rapid growth. It reveals how the dynamic power of the Holy Spirit transformed a diverse group of fishermen, tax collectors, and other ordinary folks into people who turned their world upside-down with the gospel of Jesus Christ.

ROMANS

Author: Paul; *Date:* Around A.D. 58; *Genre:* Letter.
Summary: This epistle contains some of the prime secrets of the Christian life. It is a hard-hitting diagnosis of the primary source of man's problems: sin. It also shows the futility of thinking that the answers to our problems lie within our own selves.

1 CORINTHIANS

Author: Paul; *Date:* Around A.D. 56; *Genre:* Letter.
Summary: Paul wrote this epistle in response to certain situations that arose in the Corinthian church. He straightforwardly dealt with many of the errors that the people of this church believed and practiced. Among the pitfalls were sins of immorality, false teachings, problems regarding marriage, and lawsuits.

2 CORINTHIANS

Author: Paul; *Date:* Around A.D. 57; *Genre:* Letter.
Summary: Some of the Corinthians who were still living in sin after Paul's first letter denied Paul's authority. Paul wrote this second letter to deal with the problems that persisted within the Corinthian church.

GALATIANS

Author: Paul; *Date:* Around A.D. 49; *Genre:* Letter.
Summary: Galatians is a foundational study that shows how complete the work of Jesus' death on the cross was for our salvation. Nothing needs to be added to that work, nor does it need to be improved upon, because that work was perfect.

EPHESIANS

Author: Paul; *Date:* Around A.D. 61; *Genre:* Letter.

Summary: The book of Ephesians shows us our rightful position as children of God "in the heavenly realms" with Jesus Christ. It tells us of all that God has done for us, as well as how to fully appreciate and implement it practically in our lives.

PHILIPPIANS
Author: Paul; *Date:* Around A.D. 61; *Genre:* Letter.
Summary: This book explains the mindset, attitude, and outlook the believer must have if he or she is going to experience the joy of the Lord in a troubled world.

COLOSSIANS
Author: Paul; *Date:* Around A.D. 61; *Genre:* Letter.
Summary: Paul wrote this epistle to refute certain false teachings that had found their way into the church. A common theme of this book is the superiority of Jesus Christ.

1 THESSALONIANS
Author: Paul; *Date:* Around A.D. 51; *Genre:* Letter.
Summary: The theme of this book focuses on living a godly and holy life as we await the return of Jesus Christ. Paul also offered words of comfort concerning Christian loved ones who died.

2 THESSALONIANS
Author: Paul; *Date:* Around A.D. 51; *Genre:* Letter.
Summary: This letter offers encouragement to the believers who were facing persecution. It also offers correct teaching on the subject of "the day of the Lord," a confusing matter for some of the Thessalonian believers. In addition, some were not living as they should have been in light of the return of the Lord, so Paul addressed that issue, as well.

1 TIMOTHY
Author: Paul; *Date:* Around A.D. 64; *Genre:* Letter.
Summary: Paul, under the inspiration of the Holy Spirit, laid out what the conduct of the church and its leaders should be. Though Timothy himself was a pastor, these words apply to all who want to be used by God and have their lives make a difference.

2 TIMOTHY
Author: Paul; *Date:* Around A.D. 67; *Genre:* Letter.
Summary: Paul wrote this second letter to Timothy to encourage him to be faithful to Christ. Paul also included a glimpse of what the last days would look like.

TITUS
Author: Paul; *Date:* Around A.D. 64; *Genre:* Letter.

Summary: Paul wrote this letter to address the challenges facing Titus as an overseer of the churches on the island of Crete. He included criteria for qualifications of leadership, sound teaching, and good works.

PHILEMON

Author: Paul; *Date:* Around A.D. 61; *Genre:* Letter.
Summary: This short but profound epistle contains a wonderful story of the importance of forgiveness among Christians.

HEBREWS

Author: Uncertain; perhaps Paul, Barnabas, Apollos, Priscilla, or Luke; *Date:* Around A.D. 68; *Genre:* Letter.
Summary: The book of Hebrews was written for the Jews who had accepted Jesus as their Messiah. They were in danger of slipping back into the traditions of Judaism because they had not put their roots down in the soil of Christianity.

JAMES

Author: James, Jesus' half-brother; *Date:* Around A.D. 49; *Genre:* Letter.
Summary: James spoke about faith in his book, with an emphasis on results. He stressed the need to live a practical, working faith.

1 PETER

Author: Peter; *Date:* Around A.D. 63; *Genre:* Letter.
Summary: The theme of Peter's first epistle is suffering. He brought inspired words of comfort to those who suffered under persecution.

2 PETER

Author: Peter; *Date:* Around A.D. 67; *Genre:* Letter.
Summary: In this epistle, Peter wanted to remind the believers of certain important spiritual truths. Peter also warned of false teachers and spoke of the hope in the Lord's coming.

1 JOHN

Author: John; *Date:* A.D. 85–90; *Genre:* Letter.
Summary: In this letter, John pointed out that a person either is or is not a child of God. There is no middle ground. John clearly emphasized that if one is really a child of God, it will become evident in one's habitual behavior.

2 JOHN

Author: John; *Date:* Around A.D. 90; *Genre:* Letter.
Summary: In this letter John pointed out that true Christian love involves more than just an emotional feeling. It is grounded in what

is true. John also warned of false teachers, urging the believers not to receive them.

3 JOHN

Author: John; *Date:* Around A.D. 90; *Genre:* Letter.
Summary: John wrote this letter to commend Gaius, a fellow believer, for the hospitality he showed to traveling teachers of the gospel.

JUDE

Author: Jude, Jesus' half-brother; *Date:* Around A.D. 65;
Genre: Letter.
Summary: Jude centers around the great apostasy, or falling away from the faith, that will happen on earth before the return of Jesus Christ.

REVELATION

Author: John; *Date:* Around A.D. 95; *Genre:* Apocalypse.
Summary: In this book, we learn of Jesus Christ's return to the earth, as well as the events preceding that climactic moment.

PSALMS

Authors: David, Asaph, the sons of Korah, Solomon, Heman, Ethan, and Moses; *Date:* Between the time of Moses (around 1440 B.C.) and the Babylonian captivity (586 B.C.); *Genre:* Poetry.
Summary: Psalms contains a variety of themes that touch on every area of life. The central theme, however, is the praise and worship of a sovereign and loving God. Besides being a source of comfort and worship, the Psalms are filled with prophecies about Jesus Christ.

A NOTE TO READERS

The *Holy Bible*, New Living Translation, was first published in 1996. It quickly became one of the most popular Bible translations in the English-speaking world. While the NLT's influence was rapidly growing, the Bible Translation Committee determined that an additional investment in scholarly review and text refinement could make it even better. So shortly after its initial publication, the committee began an eight-year process with the purpose of increasing the level of the NLT's precision without sacrificing its easy-to-understand quality. This second-generation text was completed in 2004, with minor changes subsequently introduced in 2007, 2013, and 2015.

The goal of any Bible translation is to convey the meaning and content of the ancient Hebrew, Aramaic, and Greek texts as accurately as possible to contemporary readers. The challenge for our translators was to create a text that would communicate as clearly and powerfully to today's readers as the original texts did to readers and listeners in the ancient biblical world. The resulting translation is easy to read and understand, while also accurately communicating the meaning and content of the original biblical texts. The NLT is a general-purpose text especially good for study, devotional reading, and reading aloud in worship services.

We believe that the New Living Translation—which combines the latest biblical scholarship with a clear, dynamic writing style—will communicate God's word powerfully to all who read it. We publish it with the prayer that God will use it to speak his timeless truth to the church and the world in a fresh, new way.

The Publishers

Matthew

The Ancestors of Jesus the Messiah

1 This is a record of the ancestors of Jesus the Messiah, a descendant of David and of Abraham*:

2 Abraham was the father of Isaac.
Isaac was the father of Jacob.
Jacob was the father of Judah and his brothers.

3 Judah was the father of Perez and Zerah (whose mother was Tamar).
Perez was the father of Hezron.
Hezron was the father of Ram.*

4 Ram was the father of Amminadab.
Amminadab was the father of Nahshon.
Nahshon was the father of Salmon.

5 Salmon was the father of Boaz (whose mother was Rahab).
Boaz was the father of Obed (whose mother was Ruth).
Obed was the father of Jesse.

6 Jesse was the father of King David.
David was the father of Solomon (whose mother was Bathsheba, the widow of Uriah).

7 Solomon was the father of Rehoboam.
Rehoboam was the father of Abijah.
Abijah was the father of Asa.*

8 Asa was the father of Jehoshaphat.
Jehoshaphat was the father of Jehoram.*
Jehoram was the father* of Uzziah.

9 Uzziah was the father of Jotham.
Jotham was the father of Ahaz.
Ahaz was the father of Hezekiah.

10 Hezekiah was the father of Manasseh.
Manasseh was the father of Amon.*
Amon was the father of Josiah.

11 Josiah was the father of Jehoiachin* and his brothers (born at the time of the exile to Babylon).

12 After the Babylonian exile:
Jehoiachin was the father of Shealtiel.

1:1 Greek *Jesus the Messiah, Son of David and son of Abraham.* **1:3** Greek *Aram,* a variant spelling of Ram; also in 1:4. See Chr 2:9-10. **1:7** Greek *Asaph,* a variant spelling of Asa; also in 1:8. See 1 Chr 3:10. **1:8a** Greek *Joram,* a variant spelling of Jehoram; also in 1:8b. See 1 Kgs 22:50 and note at 1 Chr 3:11. **1:8b** Or *ancestor;* also in 1:11. **1:10** Greek *Amos,* a variant spelling of Amon; also in 1:10b. See 1 Chr 3:14. **1:11** Greek *Jeconiah,* a variant spelling of Jehoiachin; also in 1:12. See 2 Kgs 24:6 and note at 1 Chr 3:16.

Shealtiel was the father of
Zerubbabel.
13 Zerubbabel was the father
of Abiud.
Abiud was the father of Eliakim.
Eliakim was the father of Azor.
14 Azor was the father of Zadok.
Zadok was the father of Akim.
Akim was the father of Eliud.
15 Eliud was the father of Eleazar.
Eleazar was the father of Matthan.
Matthan was the father of Jacob.
16 Jacob was the father of Joseph,
the husband of Mary.
Mary gave birth to Jesus, who
is called the Messiah.

17All those listed above include fourteen generations from Abraham to David, fourteen from David to the Babylonian exile, and fourteen from the Babylonian exile to the Messiah.

The Birth of Jesus the Messiah

18This is how Jesus the Messiah was born. His mother, Mary, was engaged to be married to Joseph. But before the marriage took place, while she was still a virgin, she became pregnant through the power of the Holy Spirit. 19Joseph, to whom she was engaged, was a righteous man and did not want to disgrace her publicly, so he decided to break the engagement* quietly.

20As he considered this, an angel of the Lord appeared to him in a dream. "Joseph, son of David," the angel said, "do not be afraid to take Mary as your wife. For the child within her was conceived by the Holy Spirit. 21And she will have a son, and you are to name him Jesus,* for he will save his people from their sins."

22All of this occurred to fulfill the Lord's message through his prophet:

23 "Look! The virgin will conceive
a child!
She will give birth to a son,
and they will call him Immanuel,*
which means 'God is with us.'"

24When Joseph woke up, he did as the angel of the Lord commanded and took Mary as his wife. 25But he did not have sexual relations with her until her son was born. And Joseph named him Jesus.

Visitors from the East

2 Jesus was born in Bethlehem in Judea, during the reign of King Herod. About that time some wise men* from eastern lands arrived in Jerusalem, asking, 2"Where is the newborn king of the Jews? We saw his star as it rose,* and we have come to worship him."

3King Herod was deeply disturbed when he heard this, as was everyone in Jerusalem. 4He called a meeting of the leading priests and teachers of religious law and asked, "Where is the Messiah supposed to be born?"

5"In Bethlehem in Judea," they said, "for this is what the prophet wrote:

1:19 Greek *to divorce her.* 1:21 *Jesus* means "The LORD saves." 1:23 Isa 7:14; 8:8, 10 (Greek version). 2:1 Or *royal astrologers;* Greek reads *magi;* also in 2:7, 16. 2:2 Or *star in the east.*

⁶ 'And you, O Bethlehem in the land of Judah,
are not least among the ruling cities* of Judah,
for a ruler will come from you
who will be the shepherd for my people Israel.'*"

⁷Then Herod called for a private meeting with the wise men, and he learned from them the time when the star first appeared. ⁸Then he told them, "Go to Bethlehem and search carefully for the child. And when you find him, come back and tell me so that I can go and worship him, too!"

⁹After this interview the wise men went their way. And the star they had seen in the east guided them to Bethlehem. It went ahead of them and stopped over the place where the child was. ¹⁰When they saw the star, they were filled with joy! ¹¹They entered the house and saw the child with his mother, Mary, and they bowed down and worshiped him. Then they opened their treasure chests and gave him gifts of gold, frankincense, and myrrh.

¹²When it was time to leave, they returned to their own country by another route, for God had warned them in a dream not to return to Herod.

The Escape to Egypt

¹³After the wise men were gone, an angel of the Lord appeared to Joseph in a dream. "Get up! Flee to Egypt with the child and his mother," the angel said. "Stay there until I tell you to return, because Herod is going to search for the child to kill him."

¹⁴That night Joseph left for Egypt with the child and Mary, his mother, ¹⁵and they stayed there until Herod's death. This fulfilled what the Lord had spoken through the prophet: "I called my Son out of Egypt."*

¹⁶Herod was furious when he realized that the wise men had outwitted him. He sent soldiers to kill all the boys in and around Bethlehem who were two years old and under, based on the wise men's report of the star's first appearance. ¹⁷Herod's brutal action fulfilled what God had spoken through the prophet Jeremiah:

¹⁸ "A cry was heard in Ramah—
weeping and great mourning.
Rachel weeps for her children,
refusing to be comforted,
for they are dead."*

The Return to Nazareth

¹⁹When Herod died, an angel of the Lord appeared in a dream to Joseph in Egypt. ²⁰"Get up!" the angel said. "Take the child and his mother back to the land of Israel, because those who were trying to kill the child are dead."

²¹So Joseph got up and returned to the land of Israel with Jesus and his mother. ²²But when he learned

2:6a Greek *the rulers.* 2:6b Mic 5:2; 2 Sam 5:2. 2:15 Hos 11:1. 2:18 Jer 31:15.

that the new ruler of Judea was Herod's son Archelaus, he was afraid to go there. Then, after being warned in a dream, he left for the region of Galilee. 23So the family went and lived in a town called Nazareth. This fulfilled what the prophets had said: "He will be called a Nazarene."

John the Baptist Prepares the Way

3 In those days John the Baptist came to the Judean wilderness and began preaching. His message was, 2"Repent of your sins and turn to God, for the Kingdom of Heaven is near.*" 3The prophet Isaiah was speaking about John when he said,

"He is a voice shouting in the wilderness,
'Prepare the way for the LORD's coming!
Clear the road for him!'"*

4John's clothes were woven from coarse camel hair, and he wore a leather belt around his waist. For food he ate locusts and wild honey. 5People from Jerusalem and from all of Judea and all over the Jordan Valley went out to see and hear John. 6And when they confessed their sins, he baptized them in the Jordan River.

7But when he saw many Pharisees and Sadducees coming to watch him baptize,* he denounced them. "You brood of snakes!" he exclaimed. "Who warned you to flee the coming wrath? 8Prove by the way you live that you have repented of your sins and turned to God. 9Don't just say to each other, 'We're safe, for we are descendants of Abraham.' That means nothing, for I tell you, God can create children of Abraham from these very stones. 10Even now the ax of God's judgment is poised, ready to sever the roots of the trees. Yes, every tree that does not produce good fruit will be chopped down and thrown into the fire.

11"I baptize with* water those who repent of their sins and turn to God. But someone is coming soon who is greater than I am—so much greater that I'm not worthy even to be his slave and carry his sandals. He will baptize you with the Holy Spirit and with fire.* 12He is ready to separate the chaff from the wheat with his winnowing fork. Then he will clean up the threshing area, gathering the wheat into his barn but burning the chaff with never-ending fire."

The Baptism of Jesus

13Then Jesus went from Galilee to the Jordan River to be baptized by John. 14But John tried to talk him out of it. "I am the one who needs to be baptized by you," he said, "so why are you coming to me?"

15But Jesus said, "It should be done, for we must carry out all that God requires.*" So John agreed to baptize him.

3:2 Or has come, or is coming soon. 3:3 Isa 40:3 (Greek version). 3:7 Or coming to be baptized. 3:11a Or in. 3:11b Or in the Holy Spirit and in fire. 3:15 Or for we must fulfill all righteousness.

[16]After his baptism, as Jesus came up out of the water, the heavens were opened* and he saw the Spirit of God descending like a dove and settling on him. [17]And a voice from heaven said, "This is my dearly loved Son, who brings me great joy."

The Temptation of Jesus

4 Then Jesus was led by the Spirit into the wilderness to be tempted there by the devil. [2]For forty days and forty nights he fasted and became very hungry.

[3]During that time the devil* came and said to him, "If you are the Son of God, tell these stones to become loaves of bread."

[4]But Jesus told him, "No! The Scriptures say,

'People do not live by bread
    alone,
  but by every word that
    comes from the mouth
    of God.'* "

[5]Then the devil took him to the holy city, Jerusalem, to the highest point of the Temple, [6]and said, "If you are the Son of God, jump off! For the Scriptures say,

'He will order his angels to
    protect you.
And they will hold you up with
    their hands
  so you won't even hurt your
    foot on a stone.'*"

[7]Jesus responded, "The Scriptures also say, 'You must not test the LORD your God.'* "

[8]Next the devil took him to the peak of a very high mountain and showed him all the kingdoms of the world and their glory. [9]"I will give it all to you," he said, "if you will kneel down and worship me."

[10]"Get out of here, Satan," Jesus told him. "For the Scriptures say,

'You must worship the LORD your
    God
  and serve only him.'* "

[11]Then the devil went away, and angels came and took care of Jesus.

The Ministry of Jesus Begins

[12]When Jesus heard that John had been arrested, he left Judea and returned to Galilee. [13]He went first to Nazareth, then left there and moved to Capernaum, beside the Sea of Galilee, in the region of Zebulun and Naphtali. [14]This fulfilled what God said through the prophet Isaiah:

[15] "In the land of Zebulun and
    of Naphtali,
  beside the sea, beyond the
    Jordan River,
  in Galilee where so many
    Gentiles live,
[16] the people who sat in darkness
    have seen a great light.
And for those who lived in the

3:16 Some manuscripts read *opened to him.* **4:3** Greek *the tempter.* **4:4** Deut 8:3. **4:6** Ps 91:11-12. **4:7** Deut 6:16. **4:10** Deut 6:13.

land where death casts
  its shadow,
   a light has shined."*

[17] From then on Jesus began to preach, "Repent of your sins and turn to God, for the Kingdom of Heaven is near.*"

The First Disciples

[18] One day as Jesus was walking along the shore of the Sea of Galilee, he saw two brothers—Simon, also called Peter, and Andrew—throwing a net into the water, for they fished for a living. [19] Jesus called out to them, "Come, follow me, and I will show you how to fish for people!" [20] And they left their nets at once and followed him.

[21] A little farther up the shore he saw two other brothers, James and John, sitting in a boat with their father, Zebedee, repairing their nets. And he called them to come, too. [22] They immediately followed him, leaving the boat and their father behind.

Crowds Follow Jesus

[23] Jesus traveled throughout the region of Galilee, teaching in the synagogues and announcing the Good News about the Kingdom. And he healed every kind of disease and illness. [24] News about him spread as far as Syria, and people soon began bringing to him all who were sick. And whatever their sickness or disease, or if they were demon possessed or epileptic or paralyzed—he healed them all. [25] Large crowds followed him wherever he went—people from Galilee, the Ten Towns,* Jerusalem, from all over Judea, and from east of the Jordan River.

The Sermon on the Mount

5 One day as he saw the crowds gathering, Jesus went up on the mountainside and sat down. His disciples gathered around him, [2] and he began to teach them.

The Beatitudes

[3] "God blesses those who are poor
   and realize their need for
   him,*
  for the Kingdom of Heaven
   is theirs.
[4] God blesses those who mourn,
  for they will be comforted.
[5] God blesses those who are
   humble,
  for they will inherit the whole
   earth.
[6] God blesses those who hunger
   and thirst for justice,*
  for they will be satisfied.
[7] God blesses those who are
   merciful,
  for they will be shown
   mercy.
[8] God blesses those whose hearts
   are pure,

4:15-16 Isa 9:1-2 (Greek version). **4:17** Or *has come,* or *is coming soon.* **4:25** Greek *Decapolis.* **5:3** Greek *poor in spirit.* **5:6** Or *for righteousness.*

for they will see God.
9 God blesses those who work
    for peace,
    for they will be called the
    children of God.
10 God blesses those who are
    persecuted for doing
    right,
    for the Kingdom of Heaven
    is theirs.

11"God blesses you when people mock you and persecute you and lie about you and say all sorts of evil things against you because you are my followers. 12Be happy about it! Be very glad! For a great reward awaits you in heaven. And remember, the ancient prophets were persecuted in the same way.

Teaching about Salt and Light
13"You are the salt of the earth. But what good is salt if it has lost its flavor? Can you make it salty again? It will be thrown out and trampled underfoot as worthless.

14"You are the light of the world—like a city on a hilltop that cannot be hidden. 15No one lights a lamp and then puts it under a basket. Instead, a lamp is placed on a stand, where it gives light to everyone in the house. 16In the same way, let your good deeds shine out for all to see, so that everyone will praise your heavenly Father.

Teaching about the Law
17"Don't misunderstand why I have come. I did not come to abolish the law of Moses or the writings of the prophets. No, I came to accomplish their purpose. 18I tell you the truth, until heaven and earth disappear, not even the smallest detail of God's law will disappear until its purpose is achieved. 19So if you ignore the least commandment and teach others to do the same, you will be called the least in the Kingdom of Heaven. But anyone who obeys God's laws and teaches them will be called great in the Kingdom of Heaven.

20"But I warn you—unless your righteousness is better than the righteousness of the teachers of religious law and the Pharisees, you will never enter the Kingdom of Heaven!

Teaching about Anger
21"You have heard that our ancestors were told, 'You must not murder. If you commit murder, you are subject to judgment.'* 22But I say, if you are even angry with someone,* you are subject to judgment! If you call someone an idiot,* you are in danger of being brought before the court. And if you curse someone,* you are in danger of the fires of hell.*

23"So if you are presenting a

5:21 Exod 20:13; Deut 5:17. **5:22a** Some manuscripts add *without cause.* **5:22b** Greek uses an Aramaic term of contempt: *If you say to your brother, 'Raca.'* **5:22c** Greek *if you say, 'You fool.'* **5:22d** Greek *Gehenna;*also in 5:29, 30.

sacrifice* at the altar in the Temple and you suddenly remember that someone has something against you, ²⁴leave your sacrifice there at the altar. Go and be reconciled to that person. Then come and offer your sacrifice to God.

²⁵"When you are on the way to court with your adversary, settle your differences quickly. Otherwise, your accuser may hand you over to the judge, who will hand you over to an officer, and you will be thrown into prison. ²⁶And if that happens, you surely won't be free again until you have paid the last penny.*

Teaching about Adultery

²⁷"You have heard the commandment that says, 'You must not commit adultery.'* ²⁸But I say, anyone who even looks at a woman with lust has already committed adultery with her in his heart. ²⁹So if your eye—even your good eye*—causes you to lust, gouge it out and throw it away. It is better for you to lose one part of your body than for your whole body to be thrown into hell. ³⁰And if your hand—even your stronger hand*—causes you to sin, cut it off and throw it away. It is better for you to lose one part of your body than for your whole body to be thrown into hell.

Teaching about Divorce

³¹"You have heard the law that says, 'A man can divorce his wife by merely giving her a written notice of divorce.'* ³²But I say that a man who divorces his wife, unless she has been unfaithful, causes her to commit adultery. And anyone who marries a divorced woman also commits adultery.

Teaching about Vows

³³"You have also heard that our ancestors were told, 'You must not break your vows; you must carry out the vows you make to the LORD.'* ³⁴But I say, do not make any vows! Do not say, 'By heaven!' because heaven is God's throne. ³⁵And do not say, 'By the earth!' because the earth is his footstool. And do not say, 'By Jerusalem!' for Jerusalem is the city of the great King. ³⁶Do not even say, 'By my head!' for you can't turn one hair white or black. ³⁷Just say a simple, 'Yes, I will,' or 'No, I won't.' Anything beyond this is from the evil one.

Teaching about Revenge

³⁸"You have heard the law that says the punishment must match the injury: 'An eye for an eye, and a tooth for a tooth.'* ³⁹But I say, do not resist an evil person! If someone slaps you on the right cheek, offer the other

5:23 Greek *gift;* also in 5:24. 5:26 Greek *the last kodrantes* [i.e., quadrans]. 5:27 Exod 20:14; Deut 5:18. 5:29 Greek *your right eye.* 5:30 Greek *your right hand.* 5:31 Deut 24:1. 5:33 Num 30:2. 5:38 Greek *the law that says: 'An eye for an eye and a tooth for a tooth.'* Exod 21:24; Lev 24:20; Deut 19:21.

cheek also. ⁴⁰If you are sued in court and your shirt is taken from you, give your coat, too. ⁴¹If a soldier demands that you carry his gear for a mile,* carry it two miles. ⁴²Give to those who ask, and don't turn away from those who want to borrow.

Teaching about Love for Enemies

⁴³"You have heard the law that says, 'Love your neighbor'* and hate your enemy. ⁴⁴But I say, love your enemies!* Pray for those who persecute you! ⁴⁵In that way, you will be acting as true children of your Father in heaven. For he gives his sunlight to both the evil and the good, and he sends rain on the just and the unjust alike. ⁴⁶If you love only those who love you, what reward is there for that? Even corrupt tax collectors do that much. ⁴⁷If you are kind only to your friends,* how are you different from anyone else? Even pagans do that. ⁴⁸But you are to be perfect, even as your Father in heaven is perfect.

Teaching about Giving to the Needy

6 "Watch out! Don't do your good deeds publicly, to be admired by others, for you will lose the reward from your Father in heaven. ²When you give to someone in need, don't do as the hypocrites do—blowing trumpets in the syna-

gogues and streets to call attention to their acts of charity! I tell you the truth, they have received all the reward they will ever get. ³But when you give to someone in need, don't let your left hand know what your right hand is doing. ⁴Give your gifts in private, and your Father, who sees everything, will reward you.

Teaching about Prayer and Fasting

⁵"When you pray, don't be like the hypocrites who love to pray publicly on street corners and in the synagogues where everyone can see them. I tell you the truth, that is all the reward they will ever get. ⁶But when you pray, go away by yourself, shut the door behind you, and pray to your Father in private. Then your Father, who sees everything, will reward you.

⁷"When you pray, don't babble on and on as the Gentiles do. They think their prayers are answered merely by repeating their words again and again. ⁸Don't be like them, for your Father knows exactly what you need even before you ask him! ⁹Pray like this:

Our Father in heaven,
    may your name be kept holy.
¹⁰ May your Kingdom come soon.
    May your will be done on earth,
        as it is in heaven.
¹¹ Give us today the food we need,*

¹² and forgive us our sins,
   as we have forgiven those
   who sin against us.
¹³ And don't let us yield to
   temptation,*
   but rescue us from the evil
   one.*

¹⁴"If you forgive those who sin against you, your heavenly Father will forgive you. ¹⁵But if you refuse to forgive others, your Father will not forgive your sins.

¹⁶"And when you fast, don't make it obvious, as the hypocrites do, for they try to look miserable and disheveled so people will admire them for their fasting. I tell you the truth, that is the only reward they will ever get. ¹⁷But when you fast, comb your hair* and wash your face. ¹⁸Then no one will notice that you are fasting, except your Father, who knows what you do in private. And your Father, who sees everything, will reward you.

Teaching about Money and Possessions

¹⁹"Don't store up treasures here on earth, where moths eat them and rust destroys them, and where thieves break in and steal. ²⁰Store your treasures in heaven, where moths and rust cannot destroy, and thieves do not break in and steal. ²¹Wherever your treasure is, there the desires of your heart will also be.

²²"Your eye is like a lamp that provides light for your body. When your eye is healthy, your whole body is filled with light. ²³But when your eye is unhealthy, your whole body is filled with darkness. And if the light you think you have is actually darkness, how deep that darkness is!

²⁴"No one can serve two masters. For you will hate one and love the other; you will be devoted to one and despise the other. You cannot serve God and be enslaved to money.

²⁵"That is why I tell you not to worry about everyday life—whether you have enough food and drink, or enough clothes to wear. Isn't life more than food, and your body more than clothing? ²⁶Look at the birds. They don't plant or harvest or store food in barns, for your heavenly Father feeds them. And aren't you far more valuable to him than they are? ²⁷Can all your worries add a single moment to your life?

²⁸"And why worry about your clothing? Look at the lilies of the field and how they grow. They don't work or make their clothing, ²⁹yet Solomon in all his glory was not dressed as beautifully as they are. ³⁰And if God cares so wonderfully for wildflowers that are here today and thrown into the fire tomorrow, he will certainly care for you. Why do you have so little faith?

³¹"So don't worry about these things, saying, 'What will we eat?

6:13a Or *And keep us from being tested.* 6:13b Or *from evil.* Some manuscripts add *For yours is the kingdom and the power and the glory forever. Amen.* 6:17 Greek *anoint your head.*

What will we drink? What will we wear?' ³²These things dominate the thoughts of unbelievers, but your heavenly Father already knows all your needs. ³³Seek the Kingdom of God* above all else, and live righteously, and he will give you everything you need.

³⁴"So don't worry about tomorrow, for tomorrow will bring its own worries. Today's trouble is enough for today.

Do Not Judge Others

7 "Do not judge others, and you will not be judged. ²For you will be treated as you treat others.* The standard you use in judging is the standard by which you will be judged.*

³"And why worry about a speck in your friend's eye* when you have a log in your own? ⁴How can you think of saying to your friend,* 'Let me help you get rid of that speck in your eye,' when you can't see past the log in your own eye? ⁵Hypocrite! First get rid of the log in your own eye; then you will see well enough to deal with the speck in your friend's eye.

⁶"Don't waste what is holy on people who are unholy.* Don't throw your pearls to pigs! They will trample the pearls, then turn and attack you.

Effective Prayer

⁷"Keep on asking, and you will receive what you ask for. Keep on seeking, and you will find. Keep on knocking, and the door will be opened to you. ⁸For everyone who asks, receives. Everyone who seeks, finds. And to everyone who knocks, the door will be opened.

⁹"You parents—if your children ask for a loaf of bread, do you give them a stone instead? ¹⁰Or if they ask for a fish, do you give them a snake? Of course not! ¹¹So if you sinful people know how to give good gifts to your children, how much more will your heavenly Father give good gifts to those who ask him.

The Golden Rule

¹²"Do to others whatever you would like them to do to you. This is the essence of all that is taught in the law and the prophets.

The Narrow Gate

¹³"You can enter God's Kingdom only through the narrow gate. The highway to hell* is broad, and its gate is wide for the many who choose that way. ¹⁴But the gateway to life is very narrow and the road is difficult, and only a few ever find it.

The Tree and Its Fruit

¹⁵"Beware of false prophets who come disguised as harmless sheep

6:33 Some manuscripts do not include *of God.* **7:2a** Or *For God will judge you as you judge others.* **7:2b** Or *The measure you give will be the measure you get back.* **7:3** Greek *your brother's eye;* also in 7:5. **7:4** Greek *your brother.* **7:6** Greek *Don't give the sacred to dogs.* **7:13** Greek *The road that leads to destruction.*

but are really vicious wolves. [16]You can identify them by their fruit, that is, by the way they act. Can you pick grapes from thornbushes, or figs from thistles? [17]A good tree produces good fruit, and a bad tree produces bad fruit. [18]A good tree can't produce bad fruit, and a bad tree can't produce good fruit. [19]So every tree that does not produce good fruit is chopped down and thrown into the fire. [20]Yes, just as you can identify a tree by its fruit, so you can identify people by their actions.

True Disciples

[21]"Not everyone who calls out to me, 'Lord! Lord!' will enter the Kingdom of Heaven. Only those who actually do the will of my Father in heaven will enter. [22]On judgment day many will say to me, 'Lord! Lord! We prophesied in your name and cast out demons in your name and performed many miracles in your name.' [23]But I will reply, 'I never knew you. Get away from me, you who break God's laws.'

Building on a Solid Foundation

[24]"Anyone who listens to my teaching and follows it is wise, like a person who builds a house on solid rock. [25]Though the rain comes in torrents and the floodwaters rise and the winds beat against that house, it won't collapse because it is built on bedrock. [26]But anyone who hears my teaching and doesn't obey it is foolish, like a person who builds a house on sand. [27]When the rains and floods come and the winds beat against that house, it will collapse with a mighty crash."

[28]When Jesus had finished saying these things, the crowds were amazed at his teaching, [29]for he taught with real authority—quite unlike their teachers of religious law.

Jesus Heals a Man with Leprosy

8 Large crowds followed Jesus as he came down the mountainside. [2]Suddenly, a man with leprosy approached him and knelt before him. "Lord," the man said, "if you are willing, you can heal me and make me clean."

[3]Jesus reached out and touched him. "I am willing," he said. "Be healed!" And instantly the leprosy disappeared. [4]Then Jesus said to him, "Don't tell anyone about this. Instead, go to the priest and let him examine you. Take along the offering required in the law of Moses for those who have been healed of leprosy.* This will be a public testimony that you have been cleansed."

The Faith of a Roman Officer

[5]When Jesus returned to Capernaum, a Roman officer* came and pleaded with him, [6]"Lord, my young servant* lies in bed, paralyzed and in terrible pain."

8:4 See Lev 14:2-32.   8:5 Greek *a centurion;* similarly in 8:8, 13.   8:6 Or *child;* also in 8:13.

⁷Jesus said, "I will come and heal him."

⁸But the officer said, "Lord, I am not worthy to have you come into my home. Just say the word from where you are, and my servant will be healed. ⁹I know this because I am under the authority of my superior officers, and I have authority over my soldiers. I only need to say, 'Go,' and they go, or 'Come,' and they come. And if I say to my slaves, 'Do this,' they do it."

¹⁰When Jesus heard this, he was amazed. Turning to those who were following him, he said, "I tell you the truth, I haven't seen faith like this in all Israel! ¹¹And I tell you this, that many Gentiles will come from all over the world—from east and west—and sit down with Abraham, Isaac, and Jacob at the feast in the Kingdom of Heaven. ¹²But many Israelites—those for whom the Kingdom was prepared—will be thrown into outer darkness, where there will be weeping and gnashing of teeth."

¹³Then Jesus said to the Roman officer, "Go back home. Because you believed, it has happened." And the young servant was healed that same hour.

Jesus Heals Many People

¹⁴When Jesus arrived at Peter's house, Peter's mother-in-law was sick in bed with a high fever. ¹⁵But when Jesus touched her hand, the fever left her. Then she got up and prepared a meal for him.

¹⁶That evening many demon-possessed people were brought to Jesus. He cast out the evil spirits with a simple command, and he healed all the sick. ¹⁷This fulfilled the word of the Lord through the prophet Isaiah, who said,

"He took our sicknesses
    and removed our diseases."*

The Cost of Following Jesus

¹⁸When Jesus saw the crowd around him, he instructed his disciples to cross to the other side of the lake.

¹⁹Then one of the teachers of religious law said to him, "Teacher, I will follow you wherever you go."

²⁰But Jesus replied, "Foxes have dens to live in, and birds have nests, but the Son of Man* has no place even to lay his head."

²¹Another of his disciples said, "Lord, first let me return home and bury my father."

²²But Jesus told him, "Follow me now. Let the spiritually dead bury their own dead.*"

Jesus Calms the Storm

²³Then Jesus got into the boat and started across the lake with his disciples. ²⁴Suddenly, a fierce storm struck the lake, with waves

8:17 Isa 53:4. 8:20 "Son of Man" is a title Jesus used for himself. 8:22 Greek *Let the dead bury their own dead.*

breaking into the boat. But Jesus was sleeping. 25The disciples went and woke him up, shouting, "Lord, save us! We're going to drown!"

26Jesus responded, "Why are you afraid? You have so little faith!" Then he got up and rebuked the wind and waves, and suddenly there was a great calm.

27The disciples were amazed. "Who is this man?" they asked. "Even the winds and waves obey him!"

Jesus Heals Two Demon-Possessed Men

28When Jesus arrived on the other side of the lake, in the region of the Gadarenes,* two men who were possessed by demons met him. They came out of the tombs and were so violent that no one could go through that area.

29They began screaming at him, "Why are you interfering with us, Son of God? Have you come here to torture us before God's appointed time?"

30There happened to be a large herd of pigs feeding in the distance. 31So the demons begged, "If you cast us out, send us into that herd of pigs."

32"All right, go!" Jesus commanded them. So the demons came out of the men and entered the pigs, and the whole herd plunged down the steep hillside into the lake and drowned in the water.

33The herdsmen fled to the nearby town, telling everyone what happened to the demon-possessed men. 34Then the entire town came out to meet Jesus, but they begged him to go away and leave them alone.

Jesus Heals a Paralyzed Man

9 Jesus climbed into a boat and went back across the lake to his own town. 2Some people brought to him a paralyzed man on a mat. Seeing their faith, Jesus said to the paralyzed man, "Be encouraged, my child! Your sins are forgiven."

3But some of the teachers of religious law said to themselves, "That's blasphemy! Does he think he's God?"

4Jesus knew* what they were thinking, so he asked them, "Why do you have such evil thoughts in your hearts? 5Is it easier to say 'Your sins are forgiven,' or 'Stand up and walk'? 6So I will prove to you that the Son of Man* has the authority on earth to forgive sins." Then Jesus turned to the paralyzed man and said, "Stand up, pick up your mat, and go home!"

7And the man jumped up and went home! 8Fear swept through the crowd as they saw this happen. And they praised God for giving humans such authority.

8:28 Other manuscripts read *Gerasenes;* still others read *Gergesenes.* Compare Mark 5:1; Luke 8:26. 9:4 Some manuscripts read *saw.* 9:6 "Son of Man" is a title Jesus used for himself.

Jesus Calls Matthew

[9]As Jesus was walking along, he saw a man named Matthew sitting at his tax collector's booth. "Follow me and be my disciple," Jesus said to him. So Matthew got up and followed him.

[10]Later, Matthew invited Jesus and his disciples to his home as dinner guests, along with many tax collectors and other disreputable sinners. [11]But when the Pharisees saw this, they asked his disciples, "Why does your teacher eat with such scum?*"

[12]When Jesus heard this, he said, "Healthy people don't need a doctor—sick people do." [13]Then he added, "Now go and learn the meaning of this Scripture: 'I want you to show mercy, not offer sacrifices.'* For I have come to call not those who think they are righteous, but those who know they are sinners."

A Discussion about Fasting

[14]One day the disciples of John the Baptist came to Jesus and asked him, "Why don't your disciples fast* like we do and the Pharisees do?"

[15]Jesus replied, "Do wedding guests mourn while celebrating with the groom? Of course not. But someday the groom will be taken away from them, and then they will fast.

[16]"Besides, who would patch old clothing with new cloth? For the new patch would shrink and rip away from the old cloth, leaving an even bigger tear than before.

[17]"And no one puts new wine into old wineskins. For the old skins would burst from the pressure, spilling the wine and ruining the skins. New wine is stored in new wineskins so that both are preserved."

Jesus Heals in Response to Faith

[18]As Jesus was saying this, the leader of a synagogue came and knelt before him. "My daughter has just died," he said, "but you can bring her back to life again if you just come and lay your hand on her."

[19]So Jesus and his disciples got up and went with him. [20]Just then a woman who had suffered for twelve years with constant bleeding came up behind him. She touched the fringe of his robe, [21]for she thought, "If I can just touch his robe, I will be healed."

[22]Jesus turned around, and when he saw her he said, "Daughter, be encouraged! Your faith has made you well." And the woman was healed at that moment.

[23]When Jesus arrived at the official's home, he saw the noisy crowd and heard the funeral music. [24]"Get out!" he told them. "The girl isn't dead; she's only asleep." But the

9:11 Greek with tax collectors and sinners?   9:13 Hos 6:6 (Greek version).   9:14 Some manuscripts read fast often.

crowd laughed at him. [25]After the crowd was put outside, however, Jesus went in and took the girl by the hand, and she stood up! [26]The report of this miracle swept through the entire countryside.

Jesus Heals the Blind

[27]After Jesus left the girl's home, two blind men followed along behind him, shouting, "Son of David, have mercy on us!"

[28]They went right into the house where he was staying, and Jesus asked them, "Do you believe I can make you see?"

"Yes, Lord," they told him, "we do."

[29]Then he touched their eyes and said, "Because of your faith, it will happen." [30]Then their eyes were opened, and they could see! Jesus sternly warned them, "Don't tell anyone about this." [31]But instead, they went out and spread his fame all over the region.

[32]When they left, a demon-possessed man who couldn't speak was brought to Jesus. [33]So Jesus cast out the demon, and then the man began to speak. The crowds were amazed. "Nothing like this has ever happened in Israel!" they exclaimed.

[34]But the Pharisees said, "He can cast out demons because he is empowered by the prince of demons."

The Need for Workers

[35]Jesus traveled through all the towns and villages of that area, teaching in the synagogues and announcing the Good News about the Kingdom. And he healed every kind of disease and illness. [36]When he saw the crowds, he had compassion on them because they were confused and helpless, like sheep without a shepherd. [37]He said to his disciples, "The harvest is great, but the workers are few. [38]So pray to the Lord who is in charge of the harvest; ask him to send more workers into his fields."

Jesus Sends Out the Twelve Apostles

10 Jesus called his twelve disciples together and gave them authority to cast out evil* spirits and to heal every kind of disease and illness. [2]Here are the names of the twelve apostles:

first, Simon (also called Peter),
then Andrew (Peter's brother),
James (son of Zebedee),
John (James's brother),
[3] Philip,
Bartholomew,
Thomas,
Matthew (the tax collector),
James (son of Alphaeus),
Thaddaeus,*
[4] Simon (the zealot*),
Judas Iscariot (who later betrayed him).

10:1 Greek *unclean*. **10:3** Other manuscripts read *Lebbaeus;* still others read *Lebbaeus who is called Thaddaeus*. **10:4** Greek *the Cananean,* an Aramaic term for Jewish nationalists.

⁵Jesus sent out the twelve apostles with these instructions: "Don't go to the Gentiles or the Samaritans, ⁶but only to the people of Israel—God's lost sheep. ⁷Go and announce to them that the Kingdom of Heaven is near.* ⁸Heal the sick, raise the dead, cure those with leprosy, and cast out demons. Give as freely as you have received!

⁹"Don't take any money in your money belts—no gold, silver, or even copper coins. ¹⁰Don't carry a traveler's bag with a change of clothes and sandals or even a walking stick. Don't hesitate to accept hospitality, because those who work deserve to be fed.

¹¹"Whenever you enter a city or village, search for a worthy person and stay in his home until you leave town. ¹²When you enter the home, give it your blessing. ¹³If it turns out to be a worthy home, let your blessing stand; if it is not, take back the blessing. ¹⁴If any household or town refuses to welcome you or listen to your message, shake its dust from your feet as you leave. ¹⁵I tell you the truth, the wicked cities of Sodom and Gomorrah will be better off than such a town on the judgment day.

¹⁶"Look, I am sending you out as sheep among wolves. So be as shrewd as snakes and harmless as doves. ¹⁷But beware! For you will be handed over to the courts and will be flogged with whips in the synagogues. ¹⁸You will stand trial before governors and kings because you are my followers. But this will be your opportunity to tell the rulers and other unbelievers about me.* ¹⁹When you are arrested, don't worry about how to respond or what to say. God will give you the right words at the right time. ²⁰For it is not you who will be speaking—it will be the Spirit of your Father speaking through you.

²¹"A brother will betray his brother to death, a father will betray his own child, and children will rebel against their parents and cause them to be killed. ²²And all nations will hate you because you are my followers.* But everyone who endures to the end will be saved. ²³When you are persecuted in one town, flee to the next. I tell you the truth, the Son of Man* will return before you have reached all the towns of Israel.

²⁴"Students* are not greater than their teacher, and slaves are not greater than their master. ²⁵Students are to be like their teacher, and slaves are to be like their master. And since I, the master of the household, have been called the prince of demons,* the members of

10:7 Or *has come,* or *is coming soon.*   **10:18** Or *But this will be your testimony against the rulers and other unbelievers.*   **10:22** Greek *on account of my name.*   **10:23** "Son of Man" is a title Jesus used for himself.   **10:24** Or *Disciples.*   **10:25** Greek *Beelzeboul;* other manuscripts read *Beezeboul;* Latin version reads *Beelzebub.*

my household will be called by even worse names!

26"But don't be afraid of those who threaten you. For the time is coming when everything that is covered will be revealed, and all that is secret will be made known to all. 27What I tell you now in the darkness, shout abroad when daybreak comes. What I whisper in your ear, shout from the housetops for all to hear!

28"Don't be afraid of those who want to kill your body; they cannot touch your soul. Fear only God, who can destroy both soul and body in hell.* 29What is the price of two sparrows—one copper coin*? But not a single sparrow can fall to the ground without your Father knowing it. 30And the very hairs on your head are all numbered. 31So don't be afraid; you are more valuable to God than a whole flock of sparrows.

32"Everyone who acknowledges me publicly here on earth, I will also acknowledge before my Father in heaven. 33But everyone who denies me here on earth, I will also deny before my Father in heaven.

34"Don't imagine that I came to bring peace to the earth! I came not to bring peace, but a sword.

35 'I have come to set a man against
  his father,
    a daughter against her
    mother,

and a daughter-in-law against
  her mother-in-law.
36   Your enemies will be right in
    your own household!'*

37"If you love your father or mother more than you love me, you are not worthy of being mine; or if you love your son or daughter more than me, you are not worthy of being mine. 38If you refuse to take up your cross and follow me, you are not worthy of being mine. 39If you cling to your life, you will lose it; but if you give up your life for me, you will find it.

40"Anyone who receives you receives me, and anyone who receives me receives the Father who sent me. 41If you receive a prophet as one who speaks for God,* you will be given the same reward as a prophet. And if you receive righteous people because of their righteousness, you will be given a reward like theirs. 42And if you give even a cup of cold water to one of the least of my followers, you will surely be rewarded."

Jesus and John the Baptist

11 When Jesus had finished giving these instructions to his twelve disciples, he went out to teach and preach in towns throughout the region.

2John the Baptist, who was in prison, heard about all the things

10:28 Greek *Gehenna.* 10:29 Greek *one assarion* [i.e., one "as," a Roman coin equal to ¹⁄₁₆ of a denarius]. 10:35-36 Mic 7:6. 10:41 Greek *receive a prophet in the name of a prophet.*

the Messiah was doing. So he sent his disciples to ask Jesus, ³"Are you the Messiah we've been expecting,* or should we keep looking for someone else?"

⁴Jesus told them, "Go back to John and tell him what you have heard and seen—⁵the blind see, the lame walk, those with leprosy are cured, the deaf hear, the dead are raised to life, and the Good News is being preached to the poor." ⁶And he added, "God blesses those who do not fall away because of me.*"

⁷As John's disciples were leaving, Jesus began talking about him to the crowds. "What kind of man did you go into the wilderness to see? Was he a weak reed, swayed by every breath of wind? ⁸Or were you expecting to see a man dressed in expensive clothes? No, people with expensive clothes live in palaces. ⁹Were you looking for a prophet? Yes, and he is more than a prophet. ¹⁰John is the man to whom the Scriptures refer when they say,

'Look, I am sending my
    messenger ahead of you,
    and he will prepare your way
    before you.'*

¹¹"I tell you the truth, of all who have ever lived, none is greater than John the Baptist. Yet even the least person in the Kingdom of Heaven is greater than he is! ¹²And from the time John the Baptist began preaching until now, the Kingdom of Heaven has been forcefully advancing,* and violent people are attacking it. ¹³For before John came, all the prophets and the law of Moses looked forward to this present time. ¹⁴And if you are willing to accept what I say, he is Elijah, the one the prophets said would come.* ¹⁵Anyone with ears to hear should listen and understand!

¹⁶"To what can I compare this generation? It is like children playing a game in the public square. They complain to their friends,

¹⁷ 'We played wedding songs,
    and you didn't dance,
so we played funeral songs,
    and you didn't mourn.'

¹⁸For John didn't spend his time eating and drinking, and you say, 'He's possessed by a demon.' ¹⁹The Son of Man,* on the other hand, feasts and drinks, and you say, 'He's a glutton and a drunkard, and a friend of tax collectors and other sinners!' But wisdom is shown to be right by its results."

Judgment for the Unbelievers

²⁰Then Jesus began to denounce the towns where he had done so many of his miracles, because they hadn't repented of their sins and turned to God. ²¹"What sorrow awaits you,

---

11:3 Greek *Are you the one who is coming?*   **11:6** Or *who are not offended by me.*   **11:10** Mal 3:1.
11:12 Or *the Kingdom of Heaven has suffered from violence.*   **11:14** See Mal 4:5.   **11:19** "Son of Man" is a title Jesus used for himself.

Korazin and Bethsaida! For if the miracles I did in you had been done in wicked Tyre and Sidon, their people would have repented of their sins long ago, clothing themselves in burlap and throwing ashes on their heads to show their remorse. 22I tell you, Tyre and Sidon will be better off on judgment day than you.

23"And you people of Capernaum, will you be honored in heaven? No, you will go down to the place of the dead.* For if the miracles I did for you had been done in wicked Sodom, it would still be here today. 24I tell you, even Sodom will be better off on judgment day than you."

Jesus' Prayer of Thanksgiving

25At that time Jesus prayed this prayer: "O Father, Lord of heaven and earth, thank you for hiding these things from those who think themselves wise and clever, and for revealing them to the childlike. 26Yes, Father, it pleased you to do it this way!

27"My Father has entrusted everything to me. No one truly knows the Son except the Father, and no one truly knows the Father except the Son and those to whom the Son chooses to reveal him."

28Then Jesus said, "Come to me, all of you who are weary and carry heavy burdens, and I will give you rest. 29Take my yoke upon you. Let me teach you, because I am humble and gentle at heart, and you will find rest for your souls. 30For my yoke is easy to bear, and the burden I give you is light."

A Discussion about the Sabbath

12 At about that time Jesus was walking through some grainfields on the Sabbath. His disciples were hungry, so they began breaking off some heads of grain and eating them. 2But some Pharisees saw them do it and protested, "Look, your disciples are breaking the law by harvesting grain on the Sabbath."

3Jesus said to them, "Haven't you read in the Scriptures what David did when he and his companions were hungry? 4He went into the house of God, and he and his companions broke the law by eating the sacred loaves of bread that only the priests are allowed to eat. 5And haven't you read in the law of Moses that the priests on duty in the Temple may work on the Sabbath? 6I tell you, there is one here who is even greater than the Temple! 7But you would not have condemned my innocent disciples if you knew the meaning of this Scripture: 'I want you to show mercy, not offer sacrifices.'* 8For the Son of Man* is Lord, even over the Sabbath!"

Jesus Heals on the Sabbath

9Then Jesus went over to their synagogue, 10where he noticed a man

11:23 Greek *to Hades.*   **12:7** Hos 6:6 (Greek version).   **12:8** "Son of Man" is a title Jesus used for himself.

with a deformed hand. The Pharisees asked Jesus, "Does the law permit a person to work by healing on the Sabbath?" (They were hoping he would say yes, so they could bring charges against him.)

¹¹And he answered, "If you had a sheep that fell into a well on the Sabbath, wouldn't you work to pull it out? Of course you would. ¹²And how much more valuable is a person than a sheep! Yes, the law permits a person to do good on the Sabbath."

¹³Then he said to the man, "Hold out your hand." So the man held out his hand, and it was restored, just like the other one! ¹⁴Then the Pharisees called a meeting to plot how to kill Jesus.

Jesus, God's Chosen Servant

¹⁵But Jesus knew what they were planning. So he left that area, and many people followed him. He healed all the sick among them, ¹⁶but he warned them not to reveal who he was. ¹⁷This fulfilled the prophecy of Isaiah concerning him:

¹⁸ "Look at my Servant, whom
      I have chosen.
   He is my Beloved, who
      pleases me.
   I will put my Spirit upon him,
      and he will proclaim justice
      to the nations.
¹⁹ He will not fight or shout

or raise his voice in public.
²⁰ He will not crush the weakest
      reed
   or put out a flickering candle.
   Finally he will cause justice
      to be victorious.
²¹ And his name will be the hope
      of all the world."*

Jesus and the Prince of Demons

²²Then a demon-possessed man, who was blind and couldn't speak, was brought to Jesus. He healed the man so that he could both speak and see. ²³The crowd was amazed and asked, "Could it be that Jesus is the Son of David, the Messiah?"

²⁴But when the Pharisees heard about the miracle, they said, "No wonder he can cast out demons. He gets his power from Satan,* the prince of demons."

²⁵Jesus knew their thoughts and replied, "Any kingdom divided by civil war is doomed. A town or family splintered by feuding will fall apart. ²⁶And if Satan is casting out Satan, he is divided and fighting against himself. His own kingdom will not survive. ²⁷And if I am empowered by Satan, what about your own exorcists? They cast out demons, too, so they will condemn you for what you have said. ²⁸But if I am casting out demons by the Spirit of God, then the Kingdom of God has arrived among you. ²⁹For who is powerful enough to enter the house

12:18-21 Isa 42:1-4 (Greek version for 42:4).   **12:24** Greek *Beelzeboul;* also in 12:27. Other manuscripts read *Beezeboul;* Latin version reads *Beelzebub.*

of a strong man and plunder his goods? Only someone even stronger—someone who could tie him up and then plunder his house.

³⁰"Anyone who isn't with me opposes me, and anyone who isn't working with me is actually working against me.

³¹"So I tell you, every sin and blasphemy can be forgiven—except blasphemy against the Holy Spirit, which will never be forgiven. ³²Anyone who speaks against the Son of Man can be forgiven, but anyone who speaks against the Holy Spirit will never be forgiven, either in this world or in the world to come.

³³"A tree is identified by its fruit. If a tree is good, its fruit will be good. If a tree is bad, its fruit will be bad. ³⁴You brood of snakes! How could evil men like you speak what is good and right? For whatever is in your heart determines what you say. ³⁵A good person produces good things from the treasury of a good heart, and an evil person produces evil things from the treasury of an evil heart. ³⁶And I tell you this, you must give an account on judgment day for every idle word you speak. ³⁷The words you say will either acquit you or condemn you."

The Sign of Jonah

³⁸One day some teachers of religious law and Pharisees came to Jesus and said, "Teacher, we want you to show us a miraculous sign to prove your authority."

³⁹But Jesus replied, "Only an evil, adulterous generation would demand a miraculous sign; but the only sign I will give them is the sign of the prophet Jonah. ⁴⁰For as Jonah was in the belly of the great fish for three days and three nights, so will the Son of Man be in the heart of the earth for three days and three nights.

⁴¹"The people of Nineveh will stand up against this generation on judgment day and condemn it, for they repented of their sins at the preaching of Jonah. Now someone greater than Jonah is here—but you refuse to repent. ⁴²The queen of Sheba* will also stand up against this generation on judgment day and condemn it, for she came from a distant land to hear the wisdom of Solomon. Now someone greater than Solomon is here—but you refuse to listen.

⁴³"When an evil* spirit leaves a person, it goes into the desert, seeking rest but finding none. ⁴⁴Then it says, 'I will return to the person I came from.' So it returns and finds its former home empty, swept, and in order. ⁴⁵Then the spirit finds seven other spirits more evil than itself, and they all enter the person and live there. And so that person is worse off than before. That will be the experience of this evil generation."

12:42 Greek *The queen of the south.*   **12:43** Greek *unclean.*

The True Family of Jesus

⁴⁶As Jesus was speaking to the crowd, his mother and brothers stood outside, asking to speak to him. ⁴⁷Someone told Jesus, "Your mother and your brothers are standing outside, and they want to speak to you."*

⁴⁸Jesus asked, "Who is my mother? Who are my brothers?" ⁴⁹Then he pointed to his disciples and said, "Look, these are my mother and brothers. ⁵⁰Anyone who does the will of my Father in heaven is my brother and sister and mother!"

Parable of the Farmer Scattering Seed

13 Later that same day Jesus left the house and sat beside the lake. ²A large crowd soon gathered around him, so he got into a boat. Then he sat there and taught as the people stood on the shore. ³He told many stories in the form of parables, such as this one:

"Listen! A farmer went out to plant some seeds. ⁴As he scattered them across his field, some seeds fell on a footpath, and the birds came and ate them. ⁵Other seeds fell on shallow soil with underlying rock. The seeds sprouted quickly because the soil was shallow. ⁶But the plants soon wilted under the hot sun, and since they didn't have deep roots, they died. ⁷Other seeds fell among thorns that grew up and choked out the tender plants. ⁸Still other seeds fell on fertile soil, and they produced a crop that was thirty, sixty, and even a hundred times as much as had been planted! ⁹Anyone with ears to hear should listen and understand."

¹⁰His disciples came and asked him, "Why do you use parables when you talk to the people?"

¹¹He replied, "You are permitted to understand the secrets* of the Kingdom of Heaven, but others are not. ¹²To those who listen to my teaching, more understanding will be given, and they will have an abundance of knowledge. But for those who are not listening, even what little understanding they have will be taken away from them. ¹³That is why I use these parables,

For they look, but they don't
    really see.
They hear, but they don't really
    listen or understand.

¹⁴This fulfills the prophecy of Isaiah that says,

'When you hear what I say,
    you will not understand.
When you see what I do,
    you will not comprehend.
¹⁵ For the hearts of these people
    are hardened,
and their ears cannot hear,
and they have closed their eyes—
    so their eyes cannot see,
and their ears cannot hear,

12:47 Some manuscripts do not include verse 47. Compare Mark 3:32 and Luke 8:20. **13:11** Greek *the mysteries.*

and their hearts cannot
     understand,
and they cannot turn to me
     and let me heal them.'*

[16]"But blessed are your eyes, because they see; and your ears, because they hear. [17]I tell you the truth, many prophets and righteous people longed to see what you see, but they didn't see it. And they longed to hear what you hear, but they didn't hear it.

[18]"Now listen to the explanation of the parable about the farmer planting seeds: [19]The seed that fell on the footpath represents those who hear the message about the Kingdom and don't understand it. Then the evil one comes and snatches away the seed that was planted in their hearts. [20]The seed on the rocky soil represents those who hear the message and immediately receive it with joy. [21]But since they don't have deep roots, they don't last long. They fall away as soon as they have problems or are persecuted for believing God's word. [22]The seed that fell among the thorns represents those who hear God's word, but all too quickly the message is crowded out by the worries of this life and the lure of wealth, so no fruit is produced. [23]The seed that fell on good soil represents those who truly hear and understand God's word and produce a harvest of thirty, sixty, or even a hundred times as much as had been planted!"

Parable of the Wheat and Weeds

[24]Here is another story Jesus told: "The Kingdom of Heaven is like a farmer who planted good seed in his field. [25]But that night as the workers slept, his enemy came and planted weeds among the wheat, then slipped away. [26]When the crop began to grow and produce grain, the weeds also grew.

[27]"The farmer's workers went to him and said, 'Sir, the field where you planted that good seed is full of weeds! Where did they come from?'

[28]"'An enemy has done this!' the farmer exclaimed.

"'Should we pull out the weeds?' they asked.

[29]"'No,' he replied, 'you'll uproot the wheat if you do. [30]Let both grow together until the harvest. Then I will tell the harvesters to sort out the weeds, tie them into bundles, and burn them, and to put the wheat in the barn.'"

Parable of the Mustard Seed

[31]Here is another illustration Jesus used: "The Kingdom of Heaven is like a mustard seed planted in a field. [32]It is the smallest of all seeds, but it becomes the largest of garden plants; it grows into a tree, and birds come and make nests in its branches."

13:14-15 Isa 6:9-10 (Greek version).

Parable of the Yeast

³³Jesus also used this illustration: "The Kingdom of Heaven is like the yeast a woman used in making bread. Even though she put only a little yeast in three measures of flour, it permeated every part of the dough."

³⁴Jesus always used stories and illustrations like these when speaking to the crowds. In fact, he never spoke to them without using such parables. ³⁵This fulfilled what God had spoken through the prophet:

> "I will speak to you in parables.
> I will explain things hidden
> since the creation of the
> world.*"

Parable of the Wheat and Weeds Explained

³⁶Then, leaving the crowds outside, Jesus went into the house. His disciples said, "Please explain to us the story of the weeds in the field."

³⁷Jesus replied, "The Son of Man* is the farmer who plants the good seed. ³⁸The field is the world, and the good seed represents the people of the Kingdom. The weeds are the people who belong to the evil one. ³⁹The enemy who planted the weeds among the wheat is the devil. The harvest is the end of the world,* and the harvesters are the angels.

⁴⁰"Just as the weeds are sorted out and burned in the fire, so it will be at the end of the world. ⁴¹The Son of Man will send his angels, and they will remove from his Kingdom everything that causes sin and all who do evil. ⁴²And the angels will throw them into the fiery furnace, where there will be weeping and gnashing of teeth. ⁴³Then the righteous will shine like the sun in their Father's Kingdom. Anyone with ears to hear should listen and understand!

Parables of the Hidden Treasure and the Pearl

⁴⁴"The Kingdom of Heaven is like a treasure that a man discovered hidden in a field. In his excitement, he hid it again and sold everything he owned to get enough money to buy the field.

⁴⁵"Again, the Kingdom of Heaven is like a merchant on the lookout for choice pearls. ⁴⁶When he discovered a pearl of great value, he sold everything he owned and bought it!

Parable of the Fishing Net

⁴⁷"Again, the Kingdom of Heaven is like a fishing net that was thrown into the water and caught fish of every kind. ⁴⁸When the net was full, they dragged it up onto the shore, sat down, and sorted the good fish into crates, but threw the bad ones away. ⁴⁹That is the way it will be at the end of the world. The angels will come and separate the wicked

13:35 Some manuscripts do not include *of the world.* Ps 78:2. **13:37** "Son of Man" is a title Jesus used for himself. **13:39** Or *the age;* also in 13:40, 49.

people from the righteous, ⁵⁰throwing the wicked into the fiery furnace, where there will be weeping and gnashing of teeth. ⁵¹Do you understand all these things?"

"Yes," they said, "we do."

⁵²Then he added, "Every teacher of religious law who becomes a disciple in the Kingdom of Heaven is like a homeowner who brings from his storeroom new gems of truth as well as old."

Jesus Rejected at Nazareth

⁵³When Jesus had finished telling these stories and illustrations, he left that part of the country. ⁵⁴He returned to Nazareth, his hometown. When he taught there in the synagogue, everyone was amazed and said, "Where does he get this wisdom and the power to do miracles?" ⁵⁵Then they scoffed, "He's just the carpenter's son, and we know Mary, his mother, and his brothers—James, Joseph,* Simon, and Judas. ⁵⁶All his sisters live right here among us. Where did he learn all these things?" ⁵⁷And they were deeply offended and refused to believe in him.

Then Jesus told them, "A prophet is honored everywhere except in his own hometown and among his own family." ⁵⁸And so he did only a few miracles there because of their unbelief.

The Death of John the Baptist

14 When Herod Antipas, the ruler of Galilee,* heard about Jesus, ²he said to his advisers, "This must be John the Baptist raised from the dead! That is why he can do such miracles."

³For Herod had arrested and imprisoned John as a favor to his wife Herodias (the former wife of Herod's brother Philip). ⁴John had been telling Herod, "It is against God's law for you to marry her." ⁵Herod wanted to kill John, but he was afraid of a riot, because all the people believed John was a prophet.

⁶But at a birthday party for Herod, Herodias's daughter performed a dance that greatly pleased him, ⁷so he promised with a vow to give her anything she wanted. ⁸At her mother's urging, the girl said, "I want the head of John the Baptist on a tray!" ⁹Then the king regretted what he had said; but because of the vow he had made in front of his guests, he issued the necessary orders. ¹⁰So John was beheaded in the prison, ¹¹and his head was brought on a tray and given to the girl, who took it to her mother. ¹²Later, John's disciples came for his body and buried it. Then they went and told Jesus what had happened.

Jesus Feeds Five Thousand

¹³As soon as Jesus heard the news, he left in a boat to a remote area to

13:55 Other manuscripts read *Joses;* still others read *John.* **14:1** Greek *Herod the tetrarch.* Herod Antipas was a son of King Herod and was ruler over Galilee.

be alone. But the crowds heard where he was headed and followed on foot from many towns. ¹⁴Jesus saw the huge crowd as he stepped from the boat, and he had compassion on them and healed their sick.

¹⁵That evening the disciples came to him and said, "This is a remote place, and it's already getting late. Send the crowds away so they can go to the villages and buy food for themselves."

¹⁶But Jesus said, "That isn't necessary—you feed them."

¹⁷"But we have only five loaves of bread and two fish!" they answered.

¹⁸"Bring them here," he said. ¹⁹Then he told the people to sit down on the grass. Jesus took the five loaves and two fish, looked up toward heaven, and blessed them. Then, breaking the loaves into pieces, he gave the bread to the disciples, who distributed it to the people. ²⁰They all ate as much as they wanted, and afterward, the disciples picked up twelve baskets of leftovers. ²¹About 5,000 men were fed that day, in addition to all the women and children!

Jesus Walks on Water

²²Immediately after this, Jesus insisted that his disciples get back into the boat and cross to the other side of the lake, while he sent the people home. ²³After sending them home, he went up into the hills by himself to pray. Night fell while he was there alone.

²⁴Meanwhile, the disciples were in trouble far away from land, for a strong wind had risen, and they were fighting heavy waves. ²⁵About three o'clock in the morning* Jesus came toward them, walking on the water. ²⁶When the disciples saw him walking on the water, they were terrified. In their fear, they cried out, "It's a ghost!"

²⁷But Jesus spoke to them at once. "Don't be afraid," he said. "Take courage. I am here!*"

²⁸Then Peter called to him, "Lord, if it's really you, tell me to come to you, walking on the water."

²⁹"Yes, come," Jesus said.

So Peter went over the side of the boat and walked on the water toward Jesus. ³⁰But when he saw the strong* wind and the waves, he was terrified and began to sink. "Save me, Lord!" he shouted.

³¹Jesus immediately reached out and grabbed him. "You have so little faith," Jesus said. "Why did you doubt me?"

³²When they climbed back into the boat, the wind stopped. ³³Then the disciples worshiped him. "You really are the Son of God!" they exclaimed.

³⁴After they had crossed the lake, they landed at Gennesaret. ³⁵When the people recognized Jesus, the news of his arrival spread quickly

14:25 Greek *In the fourth watch of the night.* **14:27** Or *The 'I Am' is here;* Greek reads *I am.* See Exod 3:14. **14:30** Some manuscripts do not include *strong.*

throughout the whole area, and soon people were bringing all their sick to be healed. [36]They begged him to let the sick touch at least the fringe of his robe, and all who touched him were healed.

Jesus Teaches about Inner Purity

15 Some Pharisees and teachers of religious law now arrived from Jerusalem to see Jesus. They asked him, [2]"Why do your disciples disobey our age-old tradition? For they ignore our tradition of ceremonial hand washing before they eat."

[3]Jesus replied, "And why do you, by your traditions, violate the direct commandments of God? [4]For instance, God says, 'Honor your father and mother,'* and 'Anyone who speaks disrespectfully of father or mother must be put to death.'* [5]But you say it is all right for people to say to their parents, 'Sorry, I can't help you. For I have vowed to give to God what I would have given to you.' [6]In this way, you say they don't need to honor their parents.* And so you cancel the word of God for the sake of your own tradition. [7]You hypocrites! Isaiah was right when he prophesied about you, for he wrote,

[8] 'These people honor me with
    their lips,
but their hearts are far
    from me.
[9] Their worship is a farce,
    for they teach man-made ideas
    as commands from God.'* "

[10]Then Jesus called to the crowd to come and hear. "Listen," he said, "and try to understand. [11]It's not what goes into your mouth that defiles you; you are defiled by the words that come out of your mouth."

[12]Then the disciples came to him and asked, "Do you realize you offended the Pharisees by what you just said?"

[13]Jesus replied, "Every plant not planted by my heavenly Father will be uprooted, [14]so ignore them. They are blind guides leading the blind, and if one blind person guides another, they will both fall into a ditch."

[15]Then Peter said to Jesus, "Explain to us the parable that says people aren't defiled by what they eat."

[16]"Don't you understand yet?" Jesus asked. [17]"Anything you eat passes through the stomach and then goes into the sewer. [18]But the words you speak come from the heart—that's what defiles you. [19]For from the heart come evil thoughts, murder, adultery, all sexual immorality, theft, lying, and slander.

15:4a Exod 20:12; Deut 5:16.   **15:4b** Exod 21:17 (Greek version); Lev 20:9 (Greek version). **15:6** Greek *their father;* other manuscripts read *their father or their mother.* **15:8-9** Isa 29:13 (Greek version).

[20]These are what defile you. Eating with unwashed hands will never defile you."

The Faith of a Gentile Woman

[21]Then Jesus left Galilee and went north to the region of Tyre and Sidon. [22]A Gentile* woman who lived there came to him, pleading, "Have mercy on me, O Lord, Son of David! For my daughter is possessed by a demon that torments her severely."

[23]But Jesus gave her no reply, not even a word. Then his disciples urged him to send her away. "Tell her to go away," they said. "She is bothering us with all her begging."

[24]Then Jesus said to the woman, "I was sent only to help God's lost sheep—the people of Israel."

[25]But she came and worshiped him, pleading again, "Lord, help me!"

[26]Jesus responded, "It isn't right to take food from the children and throw it to the dogs."

[27]She replied, "That's true, Lord, but even dogs are allowed to eat the scraps that fall beneath their masters' table."

[28]"Dear woman," Jesus said to her, "your faith is great. Your request is granted." And her daughter was instantly healed.

Jesus Heals Many People

[29]Jesus returned to the Sea of Galilee and climbed a hill and sat down. [30]A vast crowd brought to him people who were lame, blind, crippled, those who couldn't speak, and many others. They laid them before Jesus, and he healed them all. [31]The crowd was amazed! Those who hadn't been able to speak were talking, the crippled were made well, the lame were walking, and the blind could see again! And they praised the God of Israel.

Jesus Feeds Four Thousand

[32]Then Jesus called his disciples and told them, "I feel sorry for these people. They have been here with me for three days, and they have nothing left to eat. I don't want to send them away hungry, or they will faint along the way."

[33]The disciples replied, "Where would we get enough food here in the wilderness for such a huge crowd?"

[34]Jesus asked, "How much bread do you have?"

They replied, "Seven loaves, and a few small fish."

[35]So Jesus told all the people to sit down on the ground. [36]Then he took the seven loaves and the fish, thanked God for them, and broke them into pieces. He gave them to the disciples, who distributed the food to the crowd.

[37]They all ate as much as they wanted. Afterward, the disciples picked up seven large baskets of leftover food. [38]There were 4,000 men who were fed that day, in addition to all the women and children.

15:22 Greek *Canaanite.*

[39]Then Jesus sent the people home, and he got into a boat and crossed over to the region of Magadan.

Leaders Demand a Miraculous Sign

16 One day the Pharisees and Sadducees came to test Jesus, demanding that he show them a miraculous sign from heaven to prove his authority.

[2]He replied, "You know the saying, 'Red sky at night means fair weather tomorrow; [3]red sky in the morning means foul weather all day.' You know how to interpret the weather signs in the sky, but you don't know how to interpret the signs of the times!* [4]Only an evil, adulterous generation would demand a miraculous sign, but the only sign I will give them is the sign of the prophet Jonah.*" Then Jesus left them and went away.

Yeast of the Pharisees and Sadducees

[5]Later, after they crossed to the other side of the lake, the disciples discovered they had forgotten to bring any bread. [6]"Watch out!" Jesus warned them. "Beware of the yeast of the Pharisees and Sadducees."

[7]At this they began to argue with each other because they hadn't brought any bread. [8]Jesus knew what they were saying, so he said, "You have so little faith! Why are you arguing with each other about having no bread? [9]Don't you understand even yet? Don't you remember the 5,000 I fed with five loaves, and the baskets of leftovers you picked up? [10]Or the 4,000 I fed with seven loaves, and the large baskets of leftovers you picked up? [11]Why can't you understand that I'm not talking about bread? So again I say, 'Beware of the yeast of the Pharisees and Sadducees.'"

[12]Then at last they understood that he wasn't speaking about the yeast in bread, but about the deceptive teaching of the Pharisees and Sadducees.

Peter's Declaration about Jesus

[13]When Jesus came to the region of Caesarea Philippi, he asked his disciples, "Who do people say that the Son of Man is?"*

[14]"Well," they replied, "some say John the Baptist, some say Elijah, and others say Jeremiah or one of the other prophets."

[15]Then he asked them, "But who do you say I am?"

[16]Simon Peter answered, "You are the Messiah,* the Son of the living God."

[17]Jesus replied, "You are blessed, Simon son of John,* because my

---

16:2-3 Several manuscripts do not include any of the words in 16:2-3 after *He replied.* **16:4** Greek *the sign of Jonah.* **16:13** "Son of Man" is a title Jesus used for himself. **16:16** Or *the Christ. Messiah* (a Hebrew term) and *Christ* (a Greek term) both mean "anointed one." **16:17** Greek *Simon bar-Jonah;* see John 1:42; 21:15-17.

Father in heaven has revealed this to you. You did not learn this from any human being. [18]Now I say to you that you are Peter (which means 'rock'),* and upon this rock I will build my church, and all the powers of hell* will not conquer it. [19]And I will give you the keys of the Kingdom of Heaven. Whatever you forbid* on earth will be forbidden in heaven, and whatever you permit* on earth will be permitted in heaven."

[20]Then he sternly warned the disciples not to tell anyone that he was the Messiah.

Jesus Predicts His Death

[21]From then on Jesus* began to tell his disciples plainly that it was necessary for him to go to Jerusalem, and that he would suffer many terrible things at the hands of the elders, the leading priests, and the teachers of religious law. He would be killed, but on the third day he would be raised from the dead.

[22]But Peter took him aside and began to reprimand him* for saying such things. "Heaven forbid, Lord," he said. "This will never happen to you!"

[23]Jesus turned to Peter and said, "Get away from me, Satan! You are a dangerous trap to me. You are seeing things merely from a human point of view, not from God's."

[24]Then Jesus said to his disciples, "If any of you wants to be my follower, you must give up your own way, take up your cross, and follow me. [25]If you try to hang on to your life, you will lose it. But if you give up your life for my sake, you will save it. [26]And what do you benefit if you gain the whole world but lose your own soul?* Is anything worth more than your soul? [27]For the Son of Man will come with his angels in the glory of his Father and will judge all people according to their deeds. [28]And I tell you the truth, some standing here right now will not die before they see the Son of Man coming in his Kingdom."

The Transfiguration

17 Six days later Jesus took Peter and the two brothers, James and John, and led them up a high mountain to be alone. [2]As the men watched, Jesus' appearance was transformed so that his face shone like the sun, and his clothes became as white as light. [3]Suddenly, Moses and Elijah appeared and began talking with Jesus.

[4]Peter exclaimed, "Lord, it's wonderful for us to be here! If you want, I'll make three shelters as memorials*—one for you, one for Moses, and one for Elijah."

[5]But even as he spoke, a bright cloud overshadowed them, and a voice from the cloud said, "This is

16:18a Greek *that you are Peter.* **16:18b** Greek *and the gates of Hades.* **16:19a** Or *bind,* or *lock.* **16:19b** Or *loose,* or *open.* **16:21** Some manuscripts read *Jesus the Messiah.* **16:22** Or *began to correct him.* **16:26** Or *your self?* also in 16:26b. **17:4** Greek *three tabernacles.*

my dearly loved Son, who brings me great joy. Listen to him." ⁶The disciples were terrified and fell face down on the ground.

⁷Then Jesus came over and touched them. "Get up," he said. "Don't be afraid." ⁸And when they looked up, Moses and Elijah were gone, and they saw only Jesus.

⁹As they went back down the mountain, Jesus commanded them, "Don't tell anyone what you have seen until the Son of Man* has been raised from the dead."

¹⁰Then his disciples asked him, "Why do the teachers of religious law insist that Elijah must return before the Messiah comes?*"

¹¹Jesus replied, "Elijah is indeed coming first to get everything ready. ¹²But I tell you, Elijah has already come, but he wasn't recognized, and they chose to abuse him. And in the same way they will also make the Son of Man suffer." ¹³Then the disciples realized he was talking about John the Baptist.

Jesus Heals a Demon-Possessed Boy

¹⁴At the foot of the mountain, a large crowd was waiting for them. A man came and knelt before Jesus and said, ¹⁵"Lord, have mercy on my son. He has seizures and suffers terribly. He often falls into the fire or into the water. ¹⁶So I brought him to your disciples, but they couldn't heal him."

¹⁷Jesus said, "You faithless and corrupt people! How long must I be with you? How long must I put up with you? Bring the boy here to me." ¹⁸Then Jesus rebuked the demon in the boy, and it left him. From that moment the boy was well.

¹⁹Afterward the disciples asked Jesus privately, "Why couldn't we cast out that demon?"

²⁰"You don't have enough faith," Jesus told them. "I tell you the truth, if you had faith even as small as a mustard seed, you could say to this mountain, 'Move from here to there,' and it would move. Nothing would be impossible.*"

Jesus Again Predicts His Death

²²After they gathered again in Galilee, Jesus told them, "The Son of Man is going to be betrayed into the hands of his enemies. ²³He will be killed, but on the third day he will be raised from the dead." And the disciples were filled with grief.

Payment of the Temple Tax

²⁴On their arrival in Capernaum, the collectors of the Temple tax* came to Peter and asked him, "Doesn't your teacher pay the Temple tax?"

²⁵"Yes, he does," Peter replied. Then he went into the house.

17:9 "Son of Man" is a title Jesus used for himself. 17:10 Greek *that Elijah must come first?*
17:20 Some manuscripts add verse 21, *But this kind of demon won't leave except by prayer and fasting.* Compare Mark 9:29. 17:24 Greek *the two-drachma [tax];* also in 17:24b. See Exod 30:13-16; Neh 10:32-33.

But before he had a chance to speak, Jesus asked him, "What do you think, Peter?* Do kings tax their own people or the people they have conquered?*"

²⁶"They tax the people they have conquered," Peter replied.

"Well, then," Jesus said, "the citizens are free! ²⁷However, we don't want to offend them, so go down to the lake and throw in a line. Open the mouth of the first fish you catch, and you will find a large silver coin.* Take it and pay the tax for both of us."

The Greatest in the Kingdom

18 About that time the disciples came to Jesus and asked, "Who is greatest in the Kingdom of Heaven?"

²Jesus called a little child to him and put the child among them. ³Then he said, "I tell you the truth, unless you turn from your sins and become like little children, you will never get into the Kingdom of Heaven. ⁴So anyone who becomes as humble as this little child is the greatest in the Kingdom of Heaven.

⁵"And anyone who welcomes a little child like this on my behalf* is welcoming me. ⁶But if you cause one of these little ones who trusts in me to fall into sin, it would be better for you to have a large millstone tied around your neck and be drowned in the depths of the sea.

⁷"What sorrow awaits the world, because it tempts people to sin. Temptations are inevitable, but what sorrow awaits the person who does the tempting. ⁸So if your hand or foot causes you to sin, cut it off and throw it away. It's better to enter eternal life with only one hand or one foot than to be thrown into eternal fire with both of your hands and feet. ⁹And if your eye causes you to sin, gouge it out and throw it away. It's better to enter eternal life with only one eye than to have two eyes and be thrown into the fire of hell.*

¹⁰"Beware that you don't look down on any of these little ones. For I tell you that in heaven their angels are always in the presence of my heavenly Father.*

Parable of the Lost Sheep

¹²"If a man has a hundred sheep and one of them wanders away, what will he do? Won't he leave the ninety-nine others on the hills and go out to search for the one that is lost? ¹³And if he finds it, I tell you the truth, he will rejoice over it more than over the ninety-nine that didn't wander away! ¹⁴In the same way, it is not my heavenly Father's will that even one of these little ones should perish.

17:25a Greek *Simon?* **17:25b** Greek *their sons or others?* **17:27** Greek *a stater* [a Greek coin equivalent to four drachmas]. **18:5** Greek *in my name.* **18:9** Greek *the Gehenna of fire.* **18:10** Some manuscripts add verse 11, *And the Son of Man came to save those who are lost.* Compare Luke 19:10.

Correcting Another Believer

[15]"If another believer* sins against you,* go privately and point out the offense. If the other person listens and confesses it, you have won that person back. [16]But if you are unsuccessful, take one or two others with you and go back again, so that everything you say may be confirmed by two or three witnesses. [17]If the person still refuses to listen, take your case to the church. Then if he or she won't accept the church's decision, treat that person as a pagan or a corrupt tax collector.

[18]"I tell you the truth, whatever you forbid* on earth will be forbidden in heaven, and whatever you permit* on earth will be permitted in heaven.

[19]"I also tell you this: If two of you agree here on earth concerning anything you ask, my Father in heaven will do it for you. [20]For where two or three gather together as my followers,* I am there among them."

Parable of the Unforgiving Debtor

[21]Then Peter came to him and asked, "Lord, how often should I forgive someone* who sins against me? Seven times?"

[22]"No, not seven times," Jesus replied, "but seventy times seven!*

[23]"Therefore, the Kingdom of Heaven can be compared to a king who decided to bring his accounts up to date with servants who had borrowed money from him. [24]In the process, one of his debtors was brought in who owed him millions of dollars.* [25]He couldn't pay, so his master ordered that he be sold—along with his wife, his children, and everything he owned—to pay the debt.

[26]"But the man fell down before his master and begged him, 'Please, be patient with me, and I will pay it all.' [27]Then his master was filled with pity for him, and he released him and forgave his debt.

[28]"But when the man left the king, he went to a fellow servant who owed him a few thousand dollars.* He grabbed him by the throat and demanded instant payment.

[29]"His fellow servant fell down before him and begged for a little more time. 'Be patient with me, and I will pay it,' he pleaded. [30]But his creditor wouldn't wait. He had the man arrested and put in prison until the debt could be paid in full.

[31]"When some of the other servants saw this, they were very upset. They went to the king and told him everything that had happened. [32]Then the king called in the man he had forgiven and said, 'You evil servant! I forgave you that tremendous debt because you pleaded with me.

18:15a Greek *If your brother.* 18:15b Some manuscripts do not include *against you.* 18:18a Or *bind,* or *lock.* 18:18b Or *loose,* or *open.* 18:20 Greek *gather together in my name.* 18:21 Greek *my brother.* 18:22 Or *seventy-seven times.* 18:24 Greek *10,000 talents* [375 tons or 340 metric tons of silver]. 18:28 Greek *100 denarii.* A denarius was equivalent to a laborer's full day's wage.

³³Shouldn't you have mercy on your fellow servant, just as I had mercy on you?' ³⁴Then the angry king sent the man to prison to be tortured until he had paid his entire debt.

³⁵"That's what my heavenly Father will do to you if you refuse to forgive your brothers and sisters* from your heart."

Discussion about Divorce and Marriage

19 When Jesus had finished saying these things, he left Galilee and went down to the region of Judea east of the Jordan River. ²Large crowds followed him there, and he healed their sick.

³Some Pharisees came and tried to trap him with this question: "Should a man be allowed to divorce his wife for just any reason?"

⁴"Haven't you read the Scriptures?" Jesus replied. "They record that from the beginning 'God made them male and female.'*" ⁵And he said, "'This explains why a man leaves his father and mother and is joined to his wife, and the two are united into one.'* ⁶Since they are no longer two but one, let no one split apart what God has joined together."

⁷"Then why did Moses say in the law that a man could give his wife a written notice of divorce and send her away?"* they asked.

⁸Jesus replied, "Moses permitted divorce only as a concession to your hard hearts, but it was not what God had originally intended. ⁹And I tell you this, whoever divorces his wife and marries someone else commits adultery—unless his wife has been unfaithful.*"

¹⁰Jesus' disciples then said to him, "If this is the case, it is better not to marry!"

¹¹"Not everyone can accept this statement," Jesus said. "Only those whom God helps. ¹²Some are born as eunuchs, some have been made eunuchs by others, and some choose not to marry* for the sake of the Kingdom of Heaven. Let anyone accept this who can."

Jesus Blesses the Children

¹³One day some parents brought their children to Jesus so he could lay his hands on them and pray for them. But the disciples scolded the parents for bothering him.

¹⁴But Jesus said, "Let the children come to me. Don't stop them! For the Kingdom of Heaven belongs to those who are like these children." ¹⁵And he placed his hands on their heads and blessed them before he left.

The Rich Man

¹⁶Someone came to Jesus with this question: "Teacher,* what good deed must I do to have eternal life?"

18:35 Greek *your brother.* **19:4** Gen 1:27; 5:2. **19:5** Gen 2:24. **19:7** See Deut 24:1. **19:9** Some manuscripts add *And anyone who marries a divorced woman commits adultery.* Compare Matt 5:32. **19:12** Greek *and some make themselves eunuchs.* **19:16** Some manuscripts read *Good Teacher.*

[17]"Why ask me about what is good?" Jesus replied. "There is only One who is good. But to answer your question—if you want to receive eternal life, keep* the commandments."

[18]"Which ones?" the man asked.

And Jesus replied: " 'You must not murder. You must not commit adultery. You must not steal. You must not testify falsely. [19]Honor your father and mother. Love your neighbor as yourself.'* "

[20]"I've obeyed all these commandments," the young man replied. "What else must I do?"

[21]Jesus told him, "If you want to be perfect, go and sell all your possessions and give the money to the poor, and you will have treasure in heaven. Then come, follow me."

[22]But when the young man heard this, he went away sad, for he had many possessions.

[23]Then Jesus said to his disciples, "I tell you the truth, it is very hard for a rich person to enter the Kingdom of Heaven. [24]I'll say it again—it is easier for a camel to go through the eye of a needle than for a rich person to enter the Kingdom of God!"

[25]The disciples were astounded. "Then who in the world can be saved?" they asked.

[26]Jesus looked at them intently and said, "Humanly speaking, it is impossible. But with God everything is possible."

[27]Then Peter said to him, "We've given up everything to follow you. What will we get?"

[28]Jesus replied, "I assure you that when the world is made new* and the Son of Man* sits upon his glorious throne, you who have been my followers will also sit on twelve thrones, judging the twelve tribes of Israel. [29]And everyone who has given up houses or brothers or sisters or father or mother or children or property, for my sake, will receive a hundred times as much in return and will inherit eternal life. [30]But many who are the greatest now will be least important then, and those who seem least important now will be the greatest then.*

Parable of the Vineyard Workers

20 "For the Kingdom of Heaven is like the landowner who went out early one morning to hire workers for his vineyard. [2]He agreed to pay the normal daily wage* and sent them out to work.

[3]"At nine o'clock in the morning he was passing through the marketplace and saw some people standing around doing nothing. [4]So he hired them, telling them he would pay them whatever was right at the

---

19:17 Some manuscripts read *continue to keep.* **19:18-19** Exod 20:12-16; Deut 5:16-20; Lev 19:18. **19:28a** Or *in the regeneration.* **19:28b** "Son of Man" is a title Jesus used for himself. **19:30** Greek *But many who are first will be last; and the last, first.* **20:2** Greek *a denarius,* the payment for a full day's labor; similarly in 20:9, 10, 13.

end of the day. ⁵So they went to work in the vineyard. At noon and again at three o'clock he did the same thing.

⁶"At five o'clock that afternoon he was in town again and saw some more people standing around. He asked them, 'Why haven't you been working today?'

⁷"They replied, 'Because no one hired us.'

"The landowner told them, 'Then go out and join the others in my vineyard.'

⁸"That evening he told the foreman to call the workers in and pay them, beginning with the last workers first. ⁹When those hired at five o'clock were paid, each received a full day's wage. ¹⁰When those hired first came to get their pay, they assumed they would receive more. But they, too, were paid a day's wage. ¹¹When they received their pay, they protested to the owner, ¹²'Those people worked only one hour, and yet you've paid them just as much as you paid us who worked all day in the scorching heat.'

¹³"He answered one of them, 'Friend, I haven't been unfair! Didn't you agree to work all day for the usual wage? ¹⁴Take your money and go. I wanted to pay this last worker the same as you. ¹⁵Is it against the law for me to do what I want with my money? Should you be jealous because I am kind to others?'

¹⁶"So those who are last now will be first then, and those who are first will be last."

Jesus Again Predicts His Death

¹⁷As Jesus was going up to Jerusalem, he took the twelve disciples aside privately and told them what was going to happen to him. ¹⁸"Listen," he said, "we're going up to Jerusalem, where the Son of Man* will be betrayed to the leading priests and the teachers of religious law. They will sentence him to die. ¹⁹Then they will hand him over to the Romans* to be mocked, flogged with a whip, and crucified. But on the third day he will be raised from the dead."

Jesus Teaches about Serving Others

²⁰Then the mother of James and John, the sons of Zebedee, came to Jesus with her sons. She knelt respectfully to ask a favor. ²¹"What is your request?" he asked.

She replied, "In your Kingdom, please let my two sons sit in places of honor next to you, one on your right and the other on your left."

²²But Jesus answered by saying to them, "You don't know what you are asking! Are you able to drink from the bitter cup of suffering I am about to drink?"

"Oh yes," they replied, "we are able!"

²³Jesus told them, "You will indeed

20:18 "Son of Man" is a title Jesus used for himself. 20:19 Greek *the Gentiles.*

drink from my bitter cup. But I have no right to say who will sit on my right or my left. My Father has prepared those places for the ones he has chosen."

[24]When the ten other disciples heard what James and John had asked, they were indignant. [25]But Jesus called them together and said, "You know that the rulers in this world lord it over their people, and officials flaunt their authority over those under them. [26]But among you it will be different. Whoever wants to be a leader among you must be your servant, [27]and whoever wants to be first among you must become your slave. [28]For even the Son of Man came not to be served but to serve others and to give his life as a ransom for many."

Jesus Heals Two Blind Men

[29]As Jesus and the disciples left the town of Jericho, a large crowd followed behind. [30]Two blind men were sitting beside the road. When they heard that Jesus was coming that way, they began shouting, "Lord, Son of David, have mercy on us!"

[31]"Be quiet!" the crowd yelled at them.

But they only shouted louder, "Lord, Son of David, have mercy on us!"

[32]When Jesus heard them, he stopped and called, "What do you want me to do for you?"

[33]"Lord," they said, "we want to see!" [34]Jesus felt sorry for them and touched their eyes. Instantly they could see! Then they followed him.

Jesus' Triumphant Entry

21 As Jesus and the disciples approached Jerusalem, they came to the town of Bethphage on the Mount of Olives. Jesus sent two of them on ahead. [2]"Go into the village over there," he said. "As soon as you enter it, you will see a donkey tied there, with its colt beside it. Untie them and bring them to me. [3]If anyone asks what you are doing, just say, 'The Lord needs them,' and he will immediately let you take them."

[4]This took place to fulfill the prophecy that said,

[5] "Tell the people of Jerusalem,*
    'Look, your King is coming
        to you.
He is humble, riding on
    a donkey—
    riding on a donkey's colt.'"*

[6]The two disciples did as Jesus commanded. [7]They brought the donkey and the colt to him and threw their garments over the colt, and he sat on it.*

[8]Most of the crowd spread their garments on the road ahead of him, and others cut branches from the

21:5a Greek *Tell the daughter of Zion.* Isa 62:11. **21:5b** Zech 9:9. **21:7** Greek *over them, and he sat on them.*

trees and spread them on the road. ⁹Jesus was in the center of the procession, and the people all around him were shouting,

> "Praise God* for the Son of
>   David!
> Blessings on the one who
>   comes in the name of the
>   LORD!
> Praise God in highest
>   heaven!"*

¹⁰The entire city of Jerusalem was in an uproar as he entered. "Who is this?" they asked.

¹¹And the crowds replied, "It's Jesus, the prophet from Nazareth in Galilee."

Jesus Clears the Temple

¹²Jesus entered the Temple and began to drive out all the people buying and selling animals for sacrifice. He knocked over the tables of the money changers and the chairs of those selling doves. ¹³He said to them, "The Scriptures declare, 'My Temple will be called a house of prayer,' but you have turned it into a den of thieves!"*

¹⁴The blind and the lame came to him in the Temple, and he healed them. ¹⁵The leading priests and the teachers of religious law saw these wonderful miracles and heard even the children in the Temple shouting, "Praise God for the Son of David."

But the leaders were indignant. ¹⁶They asked Jesus, "Do you hear what these children are saying?"

"Yes," Jesus replied. "Haven't you ever read the Scriptures? For they say, 'You have taught children and infants to give you praise.'* " ¹⁷Then he returned to Bethany, where he stayed overnight.

Jesus Curses the Fig Tree

¹⁸In the morning, as Jesus was returning to Jerusalem, he was hungry, ¹⁹and he noticed a fig tree beside the road. He went over to see if there were any figs, but there were only leaves. Then he said to it, "May you never bear fruit again!" And immediately the fig tree withered up.

²⁰The disciples were amazed when they saw this and asked, "How did the fig tree wither so quickly?"

²¹Then Jesus told them, "I tell you the truth, if you have faith and don't doubt, you can do things like this and much more. You can even say to this mountain, 'May you be lifted up and thrown into the sea,' and it will happen. ²²You can pray for anything, and if you have faith, you will receive it."

The Authority of Jesus Challenged

²³When Jesus returned to the Temple and began teaching, the leading priests and elders came up to him. They demanded, "By what authority

---

21:9a Greek *Hosanna*, an exclamation of praise that literally means "save now"; also in 21:9b, 15. **21:9b** Pss 118:25-26; 148:1. **21:13** Isa 56:7; Jer 7:11. **21:16** Ps 8:2 (Greek version).

are you doing all these things? Who gave you the right?"

[24]"I'll tell you by what authority I do these things if you answer one question," Jesus replied. [25]"Did John's authority to baptize come from heaven, or was it merely human?"

They talked it over among themselves. "If we say it was from heaven, he will ask us why we didn't believe John. [26]But if we say it was merely human, we'll be mobbed because the people believe John was a prophet." [27]So they finally replied, "We don't know."

And Jesus responded, "Then I won't tell you by what authority I do these things.

Parable of the Two Sons

[28]"But what do you think about this? A man with two sons told the older boy, 'Son, go out and work in the vineyard today.' [29]The son answered, 'No, I won't go,' but later he changed his mind and went anyway. [30]Then the father told the other son, 'You go,' and he said, 'Yes, sir, I will.' But he didn't go.

[31]"Which of the two obeyed his father?"

They replied, "The first."*

Then Jesus explained his meaning: "I tell you the truth, corrupt tax collectors and prostitutes will get into the Kingdom of God before you do. [32]For John the Baptist came and showed you the right way to live, but you didn't believe him, while tax collectors and prostitutes did. And even when you saw this happening, you refused to believe him and repent of your sins.

Parable of the Evil Farmers

[33]"Now listen to another story. A certain landowner planted a vineyard, built a wall around it, dug a pit for pressing out the grape juice, and built a lookout tower. Then he leased the vineyard to tenant farmers and moved to another country. [34]At the time of the grape harvest, he sent his servants to collect his share of the crop. [35]But the farmers grabbed his servants, beat one, killed one, and stoned another. [36]So the landowner sent a larger group of his servants to collect for him, but the results were the same.

[37]"Finally, the owner sent his son, thinking, 'Surely they will respect my son.'

[38]"But when the tenant farmers saw his son coming, they said to one another, 'Here comes the heir to this estate. Come on, let's kill him and get the estate for ourselves!' [39]So they grabbed him, dragged him out of the vineyard, and murdered him.

[40]"When the owner of the vineyard returns," Jesus asked, "what

21:29-31 Other manuscripts read *"The second."* In still other manuscripts the first son says "Yes" but does nothing, the second son says "No" but then repents and goes, and the answer to Jesus' question is that the second son obeyed his father.

do you think he will do to those farmers?"

[41]The religious leaders replied, "He will put the wicked men to a horrible death and lease the vineyard to others who will give him his share of the crop after each harvest."

[42]Then Jesus asked them, "Didn't you ever read this in the Scriptures?

'The stone that the builders
    rejected
  has now become the
    cornerstone.
This is the Lord's doing,
  and it is wonderful to see.'*

[43]I tell you, the Kingdom of God will be taken away from you and given to a nation that will produce the proper fruit. [44]Anyone who stumbles over that stone will be broken to pieces, and it will crush anyone it falls on.*"

[45]When the leading priests and Pharisees heard this parable, they realized he was telling the story against them—they were the wicked farmers. [46]They wanted to arrest him, but they were afraid of the crowds, who considered Jesus to be a prophet.

Parable of the Great Feast

22 Jesus also told them other parables. He said, [2]"The Kingdom of Heaven can be illustrated by the story of a king who prepared a great wedding feast for his son. [3]When the banquet was ready, he sent his servants to notify those who were invited. But they all refused to come!

[4]"So he sent other servants to tell them, 'The feast has been prepared. The bulls and fattened cattle have been killed, and everything is ready. Come to the banquet!' [5]But the guests he had invited ignored them and went their own way, one to his farm, another to his business. [6]Others seized his messengers and insulted them and killed them.

[7]"The king was furious, and he sent out his army to destroy the murderers and burn their town. [8]And he said to his servants, 'The wedding feast is ready, and the guests I invited aren't worthy of the honor. [9]Now go out to the street corners and invite everyone you see.' [10]So the servants brought in everyone they could find, good and bad alike, and the banquet hall was filled with guests.

[11]"But when the king came in to meet the guests, he noticed a man who wasn't wearing the proper clothes for a wedding. [12]'Friend,' he asked, 'how is it that you are here without wedding clothes?' But the man had no reply. [13]Then the king said to his aides, 'Bind his hands and feet and throw him into the outer darkness, where there will be weeping and gnashing of teeth.'

[14]"For many are called, but few are chosen."

21:42 Ps 118:22-23. **21:44** This verse is not included in some early manuscripts. Compare Luke 20:18.

Taxes for Caesar

¹⁵Then the Pharisees met together to plot how to trap Jesus into saying something for which he could be arrested. ¹⁶They sent some of their disciples, along with the supporters of Herod, to meet with him. "Teacher," they said, "we know how honest you are. You teach the way of God truthfully. You are impartial and don't play favorites. ¹⁷Now tell us what you think about this: Is it right to pay taxes to Caesar or not?"

¹⁸But Jesus knew their evil motives. "You hypocrites!" he said. "Why are you trying to trap me? ¹⁹Here, show me the coin used for the tax." When they handed him a Roman coin,* ²⁰he asked, "Whose picture and title are stamped on it?"

²¹"Caesar's," they replied.

"Well, then," he said, "give to Caesar what belongs to Caesar, and give to God what belongs to God."

²²His reply amazed them, and they went away.

Discussion about Resurrection

²³That same day Jesus was approached by some Sadducees—religious leaders who say there is no resurrection from the dead. They posed this question: ²⁴"Teacher, Moses said, 'If a man dies without children, his brother should marry the widow and have a child who will carry on the brother's name.'* ²⁵Well, suppose there were seven brothers. The oldest one married and then died without children, so his brother married the widow. ²⁶But the second brother also died, and the third brother married her. This continued with all seven of them. ²⁷Last of all, the woman also died. ²⁸So tell us, whose wife will she be in the resurrection? For all seven were married to her."

²⁹Jesus replied, "Your mistake is that you don't know the Scriptures, and you don't know the power of God. ³⁰For when the dead rise, they will neither marry nor be given in marriage. In this respect they will be like the angels in heaven.

³¹"But now, as to whether there will be a resurrection of the dead—haven't you ever read about this in the Scriptures? Long after Abraham, Isaac, and Jacob had died, God said,* ³²'I am the God of Abraham, the God of Isaac, and the God of Jacob.'* So he is the God of the living, not the dead."

³³When the crowds heard him, they were astounded at his teaching.

The Most Important Commandment

³⁴But when the Pharisees heard that he had silenced the Sadducees with his reply, they met together to question him again. ³⁵One of them, an expert in religious law, tried to trap him with this question: ³⁶"Teacher, which is the most im-

22:19 Greek *a denarius*.   22:24 Deut 25:5-6.   22:31 Greek *read about this? God said*.
22:32 Exod 3:6.

portant commandment in the law of Moses?"

37Jesus replied, "'You must love the LORD your God with all your heart, all your soul, and all your mind.'* 38This is the first and greatest commandment. 39A second is equally important: 'Love your neighbor as yourself.'* 40The entire law and all the demands of the prophets are based on these two commandments."

Whose Son Is the Messiah?

41Then, surrounded by the Pharisees, Jesus asked them a question: 42"What do you think about the Messiah? Whose son is he?"

They replied, "He is the son of David."

43Jesus responded, "Then why does David, speaking under the inspiration of the Spirit, call the Messiah 'my Lord'? For David said,

44 'The LORD said to my Lord,
    Sit in the place of honor at my
        right hand
        until I humble your enemies
            beneath your feet.'*

45Since David called the Messiah 'my Lord,' how can the Messiah be his son?"

46No one could answer him. And after that, no one dared to ask him any more questions.

Jesus Criticizes the Religious Leaders

23 Then Jesus said to the crowds and to his disciples, 2"The teachers of religious law and the Pharisees are the official interpreters of the law of Moses.* 3So practice and obey whatever they tell you, but don't follow their example. For they don't practice what they teach. 4They crush people with unbearable religious demands and never lift a finger to ease the burden.

5"Everything they do is for show. On their arms they wear extra wide prayer boxes with Scripture verses inside, and they wear robes with extra long tassels.* 6And they love to sit at the head table at banquets and in the seats of honor in the synagogues. 7They love to receive respectful greetings as they walk in the marketplaces, and to be called 'Rabbi.'*

8"Don't let anyone call you 'Rabbi,' for you have only one teacher, and all of you are equal as brothers and sisters.* 9And don't address anyone here on earth as 'Father,' for only God in heaven is your Father. 10And don't let anyone call you 'Teacher,' for you have only one teacher, the Messiah. 11The greatest among you must be a servant. 12But those who exalt themselves will be humbled, and those who humble themselves will be exalted.

22:37 Deut 6:5. 22:39 Lev 19:18. 22:44 Ps 110:1. 23:2 Greek and the Pharisees sit in the seat of Moses. 23:5 Greek They enlarge their phylacteries and lengthen their tassels. 23:7 Rabbi, from Aramaic, means "master" or "teacher." 23:8 Greek brothers.

¹³"What sorrow awaits you teachers of religious law and you Pharisees. Hypocrites! For you shut the door of the Kingdom of Heaven in people's faces. You won't go in yourselves, and you don't let others enter either.*

¹⁵"What sorrow awaits you teachers of religious law and you Pharisees. Hypocrites! For you cross land and sea to make one convert, and then you turn that person into twice the child of hell* you yourselves are!

¹⁶"Blind guides! What sorrow awaits you! For you say that it means nothing to swear 'by God's Temple,' but that it is binding to swear 'by the gold in the Temple.' ¹⁷Blind fools! Which is more important—the gold or the Temple that makes the gold sacred? ¹⁸And you say that to swear 'by the altar' is not binding, but to swear 'by the gifts on the altar' is binding. ¹⁹How blind! For which is more important—the gift on the altar or the altar that makes the gift sacred? ²⁰When you swear 'by the altar,' you are swearing by it and by everything on it. ²¹And when you swear 'by the Temple,' you are swearing by it and by God, who lives in it. ²²And when you swear 'by heaven,' you are swearing by the throne of God and by God, who sits on the throne.

²³"What sorrow awaits you teachers of religious law and you Pharisees. Hypocrites! For you are careful to tithe even the tiniest income from your herb gardens,* but you ignore the more important aspects of the law—justice, mercy, and faith. You should tithe, yes, but do not neglect the more important things. ²⁴Blind guides! You strain your water so you won't accidentally swallow a gnat, but you swallow a camel!*

²⁵"What sorrow awaits you teachers of religious law and you Pharisees. Hypocrites! For you are so careful to clean the outside of the cup and the dish, but inside you are filthy—full of greed and self-indulgence! ²⁶You blind Pharisee! First wash the inside of the cup and the dish,* and then the outside will become clean, too.

²⁷"What sorrow awaits you teachers of religious law and you Pharisees. Hypocrites! For you are like whitewashed tombs—beautiful on the outside but filled on the inside with dead people's bones and all sorts of impurity. ²⁸Outwardly you look like righteous people, but inwardly your hearts are filled with hypocrisy and lawlessness.

23:13 Some manuscripts add verse 14, *What sorrow awaits you teachers of religious law and you Pharisees. Hypocrites! You shamelessly cheat widows out of their property and then pretend to be pious by making long prayers in public. Because of this, you will be severely punished.* Compare Mark 12:40 and Luke 20:47. 23:15 Greek *of Gehenna;* also in 23:33. 23:23 Greek *tithe the mint, the dill, and the cumin.* 23:24 See Lev 11:4, 23, where gnats and camels are both forbidden as food. 23:26 Some manuscripts do not include *and the dish.*

²⁹"What sorrow awaits you teachers of religious law and you Pharisees. Hypocrites! For you build tombs for the prophets your ancestors killed, and you decorate the monuments of the godly people your ancestors destroyed. ³⁰Then you say, 'If we had lived in the days of our ancestors, we would never have joined them in killing the prophets.'

³¹"But in saying that, you testify against yourselves that you are indeed the descendants of those who murdered the prophets. ³²Go ahead and finish what your ancestors started. ³³Snakes! Sons of vipers! How will you escape the judgment of hell?

³⁴"Therefore, I am sending you prophets and wise men and teachers of religious law. But you will kill some by crucifixion, and you will flog others with whips in your synagogues, chasing them from city to city. ³⁵As a result, you will be held responsible for the murder of all godly people of all time—from the murder of righteous Abel to the murder of Zechariah son of Berekiah, whom you killed in the Temple between the sanctuary and the altar. ³⁶I tell you the truth, this judgment will fall on this very generation.

Jesus Grieves over Jerusalem

³⁷"O Jerusalem, Jerusalem, the city that kills the prophets and stones God's messengers! How often I have wanted to gather your children together as a hen protects her chicks beneath her wings, but you wouldn't let me. ³⁸And now, look, your house is abandoned and desolate.* ³⁹For I tell you this, you will never see me again until you say, 'Blessings on the one who comes in the name of the LORD!'* "

Jesus Speaks about the Future

24 As Jesus was leaving the Temple grounds, his disciples pointed out to him the various Temple buildings. ²But he responded, "Do you see all these buildings? I tell you the truth, they will be completely demolished. Not one stone will be left on top of another!"

³Later, Jesus sat on the Mount of Olives. His disciples came to him privately and said, "Tell us, when will all this happen? What sign will signal your return and the end of the world?*"

⁴Jesus told them, "Don't let anyone mislead you, ⁵for many will come in my name, claiming, 'I am the Messiah.' They will deceive many. ⁶And you will hear of wars and threats of wars, but don't panic. Yes, these things must take place, but the end won't follow immediately. ⁷Nation will go to war against nation, and kingdom against kingdom. There will be famines and earthquakes in many parts of the world. ⁸But all this is only the first of the birth pains, with more to come.

23:38 Some manuscripts do not include *and desolate.* 23:39 Ps 118:26. 24:3 Or *the age?*

9"Then you will be arrested, persecuted, and killed. You will be hated all over the world because you are my followers.* 10And many will turn away from me and betray and hate each other. 11And many false prophets will appear and will deceive many people. 12Sin will be rampant everywhere, and the love of many will grow cold. 13But the one who endures to the end will be saved. 14And the Good News about the Kingdom will be preached throughout the whole world, so that all nations* will hear it; and then the end will come.

15"The day is coming when you will see what Daniel the prophet spoke about—the sacrilegious object that causes desecration* standing in the Holy Place." (Reader, pay attention!) 16"Then those in Judea must flee to the hills. 17A person out on the deck of a roof must not go down into the house to pack. 18A person out in the field must not return even to get a coat. 19How terrible it will be for pregnant women and for nursing mothers in those days. 20And pray that your flight will not be in winter or on the Sabbath. 21For there will be greater anguish than at any time since the world began. And it will never be so great again. 22In fact, unless that time of calamity is shortened, not a single person will survive. But it will be shortened for the sake of God's chosen ones.

23"Then if anyone tells you, 'Look, here is the Messiah,' or 'There he is,' don't believe it. 24For false messiahs and false prophets will rise up and perform great signs and wonders so as to deceive, if possible, even God's chosen ones. 25See, I have warned you about this ahead of time.

26"So if someone tells you, 'Look, the Messiah is out in the desert,' don't bother to go and look. Or, 'Look, he is hiding here,' don't believe it! 27For as the lightning flashes in the east and shines to the west, so it will be when the Son of Man* comes. 28Just as the gathering of vultures shows there is a carcass nearby, so these signs indicate that the end is near.*

29"Immediately after the anguish of those days,

the sun will be darkened,
the moon will give no light,
the stars will fall from the sky,
and the powers in the heavens will be shaken.*

30And then at last, the sign that the Son of Man is coming will appear in the heavens, and there will be deep mourning among all the peoples of the earth. And they will see the Son of Man coming on the clouds of heaven with power and great glory.*

³¹And he will send out his angels with the mighty blast of a trumpet, and they will gather his chosen ones from all over the world*—from the farthest ends of the earth and heaven.

³²"Now learn a lesson from the fig tree. When its branches bud and its leaves begin to sprout, you know that summer is near. ³³In the same way, when you see all these things, you can know his return is very near, right at the door. ³⁴I tell you the truth, this generation* will not pass from the scene until all these things take place. ³⁵Heaven and earth will disappear, but my words will never disappear.

³⁶"However, no one knows the day or hour when these things will happen, not even the angels in heaven or the Son himself.* Only the Father knows.

³⁷"When the Son of Man returns, it will be like it was in Noah's day. ³⁸In those days before the flood, the people were enjoying banquets and parties and weddings right up to the time Noah entered his boat. ³⁹People didn't realize what was going to happen until the flood came and swept them all away. That is the way it will be when the Son of Man comes.

⁴⁰"Two men will be working together in the field; one will be taken, the other left. ⁴¹Two women will be grinding flour at the mill; one will be taken, the other left.

⁴²"So you, too, must keep watch! For you don't know what day your Lord is coming. ⁴³Understand this: If a homeowner knew exactly when a burglar was coming, he would keep watch and not permit his house to be broken into. ⁴⁴You also must be ready all the time, for the Son of Man will come when least expected.

⁴⁵"A faithful, sensible servant is one to whom the master can give the responsibility of managing his other household servants and feeding them. ⁴⁶If the master returns and finds that the servant has done a good job, there will be a reward. ⁴⁷I tell you the truth, the master will put that servant in charge of all he owns. ⁴⁸But what if the servant is evil and thinks, 'My master won't be back for a while,' ⁴⁹and he begins beating the other servants, partying, and getting drunk? ⁵⁰The master will return unannounced and unexpected, ⁵¹and he will cut the servant to pieces and assign him a place with the hypocrites. In that place there will be weeping and gnashing of teeth.

Parable of the Ten Bridesmaids

25 "Then the Kingdom of Heaven will be like ten bridesmaids* who took their lamps and went to meet the bridegroom. ²Five of them were foolish, and five were wise. ³The five who were foolish didn't take enough olive oil for their

---

24:31 Greek *from the four winds.* **24:34** Or *this age,* or *this nation.* **24:36** Some manuscripts do not include *or the Son himself.* **25:1** Or *virgins;* also in 25:7, 11.

lamps, 4but the other five were wise enough to take along extra oil. 5When the bridegroom was delayed, they all became drowsy and fell asleep.

6"At midnight they were roused by the shout, 'Look, the bridegroom is coming! Come out and meet him!'

7"All the bridesmaids got up and prepared their lamps. 8Then the five foolish ones asked the others, 'Please give us some of your oil because our lamps are going out.'

9"But the others replied, 'We don't have enough for all of us. Go to a shop and buy some for yourselves.'

10"But while they were gone to buy oil, the bridegroom came. Then those who were ready went in with him to the marriage feast, and the door was locked. 11Later, when the other five bridesmaids returned, they stood outside, calling, 'Lord! Lord! Open the door for us!'

12"But he called back, 'Believe me, I don't know you!'

13"So you, too, must keep watch! For you do not know the day or hour of my return.

Parable of the Three Servants
14"Again, the Kingdom of Heaven can be illustrated by the story of a man going on a long trip. He called together his servants and entrusted his money to them while he was gone. 15He gave five bags of silver* to one, two bags of silver to another, and one bag of silver to the last—dividing it in proportion to their abilities. He then left on his trip.

16"The servant who received the five bags of silver began to invest the money and earned five more. 17The servant with two bags of silver also went to work and earned two more. 18But the servant who received the one bag of silver dug a hole in the ground and hid the master's money.

19"After a long time their master returned from his trip and called them to give an account of how they had used his money. 20The servant to whom he had entrusted the five bags of silver came forward with five more and said, 'Master, you gave me five bags of silver to invest, and I have earned five more.'

21"The master was full of praise. 'Well done, my good and faithful servant. You have been faithful in handling this small amount, so now I will give you many more responsibilities. Let's celebrate together!*'

22"The servant who had received the two bags of silver came forward and said, 'Master, you gave me two bags of silver to invest, and I have earned two more.'

23"The master said, 'Well done, my good and faithful servant. You have been faithful in handling this small amount, so now I will give you many more responsibilities. Let's celebrate together!'

25:15 Greek *talents;* also throughout the story. A talent is equal to 75 pounds or 34 kilograms.
25:21 Greek *Enter into the joy of your master* [or *your Lord*]; also in 25:23.

²⁴"Then the servant with the one bag of silver came and said, 'Master, I knew you were a harsh man, harvesting crops you didn't plant and gathering crops you didn't cultivate. ²⁵I was afraid I would lose your money, so I hid it in the earth. Look, here is your money back.'

²⁶"But the master replied, 'You wicked and lazy servant! If you knew I harvested crops I didn't plant and gathered crops I didn't cultivate, ²⁷why didn't you deposit my money in the bank? At least I could have gotten some interest on it.'

²⁸"Then he ordered, 'Take the money from this servant, and give it to the one with the ten bags of silver. ²⁹To those who use well what they are given, even more will be given, and they will have an abundance. But from those who do nothing, even what little they have will be taken away. ³⁰Now throw this useless servant into outer darkness, where there will be weeping and gnashing of teeth.'

The Final Judgment

³¹"But when the Son of Man* comes in his glory, and all the angels with him, then he will sit upon his glorious throne. ³²All the nations* will be gathered in his presence, and he will separate the people as a shepherd separates the sheep from the goats. ³³He will place the sheep at his right hand and the goats at his left.

³⁴"Then the King will say to those on his right, 'Come, you who are blessed by my Father, inherit the Kingdom prepared for you from the creation of the world. ³⁵For I was hungry, and you fed me. I was thirsty, and you gave me a drink. I was a stranger, and you invited me into your home. ³⁶I was naked, and you gave me clothing. I was sick, and you cared for me. I was in prison, and you visited me.'

³⁷"Then these righteous ones will reply, 'Lord, when did we ever see you hungry and feed you? Or thirsty and give you something to drink? ³⁸Or a stranger and show you hospitality? Or naked and give you clothing? ³⁹When did we ever see you sick or in prison and visit you?'

⁴⁰"And the King will say, 'I tell you the truth, when you did it to one of the least of these my brothers and sisters,* you were doing it to me!'

⁴¹"Then the King will turn to those on the left and say, 'Away with you, you cursed ones, into the eternal fire prepared for the devil and his demons.* ⁴²For I was hungry, and you didn't feed me. I was thirsty, and you didn't give me a drink. ⁴³I was a stranger, and you didn't invite me into your home. I was naked, and you didn't give me clothing. I was sick and in prison, and you didn't visit me.'

25:31 "Son of Man" is a title Jesus used for himself. 25:32 Or *peoples.* 25:40 Greek *my brothers.* 25:41 Greek *his angels.*

44"Then they will reply, 'Lord, when did we ever see you hungry or thirsty or a stranger or naked or sick or in prison, and not help you?'

45"And he will answer, 'I tell you the truth, when you refused to help the least of these my brothers and sisters, you were refusing to help me.'

46"And they will go away into eternal punishment, but the righteous will go into eternal life."

The Plot to Kill Jesus

26 When Jesus had finished saying all these things, he said to his disciples, 2"As you know, Passover begins in two days, and the Son of Man* will be handed over to be crucified."

3At that same time the leading priests and elders were meeting at the residence of Caiaphas, the high priest, 4plotting how to capture Jesus secretly and kill him. 5"But not during the Passover celebration," they agreed, "or the people may riot."

Jesus Anointed at Bethany

6Meanwhile, Jesus was in Bethany at the home of Simon, a man who had previously had leprosy. 7While he was eating,* a woman came in with a beautiful alabaster jar of expensive perfume and poured it over his head.

8The disciples were indignant when they saw this. "What a waste!" they said. 9"It could have been sold for a high price and the money given to the poor."

10But Jesus, aware of this, replied, "Why criticize this woman for doing such a good thing to me? 11You will always have the poor among you, but you will not always have me. 12She has poured this perfume on me to prepare my body for burial. 13I tell you the truth, wherever the Good News is preached throughout the world, this woman's deed will be remembered and discussed."

Judas Agrees to Betray Jesus

14Then Judas Iscariot, one of the twelve disciples, went to the leading priests 15and asked, "How much will you pay me to betray Jesus to you?" And they gave him thirty pieces of silver. 16From that time on, Judas began looking for an opportunity to betray Jesus.

The Last Supper

17On the first day of the Festival of Unleavened Bread, the disciples came to Jesus and asked, "Where do you want us to prepare the Passover meal for you?"

18"As you go into the city," he told them, "you will see a certain man. Tell him, 'The Teacher says: My time has come, and I will eat the Passover meal with my disciples at your house.'" 19So the disciples did as Jesus told them and prepared the Passover meal there.

26:2 "Son of Man" is a title Jesus used for himself. **26:7** Or *reclining.*

[20]When it was evening, Jesus sat down at the table* with the Twelve. [21]While they were eating, he said, "I tell you the truth, one of you will betray me."

[22]Greatly distressed, each one asked in turn, "Am I the one, Lord?"

[23]He replied, "One of you who has just eaten from this bowl with me will betray me. [24]For the Son of Man must die, as the Scriptures declared long ago. But how terrible it will be for the one who betrays him. It would be far better for that man if he had never been born!"

[25]Judas, the one who would betray him, also asked, "Rabbi, am I the one?"

And Jesus told him, "You have said it."

[26]As they were eating, Jesus took some bread and blessed it. Then he broke it in pieces and gave it to the disciples, saying, "Take this and eat it, for this is my body."

[27]And he took a cup of wine and gave thanks to God for it. He gave it to them and said, "Each of you drink from it, [28]for this is my blood, which confirms the covenant* between God and his people. It is poured out as a sacrifice to forgive the sins of many. [29]Mark my words—I will not drink wine again until the day I drink it new with you in my Father's Kingdom."

[30]Then they sang a hymn and went out to the Mount of Olives.

Jesus Predicts Peter's Denial

[31]On the way, Jesus told them, "Tonight all of you will desert me. For the Scriptures say,

'God will strike* the Shepherd,
    and the sheep of the flock will
        be scattered.'

[32]But after I have been raised from the dead, I will go ahead of you to Galilee and meet you there."

[33]Peter declared, "Even if everyone else deserts you, I will never desert you."

[34]Jesus replied, "I tell you the truth, Peter—this very night, before the rooster crows, you will deny three times that you even know me."

[35]"No!" Peter insisted. "Even if I have to die with you, I will never deny you!" And all the other disciples vowed the same.

Jesus Prays in Gethsemane

[36]Then Jesus went with them to the olive grove called Gethsemane, and he said, "Sit here while I go over there to pray." [37]He took Peter and Zebedee's two sons, James and John, and he became anguished and distressed. [38]He told them, "My soul is crushed with grief to the point of death. Stay here and keep watch with me."

[39]He went on a little farther and bowed with his face to the ground, praying, "My Father! If it is possible,

26:20 Or *Jesus reclined.*   26:28 Some manuscripts read *the new covenant.*   26:31 Greek *I will strike.* Zech 13:7.

let this cup of suffering be taken away from me. Yet I want your will to be done, not mine."

40Then he returned to the disciples and found them asleep. He said to Peter, "Couldn't you watch with me even one hour? 41Keep watch and pray, so that you will not give in to temptation. For the spirit is willing, but the body is weak!"

42Then Jesus left them a second time and prayed, "My Father! If this cup cannot be taken away* unless I drink it, your will be done." 43When he returned to them again, he found them sleeping, for they couldn't keep their eyes open.

44So he went to pray a third time, saying the same things again. 45Then he came to the disciples and said, "Go ahead and sleep. Have your rest. But look—the time has come. The Son of Man is betrayed into the hands of sinners. 46Up, let's be going. Look, my betrayer is here!"

Jesus Is Betrayed and Arrested

47And even as Jesus said this, Judas, one of the twelve disciples, arrived with a crowd of men armed with swords and clubs. They had been sent by the leading priests and elders of the people. 48The traitor, Judas, had given them a prearranged signal: "You will know which one to arrest when I greet him with a kiss." 49So Judas came straight to Jesus.

"Greetings, Rabbi!" he exclaimed and gave him the kiss.

50Jesus said, "My friend, go ahead and do what you have come for."

Then the others grabbed Jesus and arrested him. 51But one of the men with Jesus pulled out his sword and struck the high priest's slave, slashing off his ear.

52"Put away your sword," Jesus told him. "Those who use the sword will die by the sword. 53Don't you realize that I could ask my Father for thousands* of angels to protect us, and he would send them instantly? 54But if I did, how would the Scriptures be fulfilled that describe what must happen now?"

55Then Jesus said to the crowd, "Am I some dangerous revolutionary, that you come with swords and clubs to arrest me? Why didn't you arrest me in the Temple? I was there teaching every day. 56But this is all happening to fulfill the words of the prophets as recorded in the Scriptures." At that point, all the disciples deserted him and fled.

Jesus before the Council

57Then the people who had arrested Jesus led him to the home of Caiaphas, the high priest, where the teachers of religious law and the elders had gathered. 58Meanwhile, Peter followed him at a distance and came to the high priest's courtyard. He went in and sat with the

26:42 Greek *If this cannot pass.*   26:53 Greek *twelve legions.*

guards and waited to see how it would all end.

⁵⁹Inside, the leading priests and the entire high council* were trying to find witnesses who would lie about Jesus, so they could put him to death. ⁶⁰But even though they found many who agreed to give false witness, they could not use anyone's testimony. Finally, two men came forward ⁶¹who declared, "This man said, 'I am able to destroy the Temple of God and rebuild it in three days.'"

⁶²Then the high priest stood up and said to Jesus, "Well, aren't you going to answer these charges? What do you have to say for yourself?" ⁶³But Jesus remained silent. Then the high priest said to him, "I demand in the name of the living God—tell us if you are the Messiah, the Son of God."

⁶⁴Jesus replied, "You have said it. And in the future you will see the Son of Man seated in the place of power at God's right hand* and coming on the clouds of heaven."*

⁶⁵Then the high priest tore his clothing to show his horror and said, "Blasphemy! Why do we need other witnesses? You have all heard his blasphemy. ⁶⁶What is your verdict?"

"Guilty!" they shouted. "He deserves to die!"

⁶⁷Then they began to spit in Jesus' face and beat him with their fists. And some slapped him, ⁶⁸jeering, "Prophesy to us, you Messiah! Who hit you that time?"

Peter Denies Jesus

⁶⁹Meanwhile, Peter was sitting outside in the courtyard. A servant girl came over and said to him, "You were one of those with Jesus the Galilean."

⁷⁰But Peter denied it in front of everyone. "I don't know what you're talking about," he said.

⁷¹Later, out by the gate, another servant girl noticed him and said to those standing around, "This man was with Jesus of Nazareth.*"

⁷²Again Peter denied it, this time with an oath. "I don't even know the man," he said.

⁷³A little later some of the other bystanders came over to Peter and said, "You must be one of them; we can tell by your Galilean accent."

⁷⁴Peter swore, "A curse on me if I'm lying—I don't know the man!" And immediately the rooster crowed.

⁷⁵Suddenly, Jesus' words flashed through Peter's mind: "Before the rooster crows, you will deny three times that you even know me." And he went away, weeping bitterly.

Judas Hangs Himself

27 Very early in the morning the leading priests and the elders of the people met again to lay plans for putting Jesus to death.

26:59 Greek *the Sanhedrin*. 26:64a Greek *seated at the right hand of the power*. See Ps 110:1. 26:64b See Dan 7:13. 26:71 Or *Jesus the Nazarene*.

²Then they bound him, led him away, and took him to Pilate, the Roman governor.

³When Judas, who had betrayed him, realized that Jesus had been condemned to die, he was filled with remorse. So he took the thirty pieces of silver back to the leading priests and the elders. ⁴"I have sinned," he declared, "for I have betrayed an innocent man."

"What do we care?" they retorted. "That's your problem."

⁵Then Judas threw the silver coins down in the Temple and went out and hanged himself.

⁶The leading priests picked up the coins. "It wouldn't be right to put this money in the Temple treasury," they said, "since it was payment for murder."* ⁷After some discussion they finally decided to buy the potter's field, and they made it into a cemetery for foreigners. ⁸That is why the field is still called the Field of Blood. ⁹This fulfilled the prophecy of Jeremiah that says,

"They took* the thirty pieces
    of silver—
  the price at which he was
    valued by the people of
    Israel,
¹⁰ and purchased the potter's field,
    as the LORD directed.*"

Jesus' Trial before Pilate

¹¹Now Jesus was standing before Pilate, the Roman governor. "Are you the king of the Jews?" the governor asked him.

Jesus replied, "You have said it."

¹²But when the leading priests and the elders made their accusations against him, Jesus remained silent. ¹³"Don't you hear all these charges they are bringing against you?" Pilate demanded. ¹⁴But Jesus made no response to any of the charges, much to the governor's surprise.

¹⁵Now it was the governor's custom each year during the Passover celebration to release one prisoner to the crowd—anyone they wanted. ¹⁶This year there was a notorious prisoner, a man named Barabbas.* ¹⁷As the crowds gathered before Pilate's house that morning, he asked them, "Which one do you want me to release to you—Barabbas, or Jesus who is called the Messiah?" ¹⁸(He knew very well that the religious leaders had arrested Jesus out of envy.)

¹⁹Just then, as Pilate was sitting on the judgment seat, his wife sent him this message: "Leave that innocent man alone. I suffered through a terrible nightmare about him last night."

²⁰Meanwhile, the leading priests and the elders persuaded the crowd to ask for Barabbas to be released and for Jesus to be put to death. ²¹So the governor asked again, "Which

27:6 Greek *since it is the price for blood.* **27:9** Or *I took.* **27:9-10** Greek *as the* LORD *directed me.* Zech 11:12-13; Jer 32:6-9. **27:16** Some manuscripts read *Jesus Barabbas;* also in 27:17.

of these two do you want me to release to you?"

The crowd shouted back, "Barabbas!"

22Pilate responded, "Then what should I do with Jesus who is called the Messiah?"

They shouted back, "Crucify him!"

23"Why?" Pilate demanded. "What crime has he committed?"

But the mob roared even louder, "Crucify him!"

24Pilate saw that he wasn't getting anywhere and that a riot was developing. So he sent for a bowl of water and washed his hands before the crowd, saying, "I am innocent of this man's blood. The responsibility is yours!"

25And all the people yelled back, "We will take responsibility for his death—we and our children!"*

26So Pilate released Barabbas to them. He ordered Jesus flogged with a lead-tipped whip, then turned him over to the Roman soldiers to be crucified.

The Soldiers Mock Jesus

27Some of the governor's soldiers took Jesus into their headquarters* and called out the entire regiment. 28They stripped him and put a scarlet robe on him. 29They wove thorn branches into a crown and put it on his head, and they placed a reed stick in his right hand as a scepter. Then they knelt before him in mockery and taunted, "Hail! King of the Jews!" 30And they spit on him and grabbed the stick and struck him on the head with it. 31When they were finally tired of mocking him, they took off the robe and put his own clothes on him again. Then they led him away to be crucified.

The Crucifixion

32Along the way, they came across a man named Simon, who was from Cyrene,* and the soldiers forced him to carry Jesus' cross. 33And they went out to a place called Golgotha (which means "Place of the Skull"). 34The soldiers gave Jesus wine mixed with bitter gall, but when he had tasted it, he refused to drink it.

35After they had nailed him to the cross, the soldiers gambled for his clothes by throwing dice.* 36Then they sat around and kept guard as he hung there. 37A sign was fastened above Jesus' head, announcing the charge against him. It read: "This is Jesus, the King of the Jews." 38Two revolutionaries* were crucified with him, one on his right and one on his left.

39The people passing by shouted abuse, shaking their heads in mockery. 40"Look at you now!" they yelled at him. "You said you were going to

---

27:25 Greek "His blood be on us and on our children." 27:27 Or into the Praetorium. 27:32 Cyrene was a city in northern Africa. 27:35 Greek by casting lots. A few late manuscripts add This fulfilled the word of the prophet: "They divided my garments among themselves and cast lots for my robe." See Ps 22:18. 27:38 Or criminals; also in 27:44.

destroy the Temple and rebuild it in three days. Well then, if you are the Son of God, save yourself and come down from the cross!"

⁴¹The leading priests, the teachers of religious law, and the elders also mocked Jesus. ⁴²"He saved others," they scoffed, "but he can't save himself! So he is the King of Israel, is he? Let him come down from the cross right now, and we will believe in him! ⁴³He trusted God, so let God rescue him now if he wants him! For he said, 'I am the Son of God.'" ⁴⁴Even the revolutionaries who were crucified with him ridiculed him in the same way.

The Death of Jesus
⁴⁵At noon, darkness fell across the whole land until three o'clock. ⁴⁶At about three o'clock, Jesus called out with a loud voice, *"Eli, Eli,* lema sabachthani?"* which means "My God, my God, why have you abandoned me?"*

⁴⁷Some of the bystanders misunderstood and thought he was calling for the prophet Elijah. ⁴⁸One of them ran and filled a sponge with sour wine, holding it up to him on a reed stick so he could drink. ⁴⁹But the rest said, "Wait! Let's see whether Elijah comes to save him."*

⁵⁰Then Jesus shouted out again, and he released his spirit. ⁵¹At that moment the curtain in the sanctuary of the Temple was torn in two, from top to bottom. The earth shook, rocks split apart, ⁵²and tombs opened. The bodies of many godly men and women who had died were raised from the dead. ⁵³They left the cemetery after Jesus' resurrection, went into the holy city of Jerusalem, and appeared to many people.

⁵⁴The Roman officer* and the other soldiers at the crucifixion were terrified by the earthquake and all that had happened. They said, "This man truly was the Son of God!"

⁵⁵And many women who had come from Galilee with Jesus to care for him were watching from a distance. ⁵⁶Among them were Mary Magdalene, Mary (the mother of James and Joseph), and the mother of James and John, the sons of Zebedee.

The Burial of Jesus
⁵⁷As evening approached, Joseph, a rich man from Arimathea who had become a follower of Jesus, ⁵⁸went to Pilate and asked for Jesus' body. And Pilate issued an order to release it to him. ⁵⁹Joseph took the body and wrapped it in a long sheet of clean linen cloth. ⁶⁰He placed it in his own new tomb, which had been carved out of the rock. Then he

27:46a Some manuscripts read *Eloi, Eloi.* **27:46b** Ps 22:1. **27:49** Some manuscripts add *And another took a spear and pierced his side, and out flowed water and blood.* Compare John 19:34. **27:54** Greek *The centurion.*

rolled a great stone across the entrance and left. ⁶¹Both Mary Magdalene and the other Mary were sitting across from the tomb and watching.

The Guard at the Tomb

⁶²The next day, on the Sabbath,* the leading priests and Pharisees went to see Pilate. ⁶³They told him, "Sir, we remember what that deceiver once said while he was still alive: 'After three days I will rise from the dead.' ⁶⁴So we request that you seal the tomb until the third day. This will prevent his disciples from coming and stealing his body and then telling everyone he was raised from the dead! If that happens, we'll be worse off than we were at first."

⁶⁵Pilate replied, "Take guards and secure it the best you can." ⁶⁶So they sealed the tomb and posted guards to protect it.

The Resurrection

28 Early on Sunday morning,* as the new day was dawning, Mary Magdalene and the other Mary went out to visit the tomb.

²Suddenly there was a great earthquake! For an angel of the Lord came down from heaven, rolled aside the stone, and sat on it. ³His face shone like lightning, and his clothing was as white as snow. ⁴The guards shook with fear when they saw him, and they fell into a dead faint.

⁵Then the angel spoke to the women. "Don't be afraid!" he said. "I know you are looking for Jesus, who was crucified. ⁶He isn't here! He is risen from the dead, just as he said would happen. Come, see where his body was lying. ⁷And now, go quickly and tell his disciples that he has risen from the dead, and he is going ahead of you to Galilee. You will see him there. Remember what I have told you."

⁸The women ran quickly from the tomb. They were very frightened but also filled with great joy, and they rushed to give the disciples the angel's message. ⁹And as they went, Jesus met them and greeted them. And they ran to him, grasped his feet, and worshiped him. ¹⁰Then Jesus said to them, "Don't be afraid! Go tell my brothers to leave for Galilee, and they will see me there."

The Report of the Guard

¹¹As the women were on their way, some of the guards went into the city and told the leading priests what had happened. ¹²A meeting with the elders was called, and they decided to give the soldiers a large bribe. ¹³They told the soldiers, "You must say, 'Jesus' disciples came during the night while we were sleeping, and they stole his body.' ¹⁴If the governor hears about it, we'll stand up for you so you won't get in trouble." ¹⁵So the guards accepted the

27:62 Or *On the next day, which is after the Preparation.* **28:1** Greek *After the Sabbath, on the first day of the week.*

bribe and said what they were told to say. Their story spread widely among the Jews, and they still tell it today.

The Great Commission

[16]Then the eleven disciples left for Galilee, going to the mountain where Jesus had told them to go. [17]When they saw him, they worshiped him—but some of them doubted!

28:19 Or *all peoples.*

[18]Jesus came and told his disciples, "I have been given all authority in heaven and on earth. [19]Therefore, go and make disciples of all the nations,* baptizing them in the name of the Father and the Son and the Holy Spirit. [20]Teach these new disciples to obey all the commands I have given you. And be sure of this: I am with you always, even to the end of the age."

Mark

John the Baptist Prepares the Way

1 This is the Good News about Jesus the Messiah, the Son of God.* It began ²just as the prophet Isaiah had written:

"Look, I am sending my
    messenger ahead of you,
    and he will prepare your way.*
³ He is a voice shouting in the
    wilderness,
'Prepare the way for the Lord's
    coming!
Clear the road for him!'*"

⁴This messenger was John the Baptist. He was in the wilderness and preached that people should be baptized to show that they had repented of their sins and turned to God to be forgiven. ⁵All of Judea, including all the people of Jerusalem, went out to see and hear John. And when they confessed their sins, he baptized them in the Jordan River. ⁶His clothes were woven from coarse camel hair, and he wore a leather belt around his waist. For food he ate locusts and wild honey.

⁷John announced: "Someone is coming soon who is greater than I am—so much greater that I'm not even worthy to stoop down like a slave and untie the straps of his sandals. ⁸I baptize you with* water, but he will baptize you with the Holy Spirit!"

The Baptism and Temptation of Jesus

⁹One day Jesus came from Nazareth in Galilee, and John baptized him in the Jordan River. ¹⁰As Jesus came up out of the water, he saw the heavens splitting apart and the Holy Spirit descending on him* like a dove. ¹¹And a voice from heaven said, "You are my dearly loved Son, and you bring me great joy."

¹²The Spirit then compelled Jesus to go into the wilderness, ¹³where he was tempted by Satan for forty days. He was out among the wild animals, and angels took care of him.

¹⁴Later on, after John was arrested, Jesus went into Galilee, where he preached God's Good News.* ¹⁵"The time promised by God has come at last!" he announced. "The Kingdom of God is near! Repent of your sins and believe the Good News!"

1:1 Some manuscripts do not include *the Son of God*. **1:2** Mal 3:1. **1:3** Isa 40:3 (Greek version). **1:8** Or *in;* also in 1:8b. **1:10** Or *toward him,* or *into him.* **1:14** Some manuscripts read *the Good News of the Kingdom of God*.

The First Disciples

[16] One day as Jesus was walking along the shore of the Sea of Galilee, he saw Simon* and his brother Andrew throwing a net into the water, for they fished for a living. [17] Jesus called out to them, "Come, follow me, and I will show you how to fish for people!" [18] And they left their nets at once and followed him.

[19] A little farther up the shore Jesus saw Zebedee's sons, James and John, in a boat repairing their nets. [20] He called them at once, and they also followed him, leaving their father, Zebedee, in the boat with the hired men.

Jesus Casts Out an Evil Spirit

[21] Jesus and his companions went to the town of Capernaum. When the Sabbath day came, he went into the synagogue and began to teach. [22] The people were amazed at his teaching, for he taught with real authority—quite unlike the teachers of religious law.

[23] Suddenly, a man in the synagogue who was possessed by an evil* spirit cried out, [24] "Why are you interfering with us, Jesus of Nazareth? Have you come to destroy us? I know who you are—the Holy One of God!"

[25] But Jesus reprimanded him. "Be quiet! Come out of the man," he ordered. [26] At that, the evil spirit screamed, threw the man into a convulsion, and then came out of him.

[27] Amazement gripped the audience, and they began to discuss what had happened. "What sort of new teaching is this?" they asked excitedly. "It has such authority! Even evil spirits obey his orders!" [28] The news about Jesus spread quickly throughout the entire region of Galilee.

Jesus Heals Many People

[29] After Jesus left the synagogue with James and John, they went to Simon and Andrew's home. [30] Now Simon's mother-in-law was sick in bed with a high fever. They told Jesus about her right away. [31] So he went to her bedside, took her by the hand, and helped her sit up. Then the fever left her, and she prepared a meal for them.

[32] That evening after sunset, many sick and demon-possessed people were brought to Jesus. [33] The whole town gathered at the door to watch. [34] So Jesus healed many people who were sick with various diseases, and he cast out many demons. But because the demons knew who he was, he did not allow them to speak.

Jesus Preaches in Galilee

[35] Before daybreak the next morning, Jesus got up and went out to an isolated place to pray. [36] Later Simon and the others went out to find him. [37] When they found him, they said, "Everyone is looking for you."

[38] But Jesus replied, "We must go on to other towns as well, and I will

1:16 *Simon* is called "Peter" in 3:16 and thereafter.   **1:23** Greek *unclean;* also in 1:26, 27.

preach to them, too. That is why I came." [39]So he traveled throughout the region of Galilee, preaching in the synagogues and casting out demons.

Jesus Heals a Man with Leprosy

[40]A man with leprosy came and knelt in front of Jesus, begging to be healed. "If you are willing, you can heal me and make me clean," he said.

[41]Moved with compassion,* Jesus reached out and touched him. "I am willing," he said. "Be healed!" [42]Instantly the leprosy disappeared, and the man was healed. [43]Then Jesus sent him on his way with a stern warning: [44]"Don't tell anyone about this. Instead, go to the priest and let him examine you. Take along the offering required in the law of Moses for those who have been healed of leprosy.* This will be a public testimony that you have been cleansed."

[45]But the man went and spread the word, proclaiming to everyone what had happened. As a result, large crowds soon surrounded Jesus, and he couldn't publicly enter a town anywhere. He had to stay out in the secluded places, but people from everywhere kept coming to him.

Jesus Heals a Paralyzed Man

2 When Jesus returned to Capernaum several days later, the news spread quickly that he was back home. [2]Soon the house where he was staying was so packed with visitors that there was no more room, even outside the door. While he was preaching God's word to them, [3]four men arrived carrying a paralyzed man on a mat. [4]They couldn't bring him to Jesus because of the crowd, so they dug a hole through the roof above his head. Then they lowered the man on his mat, right down in front of Jesus. [5]Seeing their faith, Jesus said to the paralyzed man, "My child, your sins are forgiven."

[6]But some of the teachers of religious law who were sitting there thought to themselves, [7]"What is he saying? This is blasphemy! Only God can forgive sins!"

[8]Jesus knew immediately what they were thinking, so he asked them, "Why do you question this in your hearts? [9]Is it easier to say to the paralyzed man 'Your sins are forgiven,' or 'Stand up, pick up your mat, and walk'? [10]So I will prove to you that the Son of Man* has the authority on earth to forgive sins." Then Jesus turned to the paralyzed man and said, [11]"Stand up, pick up your mat, and go home!"

[12]And the man jumped up, grabbed his mat, and walked out through the stunned onlookers. They were all amazed and praised God, exclaiming, "We've never seen anything like this before!"

1:41 Some manuscripts read *Moved with anger.* **1:44** See Lev 14:2-32. **2:10** "Son of Man" is a title Jesus used for himself.

Jesus Calls Levi (Matthew)

[13]Then Jesus went out to the lakeshore again and taught the crowds that were coming to him. [14]As he walked along, he saw Levi son of Alphaeus sitting at his tax collector's booth. "Follow me and be my disciple," Jesus said to him. So Levi got up and followed him.

[15]Later, Levi invited Jesus and his disciples to his home as dinner guests, along with many tax collectors and other disreputable sinners. (There were many people of this kind among Jesus' followers.) [16]But when the teachers of religious law who were Pharisees* saw him eating with tax collectors and other sinners, they asked his disciples, "Why does he eat with such scum?*"

[17]When Jesus heard this, he told them, "Healthy people don't need a doctor—sick people do. I have come to call not those who think they are righteous, but those who know they are sinners."

A Discussion about Fasting

[18]Once when John's disciples and the Pharisees were fasting, some people came to Jesus and asked, "Why don't your disciples fast like John's disciples and the Pharisees do?"

[19]Jesus replied, "Do wedding guests fast while celebrating with the groom? Of course not. They can't fast while the groom is with them. [20]But someday the groom will be taken away from them, and then they will fast.

[21]"Besides, who would patch old clothing with new cloth? For the new patch would shrink and rip away from the old cloth, leaving an even bigger tear than before.

[22]"And no one puts new wine into old wineskins. For the wine would burst the wineskins, and the wine and the skins would both be lost. New wine calls for new wineskins."

A Discussion about the Sabbath

[23]One Sabbath day as Jesus was walking through some grainfields, his disciples began breaking off heads of grain to eat. [24]But the Pharisees said to Jesus, "Look, why are they breaking the law by harvesting grain on the Sabbath?"

[25]Jesus said to them, "Haven't you ever read in the Scriptures what David did when he and his companions were hungry? [26]He went into the house of God (during the days when Abiathar was high priest) and broke the law by eating the sacred loaves of bread that only the priests are allowed to eat. He also gave some to his companions."

[27]Then Jesus said to them, "The Sabbath was made to meet the needs of people, and not people to meet the requirements of the Sabbath. [28]So the Son of Man is Lord, even over the Sabbath!"

2:16a Greek *the scribes of the Pharisees.*   2:16b Greek *with tax collectors and sinners?*

Jesus Heals on the Sabbath

3 Jesus went into the synagogue again and noticed a man with a deformed hand. ²Since it was the Sabbath, Jesus' enemies watched him closely. If he healed the man's hand, they planned to accuse him of working on the Sabbath.

³Jesus said to the man with the deformed hand, "Come and stand in front of everyone." ⁴Then he turned to his critics and asked, "Does the law permit good deeds on the Sabbath, or is it a day for doing evil? Is this a day to save life or to destroy it?" But they wouldn't answer him.

⁵He looked around at them angrily and was deeply saddened by their hard hearts. Then he said to the man, "Hold out your hand." So the man held out his hand, and it was restored! ⁶At once the Pharisees went away and met with the supporters of Herod to plot how to kill Jesus.

Crowds Follow Jesus

⁷Jesus went out to the lake with his disciples, and a large crowd followed him. They came from all over Galilee, Judea, ⁸Jerusalem, Idumea, from east of the Jordan River, and even from as far north as Tyre and Sidon. The news about his miracles had spread far and wide, and vast numbers of people came to see him. ⁹Jesus instructed his disciples to have a boat ready so the crowd would

not crush him. ¹⁰He had healed many people that day, so all the sick people eagerly pushed forward to touch him. ¹¹And whenever those possessed by evil* spirits caught sight of him, the spirits would throw them to the ground in front of him shrieking, "You are the Son of God!" ¹²But Jesus sternly commanded the spirits not to reveal who he was.

Jesus Chooses the Twelve Apostles

¹³Afterward Jesus went up on a mountain and called out the ones he wanted to go with him. And they came to him. ¹⁴Then he appointed twelve of them and called them his apostles.* They were to accompany him, and he would send them out to preach, ¹⁵giving them authority to cast out demons. ¹⁶These are the twelve he chose:

Simon (whom he named Peter),
¹⁷ James and John (the sons of Zebedee, but Jesus nicknamed them "Sons of Thunder"*),
¹⁸ Andrew,
    Philip,
    Bartholomew,
    Matthew,
    Thomas,
    James (son of Alphaeus),
    Thaddaeus,
    Simon (the zealot*),
¹⁹ Judas Iscariot (who later betrayed him).

3:11 Greek *unclean;* also in 3:30.   3:14 Some manuscripts do not include *and called them his apostles.*   3:17 Greek *whom he named Boanerges, which means Sons of Thunder.*   3:18 Greek *the Cananean,* an Aramaic term for Jewish nationalists.

Jesus and the Prince of Demons

20One time Jesus entered a house, and the crowds began to gather again. Soon he and his disciples couldn't even find time to eat. 21When his family heard what was happening, they tried to take him away. "He's out of his mind," they said.

22But the teachers of religious law who had arrived from Jerusalem said, "He's possessed by Satan,* the prince of demons. That's where he gets the power to cast out demons."

23Jesus called them over and responded with an illustration. "How can Satan cast out Satan?" he asked. 24"A kingdom divided by civil war will collapse. 25Similarly, a family splintered by feuding will fall apart. 26And if Satan is divided and fights against himself, how can he stand? He would never survive. 27Let me illustrate this further. Who is powerful enough to enter the house of a strong man and plunder his goods? Only someone even stronger— someone who could tie him up and then plunder his house.

28"I tell you the truth, all sin and blasphemy can be forgiven, 29but anyone who blasphemes the Holy Spirit will never be forgiven. This is a sin with eternal consequences." 30He told them this because they were saying, "He's possessed by an evil spirit."

The True Family of Jesus

31Then Jesus' mother and brothers came to see him. They stood outside and sent word for him to come out and talk with them. 32There was a crowd sitting around Jesus, and someone said, "Your mother and your brothers* are outside asking for you."

33Jesus replied, "Who is my mother? Who are my brothers?" 34Then he looked at those around him and said, "Look, these are my mother and brothers. 35Anyone who does God's will is my brother and sister and mother."

Parable of the Farmer Scattering Seed

4 Once again Jesus began teaching by the lakeshore. A very large crowd soon gathered around him, so he got into a boat. Then he sat in the boat while all the people remained on the shore. 2He taught them by telling many stories in the form of parables, such as this one:

3"Listen! A farmer went out to plant some seed. 4As he scattered it across his field, some of the seed fell on a footpath, and the birds came and ate it. 5Other seed fell on shallow soil with underlying rock. The seed sprouted quickly because the soil was shallow. 6But the plant soon wilted under the hot sun, and since it didn't have deep roots, it died. 7Other seed fell among thorns

---

3:22 Greek Beelzeboul; other manuscripts read Beezeboul; Latin version reads Beelzebub.
3:32 Some manuscripts add and sisters.

that grew up and choked out the tender plants so they produced no grain. ⁸Still other seeds fell on fertile soil, and they sprouted, grew, and produced a crop that was thirty, sixty, and even a hundred times as much as had been planted!" ⁹Then he said, "Anyone with ears to hear should listen and understand."

¹⁰Later, when Jesus was alone with the twelve disciples and with the others who were gathered around, they asked him what the parables meant.

¹¹He replied, "You are permitted to understand the secret* of the Kingdom of God. But I use parables for everything I say to outsiders, ¹²so that the Scriptures might be fulfilled:

'When they see what I do,
     they will learn nothing.
When they hear what I say,
     they will not understand.
Otherwise, they will turn to me
     and be forgiven.'* "

¹³Then Jesus said to them, "If you can't understand the meaning of this parable, how will you understand all the other parables? ¹⁴The farmer plants seed by taking God's word to others. ¹⁵The seed that fell on the footpath represents those who hear the message, only to have Satan come at once and take it away. ¹⁶The seed on the rocky soil represents those who hear the message

and immediately receive it with joy. ¹⁷But since they don't have deep roots, they don't last long. They fall away as soon as they have problems or are persecuted for believing God's word. ¹⁸The seed that fell among the thorns represents others who hear God's word, ¹⁹but all too quickly the message is crowded out by the worries of this life, the lure of wealth, and the desire for other things, so no fruit is produced. ²⁰And the seed that fell on good soil represents those who hear and accept God's word and produce a harvest of thirty, sixty, or even a hundred times as much as had been planted!"

Parable of the Lamp

²¹Then Jesus asked them, "Would anyone light a lamp and then put it under a basket or under a bed? Of course not! A lamp is placed on a stand, where its light will shine. ²²For everything that is hidden will eventually be brought into the open, and every secret will be brought to light. ²³Anyone with ears to hear should listen and understand."

²⁴Then he added, "Pay close attention to what you hear. The closer you listen, the more understanding you will be given*—and you will receive even more. ²⁵To those who listen to my teaching, more understanding will be given. But for those

4:11 Greek mystery.   4:12 Isa 6:9-10 (Greek version).   4:24 Or The measure you give will be the measure you get back.

who are not listening, even what little understanding they have will be taken away from them."

Parable of the Growing Seed

²⁶Jesus also said, "The Kingdom of God is like a farmer who scatters seed on the ground. ²⁷Night and day, while he's asleep or awake, the seed sprouts and grows, but he does not understand how it happens. ²⁸The earth produces the crops on its own. First a leaf blade pushes through, then the heads of wheat are formed, and finally the grain ripens. ²⁹And as soon as the grain is ready, the farmer comes and harvests it with a sickle, for the harvest time has come."

Parable of the Mustard Seed

³⁰Jesus said, "How can I describe the Kingdom of God? What story should I use to illustrate it? ³¹It is like a mustard seed planted in the ground. It is the smallest of all seeds, ³²but it becomes the largest of all garden plants; it grows long branches, and birds can make nests in its shade."

³³Jesus used many similar stories and illustrations to teach the people as much as they could understand. ³⁴In fact, in his public ministry he never taught without using parables; but afterward, when he was alone with his disciples, he explained everything to them.

Jesus Calms the Storm

³⁵As evening came, Jesus said to his disciples, "Let's cross to the other side of the lake." ³⁶So they took Jesus in the boat and started out, leaving the crowds behind (although other boats followed). ³⁷But soon a fierce storm came up. High waves were breaking into the boat, and it began to fill with water.

³⁸Jesus was sleeping at the back of the boat with his head on a cushion. The disciples woke him up, shouting, "Teacher, don't you care that we're going to drown?"

³⁹When Jesus woke up, he rebuked the wind and said to the waves, "Silence! Be still!" Suddenly the wind stopped, and there was a great calm. ⁴⁰Then he asked them, "Why are you afraid? Do you still have no faith?"

⁴¹The disciples were absolutely terrified. "Who is this man?" they asked each other. "Even the wind and waves obey him!"

Jesus Heals a Demon-Possessed Man

5 So they arrived at the other side of the lake, in the region of the Gerasenes.* ²When Jesus climbed out of the boat, a man possessed by an evil* spirit came out from the tombs to meet him. ³This man lived in the burial caves and could no longer be restrained, even with a chain. ⁴Whenever he was put into chains

5:1 Other manuscripts read *Gadarenes;* still others read *Gergesenes.* See Matt 8:28; Luke 8:26.
5:2 Greek *unclean;* also in 5:8, 13.

and shackles—as he often was—he snapped the chains from his wrists and smashed the shackles. No one was strong enough to subdue him. ⁵Day and night he wandered among the burial caves and in the hills, howling and cutting himself with sharp stones.

⁶When Jesus was still some distance away, the man saw him, ran to meet him, and bowed low before him. ⁷With a shriek, he screamed, "Why are you interfering with me, Jesus, Son of the Most High God? In the name of God, I beg you, don't torture me!" ⁸For Jesus had already said to the spirit, "Come out of the man, you evil spirit."

⁹Then Jesus demanded, "What is your name?"

And he replied, "My name is Legion, because there are many of us inside this man." ¹⁰Then the evil spirits begged him again and again not to send them to some distant place.

¹¹There happened to be a large herd of pigs feeding on the hillside nearby. ¹²"Send us into those pigs," the spirits begged. "Let us enter them."

¹³So Jesus gave them permission. The evil spirits came out of the man and entered the pigs, and the entire herd of about 2,000 pigs plunged down the steep hillside into the lake and drowned in the water.

¹⁴The herdsmen fled to the nearby town and the surrounding countryside, spreading the news as they ran. People rushed out to see what had happened. ¹⁵A crowd soon gathered around Jesus, and they saw the man who had been possessed by the legion of demons. He was sitting there fully clothed and perfectly sane, and they were all afraid. ¹⁶Then those who had seen what happened told the others about the demon-possessed man and the pigs. ¹⁷And the crowd began pleading with Jesus to go away and leave them alone.

¹⁸As Jesus was getting into the boat, the man who had been demon possessed begged to go with him. ¹⁹But Jesus said, "No, go home to your family, and tell them everything the Lord has done for you and how merciful he has been." ²⁰So the man started off to visit the Ten Towns* of that region and began to proclaim the great things Jesus had done for him; and everyone was amazed at what he told them.

Jesus Heals in Response to Faith
²¹Jesus got into the boat again and went back to the other side of the lake, where a large crowd gathered around him on the shore. ²²Then a leader of the local synagogue, whose name was Jairus, arrived. When he saw Jesus, he fell at his feet, ²³pleading fervently with him. "My little daughter is dying," he said. "Please come and lay your hands on her; heal her so she can live."

²⁴Jesus went with him, and all the

people followed, crowding around him. ²⁵A woman in the crowd had suffered for twelve years with constant bleeding. ²⁶She had suffered a great deal from many doctors, and over the years she had spent everything she had to pay them, but she had gotten no better. In fact, she had gotten worse. ²⁷She had heard about Jesus, so she came up behind him through the crowd and touched his robe. ²⁸For she thought to herself, "If I can just touch his robe, I will be healed." ²⁹Immediately the bleeding stopped, and she could feel in her body that she had been healed of her terrible condition.

³⁰Jesus realized at once that healing power had gone out from him, so he turned around in the crowd and asked, "Who touched my robe?"

³¹His disciples said to him, "Look at this crowd pressing around you. How can you ask, 'Who touched me?'"

³²But he kept on looking around to see who had done it. ³³Then the frightened woman, trembling at the realization of what had happened to her, came and fell to her knees in front of him and told him what she had done. ³⁴And he said to her, "Daughter, your faith has made you well. Go in peace. Your suffering is over."

³⁵While he was still speaking to her, messengers arrived from the home of Jairus, the leader of the synagogue. They told him, "Your daughter is dead. There's no use troubling the Teacher now."

³⁶But Jesus overheard* them and said to Jairus, "Don't be afraid. Just have faith."

³⁷Then Jesus stopped the crowd and wouldn't let anyone go with him except Peter, James, and John (the brother of James). ³⁸When they came to the home of the synagogue leader, Jesus saw much commotion and weeping and wailing. ³⁹He went inside and asked, "Why all this commotion and weeping? The child isn't dead; she's only asleep."

⁴⁰The crowd laughed at him. But he made them all leave, and he took the girl's father and mother and his three disciples into the room where the girl was lying. ⁴¹Holding her hand, he said to her, *"Talitha koum,"* which means "Little girl, get up!" ⁴²And the girl, who was twelve years old, immediately stood up and walked around! They were overwhelmed and totally amazed. ⁴³Jesus gave them strict orders not to tell anyone what had happened, and then he told them to give her something to eat.

Jesus Rejected at Nazareth

6 Jesus left that part of the country and returned with his disciples to Nazareth, his hometown. ²The next Sabbath he began teaching in the synagogue, and many who heard him were amazed. They

5:36 Or *ignored.*

asked, "Where did he get all this wisdom and the power to perform such miracles?" ³Then they scoffed, "He's just a carpenter, the son of Mary* and the brother of James, Joseph,* Judas, and Simon. And his sisters live right here among us." They were deeply offended and refused to believe in him.

⁴Then Jesus told them, "A prophet is honored everywhere except in his own hometown and among his relatives and his own family." ⁵And because of their unbelief, he couldn't do any miracles among them except to place his hands on a few sick people and heal them. ⁶And he was amazed at their unbelief.

Jesus Sends Out the Twelve Disciples

Then Jesus went from village to village, teaching the people. ⁷And he called his twelve disciples together and began sending them out two by two, giving them authority to cast out evil* spirits. ⁸He told them to take nothing for their journey except a walking stick—no food, no traveler's bag, no money.* ⁹He allowed them to wear sandals but not to take a change of clothes.

¹⁰"Wherever you go," he said, "stay in the same house until you leave town. ¹¹But if any place refuses to welcome you or listen to you, shake its dust from your feet as you leave to show that you have abandoned those people to their fate."

¹²So the disciples went out, telling everyone they met to repent of their sins and turn to God. ¹³And they cast out many demons and healed many sick people, anointing them with olive oil.

The Death of John the Baptist

¹⁴Herod Antipas, the king, soon heard about Jesus, because everyone was talking about him. Some were saying,* "This must be John the Baptist raised from the dead. That is why he can do such miracles." ¹⁵Others said, "He's the prophet Elijah." Still others said, "He's a prophet like the other great prophets of the past."

¹⁶When Herod heard about Jesus, he said, "John, the man I beheaded, has come back from the dead."

¹⁷For Herod had sent soldiers to arrest and imprison John as a favor to Herodias. She had been his brother Philip's wife, but Herod had married her. ¹⁸John had been telling Herod, "It is against God's law for you to marry your brother's wife." ¹⁹So Herodias bore a grudge against John and wanted to kill him. But without Herod's approval she was powerless, ²⁰for Herod respected John; and knowing that he was a good and holy man, he protected

6:3a Some manuscripts read *He's just the son of the carpenter and of Mary.* 6:3b Most manuscripts read *Joses;* see Matt 13:55. 6:7 Greek *unclean.* 6:8 Greek *no copper coins in their money belts.* 6:14 Some manuscripts read *He was saying.*

him. Herod was greatly disturbed whenever he talked with John, but even so, he liked to listen to him.

²¹Herodias's chance finally came on Herod's birthday. He gave a party for his high government officials, army officers, and the leading citizens of Galilee. ²²Then his daughter, also named Herodias,* came in and performed a dance that greatly pleased Herod and his guests. "Ask me for anything you like," the king said to the girl, "and I will give it to you." ²³He even vowed, "I will give you whatever you ask, up to half my kingdom!"

²⁴She went out and asked her mother, "What should I ask for?"

Her mother told her, "Ask for the head of John the Baptist!"

²⁵So the girl hurried back to the king and told him, "I want the head of John the Baptist, right now, on a tray!"

²⁶Then the king deeply regretted what he had said; but because of the vows he had made in front of his guests, he couldn't refuse her. ²⁷So he immediately sent an executioner to the prison to cut off John's head and bring it to him. The soldier beheaded John in the prison, ²⁸brought his head on a tray, and gave it to the girl, who took it to her mother. ²⁹When John's disciples heard what had happened, they came to get his body and buried it in a tomb.

Jesus Feeds Five Thousand

³⁰The apostles returned to Jesus from their ministry tour and told him all they had done and taught. ³¹Then Jesus said, "Let's go off by ourselves to a quiet place and rest awhile." He said this because there were so many people coming and going that Jesus and his apostles didn't even have time to eat.

³²So they left by boat for a quiet place, where they could be alone. ³³But many people recognized them and saw them leaving, and people from many towns ran ahead along the shore and got there ahead of them. ³⁴Jesus saw the huge crowd as he stepped from the boat, and he had compassion on them because they were like sheep without a shepherd. So he began teaching them many things.

³⁵Late in the afternoon his disciples came to him and said, "This is a remote place, and it's already getting late. ³⁶Send the crowds away so they can go to the nearby farms and villages and buy something to eat."

³⁷But Jesus said, "You feed them."

"With what?" they asked. "We'd have to work for months to earn enough money* to buy food for all these people!"

³⁸"How much bread do you have?" he asked. "Go and find out."

They came back and reported, "We have five loaves of bread and two fish."

6:22 Some manuscripts read *the daughter of Herodias herself.* 6:37 Greek *It would take 200 denarii.* A denarius was equivalent to a laborer's full day's wage.

³⁹Then Jesus told the disciples to have the people sit down in groups on the green grass. ⁴⁰So they sat down in groups of fifty or a hundred.

⁴¹Jesus took the five loaves and two fish, looked up toward heaven, and blessed them. Then, breaking the loaves into pieces, he kept giving the bread to the disciples so they could distribute it to the people. He also divided the fish for everyone to share. ⁴²They all ate as much as they wanted, ⁴³and afterward, the disciples picked up twelve baskets of leftover bread and fish. ⁴⁴A total of 5,000 men and their families were fed.*

Jesus Walks on Water

⁴⁵Immediately after this, Jesus insisted that his disciples get back into the boat and head across the lake to Bethsaida, while he sent the people home. ⁴⁶After telling everyone good-bye, he went up into the hills by himself to pray.

⁴⁷Late that night, the disciples were in their boat in the middle of the lake, and Jesus was alone on land. ⁴⁸He saw that they were in serious trouble, rowing hard and struggling against the wind and waves. About three o'clock in the morning* Jesus came toward them, walking on the water. He intended to go past them, ⁴⁹but when they saw him walking on the water, they cried out in terror, thinking he was a ghost. ⁵⁰They were all terrified when they saw him.

But Jesus spoke to them at once. "Don't be afraid," he said. "Take courage! I am here!*" ⁵¹Then he climbed into the boat, and the wind stopped. They were totally amazed, ⁵²for they still didn't understand the significance of the miracle of the loaves. Their hearts were too hard to take it in.

⁵³After they had crossed the lake, they landed at Gennesaret. They brought the boat to shore ⁵⁴and climbed out. The people recognized Jesus at once, ⁵⁵and they ran throughout the whole area, carrying sick people on mats to wherever they heard he was. ⁵⁶Wherever he went—in villages, cities, or the countryside—they brought the sick out to the marketplaces. They begged him to let the sick touch at least the fringe of his robe, and all who touched him were healed.

Jesus Teaches about Inner Purity

7 One day some Pharisees and teachers of religious law arrived from Jerusalem to see Jesus. ²They noticed that some of his disciples failed to follow the Jewish ritual of hand washing before eating. ³(The Jews, especially the Pharisees, do not eat until they have poured water over their cupped hands,* as required by their ancient traditions. ⁴Similarly, they

6:44 Some manuscripts read *fed from the loaves.* 6:48 Greek *About the fourth watch of the night.* 6:50 Or *The 'I Am' is here;* Greek reads *I am.* See Exod 3:14. 7:3 Greek *have washed with the fist.*

don't eat anything from the market until they immerse their hands* in water. This is but one of many traditions they have clung to—such as their ceremonial washing of cups, pitchers, and kettles.*)

⁵So the Pharisees and teachers of religious law asked him, "Why don't your disciples follow our age-old tradition? They eat without first performing the hand-washing ceremony."

⁶Jesus replied, "You hypocrites! Isaiah was right when he prophesied about you, for he wrote,

'These people honor me with
     their lips,
  but their hearts are far
     from me.
⁷ Their worship is a farce,
  for they teach man-made ideas
     as commands from God.'*

⁸For you ignore God's law and substitute your own tradition."

⁹Then he said, "You skillfully sidestep God's law in order to hold on to your own tradition. ¹⁰For instance, Moses gave you this law from God: 'Honor your father and mother,'* and 'Anyone who speaks disrespectfully of father or mother must be put to death.'* ¹¹But you say it is all right for people to say to their parents, 'Sorry, I can't help you. For I have vowed to give to God what I would have given to you.'* ¹²In this way, you let them disregard their needy parents. ¹³And so you cancel the word of God in order to hand down your own tradition. And this is only one example among many others."

¹⁴Then Jesus called to the crowd to come and hear. "All of you listen," he said, "and try to understand. ¹⁵It's not what goes into your body that defiles you; you are defiled by what comes from your heart.*"

¹⁷Then Jesus went into a house to get away from the crowd, and his disciples asked him what he meant by the parable he had just used. ¹⁸"Don't you understand either?" he asked. "Can't you see that the food you put into your body cannot defile you? ¹⁹Food doesn't go into your heart, but only passes through the stomach and then goes into the sewer." (By saying this, he declared that every kind of food is acceptable in God's eyes.)

²⁰And then he added, "It is what comes from inside that defiles you. ²¹For from within, out of a person's heart, come evil thoughts, sexual immorality, theft, murder, ²²adultery, greed, wickedness, deceit, lustful desires, envy, slander, pride, and foolishness. ²³All these vile things come from within; they are what defile you."

7:4a Some manuscripts read *sprinkle themselves.* 7:4b Some manuscripts add *and dining couches.* 7:7 Isa 29:13 (Greek version). 7:10a Exod 20:12; Deut 5:16. 7:10b Exod 21:17 (Greek version); Lev 20:9 (Greek version). 7:11 Greek *'What I would have given to you is Corban'* (that is, a gift). 7:15 Some manuscripts add verse 16, *Anyone with ears to hear should listen and understand.* Compare 4:9, 23.

The Faith of a Gentile Woman

24Then Jesus left Galilee and went north to the region of Tyre.* He didn't want anyone to know which house he was staying in, but he couldn't keep it a secret. 25Right away a woman who had heard about him came and fell at his feet. Her little girl was possessed by an evil* spirit, 26and she begged him to cast out the demon from her daughter.

Since she was a Gentile, born in Syrian Phoenicia, 27Jesus told her, "First I should feed the children— my own family, the Jews.* It isn't right to take food from the children and throw it to the dogs."

28She replied, "That's true, Lord, but even the dogs under the table are allowed to eat the scraps from the children's plates."

29"Good answer!" he said. "Now go home, for the demon has left your daughter." 30And when she arrived home, she found her little girl lying quietly in bed, and the demon was gone.

Jesus Heals a Deaf Man

31Jesus left Tyre and went up to Sidon before going back to the Sea of Galilee and the region of the Ten Towns.* 32A deaf man with a speech impediment was brought to him, and the people begged Jesus to lay his hands on the man to heal him. 33Jesus led him away from the crowd so they could be alone. He put his fingers into the man's ears. Then, spitting on his own fingers, he touched the man's tongue. 34Looking up to heaven, he sighed and said, *"Ephphatha,"* which means, "Be opened!" 35Instantly the man could hear perfectly, and his tongue was freed so he could speak plainly!

36Jesus told the crowd not to tell anyone, but the more he told them not to, the more they spread the news. 37They were completely amazed and said again and again, "Everything he does is wonderful. He even makes the deaf to hear and gives speech to those who cannot speak."

Jesus Feeds Four Thousand

8 About this time another large crowd had gathered, and the people ran out of food again. Jesus called his disciples and told them, 2"I feel sorry for these people. They have been here with me for three days, and they have nothing left to eat. 3If I send them home hungry, they will faint along the way. For some of them have come a long distance."

4His disciples replied, "How are we supposed to find enough food to feed them out here in the wilderness?"

5Jesus asked, "How much bread do you have?"

"Seven loaves," they replied.

7:24 Some manuscripts add *and Sidon.* 7:25 Greek *unclean.* 7:27 Greek *Let the children eat first.*
7:31 Greek *Decapolis.*

⁶So Jesus told all the people to sit down on the ground. Then he took the seven loaves, thanked God for them, and broke them into pieces. He gave them to his disciples, who distributed the bread to the crowd. ⁷A few small fish were found, too, so Jesus also blessed these and told the disciples to distribute them.

⁸They ate as much as they wanted. Afterward, the disciples picked up seven large baskets of leftover food. ⁹There were about 4,000 people in the crowd that day, and Jesus sent them home after they had eaten. ¹⁰Immediately after this, he got into a boat with his disciples and crossed over to the region of Dalmanutha.

Pharisees Demand a Miraculous Sign

¹¹When the Pharisees heard that Jesus had arrived, they came and started to argue with him. Testing him, they demanded that he show them a miraculous sign from heaven to prove his authority.

¹²When he heard this, he sighed deeply in his spirit and said, "Why do these people keep demanding a miraculous sign? I tell you the truth, I will not give this generation any such sign." ¹³So he got back into the boat and left them, and he crossed to the other side of the lake.

Yeast of the Pharisees and Herod

¹⁴But the disciples had forgotten to bring any food. They had only one loaf of bread with them in the boat. ¹⁵As they were crossing the lake, Jesus warned them, "Watch out! Beware of the yeast of the Pharisees and of Herod."

¹⁶At this they began to argue with each other because they hadn't brought any bread. ¹⁷Jesus knew what they were saying, so he said, "Why are you arguing about having no bread? Don't you know or understand even yet? Are your hearts too hard to take it in? ¹⁸'You have eyes—can't you see? You have ears—can't you hear?'* Don't you remember anything at all? ¹⁹When I fed the 5,000 with five loaves of bread, how many baskets of leftovers did you pick up afterward?"

"Twelve," they said.

²⁰"And when I fed the 4,000 with seven loaves, how many large baskets of leftovers did you pick up?"

"Seven," they said.

²¹"Don't you understand yet?" he asked them.

Jesus Heals a Blind Man

²²When they arrived at Bethsaida, some people brought a blind man to Jesus, and they begged him to touch the man and heal him. ²³Jesus took the blind man by the hand and led him out of the village. Then, spitting on the man's eyes, he laid his hands on him and asked, "Can you see anything now?"

²⁴The man looked around. "Yes," he said, "I see people, but I can't see

8:18 Jer 5:21.

them very clearly. They look like trees walking around."

²⁵Then Jesus placed his hands on the man's eyes again, and his eyes were opened. His sight was completely restored, and he could see everything clearly. ²⁶Jesus sent him away, saying, "Don't go back into the village on your way home."

Peter's Declaration about Jesus

²⁷Jesus and his disciples left Galilee and went up to the villages near Caesarea Philippi. As they were walking along, he asked them, "Who do people say I am?"

²⁸"Well," they replied, "some say John the Baptist, some say Elijah, and others say you are one of the other prophets."

²⁹Then he asked them, "But who do you say I am?"

Peter replied, "You are the Messiah.*"

³⁰But Jesus warned them not to tell anyone about him.

Jesus Predicts His Death

³¹Then Jesus began to tell them that the Son of Man* must suffer many terrible things and be rejected by the elders, the leading priests, and the teachers of religious law. He would be killed, but three days later he would rise from the dead. ³²As he talked about this openly with his disciples, Peter took him aside and began to reprimand him for saying such things.*

³³Jesus turned around and looked at his disciples, then reprimanded Peter. "Get away from me, Satan!" he said. "You are seeing things merely from a human point of view, not from God's."

³⁴Then, calling the crowd to join his disciples, he said, "If any of you wants to be my follower, you must give up your own way, take up your cross, and follow me. ³⁵If you try to hang on to your life, you will lose it. But if you give up your life for my sake and for the sake of the Good News, you will save it. ³⁶And what do you benefit if you gain the whole world but lose your own soul?* ³⁷Is anything worth more than your soul? ³⁸If anyone is ashamed of me and my message in these adulterous and sinful days, the Son of Man will be ashamed of that person when he returns in the glory of his Father with the holy angels."

9 Jesus went on to say, "I tell you the truth, some standing here right now will not die before they see the Kingdom of God arrive in great power!"

The Transfiguration

²Six days later Jesus took Peter, James, and John, and led them up a

high mountain to be alone. As the men watched, Jesus' appearance was transformed, ³and his clothes became dazzling white, far whiter than any earthly bleach could ever make them. ⁴Then Elijah and Moses appeared and began talking with Jesus.

⁵Peter exclaimed, "Rabbi, it's wonderful for us to be here! Let's make three shelters as memorials*—one for you, one for Moses, and one for Elijah." ⁶He said this because he didn't really know what else to say, for they were all terrified.

⁷Then a cloud overshadowed them, and a voice from the cloud said, "This is my dearly loved Son. Listen to him." ⁸Suddenly, when they looked around, Moses and Elijah were gone, and they saw only Jesus with them.

⁹As they went back down the mountain, he told them not to tell anyone what they had seen until the Son of Man* had risen from the dead. ¹⁰So they kept it to themselves, but they often asked each other what he meant by "rising from the dead."

¹¹Then they asked him, "Why do the teachers of religious law insist that Elijah must return before the Messiah comes?*"

¹²Jesus responded, "Elijah is indeed coming first to get everything ready. Yet why do the Scriptures say that the Son of Man must suffer greatly and be treated with utter contempt? ¹³But I tell you, Elijah has already come, and they chose to abuse him, just as the Scriptures predicted."

Jesus Heals a Demon-Possessed Boy

¹⁴When they returned to the other disciples, they saw a large crowd surrounding them, and some teachers of religious law were arguing with them. ¹⁵When the crowd saw Jesus, they were overwhelmed with awe, and they ran to greet him.

¹⁶"What is all this arguing about?" Jesus asked.

¹⁷One of the men in the crowd spoke up and said, "Teacher, I brought my son so you could heal him. He is possessed by an evil spirit that won't let him talk. ¹⁸And whenever this spirit seizes him, it throws him violently to the ground. Then he foams at the mouth and grinds his teeth and becomes rigid.* So I asked your disciples to cast out the evil spirit, but they couldn't do it."

¹⁹Jesus said to them,* "You faithless people! How long must I be with you? How long must I put up with you? Bring the boy to me."

²⁰So they brought the boy. But when the evil spirit saw Jesus, it threw the child into a violent convulsion, and he fell to the ground, writhing and foaming at the mouth.

9:5 Greek three tabernacles. 9:9 "Son of Man" is a title Jesus used for himself. 9:11 Greek that Elijah must come first? 9:18 Or becomes weak. 9:19 Or said to his disciples.

²¹"How long has this been happening?" Jesus asked the boy's father.

He replied, "Since he was a little boy. ²²The spirit often throws him into the fire or into water, trying to kill him. Have mercy on us and help us, if you can."

²³"What do you mean, 'If I can'?" Jesus asked. "Anything is possible if a person believes."

²⁴The father instantly cried out, "I do believe, but help me overcome my unbelief!"

²⁵When Jesus saw that the crowd of onlookers was growing, he rebuked the evil* spirit. "Listen, you spirit that makes this boy unable to hear and speak," he said. "I command you to come out of this child and never enter him again!"

²⁶Then the spirit screamed and threw the boy into another violent convulsion and left him. The boy appeared to be dead. A murmur ran through the crowd as people said, "He's dead." ²⁷But Jesus took him by the hand and helped him to his feet, and he stood up.

²⁸Afterward, when Jesus was alone in the house with his disciples, they asked him, "Why couldn't we cast out that evil spirit?"

²⁹Jesus replied, "This kind can be cast out only by prayer.*"

Jesus Again Predicts His Death

³⁰Leaving that region, they traveled through Galilee. Jesus didn't want anyone to know he was there, ³¹for he wanted to spend more time with his disciples and teach them. He said to them, "The Son of Man is going to be betrayed into the hands of his enemies. He will be killed, but three days later he will rise from the dead." ³²They didn't understand what he was saying, however, and they were afraid to ask him what he meant.

The Greatest in the Kingdom

³³After they arrived at Capernaum and settled in a house, Jesus asked his disciples, "What were you discussing out on the road?" ³⁴But they didn't answer, because they had been arguing about which of them was the greatest. ³⁵He sat down, called the twelve disciples over to him, and said, "Whoever wants to be first must take last place and be the servant of everyone else."

³⁶Then he put a little child among them. Taking the child in his arms, he said to them, ³⁷"Anyone who welcomes a little child like this on my behalf* welcomes me, and anyone who welcomes me welcomes not only me but also my Father who sent me."

Using the Name of Jesus

³⁸John said to Jesus, "Teacher, we saw someone using your name to cast out demons, but we told him to stop because he wasn't in our group."

³⁹"Don't stop him!" Jesus said.

9:25 Greek *unclean.* 9:29 Some manuscripts read *by prayer and fasting.* 9:37 Greek *in my name.*

"No one who performs a miracle in my name will soon be able to speak evil of me. ⁴⁰Anyone who is not against us is for us. ⁴¹If anyone gives you even a cup of water because you belong to the Messiah, I tell you the truth, that person will surely be rewarded.

⁴²"But if you cause one of these little ones who trusts in me to fall into sin, it would be better for you to be thrown into the sea with a large millstone hung around your neck. ⁴³If your hand causes you to sin, cut it off. It's better to enter eternal life with only one hand than to go into the unquenchable fires of hell* with two hands.* ⁴⁵If your foot causes you to sin, cut it off. It's better to enter eternal life with only one foot than to be thrown into hell with two feet.* ⁴⁷And if your eye causes you to sin, gouge it out. It's better to enter the Kingdom of God with only one eye than to have two eyes and be thrown into hell, ⁴⁸'where the maggots never die and the fire never goes out.'*

⁴⁹"For everyone will be tested with fire.* ⁵⁰Salt is good for seasoning. But if it loses its flavor, how do you make it salty again? You must have the qualities of salt among yourselves and live in peace with each other."

Discussion about Divorce and Marriage

10 Then Jesus left Capernaum and went down to the region of Judea and into the area east of the Jordan River. Once again crowds gathered around him, and as usual he was teaching them.

²Some Pharisees came and tried to trap him with this question: "Should a man be allowed to divorce his wife?"

³Jesus answered them with a question: "What did Moses say in the law about divorce?"

⁴"Well, he permitted it," they replied. "He said a man can give his wife a written notice of divorce and send her away."*

⁵But Jesus responded, "He wrote this commandment only as a concession to your hard hearts. ⁶But 'God made them male and female'* from the beginning of creation. ⁷'This explains why a man leaves his father and mother and is joined to his wife,* ⁸and the two are united into one.'* Since they are no longer two but one, ⁹let no one split apart what God has joined together."

¹⁰Later, when he was alone with his disciples in the house, they brought up the subject again. ¹¹He told them, "Whoever divorces his wife and marries someone else

---

9:43a Greek *Gehenna;* also in 9:45, 47. **9:43b** Some manuscripts add verse 44, *'where the maggots never die and the fire never goes out.'* See 9:48. **9:45** Some manuscripts add verse 46, *'where the maggots never die and the fire never goes out.'* See 9:48. **9:48** Isa 66:24. **9:49** Greek *salted with fire;* other manuscripts add *and every sacrifice will be salted with salt.* **10:4** See Deut 24:1.
10:6 Gen 1:27; 5:2. **10:7** Some manuscripts do not include *and is joined to his wife.*
10:7-8 Gen 2:24.

commits adultery against her. ¹²And if a woman divorces her husband and marries someone else, she commits adultery."

Jesus Blesses the Children

¹³One day some parents brought their children to Jesus so he could touch and bless them. But the disciples scolded the parents for bothering him.

¹⁴When Jesus saw what was happening, he was angry with his disciples. He said to them, "Let the children come to me. Don't stop them! For the Kingdom of God belongs to those who are like these children. ¹⁵I tell you the truth, anyone who doesn't receive the Kingdom of God like a child will never enter it." ¹⁶Then he took the children in his arms and placed his hands on their heads and blessed them.

The Rich Man

¹⁷As Jesus was starting out on his way to Jerusalem, a man came running up to him, knelt down, and asked, "Good Teacher, what must I do to inherit eternal life?"

¹⁸"Why do you call me good?" Jesus asked. "Only God is truly good. ¹⁹But to answer your question, you know the commandments: 'You must not murder. You must not commit adultery. You must not steal. You must not testify falsely. You must not cheat anyone. Honor your father and mother.'* "

²⁰"Teacher," the man replied, "I've obeyed all these commandments since I was young."

²¹Looking at the man, Jesus felt genuine love for him. "There is still one thing you haven't done," he told him. "Go and sell all your possessions and give the money to the poor, and you will have treasure in heaven. Then come, follow me."

²²At this the man's face fell, and he went away sad, for he had many possessions.

²³Jesus looked around and said to his disciples, "How hard it is for the rich to enter the Kingdom of God!" ²⁴This amazed them. But Jesus said again, "Dear children, it is very hard* to enter the Kingdom of God. ²⁵In fact, it is easier for a camel to go through the eye of a needle than for a rich person to enter the Kingdom of God!"

²⁶The disciples were astounded. "Then who in the world can be saved?" they asked.

²⁷Jesus looked at them intently and said, "Humanly speaking, it is impossible. But not with God. Everything is possible with God."

²⁸Then Peter began to speak up. "We've given up everything to follow you," he said.

²⁹"Yes," Jesus replied, "and I assure you that everyone who has given up house or brothers or sisters or

10:19 Exod 20:12-16; Deut 5:16-20.   **10:24** Some manuscripts read *very hard for those who trust in riches.*

mother or father or children or property, for my sake and for the Good News, ³⁰will receive now in return a hundred times as many houses, brothers, sisters, mothers, children, and property—along with persecution. And in the world to come that person will have eternal life. ³¹But many who are the greatest now will be least important then, and those who seem least important now will be the greatest then.*"

Jesus Again Predicts His Death

³²They were now on the way up to Jerusalem, and Jesus was walking ahead of them. The disciples were filled with awe, and the people following behind were overwhelmed with fear. Taking the twelve disciples aside, Jesus once more began to describe everything that was about to happen to him. ³³"Listen," he said, "we're going up to Jerusalem, where the Son of Man* will be betrayed to the leading priests and the teachers of religious law. They will sentence him to die and hand him over to the Romans.* ³⁴They will mock him, spit on him, flog him with a whip, and kill him, but after three days he will rise again."

Jesus Teaches about Serving Others

³⁵Then James and John, the sons of Zebedee, came over and spoke to him. "Teacher," they said, "we want you to do us a favor."

³⁶"What is your request?" he asked.

³⁷They replied, "When you sit on your glorious throne, we want to sit in places of honor next to you, one on your right and the other on your left."

³⁸But Jesus said to them, "You don't know what you are asking! Are you able to drink from the bitter cup of suffering I am about to drink? Are you able to be baptized with the baptism of suffering I must be baptized with?"

³⁹"Oh yes," they replied, "we are able!"

Then Jesus told them, "You will indeed drink from my bitter cup and be baptized with my baptism of suffering. ⁴⁰But I have no right to say who will sit on my right or my left. God has prepared those places for the ones he has chosen."

⁴¹When the ten other disciples heard what James and John had asked, they were indignant. ⁴²So Jesus called them together and said, "You know that the rulers in this world lord it over their people, and officials flaunt their authority over those under them. ⁴³But among you it will be different. Whoever wants to be a leader among you must be your servant, ⁴⁴and whoever wants to be first among you must be the slave of everyone else. ⁴⁵For even the Son of Man came not to be served but to

10:31 Greek *But many who are first will be last; and the last, first.* 10:33a "Son of Man" is a title Jesus used for himself. 10:33b Greek *the Gentiles.*

serve others and to give his life as a ransom for many."

Jesus Heals Blind Bartimaeus

⁴⁶Then they reached Jericho, and as Jesus and his disciples left town, a large crowd followed him. A blind beggar named Bartimaeus (son of Timaeus) was sitting beside the road. ⁴⁷When Bartimaeus heard that Jesus of Nazareth was nearby, he began to shout, "Jesus, Son of David, have mercy on me!"

⁴⁸"Be quiet!" many of the people yelled at him.

But he only shouted louder, "Son of David, have mercy on me!"

⁴⁹When Jesus heard him, he stopped and said, "Tell him to come here."

So they called the blind man. "Cheer up," they said. "Come on, he's calling you!" ⁵⁰Bartimaeus threw aside his coat, jumped up, and came to Jesus.

⁵¹"What do you want me to do for you?" Jesus asked.

"My Rabbi,*" the blind man said, "I want to see!"

⁵²And Jesus said to him, "Go, for your faith has healed you." Instantly the man could see, and he followed Jesus down the road.*

Jesus' Triumphant Entry

11 As Jesus and his disciples approached Jerusalem, they came to the towns of Bethphage and Bethany on the Mount of Olives. Jesus sent two of them on ahead. ²"Go into that village over there," he told them. "As soon as you enter it, you will see a young donkey tied there that no one has ever ridden. Untie it and bring it here. ³If anyone asks, 'What are you doing?' just say, 'The Lord needs it and will return it soon.'"

⁴The two disciples left and found the colt standing in the street, tied outside the front door. ⁵As they were untying it, some bystanders demanded, "What are you doing, untying that colt?" ⁶They said what Jesus had told them to say, and they were permitted to take it. ⁷Then they brought the colt to Jesus and threw their garments over it, and he sat on it.

⁸Many in the crowd spread their garments on the road ahead of him, and others spread leafy branches they had cut in the fields. ⁹Jesus was in the center of the procession, and the people all around him were shouting,

"Praise God!*
Blessings on the one who
    comes in the name of the
    LORD!
¹⁰ Blessings on the coming
    Kingdom of our ancestor
    David!
Praise God in highest
    heaven!"*

10:51 Greek uses the Hebrew term *Rabboni.* **10:52** Or *on the way.* **11:9** Greek *Hosanna,* an exclamation of praise that literally means "save now"; also in 11:10. **11:9-10** Pss 118:25-26; 148:1.

¹¹So Jesus came to Jerusalem and went into the Temple. After looking around carefully at everything, he left because it was late in the afternoon. Then he returned to Bethany with the twelve disciples.

Jesus Curses the Fig Tree

¹²The next morning as they were leaving Bethany, Jesus was hungry. ¹³He noticed a fig tree in full leaf a little way off, so he went over to see if he could find any figs. But there were only leaves because it was too early in the season for fruit. ¹⁴Then Jesus said to the tree, "May no one ever eat your fruit again!" And the disciples heard him say it.

Jesus Clears the Temple

¹⁵When they arrived back in Jerusalem, Jesus entered the Temple and began to drive out the people buying and selling animals for sacrifices. He knocked over the tables of the money changers and the chairs of those selling doves, ¹⁶and he stopped everyone from using the Temple as a marketplace.* ¹⁷He said to them, "The Scriptures declare, 'My Temple will be called a house of prayer for all nations,' but you have turned it into a den of thieves."*

¹⁸When the leading priests and teachers of religious law heard what Jesus had done, they began planning how to kill him. But they were afraid of him because the people were so amazed at his teaching.

¹⁹That evening Jesus and the disciples left* the city.

²⁰The next morning as they passed by the fig tree he had cursed, the disciples noticed it had withered from the roots up. ²¹Peter remembered what Jesus had said to the tree on the previous day and exclaimed, "Look, Rabbi! The fig tree you cursed has withered and died!"

²²Then Jesus said to the disciples, "Have faith in God. ²³I tell you the truth, you can say to this mountain, 'May you be lifted up and thrown into the sea,' and it will happen. But you must really believe it will happen and have no doubt in your heart. ²⁴I tell you, you can pray for anything, and if you believe that you've received it, it will be yours. ²⁵But when you are praying, first forgive anyone you are holding a grudge against, so that your Father in heaven will forgive your sins, too.*"

The Authority of Jesus Challenged

²⁷Again they entered Jerusalem. As Jesus was walking through the Temple area, the leading priests, the teachers of religious law, and the elders came up to him. ²⁸They demanded, "By what authority are you

---

11:16 Or *from carrying merchandise through the Temple.*   11:17 Isa 56:7; Jer 7:11.   11:19 Greek *they left;* other manuscripts read *he left.*   11:25 Some manuscripts add verse 26, *But if you refuse to forgive, your Father in heaven will not forgive your sins.* Compare Matt 6:15.

doing all these things? Who gave you the right to do them?"

²⁹"I'll tell you by what authority I do these things if you answer one question," Jesus replied. ³⁰"Did John's authority to baptize come from heaven, or was it merely human? Answer me!"

³¹They talked it over among themselves. "If we say it was from heaven, he will ask why we didn't believe John. ³²But do we dare say it was merely human?" For they were afraid of what the people would do, because everyone believed that John was a prophet. ³³So they finally replied, "We don't know."

And Jesus responded, "Then I won't tell you by what authority I do these things."

Parable of the Evil Farmers

12 Then Jesus began teaching them with stories: "A man planted a vineyard. He built a wall around it, dug a pit for pressing out the grape juice, and built a lookout tower. Then he leased the vineyard to tenant farmers and moved to another country. ²At the time of the grape harvest, he sent one of his servants to collect his share of the crop. ³But the farmers grabbed the servant, beat him up, and sent him back empty-handed. ⁴The owner then sent another servant, but they insulted him and beat him over the head. ⁵The next servant he sent was killed. Others he sent were either beaten or killed, ⁶until there was only one left—his son whom he loved dearly. The owner finally sent him, thinking, 'Surely they will respect my son.'

⁷"But the tenant farmers said to one another, 'Here comes the heir to this estate. Let's kill him and get the estate for ourselves!' ⁸So they grabbed him and murdered him and threw his body out of the vineyard.

⁹"What do you suppose the owner of the vineyard will do?" Jesus asked. "I'll tell you—he will come and kill those farmers and lease the vineyard to others. ¹⁰Didn't you ever read this in the Scriptures?

'The stone that the builders
    rejected
has now become the
    cornerstone.
¹¹ This is the Lᴏʀᴅ's doing,
    and it is wonderful to see.'*"

¹²The religious leaders* wanted to arrest Jesus because they realized he was telling the story against them—they were the wicked farmers. But they were afraid of the crowd, so they left him and went away.

Taxes for Caesar

¹³Later the leaders sent some Pharisees and supporters of Herod to trap Jesus into saying something for which he could be arrested.

12:10-11 Ps 118:22-23.   **12:12** Greek *They.*

[14]"Teacher," they said, "we know how honest you are. You are impartial and don't play favorites. You teach the way of God truthfully. Now tell us—is it right to pay taxes to Caesar or not? [15]Should we pay them, or shouldn't we?"

Jesus saw through their hypocrisy and said, "Why are you trying to trap me? Show me a Roman coin,* and I'll tell you." [16]When they handed it to him, he asked, "Whose picture and title are stamped on it?"

"Caesar's," they replied.

[17]"Well, then," Jesus said, "give to Caesar what belongs to Caesar, and give to God what belongs to God."

His reply completely amazed them.

Discussion about Resurrection

[18]Then Jesus was approached by some Sadducees—religious leaders who say there is no resurrection from the dead. They posed this question: [19]"Teacher, Moses gave us a law that if a man dies, leaving a wife without children, his brother should marry the widow and have a child who will carry on the brother's name.* [20]Well, suppose there were seven brothers. The oldest one married and then died without children. [21]So the second brother married the widow, but he also died without children. Then the third brother married her. [22]This continued with all seven of them, and still there were no children. Last of all, the woman also died. [23]So tell us, whose wife will she be in the resurrection? For all seven were married to her."

[24]Jesus replied, "Your mistake is that you don't know the Scriptures, and you don't know the power of God. [25]For when the dead rise, they will neither marry nor be given in marriage. In this respect they will be like the angels in heaven.

[26]"But now, as to whether the dead will be raised—haven't you ever read about this in the writings of Moses, in the story of the burning bush? Long after Abraham, Isaac, and Jacob had died, God said to Moses,* 'I am the God of Abraham, the God of Isaac, and the God of Jacob.'* [27]So he is the God of the living, not the dead. You have made a serious error."

The Most Important Commandment

[28]One of the teachers of religious law was standing there listening to the debate. He realized that Jesus had answered well, so he asked, "Of all the commandments, which is the most important?"

[29]Jesus replied, "The most important commandment is this: 'Listen, O Israel! The LORD our God is the one and only LORD. [30]And you must love the LORD your God with all your heart, all your soul, all your mind, and all your strength.'* [31]The second is

12:15 Greek *a denarius.* 12:19 See Deut 25:5-6. 12:26a Greek *in the story of the bush? God said to him.* 12:26b Exod 3:6. 12:29-30 Deut 6:4-5.

equally important: 'Love your neighbor as yourself.'* No other commandment is greater than these."

³²The teacher of religious law replied, "Well said, Teacher. You have spoken the truth by saying that there is only one God and no other. ³³And I know it is important to love him with all my heart and all my understanding and all my strength, and to love my neighbor as myself. This is more important than to offer all of the burnt offerings and sacrifices required in the law."

³⁴Realizing how much the man understood, Jesus said to him, "You are not far from the Kingdom of God." And after that, no one dared to ask him any more questions.

Whose Son Is the Messiah?

³⁵Later, as Jesus was teaching the people in the Temple, he asked, "Why do the teachers of religious law claim that the Messiah is the son of David? ³⁶For David himself, speaking under the inspiration of the Holy Spirit, said,

'The LORD said to my Lord,
　Sit in the place of honor at my
　　right hand
　until I humble your enemies
　　beneath your feet.'*

³⁷Since David himself called the Messiah 'my Lord,' how can the Messiah be his son?" The large crowd listened to him with great delight.

³⁸Jesus also taught: "Beware of these teachers of religious law! For they like to parade around in flowing robes and receive respectful greetings as they walk in the marketplaces. ³⁹And how they love the seats of honor in the synagogues and the head table at banquets. ⁴⁰Yet they shamelessly cheat widows out of their property and then pretend to be pious by making long prayers in public. Because of this, they will be more severely punished."

The Widow's Offering

⁴¹Jesus sat down near the collection box in the Temple and watched as the crowds dropped in their money. Many rich people put in large amounts. ⁴²Then a poor widow came and dropped in two small coins.*

⁴³Jesus called his disciples to him and said, "I tell you the truth, this poor widow has given more than all the others who are making contributions. ⁴⁴For they gave a tiny part of their surplus, but she, poor as she is, has given everything she had to live on."

Jesus Speaks about the Future

13 As Jesus was leaving the Temple that day, one of his disciples said, "Teacher, look at these magnificent buildings! Look at the impressive stones in the walls."

²Jesus replied, "Yes, look at these

12:31 Lev 19:18. **12:36** Ps 110:1. **12:42** Greek *two lepta, which is a kodrantes* [i.e., a quadrans].

great buildings. But they will be completely demolished. Not one stone will be left on top of another!"

³Later, Jesus sat on the Mount of Olives across the valley from the Temple. Peter, James, John, and Andrew came to him privately and asked him, ⁴"Tell us, when will all this happen? What sign will show us that these things are about to be fulfilled?"

⁵Jesus replied, "Don't let anyone mislead you, ⁶for many will come in my name, claiming, 'I am the Messiah.'* They will deceive many. ⁷And you will hear of wars and threats of wars, but don't panic. Yes, these things must take place, but the end won't follow immediately. ⁸Nation will go to war against nation, and kingdom against kingdom. There will be earthquakes in many parts of the world, as well as famines. But this is only the first of the birth pains, with more to come.

⁹"When these things begin to happen, watch out! You will be handed over to the local councils and beaten in the synagogues. You will stand trial before governors and kings because you are my followers. But this will be your opportunity to tell them about me.* ¹⁰For the Good News must first be preached to all nations.* ¹¹But when you are arrested and stand trial, don't worry in advance about what to say. Just say

what God tells you at that time, for it is not you who will be speaking, but the Holy Spirit.

¹²"A brother will betray his brother to death, a father will betray his own child, and children will rebel against their parents and cause them to be killed. ¹³And everyone will hate you because you are my followers.* But the one who endures to the end will be saved.

¹⁴"The day is coming when you will see the sacrilegious object that causes desecration* standing where he* should not be." (Reader, pay attention!) "Then those in Judea must flee to the hills. ¹⁵A person out on the deck of a roof must not go down into the house to pack. ¹⁶A person out in the field must not return even to get a coat. ¹⁷How terrible it will be for pregnant women and for nursing mothers in those days. ¹⁸And pray that your flight will not be in winter. ¹⁹For there will be greater anguish in those days than at any time since God created the world. And it will never be so great again. ²⁰In fact, unless the Lord shortens that time of calamity, not a single person will survive. But for the sake of his chosen ones he has shortened those days.

²¹"Then if anyone tells you, 'Look, here is the Messiah,' or 'There he is,' don't believe it. ²²For false messiahs and false prophets will rise up and

13:6 Greek *claiming, 'I am.'*   13:9 Or *But this will be your testimony against them.*   13:10 Or *all peoples.*   13:13 Greek *on account of my name.*   13:14a Greek *the abomination of desolation.* See Dan 9:27; 11:31; 12:11.   13:14b Or *it.*

perform signs and wonders so as to deceive, if possible, even God's chosen ones. [23]Watch out! I have warned you about this ahead of time!

[24]"At that time, after the anguish of those days,

> the sun will be darkened,
>   the moon will give no light,
> [25] the stars will fall from the sky,
>   and the powers in the heavens
>   will be shaken.*

[26]Then everyone will see the Son of Man* coming on the clouds with great power and glory.* [27]And he will send out his angels to gather his chosen ones from all over the world*—from the farthest ends of the earth and heaven.

[28]"Now learn a lesson from the fig tree. When its branches bud and its leaves begin to sprout, you know that summer is near. [29]In the same way, when you see all these things taking place, you can know that his return is very near, right at the door. [30]I tell you the truth, this generation* will not pass from the scene before all these things take place. [31]Heaven and earth will disappear, but my words will never disappear.

[32]"However, no one knows the day or hour when these things will happen, not even the angels in heaven or the Son himself. Only the Father knows. [33]And since you don't know when that time will come, be on guard! Stay alert*!

[34]"The coming of the Son of Man can be illustrated by the story of a man going on a long trip. When he left home, he gave each of his slaves instructions about the work they were to do, and he told the gatekeeper to watch for his return. [35]You, too, must keep watch! For you don't know when the master of the household will return—in the evening, at midnight, before dawn, or at daybreak. [36]Don't let him find you sleeping when he arrives without warning. [37]I say to you what I say to everyone: Watch for him!"

Jesus Anointed at Bethany

14 It was now two days before Passover and the Festival of Unleavened Bread. The leading priests and the teachers of religious law were still looking for an opportunity to capture Jesus secretly and kill him. [2]"But not during the Passover celebration," they agreed, "or the people may riot."

[3]Meanwhile, Jesus was in Bethany at the home of Simon, a man who had previously had leprosy. While he was eating,* a woman came in with a beautiful alabaster jar of expensive perfume made from essence of nard. She broke open the jar and poured the perfume over his head.

13:24-25 See Isa 13:10; 34:4; Joel 2:10.   **13:26a** "Son of Man" is a title Jesus used for himself.
13:26b See Dan 7:13.   **13:27** Greek *from the four winds.*   **13:30** Or *this age,* or *this nation.*
13:33 Some manuscripts add *and pray.*   **14:3** Or *reclining.*

4Some of those at the table were indignant. "Why waste such expensive perfume?" they asked. 5"It could have been sold for a year's wages* and the money given to the poor!" So they scolded her harshly.

6But Jesus replied, "Leave her alone. Why criticize her for doing such a good thing to me? 7You will always have the poor among you, and you can help them whenever you want to. But you will not always have me. 8She has done what she could and has anointed my body for burial ahead of time. 9I tell you the truth, wherever the Good News is preached throughout the world, this woman's deed will be remembered and discussed."

Judas Agrees to Betray Jesus
10Then Judas Iscariot, one of the twelve disciples, went to the leading priests to arrange to betray Jesus to them. 11They were delighted when they heard why he had come, and they promised to give him money. So he began looking for an opportunity to betray Jesus.

The Last Supper
12On the first day of the Festival of Unleavened Bread, when the Passover lamb is sacrificed, Jesus' disciples asked him, "Where do you want us to go to prepare the Passover meal for you?"

13So Jesus sent two of them into Jerusalem with these instructions: "As you go into the city, a man carrying a pitcher of water will meet you. Follow him. 14At the house he enters, say to the owner, 'The Teacher asks: Where is the guest room where I can eat the Passover meal with my disciples?' 15He will take you upstairs to a large room that is already set up. That is where you should prepare our meal." 16So the two disciples went into the city and found everything just as Jesus had said, and they prepared the Passover meal there.

17In the evening Jesus arrived with the Twelve. 18As they were at the table* eating, Jesus said, "I tell you the truth, one of you eating with me here will betray me."

19Greatly distressed, each one asked in turn, "Am I the one?"

20He replied, "It is one of you twelve who is eating from this bowl with me. 21For the Son of Man* must die, as the Scriptures declared long ago. But how terrible it will be for the one who betrays him. It would be far better for that man if he had never been born!"

22As they were eating, Jesus took some bread and blessed it. Then he broke it in pieces and gave it to the disciples, saying, "Take it, for this is my body."

23And he took a cup of wine and gave thanks to God for it. He gave it

14:5 Greek for 300 denarii. A denarius was equivalent to a laborer's full day's wage. 14:18 Or As they reclined. 14:21 "Son of Man" is a title Jesus used for himself.

to them, and they all drank from it. [24]And he said to them, "This is my blood, which confirms the covenant* between God and his people. It is poured out as a sacrifice for many. [25]I tell you the truth, I will not drink wine again until the day I drink it new in the Kingdom of God."

[26]Then they sang a hymn and went out to the Mount of Olives.

Jesus Predicts Peter's Denial

[27]On the way, Jesus told them, "All of you will desert me. For the Scriptures say,

'God will strike* the Shepherd,
    and the sheep will be scattered.'

[28]But after I am raised from the dead, I will go ahead of you to Galilee and meet you there."

[29]Peter said to him, "Even if everyone else deserts you, I never will."

[30]Jesus replied, "I tell you the truth, Peter—this very night, before the rooster crows twice, you will deny three times that you even know me."

[31]"No!" Peter declared emphatically. "Even if I have to die with you, I will never deny you!" And all the others vowed the same.

Jesus Prays in Gethsemane

[32]They went to the olive grove called Gethsemane, and Jesus said, "Sit here while I go and pray." [33]He took Peter, James, and John with him, and he became deeply troubled and distressed. [34]He told them, "My soul is crushed with grief to the point of death. Stay here and keep watch with me."

[35]He went on a little farther and fell to the ground. He prayed that, if it were possible, the awful hour awaiting him might pass him by. [36]"Abba, Father,"* he cried out, "everything is possible for you. Please take this cup of suffering away from me. Yet I want your will to be done, not mine."

[37]Then he returned and found the disciples asleep. He said to Peter, "Simon, are you asleep? Couldn't you watch with me even one hour? [38]Keep watch and pray, so that you will not give in to temptation. For the spirit is willing, but the body is weak."

[39]Then Jesus left them again and prayed the same prayer as before. [40]When he returned to them again, he found them sleeping, for they couldn't keep their eyes open. And they didn't know what to say.

[41]When he returned to them the third time, he said, "Go ahead and sleep. Have your rest. But no—the time has come. The Son of Man is betrayed into the hands of sinners. [42]Up, let's be going. Look, my betrayer is here!"

14:24 Some manuscripts read *the new covenant.* **14:27** Greek *I will strike.* Zech 13:7. **14:36** *Abba* is an Aramaic term for "father."

Jesus Is Betrayed and Arrested

⁴³And immediately, even as Jesus said this, Judas, one of the twelve disciples, arrived with a crowd of men armed with swords and clubs. They had been sent by the leading priests, the teachers of religious law, and the elders. ⁴⁴The traitor, Judas, had given them a prearranged signal: "You will know which one to arrest when I greet him with a kiss. Then you can take him away under guard." ⁴⁵As soon as they arrived, Judas walked up to Jesus. "Rabbi!" he exclaimed, and gave him the kiss.

⁴⁶Then the others grabbed Jesus and arrested him. ⁴⁷But one of the men with Jesus pulled out his sword and struck the high priest's slave, slashing off his ear.

⁴⁸Jesus asked them, "Am I some dangerous revolutionary, that you come with swords and clubs to arrest me? ⁴⁹Why didn't you arrest me in the Temple? I was there among you teaching every day. But these things are happening to fulfill what the Scriptures say about me."

⁵⁰Then all his disciples deserted him and ran away. ⁵¹One young man following behind was clothed only in a long linen shirt. When the mob tried to grab him, ⁵²he slipped out of his shirt and ran away naked.

Jesus before the Council

⁵³They took Jesus to the high priest's home where the leading priests, the elders, and the teachers of religious law had gathered. ⁵⁴Meanwhile, Peter followed him at a distance and went right into the high priest's courtyard. There he sat with the guards, warming himself by the fire.

⁵⁵Inside, the leading priests and the entire high council* were trying to find evidence against Jesus, so they could put him to death. But they couldn't find any. ⁵⁶Many false witnesses spoke against him, but they contradicted each other. ⁵⁷Finally, some men stood up and gave this false testimony: ⁵⁸"We heard him say, 'I will destroy this Temple made with human hands, and in three days I will build another, made without human hands.'" ⁵⁹But even then they didn't get their stories straight!

⁶⁰Then the high priest stood up before the others and asked Jesus, "Well, aren't you going to answer these charges? What do you have to say for yourself?" ⁶¹But Jesus was silent and made no reply. Then the high priest asked him, "Are you the Messiah, the Son of the Blessed One?"

⁶²Jesus said, "I AM.* And you will see the Son of Man seated in the place of power at God's right hand* and coming on the clouds of heaven.*"

⁶³Then the high priest tore his clothing to show his horror and said, "Why do we need other wit-

14:55 Greek *the Sanhedrin.*   14:62a Or *The 'I AM' is here;* or *I am the LORD.* See Exod 3:14.
14:62b Greek *seated at the right hand of the power.* See Ps 110:1.   14:62c See Dan 7:13.

nesses? ⁶⁴You have all heard his blasphemy. What is your verdict?"

"Guilty!" they all cried. "He deserves to die!"

⁶⁵Then some of them began to spit at him, and they blindfolded him and beat him with their fists. "Prophesy to us," they jeered. And the guards slapped him as they took him away.

Peter Denies Jesus

⁶⁶Meanwhile, Peter was in the courtyard below. One of the servant girls who worked for the high priest came by ⁶⁷and noticed Peter warming himself at the fire. She looked at him closely and said, "You were one of those with Jesus of Nazareth.*"

⁶⁸But Peter denied it. "I don't know what you're talking about," he said, and he went out into the entryway. Just then, a rooster crowed.*

⁶⁹When the servant girl saw him standing there, she began telling the others, "This man is definitely one of them!" ⁷⁰But Peter denied it again.

A little later some of the other bystanders confronted Peter and said, "You must be one of them, because you are a Galilean."

⁷¹Peter swore, "A curse on me if I'm lying—I don't know this man you're talking about!" ⁷²And immediately the rooster crowed the second time.

Suddenly, Jesus' words flashed through Peter's mind: "Before the rooster crows twice, you will deny three times that you even know me." And he broke down and wept.

Jesus' Trial before Pilate

15 Very early in the morning the leading priests, the elders, and the teachers of religious law—the entire high council*—met to discuss their next step. They bound Jesus, led him away, and took him to Pilate, the Roman governor.

²Pilate asked Jesus, "Are you the king of the Jews?"

Jesus replied, "You have said it."

³Then the leading priests kept accusing him of many crimes, ⁴and Pilate asked him, "Aren't you going to answer them? What about all these charges they are bringing against you?" ⁵But Jesus said nothing, much to Pilate's surprise.

⁶Now it was the governor's custom each year during the Passover celebration to release one prisoner—anyone the people requested. ⁷One of the prisoners at that time was Barabbas, a revolutionary who had committed murder in an uprising. ⁸The crowd went to Pilate and asked him to release a prisoner as usual.

⁹"Would you like me to release to you this 'King of the Jews'?" Pilate asked. ¹⁰(For he realized by now that the leading priests had arrested Jesus out of envy.) ¹¹But at this point the leading priests stirred

14:67 Or *Jesus the Nazarene.* 14:68 Some manuscripts do not include *Just then, a rooster crowed.* 15:1 Greek *the Sanhedrin;* also in 15:43.

up the crowd to demand the release of Barabbas instead of Jesus. ¹²Pilate asked them, "Then what should I do with this man you call the king of the Jews?"

¹³They shouted back, "Crucify him!"

¹⁴"Why?" Pilate demanded. "What crime has he committed?"

But the mob roared even louder, "Crucify him!"

¹⁵So to pacify the crowd, Pilate released Barabbas to them. He ordered Jesus flogged with a lead-tipped whip, then turned him over to the Roman soldiers to be crucified.

The Soldiers Mock Jesus

¹⁶The soldiers took Jesus into the courtyard of the governor's headquarters (called the Praetorium) and called out the entire regiment. ¹⁷They dressed him in a purple robe, and they wove thorn branches into a crown and put it on his head. ¹⁸Then they saluted him and taunted, "Hail! King of the Jews!" ¹⁹And they struck him on the head with a reed stick, spit on him, and dropped to their knees in mock worship. ²⁰When they were finally tired of mocking him, they took off the purple robe and put his own clothes on him again. Then they led him away to be crucified.

The Crucifixion

²¹A passerby named Simon, who was from Cyrene,* was coming in from the countryside just then, and the soldiers forced him to carry Jesus' cross. (Simon was the father of Alexander and Rufus.) ²²And they brought Jesus to a place called Golgotha (which means "Place of the Skull"). ²³They offered him wine drugged with myrrh, but he refused it.

²⁴Then the soldiers nailed him to the cross. They divided his clothes and threw dice* to decide who would get each piece. ²⁵It was nine o'clock in the morning when they crucified him. ²⁶A sign announced the charge against him. It read, "The King of the Jews." ²⁷Two revolutionaries* were crucified with him, one on his right and one on his left.*

²⁹The people passing by shouted abuse, shaking their heads in mockery. "Ha! Look at you now!" they yelled at him. "You said you were going to destroy the Temple and rebuild it in three days. ³⁰Well then, save yourself and come down from the cross!"

³¹The leading priests and teachers of religious law also mocked Jesus. "He saved others," they scoffed, "but he can't save himself! ³²Let this Messiah, this King of Israel, come down from the cross so we can see it and believe him!" Even

15:21 Cyrene was a city in northern Africa. 15:24 Greek cast lots. See Ps 22:18. 15:27a Or Two criminals. 15:27b Some manuscripts add verse 28, And the Scripture was fulfilled that said, "He was counted among those who were rebels." See Isa 53:12; also compare Luke 22:37.

the men who were crucified with Jesus ridiculed him.

The Death of Jesus

³³At noon, darkness fell across the whole land until three o'clock. ³⁴Then at three o'clock Jesus called out with a loud voice, *"Eloi, Eloi, lema sabachthani?"* which means "My God, my God, why have you abandoned me?"*

³⁵Some of the bystanders misunderstood and thought he was calling for the prophet Elijah. ³⁶One of them ran and filled a sponge with sour wine, holding it up to him on a reed stick so he could drink. "Wait!" he said. "Let's see whether Elijah comes to take him down!"

³⁷Then Jesus uttered another loud cry and breathed his last. ³⁸And the curtain in the sanctuary of the Temple was torn in two, from top to bottom.

³⁹When the Roman officer* who stood facing him* saw how he had died, he exclaimed, "This man truly was the Son of God!"

⁴⁰Some women were there, watching from a distance, including Mary Magdalene, Mary (the mother of James the younger and of Joseph*), and Salome. ⁴¹They had been followers of Jesus and had cared for him while he was in Galilee. Many other women who had come with him to Jerusalem were also there.

The Burial of Jesus

⁴²This all happened on Friday, the day of preparation,* the day before the Sabbath. As evening approached, ⁴³Joseph of Arimathea took a risk and went to Pilate and asked for Jesus' body. (Joseph was an honored member of the high council, and he was waiting for the Kingdom of God to come.) ⁴⁴Pilate couldn't believe that Jesus was already dead, so he called for the Roman officer and asked if he had died yet. ⁴⁵The officer confirmed that Jesus was dead, so Pilate told Joseph he could have the body. ⁴⁶Joseph bought a long sheet of linen cloth. Then he took Jesus' body down from the cross, wrapped it in the cloth, and laid it in a tomb that had been carved out of the rock. Then he rolled a stone in front of the entrance. ⁴⁷Mary Magdalene and Mary the mother of Joseph saw where Jesus' body was laid.

The Resurrection

16 Saturday evening, when the Sabbath ended, Mary Magdalene, Mary the mother of James, and Salome went out and purchased burial spices so they could anoint Jesus' body. ²Very early on Sunday morning,* just at sunrise, they went to the tomb. ³On the way they were asking each other, "Who will roll away the stone for us from the

15:34 Ps 22:1. **15:39a** Greek *the centurion;* similarly in 15:44, 45. **15:39b** Some manuscripts add *heard his cry and.* **15:40** Greek *Joses;* also in 15:47. See Matt 27:56. **15:42** Greek *It was the day of preparation.* **16:2** Greek *on the first day of the week;* also in 16:9.

entrance to the tomb?" [4]But as they arrived, they looked up and saw that the stone, which was very large, had already been rolled aside.

[5]When they entered the tomb, they saw a young man clothed in a white robe sitting on the right side. The women were shocked, [6]but the angel said, "Don't be alarmed. You are looking for Jesus of Nazareth,* who was crucified. He isn't here! He is risen from the dead! Look, this is where they laid his body. [7]Now go and tell his disciples, including Peter, that Jesus is going ahead of you to Galilee. You will see him there, just as he told you before he died."

[8]The women fled from the tomb, trembling and bewildered, and they said nothing to anyone because they were too frightened.*

[The most ancient manuscripts of Mark conclude with verse 16:8. Later manuscripts add one or both of the following endings.]

[Shorter Ending of Mark]

Then they briefly reported all this to Peter and his companions. Afterward Jesus himself sent them out from east to west with the sacred and unfailing message of salvation that gives eternal life. Amen.

[Longer Ending of Mark]

[9]After Jesus rose from the dead early on Sunday morning, the first person who saw him was Mary Magdalene, the woman from whom he had cast out seven demons. [10]She went to the disciples, who were grieving and weeping, and told them what had happened. [11]But when she told them that Jesus was alive and she had seen him, they didn't believe her.

[12]Afterward he appeared in a different form to two of his followers who were walking from Jerusalem into the country. [13]They rushed back to tell the others, but no one believed them.

[14]Still later he appeared to the eleven disciples as they were eating together. He rebuked them for their stubborn unbelief because they refused to believe those who had seen him after he had been raised from the dead.*

[15]And then he told them, "Go into

16:6 Or *Jesus the Nazarene.*   16:8 The most reliable early manuscripts of the Gospel of Mark end at verse 8. Other manuscripts include various endings to the Gospel. A few include both the "shorter ending" and the "longer ending." The majority of manuscripts include the "longer ending" immediately after verse 8.   16:14 Some early manuscripts add: *And they excused themselves, saying, "This age of lawlessness and unbelief is under Satan, who does not permit God's truth and power to conquer the evil [unclean] spirits. Therefore, reveal your justice now." This is what they said to Christ. And Christ replied to them, "The period of years of Satan's power has been fulfilled, but other dreadful things will happen soon. And I was handed over to death for those who have sinned, so that they may return to the truth and sin no more, and so that they may inherit the spiritual, incorruptible, and righteous glory in heaven."*

all the world and preach the Good News to everyone. [16]Anyone who believes and is baptized will be saved. But anyone who refuses to believe will be condemned. [17]These miraculous signs will accompany those who believe: They will cast out demons in my name, and they will speak in new languages.* [18]They will be able to handle snakes with safety, and if they drink anything poisonous, it won't hurt them.

They will be able to place their hands on the sick, and they will be healed."

[19]When the Lord Jesus had finished talking with them, he was taken up into heaven and sat down in the place of honor at God's right hand. [20]And the disciples went everywhere and preached, and the Lord worked through them, confirming what they said by many miraculous signs.

16:17 Or *new tongues*; some manuscripts do not include *new*.

Luke

Introduction

1 Many people have set out to write accounts about the events that have been fulfilled among us. [2] They used the eyewitness reports circulating among us from the early disciples.* [3] Having carefully investigated everything from the beginning, I also have decided to write an accurate account for you, most honorable Theophilus, [4] so you can be certain of the truth of everything you were taught.

The Birth of John the Baptist Foretold

[5] When Herod was king of Judea, there was a Jewish priest named Zechariah. He was a member of the priestly order of Abijah, and his wife, Elizabeth, was also from the priestly line of Aaron. [6] Zechariah and Elizabeth were righteous in God's eyes, careful to obey all of the Lord's commandments and regulations. [7] They had no children because Elizabeth was unable to conceive, and they were both very old.

[8] One day Zechariah was serving God in the Temple, for his order was on duty that week. [9] As was the custom of the priests, he was chosen by lot to enter the sanctuary of the Lord and burn incense. [10] While the incense was being burned, a great crowd stood outside, praying.

[11] While Zechariah was in the sanctuary, an angel of the Lord appeared to him, standing to the right of the incense altar. [12] Zechariah was shaken and overwhelmed with fear when he saw him. [13] But the angel said, "Don't be afraid, Zechariah! God has heard your prayer. Your wife, Elizabeth, will give you a son, and you are to name him John. [14] You will have great joy and gladness, and many will rejoice at his birth, [15] for he will be great in the eyes of the Lord. He must never touch wine or other alcoholic drinks. He will be filled with the Holy Spirit, even before his birth.* [16] And he will turn many Israelites to the Lord their God. [17] He will be a man with the spirit and power of Elijah. He will prepare the people for the coming of the Lord. He will turn the hearts of the fathers to their children,* and he will cause those who are rebellious to accept the wisdom of the godly."

1:2 Greek *from those who from the beginning were servants of the word.*   **1:15** Or *even from birth.*
1:17 See Mal 4:5-6.

[18]Zechariah said to the angel, "How can I be sure this will happen? I'm an old man now, and my wife is also well along in years."

[19]Then the angel said, "I am Gabriel! I stand in the very presence of God. It was he who sent me to bring you this good news! [20]But now, since you didn't believe what I said, you will be silent and unable to speak until the child is born. For my words will certainly be fulfilled at the proper time."

[21]Meanwhile, the people were waiting for Zechariah to come out of the sanctuary, wondering why he was taking so long. [22]When he finally did come out, he couldn't speak to them. Then they realized from his gestures and his silence that he must have seen a vision in the sanctuary.

[23]When Zechariah's week of service in the Temple was over, he returned home. [24]Soon afterward his wife, Elizabeth, became pregnant and went into seclusion for five months. [25]"How kind the Lord is!" she exclaimed. "He has taken away my disgrace of having no children."

The Birth of Jesus Foretold

[26]In the sixth month of Elizabeth's pregnancy, God sent the angel Gabriel to Nazareth, a village in Galilee, [27]to a virgin named Mary. She was engaged to be married to a man named Joseph, a descendant of King David. [28]Gabriel appeared to her and said, "Greetings,* favored woman! The Lord is with you!*"

[29]Confused and disturbed, Mary tried to think what the angel could mean. [30]"Don't be afraid, Mary," the angel told her, "for you have found favor with God! [31]You will conceive and give birth to a son, and you will name him Jesus. [32]He will be very great and will be called the Son of the Most High. The Lord God will give him the throne of his ancestor David. [33]And he will reign over Israel* forever; his Kingdom will never end!"

[34]Mary asked the angel, "But how can this happen? I am a virgin."

[35]The angel replied, "The Holy Spirit will come upon you, and the power of the Most High will overshadow you. So the baby to be born will be holy, and he will be called the Son of God. [36]What's more, your relative Elizabeth has become pregnant in her old age! People used to say she was barren, but she has conceived a son and is now in her sixth month. [37]For the word of God will never fail.*"

[38]Mary responded, "I am the Lord's servant. May everything you have said about me come true." And then the angel left her.

Mary Visits Elizabeth

[39]A few days later Mary hurried to the hill country of Judea, to the town [40]where Zechariah lived. She

---

1:28a Or *Rejoice.*   **1:28b** Some manuscripts add *Blessed are you among women.*   **1:33** Greek *over the house of Jacob.*   **1:37** Some manuscripts read *For nothing is impossible with God.*

entered the house and greeted Elizabeth. [41]At the sound of Mary's greeting, Elizabeth's child leaped within her, and Elizabeth was filled with the Holy Spirit.

[42]Elizabeth gave a glad cry and exclaimed to Mary, "God has blessed you above all women, and your child is blessed. [43]Why am I so honored, that the mother of my Lord should visit me? [44]When I heard your greeting, the baby in my womb jumped for joy. [45]You are blessed because you believed that the Lord would do what he said."

The Magnificat:
Mary's Song of Praise

[46]Mary responded,

"Oh, how my soul praises
      the Lord.
[47]   How my spirit rejoices in
      God my Savior!
[48] For he took notice of his lowly
      servant girl,
      and from now on all
      generations will call me
      blessed.
[49] For the Mighty One is holy,
      and he has done great things
      for me.
[50] He shows mercy from
      generation to generation
      to all who fear him.
[51] His mighty arm has done
      tremendous things!
      He has scattered the proud
      and haughty ones.
[52] He has brought down princes
      from their thrones
      and exalted the humble.
[53] He has filled the hungry with
      good things
      and sent the rich away with
      empty hands.
[54] He has helped his servant Israel
      and remembered to be
      merciful.
[55] For he made this promise to
      our ancestors,
      to Abraham and his children
      forever."

[56]Mary stayed with Elizabeth about three months and then went back to her own home.

The Birth of John the Baptist

[57]When it was time for Elizabeth's baby to be born, she gave birth to a son. [58]And when her neighbors and relatives heard that the Lord had been very merciful to her, everyone rejoiced with her.

[59]When the baby was eight days old, they all came for the circumcision ceremony. They wanted to name him Zechariah, after his father. [60]But Elizabeth said, "No! His name is John!"

[61]"What?" they exclaimed. "There is no one in all your family by that name." [62]So they used gestures to ask the baby's father what he wanted to name him. [63]He motioned for a writing tablet, and to everyone's surprise he wrote, "His name is John."

64Instantly Zechariah could speak again, and he began praising God.

65Awe fell upon the whole neighborhood, and the news of what had happened spread throughout the Judean hills. 66Everyone who heard about it reflected on these events and asked, "What will this child turn out to be?" For the hand of the Lord was surely upon him in a special way.

Zechariah's Prophecy

67Then his father, Zechariah, was filled with the Holy Spirit and gave this prophecy:

68 "Praise the Lord, the God of
        Israel,
    because he has visited and
        redeemed his people.
69 He has sent us a mighty Savior*
        from the royal line of his
        servant David,
70 just as he promised
        through his holy prophets
        long ago.
71 Now we will be saved from our
        enemies
    and from all who hate us.
72 He has been merciful to our
        ancestors
    by remembering his sacred
        covenant—
73 the covenant he swore with
        an oath
    to our ancestor Abraham.
74 We have been rescued from
        our enemies

so we can serve God without
        fear,
75 in holiness and righteousness
        for as long as we live.

76 "And you, my little son,
        will be called the prophet
        of the Most High,
    because you will prepare the
        way for the Lord.
77 You will tell his people how to
        find salvation
    through forgiveness of their
        sins.
78 Because of God's tender mercy,
        the morning light from heaven
        is about to break upon us,*
79 to give light to those who sit in
        darkness and in the shadow
        of death,
    and to guide us to the path of
        peace."

80John grew up and became strong in spirit. And he lived in the wilderness until he began his public ministry to Israel.

The Birth of Jesus

2 At that time the Roman emperor, Augustus, decreed that a census should be taken throughout the Roman Empire. 2(This was the first census taken when Quirinius was governor of Syria.) 3All returned to their own ancestral towns to register for this census. 4And because Joseph was a descendant of King David, he had to go to Bethlehem in

---

1:69 Greek *has raised up a horn of salvation for us.*   1:78 Or *the Morning Light from Heaven is*
about to visit us.

Judea, David's ancient home. He traveled there from the village of Nazareth in Galilee. [5]He took with him Mary, to whom he was engaged, who was now expecting a child.

[6]And while they were there, the time came for her baby to be born. [7]She gave birth to her firstborn son. She wrapped him snugly in strips of cloth and laid him in a manger, because there was no lodging available for them.

The Shepherds and Angels

[8]That night there were shepherds staying in the fields nearby, guarding their flocks of sheep. [9]Suddenly, an angel of the Lord appeared among them, and the radiance of the Lord's glory surrounded them. They were terrified, [10]but the angel reassured them. "Don't be afraid!" he said. "I bring you good news that will bring great joy to all people. [11]The Savior—yes, the Messiah, the Lord—has been born today in Bethlehem, the city of David! [12]And you will recognize him by this sign: You will find a baby wrapped snugly in strips of cloth, lying in a manger."

[13]Suddenly, the angel was joined by a vast host of others—the armies of heaven—praising God and saying,

[14] "Glory to God in highest
        heaven,
    and peace on earth
        to those with whom
        God is pleased."

[15]When the angels had returned to heaven, the shepherds said to each other, "Let's go to Bethlehem! Let's see this thing that has happened, which the Lord has told us about."

[16]They hurried to the village and found Mary and Joseph. And there was the baby, lying in the manger. [17]After seeing him, the shepherds told everyone what had happened and what the angel had said to them about this child. [18]All who heard the shepherds' story were astonished, [19]but Mary kept all these things in her heart and thought about them often. [20]The shepherds went back to their flocks, glorifying and praising God for all they had heard and seen. It was just as the angel had told them.

Jesus Is Presented in the Temple

[21]Eight days later, when the baby was circumcised, he was named Jesus, the name given him by the angel even before he was conceived.

[22]Then it was time for their purification offering, as required by the law of Moses after the birth of a child; so his parents took him to Jerusalem to present him to the Lord. [23]The law of the Lord says, "If a woman's first child is a boy, he must be dedicated to the LORD."* [24]So they offered the sacrifice required in the law of the Lord—"either a pair of turtledoves or two young pigeons."*

2:23 Exod 13:2.   **2:24** Lev 12:8.

The Prophecy of Simeon

[25] At that time there was a man in Jerusalem named Simeon. He was righteous and devout and was eagerly waiting for the Messiah to come and rescue Israel. The Holy Spirit was upon him [26] and had revealed to him that he would not die until he had seen the Lord's Messiah. [27] That day the Spirit led him to the Temple. So when Mary and Joseph came to present the baby Jesus to the Lord as the law required, [28] Simeon was there. He took the child in his arms and praised God, saying,

[29] "Sovereign Lord, now let your
          servant die in peace,
       as you have promised.
[30] I have seen your salvation,
[31]   which you have prepared for
          all people.
[32] He is a light to reveal God to
          the nations,
       and he is the glory of your
          people Israel!"

[33] Jesus' parents were amazed at what was being said about him. [34] Then Simeon blessed them, and he said to Mary, the baby's mother, "This child is destined to cause many in Israel to fall, and many others to rise. He has been sent as a sign from God, but many will oppose him. [35] As a result, the deepest thoughts of many hearts will be revealed. And a sword will pierce your very soul."

The Prophecy of Anna

[36] Anna, a prophet, was also there in the Temple. She was the daughter of Phanuel from the tribe of Asher, and she was very old. Her husband died when they had been married only seven years. [37] Then she lived as a widow to the age of eighty-four.* She never left the Temple but stayed there day and night, worshiping God with fasting and prayer. [38] She came along just as Simeon was talking with Mary and Joseph, and she began praising God. She talked about the child to everyone who had been waiting expectantly for God to rescue Jerusalem.

[39] When Jesus' parents had fulfilled all the requirements of the law of the Lord, they returned home to Nazareth in Galilee. [40] There the child grew up healthy and strong. He was filled with wisdom, and God's favor was on him.

Jesus Speaks with the Teachers

[41] Every year Jesus' parents went to Jerusalem for the Passover festival. [42] When Jesus was twelve years old, they attended the festival as usual. [43] After the celebration was over, they started home to Nazareth, but Jesus stayed behind in Jerusalem. His parents didn't miss him at first, [44] because they assumed he was among the other travelers. But when he didn't show up that evening, they

2:37 Or *She had been a widow for eighty-four years.*

started looking for him among their relatives and friends.

[45]When they couldn't find him, they went back to Jerusalem to search for him there. [46]Three days later they finally discovered him in the Temple, sitting among the religious teachers, listening to them and asking questions. [47]All who heard him were amazed at his understanding and his answers.

[48]His parents didn't know what to think. "Son," his mother said to him, "why have you done this to us? Your father and I have been frantic, searching for you everywhere."

[49]"But why did you need to search?" he asked. "Didn't you know that I must be in my Father's house?"* [50]But they didn't understand what he meant.

[51]Then he returned to Nazareth with them and was obedient to them. And his mother stored all these things in her heart.

[52]Jesus grew in wisdom and in stature and in favor with God and all the people.

John the Baptist Prepares the Way

3 It was now the fifteenth year of the reign of Tiberius, the Roman emperor. Pontius Pilate was governor over Judea; Herod Antipas was ruler* over Galilee; his brother Philip was ruler* over Iturea and Traconitis; Lysanias was ruler over Abilene. [2]An-

nas and Caiaphas were the high priests. At this time a message from God came to John son of Zechariah, who was living in the wilderness. [3]Then John went from place to place on both sides of the Jordan River, preaching that people should be baptized to show that they had repented of their sins and turned to God to be forgiven. [4]Isaiah had spoken of John when he said,

"He is a voice shouting in the
wilderness,
'Prepare the way for the LORD's
coming!
Clear the road for him!
[5] The valleys will be filled,
and the mountains and hills
made level.
The curves will be straightened,
and the rough places made
smooth.
[6] And then all people will see
the salvation sent from God.'"*

[7]When the crowds came to John for baptism, he said, "You brood of snakes! Who warned you to flee the coming wrath? [8]Prove by the way you live that you have repented of your sins and turned to God. Don't just say to each other, 'We're safe, for we are descendants of Abraham.' That means nothing, for I tell you, God can create children of Abraham from these very stones. [9]Even now the ax of God's judgment

2:49 Or *"Didn't you realize that I should be involved with my Father's affairs?"* **3:1a** Greek *Herod was tetrarch.* Herod Antipas was a son of King Herod. **3:1b** Greek *tetrarch;* also in 3:1c. **3:4-6** Isa 40:3-5 (Greek version).

is poised, ready to sever the roots of the trees. Yes, every tree that does not produce good fruit will be chopped down and thrown into the fire."

[10]The crowds asked, "What should we do?"

[11]John replied, "If you have two shirts, give one to the poor. If you have food, share it with those who are hungry."

[12]Even corrupt tax collectors came to be baptized and asked, "Teacher, what should we do?"

[13]He replied, "Collect no more taxes than the government requires."

[14]"What should we do?" asked some soldiers.

John replied, "Don't extort money or make false accusations. And be content with your pay."

[15]Everyone was expecting the Messiah to come soon, and they were eager to know whether John might be the Messiah. [16]John answered their questions by saying, "I baptize you with* water; but someone is coming soon who is greater than I am—so much greater that I'm not even worthy to be his slave and untie the straps of his sandals. He will baptize you with the Holy Spirit and with fire.* [17]He is ready to separate the chaff from the wheat with his winnowing fork. Then he will clean up the threshing area, gathering the wheat into his barn but burning the chaff with never-ending fire." [18]John used many such warnings as he announced the Good News to the people.

[19]John also publicly criticized Herod Antipas, the ruler of Galilee,* for marrying Herodias, his brother's wife, and for many other wrongs he had done. [20]So Herod put John in prison, adding this sin to his many others.

The Baptism of Jesus

[21]One day when the crowds were being baptized, Jesus himself was baptized. As he was praying, the heavens opened, [22]and the Holy Spirit, in bodily form, descended on him like a dove. And a voice from heaven said, "You are my dearly loved Son, and you bring me great joy.*"

The Ancestors of Jesus

[23]Jesus was about thirty years old when he began his public ministry.

Jesus was known as the son of Joseph.
Joseph was the son of Heli.
[24] Heli was the son of Matthat.
Matthat was the son of Levi.
Levi was the son of Melki.
Melki was the son of Jannai.
Jannai was the son of Joseph.
[25] Joseph was the son of Mattathias.
Mattathias was the son of Amos.
Amos was the son of Nahum.
Nahum was the son of Esli.

3:16a Or *in.* **3:16b** Or *in the Holy Spirit and in fire.* **3:19** Greek *Herod the tetrarch.* **3:22** Some manuscripts read *my Son, and today I have become your Father.*

Esli was the son of Naggai.
26 Naggai was the son of Maath.
Maath was the son of Mattathias.
Mattathias was the son of
    Semein.
Semein was the son of Josech.
Josech was the son of Joda.
27 Joda was the son of Joanan.
Joanan was the son of Rhesa.
Rhesa was the son of
    Zerubbabel.
Zerubbabel was the son of
    Shealtiel.
Shealtiel was the son of Neri.
28 Neri was the son of Melki.
Melki was the son of Addi.
Addi was the son of Cosam.
Cosam was the son of Elmadam.
Elmadam was the son of Er.
29 Er was the son of Joshua.
Joshua was the son of Eliezer.
Eliezer was the son of Jorim.
Jorim was the son of Matthat.
Matthat was the son of Levi.
30 Levi was the son of Simeon.
Simeon was the son of Judah.
Judah was the son of Joseph.
Joseph was the son of Jonam.
Jonam was the son of Eliakim.
31 Eliakim was the son of Melea.
Melea was the son of Menna.
Menna was the son of Mattatha.
Mattatha was the son of Nathan.
Nathan was the son of David.
32 David was the son of Jesse.
Jesse was the son of Obed.
Obed was the son of Boaz.

Boaz was the son of Salmon.*
Salmon was the son of Nahshon.
33 Nahshon was the son of
    Amminadab.
Amminadab was the son of
    Admin.
Admin was the son of Arni.*
Arni was the son of Hezron.
Hezron was the son of Perez.
Perez was the son of Judah.
34 Judah was the son of Jacob.
Jacob was the son of Isaac.
Isaac was the son of Abraham.
Abraham was the son of Terah.
Terah was the son of Nahor.
35 Nahor was the son of Serug.
Serug was the son of Reu.
Reu was the son of Peleg.
Peleg was the son of Eber.
Eber was the son of Shelah.
36 Shelah was the son of Cainan.
Cainan was the son of
    Arphaxad.
Arphaxad was the son of Shem.
Shem was the son of Noah.
Noah was the son of Lamech.
37 Lamech was the son of
    Methuselah.
Methuselah was the son of
    Enoch.
Enoch was the son of Jared.
Jared was the son of Mahalalel.
Mahalalel was the son of Kenan.
38 Kenan was the son of Enosh.*
Enosh was the son of Seth.
Seth was the son of Adam.
Adam was the son of God.

3:32 Greek *Sala,* a variant spelling of Salmon; also in 3:32b. See Ruth 4:20-21. **3:33** Some manuscripts read *Amminadab was the son of Aram. Arni* and *Aram* are alternate spellings of Ram. See 1 Chr 2:9-10. **3:38** Greek *Enos,* a variant spelling of Enosh; also in 3:38b. See Gen 5:6.

The Temptation of Jesus

4 Then Jesus, full of the Holy Spirit, returned from the Jordan River. He was led by the Spirit in the wilderness,* ²where he was tempted by the devil for forty days. Jesus ate nothing all that time and became very hungry.

³Then the devil said to him, "If you are the Son of God, tell this stone to become a loaf of bread."

⁴But Jesus told him, "No! The Scriptures say, 'People do not live by bread alone.'*"

⁵Then the devil took him up and revealed to him all the kingdoms of the world in a moment of time. ⁶"I will give you the glory of these kingdoms and authority over them," the devil said, "because they are mine to give to anyone I please. ⁷I will give it all to you if you will worship me."

⁸Jesus replied, "The Scriptures say,

'You must worship the Lord
　your God
　and serve only him.'*"

⁹Then the devil took him to Jerusalem, to the highest point of the Temple, and said, "If you are the Son of God, jump off! ¹⁰For the Scriptures say,

'He will order his angels to
　protect and guard you.
¹¹ And they will hold you up with
　their hands

so you won't even hurt your
　foot on a stone.'*"

¹²Jesus responded, "The Scriptures also say, 'You must not test the Lord your God.'*"

¹³When the devil had finished tempting Jesus, he left him until the next opportunity came.

Jesus Rejected at Nazareth

¹⁴Then Jesus returned to Galilee, filled with the Holy Spirit's power. Reports about him spread quickly through the whole region. ¹⁵He taught regularly in their synagogues and was praised by everyone.

¹⁶When he came to the village of Nazareth, his boyhood home, he went as usual to the synagogue on the Sabbath and stood up to read the Scriptures. ¹⁷The scroll of Isaiah the prophet was handed to him. He unrolled the scroll and found the place where this was written:

¹⁸ "The Spirit of the Lord is
　upon me,
　for he has anointed me to
　　bring Good News to the
　　poor.
He has sent me to proclaim that
　captives will be released,
　that the blind will see,
that the oppressed will be
　set free,
¹⁹　and that the time of the Lord's
　favor has come.*"

4:1 Some manuscripts read *into the wilderness.* **4:4** Deut 8:3. **4:8** Deut 6:13. **4:10-11** Ps 91:11-12. **4:12** Deut 6:16. **4:18-19** Or *and to proclaim the acceptable year of the Lord.* Isa 61:1-2 (Greek version); 58:6.

²⁰He rolled up the scroll, handed it back to the attendant, and sat down. All eyes in the synagogue looked at him intently. ²¹Then he began to speak to them. "The Scripture you've just heard has been fulfilled this very day!"

²²Everyone spoke well of him and was amazed by the gracious words that came from his lips. "How can this be?" they asked. "Isn't this Joseph's son?"

²³Then he said, "You will undoubtedly quote me this proverb: 'Physician, heal yourself'—meaning, 'Do miracles here in your hometown like those you did in Capernaum.' ²⁴But I tell you the truth, no prophet is accepted in his own hometown.

²⁵"Certainly there were many needy widows in Israel in Elijah's time, when the heavens were closed for three and a half years, and a severe famine devastated the land. ²⁶Yet Elijah was not sent to any of them. He was sent instead to a foreigner—a widow of Zarephath in the land of Sidon. ²⁷And many in Israel had leprosy in the time of the prophet Elisha, but the only one healed was Naaman, a Syrian."

²⁸When they heard this, the people in the synagogue were furious. ²⁹Jumping up, they mobbed him and forced him to the edge of the hill on which the town was built. They intended to push him over the cliff, ³⁰but he passed right through the crowd and went on his way.

Jesus Casts Out a Demon

³¹Then Jesus went to Capernaum, a town in Galilee, and taught there in the synagogue every Sabbath day. ³²There, too, the people were amazed at his teaching, for he spoke with authority.

³³Once when he was in the synagogue, a man possessed by a demon—an evil* spirit—cried out, shouting, ³⁴"Go away! Why are you interfering with us, Jesus of Nazareth? Have you come to destroy us? I know who you are—the Holy One of God!"

³⁵But Jesus reprimanded him. "Be quiet! Come out of the man," he ordered. At that, the demon threw the man to the floor as the crowd watched; then it came out of him without hurting him further.

³⁶Amazed, the people exclaimed, "What authority and power this man's words possess! Even evil spirits obey him, and they flee at his command!" ³⁷The news about Jesus spread through every village in the entire region.

Jesus Heals Many People

³⁸After leaving the synagogue that day, Jesus went to Simon's home, where he found Simon's mother-in-law very sick with a high fever. "Please heal her," everyone begged. ³⁹Standing at her bedside, he rebuked the fever, and it left her. And she got up at once and prepared a meal for them.

4:33 Greek *unclean;* also in 4:36.

⁴⁰As the sun went down that evening, people throughout the village brought sick family members to Jesus. No matter what their diseases were, the touch of his hand healed every one. ⁴¹Many were possessed by demons; and the demons came out at his command, shouting, "You are the Son of God!" But because they knew he was the Messiah, he rebuked them and refused to let them speak.

Jesus Continues to Preach
⁴²Early the next morning Jesus went out to an isolated place. The crowds searched everywhere for him, and when they finally found him, they begged him not to leave them. ⁴³But he replied, "I must preach the Good News of the Kingdom of God in other towns, too, because that is why I was sent." ⁴⁴So he continued to travel around, preaching in synagogues throughout Judea.*

The First Disciples
5 One day as Jesus was preaching on the shore of the Sea of Galilee,* great crowds pressed in on him to listen to the word of God. ²He noticed two empty boats at the water's edge, for the fishermen had left them and were washing their nets. ³Stepping into one of the boats, Jesus asked Simon,* its owner, to push it out into the water. So he sat in the boat and taught the crowds from there.

⁴When he had finished speaking, he said to Simon, "Now go out where it is deeper, and let down your nets to catch some fish."

⁵"Master," Simon replied, "we worked hard all last night and didn't catch a thing. But if you say so, I'll let the nets down again." ⁶And this time their nets were so full of fish they began to tear! ⁷A shout for help brought their partners in the other boat, and soon both boats were filled with fish and on the verge of sinking.

⁸When Simon Peter realized what had happened, he fell to his knees before Jesus and said, "Oh, Lord, please leave me—I'm such a sinful man." ⁹For he was awestruck by the number of fish they had caught, as were the others with him. ¹⁰His partners, James and John, the sons of Zebedee, were also amazed.

Jesus replied to Simon, "Don't be afraid! From now on you'll be fishing for people!" ¹¹And as soon as they landed, they left everything and followed Jesus.

Jesus Heals a Man with Leprosy
¹²In one of the villages, Jesus met a man with an advanced case of leprosy. When the man saw Jesus, he bowed with his face to the ground, begging to be healed. "Lord," he

4:44 Some manuscripts read *Galilee.*   5:1 Greek *Lake Gennesaret,* another name for the Sea of Galilee.   5:3 *Simon* is called "Peter" in 6:14 and thereafter.

said, "if you are willing, you can heal me and make me clean."

¹³Jesus reached out and touched him. "I am willing," he said. "Be healed!" And instantly the leprosy disappeared. ¹⁴Then Jesus instructed him not to tell anyone what had happened. He said, "Go to the priest and let him examine you. Take along the offering required in the law of Moses for those who have been healed of leprosy.* This will be a public testimony that you have been cleansed."

¹⁵But despite Jesus' instructions, the report of his power spread even faster, and vast crowds came to hear him preach and to be healed of their diseases. ¹⁶But Jesus often withdrew to the wilderness for prayer.

Jesus Heals a Paralyzed Man

¹⁷One day while Jesus was teaching, some Pharisees and teachers of religious law were sitting nearby. (It seemed that these men showed up from every village in all Galilee and Judea, as well as from Jerusalem.) And the Lord's healing power was strongly with Jesus.

¹⁸Some men came carrying a paralyzed man on a sleeping mat. They tried to take him inside to Jesus, ¹⁹but they couldn't reach him because of the crowd. So they went up to the roof and took off some tiles. Then they lowered the sick man on his mat down into the crowd, right in front of Jesus. ²⁰Seeing their faith, Jesus said to the man, "Young man, your sins are forgiven."

²¹But the Pharisees and teachers of religious law said to themselves, "Who does he think he is? That's blasphemy! Only God can forgive sins!"

²²Jesus knew what they were thinking, so he asked them, "Why do you question this in your hearts? ²³Is it easier to say 'Your sins are forgiven,' or 'Stand up and walk'? ²⁴So I will prove to you that the Son of Man* has the authority on earth to forgive sins." Then Jesus turned to the paralyzed man and said, "Stand up, pick up your mat, and go home!"

²⁵And immediately, as everyone watched, the man jumped up, picked up his mat, and went home praising God. ²⁶Everyone was gripped with great wonder and awe, and they praised God, exclaiming, "We have seen amazing things today!"

Jesus Calls Levi (Matthew)

²⁷Later, as Jesus left the town, he saw a tax collector named Levi sitting at his tax collector's booth. "Follow me and be my disciple," Jesus said to him. ²⁸So Levi got up, left everything, and followed him.

²⁹Later, Levi held a banquet in his home with Jesus as the guest of honor. Many of Levi's fellow tax collectors and other guests also ate with them. ³⁰But the Pharisees and their teachers of religious law complained bitterly to Jesus' disciples,

5:14 See Lev 14:2-32. 5:24 "Son of Man" is a title Jesus used for himself.

"Why do you eat and drink with such scum?*"

³¹Jesus answered them, "Healthy people don't need a doctor—sick people do. ³²I have come to call not those who think they are righteous, but those who know they are sinners and need to repent."

A Discussion about Fasting

³³One day some people said to Jesus, "John the Baptist's disciples fast and pray regularly, and so do the disciples of the Pharisees. Why are your disciples always eating and drinking?"

³⁴Jesus responded, "Do wedding guests fast while celebrating with the groom? Of course not. ³⁵But someday the groom will be taken away from them, and then they will fast."

³⁶Then Jesus gave them this illustration: "No one tears a piece of cloth from a new garment and uses it to patch an old garment. For then the new garment would be ruined, and the new patch wouldn't even match the old garment.

³⁷"And no one puts new wine into old wineskins. For the new wine would burst the wineskins, spilling the wine and ruining the skins. ³⁸New wine must be stored in new wineskins. ³⁹But no one who drinks the old wine seems to want the new wine. 'The old is just fine,' they say."

A Discussion about the Sabbath

6 One Sabbath day as Jesus was walking through some grain-fields, his disciples broke off heads of grain, rubbed off the husks in their hands, and ate the grain. ²But some Pharisees said, "Why are you breaking the law by harvesting grain on the Sabbath?"

³Jesus replied, "Haven't you read in the Scriptures what David did when he and his companions were hungry? ⁴He went into the house of God and broke the law by eating the sacred loaves of bread that only the priests can eat. He also gave some to his companions." ⁵And Jesus added, "The Son of Man* is Lord, even over the Sabbath."

Jesus Heals on the Sabbath

⁶On another Sabbath day, a man with a deformed right hand was in the synagogue while Jesus was teaching. ⁷The teachers of religious law and the Pharisees watched Jesus closely. If he healed the man's hand, they planned to accuse him of working on the Sabbath.

⁸But Jesus knew their thoughts. He said to the man with the deformed hand, "Come and stand in front of everyone." So the man came forward. ⁹Then Jesus said to his critics, "I have a question for you. Does the law permit good deeds on the Sabbath, or is it a day for doing evil? Is this a day to save life or to destroy it?"

5:30 Greek *with tax collectors and sinners?*   **6:5** "Son of Man" is a title Jesus used for himself.

¹⁰He looked around at them one by one and then said to the man, "Hold out your hand." So the man held out his hand, and it was restored! ¹¹At this, the enemies of Jesus were wild with rage and began to discuss what to do with him.

Jesus Chooses the Twelve Apostles
¹²One day soon afterward Jesus went up on a mountain to pray, and he prayed to God all night. ¹³At daybreak he called together all of his disciples and chose twelve of them to be apostles. Here are their names:

¹⁴ Simon (whom he named Peter),
Andrew (Peter's brother),
James,
John,
Philip,
Bartholomew,
¹⁵ Matthew,
Thomas,
James (son of Alphaeus),
Simon (who was called the zealot),
¹⁶ Judas (son of James),
Judas Iscariot (who later betrayed him).

Crowds Follow Jesus
¹⁷When they came down from the mountain, the disciples stood with Jesus on a large, level area, surrounded by many of his followers and by the crowds. There were people from all over Judea and from Jerusalem and from as far north as

the seacoasts of Tyre and Sidon. ¹⁸They had come to hear him and to be healed of their diseases; and those troubled by evil* spirits were healed. ¹⁹Everyone tried to touch him, because healing power went out from him, and he healed everyone.

The Beatitudes
²⁰Then Jesus turned to his disciples and said,

"God blesses you who are poor,
for the Kingdom of God is yours.
²¹ God blesses you who are hungry now,
for you will be satisfied.
God blesses you who weep now,
for in due time you will laugh.

²²What blessings await you when people hate you and exclude you and mock you and curse you as evil because you follow the Son of Man. ²³When that happens, be happy! Yes, leap for joy! For a great reward awaits you in heaven. And remember, their ancestors treated the ancient prophets that same way.

Sorrows Foretold
²⁴ "What sorrow awaits you who are rich,
for you have your only happiness now.
²⁵ What sorrow awaits you who are fat and prosperous now,
for a time of awful hunger awaits you.

What sorrow awaits you who
  laugh now,
  for your laughing will turn to
    mourning and sorrow.
26 What sorrow awaits you who are
  praised by the crowds,
  for their ancestors also praised
    false prophets.

Love for Enemies

27"But to you who are willing to listen, I say, love your enemies! Do good to those who hate you. 28Bless those who curse you. Pray for those who hurt you. 29If someone slaps you on one cheek, offer the other cheek also. If someone demands your coat, offer your shirt also. 30Give to anyone who asks; and when things are taken away from you, don't try to get them back. 31Do to others as you would like them to do to you.

32"If you love only those who love you, why should you get credit for that? Even sinners love those who love them! 33And if you do good only to those who do good to you, why should you get credit? Even sinners do that much! 34And if you lend money only to those who can repay you, why should you get credit? Even sinners will lend to other sinners for a full return.

35"Love your enemies! Do good to them. Lend to them without expecting to be repaid. Then your reward from heaven will be very great, and you will truly be acting as children of the Most High, for he is kind to those who are unthankful and wicked. 36You must be compassionate, just as your Father is compassionate.

Do Not Judge Others

37"Do not judge others, and you will not be judged. Do not condemn others, or it will all come back against you. Forgive others, and you will be forgiven. 38Give, and you will receive. Your gift will return to you in full—pressed down, shaken together to make room for more, running over, and poured into your lap. The amount you give will determine the amount you get back.*"

39Then Jesus gave the following illustration: "Can one blind person lead another? Won't they both fall into a ditch? 40Students* are not greater than their teacher. But the student who is fully trained will become like the teacher.

41"And why worry about a speck in your friend's eye* when you have a log in your own? 42How can you think of saying, 'Friend,* let me help you get rid of that speck in your eye,' when you can't see past the log in your own eye? Hypocrite! First get rid of the log in your own eye; then you will see well enough to deal with the speck in your friend's eye.

6:38 Or *The measure you give will be the measure you get back.* 6:40 Or *Disciples.* 6:41 Greek *your brother's eye;* also in 6:42. 6:42 Greek *Brother.*

The Tree and Its Fruit

43"A good tree can't produce bad fruit, and a bad tree can't produce good fruit. 44A tree is identified by its fruit. Figs are never gathered from thornbushes, and grapes are not picked from bramble bushes. 45A good person produces good things from the treasury of a good heart, and an evil person produces evil things from the treasury of an evil heart. What you say flows from what is in your heart."

Building on a Solid Foundation

46"So why do you keep calling me 'Lord, Lord!' when you don't do what I say? 47I will show you what it's like when someone comes to me, listens to my teaching, and then follows it. 48It is like a person building a house who digs deep and lays the foundation on solid rock. When the floodwaters rise and break against that house, it stands firm because it is well built. 49But anyone who hears and doesn't obey is like a person who builds a house right on the ground, without a foundation. When the floods sweep down against that house, it will collapse into a heap of ruins."

The Faith of a Roman Officer

7 When Jesus had finished saying all this to the people, he returned to Capernaum. 2At that time the highly valued slave of a Roman officer* was sick and near death. 3When the officer heard about Jesus, he sent some respected Jewish elders to ask him to come and heal his slave. 4So they earnestly begged Jesus to help the man. "If anyone deserves your help, he does," they said, 5"for he loves the Jewish people and even built a synagogue for us."

6So Jesus went with them. But just before they arrived at the house, the officer sent some friends to say, "Lord, don't trouble yourself by coming to my home, for I am not worthy of such an honor. 7I am not even worthy to come and meet you. Just say the word from where you are, and my servant will be healed. 8I know this because I am under the authority of my superior officers, and I have authority over my soldiers. I only need to say, 'Go,' and they go, or 'Come,' and they come. And if I say to my slaves, 'Do this,' they do it."

9When Jesus heard this, he was amazed. Turning to the crowd that was following him, he said, "I tell you, I haven't seen faith like this in all Israel!" 10And when the officer's friends returned to his house, they found the slave completely healed.

Jesus Raises a Widow's Son

11Soon afterward Jesus went with his disciples to the village of Nain, and a a large crowd followed him. 12A funeral procession was coming out as he approached the village gate. The young man who had died was a

7:2 Greek *a centurion;* similarly in 7:6.

widow's only son, and a large crowd from the village was with her. [13]When the Lord saw her, his heart overflowed with compassion. "Don't cry!" he said. [14]Then he walked over to the coffin and touched it, and the bearers stopped. "Young man," he said, "I tell you, get up." [15]Then the dead boy sat up and began to talk! And Jesus gave him back to his mother.

[16]Great fear swept the crowd, and they praised God, saying, "A mighty prophet has risen among us," and "God has visited his people today." [17]And the news about Jesus spread throughout Judea and the surrounding countryside.

Jesus and John the Baptist

[18]The disciples of John the Baptist told John about everything Jesus was doing. So John called for two of his disciples, [19]and he sent them to the Lord to ask him, "Are you the Messiah we've been expecting,* or should we keep looking for someone else?"

[20]John's two disciples found Jesus and said to him, "John the Baptist sent us to ask, 'Are you the Messiah we've been expecting, or should we keep looking for someone else?'"

[21]At that very time, Jesus cured many people of their diseases, illnesses, and evil spirits, and he restored sight to many who were blind. [22]Then he told John's disciples, "Go back to John and tell him what you have seen and heard—the blind see, the lame walk, those with leprosy are cured, the deaf hear, the dead are raised to life, and the Good News is being preached to the poor." [23]And he added, "God blesses those who do not fall away because of me.*"

[24]After John's disciples left, Jesus began talking about him to the crowds. "What kind of man did you go into the wilderness to see? Was he a weak reed, swayed by every breath of wind? [25]Or were you expecting to see a man dressed in expensive clothes? No, people who wear beautiful clothes and live in luxury are found in palaces. [26]Were you looking for a prophet? Yes, and he is more than a prophet. [27]John is the man to whom the Scriptures refer when they say,

'Look, I am sending my
    messenger ahead of you,
and he will prepare your way
    before you.'*

[28]I tell you, of all who have ever lived, none is greater than John. Yet even the least person in the Kingdom of God is greater than he is!"

[29]When they heard this, all the people—even the tax collectors—agreed that God's way was right,* for they had been baptized by John. [30]But the Pharisees and experts in religious law rejected God's plan for them, for they had refused John's baptism.

7:19 Greek *Are you the one who is coming?* Also in 7:20. 7:23 Or *who are not offended by me.*
7:27 Mal 3:1. 7:29 Or *praised God for his justice.*

³¹"To what can I compare the people of this generation?" Jesus asked. "How can I describe them? ³²They are like children playing a game in the public square. They complain to their friends,

'We played wedding songs,
      and you didn't dance,
so we played funeral songs,
      and you didn't weep.'

³³For John the Baptist didn't spend his time eating bread or drinking wine, and you say, 'He's possessed by a demon.' ³⁴The Son of Man,* on the other hand, feasts and drinks, and you say, 'He's a glutton and a drunkard, and a friend of tax collectors and other sinners!' ³⁵But wisdom is shown to be right by the lives of those who follow it.*"

Jesus Anointed by a Sinful Woman

³⁶One of the Pharisees asked Jesus to have dinner with him, so Jesus went to his home and sat down to eat.* ³⁷When a certain immoral woman from that city heard he was eating there, she brought a beautiful alabaster jar filled with expensive perfume. ³⁸Then she knelt behind him at his feet, weeping. Her tears fell on his feet, and she wiped them off with her hair. Then she kept kissing his feet and putting perfume on them. ³⁹When the Pharisee who had in-

vited him saw this, he said to himself, "If this man were a prophet, he would know what kind of woman is touching him. She's a sinner!"

⁴⁰Then Jesus answered his thoughts. "Simon," he said to the Pharisee, "I have something to say to you."

"Go ahead, Teacher," Simon replied.

⁴¹Then Jesus told him this story: "A man loaned money to two people—500 pieces of silver* to one and 50 pieces to the other. ⁴²But neither of them could repay him, so he kindly forgave them both, canceling their debts. Who do you suppose loved him more after that?"

⁴³Simon answered, "I suppose the one for whom he canceled the larger debt."

"That's right," Jesus said. ⁴⁴Then he turned to the woman and said to Simon, "Look at this woman kneeling here. When I entered your home, you didn't offer me water to wash the dust from my feet, but she has washed them with her tears and wiped them with her hair. ⁴⁵You didn't greet me with a kiss, but from the time I first came in, she has not stopped kissing my feet. ⁴⁶You neglected the courtesy of olive oil to anoint my head, but she has anointed my feet with rare perfume.

⁴⁷"I tell you, her sins—and they are many—have been forgiven, so she has shown me much love. But a per-

7:34 "Son of Man" is a title Jesus used for himself. 7:35 Or *But wisdom is justified by all her children.* 7:36 Or *and reclined.* 7:41 Greek *500 denarii.* A denarius was equivalent to a laborer's full day's wage.

son who is forgiven little shows only little love." ⁴⁸Then Jesus said to the woman, "Your sins are forgiven."

⁴⁹The men at the table said among themselves, "Who is this man, that he goes around forgiving sins?"

⁵⁰And Jesus said to the woman, "Your faith has saved you; go in peace."

Women Who Followed Jesus

8 Soon afterward Jesus began a tour of the nearby towns and villages, preaching and announcing the Good News about the Kingdom of God. He took his twelve disciples with him, ²along with some women who had been cured of evil spirits and diseases. Among them were Mary Magdalene, from whom he had cast out seven demons; ³Joanna, the wife of Chuza, Herod's business manager; Susanna; and many others who were contributing from their own resources to support Jesus and his disciples.

Parable of the Farmer Scattering Seed

⁴One day Jesus told a story in the form of a parable to a large crowd that had gathered from many towns to hear him: ⁵"A farmer went out to plant his seed. As he scattered it across his field, some seed fell on a footpath, where it was stepped on, and the birds ate it. ⁶Other seed fell among rocks. It began to grow, but the plant soon wilted and died for lack of moisture. ⁷Other seed fell among thorns that grew up with it and choked out the tender plants. ⁸Still other seed fell on fertile soil. This seed grew and produced a crop that was a hundred times as much as had been planted!" When he had said this, he called out, "Anyone with ears to hear should listen and understand."

⁹His disciples asked him what this parable meant. ¹⁰He replied, "You are permitted to understand the secrets* of the Kingdom of God. But I use parables to teach the others so that the Scriptures might be fulfilled:

'When they look, they won't
    really see.
When they hear, they won't
    understand.'*

¹¹"This is the meaning of the parable: The seed is God's word. ¹²The seeds that fell on the footpath represent those who hear the message, only to have the devil come and take it away from their hearts and prevent them from believing and being saved. ¹³The seeds on the rocky soil represent those who hear the message and receive it with joy. But since they don't have deep roots, they believe for a while, then they fall away when they face temptation. ¹⁴The seeds that fell among the thorns represent those who hear the message, but all too quickly the

8:10a Greek *mysteries.*   8:10b Isa 6:9 (Greek version).

message is crowded out by the cares and riches and pleasures of this life. And so they never grow into maturity. [15]And the seeds that fell on the good soil represent honest, good-hearted people who hear God's word, cling to it, and patiently produce a huge harvest.

Parable of the Lamp

[16]"No one lights a lamp and then covers it with a bowl or hides it under a bed. A lamp is placed on a stand, where its light can be seen by all who enter the house. [17]For all that is secret will eventually be brought into the open, and everything that is concealed will be brought to light and made known to all.

[18]"So pay attention to how you hear. To those who listen to my teaching, more understanding will be given. But for those who are not listening, even what they think they understand will be taken away from them."

The True Family of Jesus

[19]Then Jesus' mother and brothers came to see him, but they couldn't get to him because of the crowd. [20]Someone told Jesus, "Your mother and your brothers are standing outside, and they want to see you."

[21]Jesus replied, "My mother and my brothers are all those who hear God's word and obey it."

Jesus Calms the Storm

[22]One day Jesus said to his disciples, "Let's cross to the other side of the lake." So they got into a boat and started out. [23]As they sailed across, Jesus settled down for a nap. But soon a fierce storm came down on the lake. The boat was filling with water, and they were in real danger.

[24]The disciples went and woke him up, shouting, "Master, Master, we're going to drown!"

When Jesus woke up, he rebuked the wind and the raging waves. Suddenly the storm stopped and all was calm. [25]Then he asked them, "Where is your faith?"

The disciples were terrified and amazed. "Who is this man?" they asked each other. "When he gives a command, even the wind and waves obey him!"

Jesus Heals a Demon-Possessed Man

[26]So they arrived in the region of the Gerasenes,* across the lake from Galilee. [27]As Jesus was climbing out of the boat, a man who was possessed by demons came out to meet him. For a long time he had been homeless and naked, living in the tombs outside the town.

[28]As soon as he saw Jesus, he shrieked and fell down in front of him. Then he screamed, "Why are you interfering with me, Jesus, Son of the Most High God? Please, I beg you,

8:26 Other manuscripts read *Gadarenes;* still others read *Gergesenes;* also in 8:37. See Matt 8:28; Mark 5:1.

don't torture me!" ²⁹For Jesus had already commanded the evil* spirit to come out of him. This spirit had often taken control of the man. Even when he was placed under guard and put in chains and shackles, he simply broke them and rushed out into the wilderness, completely under the demon's power.

³⁰Jesus demanded, "What is your name?"

"Legion," he replied, for he was filled with many demons. ³¹The demons kept begging Jesus not to send them into the bottomless pit.*

³²There happened to be a large herd of pigs feeding on the hillside nearby, and the demons begged him to let them enter into the pigs.

So Jesus gave them permission. ³³Then the demons came out of the man and entered the pigs, and the entire herd plunged down the steep hillside into the lake and drowned.

³⁴When the herdsmen saw it, they fled to the nearby town and the surrounding countryside, spreading the news as they ran. ³⁵People rushed out to see what had happened. A crowd soon gathered around Jesus, and they saw the man who had been freed from the demons. He was sitting at Jesus' feet, fully clothed and perfectly sane, and they were all afraid. ³⁶Then those who had seen what happened told the others how the demon-possessed man had been healed.

³⁷And all the people in the region of the Gerasenes begged Jesus to go away and leave them alone, for a great wave of fear swept over them.

So Jesus returned to the boat and left, crossing back to the other side of the lake. ³⁸The man who had been freed from the demons begged to go with him. But Jesus sent him home, saying, ³⁹"No, go back to your family, and tell them everything God has done for you." So he went all through the town proclaiming the great things Jesus had done for him.

Jesus Heals in Response to Faith

⁴⁰On the other side of the lake the crowds welcomed Jesus, because they had been waiting for him. ⁴¹Then a man named Jairus, a leader of the local synagogue, came and fell at Jesus' feet, pleading with him to come home with him. ⁴²His only daughter,* who was about twelve years old, was dying.

As Jesus went with him, he was surrounded by the crowds. ⁴³A woman in the crowd had suffered for twelve years with constant bleeding,* and she could find no cure. ⁴⁴Coming up behind Jesus, she touched the fringe of his robe. Immediately, the bleeding stopped.

⁴⁵"Who touched me?" Jesus asked.

Everyone denied it, and Peter said, "Master, this whole crowd is pressing up against you."

8:29 Greek *unclean.* 8:31 Or *the abyss,* or *the underworld.* 8:42 Or *His only child, a daughter.*
8:43 Some manuscripts add *having spent everything she had on doctors.*

⁴⁶But Jesus said, "Someone deliberately touched me, for I felt healing power go out from me." ⁴⁷When the woman realized that she could not stay hidden, she began to tremble and fell to her knees in front of him. The whole crowd heard her explain why she had touched him and that she had been immediately healed. ⁴⁸"Daughter," he said to her, "your faith has made you well. Go in peace."

⁴⁹While he was still speaking to her, a messenger arrived from the home of Jairus, the leader of the synagogue. He told him, "Your daughter is dead. There's no use troubling the Teacher now."

⁵⁰But when Jesus heard what had happened, he said to Jairus, "Don't be afraid. Just have faith, and she will be healed."

⁵¹When they arrived at the house, Jesus wouldn't let anyone go in with him except Peter, John, James, and the little girl's father and mother. ⁵²The house was filled with people weeping and wailing, but he said, "Stop the weeping! She isn't dead; she's only asleep."

⁵³But the crowd laughed at him because they all knew she had died. ⁵⁴Then Jesus took her by the hand and said in a loud voice, "My child, get up!" ⁵⁵And at that moment her life* returned, and she immediately stood up! Then Jesus told them to give her something to eat. ⁵⁶Her parents were overwhelmed, but Jesus insisted that they not tell anyone what had happened.

Jesus Sends Out the Twelve Disciples

9 One day Jesus called together his twelve disciples* and gave them power and authority to cast out all demons and to heal all diseases. ²Then he sent them out to tell everyone about the Kingdom of God and to heal the sick. ³"Take nothing for your journey," he instructed them. "Don't take a walking stick, a traveler's bag, food, money,* or even a change of clothes. ⁴Wherever you go, stay in the same house until you leave town. ⁵And if a town refuses to welcome you, shake its dust from your feet as you leave to show that you have abandoned those people to their fate."

⁶So they began their circuit of the villages, preaching the Good News and healing the sick.

Herod's Confusion

⁷When Herod Antipas, the ruler of Galilee,* heard about everything Jesus was doing, he was puzzled. Some were saying that John the Baptist had been raised from the dead. ⁸Others thought Jesus was Elijah or one of the other prophets risen from the dead.

8:55 Or *her spirit.* **9:1** Greek *the Twelve;* other manuscripts read *the twelve apostles.* **9:3** Or *silver coins.* **9:7** Greek *Herod the tetrarch.* Herod Antipas was a son of King Herod and was ruler over Galilee.

[9]"I beheaded John," Herod said, "so who is this man about whom I hear such stories?" And he kept trying to see him.

Jesus Feeds Five Thousand

[10]When the apostles returned, they told Jesus everything they had done. Then he slipped quietly away with them toward the town of Bethsaida. [11]But the crowds found out where he was going, and they followed him. He welcomed them and taught them about the Kingdom of God, and he healed those who were sick.

[12]Late in the afternoon the twelve disciples came to him and said, "Send the crowds away to the nearby villages and farms, so they can find food and lodging for the night. There is nothing to eat here in this remote place."

[13]But Jesus said, "You feed them."

"But we have only five loaves of bread and two fish," they answered. "Or are you expecting us to go and buy enough food for this whole crowd?" [14]For there were about 5,000 men there.

Jesus replied, "Tell them to sit down in groups of about fifty each." [15]So the people all sat down. [16]Jesus took the five loaves and two fish, looked up toward heaven, and blessed them. Then, breaking the loaves into pieces, he kept giving the bread and fish to the disciples so they could distribute it to the people. [17]They all ate as much as they wanted, and afterward, the disciples picked up twelve baskets of leftovers!

Peter's Declaration about Jesus

[18]One day Jesus left the crowds to pray alone. Only his disciples were with him, and he asked them, "Who do people say I am?"

[19]"Well," they replied, "some say John the Baptist, some say Elijah, and others say you are one of the other ancient prophets risen from the dead."

[20]Then he asked them, "But who do you say I am?"

Peter replied, "You are the Messiah* sent from God!"

Jesus Predicts His Death

[21]Jesus warned his disciples not to tell anyone who he was. [22]"The Son of Man* must suffer many terrible things," he said. "He will be rejected by the elders, the leading priests, and the teachers of religious law. He will be killed, but on the third day he will be raised from the dead."

[23]Then he said to the crowd, "If any of you wants to be my follower, you must give up you own way, take up your cross daily, and follow me. [24]If you try to hang on to your life, you will lose it. But if you give up your life for my sake, you will save it. [25]And what do you benefit if you gain the whole world but are

9:20 Or *the Christ. Messiah* (a Hebrew term) and *Christ* (a Greek term) both mean "anointed one."
9:22 "Son of Man" is a title Jesus used for himself.

yourself lost or destroyed? ²⁶If anyone is ashamed of me and my message, the Son of Man will be ashamed of that person when he returns in his glory and in the glory of the Father and the holy angels. ²⁷I tell you the truth, some standing here right now will not die before they see the Kingdom of God."

The Transfiguration

²⁸About eight days later Jesus took Peter, John, and James up on a mountain to pray. ²⁹And as he was praying, the appearance of his face was transformed, and his clothes became dazzling white. ³⁰Suddenly, two men, Moses and Elijah, appeared and began talking with Jesus. ³¹They were glorious to see. And they were speaking about his exodus from this world, which was about to be fulfilled in Jerusalem.

³²Peter and the others had fallen asleep. When they woke up, they saw Jesus' glory and the two men standing with him. ³³As Moses and Elijah were starting to leave, Peter, not even knowing what he was saying, blurted out, "Master, it's wonderful for us to be here! Let's make three shelters as memorials*—one for you, one for Moses, and one for Elijah." ³⁴But even as he was saying this, a cloud overshadowed them, and terror gripped them as the cloud covered them.

³⁵Then a voice from the cloud said, "This is my Son, my Chosen One.* Listen to him." ³⁶When the voice finished, Jesus was there alone. They didn't tell anyone at that time what they had seen.

Jesus Heals a Demon-Possessed Boy

³⁷The next day, after they had come down the mountain, a large crowd met Jesus. ³⁸A man in the crowd called out to him, "Teacher, I beg you to look at my son, my only child. ³⁹An evil spirit keeps seizing him, making him scream. It throws him into convulsions so that he foams at the mouth. It batters him and hardly ever leaves him alone. ⁴⁰I begged your disciples to cast out the spirit, but they couldn't do it."

⁴¹Jesus said, "You faithless and corrupt people! How long must I be with you and put up with you?" Then he said to the man, "Bring your son here."

⁴²As the boy came forward, the demon knocked him to the ground and threw him into a violent convulsion. But Jesus rebuked the evil* spirit and healed the boy. Then he gave him back to his father. ⁴³Awe gripped the people as they saw this majestic display of God's power.

Jesus Again Predicts His Death

While everyone was marveling at everything he was doing, Jesus said to his disciples, ⁴⁴"Listen to me and remember what I say. The Son of

9:33 Greek *three tabernacles.* 9:35 Some manuscripts read *This is my dearly loved Son.*
9:42 Greek *unclean.*

Man is going to be betrayed into the hands of his enemies." ⁴⁵But they didn't know what he meant. Its significance was hidden from them, so they couldn't understand it, and they were afraid to ask him about it.

The Greatest in the Kingdom

⁴⁶Then his disciples began arguing about which of them was the greatest. ⁴⁷But Jesus knew their thoughts, so he brought a little child to his side. ⁴⁸Then he said to them, "Anyone who welcomes a little child like this on my behalf* welcomes me, and anyone who welcomes me also welcomes my Father who sent me. Whoever is the least among you is the greatest."

Using the Name of Jesus

⁴⁹John said to Jesus, "Master, we saw someone using your name to cast out demons, but we told him to stop because he isn't in our group."

⁵⁰But Jesus said, "Don't stop him! Anyone who is not against you is for you."

Opposition from Samaritans

⁵¹As the time drew near for him to ascend to heaven, Jesus resolutely set out for Jerusalem. ⁵²He sent messengers ahead to a Samaritan village to prepare for his arrival. ⁵³But the people of the village did not welcome Jesus because he was on his way to Jerusalem. ⁵⁴When James and John saw this, they said to Jesus, "Lord, should we call down fire from heaven to burn them up*?" ⁵⁵But Jesus turned and rebuked them.* ⁵⁶So they went on to another village.

The Cost of Following Jesus

⁵⁷As they were walking along, someone said to Jesus, "I will follow you wherever you go."

⁵⁸But Jesus replied, "Foxes have dens to live in, and birds have nests, but the Son of Man has no place even to lay his head."

⁵⁹He said to another person, "Come, follow me."

The man agreed, but he said, "Lord, first let me return home and bury my father."

⁶⁰But Jesus told him, "Let the spiritually dead bury their own dead!* Your duty is to go and preach about the Kingdom of God."

⁶¹Another said, "Yes, Lord, I will follow you, but first let me say goodbye to my family."

⁶²But Jesus told him, "Anyone who puts a hand to the plow and then looks back is not fit for the Kingdom of God."

Jesus Sends Out His Disciples

10 The Lord now chose seventy-two* other disciples and sent

9:48 Greek *in my name.* 9:54 Some manuscripts add *as Elijah did.* 9:55 Some manuscripts add an expanded conclusion to verse 55 and an additional sentence in verse 56: *And he said, "You don't realize what your hearts are like.* ⁵⁶*For the Son of Man has not come to destroy people's lives, but to save them."* 9:60 Greek *Let the dead bury their own dead.* 10:1 Some manuscripts read *seventy;* also in 10:17.

them ahead in pairs to all the towns and places he planned to visit. [2]These were his instructions to them: "The harvest is great, but the workers are few. So pray to the Lord who is in charge of the harvest; ask him to send more workers into his fields. [3]Now go, and remember that I am sending you out as lambs among wolves. [4]Don't take any money with you, nor a traveler's bag, nor an extra pair of sandals. And don't stop to greet anyone on the road.

[5]"Whenever you enter someone's home, first say, 'May God's peace be on this house.' [6]If those who live there are peaceful, the blessing will stand; if they are not, the blessing will return to you. [7]Don't move around from home to home. Stay in one place, eating and drinking what they provide. Don't hesitate to accept hospitality, because those who work deserve their pay.

[8]"If you enter a town and it welcomes you, eat whatever is set before you. [9]Heal the sick, and tell them, 'The Kingdom of God is near you now.' [10]But if a town refuses to welcome you, go out into its streets and say, [11]'We wipe even the dust of your town from our feet to show that we have abandoned you to your fate. And know this—the Kingdom of God is near!' [12]I assure you, even wicked Sodom will be better off than such a town on judgment day.

[13]"What sorrow awaits you, Korazin and Bethsaida! For if the miracles I did in you had been done in wicked Tyre and Sidon, their people would have repented of their sins long ago, clothing themselves in burlap and throwing ashes on their heads to show their remorse. [14]Yes, Tyre and Sidon will be better off on judgment day than you. [15]And you people of Capernaum, will you be honored in heaven? No, you will go down to the place of the dead.*"

[16]Then he said to the disciples, "Anyone who accepts your message is also accepting me. And anyone who rejects you is rejecting me. And anyone who rejects me is rejecting God, who sent me."

[17]When the seventy-two disciples returned, they joyfully reported to him, "Lord, even the demons obey us when we use your name!"

[18]"Yes," he told them, "I saw Satan fall from heaven like lightning! [19]Look, I have given you authority over all the power of the enemy, and you can walk among snakes and scorpions and crush them. Nothing will injure you. [20]But don't rejoice because evil spirits obey you; rejoice because your names are registered in heaven."

Jesus' Prayer of Thanksgiving

[21]At that same time Jesus was filled with the joy of the Holy Spirit, and he said, "O Father, Lord of heaven and earth, thank you for hiding

10:15 Greek *to Hades.*

these things from those who think themselves wise and clever, and for revealing them to the childlike. Yes, Father, it pleased you to do it this way.

²²"My Father has entrusted everything to me. No one truly knows the Son except the Father, and no one truly knows the Father except the Son and those to whom the Son chooses to reveal him."

²³Then when they were alone, he turned to the disciples and said, "Blessed are the eyes that see what you have seen. ²⁴I tell you, many prophets and kings longed to see what you see, but they didn't see it. And they longed to hear what you hear, but they didn't hear it."

The Most Important Commandment

²⁵One day an expert in religious law stood up to test Jesus by asking him this question: "Teacher, what should I do to inherit eternal life?"

²⁶Jesus replied, "What does the law of Moses say? How do you read it?"

²⁷The man answered, " 'You must love the LORD your God with all your heart, all your soul, all your strength, and all your mind.' And, 'Love your neighbor as yourself.'"*

²⁸"Right!" Jesus told him. "Do this and you will live!"

²⁹The man wanted to justify his actions, so he asked Jesus, "And who is my neighbor?"

Parable of the Good Samaritan

³⁰Jesus replied with a story: "A Jewish man was traveling from Jerusalem down to Jericho, and he was attacked by bandits. They stripped him of his clothes, beat him up, and left him half dead beside the road.

³¹"By chance a priest came along. But when he saw the man lying there, he crossed to the other side of the road and passed him by. ³²A Temple assistant* walked over and looked at him lying there, but he also passed by on the other side.

³³"Then a despised Samaritan came along, and when he saw the man, he felt compassion for him. ³⁴Going over to him, the Samaritan soothed his wounds with olive oil and wine and bandaged them. Then he put the man on his own donkey and took him to an inn, where he took care of him. ³⁵The next day he handed the innkeeper two silver coins,* telling him, 'Take care of this man. If his bill runs higher than this, I'll pay you the next time I'm here.'

³⁶"Now which of these three would you say was a neighbor to the man who was attacked by bandits?" Jesus asked.

³⁷The man replied, "The one who showed him mercy."

Then Jesus said, "Yes, now go and do the same."

10:27 Deut 6:5; Lev 19:18. **10:32** Greek *A Levite*. **10:35** Greek *two denarii*. A denarius was equivalent to a laborer's full day's wage.

Jesus Visits Martha and Mary

[38]As Jesus and the disciples continued on their way to Jerusalem, they came to a certain village where a woman named Martha welcomed him into her home. [39]Her sister, Mary, sat at the Lord's feet, listening to what he taught. [40]But Martha was distracted by the big dinner she was preparing. She came to Jesus and said, "Lord, doesn't it seem unfair to you that my sister just sits here while I do all the work? Tell her to come and help me."

[41]But the Lord said to her, "My dear Martha, you are worried and upset over all these details! [42]There is only one thing worth being concerned about. Mary has discovered it, and it will not be taken away from her."

Teaching about Prayer

11 Once Jesus was in a certain place praying. As he finished, one of his disciples came to him and said, "Lord, teach us to pray, just as John taught his disciples."

[2]Jesus said, "This is how you should pray:*

"Father, may your name be kept holy.
May your Kingdom come soon.
[3] Give us each day the food we need,*
[4] and forgive us our sins,
as we forgive those who sin against us.
And don't let us yield to temptation.*"

[5]Then, teaching them more about prayer, he used this story: "Suppose you went to a friend's house at midnight, wanting to borrow three loaves of bread. You say to him, [6]'A friend of mine has just arrived for a visit, and I have nothing for him to eat.' [7]And suppose he calls out from his bedroom, 'Don't bother me. The door is locked for the night, and my family and I are all in bed. I can't help you.' [8]But I tell you this—though he won't do it for friendship's sake, if you keep knocking long enough, he will get up and give you whatever you need because of your shameless persistence.*

[9]"And so I tell you, keep on asking, and you will receive what you ask for. Keep on seeking, and you will find. Keep on knocking, and the door will be opened to you. [10]For everyone who asks, receives. Everyone who seeks, finds. And to everyone who knocks, the door will be opened.

[11]"You fathers—if your children ask* for a fish, do you give them a snake instead? [12]Or if they ask for an egg, do you give them a scorpion? Of course not! [13]So if you sinful people know how to give good gifts to your children, how much more will

---

11:2 Some manuscripts add additional phrases from the Lord's Prayer as it reads in Matt 6:9-13. **11:3** Or *Give us each day our food for the day;* or *Give us each day our food for tomorrow.* **11:4** Or *And keep us from being tested.* **11:8** Or *in order to avoid shame,* or *so his reputation won't be damaged.* **11:11** Some manuscripts add *for bread, do you give them a stone? Or [if they ask].*

your heavenly Father give the Holy Spirit to those who ask him."

Jesus and the Prince of Demons

[14]One day Jesus cast out a demon from a man who couldn't speak, and when the demon was gone, the man began to speak. The crowds were amazed, [15]but some of them said, "No wonder he can cast out demons. He gets his power from Satan,* the prince of demons." [16]Others, trying to test Jesus, demanded that he show them a miraculous sign from heaven to prove his authority.

[17]He knew their thoughts, so he said, "Any kingdom divided by civil war is doomed. A family splintered by feuding will fall apart. [18]You say I am empowered by Satan. But if Satan is divided and fighting against himself, how can his kingdom survive? [19]And if I am empowered by Satan, what about your own exorcists? They cast out demons, too, so they will condemn you for what you have said. [20]But if I am casting out demons by the power of God,* then the Kingdom of God has arrived among you. [21]For when a strong man is fully armed and guards his palace, his possessions are safe—[22]until someone even stronger attacks and overpowers him, strips him of his weapons, and carries off his belongings.

[23]"Anyone who isn't with me opposes me, and anyone who isn't working with me is actually working against me.

[24]"When an evil* spirit leaves a person, it goes into the desert, searching for rest. But when it finds none, it says, 'I will return to the person I came from.' [25]So it returns and finds that its former home is all swept and in order. [26]Then the spirit finds seven other spirits more evil than itself, and they all enter the person and live there. And so that person is worse off than before."

[27]As he was speaking, a woman in the crowd called out, "God bless your mother—the womb from which you came, and the breasts that nursed you!"

[28]Jesus replied, "But even more blessed are all who hear the word of God and put it into practice."

The Sign of Jonah

[29]As the crowd pressed in on Jesus, he said, "This evil generation keeps asking me to show them a miraculous sign. But the only sign I will give them is the sign of Jonah. [30]What happened to him was a sign to the people of Nineveh that God had sent him. What happens to the Son of Man* will be a sign to these people that he was sent by God.

[31]"The queen of Sheba* will stand up against this generation on judgment day and condemn it, for she came from a distant land to hear the

11:15 Greek *Beelzeboul;* also in 11:18, 19. Other manuscripts read *Beezeboul;* Latin version reads *Beelzebub.* **11:20** Greek *by the finger of God.* **11:24** Greek *unclean.* **11:30** "Son of Man" is a title Jesus used for himself. **11:31** Greek *The queen of the south.*

wisdom of Solomon. Now someone greater than Solomon is here—but you refuse to listen. ³²The people of Nineveh will also stand up against this generation on judgment day and condemn it, for they repented of their sins at the preaching of Jonah. Now someone greater than Jonah is here—but you refuse to repent.

Receiving the Light

³³"No one lights a lamp and then hides it or puts it under a basket.* Instead, a lamp is placed on a stand, where its light can be seen by all who enter the house.

³⁴"Your eye is like a lamp that provides light for your body. When your eye is healthy, your whole body is filled with light. But when it is unhealthy, your body is filled with darkness. ³⁵Make sure that the light you think you have is not actually darkness. ³⁶If you are filled with light, with no dark corners, then your whole life will be radiant, as though a floodlight were filling you with light."

Jesus Criticizes the Religious Leaders

³⁷As Jesus was speaking, one of the Pharisees invited him home for a meal. So he went in and took his place at the table.* ³⁸His host was amazed to see that he sat down to eat without first performing the hand-washing ceremony required by Jewish custom. ³⁹Then the Lord said to him, "You Pharisees are so careful to clean the outside of the cup and the dish, but inside you are filthy—full of greed and wickedness! ⁴⁰Fools! Didn't God make the inside as well as the outside? ⁴¹So clean the inside by giving gifts to the poor, and you will be clean all over.

⁴²"What sorrow awaits you Pharisees! For you are careful to tithe even the tiniest income from your herb gardens,* but you ignore justice and the love of God. You should tithe, yes, but do not neglect the more important things.

⁴³"What sorrow awaits you Pharisees! For you love to sit in the seats of honor in the synagogues and receive respectful greetings as you walk in the marketplaces. ⁴⁴Yes, what sorrow awaits you! For you are like hidden graves in a field. People walk over them without knowing the corruption they are stepping on."

⁴⁵"Teacher," said an expert in religious law, "you have insulted us, too, in what you just said."

⁴⁶"Yes," said Jesus, "what sorrow also awaits you experts in religious law! For you crush people with unbearable religious demands, and you never lift a finger to ease the burden. ⁴⁷What sorrow awaits you! For you build monuments for the prophets your own ancestors killed long ago. ⁴⁸But in fact, you stand as witnesses who agree with what your ancestors

11:33 Some manuscripts do not include *or puts it under a basket.* 11:37 Or *and reclined.*
11:42 Greek *tithe the mint, the rue, and every herb.*

did. They killed the prophets, and you join in their crime by building the monuments! [49]This is what God in his wisdom said about you:* 'I will send prophets and apostles to them, but they will kill some and persecute the others.'

[50]"As a result, this generation will be held responsible for the murder of all God's prophets from the creation of the world—[51]from the murder of Abel to the murder of Zechariah, who was killed between the altar and the sanctuary. Yes, it will certainly be charged against this generation.

[52]"What sorrow awaits you experts in religious law! For you remove the key to knowledge from the people. You don't enter the Kingdom yourselves, and you prevent others from entering."

[53]As Jesus was leaving, the teachers of religious law and the Pharisees became hostile and tried to provoke him with many questions. [54]They wanted to trap him into saying something they could use against him.

A Warning against Hypocrisy

12 Meanwhile, the crowds grew until thousands were milling about and stepping on each other. Jesus turned first to his disciples and warned them, "Beware of the yeast of the Pharisees—their hypocrisy. [2]The time is coming when everything that is covered up will be revealed, and all that is secret will be made known to all. [3]Whatever you have said in the dark will be heard in the light, and what you have whispered behind closed doors will be shouted from the housetops for all to hear!

[4]"Dear friends, don't be afraid of those who want to kill your body; they cannot do any more to you after that. [5]But I'll tell you whom to fear. Fear God, who has the power to kill you and then throw you into hell.* Yes, he's the one to fear.

[6]"What is the price of five sparrows—two copper coins*? Yet God does not forget a single one of them. [7]And the very hairs on your head are all numbered. So don't be afraid; you are more valuable to God than a whole flock of sparrows.

[8]"I tell you the truth, everyone who acknowledges me publicly here on earth, the Son of Man* will also acknowledge in the presence of God's angels. [9]But anyone who denies me here on earth will be denied before God's angels. [10]Anyone who speaks against the Son of Man can be forgiven, but anyone who blasphemes the Holy Spirit will not be forgiven.

[11]"And when you are brought to trial in the synagogues and before rulers and authorities, don't worry about how to defend yourself or what to say, [12]for the Holy Spirit will teach you at that time what needs to be said."

11:49 Greek *Therefore, the wisdom of God said.* **12:5** Greek *Gehenna.* **12:6** Greek *two assaria* [Roman coins equal to ¹/₁₆ of a denarius]. **12:8** "Son of Man" is a title Jesus used for himself.

Parable of the Rich Fool

[13]Then someone called from the crowd, "Teacher, please tell my brother to divide our father's estate with me."

[14]Jesus replied, "Friend, who made me a judge over you to decide such things as that?" [15]Then he said, "Beware! Guard against every kind of greed. Life is not measured by how much you own."

[16]Then he told them a story: "A rich man had a fertile farm that produced fine crops. [17]He said to himself, 'What should I do? I don't have room for all my crops.' [18]Then he said, 'I know! I'll tear down my barns and build bigger ones. Then I'll have room enough to store all my wheat and other goods. [19]And I'll sit back and say to myself, "My friend, you have enough stored away for years to come. Now take it easy! Eat, drink, and be merry!"'

[20]"But God said to him, 'You fool! You will die this very night. Then who will get everything you worked for?'

[21]"Yes, a person is a fool to store up earthly wealth but not have a rich relationship with God."

Teaching about Money and Possessions

[22]Then, turning to his disciples, Jesus said, "That is why I tell you not to worry about everyday life—whether you have enough food to eat or enough clothes to wear. [23]For life is more than food, and your body more than clothing. [24]Look at the ravens. They don't plant or harvest or store food in barns, for God feeds them. And you are far more valuable to him than any birds! [25]Can all your worries add a single moment to your life? [26]And if worry can't accomplish a little thing like that, what's the use of worrying over bigger things?

[27]"Look at the lilies and how they grow. They don't work or make their clothing, yet Solomon in all his glory was not dressed as beautifully as they are. [28]And if God cares so wonderfully for flowers that are here today and thrown into the fire tomorrow, he will certainly care for you. Why do you have so little faith?

[29]"And don't be concerned about what to eat and what to drink. Don't worry about such things. [30]These things dominate the thoughts of unbelievers all over the world, but your Father already knows your needs. [31]Seek the Kingdom of God above all else, and he will give you everything you need.

[32]"So don't be afraid, little flock. For it gives your Father great happiness to give you the Kingdom.

[33]"Sell your possessions and give to those in need. This will store up treasure for you in heaven! And the purses of heaven never get old or develop holes. Your treasure will be safe; no thief can steal it and no moth can destroy it. [34]Wherever your treasure is, there the desires of your heart will also be.

Be Ready for the Lord's Coming

35"Be dressed for service and keep your lamps burning, 36as though you were waiting for your master to return from the wedding feast. Then you will be ready to open the door and let him in the moment he arrives and knocks. 37The servants who are ready and waiting for his return will be rewarded. I tell you the truth, he himself will seat them, put on an apron, and serve them as they sit and eat! 38He may come in the middle of the night or just before dawn.* But whenever he comes, he will reward the servants who are ready.

39"Understand this: If a homeowner knew exactly when a burglar was coming, he would not permit his house to be broken into. 40You also must be ready all the time, for the Son of Man will come when least expected."

41Peter asked, "Lord, is that illustration just for us or for everyone?"

42And the Lord replied, "A faithful, sensible servant is one to whom the master can give the responsibility of managing his other household servants and feeding them. 43If the master returns and finds that the servant has done a good job, there will be a reward. 44I tell you the truth, the master will put that servant in charge of all he owns. 45But what if the servant thinks, 'My master won't be back for a while,' and he begins beating the other servants, partying, and getting drunk? 46The master will return unannounced and unexpected, and he will cut the servant in pieces and banish him with the unfaithful.

47"And a servant who knows what the master wants, but isn't prepared and doesn't carry out those instructions, will be severely punished. 48But someone who does not know, and then does something wrong, will be punished only lightly. When someone has been given much, much will be required in return; and when someone has been entrusted with much, even more will be required.

Jesus Causes Division

49"I have come to set the world on fire, and I wish it were already burning! 50I have a terrible baptism of suffering ahead of me, and I am under a heavy burden until it is accomplished. 51Do you think I have come to bring peace to the earth? No, I have come to divide people against each other! 52From now on families will be split apart, three in favor of me, and two against—or two in favor and three against.

53 'Father will be divided against son
    and son against father;
mother against daughter
    and daughter against mother;
and mother-in-law against
        daughter-in-law
    and daughter-in-law against
        mother-in-law.'* "

12:38 Greek *in the second or third watch.* 12:53 Mic 7:6.

⁵⁴Then Jesus turned to the crowd and said, "When you see clouds beginning to form in the west, you say, 'Here comes a shower.' And you are right. ⁵⁵When the south wind blows, you say, 'Today will be a scorcher.' And it is. ⁵⁶You fools! You know how to interpret the weather signs of the earth and sky, but you don't know how to interpret the present times.

⁵⁷"Why can't you decide for yourselves what is right? ⁵⁸When you are on the way to court with your accuser, try to settle the matter before you get there. Otherwise, your accuser may drag you before the judge, who will hand you over to an officer, who will throw you into prison. ⁵⁹And if that happens, you won't be free again until you have paid the very last penny.*"

A Call to Repentance

13 About this time Jesus was informed that Pilate had murdered some people from Galilee as they were offering sacrifices at the Temple. ²"Do you think those Galileans were worse sinners than all the other people from Galilee?" Jesus asked. "Is that why they suffered? ³Not at all! And you will perish, too, unless you repent of your sins and turn to God. ⁴And what about the eighteen people who died when the tower in Siloam fell on them? Were they the worst sinners in Jerusalem? ⁵No, and I tell you again that unless you repent, you will perish, too."

Parable of the Barren Fig Tree

⁶Then Jesus told this story: "A man planted a fig tree in his garden and came again and again to see if there was any fruit on it, but he was always disappointed. ⁷Finally, he said to his gardener, 'I've waited three years, and there hasn't been a single fig! Cut it down. It's just taking up space in the garden.'

⁸"The gardener answered, 'Sir, give it one more chance. Leave it another year, and I'll give it special attention and plenty of fertilizer. ⁹If we get figs next year, fine. If not, then you can cut it down.'"

Jesus Heals on the Sabbath

¹⁰One Sabbath day as Jesus was teaching in a synagogue, ¹¹he saw a woman who had been crippled by an evil spirit. She had been bent double for eighteen years and was unable to stand up straight. ¹²When Jesus saw her, he called her over and said, "Dear woman, you are healed of your sickness!" ¹³Then he touched her, and instantly she could stand straight. How she praised God!

¹⁴But the leader in charge of the synagogue was indignant that Jesus had healed her on the Sabbath day. "There are six days of the week for working," he said to the crowd.

12:59 Greek *last lepton* [the smallest Jewish coin].

"Come on those days to be healed, not on the Sabbath."

[15]But the Lord replied, "You hypocrites! Each of you works on the Sabbath day! Don't you untie your ox or your donkey from its stall on the Sabbath and lead it out for water? [16]This dear woman, a daughter of Abraham, has been held in bondage by Satan for eighteen years. Isn't it right that she be released, even on the Sabbath?"

[17]This shamed his enemies, but all the people rejoiced at the wonderful things he did.

Parable of the Mustard Seed

[18]Then Jesus said, "What is the Kingdom of God like? How can I illustrate it? [19]It is like a tiny mustard seed that a man planted in a garden; it grows and becomes a tree, and the birds make nests in its branches."

Parable of the Yeast

[20]He also asked, "What else is the Kingdom of God like? [21]It is like the yeast a woman used in making bread. Even though she put only a little yeast in three measures of flour, it permeated every part of the dough."

The Narrow Door

[22]Jesus went through the towns and villages, teaching as he went, always pressing on toward Jerusalem. [23]Someone asked him, "Lord, will only a few be saved?"

He replied, [24]"Work hard to enter the narrow door to God's Kingdom, for many will try to enter but will fail. [25]When the master of the house has locked the door, it will be too late. You will stand outside knocking and pleading, 'Lord, open the door for us!' But he will reply, 'I don't know you or where you come from.' [26]Then you will say, 'But we ate and drank with you, and you taught in our streets.' [27]And he will reply, 'I tell you, I don't know you or where you come from. Get away from me, all you who do evil.'

[28]"There will be weeping and gnashing of teeth, for you will see Abraham, Isaac, Jacob, and all the prophets in the Kingdom of God, but you will be thrown out. [29]And people will come from all over the world—from east and west, north and south—to take their places in the Kingdom of God. [30]And note this: Some who seem least important now will be the greatest then, and some who are the greatest now will be least important then.*"

Jesus Grieves over Jerusalem

[31]At that time some Pharisees said to him, "Get away from here if you want to live! Herod Antipas wants to kill you!"

[32]Jesus replied, "Go tell that fox that I will keep on casting out demons and healing people today and tomorrow; and the third day I will accomplish my purpose. [33]Yes, today, tomorrow, and the next day

13:30 Greek *Some are last who will be first, and some are first who will be last.*

I must proceed on my way. For it wouldn't do for a prophet of God to be killed except in Jerusalem!

³⁴"O Jerusalem, Jerusalem, the city that kills the prophets and stones God's messengers! How often I have wanted to gather your children together as a hen protects her chicks beneath her wings, but you wouldn't let me. ³⁵And now, look, your house is abandoned. And you will never see me again until you say, 'Blessings on the one who comes in the name of the Lord!'* "

Jesus Heals on the Sabbath

14 One Sabbath day Jesus went to eat dinner in the home of a leader of the Pharisees, and the people were watching him closely. ²There was a man there whose arms and legs were swollen.* ³Jesus asked the Pharisees and experts in religious law, "Is it permitted in the law to heal people on the Sabbath day, or not?" ⁴When they refused to answer, Jesus touched the sick man and healed him and sent him away. ⁵Then he turned to them and said, "Which of you doesn't work on the Sabbath? If your son* or your cow falls into a pit, don't you rush to get him out?" ⁶Again they could not answer.

Jesus Teaches about Humility

⁷When Jesus noticed that all who had come to the dinner were trying to sit in the seats of honor near the head of the table, he gave them this advice: ⁸"When you are invited to a wedding feast, don't sit in the seat of honor. What if someone who is more distinguished than you has also been invited? ⁹The host will come and say, 'Give this person your seat.' Then you will be embarrassed, and you will have to take whatever seat is left at the foot of the table!

¹⁰"Instead, take the lowest place at the foot of the table. Then when your host sees you, he will come and say, 'Friend, we have a better place for you!' Then you will be honored in front of all the other guests. ¹¹For those who exalt themselves will be humbled, and those who humble themselves will be exalted."

¹²Then he turned to his host. "When you put on a luncheon or a banquet," he said, "don't invite your friends, brothers, relatives, and rich neighbors. For they will invite you back, and that will be your only reward. ¹³Instead, invite the poor, the crippled, the lame, and the blind. ¹⁴Then at the resurrection of the righteous, God will reward you for inviting those who could not repay you."

Parable of the Great Feast

¹⁵Hearing this, a man sitting at the table with Jesus exclaimed, "What a blessing it will be to attend a banquet* in the Kingdom of God!"

¹⁶Jesus replied with this story:

13:35 Ps 118:26.   **14:2** Or *who had dropsy.*   **14:5** Some manuscripts read *donkey.*   **14:15** Greek *to eat bread.*

"A man prepared a great feast and sent out many invitations. ¹⁷When the banquet was ready, he sent his servant to tell the guests, 'Come, the banquet is ready.' ¹⁸But they all began making excuses. One said, 'I have just bought a field and must inspect it. Please excuse me.' ¹⁹Another said, 'I have just bought five pairs of oxen, and I want to try them out. Please excuse me.' ²⁰Another said, 'I just got married, so I can't come.'

²¹"The servant returned and told his master what they had said. His master was furious and said, 'Go quickly into the streets and alleys of the town and invite the poor, the crippled, the blind, and the lame.' ²²After the servant had done this, he reported, 'There is still room for more.' ²³So his master said, 'Go out into the country lanes and behind the hedges and urge anyone you find to come, so that the house will be full. ²⁴For none of those I first invited will get even the smallest taste of my banquet.'"

The Cost of Being a Disciple
²⁵A large crowd was following Jesus. He turned around and said to them, ²⁶"If you want to be my disciple, you must, by comparison, hate everyone else—your father and mother, wife and children, brothers and sisters—yes, even your own life. Otherwise, you cannot be my disciple. ²⁷And if you do not carry your own cross and follow me, you cannot be my disciple.

²⁸"But don't begin until you count the cost. For who would begin construction of a building without first calculating the cost to see if there is enough money to finish it? ²⁹Otherwise, you might complete only the foundation before running out of money, and then everyone would laugh at you. ³⁰They would say, 'There's the person who started that building and couldn't afford to finish it!'

³¹"Or what king would go to war against another king without first sitting down with his counselors to discuss whether his army of 10,000 could defeat the 20,000 soldiers marching against him? ³²And if he can't, he will send a delegation to discuss terms of peace while the enemy is still far away. ³³So you cannot become my disciple without giving up everything you own.

³⁴"Salt is good for seasoning. But if it loses its flavor, how do you make it salty again? ³⁵Flavorless salt is good neither for the soil nor for the manure pile. It is thrown away. Anyone with ears to hear should listen and understand!"

Parable of the Lost Sheep
15 Tax collectors and other notorious sinners often came to listen to Jesus teach. ²This made the Pharisees and teachers of religious law complain that he was associating with such sinful people—even eating with them!

³So Jesus told them this story: ⁴"If a man has a hundred sheep and one of them gets lost, what will he do? Won't he leave the ninety-nine others in the wilderness and go to search for the one that is lost until he finds it? ⁵And when he has found it, he will joyfully carry it home on his shoulders. ⁶When he arrives, he will call together his friends and neighbors, saying, 'Rejoice with me because I have found my lost sheep.' ⁷In the same way, there is more joy in heaven over one lost sinner who repents and returns to God than over ninety-nine others who are righteous and haven't strayed away!

Parable of the Lost Coin

⁸"Or suppose a woman has ten silver coins* and loses one. Won't she light a lamp and sweep the entire house and search carefully until she finds it? ⁹And when she finds it, she will call in her friends and neighbors and say, 'Rejoice with me because I have found my lost coin.' ¹⁰In the same way, there is joy in the presence of God's angels when even one sinner repents."

Parable of the Lost Son

¹¹To illustrate the point further, Jesus told them this story: "A man had two sons. ¹²The younger son told his father, 'I want my share of your estate now before you die.' So his father agreed to divide his wealth between his sons.

¹³"A few days later this younger son packed all his belongings and moved to a distant land, and there he wasted all his money in wild living. ¹⁴About the time his money ran out, a great famine swept over the land, and he began to starve. ¹⁵He persuaded a local farmer to hire him, and the man sent him into his fields to feed the pigs. ¹⁶The young man became so hungry that even the pods he was feeding the pigs looked good to him. But no one gave him anything.

¹⁷"When he finally came to his senses, he said to himself, 'At home even the hired servants have food enough to spare, and here I am dying of hunger! ¹⁸I will go home to my father and say, "Father, I have sinned against both heaven and you, ¹⁹and I am no longer worthy of being called your son. Please take me on as a hired servant."'

²⁰"So he returned home to his father. And while he was still a long way off, his father saw him coming. Filled with love and compassion, he ran to his son, embraced him, and kissed him. ²¹His son said to him, 'Father, I have sinned against both heaven and you, and I am no longer worthy of being called your son.*'

²²"But his father said to the servants, 'Quick! Bring the finest robe in the house and put it on him. Get a

15:8 Greek *ten drachmas*. A drachma was the equivalent of a full day's wage. **15:21** Some manuscripts add *Please take me on as a hired servant.*

ring for his finger and sandals for his feet. ²³And kill the calf we have been fattening. We must celebrate with a feast, ²⁴for this son of mine was dead and has now returned to life. He was lost, but now he is found.' So the party began.

²⁵"Meanwhile, the older son was in the fields working. When he returned home, he heard music and dancing in the house, ²⁶and he asked one of the servants what was going on. ²⁷'Your brother is back,' he was told, 'and your father has killed the fattened calf. We are celebrating because of his safe return.'

²⁸"The older brother was angry and wouldn't go in. His father came out and begged him, ²⁹but he replied, 'All these years I've slaved for you and never once refused to do a single thing you told me to. And in all that time you never gave me even one young goat for a feast with my friends. ³⁰Yet when this son of yours comes back after squandering your money on prostitutes, you celebrate by killing the fattened calf!'

³¹"His father said to him, 'Look, dear son, you have always stayed by me, and everything I have is yours. ³²We had to celebrate this happy day. For your brother was dead and has come back to life! He was lost, but now he is found!' "

Parable of the Shrewd Manager

16 Jesus told this story to his disciples: "There was a certain rich man who had a manager handling his affairs. One day a report came that the manager was wasting his employer's money. ²So the employer called him in and said, 'What's this I hear about you? Get your report in order, because you are going to be fired.'

³"The manager thought to himself, 'Now what? My boss has fired me. I don't have the strength to dig ditches, and I'm too proud to beg. ⁴Ah, I know how to ensure that I'll have plenty of friends who will give me a home when I am fired.'

⁵"So he invited each person who owed money to his employer to come and discuss the situation. He asked the first one, 'How much do you owe him?' ⁶The man replied, 'I owe him 800 gallons of olive oil.' So the manager told him, 'Take the bill and quickly change it to 400 gallons.*'

⁷" 'And how much do you owe my employer?' he asked the next man. 'I owe him 1,000 bushels of wheat,' was the reply. 'Here,' the manager said, 'take the bill and change it to 800 bushels.*'

⁸"The rich man had to admire the dishonest rascal for being so shrewd. And it is true that the children of this world are more shrewd in dealing with the world around them than are the children of the light. ⁹Here's the lesson: Use your worldly resources to benefit others and make friends. Then, when your possessions are

16:6 Greek *100 baths . . . 50 [baths].*   **16:7** Greek *100 korous . . . 80 [korous].*

gone, they will welcome you to an eternal home.*

[10]"If you are faithful in little things, you will be faithful in large ones. But if you are dishonest in little things, you won't be honest with greater responsibilities. [11]And if you are untrustworthy about worldly wealth, who will trust you with the true riches of heaven? [12]And if you are not faithful with other people's things, why should you be trusted with things of your own?

[13]"No one can serve two masters. For you will hate one and love the other; you will be devoted to one and despise the other. You cannot serve God and be enslaved to money."

[14]The Pharisees, who dearly loved their money, heard all this and scoffed at him. [15]Then he said to them, "You like to appear righteous in public, but God knows your hearts. What this world honors is detestable in the sight of God.

[16]"Until John the Baptist, the law of Moses and the messages of the prophets were your guides. But now the Good News of the Kingdom of God is preached, and everyone is eager to get in.* [17]But that doesn't mean that the law has lost its force. It is easier for heaven and earth to disappear than for the smallest point of God's law to be overturned.

[18]"For example, a man who divorces his wife and marries someone else commits adultery. And anyone who marries a woman divorced from her husband commits adultery."

Parable of the Rich Man and Lazarus

[19]Jesus said, "There was a certain rich man who was splendidly clothed in purple and fine linen and who lived each day in luxury. [20]At his gate lay a poor man named Lazarus who was covered with sores. [21]As Lazarus lay there longing for scraps from the rich man's table, the dogs would come and lick his open sores.

[22]"Finally, the poor man died and was carried by the angels to sit beside Abraham at the heavenly banquet.* The rich man also died and was buried, [23]and he went to the place of the dead.* There, in torment, he saw Abraham in the far distance with Lazarus at his side.

[24]"The rich man shouted, 'Father Abraham, have some pity! Send Lazarus over here to dip the tip of his finger in water and cool my tongue. I am in anguish in these flames.'

[25]"But Abraham said to him, 'Son, remember that during your lifetime you had everything you wanted, and Lazarus had nothing. So now he is here being comforted, and you are in anguish. [26]And besides, there is a great chasm separating us. No one can cross over to you from here, and no one can cross over to us from there.'

16:9 Or *you will be welcomed into eternal homes.* **16:16** Or *everyone is urged to enter in.*
16:22 Greek *to Abraham's bosom.* **16:23** Greek *to Hades.*

27"Then the rich man said, 'Please, Father Abraham, at least send him to my father's home. 28For I have five brothers, and I want him to warn them so they don't end up in this place of torment.'

29"But Abraham said, 'Moses and the prophets have warned them. Your brothers can read what they wrote.'

30"The rich man replied, 'No, Father Abraham! But if someone is sent to them from the dead, then they will repent of their sins and turn to God.'

31"But Abraham said, 'If they won't listen to Moses and the prophets, they won't be persuaded even if someone rises from the dead.'"

Teachings about Forgiveness and Faith

17 One day Jesus said to his disciples, "There will always be temptations to sin, but what sorrow awaits the person who does the tempting! 2It would be better to be thrown into the sea with a millstone hung around your neck than to cause one of these little ones to fall into sin. 3So watch yourselves!

"If another believer* sins, rebuke that person; then if there is repentance, forgive. 4Even if that person wrongs you seven times a day and each time turns again and asks forgiveness, you must forgive."

5The apostles said to the Lord, "Show us how to increase our faith."

6The Lord answered, "If you had faith even as small as a mustard seed, you could say to this mulberry tree, 'May you be uprooted and be planted in the sea,' and it would obey you!

7"When a servant comes in from plowing or taking care of sheep, does his master say, 'Come in and eat with me'? 8No, he says, 'Prepare my meal, put on your apron, and serve me while I eat. Then you can eat later.' 9And does the master thank the servant for doing what he was told to do? Of course not. 10In the same way, when you obey me you should say, 'We are unworthy servants who have simply done our duty.'"

Ten Healed of Leprosy

11As Jesus continued on toward Jerusalem, he reached the border between Galilee and Samaria. 12As he entered a village there, ten men with leprosy stood at a distance, 13crying out, "Jesus, Master, have mercy on us!"

14He looked at them and said, "Go show yourselves to the priests."* And as they went, they were cleansed of their leprosy.

15One of them, when he saw that he was healed, came back to Jesus, shouting, "Praise God!" 16He fell to the ground at Jesus' feet, thanking him for what he had done. This man was a Samaritan.

17Jesus asked, "Didn't I heal ten men? Where are the other nine?

17:3 Greek *If your brother.*   **17:14** See Lev 14:2-32.

[18]Has no one returned to give glory to God except this foreigner?" [19]And Jesus said to the man, "Stand up and go. Your faith has healed you.*"

The Coming of the Kingdom

[20]One day the Pharisees asked Jesus, "When will the Kingdom of God come?"

Jesus replied, "The Kingdom of God can't be detected by visible signs.* [21]You won't be able to say, 'Here it is!' or 'It's over there!' For the Kingdom of God is already among you.*"

[22]Then he said to his disciples, "The time is coming when you will long to see the day when the Son of Man returns,* but you won't see it. [23]People will tell you, 'Look, there is the Son of Man,' or 'Here he is,' but don't go out and follow them. [24]For as the lightning flashes and lights up the sky from one end to the other, so it will be on the day* when the Son of Man comes. [25]But first the Son of Man must suffer terribly* and be rejected by this generation.

[26]"When the Son of Man returns, it will be like it was in Noah's day. [27]In those days, the people enjoyed banquets and parties and weddings right up to the time Noah entered his boat and the flood came and destroyed them all.

[28]"And the world will be as it was in the days of Lot. People went about their daily business—eating and drinking, buying and selling, farming and building—[29]until the morning Lot left Sodom. Then fire and burning sulfur rained down from heaven and destroyed them all. [30]Yes, it will be 'business as usual' right up to the day when the Son of Man is revealed. [31]On that day a person out on the deck of a roof must not go down into the house to pack. A person out in the field must not return home. [32]Remember what happened to Lot's wife! [33]If you cling to your life, you will lose it, and if you let your life go, you will save it. [34]That night two people will be asleep in one bed; one will be taken, the other left. [35]Two women will be grinding flour together at the mill; one will be taken, the other left.*"

[37]"Where will this happen, Lord?"* the disciples asked.

Jesus replied, "Just as the gathering of vultures shows there is a carcass nearby, so these signs indicate that the end is near."*

Parable of the Persistent Widow

18 One day Jesus told his disciples a story to show that they should always pray and never give

---

17:19 Or *Your faith has saved you.* **17:20** Or *by your speculations.* **17:21** Or *is within you,* or *is in your grasp.* **17:22** Or *long for even one day with the Son of Man.* "Son of Man" is a title Jesus used for himself. **17:24** Some manuscripts do not include *on the day.* **17:25** Or *suffer many things.* **17:35** Some manuscripts add verse 36, *Two men will be working in the field; one will be taken, the other left.* Compare Matt 24:40. **17:37a** Greek "*Where, Lord?*" **17:37b** Greek "*Wherever the carcass is, the vultures gather.*"

up. ²"There was a judge in a certain city," he said, "who neither feared God nor cared about people. ³A widow of that city came to him repeatedly, saying, 'Give me justice in this dispute with my enemy.' ⁴The judge ignored her for a while, but finally he said to himself, 'I don't fear God or care about people, ⁵but this woman is driving me crazy. I'm going to see that she gets justice, because she is wearing me out with her constant requests!' "

⁶Then the Lord said, "Learn a lesson from this unjust judge. ⁷Even he rendered a just decision in the end. So don't you think God will surely give justice to his chosen people who cry out to him day and night? Will he keep putting them off? ⁸I tell you, he will grant justice to them quickly! But when the Son of Man* returns, how many will he find on the earth who have faith?"

Parable of the Pharisee and Tax Collector

⁹Then Jesus told this story to some who had great confidence in their own righteousness and scorned everyone else: ¹⁰"Two men went to the Temple to pray. One was a Pharisee, and the other was a despised tax collector. ¹¹The Pharisee stood by himself and prayed this prayer*: 'I thank you, God, that I am not like other people—cheaters, sinners, adulterers. I'm certainly not like that

tax collector! ¹²I fast twice a week, and I give you a tenth of my income.'

¹³"But the tax collector stood at a distance and dared not even lift his eyes to heaven as he prayed. Instead, he beat his chest in sorrow, saying, 'O God, be merciful to me, for I am a sinner.' ¹⁴I tell you, this sinner, not the Pharisee, returned home justified before God. For those who exalt themselves will be humbled, and those who humble themselves will be exalted."

Jesus Blesses the Children

¹⁵One day some parents brought their little children to Jesus so he could touch and bless them. But when the disciples saw this, they scolded the parents for bothering him.

¹⁶Then Jesus called for the children and said to the disciples, "Let the children come to me. Don't stop them! For the Kingdom of God belongs to those who are like these children. ¹⁷I tell you the truth, anyone who doesn't receive the Kingdom of God like a child will never enter it."

The Rich Man

¹⁸Once a religious leader asked Jesus this question: "Good Teacher, what should I do to inherit eternal life?"

¹⁹"Why do you call me good?" Jesus asked him. "Only God is truly good. ²⁰But to answer your question,

18:8 "Son of Man" is a title Jesus used for himself. **18:11** Some manuscripts read *stood and prayed this prayer to himself.*

you know the commandments: 'You must not commit adultery. You must not murder. You must not steal. You must not testify falsely. Honor your father and mother.'* "

²¹The man replied, "I've obeyed all these commandments since I was young."

²²When Jesus heard his answer, he said, "There is still one thing you haven't done. Sell all your possessions and give the money to the poor, and you will have treasure in heaven. Then come, follow me."

²³But when the man heard this he became very sad, for he was very rich.

²⁴When Jesus saw this,* he said, "How hard it is for the rich to enter the Kingdom of God! ²⁵In fact, it is easier for a camel to go through the eye of a needle than for a rich person to enter the Kingdom of God!"

²⁶Those who heard this said, "Then who in the world can be saved?"

²⁷He replied, "What is impossible for people is possible with God."

²⁸Peter said, "We've left our homes to follow you."

²⁹"Yes," Jesus replied, "and I assure you that everyone who has given up house or wife or brothers or parents or children, for the sake of the Kingdom of God, ³⁰will be repaid many times over in this life, and will have eternal life in the world to come."

Jesus Again Predicts His Death

³¹Taking the twelve disciples aside, Jesus said, "Listen, we're going up to Jerusalem, where all the predictions of the prophets concerning the Son of Man will come true. ³²He will be handed over to the Romans,* and he will be mocked, treated shamefully, and spit upon. ³³They will flog him with a whip and kill him, but on the third day he will rise again."

³⁴But they didn't understand any of this. The significance of his words was hidden from them, and they failed to grasp what he was talking about.

Jesus Heals a Blind Beggar

³⁵As Jesus approached Jericho, a blind beggar was sitting beside the road. ³⁶When he heard the noise of a crowd going past, he asked what was happening. ³⁷They told him that Jesus the Nazarene* was going by. ³⁸So he began shouting, "Jesus, Son of David, have mercy on me!"

³⁹"Be quiet!" the people in front yelled at him.

But he only shouted louder, "Son of David, have mercy on me!"

⁴⁰When Jesus heard him, he stopped and ordered that the man be brought to him. As the man came near, Jesus asked him, ⁴¹"What do you want me to do for you?"

"Lord," he said, "I want to see!"

⁴²And Jesus said, "All right, receive your sight! Your faith has

18:20 Exod 20:12-16; Deut 5:16-20. 18:24 Some manuscripts read *When Jesus saw how sad the man was.* 18:32 Greek *the Gentiles.* 18:37 Or *Jesus of Nazareth.*

healed you." [43]Instantly the man could see, and he followed Jesus, praising God. And all who saw it praised God, too.

Jesus and Zacchaeus

19 Jesus entered Jericho and made his way through the town. [2]There was a man there named Zacchaeus. He was the chief tax collector in the region, and he had become very rich. [3]He tried to get a look at Jesus, but he was too short to see over the crowd. [4]So he ran ahead and climbed a sycamore-fig tree beside the road, for Jesus was going to pass that way.

[5]When Jesus came by, he looked up at Zacchaeus and called him by name. "Zacchaeus!" he said. "Quick, come down! I must be a guest in your home today."

[6]Zacchaeus quickly climbed down and took Jesus to his house in great excitement and joy. [7]But the people were displeased. "He has gone to be the guest of a notorious sinner," they grumbled.

[8]Meanwhile, Zacchaeus stood before the Lord and said, "I will give half my wealth to the poor, Lord, and if I have cheated people on their taxes, I will give them back four times as much!"

[9]Jesus responded, "Salvation has come to this home today, for this man has shown himself to be a true son of Abraham. [10]For the Son of Man* came to seek and save those who are lost."

Parable of the Ten Servants

[11]The crowd was listening to everything Jesus said. And because he was nearing Jerusalem, he told them a story to correct the impression that the Kingdom of God would begin right away. [12]He said, "A nobleman was called away to a distant empire to be crowned king and then return. [13]Before he left, he called together ten of his servants and divided among them ten pounds of silver,* saying, 'Invest this for me while I am gone.' [14]But his people hated him and sent a delegation after him to say, 'We do not want him to be our king.'

[15]"After he was crowned king, he returned and called in the servants to whom he had given the money. He wanted to find out what their profits were. [16]The first servant reported, 'Master, I invested your money and made ten times the original amount!'

[17]"'Well done!' the king exclaimed. 'You are a good servant. You have been faithful with the little I entrusted to you, so you will be governor of ten cities as your reward.'

[18]"The next servant reported, 'Master, I invested your money and made five times the original amount.'

[19]"'Well done!' the king said. 'You will be governor over five cities.'

19:10 "Son of Man" is a title Jesus used for himself. **19:13** Greek *ten minas;* one mina was worth about three months' wages.

²⁰"But the third servant brought back only the original amount of money and said, 'Master, I hid your money and kept it safe. ²¹I was afraid because you are a hard man to deal with, taking what isn't yours and harvesting crops you didn't plant.'

²²" 'You wicked servant!' the king roared. 'Your own words condemn you. If you knew that I'm a hard man who takes what isn't mine and harvests crops I didn't plant, ²³why didn't you deposit my money in the bank? At least I could have gotten some interest on it.'

²⁴"Then, turning to the others standing nearby, the king ordered, 'Take the money from this servant, and give it to the one who has ten pounds.'

²⁵" 'But, master,' they said, 'he already has ten pounds!'

²⁶" 'Yes,' the king replied, 'and to those who use well what they are given, even more will be given. But from those who do nothing, even what little they have will be taken away. ²⁷And as for these enemies of mine who didn't want me to be their king—bring them in and execute them right here in front of me.' "

Jesus' Triumphant Entry

²⁸After telling this story, Jesus went on toward Jerusalem, walking ahead of his disciples. ²⁹As he came to the towns of Bethphage and Bethany on the Mount of Olives, he sent two disciples ahead. ³⁰"Go into that village over there," he told them. "As you enter it, you will see a young donkey tied there that no one has ever ridden. Untie it and bring it here. ³¹If anyone asks, 'Why are you untying that colt?' just say, 'The Lord needs it.' "

³²So they went and found the colt, just as Jesus had said. ³³And sure enough, as they were untying it, the owners asked them, "Why are you untying that colt?"

³⁴And the disciples simply replied, "The Lord needs it." ³⁵So they brought the colt to Jesus and threw their garments over it for him to ride on.

³⁶As he rode along, the crowds spread out their garments on the road ahead of him. ³⁷When he reached the place where the road started down the Mount of Olives, all of his followers began to shout and sing as they walked along, praising God for all the wonderful miracles they had seen.

³⁸ "Blessings on the King who
　　　comes in the name of
　　　the LORD!
Peace in heaven, and glory
　　　in highest heaven!"*

³⁹But some of the Pharisees among the crowd said, "Teacher, rebuke your followers for saying things like that!"

⁴⁰He replied, "If they kept quiet, the stones along the road would burst into cheers!"

19:38 Pss 118:26; 148:1.

Jesus Weeps over Jerusalem

⁴¹But as he came closer to Jerusalem and saw the city ahead, he began to weep. ⁴²"How I wish today that you of all people would understand the way to peace. But now it is too late, and peace is hidden from your eyes. ⁴³Before long your enemies will build ramparts against your walls and encircle you and close in on you from every side. ⁴⁴They will crush you into the ground, and your children with you. Your enemies will not leave a single stone in place, because you did not recognize it when God visited you.*"

Jesus Clears the Temple

⁴⁵Then Jesus entered the Temple and began to drive out the people selling animals for sacrifices. ⁴⁶He said to them, "The Scriptures declare, 'My Temple will be a house of prayer,' but you have turned it into a den of thieves."*

⁴⁷After that, he taught daily in the Temple, but the leading priests, the teachers of religious law, and the other leaders of the people began planning how to kill him. ⁴⁸But they could think of nothing, because all the people hung on every word he said.

The Authority of Jesus Challenged

20 One day as Jesus was teaching the people and preaching the Good News in the Temple, the leading priests, the teachers of religious law, and the elders came up to him. ²They demanded, "By what authority are you doing all these things? Who gave you the right?"

³"Let me ask you a question first," he replied. ⁴"Did John's authority to baptize come from heaven, or was it merely human?"

⁵They talked it over among themselves. "If we say it was from heaven, he will ask why we didn't believe John. ⁶But if we say it was merely human, the people will stone us because they are convinced John was a prophet." ⁷So they finally replied that they didn't know.

⁸And Jesus responded, "Then I won't tell you by what authority I do these things."

Parable of the Evil Farmers

⁹Now Jesus turned to the people again and told them this story: "A man planted a vineyard, leased it to tenant farmers, and moved to another country to live for several years. ¹⁰At the time of the grape harvest, he sent one of his servants to collect his share of the crop. But the farmers attacked the servant, beat him up, and sent him back empty-handed. ¹¹So the owner sent another servant, but they also insulted him, beat him up, and sent him away empty-handed. ¹²A third man was sent, and they wounded him and chased him away.

¹³"'What will I do?' the owner

19:44 Greek *did not recognize the time of your visitation,* a reference to the Messiah's coming.
19:46 Isa 56:7; Jer 7:11.

asked himself. 'I know! I'll send my cherished son. Surely they will respect him.'

¹⁴"But when the tenant farmers saw his son, they said to each other, 'Here comes the heir to this estate. Let's kill him and get the estate for ourselves!' ¹⁵So they dragged him out of the vineyard and murdered him.

"What do you suppose the owner of the vineyard will do to them?" Jesus asked. ¹⁶"I'll tell you—he will come and kill those farmers and lease the vineyard to others."

"How terrible that such a thing should ever happen," his listeners protested.

¹⁷Jesus looked at them and said, "Then what does this Scripture mean?

'The stone that the builders
    rejected
has now become the
    cornerstone.'*

¹⁸Everyone who stumbles over that stone will be broken to pieces, and it will crush anyone it falls on."

¹⁹The teachers of religious law and the leading priests wanted to arrest Jesus immediately because they realized he was telling the story against them—they were the wicked farmers. But they were afraid of the people's reaction.

Taxes for Caesar

²⁰Watching for their opportunity, the leaders sent spies pretending to be honest men. They tried to get Jesus to say something that could be reported to the Roman governor so he would arrest Jesus. ²¹"Teacher," they said, "we know that you speak and teach what is right and are not influenced by what others think. You teach the way of God truthfully. ²²Now tell us—is it right for us to pay taxes to Caesar or not?"

²³He saw through their trickery and said, ²⁴"Show me a Roman coin.* Whose picture and title are stamped on it?"

"Caesar's," they replied.

²⁵"Well then," he said, "give to Caesar what belongs to Caesar, and give to God what belongs to God."

²⁶So they failed to trap him by what he said in front of the people. Instead, they were amazed by his answer, and they became silent.

Discussion about Resurrection

²⁷Then Jesus was approached by some Sadducees—religious leaders who say there is no resurrection from the dead. ²⁸They posed this question: "Teacher, Moses gave us a law that if a man dies, leaving a wife but no children, his brother should marry the widow and have a child who will carry on the brother's name.* ²⁹Well, suppose there were seven brothers. The oldest one married and then died without children. ³⁰So the second brother married the widow, but he also

20:17 Ps 118:22. **20:24** Greek *a denarius*. **20:28** See Deut 25:5-6.

died. 31Then the third brother married her. This continued with all seven of them, who died without children. 32Finally, the woman also died. 33So tell us, whose wife will she be in the resurrection? For all seven were married to her!"

34Jesus replied, "Marriage is for people here on earth. 35But in the age to come, those worthy of being raised from the dead will neither marry nor be given in marriage. 36And they will never die again. In this respect they will be like angels. They are children of God and children of the resurrection.

37"But now, as to whether the dead will be raised—even Moses proved this when he wrote about the burning bush. Long after Abraham, Isaac, and Jacob had died, he referred to the Lord* as 'the God of Abraham, the God of Isaac, and the God of Jacob.'* 38So he is the God of the living, not the dead, for they are all alive to him."

39"Well said, Teacher!" remarked some of the teachers of religious law who were standing there. 40And then no one dared to ask him any more questions.

Whose Son Is the Messiah?

41Then Jesus presented them with a question. "Why is it," he asked, "that the Messiah is said to be the son of David? 42For David himself wrote in the book of Psalms:

'The LORD said to my Lord,
    Sit in the place of honor at my
        right hand
43 until I humble your enemies,
    making them a footstool
        under your feet.'*

44Since David called the Messiah 'Lord,' how can the Messiah be his son?"

45Then, with the crowds listening, he turned to his disciples and said, 46"Beware of these teachers of religious law! For they like to parade around in flowing robes and love to receive respectful greetings as they walk in the marketplaces. And how they love the seats of honor in the synagogues and the head table at banquets. 47Yet they shamelessly cheat widows out of their property and then pretend to be pious by making long prayers in public. Because of this, they will be severely punished."

The Widow's Offering

21 While Jesus was in the Temple, he watched the rich people dropping their gifts in the collection box. 2Then a poor widow came by and dropped in two small coins.*

3"I tell you the truth," Jesus said, "this poor widow has given more than all the rest of them. 4For they have given a tiny part of their surplus, but she, poor as she is, has given everything she has."

20:37a Greek *when he wrote about the bush. He referred to the Lord.*   20:37b Exod 3:6.
20:42-43 Ps 110:1.   21:2 Greek *two lepta* [the smallest of Jewish coins].

Jesus Speaks about the Future

⁵Some of his disciples began talking about the majestic stonework of the Temple and the memorial decorations on the walls. But Jesus said, ⁶"The time is coming when all these things will be completely demolished. Not one stone will be left on top of another!"

⁷"Teacher," they asked, "when will all this happen? What sign will show us that these things are about to take place?"

⁸He replied, "Don't let anyone mislead you, for many will come in my name, claiming, 'I am the Messiah,'* and saying, 'The time has come!' But don't believe them. ⁹And when you hear of wars and insurrections, don't panic. Yes, these things must take place first, but the end won't follow immediately."

¹⁰Then he added, "Nation will go to war against nation, and kingdom against kingdom. ¹¹There will be great earthquakes, and there will be famines and plagues in many lands, and there will be terrifying things and great miraculous signs from heaven.

¹²"But before all this occurs, there will be a time of great persecution. You will be dragged into synagogues and prisons, and you will stand trial before kings and governors because you are my followers. ¹³But this will be your opportunity to tell them about me.* ¹⁴So don't worry in advance about how to answer the charges against you, ¹⁵for I will give you the right words and such wisdom that none of your opponents will be able to reply or refute you! ¹⁶Even those closest to you—your parents, brothers, relatives, and friends—will betray you. They will even kill some of you. ¹⁷And everyone will hate you because you are my followers.* ¹⁸But not a hair of your head will perish! ¹⁹By standing firm, you will win your souls.

²⁰"And when you see Jerusalem surrounded by armies, then you will know that the time of its destruction has arrived. ²¹Then those in Judea must flee to the hills. Those in Jerusalem must get out, and those out in the country should not return to the city. ²²For those will be days of God's vengeance, and the prophetic words of the Scriptures will be fulfilled. ²³How terrible it will be for pregnant women and for nursing mothers in those days. For there will be disaster in the land and great anger against this people. ²⁴They will be killed by the sword or sent away as captives to all the nations of the world. And Jerusalem will be trampled down by the Gentiles until the period of the Gentiles comes to an end.

²⁵"And there will be strange signs in the sun, moon, and stars. And here on earth the nations will be in turmoil, perplexed by the roaring

21:8 Greek *claiming, 'I am.'* 21:13 Or *This will be your testimony against them.* 21:17 Greek *on account of my name.*

seas and strange tides. ²⁶People will be terrified at what they see coming upon the earth, for the powers in the heavens will be shaken. ²⁷Then everyone will see the Son of Man* coming on a cloud with power and great glory.* ²⁸So when all these things begin to happen, stand and look up, for your salvation is near!"

²⁹Then he gave them this illustration: "Notice the fig tree, or any other tree. ³⁰When the leaves come out, you know without being told that summer is near. ³¹In the same way, when you see all these things taking place, you can know that the Kingdom of God is near. ³²I tell you the truth, this generation will not pass from the scene until all these things have taken place. ³³Heaven and earth will disappear, but my words will never disappear.

³⁴"Watch out! Don't let your hearts be dulled by carousing and drunkenness, and by the worries of this life. Don't let that day catch you unaware, ³⁵like a trap. For that day will come upon everyone living on the earth. ³⁶Keep alert at all times. And pray that you might be strong enough to escape these coming horrors and stand before the Son of Man."

³⁷Every day Jesus went to the Temple to teach, and each evening he returned to spend the night on the Mount of Olives. ³⁸The crowds gathered at the Temple early each morning to hear him.

Judas Agrees to Betray Jesus

22 The Festival of Unleavened Bread, which is also called Passover, was approaching. ²The leading priests and teachers of religious law were plotting how to kill Jesus, but they were afraid of the people's reaction.

³Then Satan entered into Judas Iscariot, who was one of the twelve disciples, ⁴and he went to the leading priests and captains of the Temple guard to discuss the best way to betray Jesus to them. ⁵They were delighted, and they promised to give him money. ⁶So he agreed and began looking for an opportunity to betray Jesus so they could arrest him when the crowds weren't around.

The Last Supper

⁷Now the Festival of Unleavened Bread arrived, when the Passover lamb is sacrificed. ⁸Jesus sent Peter and John ahead and said, "Go and prepare the Passover meal, so we can eat it together."

⁹"Where do you want us to prepare it?" they asked him.

¹⁰He replied, "As soon as you enter Jerusalem, a man carrying a pitcher of water will meet you. Follow him. At the house he enters, ¹¹say to the owner, 'The Teacher asks: Where is the guest room where I can eat the Passover meal with my disciples?' ¹²He will take you upstairs to a large room that is already set up. That is

21:27a "Son of Man" is a title Jesus used for himself.   **21:27b** See Dan 7:13.

where you should prepare our meal." [13]They went off to the city and found everything just as Jesus had said, and they prepared the Passover meal there.

[14]When the time came, Jesus and the apostles sat down together at the table.* [15]Jesus said, "I have been very eager to eat this Passover meal with you before my suffering begins. [16]For I tell you now that I won't eat this meal again until its meaning is fulfilled in the Kingdom of God."

[17]Then he took a cup of wine and gave thanks to God for it. Then he said, "Take this and share it among yourselves. [18]For I will not drink wine again until the Kingdom of God has come."

[19]He took some bread and gave thanks to God for it. Then he broke it in pieces and gave it to the disciples, saying, "This is my body, which is given for you. Do this in remembrance of me."

[20]After supper he took another cup of wine and said, "This cup is the new covenant between God and his people—an agreement confirmed with my blood, which is poured out as a sacrifice for you.*

[21]"But here at this table, sitting among us as a friend, is the man who will betray me. [22]For it has been determined that the Son of Man* must die. But what sorrow awaits the one who betrays him." [23]The disciples began to ask each other which of them would ever do such a thing.

[24]Then they began to argue among themselves about who would be the greatest among them. [25]Jesus told them, "In this world the kings and great men lord it over their people, yet they are called 'friends of the people.' [26]But among you it will be different. Those who are the greatest among you should take the lowest rank, and the leader should be like a servant. [27]Who is more important, the one who sits at the table or the one who serves? The one who sits at the table, of course. But not here! For I am among you as one who serves.

[28]"You have stayed with me in my time of trial. [29]And just as my Father has granted me a Kingdom, I now grant you the right [30]to eat and drink at my table in my Kingdom. And you will sit on thrones, judging the twelve tribes of Israel.

Jesus Predicts Peter's Denial

[31]"Simon, Simon, Satan has asked to sift each of you like wheat. [32]But I have pleaded in prayer for you, Simon, that your faith should not fail. So when you have repented and turned to me again, strengthen your brothers."

[33]Peter said, "Lord, I am ready to go to prison with you, and even to die with you."

22:14 Or reclined together.   22:19-20 Some manuscripts do not include 22:19b-20, which is given for you . . . which is poured out as a sacrifice for you.   22:22 "Son of Man" is a title Jesus used for himself.

³⁴But Jesus said, "Peter, let me tell you something. Before the rooster crows tomorrow morning, you will deny three times that you even know me."

³⁵Then Jesus asked them, "When I sent you out to preach the Good News and you did not have money, a traveler's bag, or an extra pair of sandals, did you need anything?"

"No," they replied.

³⁶"But now," he said, "take your money and a traveler's bag. And if you don't have a sword, sell your cloak and buy one! ³⁷For the time has come for this prophecy about me to be fulfilled: 'He was counted among the rebels.'* Yes, everything written about me by the prophets will come true."

³⁸"Look, Lord," they replied, "we have two swords among us."

"That's enough," he said.

Jesus Prays on the Mount of Olives

³⁹Then, accompanied by the disciples, Jesus left the upstairs room and went as usual to the Mount of Olives. ⁴⁰There he told them, "Pray that you will not give in to temptation."

⁴¹He walked away, about a stone's throw, and knelt down and prayed, ⁴²"Father, if you are willing, please take this cup of suffering away from me. Yet I want your will to be done, not mine." ⁴³Then an angel from heaven appeared and strengthened him. ⁴⁴He prayed more fervently, and he was in such agony of spirit that his sweat fell to the ground like great drops of blood.*

⁴⁵At last he stood up again and returned to the disciples, only to find them asleep, exhausted from grief. ⁴⁶"Why are you sleeping?" he asked them. "Get up and pray, so that you will not give in to temptation."

Jesus Is Betrayed and Arrested

⁴⁷But even as Jesus said this, a crowd approached, led by Judas, one of the twelve disciples. Judas walked over to Jesus to greet him with a kiss. ⁴⁸But Jesus said, "Judas, would you betray the Son of Man with a kiss?"

⁴⁹When the other disciples saw what was about to happen, they exclaimed, "Lord, should we fight? We brought the swords!" ⁵⁰And one of them struck at the high priest's slave, slashing off his right ear.

⁵¹But Jesus said, "No more of this." And he touched the man's ear and healed him.

⁵²Then Jesus spoke to the leading priests, the captains of the Temple guard, and the elders who had come for him. "Am I some dangerous revolutionary," he asked, "that you come with swords and clubs to arrest me? ⁵³Why didn't you arrest me in the Temple? I was there every day. But this is your moment, the time when the power of darkness reigns."

Peter Denies Jesus

⁵⁴So they arrested him and led him to the high priest's home. And Peter

22:37 Isa 53:12. **22:43-44** Verses 43 and 44 are not included in the most ancient manuscripts.

followed at a distance. ⁵⁵The guards lit a fire in the middle of the courtyard and sat around it, and Peter joined them there. ⁵⁶A servant girl noticed him in the firelight and began staring at him. Finally she said, "This man was one of Jesus' followers!"

⁵⁷But Peter denied it. "Woman," he said, "I don't even know him!"

⁵⁸After a while someone else looked at him and said, "You must be one of them!"

"No, man, I'm not!" Peter retorted.

⁵⁹About an hour later someone else insisted, "This must be one of them, because he is a Galilean, too."

⁶⁰But Peter said, "Man, I don't know what you are talking about." And immediately, while he was still speaking, the rooster crowed. ⁶¹At that moment the Lord turned and looked at Peter. Suddenly, the Lord's words flashed through Peter's mind: "Before the rooster crows tomorrow morning, you will deny three times that you even know me." ⁶²And Peter left the courtyard, weeping bitterly.

⁶³The guards in charge of Jesus began mocking and beating him. ⁶⁴They blindfolded him and said, "Prophesy to us! Who hit you that time?" ⁶⁵And they hurled all sorts of terrible insults at him.

Jesus before the Council

⁶⁶At daybreak all the elders of the people assembled, including the leading priests and the teachers of religious law. Jesus was led before this high council,* ⁶⁷and they said, "Tell us, are you the Messiah?"

But he replied, "If I tell you, you won't believe me. ⁶⁸And if I ask you a question, you won't answer. ⁶⁹But from now on the Son of Man will be seated in the place of power at God's right hand.*"

⁷⁰They all shouted, "So, are you claiming to be the Son of God?"

And he replied, "You say that I am."

⁷¹"Why do we need other witnesses?" they said. "We ourselves heard him say it."

Jesus' Trial before Pilate

23 Then the entire council took Jesus to Pilate, the Roman governor. ²They began to state their case: "This man has been leading our people astray by telling them not to pay their taxes to the Roman government and by claiming he is the Messiah, a king."

³So Pilate asked him, "Are you the king of the Jews?"

Jesus replied, "You have said it."

⁴Pilate turned to the leading priests and to the crowd and said, "I find nothing wrong with this man!"

⁵Then they became insistent. "But he is causing riots by his teaching wherever he goes—all over Judea, from Galilee to Jerusalem!"

⁶"Oh, is he a Galilean?" Pilate asked. ⁷When they said that he was,

22:66 Greek *before their Sanhedrin.* 22:69 See Ps 110:1.

Pilate sent him to Herod Antipas, because Galilee was under Herod's jurisdiction, and Herod happened to be in Jerusalem at the time.

8Herod was delighted at the opportunity to see Jesus, because he had heard about him and had been hoping for a long time to see him perform a miracle. 9He asked Jesus question after question, but Jesus refused to answer. 10Meanwhile, the leading priests and the teachers of religious law stood there shouting their accusations. 11Then Herod and his soldiers began mocking and ridiculing Jesus. Finally, they put a royal robe on him and sent him back to Pilate. 12(Herod and Pilate, who had been enemies before, became friends that day.)

13Then Pilate called together the leading priests and other religious leaders, along with the people, 14and he announced his verdict. "You brought this man to me, accusing him of leading a revolt. I have examined him thoroughly on this point in your presence and find him innocent. 15Herod came to the same conclusion and sent him back to us. Nothing this man has done calls for the death penalty. 16So I will have him flogged, and then I will release him."*

18Then a mighty roar rose from the crowd, and with one voice they shouted, "Kill him, and release Barabbas to us!" 19(Barabbas was in prison for taking part in an insurrection in Jerusalem against the government, and for murder.) 20Pilate argued with them, because he wanted to release Jesus. 21But they kept shouting, "Crucify him! Crucify him!"

22For the third time he demanded, "Why? What crime has he committed? I have found no reason to sentence him to death. So I will have him flogged, and then I will release him."

23But the mob shouted louder and louder, demanding that Jesus be crucified, and their voices prevailed. 24So Pilate sentenced Jesus to die as they demanded. 25As they had requested, he released Barabbas, the man in prison for insurrection and murder. But he turned Jesus over to them to do as they wished.

The Crucifixion

26As they led Jesus away, a man named Simon, who was from Cyrene,* happened to be coming in from the countryside. The soldiers seized him and put the cross on him and made him carry it behind Jesus. 27A large crowd trailed behind, including many grief-stricken women. 28But Jesus turned and said to them, "Daughters of Jerusalem, don't weep for me, but weep for

---

23:16 Some manuscripts add verse 17, *Now it was necessary for him to release one prisoner to them during the Passover celebration.* Compare Matt 27:15; Mark 15:6; John 18:39. 23:26 *Cyrene* was a city in northern Africa.

yourselves and for your children. ²⁹For the days are coming when they will say, 'Fortunate indeed are the women who are childless, the wombs that have not borne a child and the breasts that have never nursed.' ³⁰People will beg the mountains, 'Fall on us,' and plead with the hills, 'Bury us.'* ³¹For if these things are done when the tree is green, what will happen when it is dry?*"

³²Two others, both criminals, were led out to be executed with him. ³³When they came to a place called The Skull,* they nailed him to the cross. And the criminals were also crucified—one on his right and one on his left.

³⁴Jesus said, "Father, forgive them, for they don't know what they are doing."* And the soldiers gambled for his clothes by throwing dice.*

³⁵The crowd watched and the leaders scoffed. "He saved others," they said, "let him save himself if he is really God's Messiah, the Chosen One." ³⁶The soldiers mocked him, too, by offering him a drink of sour wine. ³⁷They called out to him, "If you are the King of the Jews, save yourself!" ³⁸A sign was fastened above him with these words: "This is the King of the Jews."

³⁹One of the criminals hanging beside him scoffed, "So you're the Messiah, are you? Prove it by saving yourself—and us, too, while you're at it!"

⁴⁰But the other criminal protested, "Don't you fear God even when you have been sentenced to die? ⁴¹We deserve to die for our crimes, but this man hasn't done anything wrong." ⁴²Then he said, "Jesus, remember me when you come into your Kingdom."

⁴³And Jesus replied, "I assure you, today you will be with me in paradise."

The Death of Jesus

⁴⁴By this time it was about noon, and darkness fell across the whole land until three o'clock. ⁴⁵The light from the sun was gone. And suddenly, the curtain in the sanctuary of the Temple was torn down the middle. ⁴⁶Then Jesus shouted, "Father, I entrust my spirit into your hands!"* And with those words he breathed his last.

⁴⁷When the Roman officer* overseeing the execution saw what had happened, he worshiped God and said, "Surely this man was innocent.*" ⁴⁸And when all the crowd that came to see the crucifixion saw what had happened, they went home in deep sorrow.* ⁴⁹But Jesus' friends, including the women who had followed him from Galilee, stood at a distance watching.

23:30 Hos 10:8. 23:31 Or *If these things are done to me, the living tree, what will happen to you, the dry tree?* 23:33 Sometimes rendered *Calvary,* which comes from the Latin word for "skull." 23:34a This sentence is not included in many ancient manuscripts. 23:34b Greek *by casting lots.* See Ps 22:18. 23:46 Ps 31:5. 23:47a Greek *the centurion.* 23:47b Or *righteous.* 23:48 Greek *went home beating their breasts.*

The Burial of Jesus

50 Now there was a good and righteous man named Joseph. He was a member of the Jewish high council, 51 but he had not agreed with the decision and actions of the other religious leaders. He was from the town of Arimathea in Judea, and he was waiting for the Kingdom of God to come. 52 He went to Pilate and asked for Jesus' body. 53 Then he took the body down from the cross and wrapped it in a long sheet of linen cloth and laid it in a new tomb that had been carved out of rock. 54 This was done late on Friday afternoon, the day of preparation,* as the Sabbath was about to begin.

55 As his body was taken away, the women from Galilee followed and saw the tomb where his body was placed. 56 Then they went home and prepared spices and ointments to anoint his body. But by the time they were finished the Sabbath had begun, so they rested as required by the law.

The Resurrection

24 But very early on Sunday morning* the women went to the tomb, taking the spices they had prepared. 2 They found that the stone had been rolled away from the entrance. 3 So they went in, but they didn't find the body of the Lord Jesus. 4 As they stood there puzzled, two men suddenly appeared to them, clothed in dazzling robes.

5 The women were terrified and bowed with their faces to the ground. Then the men asked, "Why are you looking among the dead for someone who is alive? 6 He isn't here! He is risen from the dead! Remember what he told you back in Galilee, 7 that the Son of Man* must be betrayed into the hands of sinful men and be crucified, and that he would rise again on the third day."

8 Then they remembered that he had said this. 9 So they rushed back from the tomb to tell his eleven disciples—and everyone else—what had happened. 10 It was Mary Magdalene, Joanna, Mary the mother of James, and several other women who told the apostles what had happened. 11 But the story sounded like nonsense to the men, so they didn't believe it. 12 However, Peter jumped up and ran to the tomb to look. Stooping, he peered in and saw the empty linen wrappings; then he went home again, wondering what had happened.

The Walk to Emmaus

13 That same day two of Jesus' followers were walking to the village of Emmaus, seven miles* from Jerusalem. 14 As they walked along they were talking about everything that had happened. 15 As they talked

23:54 Greek *It was the day of preparation.* 24:1 Greek *But on the first day of the week, very early in the morning.* 24:7 "Son of Man" is a title Jesus used for himself. 24:13 Greek *60 stadia* [11.1 kilometers].

and discussed these things, Jesus himself suddenly came and began walking with them. [16]But God kept them from recognizing him.

[17]He asked them, "What are you discussing so intently as you walk along?"

They stopped short, sadness written across their faces. [18]Then one of them, Cleopas, replied, "You must be the only person in Jerusalem who hasn't heard about all the things that have happened there the last few days."

[19]"What things?" Jesus asked.

"The things that happened to Jesus, the man from Nazareth," they said. "He was a prophet who did powerful miracles, and he was a mighty teacher in the eyes of God and all the people. [20]But our leading priests and other religious leaders handed him over to be condemned to death, and they crucified him. [21]We had hoped he was the Messiah who had come to rescue Israel. This all happened three days ago.

[22]"Then some women from our group of his followers were at his tomb early this morning, and they came back with an amazing report. [23]They said his body was missing, and they had seen angels who told them Jesus is alive! [24]Some of our men ran out to see, and sure enough, his body was gone, just as the women had said."

[25]Then Jesus said to them, "You foolish people! You find it so hard to believe all that the prophets wrote in the Scriptures. [26]Wasn't it clearly predicted that the Messiah would have to suffer all these things before entering his glory?" [27]Then Jesus took them through the writings of Moses and all the prophets, explaining from all the Scriptures the things concerning himself.

[28]By this time they were nearing Emmaus and the end of their journey. Jesus acted as if he were going on, [29]but they begged him, "Stay the night with us, since it is getting late." So he went home with them. [30]As they sat down to eat,* he took the bread and blessed it. Then he broke it and gave it to them. [31]Suddenly, their eyes were opened, and they recognized him. And at that moment he disappeared!

[32]They said to each other, "Didn't our hearts burn within us as he talked with us on the road and explained the Scriptures to us?" [33]And within the hour they were on their way back to Jerusalem. There they found the eleven disciples and the others who had gathered with them, [34]who said, "The Lord has really risen! He appeared to Peter.*"

Jesus Appears to the Disciples

[35]Then the two from Emmaus told their story of how Jesus had appeared to them as they were walking along the road, and how they had recognized him as he was breaking the bread. [36]And just as

24:30 Or *As they reclined.* 24:34 Greek *Simon.*

they were telling about it, Jesus himself was suddenly standing there among them. "Peace be with you," he said. [37]But the whole group was startled and frightened, thinking they were seeing a ghost!

[38]"Why are you frightened?" he asked. "Why are your hearts filled with doubt? [39]Look at my hands. Look at my feet. You can see that it's really me. Touch me and make sure that I am not a ghost, because ghosts don't have bodies, as you see that I do." [40]As he spoke, he showed them his hands and his feet.

[41]Still they stood there in disbelief, filled with joy and wonder. Then he asked them, "Do you have anything here to eat?" [42]They gave him a piece of broiled fish, [43]and he ate it as they watched.

[44]Then he said, "When I was with you before, I told you that everything written about me in the law of Moses and the prophets and in the Psalms must be fulfilled." [45]Then he opened their minds to understand the Scriptures. [46]And he said, "Yes, it was written long ago that the Messiah would suffer and die and rise from the dead on the third day. [47]It was also written that this message would be proclaimed in the authority of his name to all the nations,* beginning in Jerusalem: 'There is forgiveness of sins for all who repent.' [48]You are witnesses of all these things.

[49]"And now I will send the Holy Spirit, just as my Father promised. But stay here in the city until the Holy Spirit comes and fills you with power from heaven."

The Ascension

[50]Then Jesus led them to Bethany, and lifting his hands to heaven, he blessed them. [51]While he was blessing them, he left them and was taken up to heaven. [52]So they worshiped him and then returned to Jerusalem filled with great joy. [53]And they spent all of their time in the Temple, praising God.

24:47 Or all peoples.

John

Prologue: Christ, the Eternal Word

1 ¹In the beginning the Word
already existed.
The Word was with God,
and the Word was God.
² He existed in the beginning
with God.
³ God created everything through
him,
and nothing was created
except through him.
⁴ The Word gave life to everything
that was created,*
and his life brought light to
everyone.
⁵ The light shines in the darkness,
and the darkness can never
extinguish it.*

⁶God sent a man, John the Baptist,* ⁷to tell about the light so that everyone might believe because of his testimony. ⁸John himself was not the light; he was simply a witness to tell about the light. ⁹The one who is the true light, who gives light to everyone, was coming into the world.

¹⁰He came into the very world he created, but the world didn't recognize him. ¹¹He came to his own people, and even they rejected him. ¹²But to all who believed him and accepted him, he gave the right to become children of God. ¹³They are reborn—not with a physical birth resulting from human passion or plan, but a birth that comes from God.

¹⁴So the Word became human* and made his home among us. He was full of unfailing love and faithfulness.* And we have seen his glory, the glory of the Father's one and only Son.

¹⁵John testified about him when he shouted to the crowds, "This is the one I was talking about when I said, 'Someone is coming after me who is far greater than I am, for he existed long before me.'"

¹⁶From his abundance we have all received one gracious blessing after another.* ¹⁷For the law was given through Moses, but God's unfailing love and faithfulness came through Jesus Christ. ¹⁸No one has ever seen God. But the unique One, who is himself God,* is near to the Father's heart. He has revealed God to us.

1:3-4 Or *and nothing that was created was created except through him. The Word gave life to everything.* **1:5** Or *and the darkness has not understood it.* **1:6** Greek *a man named John.* **1:14a** Greek *became flesh.* **1:14b** Or *grace and truth;* also in 1:17. **1:16** Or *received the grace of Christ rather than the grace of the law;* Greek reads *received grace upon grace.* **1:18** Some manuscripts read *But the one and only Son.*

The Testimony of John the Baptist

¹⁹This was John's testimony when the Jewish leaders sent priests and Temple assistants* from Jerusalem to ask John, "Who are you?" ²⁰He came right out and said, "I am not the Messiah."

²¹"Well then, who are you?" they asked. "Are you Elijah?"

"No," he replied.

"Are you the Prophet we are expecting?"*

"No."

²²"Then who are you? We need an answer for those who sent us. What do you have to say about yourself?"

²³John replied in the words of the prophet Isaiah:

"I am a voice shouting in the wilderness,
'Clear the way for the LORD's coming!'"*

²⁴Then the Pharisees who had been sent ²⁵asked him, "If you aren't the Messiah or Elijah or the Prophet, what right do you have to baptize?"

²⁶John told them, "I baptize with* water, but right here in the crowd is someone you do not recognize. ²⁷Though his ministry follows mine, I'm not even worthy to be his slave and untie the straps of his sandal."

²⁸This encounter took place in Bethany, an area east of the Jordan River, where John was baptizing.

Jesus, the Lamb of God

²⁹The next day John saw Jesus coming toward him and said, "Look! The Lamb of God who takes away the sin of the world! ³⁰He is the one I was talking about when I said, 'A man is coming after me who is far greater than I am, for he existed long before me.' ³¹I did not recognize him as the Messiah, but I have been baptizing with water so that he might be revealed to Israel."

³²Then John testified, "I saw the Holy Spirit descending like a dove from heaven and resting upon him. ³³I didn't know he was the one, but when God sent me to baptize with water, he told me, 'The one on whom you see the Spirit descend and rest is the one who will baptize with the Holy Spirit.' ³⁴I saw this happen to Jesus, so I testify that he is the Chosen One of God.*"

The First Disciples

³⁵The following day John was again standing with two of his disciples. ³⁶As Jesus walked by, John looked at him and declared, "Look! There is the Lamb of God!" ³⁷When John's two disciples heard this, they followed Jesus.

³⁸Jesus looked around and saw them following. "What do you want?" he asked them.

They replied, "Rabbi" (which means "Teacher"), "where are you staying?"

1:19 Greek *and Levites.* **1:21** Greek *Are you the Prophet?* See Deut 18:15, 18; Mal 4:5-6. **1:23** Isa 40:3. **1:26** Or *in;* also in 1:31, 33. **1:34** Some manuscripts read *the Son of God.*

³⁹"Come and see," he said. It was about four o'clock in the afternoon when they went with him to the place where he was staying, and they remained with him the rest of the day.

⁴⁰Andrew, Simon Peter's brother, was one of these men who heard what John said and then followed Jesus. ⁴¹Andrew went to find his brother, Simon, and told him, "We have found the Messiah" (which means "Christ"*).

⁴²Then Andrew brought Simon to meet Jesus. Looking intently at Simon, Jesus said, "Your name is Simon, son of John—but you will be called Cephas" (which means "Peter"*).

⁴³The next day Jesus decided to go to Galilee. He found Philip and said to him, "Come, follow me." ⁴⁴Philip was from Bethsaida, Andrew and Peter's hometown.

⁴⁵Philip went to look for Nathanael and told him, "We have found the very person Moses* and the prophets wrote about! His name is Jesus, the son of Joseph from Nazareth."

⁴⁶"Nazareth!" exclaimed Nathanael. "Can anything good come from Nazareth?"

"Come and see for yourself," Philip replied.

⁴⁷As they approached, Jesus said, "Now here is a genuine son of Israel—a man of complete integrity."

⁴⁸"How do you know about me?" Nathanael asked.

Jesus replied, "I could see you under the fig tree before Philip found you."

⁴⁹Then Nathanael exclaimed, "Rabbi, you are the Son of God—the King of Israel!"

⁵⁰Jesus asked him, "Do you believe this just because I told you I had seen you under the fig tree? You will see greater things than this." ⁵¹Then he said, "I tell you the truth, you will all see heaven open and the angels of God going up and down on the Son of Man, the one who is the stairway between heaven and earth.*"

The Wedding at Cana

2 The next day* there was a wedding celebration in the village of Cana in Galilee. Jesus' mother was there, ²and Jesus and his disciples were also invited to the celebration. ³The wine supply ran out during the festivities, so Jesus' mother told him, "They have no more wine."

⁴"Dear woman, that's not our problem," Jesus replied. "My time has not yet come."

⁵But his mother told the servants, "Do whatever he tells you."

⁶Standing nearby were six stone water jars, used for Jewish ceremonial washing. Each could hold

1:41 *Messiah* (a Hebrew term) and *Christ* (a Greek term) both mean "anointed one." **1:42** The names *Cephas* (from Aramaic) and *Peter* (from Greek) both mean "rock." **1:45** Greek *Moses in the law.* **1:51** Greek *going up and down on the Son of Man;* see Gen 28:10-17. "Son of Man" is a title Jesus used for himself. **2:1** Greek *On the third day;* see 1:35, 43.

twenty to thirty gallons.* 7Jesus told the servants, "Fill the jars with water." When the jars had been filled, 8he said, "Now dip some out, and take it to the master of ceremonies." So the servants followed his instructions.

9When the master of ceremonies tasted the water that was now wine, not knowing where it had come from (though, of course, the servants knew), he called the bridegroom over. 10"A host always serves the best wine first," he said. "Then, when everyone has had a lot to drink, he brings out the less expensive wine. But you have kept the best until now!"

11This miraculous sign at Cana in Galilee was the first time Jesus revealed his glory. And his disciples believed in him.

12After the wedding he went to Capernaum for a few days with his mother, his brothers, and his disciples.

Jesus Clears the Temple

13It was nearly time for the Jewish Passover celebration, so Jesus went to Jerusalem. 14In the Temple area he saw merchants selling cattle, sheep, and doves for sacrifices; he also saw dealers at tables exchanging foreign money. 15Jesus made a whip from some ropes and chased them all out of the Temple. He drove out the sheep and cattle, scattered the money changers' coins over the floor, and turned over their tables. 16Then, going over to the people who sold doves, he told them, "Get these things out of here. Stop turning my Father's house into a marketplace!"

17Then his disciples remembered this prophecy from the Scriptures: "Passion for God's house will consume me."*

18But the Jewish leaders demanded, "What are you doing? If God gave you authority to do this, show us a miraculous sign to prove it."

19"All right," Jesus replied. "Destroy this temple, and in three days I will raise it up."

20"What!" they exclaimed. "It has taken forty-six years to build this Temple, and you can rebuild it in three days?" 21But when Jesus said "this temple," he meant his own body. 22After he was raised from the dead, his disciples remembered he had said this, and they believed both the Scriptures and what Jesus had said.

Jesus and Nicodemus

23Because of the miraculous signs Jesus did in Jerusalem at the Passover celebration, many began to trust in him. 24But Jesus didn't trust them, because he knew all about people. 25No one needed to tell him about human nature, for he knew what was in each person's heart.

2:6 Greek 2 or 3 measures [75 to 113 liters]. 2:17 Or "Concern for God's house will be my undoing." Ps 69:9.

3 There was a man named Nicodemus, a Jewish religious leader who was a Pharisee. [2]After dark one evening, he came to speak with Jesus. "Rabbi," he said, "we all know that God has sent you to teach us. Your miraculous signs are evidence that God is with you."

[3]Jesus replied, "I tell you the truth, unless you are born again,* you cannot see the Kingdom of God."

[4]"What do you mean?" exclaimed Nicodemus. "How can an old man go back into his mother's womb and be born again?"

[5]Jesus replied, "I assure you, no one can enter the Kingdom of God without being born of water and the Spirit.* [6]Humans can reproduce only human life, but the Holy Spirit gives birth to spiritual life.* [7]So don't be surprised when I say, 'You* must be born again.' [8]The wind blows wherever it wants. Just as you can hear the wind but can't tell where it comes from or where it is going, so you can't explain how people are born of the Spirit."

[9]"How are these things possible?" Nicodemus asked.

[10]Jesus replied, "You are a respected Jewish teacher, and yet you don't understand these things? [11]I assure you, we tell you what we know and have seen, and yet you won't believe our testimony. [12]But if you don't believe me when I tell you about earthly things, how can you possibly believe if I tell you about heavenly things? [13]No one has ever gone to heaven and returned. But the Son of Man* has come down from heaven. [14]And as Moses lifted up the bronze snake on a pole in the wilderness, so the Son of Man must be lifted up, [15]so that everyone who believes in him will have eternal life.*

[16]"For this is how God loved the world: He gave* his one and only Son, so that everyone who believes in him will not perish but have eternal life. [17]God sent his Son into the world not to judge the world, but to save the world through him.

[18]"There is no judgment against anyone who believes in him. But anyone who does not believe in him has already been judged for not believing in God's one and only Son. [19]And the judgment is based on this fact: God's light came into the world, but people loved the darkness more than the light, for their actions were evil. [20]All who do evil hate the light and refuse to go near it for fear their sins will be exposed. [21]But those who do what is right come to the light so others can see that they are doing what God wants.*"

3:3 Or *born from above;* also in 3:7. **3:5** Or *and spirit.* The Greek word for *Spirit* can also be translated *wind;* see 3:8. **3:6** Greek *what is born of the Spirit is spirit.* **3:7** The Greek word for *you* is plural; also in 3:12. **3:13** Some manuscripts add *who lives in heaven.* "Son of Man" is a title Jesus used for himself. **3:15** Or *everyone who believes will have eternal life in him.* **3:16** Or *For God loved the world so much that he gave.* **3:21** Or *can see God at work in what he is doing.*

John the Baptist Exalts Jesus

[22]Then Jesus and his disciples left Jerusalem and went into the Judean countryside. Jesus spent some time with them there, baptizing people.

[23]At this time John the Baptist was baptizing at Aenon, near Salim, because there was plenty of water there; and people kept coming to him for baptism. [24](This was before John was thrown into prison.) [25]A debate broke out between John's disciples and a certain Jew* over ceremonial cleansing. [26]So John's disciples came to him and said, "Rabbi, the man you met on the other side of the Jordan River, the one you identified as the Messiah, is also baptizing people. And everybody is going to him instead of coming to us."

[27]John replied, "No one can receive anything unless God gives it from heaven. [28]You yourselves know how plainly I told you, 'I am not the Messiah. I am only here to prepare the way for him.' [29]It is the bridegroom who marries the bride, and the bridegroom's friend is simply glad to stand with him and hear his vows. Therefore, I am filled with joy at his success. [30]He must become greater and greater, and I must become less and less.

[31]"He has come from above and is greater than anyone else. We are of the earth, and we speak of earthly things, but he has come from heaven and is greater than anyone else.* [32]He testifies about what he has seen and heard, but how few believe what he tells them! [33]Anyone who accepts his testimony can affirm that God is true. [34]For he is sent by God. He speaks God's words, for God gives him the Spirit without limit. [35]The Father loves his Son and has put everything into his hands. [36]And anyone who believes in God's Son has eternal life. Anyone who doesn't obey the Son will never experience eternal life but remains under God's angry judgment."

Jesus and the Samaritan Woman

4 Jesus* knew the Pharisees had heard that he was baptizing and making more disciples than John [2](though Jesus himself didn't baptize them—his disciples did). [3]So he left Judea and returned to Galilee.

[4]He had to go through Samaria on the way. [5]Eventually he came to the Samaritan village of Sychar, near the field that Jacob gave to his son Joseph. [6]Jacob's well was there; and Jesus, tired from the long walk, sat wearily beside the well about noontime. [7]Soon a Samaritan woman came to draw water, and Jesus said to her, "Please give me a drink." [8]He was alone at the time because his disciples had gone into the village to buy some food.

[9]The woman was surprised, for Jews refuse to have anything to do

3:25 Some manuscripts read *some Jews.* 3:31 Some manuscripts do not include *and is greater than anyone else.* 4:1 Some manuscripts read *The Lord.*

with Samaritans.* She said to Jesus, "You are a Jew, and I am a Samaritan woman. Why are you asking me for a drink?"

[10]Jesus replied, "If you only knew the gift God has for you and who you are speaking to, you would ask me, and I would give you living water."

[11]"But sir, you don't have a rope or a bucket," she said, "and this well is very deep. Where would you get this living water? [12]And besides, do you think you're greater than our ancestor Jacob, who gave us this well? How can you offer better water than he and his sons and his animals enjoyed?"

[13]Jesus replied, "Anyone who drinks this water will soon become thirsty again. [14]But those who drink the water I give will never be thirsty again. It becomes a fresh, bubbling spring within them, giving them eternal life."

[15]"Please, sir," the woman said, "give me this water! Then I'll never be thirsty again, and I won't have to come here to get water."

[16]"Go and get your husband," Jesus told her.

[17]"I don't have a husband," the woman replied.

Jesus said, "You're right! You don't have a husband—[18]for you have had five husbands, and you aren't even married to the man you're living with now. You certainly spoke the truth!"

[19]"Sir," the woman said, "you must be a prophet. [20]So tell me, why is it that you Jews insist that Jerusalem is the only place of worship, while we Samaritans claim it is here at Mount Gerizim,* where our ancestors worshiped?"

[21]Jesus replied, "Believe me, dear woman, the time is coming when it will no longer matter whether you worship the Father on this mountain or in Jerusalem. [22]You Samaritans know very little about the one you worship, while we Jews know all about him, for salvation comes through the Jews. [23]But the time is coming—indeed it's here now—when true worshipers will worship the Father in spirit and in truth. The Father is looking for those who will worship him that way. [24]For God is Spirit, so those who worship him must worship in spirit and in truth."

[25]The woman said, "I know the Messiah is coming—the one who is called Christ. When he comes, he will explain everything to us."

[26]Then Jesus told her, "I AM the Messiah!"*

[27]Just then his disciples came back. They were shocked to find him talking to a woman, but none of them had the nerve to ask, "What do you want with her?" or "Why are you talking to her?" [28]The woman left her water jar beside the well and ran back to the village, telling everyone, [29]"Come and see a man who told me everything I ever did!

4:9 Some manuscripts do not include this sentence. 4:20 Greek *on this mountain.* 4:26 Or *"The 'I AM' is here"*; or *"I am the LORD"*; Greek reads *"I am, the one speaking to you."* See Exod 3:14.

Could he possibly be the Messiah?" ³⁰So the people came streaming from the village to see him.

³¹Meanwhile, the disciples were urging Jesus, "Rabbi, eat something."

³²But Jesus replied, "I have a kind of food you know nothing about."

³³"Did someone bring him food while we were gone?" the disciples asked each other.

³⁴Then Jesus explained: "My nourishment comes from doing the will of God, who sent me, and from finishing his work. ³⁵You know the saying, 'Four months between planting and harvest.' But I say, wake up and look around. The fields are already ripe* for harvest. ³⁶The harvesters are paid good wages, and the fruit they harvest is people brought to eternal life. What joy awaits both the planter and the harvester alike! ³⁷You know the saying, 'One plants and another harvests.' And it's true. ³⁸I sent you to harvest where you didn't plant; others had already done the work, and now you will get to gather the harvest."

Many Samaritans Believe

³⁹Many Samaritans from the village believed in Jesus because the woman had said, "He told me everything I ever did!" ⁴⁰When they came out to see him, they begged him to stay in their village. So he stayed for two days, ⁴¹long enough for many more to hear his message and believe. ⁴²Then they said to the woman, "Now we believe, not just because of what you told us, but because we have heard him ourselves. Now we know that he is indeed the Savior of the world."

Jesus Heals an Official's Son

⁴³At the end of the two days, Jesus went on to Galilee. ⁴⁴He himself had said that a prophet is not honored in his own hometown. ⁴⁵Yet the Galileans welcomed him, for they had been in Jerusalem at the Passover celebration and had seen everything he did there.

⁴⁶As he traveled through Galilee, he came to Cana, where he had turned the water into wine. There was a government official in nearby Capernaum whose son was very sick. ⁴⁷When he heard that Jesus had come from Judea to Galilee, he went and begged Jesus to come to Capernaum to heal his son, who was about to die.

⁴⁸Jesus asked, "Will you never believe in me unless you see miraculous signs and wonders?"

⁴⁹The official pleaded, "Lord, please come now before my little boy dies."

⁵⁰Then Jesus told him, "Go back home. Your son will live!" And the man believed what Jesus said and started home.

⁵¹While the man was on his way, some of his servants met him with

---

4:35 Greek *white*.

the news that his son was alive and well. [52]He asked them when the boy had begun to get better, and they replied, "Yesterday afternoon at one o'clock his fever suddenly disappeared!" [53]Then the father realized that that was the very time Jesus had told him, "Your son will live." And he and his entire household believed in Jesus. [54]This was the second miraculous sign Jesus did in Galilee after coming from Judea.

Jesus Heals a Lame Man

5 Afterward Jesus returned to Jerusalem for one of the Jewish holy days. [2]Inside the city, near the Sheep Gate, was the pool of Bethesda,* with five covered porches. [3]Crowds of sick people—blind, lame, or paralyzed—lay on the porches.* [5]One of the men lying there had been sick for thirty-eight years. [6]When Jesus saw him and knew he had been ill for a long time, he asked him, "Would you like to get well?"

[7]"I can't, sir," the sick man said, "for I have no one to put me into the pool when the water bubbles up. Someone else always gets there ahead of me."

[8]Jesus told him, "Stand up, pick up your mat, and walk!"

[9]Instantly, the man was healed! He rolled up his sleeping mat and began walking! But this miracle happened on the Sabbath, [10]so the Jewish leaders objected. They said to the man who was cured, "You can't work on the Sabbath! The law doesn't allow you to carry that sleeping mat!"

[11]But he replied, "The man who healed me told me, 'Pick up your mat and walk.'"

[12]"Who said such a thing as that?" they demanded.

[13]The man didn't know, for Jesus had disappeared into the crowd. [14]But afterward Jesus found him in the Temple and told him, "Now you are well; so stop sinning, or something even worse may happen to you." [15]Then the man went and told the Jewish leaders that it was Jesus who had healed him.

Jesus Claims to Be the Son of God

[16]So the Jewish leaders began harassing* Jesus for breaking the Sabbath rules. [17]But Jesus replied, "My Father is always working, and so am I." [18]So the Jewish leaders tried all the harder to find a way to kill him. For he not only broke the Sabbath, he called God his Father, thereby making himself equal with God.

[19]So Jesus explained, "I tell you the truth, the Son can do nothing by himself. He does only what he sees the Father doing. Whatever the Fa-

5:2 Other manuscripts read *Beth-zatha;* still others read *Bethsaida.* **5:3** Some manuscripts add an expanded conclusion to verse 3 and all of verse 4: *waiting for a certain movement of the water, [4]for an angel of the Lord came from time to time and stirred up the water. And the first person to step in after the water was stirred was healed of whatever disease he had.* **5:16** Or *persecuting.*

ther does, the Son also does. ²⁰For the Father loves the Son and shows him everything he is doing. In fact, the Father will show him how to do even greater works than healing this man. Then you will truly be astonished. ²¹For just as the Father gives life to those he raises from the dead, so the Son gives life to anyone he wants. ²²In addition, the Father judges no one. Instead, he has given the Son absolute authority to judge, ²³so that everyone will honor the Son, just as they honor the Father. Anyone who does not honor the Son is certainly not honoring the Father who sent him.

²⁴"I tell you the truth, those who listen to my message and believe in God who sent me have eternal life. They will never be condemned for their sins, but they have already passed from death into life.

²⁵"And I assure you that the time is coming, indeed it's here now, when the dead will hear my voice—the voice of the Son of God. And those who listen will live. ²⁶The Father has life in himself, and he has granted that same life-giving power to his Son. ²⁷And he has given him authority to judge everyone because he is the Son of Man.* ²⁸Don't be so surprised! Indeed, the time is coming when all the dead in their graves will hear the voice of God's Son, ²⁹and they will rise again. Those who have done good will rise to experience eternal life, and those who have continued in evil will rise to experience judgment. ³⁰I can do nothing on my own. I judge as God tells me. Therefore, my judgment is just, because I carry out the will of the one who sent me, not my own will.

Witnesses to Jesus

³¹"If I were to testify on my own behalf, my testimony would not be valid. ³²But someone else is also testifying about me, and I assure you that everything he says about me is true. ³³In fact, you sent investigators to listen to John the Baptist, and his testimony about me was true. ³⁴Of course, I have no need of human witnesses, but I say these things so you might be saved. ³⁵John was like a burning and shining lamp, and you were excited for a while about his message. ³⁶But I have a greater witness than John— my teachings and my miracles. The Father gave me these works to accomplish, and they prove that he sent me. ³⁷And the Father who sent me has testified about me himself. You have never heard his voice or seen him face to face, ³⁸and you do not have his message in your hearts, because you do not believe me—the one he sent to you.

³⁹"You search the Scriptures because you think they give you eternal life. But the Scriptures point to me! ⁴⁰Yet you refuse to come to me to receive this life.

⁴¹"Your approval means nothing

5:27 "Son of Man" is a title Jesus used for himself.

to me, ⁴²because I know you don't have God's love within you. ⁴³For I have come to you in my Father's name, and you have rejected me. Yet if others come in their own name, you gladly welcome them. ⁴⁴No wonder you can't believe! For you gladly honor each other, but you don't care about the honor that comes from the one who alone is God.*

⁴⁵"Yet it isn't I who will accuse you before the Father. Moses will accuse you! Yes, Moses, in whom you put your hopes. ⁴⁶If you really believed Moses, you would believe me, because he wrote about me. ⁴⁷But since you don't believe what he wrote, how will you believe what I say?"

Jesus Feeds Five Thousand

6 After this, Jesus crossed over to the far side of the Sea of Galilee, also known as the Sea of Tiberias. ²A huge crowd kept following him wherever he went, because they saw his miraculous signs as he healed the sick. ³Then Jesus climbed a hill and sat down with his disciples around him. ⁴(It was nearly time for the Jewish Passover celebration.) ⁵Jesus soon saw a huge crowd of people coming to look for him. Turning to Philip, he asked, "Where can we buy bread to feed all these people?" ⁶He was testing Philip, for he already knew what he was going to do.

⁷Philip replied, "Even if we worked for months, we wouldn't have enough money* to feed them!"

⁸Then Andrew, Simon Peter's brother, spoke up. ⁹"There's a young boy here with five barley loaves and two fish. But what good is that with this huge crowd?"

¹⁰"Tell everyone to sit down," Jesus said. So they all sat down on the grassy slopes. (The men alone numbered about 5,000.) ¹¹Then Jesus took the loaves, gave thanks to God, and distributed them to the people. Afterward he did the same with the fish. And they all ate as much as they wanted. ¹²After everyone was full, Jesus told his disciples, "Now gather the leftovers, so that nothing is wasted." ¹³So they picked up the pieces and filled twelve baskets with scraps left by the people who had eaten from the five barley loaves.

¹⁴When the people saw him* do this miraculous sign, they exclaimed, "Surely, he is the Prophet we have been expecting!"* ¹⁵When Jesus saw that they were ready to force him to be their king, he slipped away into the hills by himself.

Jesus Walks on Water

¹⁶That evening Jesus' disciples went down to the shore to wait for him. ¹⁷But as darkness fell and Jesus still hadn't come back, they got into the boat and headed across the lake

5:44 Some manuscripts read *from the only One.*   **6:7** Greek *Two hundred denarii would not be enough.* A denarius was equivalent to a laborer's full day's wage.   **6:14a** Some manuscripts read *Jesus.* **6:14b** See Deut 18:15, 18; Mal 4:5-6.   **6:19** Greek *25 or 30 stadia* [4.6 or 5.5 kilometers].

toward Capernaum. ¹⁸Soon a gale swept down upon them, and the sea grew very rough. ¹⁹They had rowed three or four miles* when suddenly they saw Jesus walking on the water toward the boat. They were terrified, ²⁰but he called out to them, "Don't be afraid. I am here!*" ²¹Then they were eager to let him in the boat, and immediately they arrived at their destination!

Jesus, the Bread of Life

²²The next day the crowd that had stayed on the far shore saw that the disciples had taken the only boat, and they realized Jesus had not gone with them. ²³Several boats from Tiberias landed near the place where the Lord had blessed the bread and the people had eaten. ²⁴So when the crowd saw that neither Jesus nor his disciples were there, they got into the boats and went across to Capernaum to look for him. ²⁵They found him on the other side of the lake and asked, "Rabbi, when did you get here?"

²⁶Jesus replied, "I tell you the truth, you want to be with me because I fed you, not because you understood the miraculous signs. ²⁷But don't be so concerned about perishable things like food. Spend your energy seeking the eternal life that the Son of Man* can give you. For God the Father has given me the seal of his approval."

²⁸They replied, "We want to perform God's works, too. What should we do?"

²⁹Jesus told them, "This is the only work God wants from you: Believe in the one he has sent."

³⁰They answered, "Show us a miraculous sign if you want us to believe in you. What can you do? ³¹After all, our ancestors ate manna while they journeyed through the wilderness! The Scriptures say, 'Moses gave them bread from heaven to eat.'*"

³²Jesus said, "I tell you the truth, Moses didn't give you bread from heaven. My Father did. And now he offers you the true bread from heaven. ³³The true bread of God is the one who comes down from heaven and gives life to the world."

³⁴"Sir," they said, "give us that bread every day."

³⁵Jesus replied, "I am the bread of life. Whoever comes to me will never be hungry again. Whoever believes in me will never be thirsty. ³⁶But you haven't believed in me even though you have seen me. ³⁷However, those the Father has given me will come to me, and I will never reject them. ³⁸For I have come down from heaven to do the will of God who sent me, not to do my own will. ³⁹And this is the will of God, that I should not lose even one of all those he has given me, but that I should raise them up at the last day.

6:20 Or *The 'I Am' is here;* Greek reads *I am.* See Exod 3:14.   6:27 "Son of Man" is a title Jesus used for himself.   6:31 Exod 16:4; Ps 78:24.

[40] For it is my Father's will that all who see his Son and believe in him should have eternal life. I will raise them up at the last day."

[41] Then the people* began to murmur in disagreement because he had said, "I am the bread that came down from heaven." [42] They said, "Isn't this Jesus, the son of Joseph? We know his father and mother. How can he say, 'I came down from heaven'?"

[43] But Jesus replied, "Stop complaining about what I said. [44] For no one can come to me unless the Father who sent me draws them to me, and at the last day I will raise them up. [45] As it is written in the Scriptures,* 'They will all be taught by God.' Everyone who listens to the Father and learns from him comes to me. [46] (Not that anyone has ever seen the Father; only I, who was sent from God, have seen him.)

[47] "I tell you the truth, anyone who believes has eternal life. [48] Yes, I am the bread of life! [49] Your ancestors ate manna in the wilderness, but they all died. [50] Anyone who eats the bread from heaven, however, will never die. [51] I am the living bread that came down from heaven. Anyone who eats this bread will live forever; and this bread, which I will offer so the world may live, is my flesh."

[52] Then the people began arguing with each other about what he meant. "How can this man give us his flesh to eat?" they asked.

[53] So Jesus said again, "I tell you the truth, unless you eat the flesh of the Son of Man and drink his blood, you cannot have eternal life within you. [54] But anyone who eats my flesh and drinks my blood has eternal life, and I will raise that person at the last day. [55] For my flesh is true food, and my blood is true drink. [56] Anyone who eats my flesh and drinks my blood remains in me, and I in him. [57] I live because of the living Father who sent me; in the same way, anyone who feeds on me will live because of me. [58] I am the true bread that came down from heaven. Anyone who eats this bread will not die as your ancestors did (even though they ate the manna) but will live forever."

[59] He said these things while he was teaching in the synagogue in Capernaum.

Many Disciples Desert Jesus

[60] Many of his disciples said, "This is very hard to understand. How can anyone accept it?"

[61] Jesus was aware that his disciples were complaining, so he said to them, "Does this offend you? [62] Then what will you think if you see the Son of Man ascend to heaven again? [63] The Spirit alone gives eternal life. Human effort accomplishes nothing. And the very words I have spoken to you are spirit and life. [64] But some of you do not believe me." (For Jesus knew

6:41 Greek *Jewish people;* also in 6:52.   6:45 Greek *in the prophets.* Isa 54:13.

from the beginning which ones didn't believe, and he knew who would betray him.) ⁶⁵Then he said, "That is why I said that people can't come to me unless the Father gives them to me."

⁶⁶At this point many of his disciples turned away and deserted him. ⁶⁷Then Jesus turned to the Twelve and asked, "Are you also going to leave?"

⁶⁸Simon Peter replied, "Lord, to whom would we go? You have the words that give eternal life. ⁶⁹We believe, and we know you are the Holy One of God.*"

⁷⁰Then Jesus said, "I chose the twelve of you, but one is a devil." ⁷¹He was speaking of Judas, son of Simon Iscariot, one of the Twelve, who would later betray him.

Jesus and His Brothers

7 After this, Jesus traveled around Galilee. He wanted to stay out of Judea, where the Jewish leaders were plotting his death. ²But soon it was time for the Jewish Festival of Shelters, ³and Jesus' brothers said to him, "Leave here and go to Judea, where your followers can see your miracles! ⁴You can't become famous if you hide like this! If you can do such wonderful things, show yourself to the world!" ⁵For even his brothers didn't believe in him.

⁶Jesus replied, "Now is not the right time for me to go, but you can go anytime. ⁷The world can't hate you, but it does hate me because I accuse it of doing evil. ⁸You go on. I'm not going* to this festival, because my time has not yet come." ⁹After saying these things, Jesus remained in Galilee.

Jesus Teaches Openly at the Temple

¹⁰But after his brothers left for the festival, Jesus also went, though secretly, staying out of public view. ¹¹The Jewish leaders tried to find him at the festival and kept asking if anyone had seen him. ¹²There was a lot of grumbling about him among the crowds. Some argued, "He's a good man," but others said, "He's nothing but a fraud who deceives the people." ¹³But no one had the courage to speak favorably about him in public, for they were afraid of getting in trouble with the Jewish leaders.

¹⁴Then, midway through the festival, Jesus went up to the Temple and began to teach. ¹⁵The people* were surprised when they heard him. "How does he know so much when he hasn't been trained?" they asked.

¹⁶So Jesus told them, "My message is not my own; it comes from God who sent me. ¹⁷Anyone who wants to do the will of God will know whether my teaching is from

6:69 Other manuscripts read *you are the Christ, the Holy One of God;* still others read *you are the Christ, the Son of God;* and still others read *you are the Christ, the Son of the living God.*   7:8 Some manuscripts read *not yet going.*   7:15 Greek *Jewish people.*

God or is merely my own. [18]Those who speak for themselves want glory only for themselves, but a person who seeks to honor the one who sent him speaks truth, not lies. [19]Moses gave you the law, but none of you obeys it! In fact, you are trying to kill me."

[20]The crowd replied, "You're demon possessed! Who's trying to kill you?"

[21]Jesus replied, "I did one miracle on the Sabbath, and you were amazed. [22]But you work on the Sabbath, too, when you obey Moses' law of circumcision. (Actually, this tradition of circumcision began with the patriarchs, long before the law of Moses.) [23]For if the correct time for circumcising your son falls on the Sabbath, you go ahead and do it so as not to break the law of Moses. So why should you be angry with me for healing a man on the Sabbath? [24]Look beneath the surface so you can judge correctly."

Is Jesus the Messiah?

[25]Some of the people who lived in Jerusalem started to ask each other, "Isn't this the man they are trying to kill? [26]But here he is, speaking in public, and they say nothing to him. Could our leaders possibly believe that he is the Messiah? [27]But how could he be? For we know where this man comes from. When the Messiah comes, he will simply appear; no one will know where he comes from."

[28]While Jesus was teaching in the Temple, he called out, "Yes, you know me, and you know where I come from. But I'm not here on my own. The one who sent me is true, and you don't know him. [29]But I know him because I come from him, and he sent me to you." [30]Then the leaders tried to arrest him; but no one laid a hand on him, because his time* had not yet come.

[31]Many among the crowds at the Temple believed in him. "After all," they said, "would you expect the Messiah to do more miraculous signs than this man has done?"

[32]When the Pharisees heard that the crowds were whispering such things, they and the leading priests sent Temple guards to arrest Jesus. [33]But Jesus told them, "I will be with you only a little longer. Then I will return to the one who sent me. [34]You will search for me but not find me. And you cannot go where I am going."

[35]The Jewish leaders were puzzled by this statement. "Where is he planning to go?" they asked. "Is he thinking of leaving the country and going to the Jews in other lands?* Maybe he will even teach the Greeks! [36]What does he mean when he says, 'You will search for me but not find me,' and 'You cannot go where I am going'?"

7:30 Greek *his hour.*   7:35 Or *the Jews who live among the Greeks?*

Jesus Promises Living Water

37On the last day, the climax of the festival, Jesus stood and shouted to the crowds, "Anyone who is thirsty may come to me! 38Anyone who believes in me may come and drink! For the Scriptures declare, 'Rivers of living water will flow from his heart.'"* 39(When he said "living water," he was speaking of the Spirit, who would be given to everyone believing in him. But the Spirit had not yet been given,* because Jesus had not yet entered into his glory.)

Division and Unbelief

40When the crowds heard him say this, some of them declared, "Surely this man is the Prophet we've been expecting."* 41Others said, "He is the Messiah." Still others said, "But he can't be! Will the Messiah come from Galilee? 42For the Scriptures clearly state that the Messiah will be born of the royal line of David, in Bethlehem, the village where King David was born."* 43So the crowd was divided about him. 44Some even wanted him arrested, but no one laid a hand on him.

45When the Temple guards returned without having arrested Jesus, the leading priests and Pharisees demanded, "Why didn't you bring him in?"

46"We have never heard anyone speak like this!" the guards responded.

47"Have you been led astray, too?" the Pharisees mocked. 48"Is there a single one of us rulers or Pharisees who believes in him? 49This foolish crowd follows him, but they are ignorant of the law. God's curse is on them!"

50Then Nicodemus, the leader who had met with Jesus earlier, spoke up. 51"Is it legal to convict a man before he is given a hearing?" he asked.

52They replied, "Are you from Galilee, too? Search the Scriptures and see for yourself—no prophet ever comes* from Galilee!"

[The most ancient Greek manuscripts do not include John 7:53–8:11.]

53Then the meeting broke up, and everybody went home.

A Woman Caught in Adultery

8 Jesus returned to the Mount of Olives, 2but early the next morning he was back again at the Temple. A crowd soon gathered, and he sat down and taught them. 3As he was speaking, the teachers of religious law and the Pharisees brought a woman who had been caught in the act of adultery. They put her in front of the crowd.

7:37-38 Or *"Let anyone who is thirsty come to me and drink.* 38*For the Scriptures declare, 'Rivers of living water will flow from the heart of anyone who believes in me.' "* **7:39** Several early manuscripts read *But as yet there was no Spirit.* Still others read *But as yet there was no Holy Spirit.* **7:40** See Deut 18:15, 18; Mal 4:5-6. **7:42** See Mic 5:2. **7:52** Some manuscripts read *the prophet does not come.*

4"Teacher," they said to Jesus, "this woman was caught in the act of adultery. 5The law of Moses says to stone her. What do you say?"

6They were trying to trap him into saying something they could use against him, but Jesus stooped down and wrote in the dust with his finger. 7They kept demanding an answer, so he stood up again and said, "All right, but let the one who has never sinned throw the first stone!" 8Then he stooped down again and wrote in the dust.

9When the accusers heard this, they slipped away one by one, beginning with the oldest, until only Jesus was left in the middle of the crowd with the woman. 10Then Jesus stood up again and said to the woman, "Where are your accusers? Didn't even one of them condemn you?"

11"No, Lord," she said.

And Jesus said, "Neither do I. Go and sin no more."

Jesus, the Light of the World

12Jesus spoke to the people once more and said, "I am the light of the world. If you follow me, you won't have to walk in darkness, because you will have the light that leads to life."

13The Pharisees replied, "You are making those claims about yourself! Such testimony is not valid."

14Jesus told them, "These claims are valid even though I make them about myself. For I know where I came from and where I am going, but you don't know this about me. 15You judge me by human standards, but I do not judge anyone. 16And if I did, my judgment would be correct in every respect because I am not alone. The Father* who sent me is with me. 17Your own law says that if two people agree about something, their witness is accepted as fact.* 18I am one witness, and my Father who sent me is the other."

19"Where is your father?" they asked.

Jesus answered, "Since you don't know who I am, you don't know who my Father is. If you knew me, you would also know my Father." 20Jesus made these statements while he was teaching in the section of the Temple known as the Treasury. But he was not arrested, because his time* had not yet come.

The Unbelieving People Warned

21Later Jesus said to them again, "I am going away. You will search for me but will die in your sin. You cannot come where I am going."

22The people* asked, "Is he planning to commit suicide? What does he mean, 'You cannot come where I am going'?"

23Jesus continued, "You are from below; I am from above. You belong to this world; I do not. 24That is why

8:16 Some manuscripts read *The One*. 8:17 See Deut 19:15. 8:20 Greek *his hour*. 8:22 Greek *Jewish people;* also in 8:31, 48, 52, 57.

I said that you will die in your sins; for unless you believe that I Am who I claim to be,* you will die in your sins."

25"Who are you?" they demanded.

Jesus replied, "The one I have always claimed to be.* 26I have much to say about you and much to condemn, but I won't. For I say only what I have heard from the one who sent me, and he is completely truthful." 27But they still didn't understand that he was talking about his Father.

28So Jesus said, "When you have lifted up the Son of Man on the cross, then you will understand that I Am he.* I do nothing on my own but say only what the Father taught me. 29And the one who sent me is with me—he has not deserted me. For I always do what pleases him." 30Then many who heard him say these things believed in him.

Jesus and Abraham

31Jesus said to the people who believed in him, "You are truly my disciples if you remain faithful to my teachings. 32And you will know the truth, and the truth will set you free."

33"But we are descendants of Abraham," they said. "We have never been slaves to anyone. What do you mean, 'You will be set free'?"

34Jesus replied, "I tell you the truth, everyone who sins is a slave of sin. 35A slave is not a permanent member of the family, but a son is part of the family forever. 36So if the Son sets you free, you are truly free. 37Yes, I realize that you are descendants of Abraham. And yet some of you are trying to kill me because there's no room in your hearts for my message. 38I am telling you what I saw when I was with my Father. But you are following the advice of your father."

39"Our father is Abraham!" they declared.

"No," Jesus replied, "for if you were really the children of Abraham, you would follow his example.* 40Instead, you are trying to kill me because I told you the truth, which I heard from God. Abraham never did such a thing. 41No, you are imitating your real father."

They replied, "We aren't illegitimate children! God himself is our true Father."

42Jesus told them, "If God were your Father, you would love me, because I have come to you from God. I am not here on my own, but he sent me. 43Why can't you understand what I am saying? It's because you can't even hear me! 44For you are the children of your father the devil, and you love to do the evil things he does. He was a murderer

---

8:24 Greek *unless you believe that I am.* See Exod 3:14. 8:25 Or *Why do I speak to you at all?* 8:28 Greek *When you have lifted up the Son of Man, then you will know that I am.* "Son of Man" is a title Jesus used for himself. 8:39 Some manuscripts read *if you are really the children of Abraham, follow his example.*

from the beginning. He has always hated the truth, because there is no truth in him. When he lies, it is consistent with his character; for he is a liar and the father of lies. ⁴⁵So when I tell the truth, you just naturally don't believe me! ⁴⁶Which of you can truthfully accuse me of sin? And since I am telling you the truth, why don't you believe me? ⁴⁷Anyone who belongs to God listens gladly to the words of God. But you don't listen because you don't belong to God."

⁴⁸The people retorted, "You Samaritan devil! Didn't we say all along that you were possessed by a demon?"

⁴⁹"No," Jesus said, "I have no demon in me. For I honor my Father—and you dishonor me. ⁵⁰And though I have no wish to glorify myself, God is going to glorify me. He is the true judge. ⁵¹I tell you the truth, anyone who obeys my teaching will never die!"

⁵²The people said, "Now we know you are possessed by a demon. Even Abraham and the prophets died, but you say, 'Anyone who obeys my teaching will never die!' ⁵³Are you greater than our father Abraham? He died, and so did the prophets. Who do you think you are?"

⁵⁴Jesus answered, "If I want glory for myself, it doesn't count. But it is my Father who will glorify me. You say, 'He is our God,'* ⁵⁵but you don't even know him. I know him. If I said otherwise, I would be as great a liar as you! But I do know him and obey him. ⁵⁶Your father Abraham rejoiced as he looked forward to my coming. He saw it and was glad."

⁵⁷The people said, "You aren't even fifty years old. How can you say you have seen Abraham?*"

⁵⁸Jesus answered, "I tell you the truth, before Abraham was even born, I Am!*" ⁵⁹At that point they picked up stones to throw at him. But Jesus was hidden from them and left the Temple.

Jesus Heals a Man Born Blind

9 As Jesus was walking along, he saw a man who had been blind from birth. ²"Rabbi," his disciples asked him, "why was this man born blind? Was it because of his own sins or his parents' sins?"

³"It was not because of his sins or his parents' sins," Jesus answered. "This happened so the power of God could be seen in him. ⁴We must quickly carry out the tasks assigned us by the one who sent us.* The night is coming, and then no one can work. ⁵But while I am here in the world, I am the light of the world."

⁶Then he spit on the ground, made mud with the saliva, and

8:54 Some manuscripts read *You say he is your God.* 8:57 Some manuscripts read *How can you say Abraham has seen you?* 8:58 Or *before Abraham was even born, I have always been alive;* Greek reads *before Abraham was, I am.* See Exod 3:14. 9:4 Other manuscripts read *I must quickly carry out the tasks assigned me by the one who sent me;* still others read *We must quickly carry out the tasks assigned us by the one who sent me.*

spread the mud over the blind man's eyes. [7]He told him, "Go wash yourself in the pool of Siloam" (Siloam means "sent"). So the man went and washed and came back seeing!

[8]His neighbors and others who knew him as a blind beggar asked each other, "Isn't this the man who used to sit and beg?" [9]Some said he was, and others said, "No, he just looks like him!"

But the beggar kept saying, "Yes, I am the same one!"

[10]They asked, "Who healed you? What happened?"

[11]He told them, "The man they call Jesus made mud and spread it over my eyes and told me, 'Go to the pool of Siloam and wash yourself.' So I went and washed, and now I can see!"

[12]"Where is he now?" they asked.

"I don't know," he replied.

[13]Then they took the man who had been blind to the Pharisees, [14]because it was on the Sabbath that Jesus had made the mud and healed him. [15]The Pharisees asked the man all about it. So he told them, "He put the mud over my eyes, and when I washed it away, I could see!"

[16]Some of the Pharisees said, "This man Jesus is not from God, for he is working on the Sabbath." Others said, "But how could an ordinary sinner do such miraculous signs?" So there was a deep division of opinion among them.

[17]Then the Pharisees again questioned the man who had been blind and demanded, "What's your opinion about this man who healed you?"

The man replied, "I think he must be a prophet."

[18]The Jewish leaders still refused to believe the man had been blind and could now see, so they called in his parents. [19]They asked them, "Is this your son? Was he born blind? If so, how can he now see?"

[20]His parents replied, "We know this is our son and that he was born blind, [21]but we don't know how he can see or who healed him. Ask him. He is old enough to speak for himself." [22]His parents said this because they were afraid of the Jewish leaders, who had announced that anyone saying Jesus was the Messiah would be expelled from the synagogue. [23]That's why they said, "He is old enough. Ask him."

[24]So for the second time they called in the man who had been blind and told him, "God should get the glory for this,* because we know this man Jesus is a sinner."

[25]"I don't know whether he is a sinner," the man replied. "But I know this: I was blind, and now I can see!"

[26]"But what did he do?" they asked. "How did he heal you?"

[27]"Look!" the man exclaimed. "I told you once. Didn't you listen? Why do you want to hear it again? Do you want to become his disciples, too?"

9:24 Or *Give glory to God, not to Jesus;* Greek reads *Give glory to God.*

[28]Then they cursed him and said, "You are his disciple, but we are disciples of Moses! [29]We know God spoke to Moses, but we don't even know where this man comes from."

[30]"Why, that's very strange!" the man replied. "He healed my eyes, and yet you don't know where he comes from? [31]We know that God doesn't listen to sinners, but he is ready to hear those who worship him and do his will. [32]Ever since the world began, no one has been able to open the eyes of someone born blind. [33]If this man were not from God, he couldn't have done it."

[34]"You were born a total sinner!" they answered. "Are you trying to teach us?" And they threw him out of the synagogue.

Spiritual Blindness

[35]When Jesus heard what had happened, he found the man and asked, "Do you believe in the Son of Man?*"

[36]The man answered, "Who is he, sir? I want to believe in him."

[37]"You have seen him," Jesus said, "and he is speaking to you!"

[38]"Yes, Lord, I believe!" the man said. And he worshiped Jesus.

[39]Then Jesus told him,* "I entered this world to render judgment—to give sight to the blind and to show those who think they see* that they are blind."

[40]Some Pharisees who were standing nearby heard him and asked, "Are you saying we're blind?"

[41]"If you were blind, you wouldn't be guilty," Jesus replied. "But you remain guilty because you claim you can see.

The Good Shepherd and His Sheep

10 "I tell you the truth, anyone who sneaks over the wall of a sheepfold, rather than going through the gate, must surely be a thief and a robber! [2]But the one who enters through the gate is the shepherd of the sheep. [3]The gatekeeper opens the gate for him, and the sheep recognize his voice and come to him. He calls his own sheep by name and leads them out. [4]After he has gathered his own flock, he walks ahead of them, and they follow him because they know his voice. [5]They won't follow a stranger; they will run from him because they don't know his voice."

[6]Those who heard Jesus use this illustration didn't understand what he meant, [7]so he explained it to them: "I tell you the truth, I am the gate for the sheep. [8]All who came before me* were thieves and robbers. But the true sheep did not listen to them. [9]Yes, I am the gate. Those who come in through me will be saved.* They will come and go

---

9:35 Some manuscripts read *the Son of God?* "Son of Man" is a title Jesus used for himself. **9:38-39a** Some manuscripts do not include *"Yes, Lord, I believe!" the man said. And he worshiped Jesus. Then Jesus told him.* **9:39b** Greek *those who see.* **10:8** Some manuscripts do not include *before me.* **10:9** Or *will find safety.*

freely and will find good pastures. ¹⁰The thief's purpose is to steal and kill and destroy. My purpose is to give them a rich and satisfying life.

¹¹"I am the good shepherd. The good shepherd sacrifices his life for the sheep. ¹²A hired hand will run when he sees a wolf coming. He will abandon the sheep because they don't belong to him and he isn't their shepherd. And so the wolf attacks them and scatters the flock. ¹³The hired hand runs away because he's working only for the money and doesn't really care about the sheep.

¹⁴"I am the good shepherd; I know my own sheep, and they know me, ¹⁵just as my Father knows me and I know the Father. So I sacrifice my life for the sheep. ¹⁶I have other sheep, too, that are not in this sheepfold. I must bring them also. They will listen to my voice, and there will be one flock with one shepherd.

¹⁷"The Father loves me because I sacrifice my life so I may take it back again. ¹⁸No one can take my life from me. I sacrifice it voluntarily. For I have the authority to lay it down when I want to and also to take it up again. For this is what my Father has commanded."

¹⁹When he said these things, the people* were again divided in their opinions about him. ²⁰Some said,

"He's demon possessed and out of his mind. Why listen to a man like that?" ²¹Others said, "This doesn't sound like a man possessed by a demon! Can a demon open the eyes of the blind?"

Jesus Claims to Be the Son of God

²²It was now winter, and Jesus was in Jerusalem at the time of Hanukkah, the Festival of Dedication. ²³He was in the Temple, walking through the section known as Solomon's Colonnade. ²⁴The people surrounded him and asked, "How long are you going to keep us in suspense? If you are the Messiah, tell us plainly."

²⁵Jesus replied, "I have already told you, and you don't believe me. The proof is the work I do in my Father's name. ²⁶But you don't believe me because you are not my sheep. ²⁷My sheep listen to my voice; I know them, and they follow me. ²⁸I give them eternal life, and they will never perish. No one can snatch them away from me, ²⁹for my Father has given them to me, and he is more powerful than anyone else.* No one can snatch them from the Father's hand. ³⁰The Father and I are one."

³¹Once again the people picked up stones to kill him. ³²Jesus said, "At my Father's direction I have done many good works. For which one are you going to stone me?"

10:19 Greek *Jewish people;* also in 10:24, 31. **10:29** Other manuscripts read *for what my Father has given me is more powerful than anything;* still others read *for regarding that which my Father has given me, he is greater than all.*

³³They replied, "We're stoning you not for any good work, but for blasphemy! You, a mere man, claim to be God."

³⁴Jesus replied, "It is written in your own Scriptures* that God said to certain leaders of the people, 'I say, you are gods!'* ³⁵And you know that the Scriptures cannot be altered. So if those people who received God's message were called 'gods,' ³⁶why do you call it blasphemy when I say, 'I am the Son of God'? After all, the Father set me apart and sent me into the world. ³⁷Don't believe me unless I carry out my Father's work. ³⁸But if I do his work, believe in the evidence of the miraculous works I have done, even if you don't believe me. Then you will know and understand that the Father is in me, and I am in the Father."

³⁹Once again they tried to arrest him, but he got away and left them. ⁴⁰He went beyond the Jordan River near the place where John was first baptizing and stayed there awhile. ⁴¹And many followed him. "John didn't perform miraculous signs," they remarked to one another, "but everything he said about this man has come true." ⁴²And many who were there believed in Jesus.

The Raising of Lazarus

11 A man named Lazarus was sick. He lived in Bethany with his sisters, Mary and Martha. ²This is the Mary who later poured the expensive perfume on the Lord's feet and wiped them with her hair.* Her brother, Lazarus, was sick. ³So the two sisters sent a message to Jesus telling him, "Lord, your dear friend is very sick."

⁴But when Jesus heard about it he said, "Lazarus's sickness will not end in death. No, it happened for the glory of God so that the Son of God will receive glory from this." ⁵So although Jesus loved Martha, Mary, and Lazarus, ⁶he stayed where he was for the next two days. ⁷Finally, he said to his disciples, "Let's go back to Judea."

⁸But his disciples objected. "Rabbi," they said, "only a few days ago the people* in Judea were trying to stone you. Are you going there again?"

⁹Jesus replied, "There are twelve hours of daylight every day. During the day people can walk safely. They can see because they have the light of this world. ¹⁰But at night there is danger of stumbling because they have no light." ¹¹Then he said, "Our friend Lazarus has fallen asleep, but now I will go and wake him up."

¹²The disciples said, "Lord, if he is sleeping, he will soon get better!" ¹³They thought Jesus meant Lazarus was simply sleeping, but Jesus meant Lazarus had died.

¹⁴So he told them plainly, "Lazarus is dead. ¹⁵And for your sakes,

10:34a Greek *your own law.* **10:34b** Ps 82:6. **11:2** This incident is recorded in chapter 12.
11:8 Greek *Jewish people;* also in 11:19, 31, 33, 36, 45, 54.

I'm glad I wasn't there, for now you will really believe. Come, let's go see him."

¹⁶Thomas, nicknamed the Twin,* said to his fellow disciples, "Let's go, too—and die with Jesus."

¹⁷When Jesus arrived at Bethany, he was told that Lazarus had already been in his grave for four days. ¹⁸Bethany was only a few miles* down the road from Jerusalem, ¹⁹and many of the people had come to console Martha and Mary in their loss. ²⁰When Martha got word that Jesus was coming, she went to meet him. But Mary stayed in the house. ²¹Martha said to Jesus, "Lord, if only you had been here, my brother would not have died. ²²But even now I know that God will give you whatever you ask."

²³Jesus told her, "Your brother will rise again."

²⁴"Yes," Martha said, "he will rise when everyone else rises, at the last day."

²⁵Jesus told her, "I am the resurrection and the life.* Anyone who believes in me will live, even after dying. ²⁶Everyone who lives in me and believes in me will never ever die. Do you believe this, Martha?"

²⁷"Yes, Lord," she told him. "I have always believed you are the Messiah, the Son of God, the one who has come into the world from God." ²⁸Then she returned to Mary. She called Mary aside from the mourners and told her, "The Teacher is here and wants to see you." ²⁹So Mary immediately went to him.

³⁰Jesus had stayed outside the village, at the place where Martha met him. ³¹When the people who were at the house consoling Mary saw her leave so hastily, they assumed she was going to Lazarus's grave to weep. So they followed her there. ³²When Mary arrived and saw Jesus, she fell at his feet and said, "Lord, if only you had been here, my brother would not have died."

³³When Jesus saw her weeping and saw the other people wailing with her, a deep anger welled up within him,* and he was deeply troubled. ³⁴"Where have you put him?" he asked them.

They told him, "Lord, come and see." ³⁵Then Jesus wept. ³⁶The people who were standing nearby said, "See how much he loved him!" ³⁷But some said, "This man healed a blind man. Couldn't he have kept Lazarus from dying?"

³⁸Jesus was still angry as he arrived at the tomb, a cave with a stone rolled across its entrance. ³⁹"Roll the stone aside," Jesus told them.

But Martha, the dead man's sister, protested, "Lord, he has been dead for four days. The smell will be terrible."

11:16 Greek *Thomas, who was called Didymus.* 11:18 Greek *was about 15 stadia* [about 2.8 kilometers]. 11:25 Some manuscripts do not include *and the life.* 11:33 Or *he was angry in his spirit.*

[40]Jesus responded, "Didn't I tell you that you would see God's glory if you believe?" [41]So they rolled the stone aside. Then Jesus looked up to heaven and said, "Father, thank you for hearing me. [42]You always hear me, but I said it out loud for the sake of all these people standing here, so that they will believe you sent me." [43]Then Jesus shouted, "Lazarus, come out!" [44]And the dead man came out, his hands and feet bound in graveclothes, his face wrapped in a headcloth. Jesus told them, "Unwrap him and let him go!"

The Plot to Kill Jesus

[45]Many of the people who were with Mary believed in Jesus when they saw this happen. [46]But some went to the Pharisees and told them what Jesus had done. [47]Then the leading priests and Pharisees called the high council* together. "What are we going to do?" they asked each other. "This man certainly performs many miraculous signs. [48]If we allow him to go on like this, soon everyone will believe in him. Then the Roman army will come and destroy both our Temple* and our nation."

[49]Caiaphas, who was high priest at that time,* said, "You don't know what you're talking about! [50]You don't realize that it's better for you that one man should die for the people than for the whole nation to be destroyed."

[51]He did not say this on his own; as high priest at that time he was led to prophesy that Jesus would die for the entire nation. [52]And not only for that nation, but to bring together and unite all the children of God scattered around the world.

[53]So from that time on, the Jewish leaders began to plot Jesus' death. [54]As a result, Jesus stopped his public ministry among the people and left Jerusalem. He went to a place near the wilderness, to the village of Ephraim, and stayed there with his disciples.

[55]It was now almost time for the Jewish Passover celebration, and many people from all over the country arrived in Jerusalem several days early so they could go through the purification ceremony before Passover began. [56]They kept looking for Jesus, but as they stood around in the Temple, they said to each other, "What do you think? He won't come for Passover, will he?" [57]Meanwhile, the leading priests and Pharisees had publicly ordered that anyone seeing Jesus must report it immediately so they could arrest him.

Jesus Anointed at Bethany

12 Six days before the Passover celebration began, Jesus arrived in Bethany, the home of Lazarus—the man he had raised from the dead. [2]A dinner was prepared in

---

11:47 Greek *the Sanhedrin.* **11:48** Or *our position;* Greek reads *our place.* **11:49** Greek *that year;* also in 11:51.

Jesus' honor. Martha served, and Lazarus was among those who ate* with him. ³Then Mary took a twelve-ounce jar* of expensive perfume made from essence of nard, and she anointed Jesus' feet with it, wiping his feet with her hair. The house was filled with the fragrance.

⁴But Judas Iscariot, the disciple who would soon betray him, said, ⁵"That perfume was worth a year's wages.* It should have been sold and the money given to the poor." ⁶Not that he cared for the poor—he was a thief, and since he was in charge of the disciples' money, he often stole some for himself.

⁷Jesus replied, "Leave her alone. She did this in preparation for my burial. ⁸You will always have the poor among you, but you will not always have me."

⁹When all the people* heard of Jesus' arrival, they flocked to see him and also to see Lazarus, the man Jesus had raised from the dead. ¹⁰Then the leading priests decided to kill Lazarus, too, ¹¹for it was because of him that many of the people had deserted them* and believed in Jesus.

Jesus' Triumphant Entry

¹²The next day, the news that Jesus was on the way to Jerusalem swept through the city. A large crowd of Passover visitors ¹³took palm branches and went down the road to meet him. They shouted,

"Praise God!*
Blessings on the one who comes
    in the name of the LORD!
Hail to the King of Israel!"*

¹⁴Jesus found a young donkey and rode on it, fulfilling the prophecy that said:

¹⁵ "Don't be afraid, people of
    Jerusalem.*
Look, your King is coming,
    riding on a donkey's colt."*

¹⁶His disciples didn't understand at the time that this was a fulfillment of prophecy. But after Jesus entered into his glory, they remembered what had happened and realized that these things had been written about him.

¹⁷Many in the crowd had seen Jesus call Lazarus from the tomb, raising him from the dead, and they were telling others* about it. ¹⁸That was the reason so many went out to meet him—because they had heard about this miraculous sign. ¹⁹Then the Pharisees said to each other, "There's nothing we can do. Look, everyone* has gone after him!"

12:2 Or who reclined. 12:3 Greek took 1 litra [327 grams]. 12:5 Greek worth 300 denarii. A denarius was equivalent to a laborer's full day's wage. 12:9 Greek Jewish people; also in 12:11. 12:11 Or had deserted their traditions; Greek reads had deserted. 12:13a Greek Hosanna, an exclamation of praise adapted from a Hebrew expression that means "save now." 12:13b Ps 118:25-26; Zeph 3:15. 12:15a Greek daughter of Zion. 12:15b Zech 9:9. 12:17 Greek were testifying. 12:19 Greek the world.

Jesus Predicts His Death

²⁰Some Greeks who had come to Jerusalem for the Passover celebration ²¹paid a visit to Philip, who was from Bethsaida in Galilee. They said, "Sir, we want to meet Jesus." ²²Philip told Andrew about it, and they went together to ask Jesus.

²³Jesus replied, "Now the time has come for the Son of Man* to enter into his glory. ²⁴I tell you the truth, unless a kernel of wheat is planted in the soil and dies, it remains alone. But its death will produce many new kernels—a plentiful harvest of new lives. ²⁵Those who love their life in this world will lose it. Those who care nothing for their life in this world will keep it for eternity. ²⁶Anyone who wants to serve me must follow me, because my servants must be where I am. And the Father will honor anyone who serves me.

²⁷"Now my soul is deeply troubled. Should I pray, 'Father, save me from this hour'? But this is the very reason I came! ²⁸Father, bring glory to your name."

Then a voice spoke from heaven, saying, "I have already brought glory to my name, and I will do so again." ²⁹When the crowd heard the voice, some thought it was thunder, while others declared an angel had spoken to him.

³⁰Then Jesus told them, "The voice was for your benefit, not mine. ³¹The time for judging this world has come, when Satan, the ruler of this world, will be cast out. ³²And when I am lifted up from the earth, I will draw everyone to myself." ³³He said this to indicate how he was going to die.

³⁴The crowd responded, "We understood from Scripture* that the Messiah would live forever. How can you say the Son of Man will die? Just who is this Son of Man, anyway?"

³⁵Jesus replied, "My light will shine for you just a little longer. Walk in the light while you can, so the darkness will not overtake you. Those who walk in the darkness cannot see where they are going. ³⁶Put your trust in the light while there is still time; then you will become children of the light."

After saying these things, Jesus went away and was hidden from them.

The Unbelief of the People

³⁷But despite all the miraculous signs Jesus had done, most of the people still did not believe in him. ³⁸This is exactly what Isaiah the prophet had predicted:

"LORD, who has believed our
    message?
To whom has the LORD revealed
    his powerful arm?"*

³⁹But the people couldn't believe, for as Isaiah also said,

12:23 "Son of Man" is a title Jesus used for himself.   12:34 Greek *from the law.*   12:38 Isa 53:1.

⁴⁰ "The Lord has blinded their eyes
and hardened their hearts—
so that their eyes cannot see,
and their hearts cannot
understand,
and they cannot turn to me
and have me heal them."*

⁴¹Isaiah was referring to Jesus when he said this, because he saw the future and spoke of the Messiah's glory. ⁴²Many people did believe in him, however, including some of the Jewish leaders. But they wouldn't admit it for fear that the Pharisees would expel them from the synagogue. ⁴³For they loved human praise more than the praise of God.

⁴⁴Jesus shouted to the crowds, "If you trust me, you are trusting not only me, but also God who sent me. ⁴⁵For when you see me, you are seeing the one who sent me. ⁴⁶I have come as a light to shine in this dark world, so that all who put their trust in me will no longer remain in the dark. ⁴⁷I will not judge those who hear me but don't obey me, for I have come to save the world and not to judge it. ⁴⁸But all who reject me and my message will be judged on the day of judgment by the truth I have spoken. ⁴⁹I don't speak on my own authority. The Father who sent me has commanded me what to say and how to say it. ⁵⁰And I know his commands lead to eternal life; so I say whatever the Father tells me to say."

Jesus Washes His Disciples' Feet

13 Before the Passover celebration, Jesus knew that his hour had come to leave this world and return to his Father. He had loved his disciples during his ministry on earth, and now he loved them to the very end.* ²It was time for supper, and the devil had already prompted Judas,* son of Simon Iscariot, to betray Jesus. ³Jesus knew that the Father had given him authority over everything and that he had come from God and would return to God. ⁴So he got up from the table, took off his robe, wrapped a towel around his waist, ⁵and poured water into a basin. Then he began to wash the disciples' feet, drying them with the towel he had around him.

⁶When Jesus came to Simon Peter, Peter said to him, "Lord, are you going to wash my feet?"

⁷Jesus replied, "You don't understand now what I am doing, but someday you will."

⁸"No," Peter protested, "you will never ever wash my feet!"

Jesus replied, "Unless I wash you, you won't belong to me."

⁹Simon Peter exclaimed, "Then wash my hands and head as well, Lord, not just my feet!"

¹⁰Jesus replied, "A person who has bathed all over does not need to wash, except for the feet,* to be entirely clean. And you disciples are clean, but not all of you." ¹¹For Jesus

12:40 Isa 6:10. **13:1** Or *he showed them the full extent of his love.* **13:2** Or *the devil had already intended for Judas.* **13:10** Some manuscripts do not include *except for the feet.*

knew who would betray him. That is what he meant when he said, "Not all of you are clean."

¹²After washing their feet, he put on his robe again and sat down and asked, "Do you understand what I was doing? ¹³You call me 'Teacher' and 'Lord,' and you are right, because that's what I am. ¹⁴And since I, your Lord and Teacher, have washed your feet, you ought to wash each other's feet. ¹⁵I have given you an example to follow. Do as I have done to you. ¹⁶I tell you the truth, slaves are not greater than their master. Nor is the messenger more important than the one who sends the message. ¹⁷Now that you know these things, God will bless you for doing them.

Jesus Predicts His Betrayal

¹⁸"I am not saying these things to all of you; I know the ones I have chosen. But this fulfills the Scripture that says, 'The one who eats my food has turned against me.'* ¹⁹I tell you this beforehand, so that when it happens you will believe that I AM the Messiah.* ²⁰I tell you the truth, anyone who welcomes my messenger is welcoming me, and anyone who welcomes me is welcoming the Father who sent me."

²¹Now Jesus was deeply troubled,* and he exclaimed, "I tell you the truth, one of you will betray me!"

²²The disciples looked at each other, wondering whom he could mean. ²³The disciple Jesus loved was sitting next to Jesus at the table.* ²⁴Simon Peter motioned to him to ask, "Who's he talking about?" ²⁵So that disciple leaned over to Jesus and asked, "Lord, who is it?"

²⁶Jesus responded, "It is the one to whom I give the bread I dip in the bowl." And when he had dipped it, he gave it to Judas, son of Simon Iscariot. ²⁷When Judas had eaten the bread, Satan entered into him. Then Jesus told him, "Hurry and do what you're going to do." ²⁸None of the others at the table knew what Jesus meant. ²⁹Since Judas was their treasurer, some thought Jesus was telling him to go and pay for the food or to give some money to the poor. ³⁰So Judas left at once, going out into the night.

Jesus Predicts Peter's Denial

³¹As soon as Judas left the room, Jesus said, "The time has come for the Son of Man* to enter into his glory, and God will be glorified because of him. ³²And since God receives glory because of the Son,* he will give his own glory to the Son, and he will do so at once. ³³Dear children, I will be with you only a little longer. And as I told the Jewish leaders, you will search for me, but you can't come where I am going.

13:18 Ps 41:9. **13:19** Or *that the 'I AM' has come;* or *that I am the LORD;* Greek reads *that I am.*
See Exod 3:14. **13:21** Greek *was troubled in his spirit.* **13:23** Greek *was reclining on Jesus' bosom.*
The "disciple Jesus loved" was probably John. **13:31** "Son of Man" is a title Jesus used for himself.
13:32 Several early manuscripts do not include *And since God receives glory because of the Son.*

34So now I am giving you a new commandment: Love each other. Just as I have loved you, you should love each other. 35Your love for one another will prove to the world that you are my disciples."

36Simon Peter asked, "Lord, where are you going?"

And Jesus replied, "You can't go with me now, but you will follow me later."

37"But why can't I come now, Lord?" he asked. "I'm ready to die for you."

38Jesus answered, "Die for me? I tell you the truth, Peter—before the rooster crows tomorrow morning, you will deny three times that you even know me.

Jesus, the Way to the Father

14 "Don't let your hearts be troubled. Trust in God, and trust also in me. 2There is more than enough room in my Father's home.* If this were not so, would I have told you that I am going to prepare a place for you?* 3When everything is ready, I will come and get you, so that you will always be with me where I am. 4And you know the way to where I am going."

5"No, we don't know, Lord," Thomas said. "We have no idea where you are going, so how can we know the way?"

6Jesus told him, "I am the way, the truth, and the life. No one can come to the Father except through me. 7If you had really known me, you would know who my Father is.* From now on, you do know him and have seen him!"

8Philip said, "Lord, show us the Father, and we will be satisfied."

9Jesus replied, "Have I been with you all this time, Philip, and yet you still don't know who I am? Anyone who has seen me has seen the Father! So why are you asking me to show him to you? 10Don't you believe that I am in the Father and the Father is in me? The words I speak are not my own, but my Father who lives in me does his work through me. 11Just believe that I am in the Father and the Father is in me. Or at least believe because of the work you have seen me do.

12"I tell you the truth, anyone who believes in me will do the same works I have done, and even greater works, because I am going to be with the Father. 13You can ask for anything in my name, and I will do it, so that the Son can bring glory to the Father. 14Yes, ask me for anything in my name, and I will do it!

Jesus Promises the Holy Spirit

15"If you love me, obey* my commandments. 16And I will ask the

---

14:2a Or *There are many rooms in my Father's house.* **14:2b** Or *If this were not so, I would have told you that I am going to prepare a place for you.* Some manuscripts read *If this were not so, I would have told you. I am going to prepare a place for you.* **14:7** Some manuscripts read *If you have really known me, you will know who my Father is.* **14:15** Other manuscripts read *you will obey;* still others read *you should obey.*

Father, and he will give you another Advocate,* who will never leave you. [17]He is the Holy Spirit, who leads into all truth. The world cannot receive him, because it isn't looking for him and doesn't recognize him. But you know him, because he lives with you now and later will be in you.* [18]No, I will not abandon you as orphans—I will come to you. [19]Soon the world will no longer see me, but you will see me. Since I live, you also will live. [20]When I am raised to life again, you will know that I am in my Father, and you are in me, and I am in you. [21]Those who accept my commandments and obey them are the ones who love me. And because they love me, my Father will love them. And I will love them and reveal myself to each of them."

[22]Judas (not Judas Iscariot, but the other disciple with that name) said to him, "Lord, why are you going to reveal yourself only to us and not to the world at large?"

[23]Jesus replied, "All who love me will do what I say. My Father will love them, and we will come and make our home with each of them. [24]Anyone who doesn't love me will not obey me. And remember, my words are not my own. What I am telling you is from the Father who sent me. [25]I am telling you these things now while I am still with you. [26]But when the Father sends the Advocate as my representative—that is, the Holy Spirit—he will teach you everything and will remind you of everything I have told you.

[27]"I am leaving you with a gift—peace of mind and heart. And the peace I give is a gift the world cannot give. So don't be troubled or afraid. [28]Remember what I told you: I am going away, but I will come back to you again. If you really loved me, you would be happy that I am going to the Father, who is greater than I am. [29]I have told you these things before they happen so that when they do happen, you will believe.

[30]"I don't have much more time to talk to you, because the ruler of this world approaches. He has no power over me, [31]but I will do what the Father requires of me, so that the world will know that I love the Father. Come, let's be going.

Jesus, the True Vine

15 "I am the true grapevine, and my Father is the gardener. [2]He cuts off every branch of mine that doesn't produce fruit, and he prunes the branches that do bear fruit so they will produce even more. [3]You have already been pruned and purified by the message I have given you. [4]Remain in me, and I will remain in you. For a branch cannot produce fruit if it is severed from the vine, and you cannot be fruitful unless you remain in me.

14:16 Or *Comforter,* or *Encourager,* or *Counselor.* Greek reads *Paraclete;* also in 14:26. **14:17** Some manuscripts read *and is in you.*

⁵"Yes, I am the vine; you are the branches. Those who remain in me, and I in them, will produce much fruit. For apart from me you can do nothing. ⁶Anyone who does not remain in me is thrown away like a useless branch and withers. Such branches are gathered into a pile to be burned. ⁷But if you remain in me and my words remain in you, you may ask for anything you want, and it will be granted! ⁸When you produce much fruit, you are my true disciples. This brings great glory to my Father.

⁹"I have loved you even as the Father has loved me. Remain in my love. ¹⁰When you obey my commandments, you remain in my love, just as I obey my Father's commandments and remain in his love. ¹¹I have told you these things so that you will be filled with my joy. Yes, your joy will overflow! ¹²This is my commandment: Love each other in the same way I have loved you. ¹³There is no greater love than to lay down one's life for one's friends. ¹⁴You are my friends if you do what I command. ¹⁵I no longer call you slaves, because a master doesn't confide in his slaves. Now you are my friends, since I have told you everything the Father told me. ¹⁶You didn't choose me. I chose you. I appointed you to go and produce lasting fruit, so that the Father will give you whatever you ask for, using

my name. ¹⁷This is my command: Love each other.

The World's Hatred

¹⁸"If the world hates you, remember that it hated me first. ¹⁹The world would love you as one of its own if you belonged to it, but you are no longer part of the world. I chose you to come out of the world, so it hates you. ²⁰Do you remember what I told you? 'A slave is not greater than the master.' Since they persecuted me, naturally they will persecute you. And if they had listened to me, they would listen to you. ²¹They will do all this to you because of me, for they have rejected the one who sent me. ²²They would not be guilty if I had not come and spoken to them. But now they have no excuse for their sin. ²³Anyone who hates me also hates my Father. ²⁴If I hadn't done such miraculous signs among them that no one else could do, they would not be guilty. But as it is, they have seen everything I did, yet they still hate me and my Father. ²⁵This fulfills what is written in their Scriptures*: 'They hated me without cause.'

²⁶"But I will send you the Advocate*—the Spirit of truth. He will come to you from the Father and will testify all about me. ²⁷And you must also testify about me because you have been with me from the beginning of my ministry.

15:25 Greek *in their law.* Pss 35:19; 69:4. **15:26** Or *Comforter,* or *Encourager,* or *Counselor.* Greek reads *Paraclete.*

16

"I have told you these things so that you won't abandon your faith. ²For you will be expelled from the synagogues, and the time is coming when those who kill you will think they are doing a holy service for God. ³This is because they have never known the Father or me. ⁴Yes, I'm telling you these things now, so that when they happen, you will remember my warning. I didn't tell you earlier because I was going to be with you for a while longer.

The Work of the Holy Spirit

⁵"But now I am going away to the one who sent me, and not one of you is asking where I am going. ⁶Instead, you grieve because of what I've told you. ⁷But in fact, it is best for you that I go away, because if I don't, the Advocate* won't come. If I do go away, then I will send him to you. ⁸And when he comes, he will convict the world of its sin, and of God's righteousness, and of the coming judgment. ⁹The world's sin is that it refuses to believe in me. ¹⁰Righteousness is available because I go to the Father, and you will see me no more. ¹¹Judgment will come because the ruler of this world has already been judged.

¹²"There is so much more I want to tell you, but you can't bear it now. ¹³When the Spirit of truth comes, he will guide you into all truth. He will not speak on his own but will tell you what he has heard. He will tell you about the future. ¹⁴He will bring me glory by telling you whatever he receives from me. ¹⁵All that belongs to the Father is mine; this is why I said, 'The Spirit will tell you whatever he receives from me.'

Sadness Will Be Turned to Joy

¹⁶"In a little while you won't see me anymore. But a little while after that, you will see me again."

¹⁷Some of the disciples asked each other, "What does he mean when he says, 'In a little while you won't see me, but then you will see me,' and 'I am going to the Father'? ¹⁸And what does he mean by 'a little while'? We don't understand."

¹⁹Jesus realized they wanted to ask him about it, so he said, "Are you asking yourselves what I meant? I said in a little while you won't see me, but a little while after that you will see me again. ²⁰I tell you the truth, you will weep and mourn over what is going to happen to me, but the world will rejoice. You will grieve, but your grief will suddenly turn to wonderful joy. ²¹It will be like a woman suffering the pains of labor. When her child is born, her anguish gives way to joy because she has brought a new baby into the world. ²²So you have sorrow now, but I will see you again; then you will rejoice, and no one can rob you of that joy. ²³At that time you

16:7 Or *Comforter,* or *Encourager,* or *Counselor.* Greek reads *Paraclete.*

won't need to ask me for anything. I tell you the truth, you will ask the Father directly, and he will grant your request because you use my name. ²⁴You haven't done this before. Ask, using my name, and you will receive, and you will have abundant joy.

²⁵"I have spoken of these matters in figures of speech, but soon I will stop speaking figuratively and will tell you plainly all about the Father. ²⁶Then you will ask in my name. I'm not saying I will ask the Father on your behalf, ²⁷for the Father himself loves you dearly because you love me and believe that I came from God.* ²⁸Yes, I came from the Father into the world, and now I will leave the world and return to the Father."

²⁹Then his disciples said, "At last you are speaking plainly and not figuratively. ³⁰Now we understand that you know everything, and there's no need to question you. From this we believe that you came from God."

³¹Jesus asked, "Do you finally believe? ³²But the time is coming—indeed it's here now—when you will be scattered, each one going his own way, leaving me alone. Yet I am not alone because the Father is with me. ³³I have told you all this so that you may have peace in me. Here on earth you will have many trials and sorrows. But take heart, because I have overcome the world."

The Prayer of Jesus

17 After saying all these things, Jesus looked up to heaven and said, "Father, the hour has come. Glorify your Son so he can give glory back to you. ²For you have given him authority over everyone. He gives eternal life to each one you have given him. ³And this is the way to have eternal life—to know you, the only true God, and Jesus Christ, the one you sent to earth. ⁴I brought glory to you here on earth by completing the work you gave me to do. ⁵Now, Father, bring me into the glory we shared before the world began.

⁶"I have revealed you* to the ones you gave me from this world. They were always yours. You gave them to me, and they have kept your word. ⁷Now they know that everything I have is a gift from you, ⁸for I have passed on to them the message you gave me. They accepted it and know that I came from you, and they believe you sent me.

⁹"My prayer is not for the world, but for those you have given me, because they belong to you. ¹⁰All who are mine belong to you, and you have given them to me, so they bring me glory. ¹¹Now I am departing from the world; they are staying in this world, but I am coming to you. Holy Father, you have given me your name;* now protect them by the power of your name so that they will be united just as we are. ¹²During my

16:27 Some manuscripts read *from the Father.* **17:6** Greek *have revealed your name;* also in 17:26. **17:11** Some manuscripts read *you have given me these [disciples].*

time here, I protected them by the power of the name you gave me.* I guarded them so that not one was lost, except the one headed for destruction, as the Scriptures foretold.

¹³"Now I am coming to you. I told them many things while I was with them in this world so they would be filled with my joy. ¹⁴I have given them your word. And the world hates them because they do not belong to the world, just as I do not belong to the world. ¹⁵I'm not asking you to take them out of the world, but to keep them safe from the evil one. ¹⁶They do not belong to this world any more than I do. ¹⁷Make them holy by your truth; teach them your word, which is truth. ¹⁸Just as you sent me into the world, I am sending them into the world. ¹⁹And I give myself as a holy sacrifice for them so they can be made holy by your truth.

²⁰"I am praying not only for these disciples but also for all who will ever believe in me through their message. ²¹I pray that they will all be one, just as you and I are one—as you are in me, Father, and I am in you. And may they be in us so that the world will believe you sent me. ²²"I have given them the glory you gave me, so they may be one as we are one. ²³I am in them and you are in me. May they experience such perfect unity that the world will

know that you sent me and that you love them as much as you love me. ²⁴Father, I want these whom you have given me to be with me where I am. Then they can see all the glory you gave me because you loved me even before the world began!

²⁵"O righteous Father, the world doesn't know you, but I do; and these disciples know you sent me. ²⁶I have revealed you to them, and I will continue to do so. Then your love for me will be in them, and I will be in them."

Jesus Is Betrayed and Arrested

18 After saying these things, Jesus crossed the Kidron Valley with his disciples and entered a grove of olive trees. ²Judas, the betrayer, knew this place, because Jesus had often gone there with his disciples. ³The leading priests and Pharisees had given Judas a contingent of Roman soldiers and Temple guards to accompany him. Now with blazing torches, lanterns, and weapons, they arrived at the olive grove.

⁴Jesus fully realized all that was going to happen to him, so he stepped forward to meet them. "Who are you looking for?" he asked.

⁵"Jesus the Nazarene,"* they replied.

"I AM he,"* Jesus said. (Judas, who betrayed him, was standing with

---

17:12 Some manuscripts read *I protected those you gave me, by the power of your name.* **18:5a** Or *Jesus of Nazareth;* also in 18:7. **18:5b** Or *"The 'I AM' is here";* or *"I am the LORD";* Greek reads *I am;* also in 18:6, 8. See Exod 3:14.

them.) [6]As Jesus said "I AM he," they all drew back and fell to the ground! [7]Once more he asked them, "Who are you looking for?"

And again they replied, "Jesus the Nazarene."

[8]"I told you that I AM he," Jesus said. "And since I am the one you want, let these others go." [9]He did this to fulfill his own statement: "I did not lose a single one of those you have given me."*

[10]Then Simon Peter drew a sword and slashed off the right ear of Malchus, the high priest's slave. [11]But Jesus said to Peter, "Put your sword back into its sheath. Shall I not drink from the cup of suffering the Father has given me?"

Jesus at the High Priest's House

[12]So the soldiers, their commanding officer, and the Temple guards arrested Jesus and tied him up. [13]First they took him to Annas, since he was the father-in-law of Caiaphas, the high priest at that time.* [14]Caiaphas was the one who had told the other Jewish leaders, "It's better that one man should die for the people."

Peter's First Denial

[15]Simon Peter followed Jesus, as did another of the disciples. That other disciple was acquainted with the high priest, so he was allowed to enter the high priest's courtyard with Jesus. [16]Peter had to stay outside the gate. Then the disciple who knew the high priest spoke to the woman watching at the gate, and she let Peter in. [17]The woman asked Peter, "You're not one of that man's disciples, are you?"

"No," he said, "I am not."

[18]Because it was cold, the household servants and the guards had made a charcoal fire. They stood around it, warming themselves, and Peter stood with them, warming himself.

The High Priest Questions Jesus

[19]Inside, the high priest began asking Jesus about his followers and what he had been teaching them. [20]Jesus replied, "Everyone knows what I teach. I have preached regularly in the synagogues and the Temple, where the people* gather. I have not spoken in secret. [21]Why are you asking me this question? Ask those who heard me. They know what I said."

[22]Then one of the Temple guards standing nearby slapped Jesus across the face. "Is that the way to answer the high priest?" he demanded.

[23]Jesus replied, "If I said anything wrong, you must prove it. But if I'm speaking the truth, why are you beating me?"

[24]Then Annas bound Jesus and sent him to Caiaphas, the high priest.

Peter's Second and Third Denials

[25]Meanwhile, as Simon Peter was standing by the fire warming

18:9 See John 6:39 and 17:12.   18:13 Greek *that year.*   18:20 Greek *Jewish people;* also in 18:38.

himself, they asked him again, "You're not one of his disciples, are you?"

He denied it, saying, "No, I am not."

²⁶But one of the household slaves of the high priest, a relative of the man whose ear Peter had cut off, asked, "Didn't I see you out there in the olive grove with Jesus?" ²⁷Again Peter denied it. And immediately a rooster crowed.

Jesus' Trial before Pilate

²⁸Jesus' trial before Caiaphas ended in the early hours of the morning. Then he was taken to the headquarters of the Roman governor.* His accusers didn't go inside because it would defile them, and they wouldn't be allowed to celebrate the Passover. ²⁹So Pilate, the governor, went out to them and asked, "What is your charge against this man?"

³⁰"We wouldn't have handed him over to you if he weren't a criminal!" they retorted.

³¹"Then take him away and judge him by your own law," Pilate told them.

"Only the Romans are permitted to execute someone," the Jewish leaders replied. ³²(This fulfilled Jesus' prediction about the way he would die.*)

³³Then Pilate went back into his headquarters and called for Jesus to be brought to him. "Are you the king of the Jews?" he asked him.

³⁴Jesus replied, "Is this your own question, or did others tell you about me?"

³⁵"Am I a Jew?" Pilate retorted. "Your own people and their leading priests brought you to me for trial. Why? What have you done?"

³⁶Jesus answered, "My Kingdom is not an earthly kingdom. If it were, my followers would fight to keep me from being handed over to the Jewish leaders. But my Kingdom is not of this world."

³⁷Pilate said, "So you are a king?"

Jesus responded, "You say I am a king. Actually, I was born and came into the world to testify to the truth. All who love the truth recognize that what I say is true."

³⁸"What is truth?" Pilate asked. Then he went out again to the people and told them, "He is not guilty of any crime. ³⁹But you have a custom of asking me to release one prisoner each year at Passover. Would you like me to release this 'King of the Jews'?"

⁴⁰But they shouted back, "No! Not this man. We want Barabbas!" (Barabbas was a revolutionary.)

Jesus Sentenced to Death

19 Then Pilate had Jesus flogged with a lead-tipped whip. ²The soldiers wove a crown of thorns and put it on his head, and they put a

18:28 Greek *to the Praetorium;* also in 18:33. **18:32** See John 12:32-33.

purple robe on him. ³"Hail! King of the Jews!" they mocked, as they slapped him across the face.

⁴Pilate went outside again and said to the people, "I am going to bring him out to you now, but understand clearly that I find him not guilty." ⁵Then Jesus came out wearing the crown of thorns and the purple robe. And Pilate said, "Look, here is the man!"

⁶When they saw him, the leading priests and Temple guards began shouting, "Crucify him! Crucify him!"

"Take him yourselves and crucify him," Pilate said. "I find him not guilty."

⁷The Jewish leaders replied, "By our law he ought to die because he called himself the Son of God."

⁸When Pilate heard this, he was more frightened than ever. ⁹He took Jesus back into the headquarters* again and asked him, "Where are you from?" But Jesus gave no answer. ¹⁰"Why don't you talk to me?" Pilate demanded. "Don't you realize that I have the power to release you or crucify you?"

¹¹Then Jesus said, "You would have no power over me at all unless it were given to you from above. So the one who handed me over to you has the greater sin."

¹²Then Pilate tried to release him, but the Jewish leaders shouted, "If you release this man, you are no 'friend of Caesar.'* Anyone who declares himself a king is a rebel against Caesar."

¹³When they said this, Pilate brought Jesus out to them again. Then Pilate sat down on the judgment seat on the platform that is called the Stone Pavement (in Hebrew, *Gabbatha*). ¹⁴It was now about noon on the day of preparation for the Passover. And Pilate said to the people,* "Look, here is your king!"

¹⁵"Away with him," they yelled. "Away with him! Crucify him!"

"What? Crucify your king?" Pilate asked.

"We have no king but Caesar," the leading priests shouted back.

¹⁶Then Pilate turned Jesus over to them to be crucified.

The Crucifixion

So they took Jesus away. ¹⁷Carrying the cross by himself, he went to the place called Place of the Skull (in Hebrew, *Golgotha*). ¹⁸There they nailed him to the cross. Two others were crucified with him, one on either side, with Jesus between them. ¹⁹And Pilate posted a sign on the cross that read, "Jesus of Nazareth,* the King of the Jews." ²⁰The place where Jesus was crucified was near the city, and the sign was written in Hebrew, Latin, and Greek, so that many people could read it.

²¹Then the leading priests objected and said to Pilate, "Change it

19:9 Greek *the Praetorium*. 19:12 "Friend of Caesar" is a technical term that refers to an ally of the emperor. 19:14 Greek *Jewish people;* also in 19:20. 19:19 Or *Jesus the Nazarene*.

from 'The King of the Jews' to 'He said, I am King of the Jews.'"

²²Pilate replied, "No, what I have written, I have written."

²³When the soldiers had crucified Jesus, they divided his clothes among the four of them. They also took his robe, but it was seamless, woven in one piece from top to bottom. ²⁴So they said, "Rather than tearing it apart, let's throw dice* for it." This fulfilled the Scripture that says, "They divided my garments among themselves and threw dice for my clothing."* So that is what they did.

²⁵Standing near the cross were Jesus' mother, and his mother's sister, Mary (the wife of Clopas), and Mary Magdalene. ²⁶When Jesus saw his mother standing there beside the disciple he loved, he said to her, "Dear woman, here is your son." ²⁷And he said to this disciple, "Here is your mother." And from then on this disciple took her into his home.

The Death of Jesus

²⁸Jesus knew that his mission was now finished, and to fulfill Scripture he said, "I am thirsty."* ²⁹A jar of sour wine was sitting there, so they soaked a sponge in it, put it on a hyssop branch, and held it up to his lips. ³⁰When Jesus had tasted it, he said, "It is finished!" Then he bowed his head and gave up his spirit.

³¹It was the day of preparation, and the Jewish leaders didn't want the bodies hanging there the next day, which was the Sabbath (and a very special Sabbath, because it was the Passover). So they asked Pilate to hasten their deaths by ordering that their legs be broken. Then their bodies could be taken down. ³²So the soldiers came and broke the legs of the two men crucified with Jesus. ³³But when they came to Jesus, they saw that he was already dead, so they didn't break his legs. ³⁴One of the soldiers, however, pierced his side with a spear, and immediately blood and water flowed out. ³⁵(This report is from an eyewitness giving an accurate account. He speaks the truth so that you also may continue to believe.*) ³⁶These things happened in fulfillment of the Scriptures that say, "Not one of his bones will be broken,"* ³⁷and "They will look on the one they pierced."*

The Burial of Jesus

³⁸Afterward Joseph of Arimathea, who had been a secret disciple of Jesus (because he feared the Jewish leaders), asked Pilate for permission to take down Jesus' body. When Pilate gave permission, Joseph came and took the body away. ³⁹With him came Nicodemus, the man who had come to Jesus at night. He brought about seventy-

19:24a Greek *cast lots*. 19:24b Ps 22:18. 19:28 See Pss 22:15; 69:21. 19:35 Some manuscripts read *that you also may believe*. 19:36 Exod 12:46; Num 9:12; Ps 34:20. 19:37 Zech 12:10.

five pounds* of perfumed oint-ment made from myrrh and aloes. 40Following Jewish burial custom, they wrapped Jesus' body with the spices in long sheets of linen cloth. 41The place of crucifixion was near a garden, where there was a new tomb, never used before. 42And so, because it was the day of prepara-tion for the Jewish Passover* and since the tomb was close at hand, they laid Jesus there.

The Resurrection

20 Early on Sunday morning,* while it was still dark, Mary Magdalene came to the tomb and found that the stone had been rolled away from the entrance. 2She ran and found Simon Peter and the other disciple, the one whom Jesus loved. She said, "They have taken the Lord's body out of the tomb, and we don't know where they have put him!"

3Peter and the other disciple started out for the tomb. 4They were both running, but the other disciple outran Peter and reached the tomb first. 5He stooped and looked in and saw the linen wrap-pings lying there, but he didn't go in. 6Then Simon Peter arrived and went inside. He also noticed the linen wrappings lying there, 7while the cloth that had covered Jesus' head was folded up and lying apart from the other wrappings. 8Then the disciple who had reached the tomb first also went in, and he saw and believed—9for until then they still hadn't understood the Scrip-tures that said Jesus must rise from the dead. 10Then they went home.

Jesus Appears to Mary Magdalene

11Mary was standing outside the tomb crying, and as she wept, she stooped and looked in. 12She saw two white-robed angels, one sitting at the head and the other at the foot of the place where the body of Jesus had been lying. 13"Dear woman, why are you crying?" the angels asked her.

"Because they have taken away my Lord," she replied, "and I don't know where they have put him."

14She turned to leave and saw someone standing there. It was Jesus, but she didn't recognize him. 15"Dear woman, why are you cry-ing?" Jesus asked her. "Who are you looking for?"

She thought he was the gardener. "Sir," she said, "if you have taken him away, tell me where you have put him, and I will go and get him."

16"Mary!" Jesus said.

She turned to him and cried out, "Rabboni!" (which is Hebrew for "Teacher").

17"Don't cling to me," Jesus said, "for I haven't yet ascended to the Father. But go find my brothers and tell them, 'I am ascending to my

19:39 Greek *100 litras* [32.7 kilograms]. **19:42** Greek *because of the Jewish day of preparation.* **20:1** Greek *On the first day of the week.*

Father and your Father, to my God and your God.' "

¹⁸Mary Magdalene found the disciples and told them, "I have seen the Lord!" Then she gave them his message.

Jesus Appears to His Disciples

¹⁹That Sunday evening* the disciples were meeting behind locked doors because they were afraid of the Jewish leaders. Suddenly, Jesus was standing there among them! "Peace be with you," he said. ²⁰As he spoke, he showed them the wounds in his hands and his side. They were filled with joy when they saw the Lord! ²¹Again he said, "Peace be with you. As the Father has sent me, so I am sending you." ²²Then he breathed on them and said, "Receive the Holy Spirit. ²³If you forgive anyone's sins, they are forgiven. If you do not forgive them, they are not forgiven."

Jesus Appears to Thomas

²⁴One of the twelve disciples, Thomas (nicknamed the Twin),* was not with the others when Jesus came. ²⁵They told him, "We have seen the Lord!"

But he replied, "I won't believe it unless I see the nail wounds in his hands, put my fingers into them, and place my hand into the wound in his side."

²⁶Eight days later the disciples were together again, and this time Thomas was with them. The doors were locked; but suddenly, as before, Jesus was standing among them. "Peace be with you," he said. ²⁷Then he said to Thomas, "Put your finger here, and look at my hands. Put your hand into the wound in my side. Don't be faithless any longer. Believe!"

²⁸"My Lord and my God!" Thomas exclaimed.

²⁹Then Jesus told him, "You believe because you have seen me. Blessed are those who believe without seeing me."

Purpose of the Book

³⁰The disciples saw Jesus do many other miraculous signs in addition to the ones recorded in this book. ³¹But these are written so that you may continue to believe* that Jesus is the Messiah, the Son of God, and that by believing in him you will have life by the power of his name.

Epilogue: Jesus Appears to Seven Disciples

21 Later, Jesus appeared again to the disciples beside the Sea of Galilee.* This is how it happened. ²Several of the disciples were there—Simon Peter, Thomas (nicknamed the Twin),* Nathanael

20:19 Greek *In the evening of that day, the first day of the week.* 20:24 Greek *Thomas, who was called Didymus.* 20:31 Some manuscripts read *that you may believe.* 21:1 Greek *Sea of Tiberias,* another name for the Sea of Galilee. 21:2 Greek *Thomas, who was called Didymus.*

from Cana in Galilee, the sons of Zebedee, and two other disciples.

³Simon Peter said, "I'm going fishing."

"We'll come, too," they all said. So they went out in the boat, but they caught nothing all night.

⁴At dawn Jesus was standing on the beach, but the disciples couldn't see who he was. ⁵He called out, "Fellows,* have you caught any fish?"

"No," they replied.

⁶Then he said, "Throw out your net on the right-hand side of the boat, and you'll get some!" So they did, and they couldn't haul in the net because there were so many fish in it.

⁷Then the disciple Jesus loved said to Peter, "It's the Lord!" When Simon Peter heard that it was the Lord, he put on his tunic (for he had stripped for work), jumped into the water, and headed to shore. ⁸The others stayed with the boat and pulled the loaded net to the shore, for they were only about a hundred yards* from shore. ⁹When they got there, they found breakfast waiting for them—fish cooking over a charcoal fire, and some bread.

¹⁰"Bring some of the fish you've just caught," Jesus said. ¹¹So Simon Peter went aboard and dragged the net to the shore. There were 153 large fish, and yet the net hadn't torn.

¹²"Now come and have some breakfast!" Jesus said. None of the disciples dared to ask him, "Who are you?" They knew it was the Lord. ¹³Then Jesus served them the bread and the fish. ¹⁴This was the third time Jesus had appeared to his disciples since he had been raised from the dead.

¹⁵After breakfast Jesus asked Simon Peter, "Simon son of John, do you love me more than these?*"

"Yes, Lord," Peter replied, "you know I love you."

"Then feed my lambs," Jesus told him.

¹⁶Jesus repeated the question: "Simon son of John, do you love me?"

"Yes, Lord," Peter said, "you know I love you."

"Then take care of my sheep," Jesus said.

¹⁷A third time he asked him, "Simon son of John, do you love me?"

Peter was hurt that Jesus asked the question a third time. He said, "Lord, you know everything. You know that I love you."

Jesus said, "Then feed my sheep.

¹⁸"I tell you the truth, when you were young, you were able to do as you liked; you dressed yourself and went wherever you wanted to go. But when you are old, you will stretch out your hands, and others* will dress you and take you where you don't want to go." ¹⁹Jesus said this to let him know by what kind of

21:5 Greek *Children.*   21:8 Greek *200 cubits* [90 meters].   21:15 Or *more than these others do?*
21:18 Some manuscripts read *and another one.*

death he would glorify God. Then Jesus told him, "Follow me."

²⁰Peter turned around and saw behind them the disciple Jesus loved—the one who had leaned over to Jesus during supper and asked, "Lord, who will betray you?" ²¹Peter asked Jesus, "What about him, Lord?"

²²Jesus replied, "If I want him to remain alive until I return, what is that to you? As for you, follow me." ²³So the rumor spread among the community of believers* that this

21:23 Greek *the brothers.*

disciple wouldn't die. But that isn't what Jesus said at all. He only said, "If I want him to remain alive until I return, what is that to you?"

²⁴This disciple is the one who testifies to these events and has recorded them here. And we know that his account of these things is accurate.

²⁵Jesus also did many other things. If they were all written down, I suppose the whole world could not contain the books that would be written.

Acts of the Apostles

The Promise of the Holy Spirit

1 In my first book* I told you, Theophilus, about everything Jesus began to do and teach ²until the day he was taken up to heaven after giving his chosen apostles further instructions through the Holy Spirit. ³During the forty days after he suffered and died, he appeared to the apostles from time to time, and he proved to them in many ways that he was actually alive. And he talked to them about the Kingdom of God.

⁴Once when he was eating with them, he commanded them, "Do not leave Jerusalem until the Father sends you the gift he promised, as I told you before. ⁵John baptized with* water, but in just a few days you will be baptized with the Holy Spirit."

The Ascension of Jesus

⁶So when the apostles were with Jesus, they kept asking him, "Lord, has the time come for you to free Israel and restore our kingdom?"

⁷He replied, "The Father alone has the authority to set those dates and times, and they are not for you to know. ⁸But you will receive power when the Holy Spirit comes upon you. And you will be my witnesses, telling people about me everywhere—in Jerusalem, throughout Judea, in Samaria, and to the ends of the earth."

⁹After saying this, he was taken up into a cloud while they were watching, and they could no longer see him. ¹⁰As they strained to see him rising into heaven, two white-robed men suddenly stood among them. ¹¹"Men of Galilee," they said, "why are you standing here staring into heaven? Jesus has been taken from you into heaven, but someday he will return from heaven in the same way you saw him go!"

Matthias Replaces Judas

¹²Then the apostles returned to Jerusalem from the Mount of Olives, a distance of half a mile.* ¹³When they arrived, they went to the upstairs room of the house where they were staying.

Here are the names of those who were present: Peter, John, James, Andrew, Philip, Thomas, Bartholomew, Matthew, James (son of Alphaeus), Simon (the zealot), and Judas (son of

---

1:1 The reference is to the Gospel of Luke. **1:5** Or *in;* also in 1:5b. **1:12** Greek *a Sabbath day's journey*.

James). [14]They all met together and were constantly united in prayer, along with Mary the mother of Jesus, several other women, and the brothers of Jesus.

[15]During this time, when about 120 believers* were together in one place, Peter stood up and addressed them. [16]"Brothers," he said, "the Scriptures had to be fulfilled concerning Judas, who guided those who arrested Jesus. This was predicted long ago by the Holy Spirit, speaking through King David. [17]Judas was one of us and shared in the ministry with us."

[18](Judas had bought a field with the money he received for his treachery. Falling headfirst there, his body split open, spilling out all his intestines. [19]The news of his death spread to all the people of Jerusalem, and they gave the place the Aramaic name *Akeldama,* which means "Field of Blood.")

[20]Peter continued, "This was written in the book of Psalms, where it says, 'Let his home become desolate, with no one living in it.' It also says, 'Let someone else take his position.'*

[21]"So now we must choose a replacement for Judas from among the men who were with us the entire time we were traveling with the Lord Jesus—[22]from the time he was baptized by John until the day he was taken from us. Whoever is cho-

sen will join us as a witness of Jesus' resurrection."

[23]So they nominated two men: Joseph called Barsabbas (also known as Justus) and Matthias. [24]Then they all prayed, "O Lord, you know every heart. Show us which of these men you have chosen [25]as an apostle to replace Judas in this ministry, for he has deserted us and gone where he belongs." [26]Then they cast lots, and Matthias was selected to become an apostle with the other eleven.

The Holy Spirit Comes

2 On the day of Pentecost* all the believers were meeting together in one place. [2]Suddenly, there was a sound from heaven like the roaring of a mighty windstorm, and it filled the house where they were sitting. [3]Then, what looked like flames or tongues of fire appeared and settled on each of them. [4]And everyone present was filled with the Holy Spirit and began speaking in other languages,* as the Holy Spirit gave them this ability.

[5]At that time there were devout Jews from every nation living in Jerusalem. [6]When they heard the loud noise, everyone came running, and they were bewildered to hear their own languages being spoken by the believers.

[7]They were completely amazed. "How can this be?" they exclaimed. "These people are all from Galilee,

1:15 Greek *brothers.* **1:20** Pss 69:25; 109:8. **2:1** The Festival of Pentecost came 50 days after Passover (when Jesus was crucified). **2:4** Or *in other tongues.*

8and yet we hear them speaking in our own native languages! 9Here we are—Parthians, Medes, Elamites, people from Mesopotamia, Judea, Cappadocia, Pontus, the province of Asia, 10Phrygia, Pamphylia, Egypt, and the areas of Libya around Cyrene, visitors from Rome 11(both Jews and converts to Judaism), Cretans, and Arabs. And we all hear these people speaking in our own languages about the wonderful things God has done!" 12They stood there amazed and perplexed. "What can this mean?" they asked each other.

13But others in the crowd ridiculed them, saying, "They're just drunk, that's all!"

Peter Preaches to the Crowd

14Then Peter stepped forward with the eleven other apostles and shouted to the crowd, "Listen carefully, all of you, fellow Jews and residents of Jerusalem! Make no mistake about this. 15These people are not drunk, as some of you are assuming. Nine o'clock in the morning is much too early for that. 16No, what you see was predicted long ago by the prophet Joel:

17 'In the last days,' God says,
    'I will pour out my Spirit upon all people.
  Your sons and daughters will prophesy.
  Your young men will see visions,

and your old men will dream dreams.
18 In those days I will pour out my Spirit
    even on my servants—men and women alike—
    and they will prophesy.
19 And I will cause wonders in the heavens above
    and signs on the earth below—
    blood and fire and clouds of smoke.
20 The sun will become dark,
    and the moon will turn blood red
    before that great and glorious day of the LORD arrives.
21 But everyone who calls on the name of the LORD
    will be saved.'*

22"People of Israel, listen! God publicly endorsed Jesus the Nazarene* by doing powerful miracles, wonders, and signs through him, as you well know. 23But God knew what would happen, and his prearranged plan was carried out when Jesus was betrayed. With the help of lawless Gentiles, you nailed him to a cross and killed him. 24But God released him from the horrors of death and raised him back to life, for death could not keep him in its grip. 25King David said this about him:

'I see that the LORD is always with me.
  I will not be shaken, for he is right beside me.

2:17-21 Joel 2:28-32. 2:22 Or *Jesus of Nazareth.*

26 No wonder my heart is glad,
     and my tongue shouts his
          praises!
     My body rests in hope.
27 For you will not leave my soul
          among the dead*
     or allow your Holy One to rot
          in the grave.
28 You have shown me the way
          of life,
     and you will fill me with the
          joy of your presence.'*

29 "Dear brothers, think about this! You can be sure that the patriarch David wasn't referring to himself, for he died and was buried, and his tomb is still here among us. 30But he was a prophet, and he knew God had promised with an oath that one of David's own descendants would sit on his throne. 31David was looking into the future and speaking of the Messiah's resurrection. He was saying that God would not leave him among the dead or allow his body to rot in the grave.

32 "God raised Jesus from the dead, and we are all witnesses of this. 33Now he is exalted to the place of highest honor in heaven, at God's right hand. And the Father, as he had promised, gave him the Holy Spirit to pour out upon us, just as you see and hear today. 34For David himself never ascended into heaven, yet he said,

'The Lord said to my Lord,
     "Sit in the place of honor at
          my right hand
35 until I humble your enemies,
          making them a footstool
               under your feet."'*

36 "So let everyone in Israel know for certain that God has made this Jesus, whom you crucified, to be both Lord and Messiah!"

37 Peter's words pierced their hearts, and they said to him and to the other apostles, "Brothers, what should we do?"

38 Peter replied, "Each of you must repent of your sins and turn to God, and be baptized in the name of Jesus Christ for the forgiveness of your sins. Then you will receive the gift of the Holy Spirit. 39This promise is to you, to your children, and to those far away*—all who have been called by the Lord our God." 40Then Peter continued preaching for a long time, strongly urging all his listeners, "Save yourselves from this crooked generation!"

41 Those who believed what Peter said were baptized and added to the church that day—about 3,000 in all.

The Believers Form a Community
42 All the believers devoted themselves to the apostles' teaching, and to fellowship, and to sharing in meals (including the Lord's Supper*), and to prayer.

2:27 Greek *in Hades;* also in 2:31.   2:25-28 Ps 16:8-11 (Greek version).   2:34-35 Ps 110:1.
2:39 Or *and to people far in the future,* or *and to the Gentiles.*   2:42 Greek *the breaking of bread;* also in 2:46.

43A deep sense of awe came over them all, and the apostles performed many miraculous signs and wonders. 44And all the believers met together in one place and shared everything they had. 45They sold their property and possessions and shared the money with those in need. 46They worshiped together at the Temple each day, met in homes for the Lord's Supper, and shared their meals with great joy and generosity*—47all the while praising God and enjoying the goodwill of all the people. And each day the Lord added to their fellowship those who were being saved.

Peter Heals a Crippled Beggar

3 Peter and John went to the Temple one afternoon to take part in the three o'clock prayer service. 2As they approached the Temple, a man lame from birth was being carried in. Each day he was put beside the Temple gate, the one called the Beautiful Gate, so he could beg from the people going into the Temple. 3When he saw Peter and John about to enter, he asked them for some money.

4Peter and John looked at him intently, and Peter said, "Look at us!" 5The lame man looked at them eagerly, expecting some money. 6But Peter said, "I don't have any silver or gold for you. But I'll give you what I have. In the name of Jesus Christ the Nazarene,* get up and* walk!"

7Then Peter took the lame man by the right hand and helped him up. And as he did, the man's feet and ankles were instantly healed and strengthened. 8He jumped up, stood on his feet, and began to walk! Then, walking, leaping, and praising God, he went into the Temple with them.

9All the people saw him walking and heard him praising God. 10When they realized he was the lame beggar they had seen so often at the Beautiful Gate, they were absolutely astounded! 11They all rushed out in amazement to Solomon's Colonnade, where the man was holding tightly to Peter and John.

Peter Preaches in the Temple

12Peter saw his opportunity and addressed the crowd. "People of Israel," he said, "what is so surprising about this? And why stare at us as though we had made this man walk by our own power or godliness? 13For it is the God of Abraham, Isaac, and Jacob—the God of all our ancestors—who has brought glory to his servant Jesus by doing this. This is the same Jesus whom you handed over and rejected before Pilate, despite Pilate's decision to release him. 14You rejected this holy, righteous one and instead demanded the release of a murderer. 15You killed the author of life, but

2:46 Or *and sincere hearts.* 3:6a Or *Jesus Christ of Nazareth.* 3:6b Some manuscripts do not include *get up and.*

God raised him from the dead. And we are witnesses of this fact!

¹⁶"Through faith in the name of Jesus, this man was healed—and you know how crippled he was before. Faith in Jesus' name has healed him before your very eyes.

¹⁷"Friends,* I realize that what you and your leaders did to Jesus was done in ignorance. ¹⁸But God was fulfilling what all the prophets had foretold about the Messiah—that he must suffer these things. ¹⁹Now repent of your sins and turn to God, so that your sins may be wiped away. ²⁰Then times of refreshment will come from the presence of the Lord, and he will again send you Jesus, your appointed Messiah. ²¹For he must remain in heaven until the time for the final restoration of all things, as God promised long ago through his holy prophets. ²²Moses said, 'The LORD your God will raise up for you a Prophet like me from among your own people. Listen carefully to everything he tells you.'* ²³Then Moses said, 'Anyone who will not listen to that Prophet will be completely cut off from God's people.'*

²⁴"Starting with Samuel, every prophet spoke about what is happening today. ²⁵You are the children of those prophets, and you are included in the covenant God promised to your ancestors. For God said to Abraham, 'Through your descendants* all the families on earth will be blessed.' ²⁶When God raised up his servant, Jesus, he sent him first to you people of Israel, to bless you by turning each of you back from your sinful ways."

Peter and John before the Council

4 While Peter and John were speaking to the people, they were confronted by the priests, the captain of the Temple guard, and some of the Sadducees. ²These leaders were very disturbed that Peter and John were teaching the people that through Jesus there is a resurrection of the dead. ³They arrested them and, since it was already evening, put them in jail until morning. ⁴But many of the people who heard their message believed it, so the number of men who believed now totaled about 5,000.

⁵The next day the council of all the rulers and elders and teachers of religious law met in Jerusalem. ⁶Annas the high priest was there, along with Caiaphas, John, Alexander, and other relatives of the high priest. ⁷They brought in the two disciples and demanded, "By what power, or in whose name, have you done this?"

⁸Then Peter, filled with the Holy Spirit, said to them, "Rulers and elders of our people, ⁹are we being questioned today because we've done a good deed for a crippled man? Do you want to know how he was healed? ¹⁰Let me clearly state to all of you and to all the people of

3:17 Greek *Brothers.* **3:22** Deut 18:15. **3:23** Deut 18:19; Lev 23:29. **3:25** Greek *your seed;* see Gen 12:3; 22:18.

Israel that he was healed by the powerful name of Jesus Christ the Nazarene,* the man you crucified but whom God raised from the dead. [11]For Jesus is the one referred to in the Scriptures, where it says,

'The stone that you builders
      rejected
   has now become the
      cornerstone.'*

[12]There is salvation in no one else! God has given no other name under heaven by which we must be saved."

[13]The members of the council were amazed when they saw the boldness of Peter and John, for they could see that they were ordinary men with no special training in the Scriptures. They also recognized them as men who had been with Jesus. [14]But since they could see the man who had been healed standing right there among them, there was nothing the council could say. [15]So they ordered Peter and John out of the council chamber* and conferred among themselves.

[16]"What should we do with these men?" they asked each other. "We can't deny that they have performed a miraculous sign, and everybody in Jerusalem knows about it. [17]But to keep them from spreading their propaganda any further, we must warn them not to speak to anyone in Jesus' name again." [18]So they called the apostles back in and commanded them never again to speak or teach in the name of Jesus.

[19]But Peter and John replied, "Do you think God wants us to obey you rather than him? [20]We cannot stop telling about everything we have seen and heard."

[21]The council then threatened them further, but they finally let them go because they didn't know how to punish them without starting a riot. For everyone was praising God [22]for this miraculous sign—the healing of a man who had been lame for more than forty years.

The Believers Pray for Courage
[23]As soon as they were freed, Peter and John returned to the other believers and told them what the leading priests and elders had said. [24]When they heard the report, all the believers lifted their voices together in prayer to God: "O Sovereign Lord, Creator of heaven and earth, the sea, and everything in them—[25]you spoke long ago by the Holy Spirit through our ancestor David, your servant, saying,

'Why were the nations so angry?
   Why did they waste their time
      with futile plans?
[26] The kings of the earth prepared
      for battle;
   the rulers gathered together
against the Lord
   and against his Messiah.'*

4:10 Or *Jesus Christ of Nazareth.* 4:11 Ps 118:22. 4:15 Greek *the Sanhedrin.* 4:25-26 Or *his anointed one;* or *his Christ.* Ps 2:1-2.

²⁷"In fact, this has happened here in this very city! For Herod Antipas, Pontius Pilate the governor, the Gentiles, and the people of Israel were all united against Jesus, your holy servant, whom you anointed. ²⁸But everything they did was determined beforehand according to your will. ²⁹And now, O Lord, hear their threats, and give us, your servants, great boldness in preaching your word. ³⁰Stretch out your hand with healing power; may miraculous signs and wonders be done through the name of your holy servant Jesus."

³¹After this prayer, the meeting place shook, and they were all filled with the Holy Spirit. Then they preached the word of God with boldness.

The Believers Share Their Possessions

³²All the believers were united in heart and mind. And they felt that what they owned was not their own, so they shared everything they had. ³³The apostles testified powerfully to the resurrection of the Lord Jesus, and God's great blessing was upon them all. ³⁴There were no needy people among them, because those who owned land or houses would sell them ³⁵and bring the money to the apostles to give to those in need.

³⁶For instance, there was Joseph, the one the apostles nicknamed Barnabas (which means "Son of Encouragement"). He was from the tribe of Levi and came from the island of Cyprus. ³⁷He sold a field he owned and brought the money to the apostles.

Ananias and Sapphira

5 But there was a certain man named Ananias who, with his wife, Sapphira, sold some property. ²He brought part of the money to the apostles, claiming it was the full amount. With his wife's consent, he kept the rest.

³Then Peter said, "Ananias, why have you let Satan fill your heart? You lied to the Holy Spirit, and you kept some of the money for yourself. ⁴The property was yours to sell or not sell, as you wished. And after selling it, the money was also yours to give away. How could you do a thing like this? You weren't lying to us but to God!"

⁵As soon as Ananias heard these words, he fell to the floor and died. Everyone who heard about it was terrified. ⁶Then some young men got up, wrapped him in a sheet, and took him out and buried him.

⁷About three hours later his wife came in, not knowing what had happened. ⁸Peter asked her, "Was this the price you and your husband received for your land?"

"Yes," she replied, "that was the price."

⁹And Peter said, "How could the two of you even think of conspiring to test the Spirit of the Lord like this?

The young men who buried your husband are just outside the door, and they will carry you out, too."

¹⁰Instantly, she fell to the floor and died. When the young men came in and saw that she was dead, they carried her out and buried her beside her husband. ¹¹Great fear gripped the entire church and everyone else who heard what had happened.

The Apostles Heal Many

¹²The apostles were performing many miraculous signs and wonders among the people. And all the believers were meeting regularly at the Temple in the area known as Solomon's Colonnade. ¹³But no one else dared to join them, even though all the people had high regard for them. ¹⁴Yet more and more people believed and were brought to the Lord—crowds of both men and women. ¹⁵As a result of the apostles' work, sick people were brought out into the streets on beds and mats so that Peter's shadow might fall across some of them as he went by. ¹⁶Crowds came from the villages around Jerusalem, bringing their sick and those possessed by evil* spirits, and they were all healed.

The Apostles Meet Opposition

¹⁷The high priest and his officials, who were Sadducees, were filled with jealousy. ¹⁸They arrested the apostles and put them in the public jail. ¹⁹But an angel of the Lord came at night, opened the gates of the jail, and brought them out. Then he told them, ²⁰"Go to the Temple and give the people this message of life!"

²¹So at daybreak the apostles entered the Temple, as they were told, and immediately began teaching.

When the high priest and his officials arrived, they convened the high council*—the full assembly of the elders of Israel. Then they sent for the apostles to be brought from the jail for trial. ²²But when the Temple guards went to the jail, the men were gone. So they returned to the council and reported, ²³"The jail was securely locked, with the guards standing outside, but when we opened the gates, no one was there!"

²⁴When the captain of the Temple guard and the leading priests heard this, they were perplexed, wondering where it would all end. ²⁵Then someone arrived with startling news: "The men you put in jail are standing in the Temple, teaching the people!"

²⁶The captain went with his Temple guards and arrested the apostles, but without violence, for they were afraid the people would stone them. ²⁷Then they brought the apostles before the high council, where the high priest confronted them. ²⁸"We gave you strict orders never again to teach in this man's

5:16 Greek unclean.   5:21 Greek Sanhedrin; also in 5:27, 41.

name!" he said. "Instead, you have filled all Jerusalem with your teaching about him, and you want to make us responsible for his death!"

²⁹But Peter and the apostles replied, "We must obey God rather than any human authority. ³⁰The God of our ancestors raised Jesus from the dead after you killed him by hanging him on a cross.* ³¹Then God put him in the place of honor at his right hand as Prince and Savior. He did this so the people of Israel would repent of their sins and be forgiven. ³²We are witnesses of these things and so is the Holy Spirit, who is given by God to those who obey him."

³³When they heard this, the high council was furious and decided to kill them. ³⁴But one member, a Pharisee named Gamaliel, who was an expert in religious law and respected by all the people, stood up and ordered that the men be sent outside the council chamber for a while. ³⁵Then he said to his colleagues, "Men of Israel, take care what you are planning to do to these men! ³⁶Some time ago there was that fellow Theudas, who pretended to be someone great. About 400 others joined him, but he was killed, and all his followers went their various ways. The whole movement came to nothing. ³⁷After him, at the time of the census, there was Judas of Galilee. He got people

to follow him, but he was killed, too, and all his followers were scattered.

³⁸"So my advice is, leave these men alone. Let them go. If they are planning and doing these things merely on their own, it will soon be overthrown. ³⁹But if it is from God, you will not be able to overthrow them. You may even find yourselves fighting against God!"

⁴⁰The others accepted his advice. They called in the apostles and had them flogged. Then they ordered them never again to speak in the name of Jesus, and they let them go.

⁴¹The apostles left the high council rejoicing that God had counted them worthy to suffer disgrace for the name of Jesus.* ⁴²And every day, in the Temple and from house to house, they continued to teach and preach this message: "Jesus is the Messiah."

Seven Men Chosen to Serve

6 But as the believers* rapidly multiplied, there were rumblings of discontent. The Greek-speaking believers complained about the Hebrew-speaking believers, saying that their widows were being discriminated against in the daily distribution of food.

²So the Twelve called a meeting of all the believers. They said, "We apostles should spend our time teaching the word of God, not running a food program. ³And so, brothers, select seven men who are

5:30 Greek *on a tree.* **5:41** Greek *for the name.* **6:1** Greek *disciples;* also in 6:2, 7.

well respected and are full of the Spirit and wisdom. We will give them this responsibility. [4]Then we apostles can spend our time in prayer and teaching the word."

[5]Everyone liked this idea, and they chose the following: Stephen (a man full of faith and the Holy Spirit), Philip, Procorus, Nicanor, Timon, Parmenas, and Nicolas of Antioch (an earlier convert to the Jewish faith). [6]These seven were presented to the apostles, who prayed for them as they laid their hands on them.

[7]So God's message continued to spread. The number of believers greatly increased in Jerusalem, and many of the Jewish priests were converted, too.

Stephen Is Arrested

[8]Stephen, a man full of God's grace and power, performed amazing miracles and signs among the people. [9]But one day some men from the Synagogue of Freed Slaves, as it was called, started to debate with him. They were Jews from Cyrene, Alexandria, Cilicia, and the province of Asia. [10]None of them could stand against the wisdom and the Spirit with which Stephen spoke.

[11]So they persuaded some men to lie about Stephen, saying, "We heard him blaspheme Moses, and even God." [12]This roused the people, the elders, and the teachers of religious law. So they arrested Stephen and brought him before the high council.*

[13]The lying witnesses said, "This man is always speaking against the holy Temple and against the law of Moses. [14]We have heard him say that this Jesus of Nazareth* will destroy the Temple and change the customs Moses handed down to us."

[15]At this point everyone in the high council stared at Stephen, because his face became as bright as an angel's.

Stephen Addresses the Council

7 Then the high priest asked Stephen, "Are these accusations true?"

[2]This was Stephen's reply: "Brothers and fathers, listen to me. Our glorious God appeared to our ancestor Abraham in Mesopotamia before he settled in Haran.* [3]God told him, 'Leave your native land and your relatives, and come into the land that I will show you.'* [4]So Abraham left the land of the Chaldeans and lived in Haran until his father died. Then God brought him here to the land where you now live.

[5]"But God gave him no inheritance here, not even one square foot of land. God did promise, however, that eventually the whole land would belong to Abraham and his descendants—even though he had no children yet. [6]God also told him

6:12 Greek Sanhedrin; also in 6:15. 6:14 Or Jesus the Nazarene. 7:2 Mesopotamia was the region now called Iraq. Haran was a city in what is now called Syria. 7:3 Gen 12:1.

that his descendants would live in a foreign land, where they would be oppressed as slaves for 400 years. [7]"But I will punish the nation that enslaves them,' God said, 'and in the end they will come out and worship me here in this place.'*

[8]"God also gave Abraham the covenant of circumcision at that time. So when Abraham became the father of Isaac, he circumcised him on the eighth day. And the practice was continued when Isaac became the father of Jacob, and when Jacob became the father of the twelve patriarchs of the Israelite nation.

[9]"These patriarchs were jealous of their brother Joseph, and they sold him to be a slave in Egypt. But God was with him [10]and rescued him from all his troubles. And God gave him favor before Pharaoh, king of Egypt. God also gave Joseph unusual wisdom, so that Pharaoh appointed him governor over all of Egypt and put him in charge of the palace.

[11]"But a famine came upon Egypt and Canaan. There was great misery, and our ancestors ran out of food. [12]Jacob heard that there was still grain in Egypt, so he sent his sons—our ancestors—to buy some. [13]The second time they went, Joseph revealed his identity to his brothers,* and they were introduced to Pharaoh. [14]Then Joseph sent for his father, Jacob, and all his relatives to come to Egypt, seventy-five persons in all. [15]So Jacob went to Egypt. He died there, as did our ancestors. [16]Their bodies were taken to Shechem and buried in the tomb Abraham had bought for a certain price from Hamor's sons in Shechem.

[17]"As the time drew near when God would fulfill his promise to Abraham, the number of our people in Egypt greatly increased. [18]But then a new king came to the throne of Egypt who knew nothing about Joseph. [19]This king exploited our people and oppressed them, forcing parents to abandon their newborn babies so they would die.

[20]"At that time Moses was born—a beautiful child in God's eyes. His parents cared for him at home for three months. [21]When they had to abandon him, Pharaoh's daughter adopted him and raised him as her own son. [22]Moses was taught all the wisdom of the Egyptians, and he was powerful in both speech and action.

[23]"One day when Moses was forty years old, he decided to visit his relatives, the people of Israel. [24]He saw an Egyptian mistreating an Israelite. So Moses came to the man's defense and avenged him, killing the Egyptian. [25]Moses assumed his fellow Israelites would realize that God had sent him to rescue them, but they didn't.

7:5-7 Gen 12:7; 15:13-14; Exod 3:12. **7:13** Other manuscripts read *Joseph was recognized by his brothers.*

26"The next day he visited them again and saw two men of Israel fighting. He tried to be a peacemaker. 'Men,' he said, 'you are brothers. Why are you fighting each other?'

27"But the man in the wrong pushed Moses aside. 'Who made you a ruler and judge over us?' he asked. 28'Are you going to kill me as you killed that Egyptian yesterday?' 29When Moses heard that, he fled the country and lived as a foreigner in the land of Midian. There his two sons were born.

30"Forty years later, in the desert near Mount Sinai, an angel appeared to Moses in the flame of a burning bush. 31When Moses saw it, he was amazed at the sight. As he went to take a closer look, the voice of the LORD called out to him, 32'I am the God of your ancestors—the God of Abraham, Isaac, and Jacob.' Moses shook with terror and did not dare to look.

33"Then the LORD said to him, 'Take off your sandals, for you are standing on holy ground. 34I have certainly seen the oppression of my people in Egypt. I have heard their groans and have come down to rescue them. Now go, for I am sending you back to Egypt.'*

35"So God sent back the same man his people had previously rejected when they demanded, 'Who made you a ruler and judge over us?' Through the angel who appeared to him in the burning bush, God sent Moses to be their ruler and savior. 36And by means of many wonders and miraculous signs, he led them out of Egypt, through the Red Sea, and through the wilderness for forty years.

37"Moses himself told the people of Israel, 'God will raise up for you a Prophet like me from among your own people.'* 38Moses was with our ancestors, the assembly of God's people in the wilderness, when the angel spoke to him at Mount Sinai. And there Moses received life-giving words to pass on to us.*

39"But our ancestors refused to listen to Moses. They rejected him and wanted to return to Egypt. 40They told Aaron, 'Make us some gods who can lead us, for we don't know what has become of this Moses, who brought us out of Egypt.' 41So they made an idol shaped like a calf, and they sacrificed to it and celebrated over this thing they had made. 42Then God turned away from them and abandoned them to serve the stars of heaven as their gods! In the book of the prophets it is written,

'Was it to me you were bringing
    sacrifices and offerings
during those forty years in the
    wilderness, Israel?
43 No, you carried your pagan gods—
    the shrine of Molech,
    the star of your god Rephan,

7:31-34 Exod 3:5-10.   7:37 Deut 18:15.   7:38 Some manuscripts read to you.

and the images you made to
worship them.
So I will send you into exile
as far away as Babylon.'*

⁴⁴"Our ancestors carried the Tabernacle* with them through the wilderness. It was constructed according to the plan God had shown to Moses. ⁴⁵Years later, when Joshua led our ancestors in battle against the nations that God drove out of this land, the Tabernacle was taken with them into their new territory. And it stayed there until the time of King David.

⁴⁶"David found favor with God and asked for the privilege of building a permanent Temple for the God of Jacob.* ⁴⁷But it was Solomon who actually built it. ⁴⁸However, the Most High doesn't live in temples made by human hands. As the prophet says,

⁴⁹ 'Heaven is my throne,
    and the earth is my footstool.
  Could you build me a temple
      as good as that?'
    asks the LORD.
  'Could you build me such
      a resting place?
⁵⁰   Didn't my hands make both
      heaven and earth?'*

⁵¹"You stubborn people! You are heathen* at heart and deaf to the truth. Must you forever resist the Holy Spirit? That's what your ancestors did, and so do you! ⁵²Name one prophet your ancestors didn't persecute! They even killed the ones who predicted the coming of the Righteous One—the Messiah whom you betrayed and murdered. ⁵³You deliberately disobeyed God's law, even though you received it from the hands of angels."

⁵⁴The Jewish leaders were infuriated by Stephen's accusation, and they shook their fists at him in rage.* ⁵⁵But Stephen, full of the Holy Spirit, gazed steadily into heaven and saw the glory of God, and he saw Jesus standing in the place of honor at God's right hand. ⁵⁶And he told them, "Look, I see the heavens opened and the Son of Man standing in the place of honor at God's right hand!"

⁵⁷Then they put their hands over their ears and began shouting. They rushed at him ⁵⁸and dragged him out of the city and began to stone him. His accusers took off their coats and laid them at the feet of a young man named Saul.*

⁵⁹As they stoned him, Stephen prayed, "Lord Jesus, receive my spirit." ⁶⁰He fell to his knees, shouting, "Lord, don't charge them with this sin!" And with that, he died.

8 Saul was one of the witnesses, and he agreed completely with the killing of Stephen.

7:42-43 Amos 5:25-27 (Greek version).   7:44 Greek *the tent of witness*.   7:46 Some manuscripts read *the house of Jacob*.   7:49-50 Isa 66:1-2.   7:51 Greek *uncircumcised*.   7:54 Greek *they were grinding their teeth against him*.   7:58 *Saul* is later called Paul; see 13:9.

Persecution Scatters the Believers

A great wave of persecution began that day, sweeping over the church in Jerusalem; and all the believers except the apostles were scattered through the regions of Judea and Samaria. ²(Some devout men came and buried Stephen with great mourning.) ³But Saul was going everywhere to destroy the church. He went from house to house, dragging out both men and women to throw them into prison.

Philip Preaches in Samaria

⁴But the believers who were scattered preached the Good News about Jesus wherever they went. ⁵Philip, for example, went to the city of Samaria and told the people there about the Messiah. ⁶Crowds listened intently to Philip because they were eager to hear his message and see the miraculous signs he did. ⁷Many evil* spirits were cast out, screaming as they left their victims. And many who had been paralyzed or lame were healed. ⁸So there was great joy in that city.

⁹A man named Simon had been a sorcerer there for many years, amazing the people of Samaria and claiming to be someone great. ¹⁰Everyone, from the least to the greatest, often spoke of him as "the Great One—the Power of God." ¹¹They listened closely to him because for a long time he had astounded them with his magic.

¹²But now the people believed Philip's message of Good News concerning the Kingdom of God and the name of Jesus Christ. As a result, many men and women were baptized. ¹³Then Simon himself believed and was baptized. He began following Philip wherever he went, and he was amazed by the signs and great miracles Philip performed.

¹⁴When the apostles in Jerusalem heard that the people of Samaria had accepted God's message, they sent Peter and John there. ¹⁵As soon as they arrived, they prayed for these new believers to receive the Holy Spirit. ¹⁶The Holy Spirit had not yet come upon any of them, for they had only been baptized in the name of the Lord Jesus. ¹⁷Then Peter and John laid their hands upon these believers, and they received the Holy Spirit.

¹⁸When Simon saw that the Spirit was given when the apostles laid their hands on people, he offered them money to buy this power. ¹⁹"Let me have this power, too," he exclaimed, "so that when I lay my hands on people, they will receive the Holy Spirit!"

²⁰But Peter replied, "May your money be destroyed with you for thinking God's gift can be bought! ²¹You can have no part in this, for your heart is not right with God. ²²Repent of your wickedness and pray to the Lord. Perhaps he will forgive your evil thoughts, ²³for I

8:7 Greek unclean.

can see that you are full of bitter jealousy and are held captive by sin."

²⁴"Pray to the Lord for me," Simon exclaimed, "that these terrible things you've said won't happen to me!"

²⁵After testifying and preaching the word of the Lord in Samaria, Peter and John returned to Jerusalem. And they stopped in many Samaritan villages along the way to preach the Good News.

Philip and the Ethiopian Eunuch

²⁶As for Philip, an angel of the Lord said to him, "Go south* down the desert road that runs from Jerusalem to Gaza." ²⁷So he started out, and he met the treasurer of Ethiopia, a eunuch of great authority under the Kandake, the queen of Ethiopia. The eunuch had gone to Jerusalem to worship, ²⁸and he was now returning. Seated in his carriage, he was reading aloud from the book of the prophet Isaiah.

²⁹The Holy Spirit said to Philip, "Go over and walk along beside the carriage."

³⁰Philip ran over and heard the man reading from the prophet Isaiah. Philip asked, "Do you understand what you are reading?"

³¹The man replied, "How can I, unless someone instructs me?" And he urged Philip to come up into the carriage and sit with him.

³²The passage of Scripture he had been reading was this:

"He was led like a sheep to the
　slaughter.
And as a lamb is silent before
　the shearers,
he did not open his mouth.
³³ He was humiliated and received
　no justice.
Who can speak of his
　descendants?
For his life was taken from
　the earth."*

³⁴The eunuch asked Philip, "Tell me, was the prophet talking about himself or someone else?" ³⁵So beginning with this same Scripture, Philip told him the Good News about Jesus.

³⁶As they rode along, they came to some water, and the eunuch said, "Look! There's some water! Why can't I be baptized?"* ³⁸He ordered the carriage to stop, and they went down into the water, and Philip baptized him.

³⁹When they came up out of the water, the Spirit of the Lord snatched Philip away. The eunuch never saw him again but went on his way rejoicing. ⁴⁰Meanwhile, Philip found himself farther north at the town of Azotus. He preached the Good News there and in every town along the way until he came to Caesarea.

8:26 Or *Go at noon.* 8:32-33 Isa 53:7-8 (Greek version). 8:36 Some manuscripts add verse 37, *"You can," Philip answered, "if you believe with all your heart." And the eunuch replied, "I believe that Jesus Christ is the Son of God."*

Saul's Conversion

9 Meanwhile, Saul was uttering threats with every breath and was eager to kill the Lord's followers.* So he went to the high priest. [2]He requested letters addressed to the synagogues in Damascus, asking for their cooperation in the arrest of any followers of the Way he found there. He wanted to bring them—both men and women—back to Jerusalem in chains.

[3]As he was approaching Damascus on this mission, a light from heaven suddenly shone down around him. [4]He fell to the ground and heard a voice saying to him, "Saul! Saul! Why are you persecuting me?"

[5]"Who are you, lord?" Saul asked.

And the voice replied, "I am Jesus, the one you are persecuting! [6]Now get up and go into the city, and you will be told what you must do."

[7]The men with Saul stood speechless, for they heard the sound of someone's voice but saw no one! [8]Saul picked himself up off the ground, but when he opened his eyes he was blind. So his companions led him by the hand to Damascus. [9]He remained there blind for three days and did not eat or drink.

[10]Now there was a believer* in Damascus named Ananias. The Lord spoke to him in a vision, calling, "Ananias!"

"Yes, Lord!" he replied.

[11]The Lord said, "Go over to Straight Street, to the house of Judas. When you get there, ask for a man from Tarsus named Saul. He is praying to me right now. [12]I have shown him a vision of a man named Ananias coming in and laying hands on him so he can see again."

[13]"But Lord," exclaimed Ananias, "I've heard many people talk about the terrible things this man has done to the believers* in Jerusalem! [14]And he is authorized by the leading priests to arrest everyone who calls upon your name."

[15]But the Lord said, "Go, for Saul is my chosen instrument to take my message to the Gentiles and to kings, as well as to the people of Israel. [16]And I will show him how much he must suffer for my name's sake."

[17]So Ananias went and found Saul. He laid his hands on him and said, "Brother Saul, the Lord Jesus, who appeared to you on the road, has sent me so that you might regain your sight and be filled with the Holy Spirit." [18]Instantly something like scales fell from Saul's eyes, and he regained his sight. Then he got up and was baptized. [19]Afterward he ate some food and regained his strength.

Saul in Damascus and Jerusalem

Saul stayed with the believers* in Damascus for a few days. [20]And

---

9:1 Greek *disciples.* **9:10** Greek *disciple;* also in 9:26, 36. **9:13** Greek *God's holy people;* also in 9:32, 41. **9:19** Greek *disciples;* also in 9:26, 38.

immediately he began preaching about Jesus in the synagogues, saying, "He is indeed the Son of God!"

21All who heard him were amazed. "Isn't this the same man who caused such devastation among Jesus' followers in Jerusalem?" they asked. "And didn't he come here to arrest them and take them in chains to the leading priests?"

22Saul's preaching became more and more powerful, and the Jews in Damascus couldn't refute his proofs that Jesus was indeed the Messiah. 23After a while some of the Jews plotted together to kill him. 24They were watching for him day and night at the city gate so they could murder him, but Saul was told about their plot. 25So during the night, some of the other believers* lowered him in a large basket through an opening in the city wall.

26When Saul arrived in Jerusalem, he tried to meet with the believers, but they were all afraid of him. They did not believe he had truly become a believer! 27Then Barnabas brought him to the apostles and told them how Saul had seen the Lord on the way to Damascus and how the Lord had spoken to Saul. He also told them that Saul had preached boldly in the name of Jesus in Damascus.

28So Saul stayed with the apostles and went all around Jerusalem with them, preaching boldly in the name of the Lord. 29He debated with some Greek-speaking Jews, but they tried to murder him. 30When the believers* heard about this, they took him down to Caesarea and sent him away to Tarsus, his hometown.

31The church then had peace throughout Judea, Galilee, and Samaria, and it became stronger as the believers lived in the fear of the Lord. And with the encouragement of the Holy Spirit, it also grew in numbers.

Peter Heals Aeneas and Raises Dorcas

32Meanwhile, Peter traveled from place to place, and he came down to visit the believers in the town of Lydda. 33There he met a man named Aeneas, who had been paralyzed and bedridden for eight years. 34Peter said to him, "Aeneas, Jesus Christ heals you! Get up, and roll up your sleeping mat!" And he was healed instantly. 35Then the whole population of Lydda and Sharon saw Aeneas walking around, and they turned to the Lord.

36There was a believer in Joppa named Tabitha (which in Greek is Dorcas*). She was always doing kind things for others and helping the poor. 37About this time she became ill and died. Her body was washed for burial and laid in an upstairs room. 38But the believers had heard that Peter was nearby at Lydda, so

9:25 Greek his disciples.   9:30 Greek brothers.   9:36 The names Tabitha in Aramaic and Dorcas in Greek both mean "gazelle."

they sent two men to beg him, "Please come as soon as possible!"

39So Peter returned with them; and as soon as he arrived, they took him to the upstairs room. The room was filled with widows who were weeping and showing him the coats and other clothes Dorcas had made for them. 40But Peter asked them all to leave the room; then he knelt and prayed. Turning to the body he said, "Get up, Tabitha." And she opened her eyes! When she saw Peter, she sat up! 41He gave her his hand and helped her up. Then he called in the widows and all the believers, and he presented her to them alive.

42The news spread through the whole town, and many believed in the Lord. 43And Peter stayed a long time in Joppa, living with Simon, a tanner of hides.

Cornelius Calls for Peter

10 In Caesarea there lived a Roman army officer* named Cornelius, who was a captain of the Italian Regiment. 2He was a devout, God-fearing man, as was everyone in his household. He gave generously to the poor and prayed regularly to God. 3One afternoon about three o'clock, he had a vision in which he saw an angel of God coming toward him. "Cornelius!" the angel said.

4Cornelius stared at him in terror. "What is it, sir?" he asked the angel. And the angel replied, "Your prayers and gifts to the poor have been received by God as an offering! 5Now send some men to Joppa, and summon a man named Simon Peter. 6He is staying with Simon, a tanner who lives near the seashore."

7As soon as the angel was gone, Cornelius called two of his household servants and a devout soldier, one of his personal attendants. 8He told them what had happened and sent them off to Joppa.

Peter Visits Cornelius

9The next day as Cornelius's messengers were nearing the town, Peter went up on the flat roof to pray. It was about noon, 10and he was hungry. But while a meal was being prepared, he fell into a trance. 11He saw the sky open, and something like a large sheet was let down by its four corners. 12In the sheet were all sorts of animals, reptiles, and birds. 13Then a voice said to him, "Get up, Peter; kill and eat them."

14"No, Lord," Peter declared. "I have never eaten anything that our Jewish laws have declared impure and unclean.*"

15But the voice spoke again: "Do not call something unclean if God has made it clean." 16The same vision was repeated three times. Then the sheet was suddenly pulled up to heaven.

17Peter was very perplexed. What could the vision mean? Just then the men sent by Cornelius found

10:1 Greek *a centurion;* similarly in 10:22. 10:14 Greek *anything common and unclean.*

Simon's house. Standing outside the gate, [18]they asked if a man named Simon Peter was staying there.

[19]Meanwhile, as Peter was puzzling over the vision, the Holy Spirit said to him, "Three men have come looking for you. [20]Get up, go downstairs, and go with them without hesitation. Don't worry, for I have sent them."

[21]So Peter went down and said, "I'm the man you are looking for. Why have you come?"

[22]They said, "We were sent by Cornelius, a Roman officer. He is a devout and God-fearing man, well respected by all the Jews. A holy angel instructed him to summon you to his house so that he can hear your message." [23]So Peter invited the men to stay for the night. The next day he went with them, accompanied by some of the brothers from Joppa.

[24]They arrived in Caesarea the following day. Cornelius was waiting for them and had called together his relatives and close friends. [25]As Peter entered his home, Cornelius fell at his feet and worshiped him. [26]But Peter pulled him up and said, "Stand up! I'm a human being just like you!" [27]So they talked together and went inside, where many others were assembled.

[28]Peter told them, "You know it is against our laws for a Jewish man to enter a Gentile home like this or to associate with you. But God has shown me that I should no longer think of anyone as impure or unclean. [29]So I came without objection as soon as I was sent for. Now tell me why you sent for me."

[30]Cornelius replied, "Four days ago I was praying in my house about this same time, three o'clock in the afternoon. Suddenly, a man in dazzling clothes was standing in front of me. [31]He told me, 'Cornelius, your prayer has been heard, and your gifts to the poor have been noticed by God! [32]Now send messengers to Joppa, and summon a man named Simon Peter. He is staying in the home of Simon, a tanner who lives near the seashore.' [33]So I sent for you at once, and it was good of you to come. Now we are all here, waiting before God to hear the message the Lord has given you."

The Gentiles Hear the Good News

[34]Then Peter replied, "I see very clearly that God shows no favoritism. [35]In every nation he accepts those who fear him and do what is right. [36]This is the message of Good News for the people of Israel—that there is peace with God through Jesus Christ, who is Lord of all. [37]You know what happened throughout Judea, beginning in Galilee, after John began preaching his message of baptism. [38]And you know that God anointed Jesus of Nazareth with the Holy Spirit and with power. Then Jesus went around doing good

and healing all who were oppressed by the devil, for God was with him.

[39]"And we apostles are witnesses of all he did throughout Judea and in Jerusalem. They put him to death by hanging him on a cross,* [40]but God raised him to life on the third day. Then God allowed him to appear, [41]not to the general public,* but to us whom God had chosen in advance to be his witnesses. We were those who ate and drank with him after he rose from the dead. [42]And he ordered us to preach everywhere and to testify that Jesus is the one appointed by God to be the judge of all—the living and the dead. [43]He is the one all the prophets testified about, saying that everyone who believes in him will have their sins forgiven through his name."

The Gentiles Receive the Holy Spirit

[44]Even as Peter was saying these things, the Holy Spirit fell upon all who were listening to the message. [45]The Jewish believers* who came with Peter were amazed that the gift of the Holy Spirit had been poured out on the Gentiles, too. [46]For they heard them speaking in other tongues* and praising God.

Then Peter asked, [47]"Can anyone object to their being baptized, now that they have received the Holy Spirit just as we did?" [48]So he gave orders for them to be baptized in the name of Jesus Christ. Afterward Cornelius asked him to stay with them for several days.

Peter Explains His Actions

11 Soon the news reached the apostles and other believers* in Judea that the Gentiles had received the word of God. [2]But when Peter arrived back in Jerusalem, the Jewish believers* criticized him. [3]"You entered the home of Gentiles* and even ate with them!" they said.

[4]Then Peter told them exactly what had happened. [5]"I was in the town of Joppa," he said, "and while I was praying, I went into a trance and saw a vision. Something like a large sheet was let down by its four corners from the sky. And it came right down to me. [6]When I looked inside the sheet, I saw all sorts of tame and wild animals, reptiles, and birds. [7]And I heard a voice say, 'Get up, Peter; kill and eat them.'

[8]" 'No, Lord,' I replied. 'I have never eaten anything that our Jewish laws have declared impure or unclean.*'

[9]"But the voice from heaven spoke again: 'Do not call something unclean if God has made it clean.' [10]This happened three times before the sheet and all it contained was pulled back up to heaven.

[11]"Just then three men who had

10:39 Greek *on a tree.* **10:41** Greek *the people.* **10:45** Greek *The faithful ones of the circumcision.*
10:46 Or *in other languages.* **11:1** Greek *brothers.* **11:2** Greek *those of the circumcision.*
11:3 Greek *of uncircumcised men.* **11:8** Greek *anything common or unclean.*

been sent from Caesarea arrived at the house where we were staying. [12]The Holy Spirit told me to go with them and not to worry that they were Gentiles. These six brothers here accompanied me, and we soon entered the home of the man who had sent for us. [13]He told us how an angel had appeared to him in his home and had told him, 'Send messengers to Joppa, and summon a man named Simon Peter. [14]He will tell you how you and everyone in your household can be saved!'

[15]"As I began to speak," Peter continued, "the Holy Spirit fell on them, just as he fell on us at the beginning. [16]Then I thought of the Lord's words when he said, 'John baptized with* water, but you will be baptized with the Holy Spirit.' [17]And since God gave these Gentiles the same gift he gave us when we believed in the Lord Jesus Christ, who was I to stand in God's way?"

[18]When the others heard this, they stopped objecting and began praising God. They said, "We can see that God has also given the Gentiles the privilege of repenting of their sins and receiving eternal life."

The Church in Antioch of Syria

[19]Meanwhile, the believers who had been scattered during the persecution after Stephen's death traveled as far as Phoenicia, Cyprus, and Antioch of Syria. They preached the word of God, but only to Jews. [20]However, some of the believers who went to Antioch from Cyprus and Cyrene began preaching to the Gentiles* about the Lord Jesus. [21]The power of the Lord was with them, and a large number of these Gentiles believed and turned to the Lord.

[22]When the church at Jerusalem heard what had happened, they sent Barnabas to Antioch. [23]When he arrived and saw this evidence of God's blessing, he was filled with joy, and he encouraged the believers to stay true to the Lord. [24]Barnabas was a good man, full of the Holy Spirit and strong in faith. And many people were brought to the Lord.

[25]Then Barnabas went on to Tarsus to look for Saul. [26]When he found him, he brought him back to Antioch. Both of them stayed there with the church for a full year, teaching large crowds of people. (It was at Antioch that the believers* were first called Christians.)

[27]During this time some prophets traveled from Jerusalem to Antioch. [28]One of them named Agabus stood up in one of the meetings and predicted by the Spirit that a great famine was coming upon the entire Roman world. (This was fulfilled during the reign of Claudius.) [29]So the believers in Antioch decided to send relief to the brothers and sisters* in Judea, everyone giving as

11:16 Or *in;* also in 11:16b.   **11:20** Greek *the Hellenists* (i.e., those who speak Greek); other manuscripts read *the Greeks.*   **11:26** Greek *disciples;* also in 11:29.   **11:29** Greek *the brothers.*

much as they could. ³⁰This they did, entrusting their gifts to Barnabas and Saul to take to the elders of the church in Jerusalem.

James Is Killed and Peter Is Imprisoned

12 About that time King Herod Agrippa* began to persecute some believers in the church. ²He had the apostle James (John's brother) killed with a sword. ³When Herod saw how much this pleased the Jewish people, he also arrested Peter. (This took place during the Passover celebration.*) ⁴Then he imprisoned him, placing him under the guard of four squads of four soldiers each. Herod intended to bring Peter out for public trial after the Passover. ⁵But while Peter was in prison, the church prayed very earnestly for him.

Peter's Miraculous Escape from Prison

⁶The night before Peter was to be placed on trial, he was asleep, fastened with two chains between two soldiers. Others stood guard at the prison gate. ⁷Suddenly, there was a bright light in the cell, and an angel of the Lord stood before Peter. The angel struck him on the side to awaken him and said, "Quick! Get up!" And the chains fell off his wrists. ⁸Then the angel told him, "Get dressed and put on your sandals." And he did. "Now put on your coat and follow me," the angel ordered.

⁹So Peter left the cell, following the angel. But all the time he thought it was a vision. He didn't realize it was actually happening. ¹⁰They passed the first and second guard posts and came to the iron gate leading to the city, and this opened for them all by itself. So they passed through and started walking down the street, and then the angel suddenly left him.

¹¹Peter finally came to his senses. "It's really true!" he said. "The Lord has sent his angel and saved me from Herod and from what the Jewish leaders* had planned to do to me!"

¹²When he realized this, he went to the home of Mary, the mother of John Mark, where many were gathered for prayer. ¹³He knocked at the door in the gate, and a servant girl named Rhoda came to open it. ¹⁴When she recognized Peter's voice, she was so overjoyed that, instead of opening the door, she ran back inside and told everyone, "Peter is standing at the door!"

¹⁵"You're out of your mind!" they said. When she insisted, they decided, "It must be his angel."

¹⁶Meanwhile, Peter continued knocking. When they finally opened the door and saw him, they were amazed. ¹⁷He motioned for them to

---

12:1 Greek *Herod the king.* He was the nephew of Herod Antipas and a grandson of Herod the Great. **12:3** Greek *the days of unleavened bread.* **12:11** Or *the Jewish people.*

quiet down and told them how the Lord had led him out of prison. "Tell James and the other brothers what happened," he said. And then he went to another place.

[18]At dawn there was a great commotion among the soldiers about what had happened to Peter. [19]Herod Agrippa ordered a thorough search for him. When he couldn't be found, Herod interrogated the guards and sentenced them to death. Afterward Herod left Judea to stay in Caesarea for a while.

The Death of Herod Agrippa
[20]Now Herod was very angry with the people of Tyre and Sidon. So they sent a delegation to make peace with him because their cities were dependent upon Herod's country for food. The delegates won the support of Blastus, Herod's personal assistant, [21]and an appointment with Herod was granted. When the day arrived, Herod put on his royal robes, sat on his throne, and made a speech to them. [22]The people gave him a great ovation, shouting, "It's the voice of a god, not of a man!"

[23]Instantly, an angel of the Lord struck Herod with a sickness, because he accepted the people's worship instead of giving the glory to God. So he was consumed with worms and died.

[24]Meanwhile, the word of God continued to spread, and there were many new believers.

[25]When Barnabas and Saul had finished their mission to Jerusalem, they returned,* taking John Mark with them.

Barnabas and Saul Are Commissioned
13 Among the prophets and teachers of the church at Antioch of Syria were Barnabas, Simeon (called "the black man"*), Lucius (from Cyrene), Manaen (the childhood companion of King Herod Antipas*), and Saul. [2]One day as these men were worshiping the Lord and fasting, the Holy Spirit said, "Appoint Barnabas and Saul for the special work to which I have called them." [3]So after more fasting and prayer, the men laid their hands on them and sent them on their way.

Paul's First Missionary Journey
[4]So Barnabas and Saul were sent out by the Holy Spirit. They went down to the seaport of Seleucia and then sailed for the island of Cyprus. [5]There, in the town of Salamis, they went to the Jewish synagogues and preached the word of God. John Mark went with them as their assistant.

[6]Afterward they traveled from town to town across the entire island

12:25 Or *mission, they returned to Jerusalem.* Other manuscripts read *mission, they returned from Jerusalem;* still others read *mission, they returned from Jerusalem to Antioch.* 13:1a Greek *who was called Niger.* 13:1b Greek *Herod the tetrarch.*

until finally they reached Paphos, where they met a Jewish sorcerer, a false prophet named Bar-Jesus. [7]He had attached himself to the governor, Sergius Paulus, who was an intelligent man. The governor invited Barnabas and Saul to visit him, for he wanted to hear the word of God. [8]But Elymas, the sorcerer (as his name means in Greek), interfered and urged the governor to pay no attention to what Barnabas and Saul said. He was trying to keep the governor from believing.

[9]Saul, also known as Paul, was filled with the Holy Spirit, and he looked the sorcerer in the eye. [10]Then he said, "You son of the devil, full of every sort of deceit and fraud, and enemy of all that is good! Will you never stop perverting the true ways of the Lord? [11]Watch now, for the Lord has laid his hand of punishment upon you, and you will be struck blind. You will not see the sunlight for some time." Instantly mist and darkness came over the man's eyes, and he began groping around begging for someone to take his hand and lead him.

[12]When the governor saw what had happened, he became a believer, for he was astonished at the teaching about the Lord.

Paul Preaches in Antioch of Pisidia

[13]Paul and his companions then left Paphos by ship for Pamphylia, landing at the port town of Perga. There John Mark left them and returned to Jerusalem. [14]But Paul and Barnabas traveled inland to Antioch of Pisidia.*

On the Sabbath they went to the synagogue for the services. [15]After the usual readings from the books of Moses* and the prophets, those in charge of the service sent them this message: "Brothers, if you have any word of encouragement for the people, come and give it."

[16]So Paul stood, lifted his hand to quiet them, and started speaking. "Men of Israel," he said, "and you God-fearing Gentiles, listen to me. [17]"The God of this nation of Israel chose our ancestors and made them multiply and grow strong during their stay in Egypt. Then with a powerful arm he led them out of their slavery. [18]He put up with them* through forty years of wandering in the wilderness. [19]Then he destroyed seven nations in Canaan and gave their land to Israel as an inheritance. [20]All this took about 450 years.

"After that, God gave them judges to rule until the time of Samuel the prophet. [21]Then the people begged for a king, and God gave them Saul son of Kish, a man of the tribe of Benjamin, who reigned for forty years. [22]But God removed Saul and replaced him with David, a man about whom God said, 'I have found

13:13-14 *Pamphylia* and *Pisidia* were districts in what is now Turkey. 13:15 Greek *from the law.*
13:18 Some manuscripts read *He cared for them;* compare Deut 1:31.

David son of Jesse, a man after my own heart. He will do everything I want him to do.'*

²³"And it is one of King David's descendants, Jesus, who is God's promised Savior of Israel! ²⁴Before he came, John the Baptist preached that all the people of Israel needed to repent of their sins and turn to God and be baptized. ²⁵As John was finishing his ministry he asked, 'Do you think I am the Messiah? No, I am not! But he is coming soon—and I'm not even worthy to be his slave and untie the sandals on his feet.'

²⁶"Brothers—you sons of Abraham, and also you God-fearing Gentiles—this message of salvation has been sent to us! ²⁷The people in Jerusalem and their leaders did not recognize Jesus as the one the prophets had spoken about. Instead, they condemned him, and in doing this they fulfilled the prophets' words that are read every Sabbath. ²⁸They found no legal reason to execute him, but they asked Pilate to have him killed anyway.

²⁹"When they had done all that the prophecies said about him, they took him down from the cross* and placed him in a tomb. ³⁰But God raised him from the dead! ³¹And over a period of many days he appeared to those who had gone with him from Galilee to Jerusalem. They are now his witnesses to the people of Israel.

³²"And now we are here to bring you this Good News. The promise was made to our ancestors, ³³and God has now fulfilled it for us, their descendants, by raising Jesus. This is what the second psalm says about Jesus:

'You are my Son.
    Today I have become your
        Father.*'

³⁴For God had promised to raise him from the dead, not leaving him to rot in the grave. He said, 'I will give you the sacred blessings I promised to David.'* ³⁵Another psalm explains it more fully: 'You will not allow your Holy One to rot in the grave.'* ³⁶This is not a reference to David, for after David had done the will of God in his own generation, he died and was buried with his ancestors, and his body decayed. ³⁷No, it was a reference to someone else—someone whom God raised and whose body did not decay.

³⁸*"Brothers, listen! We are here to proclaim that through this man Jesus there is forgiveness for your sins. ³⁹Everyone who believes in him is made right in God's sight—something the law of Moses could never do. ⁴⁰Be careful! Don't let the prophets' words apply to you. For they said,

⁴¹ 'Look, you mockers,
    be amazed and die!

13:22 1 Sam 13:14. 13:29 Greek *from the tree.* 13:33 Or *Today I reveal you as my Son.* Ps 2:7.
13:34 Isa 55:3. 13:35 Ps 16:10. 13:38 English translations divide verses 38 and 39 in various ways.

For I am doing something in
   your own day,
   something you wouldn't
      believe
   even if someone told you
      about it.'*"

⁴²As Paul and Barnabas left the synagogue that day, the people begged them to speak about these things again the next week. ⁴³Many Jews and devout converts to Judaism followed Paul and Barnabas, and the two men urged them to continue to rely on the grace of God.

Paul Turns to the Gentiles

⁴⁴The following week almost the entire city turned out to hear them preach the word of the Lord. ⁴⁵But when some of the Jews saw the crowds, they were jealous; so they slandered Paul and argued against whatever he said.

⁴⁶Then Paul and Barnabas spoke out boldly and declared, "It was necessary that we first preach the word of God to you Jews. But since you have rejected it and judged yourselves unworthy of eternal life, we will offer it to the Gentiles. ⁴⁷For the Lord gave us this command when he said,

'I have made you a light to
      the Gentiles,
   to bring salvation to the
      farthest corners of the
      earth.'*"

⁴⁸When the Gentiles heard this, they were very glad and thanked the Lord for his message; and all who were chosen for eternal life became believers. ⁴⁹So the Lord's message spread throughout that region.

⁵⁰Then the Jews stirred up the influential religious women and the leaders of the city, and they incited a mob against Paul and Barnabas and ran them out of town. ⁵¹So they shook the dust from their feet as a sign of rejection and went to the town of Iconium. ⁵²And the believers* were filled with joy and with the Holy Spirit.

Paul and Barnabas in Iconium

14 The same thing happened in Iconium.* Paul and Barnabas went to the Jewish synagogue and preached with such power that a great number of both Jews and Greeks became believers. ²Some of the Jews, however, spurned God's message and poisoned the minds of the Gentiles against Paul and Barnabas. ³But the apostles stayed there a long time, preaching boldly about the grace of the Lord. And the Lord proved their message was true by giving them power to do miraculous signs and wonders. ⁴But the people of the town were divided in their opinion about them. Some sided with the Jews, and some with the apostles.

⁵Then a mob of Gentiles and Jews,

13:41 Hab 1:5 (Greek version). 13:47 Isa 49:6. 13:52 Greek *the disciples*. 14:1 *Iconium*, as well as *Lystra* and *Derbe* (14:6), were towns in what is now Turkey.

along with their leaders, decided to attack and stone them. ⁶When the apostles learned of it, they fled to the region of Lycaonia—to the towns of Lystra and Derbe and the surrounding area. ⁷And there they preached the Good News.

Paul and Barnabas in Lystra and Derbe

⁸While they were at Lystra, Paul and Barnabas came upon a man with crippled feet. He had been that way from birth, so he had never walked. He was sitting ⁹and listening as Paul preached. Looking straight at him, Paul realized he had faith to be healed. ¹⁰So Paul called to him in a loud voice, "Stand up!" And the man jumped to his feet and started walking.

¹¹When the crowd saw what Paul had done, they shouted in their local dialect, "These men are gods in human form!" ¹²They decided that Barnabas was the Greek god Zeus and that Paul was Hermes, since he was the chief speaker. ¹³Now the temple of Zeus was located just outside the town. So the priest of the temple and the crowd brought bulls and wreaths of flowers to the town gates, and they prepared to offer sacrifices to the apostles.

¹⁴But when the apostles Barnabas and Paul heard what was happening, they tore their clothing in dismay and ran out among the people, shouting, ¹⁵"Friends,* why are you doing this? We are merely human beings—just like you! We have come to bring you the Good News that you should turn from these worthless things and turn to the living God, who made heaven and earth, the sea, and everything in them. ¹⁶In the past he permitted all the nations to go their own ways, ¹⁷but he never left them without evidence of himself and his goodness. For instance, he sends you rain and good crops and gives you food and joyful hearts." ¹⁸But even with these words, Paul and Barnabas could scarcely restrain the people from sacrificing to them.

¹⁹Then some Jews arrived from Antioch and Iconium and won the crowds to their side. They stoned Paul and dragged him out of town, thinking he was dead. ²⁰But as the believers* gathered around him, he got up and went back into the town. The next day he left with Barnabas for Derbe.

Paul and Barnabas Return to Antioch of Syria

²¹After preaching the Good News in Derbe and making many disciples, Paul and Barnabas returned to Lystra, Iconium, and Antioch of Pisidia, ²²where they strengthened the believers. They encouraged them to continue in the faith, reminding them that we must suffer many hardships to enter the Kingdom of God. ²³Paul and Barnabas also appointed elders in every church.

14:15 Greek *Men.* **14:20** Greek *disciples;* also in 14:22, 28.

With prayer and fasting, they turned the elders over to the care of the Lord, in whom they had put their trust. ²⁴Then they traveled back through Pisidia to Pamphylia. ²⁵They preached the word in Perga, then went down to Attalia.

²⁶Finally, they returned by ship to Antioch of Syria, where their journey had begun. The believers there had entrusted them to the grace of God to do the work they had now completed. ²⁷Upon arriving in Antioch, they called the church together and reported everything God had done through them and how he had opened the door of faith to the Gentiles, too. ²⁸And they stayed there with the believers for a long time.

The Council at Jerusalem

15 While Paul and Barnabas were at Antioch of Syria, some men from Judea arrived and began to teach the believers*: "Unless you are circumcised as required by the law of Moses, you cannot be saved." ²Paul and Barnabas disagreed with them, arguing vehemently. Finally, the church decided to send Paul and Barnabas to Jerusalem, accompanied by some local believers, to talk to the apostles and elders about this question. ³The church sent the delegates to Jerusalem, and they stopped along the way in Phoenicia and Samaria to visit the believers. They told them— much to everyone's joy—that the Gentiles, too, were being converted.

⁴When they arrived in Jerusalem, Barnabas and Paul were welcomed by the whole church, including the apostles and elders. They reported everything God had done through them. ⁵But then some of the believers who belonged to the sect of the Pharisees stood up and insisted, "The Gentile converts must be circumcised and required to follow the law of Moses."

⁶So the apostles and elders met together to resolve this issue. ⁷At the meeting, after a long discussion, Peter stood and addressed them as follows: "Brothers, you all know that God chose me from among you some time ago to preach to the Gentiles so that they could hear the Good News and believe. ⁸God knows people's hearts, and he confirmed that he accepts Gentiles by giving them the Holy Spirit, just as he did to us. ⁹He made no distinction between us and them, for he cleansed their hearts through faith. ¹⁰So why are you now challenging God by burdening the Gentile believers* with a yoke that neither we nor our ancestors were able to bear? ¹¹We believe that we are all saved the same way, by the undeserved grace of the Lord Jesus."

¹²Everyone listened quietly as Barnabas and Paul told about the miraculous signs and wonders God had done through them among the Gentiles.

¹³When they had finished, James

15:1 Greek *brothers;* also in 15:3, 23, 32, 33, 36, 40. **15:10** Greek *disciples.*

stood and said, "Brothers, listen to me. [14]Peter* has told you about the time God first visited the Gentiles to take from them a people for himself. [15]And this conversion of Gentiles is exactly what the prophets predicted. As it is written:

[16] 'Afterward I will return
    and restore the fallen house*
        of David.
    I will rebuild its ruins
        and restore it,
[17] so that the rest of humanity
        might seek the LORD,
    including the Gentiles—
    all those I have called to be
        mine.
    The LORD has spoken—
[18]   he who made these things
        known so long ago.'*

[19]"And so my judgment is that we should not make it difficult for the Gentiles who are turning to God. [20]Instead, we should write and tell them to abstain from eating food offered to idols, from sexual immorality, from eating the meat of strangled animals, and from consuming blood. [21]For these laws of Moses have been preached in Jewish synagogues in every city on every Sabbath for many generations."

The Letter for Gentile Believers

[22]Then the apostles and elders together with the whole church in Jerusalem chose delegates, and they sent them to Antioch of Syria with Paul and Barnabas to report on this decision. The men chosen were two of the church leaders*—Judas (also called Barsabbas) and Silas. [23]This is the letter they took with them:

"This letter is from the apostles and elders, your brothers in Jerusalem. It is written to the Gentile believers in Antioch, Syria, and Cilicia. Greetings!

[24]"We understand that some men from here have troubled you and upset you with their teaching, but we did not send them! [25]So we decided, having come to complete agreement, to send you official representatives, along with our beloved Barnabas and Paul, [26]who have risked their lives for the name of our Lord Jesus Christ. [27]We are sending Judas and Silas to confirm what we have decided concerning your question.

[28]"For it seemed good to the Holy Spirit and to us to lay no greater burden on you than these few requirements: [29]You must abstain from eating food offered to idols, from consuming blood or the meat of strangled animals, and from sexual immorality. If you do this, you will do well. Farewell."

[30]The messengers went at once to Antioch, where they called a gen-

15:14 Greek *Simeon*.   15:16 Or *kingdom*; Greek reads *tent*.   15:16-18 Amos 9:11-12 (Greek version); Isa 45:21.   15:22 Greek *were leaders among the brothers*.

eral meeting of the believers and delivered the letter. [31]And there was great joy throughout the church that day as they read this encouraging message.

[32]Then Judas and Silas, both being prophets, spoke at length to the believers, encouraging and strengthening their faith. [33]They stayed for a while, and then the believers sent them back to the church in Jerusalem with a blessing of peace.* [35]Paul and Barnabas stayed in Antioch. They and many others taught and preached the word of the Lord there.

Paul and Barnabas Separate

[36]After some time Paul said to Barnabas, "Let's go back and visit each city where we previously preached the word of the Lord, to see how the new believers are doing." [37]Barnabas agreed and wanted to take along John Mark. [38]But Paul disagreed strongly, since John Mark had deserted them in Pamphylia and had not continued with them in their work. [39]Their disagreement was so sharp that they separated. Barnabas took John Mark with him and sailed for Cyprus. [40]Paul chose Silas, and as he left, the believers entrusted him to the Lord's gracious care. [41]Then he traveled throughout Syria and Cilicia, strengthening the churches there.

Paul's Second Missionary Journey

16 Paul went first to Derbe and then to Lystra, where there was a young disciple named Timothy. His mother was a Jewish believer, but his father was a Greek. [2]Timothy was well thought of by the believers* in Lystra and Iconium, [3]so Paul wanted him to join them on their journey. In deference to the Jews of the area, he arranged for Timothy to be circumcised before they left, for everyone knew that his father was a Greek. [4]Then they went from town to town, instructing the believers to follow the decisions made by the apostles and elders in Jerusalem. [5]So the churches were strengthened in their faith and grew larger every day.

A Call from Macedonia

[6]Next Paul and Silas traveled through the area of Phrygia and Galatia, because the Holy Spirit had prevented them from preaching the word in the province of Asia at that time. [7]Then coming to the borders of Mysia, they headed north for the province of Bithynia,* but again the Spirit of Jesus did not allow them to go there. [8]So instead, they went on through Mysia to the seaport of Troas.

[9]That night Paul had a vision: A man from Macedonia in northern Greece was standing there, pleading with him, "Come over to Macedonia

---

15:33 Some manuscripts add verse 34, *But Silas decided to stay there.* **16:2** Greek *brothers;* also in 16:40. **16:6-7** *Phrygia, Galatia, Asia, Mysia,* and *Bithynia* were all districts in what is now Turkey.

and help us!" [10]So we* decided to leave for Macedonia at once, having concluded that God was calling us to preach the Good News there.

Lydia of Philippi Believes in Jesus

[11]We boarded a boat at Troas and sailed straight across to the island of Samothrace, and the next day we landed at Neapolis. [12]From there we reached Philippi, a major city of that district of Macedonia and a Roman colony. And we stayed there several days.

[13]On the Sabbath we went a little way outside the city to a riverbank, where we thought people would be meeting for prayer, and we sat down to speak with some women who had gathered there. [14]One of them was Lydia from Thyatira, a merchant of expensive purple cloth, who worshiped God. As she listened to us, the Lord opened her heart, and she accepted what Paul was saying. [15]She and her household were baptized, and she asked us to be her guests. "If you agree that I am a true believer in the Lord," she said, "come and stay at my home." And she urged us until we agreed.

Paul and Silas in Prison

[16]One day as we were going down to the place of prayer, we met a slave girl who had a spirit that enabled her to tell the future. She earned a lot of money for her masters by telling fortunes. [17]She followed Paul and the rest of us, shouting, "These men are servants of the Most High God, and they have come to tell you how to be saved."

[18]This went on day after day until Paul got so exasperated that he turned and said to the demon within her, "I command you in the name of Jesus Christ to come out of her." And instantly it left her.

[19]Her masters' hopes of wealth were now shattered, so they grabbed Paul and Silas and dragged them before the authorities at the marketplace. [20]"The whole city is in an uproar because of these Jews!" they shouted to the city officials. [21]"They are teaching customs that are illegal for us Romans to practice."

[22]A mob quickly formed against Paul and Silas, and the city officials ordered them stripped and beaten with wooden rods. [23]They were severely beaten, and then they were thrown into prison. The jailer was ordered to make sure they didn't escape. [24]So the jailer put them into the inner dungeon and clamped their feet in the stocks.

[25]Around midnight Paul and Silas were praying and singing hymns to God, and the other prisoners were listening. [26]Suddenly, there was a massive earthquake, and the prison was shaken to its foundations. All the doors immediately flew open, and the chains of every prisoner fell off! [27]The jailer woke up to see the prison doors wide open. He as-

16:10 Luke, the writer of this book, here joined Paul and accompanied him on his journey.

sumed the prisoners had escaped, so he drew his sword to kill himself. [28]But Paul shouted to him, "Stop! Don't kill yourself! We are all here!"

[29]The jailer called for lights and ran to the dungeon and fell down trembling before Paul and Silas. [30]Then he brought them out and asked, "Sirs, what must I do to be saved?"

[31]They replied, "Believe in the Lord Jesus and you will be saved, along with everyone in your household." [32]And they shared the word of the Lord with him and with all who lived in his household. [33]Even at that hour of the night, the jailer cared for them and washed their wounds. Then he and everyone in his household were immediately baptized. [34]He brought them into his house and set a meal before them, and he and his entire household rejoiced because they all believed in God.

[35]The next morning the city officials sent the police to tell the jailer, "Let those men go!" [36]So the jailer told Paul, "The city officials have said you and Silas are free to leave. Go in peace."

[37]But Paul replied, "They have publicly beaten us without a trial and put us in prison—and we are Roman citizens. So now they want us to leave secretly? Certainly not! Let them come themselves to release us!"

[38]When the police reported this, the city officials were alarmed to learn that Paul and Silas were Roman citizens. [39]So they came to the jail and apologized to them. Then they brought them out and begged them to leave the city. [40]When Paul and Silas left the prison, they returned to the home of Lydia. There they met with the believers and encouraged them once more. Then they left town.

Paul Preaches in Thessalonica

17 Paul and Silas then traveled through the towns of Amphipolis and Apollonia and came to Thessalonica, where there was a Jewish synagogue. [2]As was Paul's custom, he went to the synagogue service, and for three Sabbaths in a row he used the Scriptures to reason with the people. [3]He explained the prophecies and proved that the Messiah must suffer and rise from the dead. He said, "This Jesus I'm telling you about is the Messiah." [4]Some of the Jews who listened were persuaded and joined Paul and Silas, along with many God-fearing Greek men and quite a few prominent women.*

[5]But some of the Jews were jealous, so they gathered some troublemakers from the marketplace to form a mob and start a riot. They attacked the home of Jason, searching for Paul and Silas so they could drag them out to the crowd.* [6]Not finding them there, they dragged out Jason and some of the other

17:4 Some manuscripts read *quite a few of the wives of the leading men.* **17:5** Or *the city council.*

believers* instead and took them before the city council. "Paul and Silas have caused trouble all over the world," they shouted, "and now they are here disturbing our city, too. [7]And Jason has welcomed them into his home. They are all guilty of treason against Caesar, for they profess allegiance to another king, named Jesus."

[8]The people of the city, as well as the city council, were thrown into turmoil by these reports. [9]So the officials forced Jason and the other believers to post bond, and then they released them.

Paul and Silas in Berea
[10]That very night the believers sent Paul and Silas to Berea. When they arrived there, they went to the Jewish synagogue. [11]And the people of Berea were more open-minded than those in Thessalonica, and they listened eagerly to Paul's message. They searched the Scriptures day after day to see if Paul and Silas were teaching the truth. [12]As a result, many Jews believed, as did many of the prominent Greek women and men.

[13]But when some Jews in Thessalonica learned that Paul was preaching the word of God in Berea, they went there and stirred up trouble. [14]The believers acted at once, sending Paul on to the coast, while Silas and Timothy remained behind. [15]Those escorting Paul went with him all the way to Athens; then they returned to Berea with instructions for Silas and Timothy to hurry and join him.

Paul Preaches in Athens
[16]While Paul was waiting for them in Athens, he was deeply troubled by all the idols he saw everywhere in the city. [17]He went to the synagogue to reason with the Jews and the God-fearing Gentiles, and he spoke daily in the public square to all who happened to be there.

[18]He also had a debate with some of the Epicurean and Stoic philosophers. When he told them about Jesus and his resurrection, they said, "What's this babbler trying to say with these strange ideas he's picked up?" Others said, "He seems to be preaching about some foreign gods."

[19]Then they took him to the high council of the city.* "Come and tell us about this new teaching," they said. [20]"You are saying some rather strange things, and we want to know what it's all about." [21](It should be explained that all the Athenians as well as the foreigners in Athens seemed to spend all their time discussing the latest ideas.)

[22]So Paul, standing before the council,* addressed them as fol-

---

17:6 Greek *brothers;* also in 17:10, 14.   **17:19** Or *the most learned society of philosophers in the city.* Greek reads *the Areopagus.*   **17:22** Traditionally rendered *standing in the middle of Mars Hill;* Greek reads *standing in the middle of the Areopagus.*

lows: "Men of Athens, I notice that you are very religious in every way, ²³for as I was walking along I saw your many shrines. And one of your altars had this inscription on it: 'To an Unknown God.' This God, whom you worship without knowing, is the one I'm telling you about.

²⁴"He is the God who made the world and everything in it. Since he is Lord of heaven and earth, he doesn't live in man-made temples, ²⁵and human hands can't serve his needs—for he has no needs. He himself gives life and breath to everything, and he satisfies every need. ²⁶From one man* he created all the nations throughout the whole earth. He decided beforehand when they should rise and fall, and he determined their boundaries.

²⁷"His purpose was for the nations to seek after God and perhaps feel their way toward him and find him—though he is not far from any one of us. ²⁸For in him we live and move and exist. As some of your* own poets have said, 'We are his offspring.' ²⁹And since this is true, we shouldn't think of God as an idol designed by craftsmen from gold or silver or stone.

³⁰"God overlooked people's ignorance about these things in earlier times, but now he commands everyone everywhere to repent of their sins and turn to him. ³¹For he has set a day for judging the world with justice by the man he has appointed, and he proved to everyone who this is by raising him from the dead."

³²When they heard Paul speak about the resurrection of the dead, some laughed in contempt, but others said, "We want to hear more about this later." ³³That ended Paul's discussion with them, ³⁴but some joined him and became believers. Among them were Dionysius, a member of the council,* a woman named Damaris, and others with them.

Paul Meets Priscilla and Aquila in Corinth

18 Then Paul left Athens and went to Corinth.* ²There he became acquainted with a Jew named Aquila, born in Pontus, who had recently arrived from Italy with his wife, Priscilla. They had left Italy when Claudius Caesar deported all Jews from Rome. ³Paul lived and worked with them, for they were tentmakers* just as he was.

⁴Each Sabbath found Paul at the synagogue, trying to convince the Jews and Greeks alike. ⁵And after Silas and Timothy came down from Macedonia, Paul spent all his time preaching the word. He testified to the Jews that Jesus was the Messiah. ⁶But when they opposed and

17:26 Greek *From one;* other manuscripts read *From one blood.* 17:28 Some manuscripts read *our.* 17:34 Greek *an Areopagite.* 18:1 *Athens* and *Corinth* were major cities in Achaia, the region in the southern portion of the Greek peninsula. 18:3 Or *leatherworkers.*

insulted him, Paul shook the dust from his clothes and said, "Your blood is upon your own heads—I am innocent. From now on I will go preach to the Gentiles."

7Then he left and went to the home of Titius Justus, a Gentile who worshiped God and lived next door to the synagogue. 8Crispus, the leader of the synagogue, and everyone in his household believed in the Lord. Many others in Corinth also heard Paul, became believers, and were baptized.

9One night the Lord spoke to Paul in a vision and told him, "Don't be afraid! Speak out! Don't be silent! 10For I am with you, and no one will attack and harm you, for many people in this city belong to me." 11So Paul stayed there for the next year and a half, teaching the word of God.

12But when Gallio became governor of Achaia, some Jews rose up together against Paul and brought him before the governor for judgment. 13They accused Paul of "persuading people to worship God in ways that are contrary to our law."

14But just as Paul started to make his defense, Gallio turned to Paul's accusers and said, "Listen, you Jews, if this were a case involving some wrongdoing or a serious crime, I would have a reason to accept your case. 15But since it is merely a question of words and names and your Jewish law, take care of it yourselves. I refuse to judge such matters." 16And he threw them out of the courtroom.

17The crowd* then grabbed Sosthenes, the leader of the synagogue, and beat him right there in the courtroom. But Gallio paid no attention.

Paul Returns to Antioch of Syria

18Paul stayed in Corinth for some time after that, then said good-bye to the brothers and sisters* and went to nearby Cenchrea. There he shaved his head according to Jewish custom, marking the end of a vow. Then he set sail for Syria, taking Priscilla and Aquila with him.

19They stopped first at the port of Ephesus, where Paul left the others behind. While he was there, he went to the synagogue to reason with the Jews. 20They asked him to stay longer, but he declined. 21As he left, however, he said, "I will come back later,* God willing." Then he set sail from Ephesus. 22The next stop was at the port of Caesarea. From there he went up and visited the church at Jerusalem* and then went back to Antioch.

23After spending some time in Antioch, Paul went back through Galatia and Phrygia, visiting and strengthening all the believers.*

18:17 Greek *Everyone;* other manuscripts read *All the Greeks.* **18:18** Greek *brothers;* also in 18:27. **18:21** Some manuscripts read *"I must by all means be at Jerusalem for the upcoming festival, but I will come back later."* **18:22** Greek *the church.* **18:23** Greek *disciples;* also in 18:27.

Apollos Instructed at Ephesus

24Meanwhile, a Jew named Apollos, an eloquent speaker who knew the Scriptures well, had arrived in Ephesus from Alexandria in Egypt. 25He had been taught the way of the Lord, and he taught others about Jesus with an enthusiastic spirit* and with accuracy. However, he knew only about John's baptism. 26When Priscilla and Aquila heard him preaching boldly in the synagogue, they took him aside and explained the way of God even more accurately.

27Apollos had been thinking about going to Achaia, and the brothers and sisters in Ephesus encouraged him to go. They wrote to the believers in Achaia, asking them to welcome him. When he arrived there, he proved to be of great benefit to those who, by God's grace, had believed. 28He refuted the Jews with powerful arguments in public debate. Using the Scriptures, he explained to them that Jesus was the Messiah.

Paul's Third Missionary Journey

19 While Apollos was in Corinth, Paul traveled through the interior regions until he reached Ephesus, on the coast, where he found several believers.* 2"Did you receive the Holy Spirit when you believed?" he asked them.

"No," they replied, "we haven't even heard that there is a Holy Spirit."

3"Then what baptism did you experience?" he asked.

And they replied, "The baptism of John."

4Paul said, "John's baptism called for repentance from sin. But John himself told the people to believe in the one who would come later, meaning Jesus."

5As soon as they heard this, they were baptized in the name of the Lord Jesus. 6Then when Paul laid his hands on them, the Holy Spirit came on them, and they spoke in other tongues* and prophesied. 7There were about twelve men in all.

Paul Ministers in Ephesus

8Then Paul went to the synagogue and preached boldly for the next three months, arguing persuasively about the Kingdom of God. 9But some became stubborn, rejecting his message and publicly speaking against the Way. So Paul left the synagogue and took the believers with him. Then he held daily discussions at the lecture hall of Tyrannus. 10This went on for the next two years, so that people throughout the province of Asia—both Jews and Greeks—heard the word of the Lord.

11God gave Paul the power to perform unusual miracles. 12When handkerchiefs or aprons that had merely touched his skin were placed on sick people, they were

18:25 Or *with enthusiasm in the Spirit.* **19:1** Greek *disciples;* also in 19:9, 30. **19:6** Or *in other languages.*

healed of their diseases, and evil spirits were expelled.

¹³A group of Jews was traveling from town to town casting out evil spirits. They tried to use the name of the Lord Jesus in their incantation, saying, "I command you in the name of Jesus, whom Paul preaches, to come out!" ¹⁴Seven sons of Sceva, a leading priest, were doing this. ¹⁵But one time when they tried it, the evil spirit replied, "I know Jesus, and I know Paul, but who are you?" ¹⁶Then the man with the evil spirit leaped on them, overpowered them, and attacked them with such violence that they fled from the house, naked and battered.

¹⁷The story of what happened spread quickly all through Ephesus, to Jews and Greeks alike. A solemn fear descended on the city, and the name of the Lord Jesus was greatly honored. ¹⁸Many who became believers confessed their sinful practices. ¹⁹A number of them who had been practicing sorcery brought their incantation books and burned them at a public bonfire. The value of the books was several million dollars.* ²⁰So the message about the Lord spread widely and had a powerful effect.

²¹Afterward Paul felt compelled by the Spirit* to go over to Macedonia and Achaia before going to Jerusalem. "And after that," he said, "I must go on to Rome!" ²²He sent his two assistants, Timothy and Erastus, ahead to Macedonia while he stayed awhile longer in the province of Asia.

The Riot in Ephesus

²³About that time, serious trouble developed in Ephesus concerning the Way. ²⁴It began with Demetrius, a silversmith who had a large business manufacturing silver shrines of the Greek goddess Artemis.* He kept many craftsmen busy. ²⁵He called them together, along with others employed in similar trades, and addressed them as follows:

"Gentlemen, you know that our wealth comes from this business. ²⁶But as you have seen and heard, this man Paul has persuaded many people that handmade gods aren't really gods at all. And he's done this not only here in Ephesus but throughout the entire province! ²⁷Of course, I'm not just talking about the loss of public respect for our business. I'm also concerned that the temple of the great goddess Artemis will lose its influence and that Artemis—this magnificent goddess worshiped throughout the province of Asia and all around the world—will be robbed of her great prestige!"

²⁸At this their anger boiled, and they began shouting, "Great is Artemis of the Ephesians!" ²⁹Soon the whole city was filled with confusion. Everyone rushed to the amphi-

19:19 Greek *50,000 pieces of silver*, each of which was the equivalent of a day's wage. 19:21 Or *decided in his spirit.* 19:24 *Artemis* is otherwise known as Diana.

theater, dragging along Gaius and Aristarchus, who were Paul's traveling companions from Macedonia. [30]Paul wanted to go in, too, but the believers wouldn't let him. [31]Some of the officials of the province, friends of Paul, also sent a message to him, begging him not to risk his life by entering the amphitheater.

[32]Inside, the people were all shouting, some one thing and some another. Everything was in confusion. In fact, most of them didn't even know why they were there. [33]The Jews in the crowd pushed Alexander forward and told him to explain the situation. He motioned for silence and tried to speak. [34]But when the crowd realized he was a Jew, they started shouting again and kept it up for about two hours: "Great is Artemis of the Ephesians! Great is Artemis of the Ephesians!"

[35]At last the mayor was able to quiet them down enough to speak. "Citizens of Ephesus," he said. "Everyone knows that Ephesus is the official guardian of the temple of the great Artemis, whose image fell down to us from heaven. [36]Since this is an undeniable fact, you should stay calm and not do anything rash. [37]You have brought these men here, but they have stolen nothing from the temple and have not spoken against our goddess.

[38]"If Demetrius and the craftsmen have a case against them, the courts are in session and the officials can hear the case at once. Let them make formal charges. [39]And if there are complaints about other matters, they can be settled in a legal assembly. [40]I am afraid we are in danger of being charged with rioting by the Roman government, since there is no cause for all this commotion. And if Rome demands an explanation, we won't know what to say." [41]*Then he dismissed them, and they dispersed.

Paul Goes to Macedonia and Greece

20 When the uproar was over, Paul sent for the believers* and encouraged them. Then he said good-bye and left for Macedonia. [2]While there, he encouraged the believers in all the towns he passed through. Then he traveled down to Greece, [3]where he stayed for three months. He was preparing to sail back to Syria when he discovered a plot by some Jews against his life, so he decided to return through Macedonia.

[4]Several men were traveling with him. They were Sopater son of Pyrrhus from Berea; Aristarchus and Secundus from Thessalonica; Gaius from Derbe; Timothy; and Tychicus and Trophimus from the province of Asia. [5]They went on ahead and waited for us at Troas. [6]After the Passover* ended, we boarded a ship

19:41 Some translations include verse 41 as part of verse 40. 20:1 Greek *disciples.* 20:6 Greek *the days of unleavened bread.*

at Philippi in Macedonia and five days later joined them in Troas, where we stayed a week.

Paul's Final Visit to Troas

7On the first day of the week, we gathered with the local believers to share in the Lord's Supper.* Paul was preaching to them, and since he was leaving the next day, he kept talking until midnight. 8The upstairs room where we met was lighted with many flickering lamps. 9As Paul spoke on and on, a young man named Eutychus, sitting on the windowsill, became very drowsy. Finally, he fell sound asleep and dropped three stories to his death below. 10Paul went down, bent over him, and took him into his arms. "Don't worry," he said, "he's alive!" 11Then they all went back upstairs, shared in the Lord's Supper,* and ate together. Paul continued talking to them until dawn, and then he left. 12Meanwhile, the young man was taken home alive and well, and everyone was greatly relieved.

Paul Meets the Ephesian Elders

13Paul went by land to Assos, where he had arranged for us to join him, while we traveled by ship. 14He joined us there, and we sailed together to Mitylene. 15The next day we sailed past the island of Kios. The following day we crossed to the island of Samos, and* a day later we arrived at Miletus.

16Paul had decided to sail on past Ephesus, for he didn't want to spend any more time in the province of Asia. He was hurrying to get to Jerusalem, if possible, in time for the Festival of Pentecost. 17But when we landed at Miletus, he sent a message to the elders of the church at Ephesus, asking them to come and meet him.

18When they arrived he declared, "You know that from the day I set foot in the province of Asia until now 19I have done the Lord's work humbly and with many tears. I have endured the trials that came to me from the plots of the Jews. 20I never shrank back from telling you what you needed to hear, either publicly or in your homes. 21I have had one message for Jews and Greeks alike—the necessity of repenting from sin and turning to God, and of having faith in our Lord Jesus.

22"And now I am bound by the Spirit* to go to Jerusalem. I don't know what awaits me, 23except that the Holy Spirit tells me in city after city that jail and suffering lie ahead. 24But my life is worth nothing to me unless I use it for finishing the work assigned me by the Lord Jesus—the work of telling others the Good News about the wonderful grace of God.

25"And now I know that none of you to whom I have preached the Kingdom will ever see me again.

20:7 Greek *to break bread.* 20:11 Greek *broke the bread.* 20:15 Some manuscripts read *and having stayed at Trogyllium.* 20:22 Or *by my spirit,* or *by an inner compulsion;* Greek reads *by the spirit.*

26I declare today that I have been faithful. If anyone suffers eternal death, it's not my fault,* 27for I didn't shrink from declaring all that God wants you to know.

28"So guard yourselves and God's people. Feed and shepherd God's flock—his church, purchased with his own blood*—over which the Holy Spirit has appointed you as leaders.* 29I know that false teachers, like vicious wolves, will come in among you after I leave, not sparing the flock. 30Even some men from your own group will rise up and distort the truth in order to draw a following. 31Watch out! Remember the three years I was with you—my constant watch and care over you night and day, and my many tears for you.

32"And now I entrust you to God and the message of his grace that is able to build you up and give you an inheritance with all those he has set apart for himself.

33"I have never coveted anyone's silver or gold or fine clothes. 34You know that these hands of mine have worked to supply my own needs and even the needs of those who were with me. 35And I have been a constant example of how you can help those in need by working hard. You should remember the words of the Lord Jesus: 'It is more blessed to give than to receive.'"

36When he had finished speaking, he knelt and prayed with them. 37They all cried as they embraced and kissed him good-bye. 38They were sad most of all because he had said that they would never see him again. Then they escorted him down to the ship.

Paul's Journey to Jerusalem

21 After saying farewell to the Ephesian elders, we sailed straight to the island of Cos. The next day we reached Rhodes and then went to Patara. 2There we boarded a ship sailing for Phoenicia. 3We sighted the island of Cyprus, passed it on our left, and landed at the harbor of Tyre, in Syria, where the ship was to unload its cargo.

4We went ashore, found the local believers,* and stayed with them a week. These believers prophesied through the Holy Spirit that Paul should not go on to Jerusalem. 5When we returned to the ship at the end of the week, the entire congregation, including women* and children, left the city and came down to the shore with us. There we knelt, prayed, 6and said our farewells. Then we went aboard, and they returned home.

7The next stop after leaving Tyre was Ptolemais, where we greeted the brothers and sisters* and stayed for one day. 8The next day we went on to Caesarea and stayed at the

---

20:26 Greek *I am innocent of the blood of all.*　**20:28a** Or *with the blood of his own [Son].* **20:28b** Or *overseers,* or *bishops.*　**21:4** Greek *disciples;* also in 21:16.　**21:5** Or *wives.*　**21:7** Greek *brothers;* also in 21:17.

home of Philip the Evangelist, one of the seven men who had been chosen to distribute food. [9]He had four unmarried daughters who had the gift of prophecy.

[10]Several days later a man named Agabus, who also had the gift of prophecy, arrived from Judea. [11]He came over, took Paul's belt, and bound his own feet and hands with it. Then he said, "The Holy Spirit declares, 'So shall the owner of this belt be bound by the Jewish leaders in Jerusalem and turned over to the Gentiles.'" [12]When we heard this, we and the local believers all begged Paul not to go on to Jerusalem.

[13]But he said, "Why all this weeping? You are breaking my heart! I am ready not only to be jailed at Jerusalem but even to die for the sake of the Lord Jesus." [14]When it was clear that we couldn't persuade him, we gave up and said, "The Lord's will be done."

Paul Arrives at Jerusalem

[15]After this we packed our things and left for Jerusalem. [16]Some believers from Caesarea accompanied us, and they took us to the home of Mnason, a man originally from Cyprus and one of the early believers. [17]When we arrived, the brothers and sisters in Jerusalem welcomed us warmly.

[18]The next day Paul went with us to meet with James, and all the elders of the Jerusalem church were present. [19]After greeting them, Paul gave a detailed account of the things God had accomplished among the Gentiles through his ministry.

[20]After hearing this, they praised God. And then they said, "You know, dear brother, how many thousands of Jews have also believed, and they all follow the law of Moses very seriously. [21]But the Jewish believers here in Jerusalem have been told that you are teaching all the Jews who live among the Gentiles to turn their backs on the laws of Moses. They've heard that you teach them not to circumcise their children or follow other Jewish customs. [22]What should we do? They will certainly hear that you have come.

[23]"Here's what we want you to do. We have four men here who have completed their vow. [24]Go with them to the Temple and join them in the purification ceremony, paying for them to have their heads ritually shaved. Then everyone will know that the rumors are all false and that you yourself observe the Jewish laws.

[25]"As for the Gentile believers, they should do what we already told them in a letter: They should abstain from eating food offered to idols, from consuming blood or the meat of strangled animals, and from sexual immorality."

Paul Is Arrested

[26]So Paul went to the Temple the next day with the other men. They

had already started the purification ritual, so he publicly announced the date when their vows would end and sacrifices would be offered for each of them.

27The seven days were almost ended when some Jews from the province of Asia saw Paul in the Temple and roused a mob against him. They grabbed him, 28yelling, "Men of Israel, help us! This is the man who preaches against our people everywhere and tells everybody to disobey the Jewish laws. He speaks against the Temple—and even defiles this holy place by bringing in Gentiles.*" 29(For earlier that day they had seen him in the city with Trophimus, a Gentile from Ephesus,* and they assumed Paul had taken him into the Temple.)

30The whole city was rocked by these accusations, and a great riot followed. Paul was grabbed and dragged out of the Temple, and immediately the gates were closed behind him. 31As they were trying to kill him, word reached the commander of the Roman regiment that all Jerusalem was in an uproar. 32He immediately called out his soldiers and officers* and ran down among the crowd. When the mob saw the commander and the troops coming, they stopped beating Paul.

33Then the commander arrested him and ordered him bound with two chains. He asked the crowd who he was and what he had done. 34Some shouted one thing and some another. Since he couldn't find out the truth in all the uproar and confusion, he ordered that Paul be taken to the fortress. 35As Paul reached the stairs, the mob grew so violent the soldiers had to lift him to their shoulders to protect him. 36And the crowd followed behind, shouting, "Kill him, kill him!"

Paul Speaks to the Crowd

37As Paul was about to be taken inside, he said to the commander, "May I have a word with you?"

"Do you know Greek?" the commander asked, surprised. 38"Aren't you the Egyptian who led a rebellion some time ago and took 4,000 members of the Assassins out into the desert?"

39"No," Paul replied, "I am a Jew and a citizen of Tarsus in Cilicia, which is an important city. Please, let me talk to these people." 40The commander agreed, so Paul stood on the stairs and motioned to the people to be quiet. Soon a deep silence enveloped the crowd, and he addressed them in their own language, Aramaic.*

22 "Brothers and esteemed fathers," Paul said, "listen to me as I offer my defense." 2When they heard him speaking in their

21:28 Greek *Greeks.* 21:29 Greek *Trophimus, the Ephesian.* 21:32 Greek *centurions.* 21:40 Or *Hebrew.*

own language,* the silence was even greater.

³Then Paul said, "I am a Jew, born in Tarsus, a city in Cilicia, and I was brought up and educated here in Jerusalem under Gamaliel. As his student, I was carefully trained in our Jewish laws and customs. I became very zealous to honor God in everything I did, just like all of you today. ⁴And I persecuted the followers of the Way, hounding some to death, arresting both men and women and throwing them in prison. ⁵The high priest and the whole council of elders can testify that this is so. For I received letters from them to our Jewish brothers in Damascus, authorizing me to bring the followers of the Way from there to Jerusalem, in chains, to be punished.

⁶"As I was on the road, approaching Damascus about noon, a very bright light from heaven suddenly shone down around me. ⁷I fell to the ground and heard a voice saying to me, 'Saul, Saul, why are you persecuting me?'

⁸"'Who are you, lord?' I asked.

"And the voice replied, 'I am Jesus the Nazarene,* the one you are persecuting.' ⁹The people with me saw the light but didn't understand the voice speaking to me.

¹⁰"I asked, 'What should I do, Lord?'

"And the Lord told me, 'Get up and go into Damascus, and there you will be told everything you are to do.'

¹¹"I was blinded by the intense light and had to be led by the hand to Damascus by my companions. ¹²A man named Ananias lived there. He was a godly man, deeply devoted to the law, and well regarded by all the Jews of Damascus. ¹³He came and stood beside me and said, 'Brother Saul, regain your sight.' And that very moment I could see him!

¹⁴"Then he told me, 'The God of our ancestors has chosen you to know his will and to see the Righteous One and hear him speak. ¹⁵For you are to be his witness, telling everyone what you have seen and heard. ¹⁶What are you waiting for? Get up and be baptized. Have your sins washed away by calling on the name of the Lord.'

¹⁷"After I returned to Jerusalem, I was praying in the Temple and fell into a trance. ¹⁸I saw a vision of Jesus* saying to me, 'Hurry! Leave Jerusalem, for the people here won't accept your testimony about me.'

¹⁹"'But Lord,' I argued, 'they certainly know that in every synagogue I imprisoned and beat those who believed in you. ²⁰And I was in complete agreement when your witness Stephen was killed. I stood by and kept the coats they took off when they stoned him.'

²¹"But the Lord said to me, 'Go, for I will send you far away to the Gentiles!'"

²²The crowd listened until Paul said that word. Then they all began

22:2 Greek in Aramaic, or in Hebrew. 22:8 Or Jesus of Nazareth. 22:18 Greek him.

to shout, "Away with such a fellow! He isn't fit to live!" ²³They yelled, threw off their coats, and tossed handfuls of dust into the air.

Paul Reveals His Roman Citizenship

²⁴The commander brought Paul inside and ordered him lashed with whips to make him confess his crime. He wanted to find out why the crowd had become so furious. ²⁵When they tied Paul down to lash him, Paul said to the officer* standing there, "Is it legal for you to whip a Roman citizen who hasn't even been tried?"

²⁶When the officer heard this, he went to the commander and asked, "What are you doing? This man is a Roman citizen!"

²⁷So the commander went over and asked Paul, "Tell me, are you a Roman citizen?"

"Yes, I certainly am," Paul replied.

²⁸"I am, too," the commander muttered, "and it cost me plenty!"

Paul answered, "But I am a citizen by birth!"

²⁹The soldiers who were about to interrogate Paul quickly withdrew when they heard he was a Roman citizen, and the commander was frightened because he had ordered him bound and whipped.

Paul before the High Council

³⁰The next day the commander ordered the leading priests into session with the Jewish high council.* He wanted to find out what the trouble was all about, so he released Paul to have him stand before them.

23 Gazing intently at the high council,* Paul began: "Brothers, I have always lived before God with a clear conscience!"

²Instantly Ananias the high priest commanded those close to Paul to slap him on the mouth. ³But Paul said to him, "God will slap you, you corrupt hypocrite!* What kind of judge are you to break the law yourself by ordering me struck like that?"

⁴Those standing near Paul said to him, "Do you dare to insult God's high priest?"

⁵"I'm sorry, brothers. I didn't realize he was the high priest," Paul replied, "for the Scriptures say, 'You must not speak evil of any of your rulers.'*"

⁶Paul realized that some members of the high council were Sadducees and some were Pharisees, so he shouted, "Brothers, I am a Pharisee, as were my ancestors! And I am on trial because my hope is in the resurrection of the dead!"

⁷This divided the council—the Pharisees against the Sadducees—⁸for the Sadducees say there is no resurrection or angels or spirits, but the Pharisees believe in all of these.

22:25 Greek *the centurion;* also in 22:26. **22:30** Greek *Sanhedrin.* **23:1** Greek *Sanhedrin;* also in 23:6, 15, 20, 28. **23:3** Greek *you whitewashed wall.* **23:5** Exod 22:28.

⁹So there was a great uproar. Some of the teachers of religious law who were Pharisees jumped up and began to argue forcefully. "We see nothing wrong with him," they shouted. "Perhaps a spirit or an angel spoke to him." ¹⁰As the conflict grew more violent, the commander was afraid they would tear Paul apart. So he ordered his soldiers to go and rescue him by force and take him back to the fortress.

¹¹That night the Lord appeared to Paul and said, "Be encouraged, Paul. Just as you have been a witness to me here in Jerusalem, you must preach the Good News in Rome as well."

The Plan to Kill Paul
¹²The next morning a group of Jews* got together and bound themselves with an oath not to eat or drink until they had killed Paul. ¹³There were more than forty of them in the conspiracy. ¹⁴They went to the leading priests and elders and told them, "We have bound ourselves with an oath to eat nothing until we have killed Paul. ¹⁵So you and the high council should ask the commander to bring Paul back to the council again. Pretend you want to examine his case more fully. We will kill him on the way."

¹⁶But Paul's nephew—his sister's son—heard of their plan and went to the fortress and told Paul. ¹⁷Paul called for one of the Roman officers* and said, "Take this young man to the commander. He has something important to tell him."

¹⁸So the officer did, explaining, "Paul, the prisoner, called me over and asked me to bring this young man to you because he has something to tell you."

¹⁹The commander took his hand, led him aside, and asked, "What is it you want to tell me?"

²⁰Paul's nephew told him, "Some Jews are going to ask you to bring Paul before the high council tomorrow, pretending they want to get some more information. ²¹But don't do it! There are more than forty men hiding along the way ready to ambush him. They have vowed not to eat or drink anything until they have killed him. They are ready now, just waiting for your consent."

²²"Don't let anyone know you told me this," the commander warned the young man.

Paul Is Sent to Caesarea
²³Then the commander called two of his officers and ordered, "Get 200 soldiers ready to leave for Caesarea at nine o'clock tonight. Also take 200 spearmen and 70 mounted troops. ²⁴Provide horses for Paul to ride, and get him safely to Governor Felix." ²⁵Then he wrote this letter to the governor:

²⁶"From Claudius Lysias, to his Excellency, Governor Felix: Greetings!

23:12 Greek *the Jews*. **23:17** Greek *centurions;* also in 23:23.

27"This man was seized by some Jews, and they were about to kill him when I arrived with the troops. When I learned that he was a Roman citizen, I removed him to safety. 28Then I took him to their high council to try to learn the basis of the accusations against him. 29I soon discovered the charge was something regarding their religious law—certainly nothing worthy of imprisonment or death. 30But when I was informed of a plot to kill him, I immediately sent him on to you. I have told his accusers to bring their charges before you."

31So that night, as ordered, the soldiers took Paul as far as Antipatris. 32They returned to the fortress the next morning, while the mounted troops took him on to Caesarea. 33When they arrived in Caesarea, they presented Paul and the letter to Governor Felix. 34He read it and then asked Paul what province he was from. "Cilicia," Paul answered.

35"I will hear your case myself when your accusers arrive," the governor told him. Then the governor ordered him kept in the prison at Herod's headquarters.*

Paul Appears before Felix

24 Five days later Ananias, the high priest, arrived with some of the Jewish elders and the law-yer* Tertullus, to present their case against Paul to the governor. 2When Paul was called in, Tertullus present-ed the charges against Paul in the following address to the governor:

"You have provided a long period of peace for us Jews and with fore-sight have enacted reforms for us. 3For all of this, Your Excellency, we are very grateful to you. 4But I don't want to bore you, so please give me your attention for only a moment. 5We have found this man to be a troublemaker who is constantly stirring up riots among the Jews all over the world. He is a ringleader of the cult known as the Nazarenes. 6Furthermore, he was trying to dese-crate the Temple when we arrested him.* 8You can find out the truth of our accusations by examining him yourself." 9Then the other Jews chimed in, declaring that every-thing Tertullus said was true.

10The governor then motioned for Paul to speak. Paul said, "I know, sir, that you have been a judge of Jewish affairs for many years, so I gladly present my defense before you. 11You can quickly discover that I arrived in Jerusalem no more than twelve days ago to worship at the

23:35 Greek *Herod's Praetorium.* 24:1 Greek *some elders and an orator.* 24:6 Some manuscripts add an expanded conclusion to verse 6, all of verse 7, and an additional phrase in verse 8: *We would have judged him by our law, 7but Lysias, the commander of the garrison, came and violently took him away from us, 8commanding his accusers to come before you.*

Temple. ¹²My accusers never found me arguing with anyone in the Temple, nor stirring up a riot in any synagogue or on the streets of the city. ¹³These men cannot prove the things they accuse me of doing.

¹⁴"But I admit that I follow the Way, which they call a cult. I worship the God of our ancestors, and I firmly believe the Jewish law and everything written in the prophets. ¹⁵I have the same hope in God that these men have, that he will raise both the righteous and the unrighteous. ¹⁶Because of this, I always try to maintain a clear conscience before God and all people.

¹⁷"After several years away, I returned to Jerusalem with money to aid my people and to offer sacrifices to God. ¹⁸My accusers saw me in the Temple as I was completing a purification ceremony. There was no crowd around me and no rioting. ¹⁹But some Jews from the province of Asia were there—and they ought to be here to bring charges if they have anything against me! ²⁰Ask these men here what crime the Jewish high council* found me guilty of, ²¹except for the one time I shouted out, 'I am on trial before you today because I believe in the resurrection of the dead!'"

²²At that point Felix, who was quite familiar with the Way, adjourned the hearing and said, "Wait until Lysias, the garrison commander, arrives. Then I will decide the case." ²³He ordered an officer* to keep Paul in custody but to give him some freedom and allow his friends to visit him and take care of his needs.

²⁴A few days later Felix came back with his wife, Drusilla, who was Jewish. Sending for Paul, they listened as he told them about faith in Christ Jesus. ²⁵As he reasoned with them about righteousness and self-control and the coming day of judgment, Felix became frightened. "Go away for now," he replied. "When it is more convenient, I'll call for you again." ²⁶He also hoped that Paul would bribe him, so he sent for him quite often and talked with him.

²⁷After two years went by in this way, Felix was succeeded by Porcius Festus. And because Felix wanted to gain favor with the Jewish people, he left Paul in prison.

Paul Appears before Festus

25 Three days after Festus arrived in Caesarea to take over his new responsibilities, he left for Jerusalem, ²where the leading priests and other Jewish leaders met with him and made their accusations against Paul. ³They asked Festus as a favor to transfer Paul to Jerusalem (planning to ambush and kill him on the way). ⁴But Festus replied that Paul was at Caesarea and he himself would be returning there soon. ⁵So he said, "Those of you in

24:20 Greek *Sanhedrin.* **24:23** Greek *a centurion.*

authority can return with me. If Paul has done anything wrong, you can make your accusations."

⁶About eight or ten days later Festus returned to Caesarea, and on the following day he took his seat in court and ordered that Paul be brought in. ⁷When Paul arrived, the Jewish leaders from Jerusalem gathered around and made many serious accusations they couldn't prove.

⁸Paul denied the charges. "I am not guilty of any crime against the Jewish laws or the Temple or the Roman government," he said.

⁹Then Festus, wanting to please the Jews, asked him, "Are you willing to go to Jerusalem and stand trial before me there?"

¹⁰But Paul replied, "No! This is the official Roman court, so I ought to be tried right here. You know very well I am not guilty of harming the Jews. ¹¹If I have done something worthy of death, I don't refuse to die. But if I am innocent, no one has a right to turn me over to these men to kill me. I appeal to Caesar!"

¹²Festus conferred with his advisers and then replied, "Very well! You have appealed to Caesar, and to Caesar you will go!"

¹³A few days later King Agrippa arrived with his sister, Bernice,* to pay their respects to Festus. ¹⁴During their stay of several days, Festus discussed Paul's case with the king. "There is a prisoner here," he told him, "whose case was left for me by Felix. ¹⁵When I was in Jerusalem, the leading priests and Jewish elders pressed charges against him and asked me to condemn him. ¹⁶I pointed out to them that Roman law does not convict people without a trial. They must be given an opportunity to confront their accusers and defend themselves.

¹⁷"When his accusers came here for the trial, I didn't delay. I called the case the very next day and ordered Paul brought in. ¹⁸But the accusations made against him weren't any of the crimes I expected. ¹⁹Instead, it was something about their religion and a dead man named Jesus, who Paul insists is alive. ²⁰I was at a loss to know how to investigate these things, so I asked him whether he would be willing to stand trial on these charges in Jerusalem. ²¹But Paul appealed to have his case decided by the emperor. So I ordered that he be held in custody until I could arrange to send him to Caesar."

²²"I'd like to hear the man myself," Agrippa said.

And Festus replied, "You will—tomorrow!"

Paul Speaks to Agrippa

²³So the next day Agrippa and Bernice arrived at the auditorium with great pomp, accompanied by military officers and prominent men of the city. Festus ordered that Paul be brought in. ²⁴Then Festus said,

25:13 Greek *Agrippa the king and Bernice arrived.*

"King Agrippa and all who are here, this is the man whose death is demanded by all the Jews, both here and in Jerusalem. 25But in my opinion he has done nothing deserving death. However, since he appealed his case to the emperor, I have decided to send him to Rome.

26"But what shall I write the emperor? For there is no clear charge against him. So I have brought him before all of you, and especially you, King Agrippa, so that after we examine him, I might have something to write. 27For it makes no sense to send a prisoner to the emperor without specifying the charges against him!"

26 Then Agrippa said to Paul, "You may speak in your defense."

So Paul, gesturing with his hand, started his defense: 2"I am fortunate, King Agrippa, that you are the one hearing my defense today against all these accusations made by the Jewish leaders, 3for I know you are an expert on all Jewish customs and controversies. Now please listen to me patiently!

4"As the Jewish leaders are well aware, I was given a thorough Jewish training from my earliest childhood among my own people and in Jerusalem. 5If they would admit it, they know that I have been a member of the Pharisees, the strictest sect of our religion. 6Now I am on trial because of my hope in the fulfillment of God's promise made to our ancestors. 7In fact, that is why the twelve tribes of Israel zealously worship God night and day, and they share the same hope I have. Yet, Your Majesty, they accuse me for having this hope! 8Why does it seem incredible to any of you that God can raise the dead?

9"I used to believe that I ought to do everything I could to oppose the very name of Jesus the Nazarene.* 10Indeed, I did just that in Jerusalem. Authorized by the leading priests, I caused many believers* there to be sent to prison. And I cast my vote against them when they were condemned to death. 11Many times I had them punished in the synagogues to get them to curse Jesus.* I was so violently opposed to them that I even chased them down in foreign cities.

12"One day I was on such a mission to Damascus, armed with the authority and commission of the leading priests. 13About noon, Your Majesty, as I was on the road, a light from heaven brighter than the sun shone down on me and my companions. 14We all fell down, and I heard a voice saying to me in Aramaic,* 'Saul, Saul, why are you persecuting me? It is useless for you to fight against my will.*'

15"'Who are you, lord?' I asked.

"And the Lord replied, 'I am Jesus,

26:9 Or *Jesus of Nazareth.* 26:10 Greek *many of God's holy people.* 26:11 Greek *to blaspheme.* 26:14a Or *Hebrew.* 26:14b Greek *It is hard for you to kick against the oxgoads.*

the one you are persecuting. [16]Now get to your feet! For I have appeared to you to appoint you as my servant and witness. Tell people that you have seen me, and tell them what I will show you in the future. [17]And I will rescue you from both your own people and the Gentiles. Yes, I am sending you to the Gentiles [18]to open their eyes, so they may turn from darkness to light and from the power of Satan to God. Then they will receive forgiveness for their sins and be given a place among God's people, who are set apart by faith in me.'

[19]"And so, King Agrippa, I obeyed that vision from heaven. [20]I preached first to those in Damascus, then in Jerusalem and throughout all Judea, and also to the Gentiles, that all must repent of their sins and turn to God—and prove they have changed by the good things they do. [21]Some Jews arrested me in the Temple for preaching this, and they tried to kill me. [22]But God has protected me right up to this present time so I can testify to everyone, from the least to the greatest. I teach nothing except what the prophets and Moses said would happen—[23]that the Messiah would suffer and be the first to rise from the dead, and in this way announce God's light to Jews and Gentiles alike."

[24]Suddenly, Festus shouted, "Paul, you are insane. Too much study has made you crazy!"

[25]But Paul replied, "I am not insane, Most Excellent Festus. What I am saying is the sober truth. [26]And King Agrippa knows about these things. I speak boldly, for I am sure these events are all familiar to him, for they were not done in a corner! [27]King Agrippa, do you believe the prophets? I know you do—"

[28]Agrippa interrupted him. "Do you think you can persuade me to become a Christian so quickly?"*

[29]Paul replied, "Whether quickly or not, I pray to God that both you and everyone here in this audience might become the same as I am, except for these chains."

[30]Then the king, the governor, Bernice, and all the others stood and left. [31]As they went out, they talked it over and agreed, "This man hasn't done anything to deserve death or imprisonment."

[32]And Agrippa said to Festus, "He could have been set free if he hadn't appealed to Caesar."

Paul Sails for Rome

27 When the time came, we set sail for Italy. Paul and several other prisoners were placed in the custody of a Roman officer* named Julius, a captain of the Imperial Regiment. [2]Aristarchus, a Macedonian from Thessalonica, was also with us. We left on a ship whose home port was Adramyttium on the northwest coast of the province of

26:28 Or *"A little more, and your arguments would make me a Christian."* 27:1 Greek *centurion;* similarly in 27:6, 11, 31, 43.

Asia;* it was scheduled to make several stops at ports along the coast of the province.

³The next day when we docked at Sidon, Julius was very kind to Paul and let him go ashore to visit with friends so they could provide for his needs. ⁴Putting out to sea from there, we encountered strong headwinds that made it difficult to keep the ship on course, so we sailed north of Cyprus between the island and the mainland. ⁵Keeping to the open sea, we passed along the coast of Cilicia and Pamphylia, landing at Myra, in the province of Lycia. ⁶There the commanding officer found an Egyptian ship from Alexandria that was bound for Italy, and he put us on board.

⁷We had several days of slow sailing, and after great difficulty we finally neared Cnidus. But the wind was against us, so we sailed across to Crete and along the sheltered coast of the island, past the cape of Salmone. ⁸We struggled along the coast with great difficulty and finally arrived at Fair Havens, near the town of Lasea. ⁹We had lost a lot of time. The weather was becoming dangerous for sea travel because it was so late in the fall,* and Paul spoke to the ship's officers about it.

¹⁰"Men," he said, "I believe there is trouble ahead if we go on—shipwreck, loss of cargo, and danger to our lives as well." ¹¹But the officer in charge of the prisoners listened more to the ship's captain and the owner than to Paul. ¹²And since Fair Havens was an exposed harbor—a poor place to spend the winter—most of the crew wanted to go on to Phoenix, farther up the coast of Crete, and spend the winter there. Phoenix was a good harbor with only a southwest and northwest exposure.

The Storm at Sea

¹³When a light wind began blowing from the south, the sailors thought they could make it. So they pulled up anchor and sailed close to the shore of Crete. ¹⁴But the weather changed abruptly, and a wind of typhoon strength (called a "northeaster") burst across the island and blew us out to sea. ¹⁵The sailors couldn't turn the ship into the wind, so they gave up and let it run before the gale.

¹⁶We sailed along the sheltered side of a small island named Cauda,* where with great difficulty we hoisted aboard the lifeboat being towed behind us. ¹⁷Then the sailors bound ropes around the hull of the ship to strengthen it. They were afraid of being driven across to the sandbars of Syrtis off the African coast, so they lowered the sea anchor to slow the ship and were driven before the wind.

27:2 Asia was a Roman province in what is now western Turkey.   27:9 Greek because the fast was now already gone by. This fast was associated with the Day of Atonement (Yom Kippur), which occurred in late September or early October.   27:16 Some manuscripts read Clauda.

¹⁸The next day, as gale-force winds continued to batter the ship, the crew began throwing the cargo overboard. ¹⁹The following day they even took some of the ship's gear and threw it overboard. ²⁰The terrible storm raged for many days, blotting out the sun and the stars, until at last all hope was gone.

²¹No one had eaten for a long time. Finally, Paul called the crew together and said, "Men, you should have listened to me in the first place and not left Crete. You would have avoided all this damage and loss. ²²But take courage! None of you will lose your lives, even though the ship will go down. ²³For last night an angel of the God to whom I belong and whom I serve stood beside me, ²⁴and he said, 'Don't be afraid, Paul, for you will surely stand trial before Caesar! What's more, God in his goodness has granted safety to everyone sailing with you.' ²⁵So take courage! For I believe God. It will be just as he said. ²⁶But we will be shipwrecked on an island."

The Shipwreck

²⁷About midnight on the fourteenth night of the storm, as we were being driven across the Sea of Adria,* the sailors sensed land was near. ²⁸They dropped a weighted line and found that the water was 120 feet deep. But a little later they measured again and found it was only 90 feet deep.* ²⁹At this rate they were afraid we would soon be driven against the rocks along the shore, so they threw out four anchors from the back of the ship and prayed for daylight.

³⁰Then the sailors tried to abandon the ship; they lowered the lifeboat as though they were going to put out anchors from the front of the ship. ³¹But Paul said to the commanding officer and the soldiers, "You will all die unless the sailors stay aboard." ³²So the soldiers cut the ropes to the lifeboat and let it drift away.

³³Just as day was dawning, Paul urged everyone to eat. "You have been so worried that you haven't touched food for two weeks," he said. ³⁴"Please eat something now for your own good. For not a hair of your heads will perish." ³⁵Then he took some bread, gave thanks to God before them all, and broke off a piece and ate it. ³⁶Then everyone was encouraged and began to eat— ³⁷all 276 of us who were on board. ³⁸After eating, the crew lightened the ship further by throwing the cargo of wheat overboard.

³⁹When morning dawned, they didn't recognize the coastline, but they saw a bay with a beach and wondered if they could get to shore by running the ship aground. ⁴⁰So they cut off the anchors and left them in the sea. Then they lowered

27:27 The *Sea of Adria* includes the central portion of the Mediterranean. 27:28 Greek 20 fathoms . . . 15 fathoms [37 meters . . . 27 meters].

the rudders, raised the foresail, and headed toward shore. [41]But they hit a shoal and ran the ship aground too soon. The bow of the ship stuck fast, while the stern was repeatedly smashed by the force of the waves and began to break apart.

[42]The soldiers wanted to kill the prisoners to make sure they didn't swim ashore and escape. [43]But the commanding officer wanted to spare Paul, so he didn't let them carry out their plan. Then he ordered all who could swim to jump overboard first and make for land. [44]The others held on to planks or debris from the broken ship.* So everyone escaped safely to shore.

Paul on the Island of Malta

28 Once we were safe on shore, we learned that we were on the island of Malta. [2]The people of the island were very kind to us. It was cold and rainy, so they built a fire on the shore to welcome us.

[3]As Paul gathered an armful of sticks and was laying them on the fire, a poisonous snake, driven out by the heat, bit him on the hand. [4]The people of the island saw it hanging from his hand and said to each other, "A murderer, no doubt! Though he escaped the sea, justice will not permit him to live." [5]But Paul shook off the snake into the fire and was unharmed. [6]The people waited for him to swell up or suddenly drop dead. But when they had waited a long time and saw that he wasn't harmed, they changed their minds and decided he was a god.

[7]Near the shore where we landed was an estate belonging to Publius, the chief official of the island. He welcomed us and treated us kindly for three days. [8]As it happened, Publius's father was ill with fever and dysentery. Paul went in and prayed for him, and laying his hands on him, he healed him. [9]Then all the other sick people on the island came and were healed. [10]As a result we were showered with honors, and when the time came to sail, people supplied us with everything we would need for the trip.

Paul Arrives at Rome

[11]It was three months after the shipwreck that we set sail on another ship that had wintered at the island—an Alexandrian ship with the twin gods* as its figurehead. [12]Our first stop was Syracuse,* where we stayed three days. [13]From there we sailed across to Rhegium.* A day later a south wind began blowing, so the following day we sailed up the coast to Puteoli. [14]There we found some believers,* who invited us to spend a week with them. And so we came to Rome.

27:44 Or *or were helped by members of the ship's crew.* 28:11 The *twin gods* were the Roman gods Castor and Pollux. 28:12 *Syracuse* was on the island of Sicily. 28:13 *Rhegium* was on the southern tip of Italy. 28:14 Greek *brothers.*

15The brothers and sisters* in Rome had heard we were coming, and they came to meet us at the Forum* on the Appian Way. Others joined us at The Three Taverns.* When Paul saw them, he was encouraged and thanked God.

16When we arrived in Rome, Paul was permitted to have his own private lodging, though he was guarded by a soldier.

Paul Preaches at Rome under Guard

17Three days after Paul's arrival, he called together the local Jewish leaders. He said to them, "Brothers, I was arrested in Jerusalem and handed over to the Roman government, even though I had done nothing against our people or the customs of our ancestors. 18The Romans tried me and wanted to release me, because they found no cause for the death sentence. 19But when the Jewish leaders protested the decision, I felt it necessary to appeal to Caesar, even though I had no desire to press charges against my own people. 20I asked you to come here today so we could get acquainted and so I could explain to you that I am bound with this chain because I believe that the hope of Israel—the Messiah—has already come."

21They replied, "We have had no letters from Judea or reports against you from anyone who has come here. 22But we want to hear what you believe, for the only thing we know about this movement is that it is denounced everywhere."

23So a time was set, and on that day a large number of people came to Paul's lodging. He explained and testified about the Kingdom of God and tried to persuade them about Jesus from the Scriptures. Using the law of Moses and the books of the prophets, he spoke to them from morning until evening. 24Some were persuaded by the things he said, but others did not believe. 25And after they had argued back and forth among themselves, they left with this final word from Paul: "The Holy Spirit was right when he said to your ancestors through Isaiah the prophet,

26 'Go and say to this people:
When you hear what I say,
    you will not understand.
When you see what I do,
    you will not comprehend.
27 For the hearts of these people
        are hardened,
    and their ears cannot hear,
    and they have closed their
        eyes—
so their eyes cannot see,
    and their ears cannot hear,
    and their hearts cannot
        understand,

28:15a Greek brothers. 28:15b The Forum was about 43 miles (70 kilometers) from Rome.
28:15c The Three Taverns was about 35 miles (57 kilometers) from Rome.

and they cannot turn
to me
and let me heal them.'*

²⁸So I want you to know that this salvation from God has also been offered to the Gentiles, and they will accept it."*

³⁰For the next two years, Paul lived in Rome at his own expense.* He welcomed all who visited him, ³¹boldly proclaiming the Kingdom of God and teaching about the Lord Jesus Christ. And no one tried to stop him.

28:26-27 Isa 6:9-10 (Greek version).   **28:28** Some manuscripts add verse 29, *And when he had said these words, the Jews departed, greatly disagreeing with each other.*   **28:30** Or *in his own rented quarters.*

Romans

Greetings from Paul

1 This letter is from Paul, a slave of Christ Jesus, chosen by God to be an apostle and sent out to preach his Good News. [2]God promised this Good News long ago through his prophets in the holy Scriptures. [3]The Good News is about his Son. In his earthly life he was born into King David's family line, [4]and he was shown to be* the Son of God when he was raised from the dead by the power of the Holy Spirit.* He is Jesus Christ our Lord. [5]Through Christ, God has given us the privilege* and authority as apostles to tell Gentiles everywhere what God has done for them, so that they will believe and obey him, bringing glory to his name.

[6]And you are included among those Gentiles who have been called to belong to Jesus Christ. [7]I am writing to all of you in Rome who are loved by God and are called to be his own holy people.

May God our Father and the Lord Jesus Christ give you grace and peace.

God's Good News

[8]Let me say first that I thank my God through Jesus Christ for all of you, because your faith in him is being talked about all over the world. [9]God knows how often I pray for you. Day and night I bring you and your needs in prayer to God, whom I serve with all my heart* by spreading the Good News about his Son.

[10]One of the things I always pray for is the opportunity, God willing, to come at last to see you. [11]For I long to visit you so I can bring you some spiritual gift that will help you grow strong in the Lord. [12]When we get together, I want to encourage you in your faith, but I also want to be encouraged by yours.

[13]I want you to know, dear brothers and sisters,* that I planned many times to visit you, but I was prevented until now. I want to work among you and see spiritual fruit, just as I have seen among other Gentiles. [14]For I have a great sense of obligation to people in both the civilized world and the rest of the world,* to the educated and uneducated alike. [15]So I am eager to come to you in Rome, too, to preach the Good News.

[16]For I am not ashamed of this Good News about Christ. It is the

---

1:4a Or *and was designated.*   1:4b Or *by the Spirit of holiness;* or *in the new realm of the Spirit.*
1:5 Or *the grace.*   1:9 Or *in my spirit.*   1:13 Greek *brothers.*   1:14 Greek *to Greeks and barbarians.*

power of God at work, saving everyone who believes—the Jew first and also the Gentile.* [17]This Good News tells us how God makes us right in his sight. This is accomplished from start to finish by faith. As the Scriptures say, "It is through faith that a righteous person has life."*

God's Anger at Sin

[18]But God shows his anger from heaven against all sinful, wicked people who suppress the truth by their wickedness.* [19]They know the truth about God because he has made it obvious to them. [20]For ever since the world was created, people have seen the earth and sky. Through everything God made, they can clearly see his invisible qualities—his eternal power and divine nature. So they have no excuse for not knowing God.

[21]Yes, they knew God, but they wouldn't worship him as God or even give him thanks. And they began to think up foolish ideas of what God was like. As a result, their minds became dark and confused. [22]Claiming to be wise, they instead became utter fools. [23]And instead of worshiping the glorious, ever-living God, they worshiped idols made to look like mere people and birds and animals and reptiles.

[24]So God abandoned them to do whatever shameful things their hearts desired. As a result, they did vile and degrading things with each other's bodies. [25]They traded the truth about God for a lie. So they worshiped and served the things God created instead of the Creator himself, who is worthy of eternal praise! Amen. [26]That is why God abandoned them to their shameful desires. Even the women turned against the natural way to have sex and instead indulged in sex with each other. [27]And the men, instead of having normal sexual relations with women, burned with lust for each other. Men did shameful things with other men, and as a result of this sin, they suffered within themselves the penalty they deserved.

[28]Since they thought it foolish to acknowledge God, he abandoned them to their foolish thinking and let them do things that should never be done. [29]Their lives became full of every kind of wickedness, sin, greed, hate, envy, murder, quarreling, deception, malicious behavior, and gossip. [30]They are backstabbers, haters of God, insolent, proud, and boastful. They invent new ways of sinning, and they disobey their parents. [31]They refuse to understand, break their promises, are heartless, and have no mercy. [32]They know God's justice requires that those who do these things deserve to die, yet they do them anyway. Worse yet, they encourage others to do them, too.

1:16 Greek *also the Greek.* 1:17 Or *"The righteous will live by faith."* Hab 2:4. 1:18 Or *who, by their wickedness, prevent the truth from being known.*

God's Judgment of Sin

2 You may think you can condemn such people, but you are just as bad, and you have no excuse! When you say they are wicked and should be punished, you are condemning yourself, for you who judge others do these very same things. [2]And we know that God, in his justice, will punish anyone who does such things. [3]Since you judge others for doing these things, why do you think you can avoid God's judgment when you do the same things? [4]Don't you see how wonderfully kind, tolerant, and patient God is with you? Does this mean nothing to you? Can't you see that his kindness is intended to turn you from your sin?

[5]But because you are stubborn and refuse to turn from your sin, you are storing up terrible punishment for yourself. For a day of anger is coming, when God's righteous judgment will be revealed. [6]He will judge everyone according to what they have done. [7]He will give eternal life to those who keep on doing good, seeking after the glory and honor and immortality that God offers. [8]But he will pour out his anger and wrath on those who live for themselves, who refuse to obey the truth and instead live lives of wickedness. [9]There will be trouble and calamity for everyone who keeps on doing what is evil—for the Jew first and also for the Gentile.* [10]But there will

be glory and honor and peace from God for all who do good—for the Jew first and also for the Gentile. [11]For God does not show favoritism.

[12]When the Gentiles sin, they will be destroyed, even though they never had God's written law. And the Jews, who do have God's law, will be judged by that law when they fail to obey it. [13]For merely listening to the law doesn't make us right with God. It is obeying the law that makes us right in his sight. [14]Even Gentiles, who do not have God's written law, show that they know his law when they instinctively obey it, even without having heard it. [15]They demonstrate that God's law is written in their hearts, for their own conscience and thoughts either accuse them or tell them they are doing right. [16]And this is the message I proclaim—that the day is coming when God, through Christ Jesus, will judge everyone's secret life.

The Jews and the Law

[17]You who call yourselves Jews are relying on God's law, and you boast about your special relationship with him. [18]You know what he wants; you know what is right because you have been taught his law. [19]You are convinced that you are a guide for the blind and a light for people who are lost in darkness. [20]You think you can instruct the ignorant and teach

2:9 Greek *also for the Greek;* also in 2:10.

children the ways of God. For you are certain that God's law gives you complete knowledge and truth.

²¹Well then, if you teach others, why don't you teach yourself? You tell others not to steal, but do you steal? ²²You say it is wrong to commit adultery, but do you commit adultery? You condemn idolatry, but do you use items stolen from pagan temples?* ²³You are so proud of knowing the law, but you dishonor God by breaking it. ²⁴No wonder the Scriptures say, "The Gentiles blaspheme the name of God because of you."*

²⁵The Jewish ceremony of circumcision has value only if you obey God's law. But if you don't obey God's law, you are no better off than an uncircumcised Gentile. ²⁶And if the Gentiles obey God's law, won't God declare them to be his own people? ²⁷In fact, uncircumcised Gentiles who keep God's law will condemn you Jews who are circumcised and possess God's law but don't obey it.

²⁸For you are not a true Jew just because you were born of Jewish parents or because you have gone through the ceremony of circumcision. ²⁹No, a true Jew is one whose heart is right with God. And true circumcision is not merely obeying the letter of the law; rather, it is a change of heart produced by the Spirit. And a person with a changed heart seeks praise* from God, not from people.

God Remains Faithful

3 Then what's the advantage of being a Jew? Is there any value in the ceremony of circumcision? ²Yes, there are great benefits! First of all, the Jews were entrusted with the whole revelation of God.*

³True, some of them were unfaithful; but just because they were unfaithful, does that mean God will be unfaithful? ⁴Of course not! Even if everyone else is a liar, God is true. As the Scriptures say about him,

"You will be proved right in what you say,
and you will win your case in court."*

⁵"But," some might say, "our sinfulness serves a good purpose, for it helps people see how righteous God is. Isn't it unfair, then, for him to punish us?" (This is merely a human point of view.) ⁶Of course not! If God were not entirely fair, how would he be qualified to judge the world? ⁷"But," someone might still argue, "how can God condemn me as a sinner if my dishonesty highlights his truthfulness and brings him more glory?" ⁸And some people even slander us by claiming that we say, "The more we sin, the better it is!" Those who say such things deserve to be condemned.

2:22 Greek *do you steal from temples?* 2:24 Isa 52:5 (Greek version). 2:29 Or *receives praise.*
3:2 Greek *the oracles of God.* 3:4 Ps 51:4 (Greek version).

All People Are Sinners

⁹Well then, should we conclude that we Jews are better than others? No, not at all, for we have already shown that all people, whether Jews or Gentiles,* are under the power of sin. ¹⁰As the Scriptures say,

"No one is righteous—
    not even one.
¹¹ No one is truly wise;
    no one is seeking God.
¹² All have turned away;
    all have become useless.
No one does good,
    not a single one."*
¹³ "Their talk is foul, like the
        stench from an open grave.
    Their tongues are filled with
        lies."
"Snake venom drips from
        their lips."*
¹⁴ "Their mouths are full of
        cursing and bitterness."*
¹⁵ "They rush to commit murder.
¹⁶   Destruction and misery always
        follow them.
¹⁷ They don't know where to find
        peace."*
¹⁸ "They have no fear of God
        at all."*

¹⁹Obviously, the law applies to those to whom it was given, for its purpose is to keep people from having excuses, and to show that the entire world is guilty before God. ²⁰For no one can ever be made right with God by doing what the law commands. The law simply shows us how sinful we are.

Christ Took Our Punishment

²¹But now God has shown us a way to be made right with him without keeping the requirements of the law, as was promised in the writings of Moses* and the prophets long ago. ²²We are made right with God by placing our faith in Jesus Christ. And this is true for everyone who believes, no matter who we are.

²³For everyone has sinned; we all fall short of God's glorious standard. ²⁴Yet God, in his grace, freely makes us right in his sight. He did this through Christ Jesus when he freed us from the penalty for our sins. ²⁵For God presented Jesus as the sacrifice for sin. People are made right with God when they believe that Jesus sacrificed his life, shedding his blood. This sacrifice shows that God was being fair when he held back and did not punish those who sinned in times past, ²⁶for he was looking ahead and including them in what he would do in this present time. God did this to demonstrate his righteousness, for he himself is fair and just, and he makes sinners right in his sight when they believe in Jesus.

²⁷Can we boast, then, that we have done anything to be accepted by God? No, because our acquittal is

3:9 Greek *or Greeks*. 3:10-12 Pss 14:1-3; 53:1-3 (Greek version). 3:13 Pss 5:9 (Greek version); 140:3. 3:14 Ps 10:7 (Greek version). 3:15-17 Isa 59:7-8. 3:18 Ps 36:1. 3:21 Greek *in the law*.

not based on obeying the law. It is based on faith. ²⁸So we are made right with God through faith and not by obeying the law.

²⁹After all, is God the God of the Jews only? Isn't he also the God of the Gentiles? Of course he is. ³⁰There is only one God, and he makes people right with himself only by faith, whether they are Jews or Gentiles.* ³¹Well then, if we emphasize faith, does this mean that we can forget about the law? Of course not! In fact, only when we have faith do we truly fulfill the law.

The Faith of Abraham

4 Abraham was, humanly speaking, the founder of our Jewish nation. What did he discover about being made right with God? ²If his good deeds had made him acceptable to God, he would have had something to boast about. But that was not God's way. ³For the Scriptures tell us, "Abraham believed God, and God counted him as righteous because of his faith."*

⁴When people work, their wages are not a gift, but something they have earned. ⁵But people are counted as righteous, not because of their work, but because of their faith in God who forgives sinners. ⁶David also spoke of this when he described the happiness of those who are declared righteous without working for it:

⁷ "Oh, what joy for those
    whose disobedience is
        forgiven,
    whose sins are put out
        of sight.
⁸ Yes, what joy for those
    whose record the LORD has
        cleared of sin."*

⁹Now, is this blessing only for the Jews, or is it also for uncircumcised Gentiles?* Well, we have been saying that Abraham was counted as righteous by God because of his faith. ¹⁰But how did this happen? Was he counted as righteous only after he was circumcised, or was it before he was circumcised? Clearly, God accepted Abraham before he was circumcised!

¹¹Circumcision was a sign that Abraham already had faith and that God had already accepted him and declared him to be righteous—even before he was circumcised. So Abraham is the spiritual father of those who have faith but have not been circumcised. They are counted as righteous because of their faith. ¹²And Abraham is also the spiritual father of those who have been circumcised, but only if they have the same kind of faith Abraham had before he was circumcised.

¹³Clearly, God's promise to give the whole earth to Abraham and his descendants was based not on his obedience to God's law, but on a

3:30 Greek *whether they are circumcised or uncircumcised.* 4:3 Gen 15:6. 4:7-8 Ps 32:1-2 (Greek version). 4:9 Greek *is this blessing only for the circumcised, or is it also for the uncircumcised?*

right relationship with God that comes by faith. [14]If God's promise is only for those who obey the law, then faith is not necessary and the promise is pointless. [15]For the law always brings punishment on those who try to obey it. (The only way to avoid breaking the law is to have no law to break!)

[16]So the promise is received by faith. It is given as a free gift. And we are all certain to receive it, whether or not we live according to the law of Moses, if we have faith like Abraham's. For Abraham is the father of all who believe. [17]That is what the Scriptures mean when God told him, "I have made you the father of many nations."* This happened because Abraham believed in the God who brings the dead back to life and who creates new things out of nothing.

[18]Even when there was no reason for hope, Abraham kept hoping—believing that he would become the father of many nations. For God had said to him, "That's how many descendants you will have!"* [19]And Abraham's faith did not weaken, even though, at about 100 years of age, he figured his body was as good as dead—and so was Sarah's womb.

[20]Abraham never wavered in believing God's promise. In fact, his faith grew stronger, and in this he brought glory to God. [21]He was fully convinced that God is able to do whatever he promises. [22]And be-cause of Abraham's faith, God counted him as righteous. [23]And when God counted him as righteous, it wasn't just for Abraham's benefit. It was recorded [24]for our benefit, too, assuring us that God will also count us as righteous if we believe in him, the one who raised Jesus our Lord from the dead. [25]He was handed over to die because of our sins, and he was raised to life to make us right with God.

Faith Brings Joy

5 Therefore, since we have been made right in God's sight by faith, we have peace* with God because of what Jesus Christ our Lord has done for us. [2]Because of our faith, Christ has brought us into this place of undeserved privilege where we now stand, and we confidently and joyfully look forward to sharing God's glory.

[3]We can rejoice, too, when we run into problems and trials, for we know that they help us develop endurance. [4]And endurance develops strength of character, and character strengthens our confident hope of salvation. [5]And this hope will not lead to disappointment. For we know how dearly God loves us, because he has given us the Holy Spirit to fill our hearts with his love.

[6]When we were utterly helpless, Christ came at just the right time and died for us sinners. [7]Now, most people would not be willing to die

4:17 Gen 17:5.   4:18 Gen 15:5.   5:1 Some manuscripts read *let us have peace.*

for an upright person, though someone might perhaps be willing to die for a person who is especially good. [8]But God showed his great love for us by sending Christ to die for us while we were still sinners. [9]And since we have been made right in God's sight by the blood of Christ, he will certainly save us from God's condemnation. [10]For since our friendship with God was restored by the death of his Son while we were still his enemies, we will certainly be saved through the life of his Son. [11]So now we can rejoice in our wonderful new relationship with God because our Lord Jesus Christ has made us friends of God.

Adam and Christ Contrasted

[12]When Adam sinned, sin entered the world. Adam's sin brought death, so death spread to everyone, for everyone sinned. [13]Yes, people sinned even before the law was given. But it was not counted as sin because there was not yet any law to break. [14]Still, everyone died—from the time of Adam to the time of Moses—even those who did not disobey an explicit commandment of God, as Adam did. Now Adam is a symbol, a representation of Christ, who was yet to come. [15]But there is a great difference between Adam's sin and God's gracious gift. For the sin of this one man, Adam, brought death to many. But even greater is God's wonderful grace and his gift of forgiveness to many through this other man, Jesus Christ. [16]And the result of God's gracious gift is very different from the result of that one man's sin. For Adam's sin led to condemnation, but God's free gift leads to our being made right with God, even though we are guilty of many sins. [17]For the sin of this one man, Adam, caused death to rule over many. But even greater is God's wonderful grace and his gift of righteousness, for all who receive it will live in triumph over sin and death through this one man, Jesus Christ.

[18]Yes, Adam's one sin brings condemnation for everyone, but Christ's one act of righteousness brings a right relationship with God and new life for everyone. [19]Because one person disobeyed God, many became sinners. But because one other person obeyed God, many will be made righteous.

[20]God's law was given so that all people could see how sinful they were. But as people sinned more and more, God's wonderful grace became more abundant. [21]So just as sin ruled over all people and brought them to death, now God's wonderful grace rules instead, giving us right standing with God and resulting in eternal life through Jesus Christ our Lord.

Sin's Power Is Broken

6 Well then, should we keep on sinning so that God can show us more and more of his wonderful grace? [2]Of course not! Since we have died to sin, how can we continue to live in it? ³Or have you forgotten that when we were joined with Christ Jesus in baptism, we joined him in his death? ⁴For we died and were buried with Christ by baptism. And just as Christ was raised from the dead by the glorious power of the Father, now we also may live new lives.

⁵Since we have been united with him in his death, we will also be raised to life as he was. ⁶We know that our old sinful selves were crucified with Christ so that sin might lose its power in our lives. We are no longer slaves to sin. ⁷For when we died with Christ we were set free from the power of sin. ⁸And since we died with Christ, we know we will also live with him. ⁹We are sure of this because Christ was raised from the dead, and he will never die again. Death no longer has any power over him. ¹⁰When he died, he died once to break the power of sin. But now that he lives, he lives for the glory of God. ¹¹So you also should consider yourselves to be dead to the power of sin and alive to God through Christ Jesus.

¹²Do not let sin control the way you live;* do not give in to sinful desires. ¹³Do not let any part of your body become an instrument of evil to serve sin. Instead, give yourselves completely to God, for you were dead, but now you have new life. So use your whole body as an instru-ment to do what is right for the glory of God. ¹⁴Sin is no longer your master, for you no longer live under the requirements of the law. Instead, you live under the freedom of God's grace.

¹⁵Well then, since God's grace has set us free from the law, does that mean we can go on sinning? Of course not! ¹⁶Don't you realize that you become the slave of whatever you choose to obey? You can be a slave to sin, which leads to death, or you can choose to obey God, which leads to righteous living. ¹⁷Thank God! Once you were slaves of sin, but now you wholeheartedly obey this teaching we have given you. ¹⁸Now you are free from your slavery to sin, and you have become slaves to righteous living.

¹⁹Because of the weakness of your human nature, I am using the illustration of slavery to help you understand all this. Previously, you let yourselves be slaves to impurity and lawlessness, which led ever deeper into sin. Now you must give yourselves to be slaves to righteous living so that you will become holy.

²⁰When you were slaves to sin, you were free from the obligation to do right. ²¹And what was the result? You are now ashamed of the things you used to do, things that end in eternal doom. ²²But now you are free from the power of sin and have become slaves of God. Now you do those things that lead to holiness

6:12 Or *Do not let sin reign in your body, which is subject to death.*

and result in eternal life. ²³For the wages of sin is death, but the free gift of God is eternal life through Christ Jesus our Lord.

No Longer Bound to the Law

7 Now, dear brothers and sisters*—you who are familiar with the law—don't you know that the law applies only while a person is living? ²For example, when a woman marries, the law binds her to her husband as long as he is alive. But if he dies, the laws of marriage no longer apply to her. ³So while her husband is alive, she would be committing adultery if she married another man. But if her husband dies, she is free from that law and does not commit adultery when she remarries.

⁴So, my dear brothers and sisters, this is the point: You died to the power of the law when you died with Christ. And now you are united with the one who was raised from the dead. As a result, we can produce a harvest of good deeds for God. ⁵When we were controlled by our old nature,* sinful desires were at work within us, and the law aroused these evil desires that produced a harvest of sinful deeds, resulting in death. ⁶But now we have been released from the law, for we died to it and are no longer captive to its power. Now we can serve God, not in the old way of obeying the letter of the law, but in the new way of living in the Spirit.

God's Law Reveals Our Sin

⁷Well then, am I suggesting that the law of God is sinful? Of course not! In fact, it was the law that showed me my sin. I would never have known that coveting is wrong if the law had not said, "You must not covet."* ⁸But sin used this command to arouse all kinds of covetous desires within me! If there were no law, sin would not have that power. ⁹At one time I lived without understanding the law. But when I learned the command not to covet, for instance, the power of sin came to life, ¹⁰and I died. So I discovered that the law's commands, which were supposed to bring life, brought spiritual death instead. ¹¹Sin took advantage of those commands and deceived me; it used the commands to kill me. ¹²But still, the law itself is holy, and its commands are holy and right and good.

¹³But how can that be? Did the law, which is good, cause my death? Of course not! Sin used what was good to bring about my condemnation to death. So we can see how terrible sin really is. It uses God's good commands for its own evil purposes.

Struggling with Sin

¹⁴So the trouble is not with the law, for it is spiritual and good. The trouble is with me, for I am all too human, a slave to sin. ¹⁵I don't really understand myself, for I want to do what is right, but I don't do it. Instead, I do

7:1 Greek *brothers;* also in 7:4.   7:5 Greek *When we were in the flesh.*   7:7 Exod 20:17; Deut 5:21.

what I hate. ¹⁶But if I know that what I am doing is wrong, this shows that I agree that the law is good. ¹⁷So I am not the one doing wrong; it is sin living in me that does it.

¹⁸And I know that nothing good lives in me, that is, in my sinful nature.* I want to do what is right, but I can't. ¹⁹I want to do what is good, but I don't. I don't want to do what is wrong, but I do it anyway. ²⁰But if I do what I don't want to do, I am not really the one doing wrong; it is sin living in me that does it.

²¹I have discovered this principle of life—that when I want to do what is right, I inevitably do what is wrong. ²²I love God's law with all my heart. ²³But there is another power* within me that is at war with my mind. This power makes me a slave to the sin that is still within me. ²⁴Oh, what a miserable person I am! Who will free me from this life that is dominated by sin and death? ²⁵Thank God! The answer is in Jesus Christ our Lord. So you see how it is: In my mind I really want to obey God's law, but because of my sinful nature I am a slave to sin.

Life in the Spirit

8 So now there is no condemnation for those who belong to Christ Jesus. ²And because you belong to him, the power* of the life-giving Spirit has freed you* from the power of sin that leads to death.

³The law of Moses was unable to save us because of the weakness of our sinful nature.* So God did what the law could not do. He sent his own Son in a body like the bodies we sinners have. And in that body God declared an end to sin's control over us by giving his Son as a sacrifice for our sins. ⁴He did this so that the just requirement of the law would be fully satisfied for us, who no longer follow our sinful nature but instead follow the Spirit.

⁵Those who are dominated by the sinful nature think about sinful things, but those who are controlled by the Holy Spirit think about things that please the Spirit. ⁶So letting your sinful nature control your mind leads to death. But letting the Spirit control your mind leads to life and peace. ⁷For the sinful nature is always hostile to God. It never did obey God's laws, and it never will. ⁸That's why those who are still under the control of their sinful nature can never please God.

⁹But you are not controlled by your sinful nature. You are controlled by the Spirit if you have the Spirit of God living in you. (And remember that those who do not have the Spirit of Christ living in them do not belong to him at all.) ¹⁰And Christ lives within you, so even though your body will die because of sin, the Spirit gives you life*

7:18 Greek *my flesh;* also in 7:25.   **7:23** Greek *law;* also in 7:23b.   **8:2a** Greek *the law;* also in 8:2b.   **8:2b** Some manuscripts read *me.*   **8:3** Greek *our flesh;* similarly in 8:4, 5, 6, 7, 8, 9, 12.   **8:10** Or *your spirit is alive.*

because you have been made right with God. [11]The Spirit of God, who raised Jesus from the dead, lives in you. And just as God raised Christ Jesus from the dead, he will give life to your mortal bodies by this same Spirit living within you.

[12]Therefore, dear brothers and sisters,* you have no obligation to do what your sinful nature urges you to do. [13]For if you live by its dictates, you will die. But if through the power of the Spirit you put to death the deeds of your sinful nature,* you will live. [14]For all who are led by the Spirit of God are children* of God.

[15]So you have not received a spirit that makes you fearful slaves. Instead, you received God's Spirit when he adopted you as his own children.* Now we call him, "Abba, Father."* [16]For his Spirit joins with our spirit to affirm that we are God's children. [17]And since we are his children, we are his heirs. In fact, together with Christ we are heirs of God's glory. But if we are to share his glory, we must also share his suffering.

The Future Glory

[18]Yet what we suffer now is nothing compared to the glory he will reveal to us later. [19]For all creation is waiting eagerly for that future day when God will reveal who his children really are. [20]Against its will, all creation was subjected to God's curse. But with eager hope, [21]the creation looks forward to the day when it will join God's children in glorious freedom from death and decay. [22]For we know that all creation has been groaning as in the pains of childbirth right up to the present time. [23]And we believers also groan, even though we have the Holy Spirit within us as a foretaste of future glory, for we long for our bodies to be released from sin and suffering. We, too, wait with eager hope for the day when God will give us our full rights as his adopted children,* including the new bodies he has promised us. [24]We were given this hope when we were saved. (If we already have something, we don't need to hope* for it. [25]But if we look forward to something we don't yet have, we must wait patiently and confidently.)

[26]And the Holy Spirit helps us in our weakness. For example, we don't know what God wants us to pray for. But the Holy Spirit prays for us with groanings that cannot be expressed in words. [27]And the Father who knows all hearts knows what the Spirit is saying, for the Spirit pleads for us believers* in harmony with God's own will. [28]And we know that God causes every-

8:12 Greek brothers; also in 8:29.　8:13 Greek deeds of the body.　8:14 Greek sons; also in 8:19.
8:15a Greek you received a spirit of sonship.　8:15b Abba is an Aramaic term for "father."
8:23 Greek wait anxiously for sonship.　8:24 Some manuscripts read wait.　8:27 Greek for God's holy people.

thing to work together* for the good of those who love God and are called according to his purpose for them. ²⁹For God knew his people in advance, and he chose them to become like his Son, so that his Son would be the firstborn* among many brothers and sisters. ³⁰And having chosen them, he called them to come to him. And having called them, he gave them right standing with himself. And having given them right standing, he gave them his glory.

Nothing Can Separate Us from God's Love

³¹What shall we say about such wonderful things as these? If God is for us, who can ever be against us? ³²Since he did not spare even his own Son but gave him up for us all, won't he also give us everything else? ³³Who dares accuse us whom God has chosen for his own? No one—for God himself has given us right standing with himself. ³⁴Who then will condemn us? No one—for Christ Jesus died for us and was raised to life for us, and he is sitting in the place of honor at God's right hand, pleading for us.

³⁵Can anything ever separate us from Christ's love? Does it mean he no longer loves us if we have trouble or calamity, or are persecuted, or hungry, or destitute, or in danger, or threatened with death? ³⁶(As the Scriptures say, "For your sake we are killed every day; we are being slaughtered like sheep."*) ³⁷No, despite all these things, overwhelming victory is ours through Christ, who loved us.

³⁸And I am convinced that nothing can ever separate us from God's love. Neither death nor life, neither angels nor demons,* neither our fears for today nor our worries about tomorrow—not even the powers of hell can separate us from God's love. ³⁹No power in the sky above or in the earth below—indeed, nothing in all creation will ever be able to separate us from the love of God that is revealed in Christ Jesus our Lord.

God's Selection of Israel

9 With Christ as my witness, I speak with utter truthfulness. My conscience and the Holy Spirit confirm it. ²My heart is filled with bitter sorrow and unending grief ³for my people, my Jewish brothers and sisters.* I would be willing to be forever cursed—cut off from Christ!—if that would save them. ⁴They are the people of Israel, chosen to be God's adopted children.* God revealed his glory to them. He made covenants with them and gave them his law. He gave them the privilege of worshiping him and receiving his wonderful promises. ⁵Abraham, Isaac, and Jacob are their ancestors, and Christ himself was

8:28 Some manuscripts read *And we know that everything works together.*   **8:29** Or *would be supreme.*
8:36 Ps 44:22.   **8:38** Greek *nor rulers.*   **9:3** Greek *my brothers.*   **9:4** Greek *chosen for sonship.*

an Israelite as far as his human nature is concerned. And he is God, the one who rules over everything and is worthy of eternal praise! Amen.*

6Well then, has God failed to fulfill his promise to Israel? No, for not all who are born into the nation of Israel are truly members of God's people! 7Being descendants of Abraham doesn't make them truly Abraham's children. For the Scriptures say, "Isaac is the son through whom your descendants will be counted,"* though Abraham had other children, too. 8This means that Abraham's physical descendants are not necessarily children of God. Only the children of the promise are considered to be Abraham's children. 9For God had promised, "I will return about this time next year, and Sarah will have a son."*

10This son was our ancestor Isaac. When he married Rebekah, she gave birth to twins.* 11But before they were born, before they had done anything good or bad, she received a message from God. (This message shows that God chooses people according to his own purposes; 12he calls people, but not according to their good or bad works.) She was told, "Your older son will serve your younger son."* 13In the words of the Scriptures, "I loved Jacob, but I rejected Esau."*

14Are we saying, then, that God was unfair? Of course not! 15For God said to Moses,

"I will show mercy to anyone
    I choose,
and I will show compassion
    to anyone I choose."*

16So it is God who decides to show mercy. We can neither choose it nor work for it.

17For the Scriptures say that God told Pharaoh, "I have appointed you for the very purpose of displaying my power in you and to spread my fame throughout the earth."* 18So you see, God chooses to show mercy to some, and he chooses to harden the hearts of others so they refuse to listen.

19Well then, you might say, "Why does God blame people for not responding? Haven't they simply done what he makes them do?"

20No, don't say that. Who are you, a mere human being, to argue with God? Should the thing that was created say to the one who created it, "Why have you made me like this?" 21When a potter makes jars out of clay, doesn't he have a right to use the same lump of clay to make one jar for decoration and another to throw garbage into? 22In the same way, even though God has the right to show his anger and his power, he is very patient with those on whom

---

9:5 Or *May God, the one who rules over everything, be praised forever. Amen.*   9:7 Gen 21:12.
9:9 Gen 18:10, 14.   9:10 Greek *she conceived children through this one man.*   9:12 Gen 25:23.
9:13 Mal 1:2-3.   9:15 Exod 33:19.   9:17 Exod 9:16 (Greek version).

his anger falls, who are destined for destruction. ²³He does this to make the riches of his glory shine even brighter on those to whom he shows mercy, who were prepared in advance for glory. ²⁴And we are among those whom he selected, both from the Jews and from the Gentiles.

²⁵Concerning the Gentiles, God says in the prophecy of Hosea,

"Those who were not my people,
    I will now call my people.
And I will love those
    whom I did not love before."*

²⁶And,

"Then, at the place where they
        were told,
    'You are not my people,'
there they will be called
    'children of the living God.'"*

²⁷And concerning Israel, Isaiah the prophet cried out,

"Though the people of Israel are
        as numerous as the sand of
        the seashore,
    only a remnant will be saved.
²⁸ For the LORD will carry out his
        sentence upon the earth
    quickly and with finality."*

²⁹And Isaiah said the same thing in another place:

"If the LORD of Heaven's Armies
        had not spared a few of our
        children,

we would have been wiped out
        like Sodom,
    destroyed like Gomorrah."*

Israel's Unbelief

³⁰What does all this mean? Even though the Gentiles were not trying to follow God's standards, they were made right with God. And it was by faith that this took place. ³¹But the people of Israel, who tried so hard to get right with God by keeping the law, never succeeded. ³²Why not? Because they were trying to get right with God by keeping the law* instead of by trusting in him. They stumbled over the great rock in their path. ³³God warned them of this in the Scriptures when he said,

"I am placing a stone in
        Jerusalem* that makes
        people stumble,
    a rock that makes them fall.
But anyone who trusts in him
    will never be disgraced."*

10 Dear brothers and sisters,* the longing of my heart and my prayer to God is for the people of Israel to be saved. ²I know what enthusiasm they have for God, but it is misdirected zeal. ³For they don't understand God's way of making people right with himself. Refusing to accept God's way, they cling to their own way of getting right with God by trying to keep the law. ⁴For

9:25 Hos 2:23. 9:26 Greek *sons of the living God.* Hos 1:10. 9:27-28 Isa 10:22-23 (Greek version).
9:29 Isa 1:9 (Greek version). 9:32 Greek *by works.* 9:33a Greek *in Zion.* 9:33b Isa 8:14; 28:16
(Greek version). 10:1 Greek *Brothers.*

Christ has already accomplished the purpose for which the law was given.* As a result, all who believe in him are made right with God.

Salvation Is for Everyone

5For Moses writes that the law's way of making a person right with God requires obedience to all of its commands.* 6But faith's way of getting right with God says, "Don't say in your heart, 'Who will go up to heaven?' (to bring Christ down to earth). 7And don't say, 'Who will go down to the place of the dead?' (to bring Christ back to life again)." 8In fact, it says,

> "The message is very close
> at hand;
> it is on your lips and in
> your heart."*

And that message is the very message about faith that we preach: 9If you openly declare that Jesus is Lord and believe in your heart that God raised him from the dead, you will be saved. 10For it is by believing in your heart that you are made right with God, and it is by openly declaring your faith that you are saved. 11As the Scriptures tell us, "Anyone who trusts in him will never be disgraced."* 12Jew and Gentile* are the same in this respect. They have the same Lord, who gives generously to all who call on him. 13For "Everyone who calls on the name of the LORD will be saved."*

14But how can they call on him to save them unless they believe in him? And how can they believe in him if they have never heard about him? And how can they hear about him unless someone tells them? 15And how will anyone go and tell them without being sent? That is why the Scriptures say, "How beautiful are the feet of messengers who bring good news!"*

16But not everyone welcomes the Good News, for Isaiah the prophet said, "LORD, who has believed our message?"* 17So faith comes from hearing, that is, hearing the Good News about Christ. 18But I ask, have the people of Israel actually heard the message? Yes, they have:

> "The message has gone
> throughout the earth,
> and the words to all the
> world."*

19But I ask, did the people of Israel really understand? Yes, they did, for even in the time of Moses, God said,

> "I will rouse your jealousy
> through people who are not
> even a nation.
> I will provoke your anger
> through the foolish
> Gentiles."*

10:4 Or *For Christ is the end of the law.* 10:5 See Lev 18:5. 10:6-8 Deut 30:12-14. 10:11 Isa 28:16 (Greek version). 10:12 Greek *and Greek.* 10:13 Joel 2:32. 10:15 Isa 52:7. 10:16 Isa 53:1. 10:18 Ps 19:4. 10:19 Deut 32:21.

[20]And later Isaiah spoke boldly for God, saying,

> "I was found by people who were not looking for me.
> I showed myself to those who were not asking for me."*

[21]But regarding Israel, God said,

> "All day long I opened my arms to them,
> but they were disobedient and rebellious."*

God's Mercy on Israel

11 I ask, then, has God rejected his own people, the nation of Israel? Of course not! I myself am an Israelite, a descendant of Abraham and a member of the tribe of Benjamin. [2]No, God has not rejected his own people, whom he chose from the very beginning. Do you realize what the Scriptures say about this? Elijah the prophet complained to God about the people of Israel and said, [3]"Lord, they have killed your prophets and torn down your altars. I am the only one left, and now they are trying to kill me, too."* [4]And do you remember God's reply? He said, "No, I have 7,000 others who have never bowed down to Baal!"* [5]It is the same today, for a few of the people of Israel* have remained faithful because of God's grace—his undeserved kindness in choosing them. [6]And since it is through God's kindness, then it is not by their good works. For in that case, God's grace would not be what it really is—free and undeserved.

[7]So this is the situation: Most of the people of Israel have not found the favor of God they are looking for so earnestly. A few have—the ones God has chosen—but the hearts of the rest were hardened. [8]As the Scriptures say,

> "God has put them into a deep sleep.
> To this day he has shut their eyes so they do not see,
> and closed their ears so they do not hear."*

[9]Likewise, David said,

> "Let their bountiful table become a snare,
> a trap that makes them think all is well.
> Let their blessings cause them to stumble,
> and let them get what they deserve.
> [10] Let their eyes go blind so they cannot see,
> and let their backs be bent forever."*

[11]Did God's people stumble and fall beyond recovery? Of course not! They were disobedient, so God

10:20 Isa 65:1 (Greek version). **10:21** Isa 65:2 (Greek version). **11:3** 1 Kgs 19:10, 14. **11:4** 1 Kgs 19:18. **11:5** Greek *for a remnant*. **11:8** Isa 29:10; Deut 29:4. **11:9-10** Ps 69:22-23 (Greek version).

made salvation available to the Gentiles. But he wanted his own people to become jealous and claim it for themselves. ¹²Now if the Gentiles were enriched because the people of Israel turned down God's offer of salvation, think how much greater a blessing the world will share when they finally accept it.

¹³I am saying all this especially for you Gentiles. God has appointed me as the apostle to the Gentiles. I stress this, ¹⁴for I want somehow to make the people of Israel jealous of what you Gentiles have, so I might save some of them. ¹⁵For since their rejection meant that God offered salvation to the rest of the world, their acceptance will be even more wonderful. It will be life for those who were dead! ¹⁶And since Abraham and the other patriarchs were holy, their descendants will also be holy—just as the entire batch of dough is holy because the portion given as an offering is holy. For if the roots of the tree are holy, the branches will be, too.

¹⁷But some of these branches from Abraham's tree—some of the people of Israel—have been broken off. And you Gentiles, who were branches from a wild olive tree, have been grafted in. So now you also receive the blessing God has promised Abraham and his children, sharing in the rich nourishment from the root of God's special olive tree. ¹⁸But you must not brag about being grafted in to replace the branches that were broken off. You are just a branch, not the root.

¹⁹"Well," you may say, "those branches were broken off to make room for me." ²⁰Yes, but remember—those branches were broken off because they didn't believe in Christ, and you are there because you do believe. So don't think highly of yourself, but fear what could happen. ²¹For if God did not spare the original branches, he won't* spare you either.

²²Notice how God is both kind and severe. He is severe toward those who disobeyed, but kind to you if you continue to trust in his kindness. But if you stop trusting, you also will be cut off. ²³And if the people of Israel turn from their unbelief, they will be grafted in again, for God has the power to graft them back into the tree. ²⁴You, by nature, were a branch cut from a wild olive tree. So if God was willing to do something contrary to nature by grafting you into his cultivated tree, he will be far more eager to graft the original branches back into the tree where they belong.

God's Mercy Is for Everyone
²⁵I want you to understand this mystery, dear brothers and sisters,* so that you will not feel proud about yourselves. Some of the people of Israel have hard hearts, but this will last only until the full number of

11:21 Some manuscripts read *perhaps he won't.* **11:25** Greek *brothers.*

Gentiles comes to Christ. ²⁶And so all Israel will be saved. As the Scriptures say,

"The one who rescues will come
from Jerusalem,*
and he will turn Israel* away
from ungodliness.
²⁷ And this is my covenant with
them,
that I will take away their
sins."*

²⁸Many of the people of Israel are now enemies of the Good News, and this benefits you Gentiles. Yet they are still the people he loves because he chose their ancestors Abraham, Isaac, and Jacob. ²⁹For God's gifts and his call can never be withdrawn. ³⁰Once, you Gentiles were rebels against God, but when the people of Israel rebelled against him, God was merciful to you instead. ³¹Now they are the rebels, and God's mercy has come to you so that they, too, will share* in God's mercy. ³²For God has imprisoned everyone in disobedience so he could have mercy on everyone.

³³Oh, how great are God's riches and wisdom and knowledge! How impossible it is for us to understand his decisions and his ways!

³⁴ For who can know the LORD's
thoughts?

Who knows enough to give
him advice?*
³⁵ And who has given him so much
that he needs to pay it back?*

³⁶For everything comes from him and exists by his power and is intended for his glory. All glory to him forever! Amen.

A Living Sacrifice to God

12 And so, dear brothers and sisters,* I plead with you to give your bodies to God because of all he has done for you. Let them be a living and holy sacrifice—the kind he will find acceptable. This is truly the way to worship him.* ²Don't copy the behavior and customs of this world, but let God transform you into a new person by changing the way you think. Then you will learn to know God's will for you, which is good and pleasing and perfect.

³Because of the privilege and authority* God has given me, I give each of you this warning: Don't think you are better than you really are. Be honest in your evaluation of yourselves, measuring yourselves by the faith God has given us.* ⁴Just as our bodies have many parts and each part has a special function, ⁵so it is with Christ's body. We are many parts of one body, and we all belong to each other.

11:26a Greek *from Zion.*   **11:26b** Greek *Jacob.*   **11:26-27** Isa 59:20-21; 27:9 (Greek version).
11:31 Other manuscripts read *will now share;* still others read *will someday share.*   **11:34** Isa 40:13
(Greek version).   **11:35** See Job 41:11.   **12:1a** Greek *brothers.*   **12:1b** Or *This is your spiritual
worship;* or *This is your reasonable service.*   **12:3a** Or *Because of the grace;* compare 1:5.   **12:3b** Or
by the faith God has given you; or *by the standard of our God-given faith.*

[6]In his grace, God has given us different gifts for doing certain things well. So if God has given you the ability to prophesy, speak out with as much faith as God has given you. [7]If your gift is serving others, serve them well. If you are a teacher, teach well. [8]If your gift is to encourage others, be encouraging. If it is giving, give generously. If God has given you leadership ability, take the responsibility seriously. And if you have a gift for showing kindness to others, do it gladly.

[9]Don't just pretend to love others. Really love them. Hate what is wrong. Hold tightly to what is good. [10]Love each other with genuine affection,* and take delight in honoring each other. [11]Never be lazy, but work hard and serve the Lord enthusiastically.* [12]Rejoice in our confident hope. Be patient in trouble, and keep on praying. [13]When God's people are in need, be ready to help them. Always be eager to practice hospitality.

[14]Bless those who persecute you. Don't curse them; pray that God will bless them. [15]Be happy with those who are happy, and weep with those who weep. [16]Live in harmony with each other. Don't be too proud to enjoy the company of ordinary people. And don't think you know it all!

[17]Never pay back evil with more evil. Do things in such a way that everyone can see you are honorable. [18]Do all that you can to live in peace with everyone.

[19]Dear friends, never take revenge. Leave that to the righteous anger of God. For the Scriptures say,

"I will take revenge;
    I will pay them back,"*
    says the Lord.

[20]Instead,

"If your enemies are hungry,
    feed them.
If they are thirsty, give them
    something to drink.
In doing this, you will heap
    burning coals of shame on
    their heads."*

[21]Don't let evil conquer you, but conquer evil by doing good.

Respect for Authority

13 Everyone must submit to governing authorities. For all authority comes from God, and those in positions of authority have been placed there by God. [2]So anyone who rebels against authority is rebelling against what God has instituted, and they will be punished. [3]For the authorities do not strike fear in people who are doing right, but in those who are doing wrong. Would you like to live without fear of the authorities? Do what is right, and they will honor you. [4]The authorities are God's servants, sent for your good. But if you are doing

12:10 Greek *with brotherly love.* **12:11** Or *but serve the Lord with a zealous spirit;* or *but let the Spirit excite you as you serve the Lord.* **12:19** Deut 32:35. **12:20** Prov 25:21-22.

wrong, of course you should be afraid, for they have the power to punish you. They are God's servants, sent for the very purpose of punishing those who do what is wrong. [5]So you must submit to them, not only to avoid punishment, but also to keep a clear conscience.

[6]Pay your taxes, too, for these same reasons. For government workers need to be paid. They are serving God in what they do. [7]Give to everyone what you owe them: Pay your taxes and government fees to those who collect them, and give respect and honor to those who are in authority.

Love Fulfills God's Requirements

[8]Owe nothing to anyone—except for your obligation to love one another. If you love your neighbor, you will fulfill the requirements of God's law. [9]For the commandments say, "You must not commit adultery. You must not murder. You must not steal. You must not covet."* These—and other such commandments—are summed up in this one commandment: "Love your neighbor as yourself."* [10]Love does no wrong to others, so love fulfills the requirements of God's law.

[11]This is all the more urgent, for you know how late it is; time is running out. Wake up, for our salvation is nearer now than when we first believed. [12]The night is almost gone; the day of salvation will soon be here. So remove your dark deeds like dirty clothes, and put on the shining armor of right living. [13]Because we belong to the day, we must live decent lives for all to see. Don't participate in the darkness of wild parties and drunkenness, or in sexual promiscuity and immoral living, or in quarreling and jealousy. [14]Instead, clothe yourself with the presence of the Lord Jesus Christ. And don't let yourself think about ways to indulge your evil desires.

The Danger of Criticism

14 Accept other believers who are weak in faith, and don't argue with them about what they think is right or wrong. [2]For instance, one person believes it's all right to eat anything. But another believer with a sensitive conscience will eat only vegetables. [3]Those who feel free to eat anything must not look down on those who don't. And those who don't eat certain foods must not condemn those who do, for God has accepted them. [4]Who are you to condemn someone else's servants? Their own master will judge whether they stand or fall. And with the Lord's help, they will stand and receive his approval.

[5]In the same way, some think one day is more holy than another day, while others think every day is alike. You should each be fully convinced that whichever day you choose is

13:9a Exod 20:13-15, 17. **13:9b** Lev 19:18.

acceptable. 6Those who worship the Lord on a special day do it to honor him. Those who eat any kind of food do so to honor the Lord, since they give thanks to God before eating. And those who refuse to eat certain foods also want to please the Lord and give thanks to God. 7For we don't live for ourselves or die for ourselves. 8If we live, it's to honor the Lord. And if we die, it's to honor the Lord. So whether we live or die, we belong to the Lord. 9Christ died and rose again for this very purpose—to be Lord both of the living and of the dead.

10So why do you condemn another believer*? Why do you look down on another believer? Remember, we will all stand before the judgment seat of God. 11For the Scriptures say,

"'As surely as I live,' says the LORD,
'every knee will bend to me,
   and every tongue will declare
      allegiance to God.*'"

12Yes, each of us will give a personal account to God. 13So let's stop condemning each other. Decide instead to live in such a way that you will not cause another believer to stumble and fall.

14I know and am convinced on the authority of the Lord Jesus that no food, in and of itself, is wrong to eat. But if someone believes it is wrong, then for that person it is wrong. 15And if another believer is distressed by what you eat, you are not acting in love if you eat it. Don't let your eating ruin someone for whom Christ died. 16Then you will not be criticized for doing something you believe is good. 17For the Kingdom of God is not a matter of what we eat or drink, but of living a life of goodness and peace and joy in the Holy Spirit. 18If you serve Christ with this attitude, you will please God, and others will approve of you, too. 19So then, let us aim for harmony in the church and try to build each other up.

20Don't tear apart the work of God over what you eat. Remember, all foods are acceptable, but it is wrong to eat something if it makes another person stumble. 21It is better not to eat meat or drink wine or do anything else if it might cause another believer to stumble.* 22You may believe there's nothing wrong with what you are doing, but keep it between yourself and God. Blessed are those who don't feel guilty for doing something they have decided is right. 23But if you have doubts about whether or not you should eat something, you are sinning if you go ahead and do it. For you are not following your convictions. If you do anything you believe is not right, you are sinning.*

14:10 Greek *your brother;* also in 14:10b, 13, 15, 21.   14:11 Or *declare praise for God.* Isa 49:18; 45:23 (Greek version).   14:21 Some manuscripts read *to stumble or be offended or be weakened.*
14:23 Some manuscripts place the text of 16:25-27 here.

Living to Please Others

15 We who are strong must be considerate of those who are sensitive about things like this. We must not just please ourselves. ²We should help others do what is right and build them up in the Lord. ³For even Christ didn't live to please himself. As the Scriptures say, "The insults of those who insult you, O God, have fallen on me."* ⁴Such things were written in the Scriptures long ago to teach us. And the Scriptures give us hope and encouragement as we wait patiently for God's promises to be fulfilled.

⁵May God, who gives this patience and encouragement, help you live in complete harmony with each other, as is fitting for followers of Christ Jesus. ⁶Then all of you can join together with one voice, giving praise and glory to God, the Father of our Lord Jesus Christ.

⁷Therefore, accept each other just as Christ has accepted you so that God will be given glory. ⁸Remember that Christ came as a servant to the Jews* to show that God is true to the promises he made to their ancestors. ⁹He also came so that the Gentiles might give glory to God for his mercies to them. That is what the psalmist meant when he wrote:

"For this, I will praise you among
the Gentiles;

I will sing praises to your
name."*

¹⁰And in another place it is written,

"Rejoice with his people,
you Gentiles."*

¹¹And yet again,

"Praise the Lᴏʀᴅ, all you
Gentiles.
Praise him, all you people
of the earth."*

¹²And in another place Isaiah said,

"The heir to David's throne*
will come,
and he will rule over the
Gentiles.
They will place their hope
on him."*

¹³I pray that God, the source of hope, will fill you completely with joy and peace because you trust in him. Then you will overflow with confident hope through the power of the Holy Spirit.

Paul's Reason for Writing

¹⁴I am fully convinced, my dear brothers and sisters,* that you are full of goodness. You know these things so well you can teach each other all about them. ¹⁵Even so, I have been bold enough to write about some of these points, knowing that all you need is this reminder.

15:3 Greek *who insult you have fallen on me.* Ps 69:9.   **15:8** Greek *servant of circumcision.*   **15:9** Ps 18:49.   **15:10** Deut 32:43.   **15:11** Ps 117:1.   **15:12a** Greek *The root of Jesse.* David was the son of Jesse.   **15:12b** Isa 11:10 (Greek version).   **15:14** Greek *brothers;* also in 15:30.

For by God's grace, [16]I am a special messenger from Christ Jesus to you Gentiles. I bring you the Good News so that I might present you as an acceptable offering to God, made holy by the Holy Spirit. [17]So I have reason to be enthusiastic about all Christ Jesus has done through me in my service to God. [18]Yet I dare not boast about anything except what Christ has done through me, bringing the Gentiles to God by my message and by the way I worked among them. [19]They were convinced by the power of miraculous signs and wonders and by the power of God's Spirit.* In this way, I have fully presented the Good News of Christ from Jerusalem all the way to Illyricum.*

[20]My ambition has always been to preach the Good News where the name of Christ has never been heard, rather than where a church has already been started by someone else. [21]I have been following the plan spoken of in the Scriptures, where it says,

> "Those who have never been told
>   about him will see,
>   and those who have never
>   heard of him will
>   understand."*

[22]In fact, my visit to you has been delayed so long because I have been preaching in these places.

Paul's Travel Plans

[23]But now I have finished my work in these regions, and after all these long years of waiting, I am eager to visit you. [24]I am planning to go to Spain, and when I do, I will stop off in Rome. And after I have enjoyed your fellowship for a little while, you can provide for my journey.

[25]But before I come, I must go to Jerusalem to take a gift to the believers* there. [26]For you see, the believers in Macedonia and Achaia* have eagerly taken up an offering for the poor among the believers in Jerusalem. [27]They were glad to do this because they feel they owe a real debt to them. Since the Gentiles received the spiritual blessings of the Good News from the believers in Jerusalem, they feel the least they can do in return is to help them financially. [28]As soon as I have delivered this money and completed this good deed of theirs, I will come to see you on my way to Spain. [29]And I am sure that when I come, Christ will richly bless our time together.

[30]Dear brothers and sisters, I urge you in the name of our Lord Jesus Christ to join in my struggle by praying to God for me. Do this because of your love for me, given to you by the Holy Spirit. [31]Pray that I will be rescued from those in Judea who refuse to obey God. Pray also that the believers there will be will-

15:19a Other manuscripts read *the Spirit;* still others read *the Holy Spirit.* 15:19b *Illyricum* was a region northeast of Italy. 15:21 Isa 52:15 (Greek version). 15:25 Greek *God's holy people;* also in 15:26, 31. 15:26 *Macedonia* and *Achaia* were the northern and southern regions of Greece.

ing to accept the donation* I am taking to Jerusalem. ³²Then, by the will of God, I will be able to come to you with a joyful heart, and we will be an encouragement to each other.

³³And now may God, who gives us his peace, be with you all. Amen.*

Paul Greets His Friends

16 I commend to you our sister Phoebe, who is a deacon in the church in Cenchrea. ²Welcome her in the Lord as one who is worthy of honor among God's people. Help her in whatever she needs, for she has been helpful to many, and especially to me.

³Give my greetings to Priscilla and Aquila, my co-workers in the ministry of Christ Jesus. ⁴In fact, they once risked their lives for me. I am thankful to them, and so are all the Gentile churches. ⁵Also give my greetings to the church that meets in their home.

Greet my dear friend Epenetus. He was the first person from the province of Asia to become a follower of Christ. ⁶Give my greetings to Mary, who has worked so hard for your benefit. ⁷Greet Andronicus and Junia,* my fellow Jews,* who were in prison with me. They are highly respected among the apostles and became followers of Christ before I did. ⁸Greet Ampliatus, my dear friend in the Lord. ⁹Greet Urbanus, our co-worker in Christ, and my dear friend Stachys.

¹⁰Greet Apelles, a good man whom Christ approves. And give my greetings to the believers from the household of Aristobulus. ¹¹Greet Herodion, my fellow Jew.* Greet the Lord's people from the household of Narcissus. ¹²Give my greetings to Tryphena and Tryphosa, the Lord's workers, and to dear Persis, who has worked so hard for the Lord. ¹³Greet Rufus, whom the Lord picked out to be his very own; and also his dear mother, who has been a mother to me.

¹⁴Give my greetings to Asyncritus, Phlegon, Hermes, Patrobas, Hermas, and the brothers and sisters* who meet with them. ¹⁵Give my greetings to Philologus, Julia, Nereus and his sister, and to Olympas and all the believers* who meet with them. ¹⁶Greet each other with a sacred kiss. All the churches of Christ send you their greetings.

Paul's Final Instructions

¹⁷And now I make one more appeal, my dear brothers and sisters. Watch out for people who cause divisions and upset people's faith by teaching things contrary to what you have been taught. Stay away from them. ¹⁸Such people are not serving Christ our Lord; they are serving their own

15:31 Greek *the ministry;* other manuscripts read *the gift.* **15:33** Some manuscripts do not include *Amen.* One very early manuscript places 16:25-27 here. **16:7a** *Junia* is a feminine name. Some late manuscripts accent the word so it reads *Junias,* a masculine name; still others read *Julia* (feminine). **16:7b** Or *compatriots;* also in 16:21. **16:11** Or *compatriot.* **16:14** Greek *brothers;* also in 16:17. **16:15** Greek *all of God's holy people.*

personal interests. By smooth talk and glowing words they deceive innocent people. [19]But everyone knows that you are obedient to the Lord. This makes me very happy. I want you to be wise in doing right and to stay innocent of any wrong. [20]The God of peace will soon crush Satan under your feet. May the grace of our Lord Jesus* be with you.

[21]Timothy, my fellow worker, sends you his greetings, as do Lucius, Jason, and Sosipater, my fellow Jews.

[22]I, Tertius, the one writing this letter for Paul, send my greetings, too, as one of the Lord's followers.

[23]Gaius says hello to you. He is my host and also serves as host to the whole church. Erastus, the city treasurer, sends you his greetings, and so does our brother Quartus.*

[25]Now all glory to God, who is able to make you strong, just as my Good News says. This message about Jesus Christ has revealed his plan for you Gentiles, a plan kept secret from the beginning of time. [26]But now as the prophets* foretold and as the eternal God has commanded, this message is made known to all Gentiles everywhere, so that they too might believe and obey him. [27]All glory to the only wise God, through Jesus Christ, forever. Amen.*

16:20 Some manuscripts read *Lord Jesus Christ.* **16:23** Some manuscripts add verse 24, *May the grace of our Lord Jesus Christ be with you all. Amen.* Still others add this sentence after verse 27. **16:26** Greek *the prophetic writings.* **16:25-27** Various manuscripts place the doxology (shown here as 16:25-27) after 14:23 or after 15:33 or after 16:23.

1 Corinthians

Greetings from Paul

1 This letter is from Paul, chosen by the will of God to be an apostle of Christ Jesus, and from our brother Sosthenes.

²I am writing to God's church in Corinth,* to you who have been called by God to be his own holy people. He made you holy by means of Christ Jesus,* just as he did for all people everywhere who call on the name of our Lord Jesus Christ, their Lord and ours.

³May God our Father and the Lord Jesus Christ give you grace and peace.

Paul Gives Thanks to God

⁴I always thank my God for you and for the gracious gifts he has given you, now that you belong to Christ Jesus. ⁵Through him, God has enriched your church in every way—with all of your eloquent words and all of your knowledge. ⁶This confirms that what I told you about Christ is true. ⁷Now you have every spiritual gift you need as you eagerly wait for the return of our Lord Jesus Christ. ⁸He will keep you strong to the end so that you will be free from all blame on the day when our Lord Jesus Christ returns. ⁹God will do this, for he is faithful to do what he says, and he has invited you into partnership with his Son, Jesus Christ our Lord.

Divisions in the Church

¹⁰I appeal to you, dear brothers and sisters,* by the authority of our Lord Jesus Christ, to live in harmony with each other. Let there be no divisions in the church. Rather, be of one mind, united in thought and purpose. ¹¹For some members of Chloe's household have told me about your quarrels, my dear brothers and sisters. ¹²Some of you are saying, "I am a follower of Paul." Others are saying, "I follow Apollos," or "I follow Peter,*" or "I follow only Christ."

¹³Has Christ been divided into factions? Was I, Paul, crucified for you? Were any of you baptized in the name of Paul? Of course not! ¹⁴I thank God that I did not baptize any of you except Crispus and Gaius, ¹⁵for now no one can say they were baptized in my name. ¹⁶(Oh yes, I also baptized the household of Stephanas, but I don't remember baptizing anyone else.) ¹⁷For Christ

---

1:2a *Corinth* was the capital city of Achaia, the southern region of the Greek peninsula. **1:2b** Or *because you belong to Christ Jesus.* **1:10** Greek *brothers;* also in 1:11, 26. **1:12** Greek *Cephas.*

didn't send me to baptize, but to preach the Good News—and not with clever speech, for fear that the cross of Christ would lose its power.

The Wisdom of God

[18]The message of the cross is foolish to those who are headed for destruction! But we who are being saved know it is the very power of God. [19]As the Scriptures say,

> "I will destroy the wisdom of
> the wise
> and discard the intelligence
> of the intelligent."*

[20]So where does this leave the philosophers, the scholars, and the world's brilliant debaters? God has made the wisdom of this world look foolish. [21]Since God in his wisdom saw to it that the world would never know him through human wisdom, he has used our foolish preaching to save those who believe. [22]It is foolish to the Jews, who ask for signs from heaven. And it is foolish to the Greeks, who seek human wisdom. [23]So when we preach that Christ was crucified, the Jews are offended and the Gentiles say it's all nonsense.

[24]But to those called by God to salvation, both Jews and Gentiles,* Christ is the power of God and the wisdom of God. [25]This foolish plan of God is wiser than the wisest of human plans, and God's weakness is stronger than the greatest of human strength.

[26]Remember, dear brothers and sisters, that few of you were wise in the world's eyes or powerful or wealthy* when God called you. [27]Instead, God chose things the world considers foolish in order to shame those who think they are wise. And he chose things that are powerless to shame those who are powerful. [28]God chose things despised by the world,* things counted as nothing at all, and used them to bring to nothing what the world considers important. [29]As a result, no one can ever boast in the presence of God.

[30]God has united you with Christ Jesus. For our benefit God made him to be wisdom itself. Christ made us right with God; he made us pure and holy, and he freed us from sin. [31]Therefore, as the Scriptures say, "If you want to boast, boast only about the LORD."*

Paul's Message of Wisdom

2 When I first came to you, dear brothers and sisters,* I didn't use lofty words and impressive wisdom to tell you God's secret plan.* [2]For I decided that while I was with you I would forget everything except Jesus Christ, the one who was crucified. [3]I came to you in weakness—timid and trembling. [4]And my message and my preaching were very plain. Rather than using clever and persuasive speeches, I relied only on the power of the Holy Spirit. [5]I did this so you would trust not in human wisdom but in the power of God.

[6]Yet when I am among mature believers, I do speak with words of wisdom, but not the kind of wisdom that belongs to this world or to the rulers of this world, who are soon forgotten. [7]No, the wisdom we speak of is the mystery of God*— his plan that was previously hidden, even though he made it for our ultimate glory before the world began. [8]But the rulers of this world have not understood it; if they had, they would not have crucified our glorious Lord. [9]That is what the Scriptures mean when they say,

"No eye has seen, no ear has
       heard,
   and no mind has imagined
what God has prepared
   for those who love him."*

[10]But* it was to us that God revealed these things by his Spirit. For his Spirit searches out everything and shows us God's deep secrets. [11]No one can know a person's thoughts except that person's own spirit, and no one can know God's thoughts except God's own Spirit. [12]And we have received God's Spirit (not the world's spirit), so we can know the wonderful things God has freely given us.

[13]When we tell you these things, we do not use words that come from human wisdom. Instead, we speak words given to us by the Spirit, using the Spirit's words to explain spiritual truths.* [14]But people who aren't spiritual* can't receive these truths from God's Spirit. It all sounds foolish to them and they can't understand it, for only those who are spiritual can understand what the Spirit means. [15]Those who are spiritual can evaluate all things, but they themselves cannot be evaluated by others. [16]For,

"Who can know the LORD's
       thoughts?
   Who knows enough to
       teach him?"*

But we understand these things, for we have the mind of Christ.

Paul and Apollos, Servants of Christ

3 Dear brothers and sisters,* when I was with you I couldn't talk to you as I would to spiritual people.* I had to talk as though you belonged to this world or as though you were infants in Christ. [2]I had to feed you with milk, not with solid food, because you weren't ready for anything

2:7 Greek *But we speak God's wisdom in a mystery.* 2:9 Isa 64:4. 2:10 Some manuscripts read *For.* 2:13 Or *explaining spiritual truths in spiritual language,* or *explaining spiritual truths to spiritual people.* 2:14 Or *who don't have the Spirit;* or *who have only physical life.* 2:16 Isa 40:13 (Greek version). 3:1a Greek *Brothers.* 3:1b Or *to people who have the Spirit.*

stronger. And you still aren't ready, ³for you are still controlled by your sinful nature. You are jealous of one another and quarrel with each other. Doesn't that prove you are controlled by your sinful nature? Aren't you living like people of the world? ⁴When one of you says, "I am a follower of Paul," and another says, "I follow Apollos," aren't you acting just like people of the world?

⁵After all, who is Apollos? Who is Paul? We are only God's servants through whom you believed the Good News. Each of us did the work the Lord gave us. ⁶I planted the seed in your hearts, and Apollos watered it, but it was God who made it grow. ⁷It's not important who does the planting, or who does the watering. What's important is that God makes the seed grow. ⁸The one who plants and the one who waters work together with the same purpose. And both will be rewarded for their own hard work. ⁹For we are both God's workers. And you are God's field. You are God's building.

¹⁰Because of God's grace to me, I have laid the foundation like an expert builder. Now others are building on it. But whoever is building on this foundation must be very careful. ¹¹For no one can lay any foundation other than the one we already have—Jesus Christ.

¹²Anyone who builds on that foundation may use a variety of materials—gold, silver, jewels, wood, hay, or straw. ¹³But on the judgment day, fire will reveal what kind of work each builder has done. The fire will show if a person's work has any value. ¹⁴If the work survives, that builder will receive a reward. ¹⁵But if the work is burned up, the builder will suffer great loss. The builder will be saved, but like someone barely escaping through a wall of flames.

¹⁶Don't you realize that all of you together are the temple of God and that the Spirit of God lives in* you? ¹⁷God will destroy anyone who destroys this temple. For God's temple is holy, and you are that temple.

¹⁸Stop deceiving yourselves. If you think you are wise by this world's standards, you need to become a fool to be truly wise. ¹⁹For the wisdom of this world is foolishness to God. As the Scriptures say,

"He traps the wise
    in the snare of their own
        cleverness."*

²⁰And again,

"The LORD knows the thoughts
    of the wise;
he knows they are worthless."*

²¹So don't boast about following a particular human leader. For everything belongs to you—²²whether Paul or Apollos or Peter,* or the world, or life and death, or the present and the future. Everything belongs to you, ²³and you belong to Christ, and Christ belongs to God.

3:16 Or among. 3:19 Job 5:13. 3:20 Ps 94:11. 3:22 Greek Cephas.

Paul's Relationship with the Corinthians

4 So look at Apollos and me as mere servants of Christ who have been put in charge of explaining God's mysteries. [2]Now, a person who is put in charge as a manager must be faithful. [3]As for me, it matters very little how I might be evaluated by you or by any human authority. I don't even trust my own judgment on this point. [4]My conscience is clear, but that doesn't prove I'm right. It is the Lord himself who will examine me and decide.

[5]So don't make judgments about anyone ahead of time—before the Lord returns. For he will bring our darkest secrets to light and will reveal our private motives. Then God will give to each one whatever praise is due.

[6]Dear brothers and sisters,* I have used Apollos and myself to illustrate what I've been saying. If you pay attention to what I have quoted from the Scriptures,* you won't be proud of one of your leaders at the expense of another. [7]For what gives you the right to make such a judgment? What do you have that God hasn't given you? And if everything you have is from God, why boast as though it were not a gift?

[8]You think you already have everything you need. You think you are already rich. You have begun to reign in God's kingdom without us! I wish you really were reigning already, for then we would be reigning with you. [9]Instead, I sometimes think God has put us apostles on display, like prisoners of war at the end of a victor's parade, condemned to die. We have become a spectacle to the entire world—to people and angels alike.

[10]Our dedication to Christ makes us look like fools, but you claim to be so wise in Christ! We are weak, but you are so powerful! You are honored, but we are ridiculed. [11]Even now we go hungry and thirsty, and we don't have enough clothes to keep warm. We are often beaten and have no home. [12]We work wearily with our own hands to earn our living. We bless those who curse us. We are patient with those who abuse us. [13]We appeal gently when evil things are said about us. Yet we are treated like the world's garbage, like everybody's trash—right up to the present moment.

[14]I am not writing these things to shame you, but to warn you as my beloved children. [15]For even if you had ten thousand others to teach you about Christ, you have only one spiritual father. For I became your father in Christ Jesus when I preached the Good News to you. [16]So I urge you to imitate me.

[17]That's why I have sent Timothy, my beloved and faithful child in the Lord. He will remind you of how

4:6a Greek *Brothers.*   **4:6b** Or *If you learn not to go beyond "what is written."*

I follow Christ Jesus, just as I teach in all the churches wherever I go.

¹⁸Some of you have become arrogant, thinking I will not visit you again. ¹⁹But I will come—and soon—if the Lord lets me, and then I'll find out whether these arrogant people just give pretentious speeches or whether they really have God's power. ²⁰For the Kingdom of God is not just a lot of talk; it is living by God's power. ²¹Which do you choose? Should I come with a rod to punish you, or should I come with love and a gentle spirit?

Paul Condemns Spiritual Pride

5 I can hardly believe the report about the sexual immorality going on among you—something that even pagans don't do. I am told that a man in your church is living in sin with his stepmother.* ²You are so proud of yourselves, but you should be mourning in sorrow and shame. And you should remove this man from your fellowship.

³Even though I am not with you in person, I am with you in the Spirit.* And as though I were there, I have already passed judgment on this man ⁴in the name of the Lord Jesus. You must call a meeting of the church.* I will be present with you in spirit, and so will the power of our Lord Jesus. ⁵Then you must throw this man out and hand him over to Satan so that his sinful nature will be destroyed* and he himself* will be saved on the day the Lord* returns.

⁶Your boasting about this is terrible. Don't you realize that this sin is like a little yeast that spreads through the whole batch of dough? ⁷Get rid of the old "yeast" by removing this wicked person from among you. Then you will be like a fresh batch of dough made without yeast, which is what you really are. Christ, our Passover Lamb, has been sacrificed for us.* ⁸So let us celebrate the festival, not with the old bread* of wickedness and evil, but with the new bread* of sincerity and truth.

⁹When I wrote to you before, I told you not to associate with people who indulge in sexual sin. ¹⁰But I wasn't talking about unbelievers who indulge in sexual sin, or are greedy, or cheat people, or worship idols. You would have to leave this world to avoid people like that. ¹¹I meant that you are not to associate with anyone who claims to be a believer* yet indulges in sexual sin, or is greedy, or worships idols, or is abusive, or is a drunkard, or cheats people. Don't even eat with such people.

¹²It isn't my responsibility to judge outsiders, but it certainly is

5:1 Greek *his father's wife.* 5:3 Or *in spirit.* 5:4 Or *In the name of the Lord Jesus, you must call a meeting of the church.* 5:5a Or *so that his body will be destroyed;* Greek reads *for the destruction of the flesh.* 5:5b Greek *and the spirit.* 5:5c Other manuscripts read *the Lord Jesus;* still others read *our Lord Jesus Christ.* 5:7 Greek *has been sacrificed.* 5:8a Greek *not with old leaven.* 5:8b Greek *but with unleavened [bread].* 5:11 Greek *a brother.*

your responsibility to judge those inside the church who are sinning. [13]God will judge those on the outside; but as the Scriptures say, "You must remove the evil person from among you."*

Avoiding Lawsuits with Christians

6 When one of you has a dispute with another believer, how dare you file a lawsuit and ask a secular court to decide the matter instead of taking it to other believers*! [2]Don't you realize that someday we believers will judge the world? And since you are going to judge the world, can't you decide even these little things among yourselves? [3]Don't you realize that we will judge angels? So you should surely be able to resolve ordinary disputes in this life. [4]If you have legal disputes about such matters, why go to outside judges who are not respected by the church? [5]I am saying this to shame you. Isn't there anyone in all the church who is wise enough to decide these issues? [6]But instead, one believer* sues another—right in front of unbelievers!

[7]Even to have such lawsuits with one another is a defeat for you. Why not just accept the injustice and leave it at that? Why not let yourselves be cheated? [8]Instead, you yourselves are the ones who do wrong and cheat even your fellow believers.*

[9]Don't you realize that those who do wrong will not inherit the Kingdom of God? Don't fool yourselves. Those who indulge in sexual sin, or who worship idols, or commit adultery, or are male prostitutes, or practice homosexuality, [10]or are thieves, or greedy people, or drunkards, or are abusive, or cheat people—none of these will inherit the Kingdom of God. [11]Some of you were once like that. But you were cleansed; you were made holy; you were made right with God by calling on the name of the Lord Jesus Christ and by the Spirit of our God.

Avoiding Sexual Sin

[12]You say, "I am allowed to do anything"—but not everything is good for you. And even though "I am allowed to do anything," I must not become a slave to anything. [13]You say, "Food was made for the stomach, and the stomach for food." (This is true, though someday God will do away with both of them.) But you can't say that our bodies were made for sexual immorality. They were made for the Lord, and the Lord cares about our bodies. [14]And God will raise us from the dead by his power, just as he raised our Lord from the dead.

[15]Don't you realize that your bodies are actually parts of Christ? Should a man take his body, which is part of Christ, and join it to a

5:13 Deut 17:7. 6:1 Greek *God's holy people;* also in 6:2. 6:6 Greek *one brother.* 6:8 Greek *even the brothers.*

prostitute? Never! [16]And don't you realize that if a man joins himself to a prostitute, he becomes one body with her? For the Scriptures say, "The two are united into one."* [17]But the person who is joined to the Lord is one spirit with him.

[18]Run from sexual sin! No other sin so clearly affects the body as this one does. For sexual immorality is a sin against your own body. [19]Don't you realize that your body is the temple of the Holy Spirit, who lives in you and was given to you by God? You do not belong to yourself, [20]for God bought you with a high price. So you must honor God with your body.

Instruction on Marriage

7 Now regarding the questions you asked in your letter. Yes, it is good to abstain from sexual relations.* [2]But because there is so much sexual immorality, each man should have his own wife, and each woman should have her own husband.

[3]The husband should fulfill his wife's sexual needs, and the wife should fulfill her husband's needs. [4]The wife gives authority over her body to her husband, and the husband gives authority over his body to his wife.

[5]Do not deprive each other of sexual relations, unless you both agree to refrain from sexual intimacy for a limited time so you can give yourselves more completely to prayer. Afterward, you should come together again so that Satan won't be able to tempt you because of your lack of self-control. [6]I say this as a concession, not as a command. [7]But I wish everyone were single, just as I am. Yet each person has a special gift from God, of one kind or another.

[8]So I say to those who aren't married and to widows—it's better to stay unmarried, just as I am. [9]But if they can't control themselves, they should go ahead and marry. It's better to marry than to burn with lust.

[10]But for those who are married, I have a command that comes not from me, but from the Lord.* A wife must not leave her husband. [11]But if she does leave him, let her remain single or else be reconciled to him. And the husband must not leave his wife.

[12]Now, I will speak to the rest of you, though I do not have a direct command from the Lord. If a fellow believer* has a wife who is not a believer and she is willing to continue living with him, he must not leave her. [13]And if a believing woman has a husband who is not a believer and he is willing to continue living with her, she must not leave him. [14]For the believing wife brings holiness to her marriage, and the believing husband* brings holiness to his mar-

6:16 Gen 2:24. **7:1** Or *to live a celibate life;* Greek reads *It is good for a man not to touch a woman.* **7:10** See Matt 5:32; 19:9; Mark 10:11-12; Luke 16:18. **7:12** Greek *a brother.* **7:14** Greek *the brother.*

riage. Otherwise, your children would not be holy, but now they are holy. [15](But if the husband or wife who isn't a believer insists on leaving, let them go. In such cases the believing husband or wife* is no longer bound to the other, for God has called you* to live in peace.) [16]Don't you wives realize that your husbands might be saved because of you? And don't you husbands realize that your wives might be saved because of you?

[17]Each of you should continue to live in whatever situation the Lord has placed you, and remain as you were when God first called you. This is my rule for all the churches. [18]For instance, a man who was circumcised before he became a believer should not try to reverse it. And the man who was uncircumcised when he became a believer should not be circumcised now. [19]For it makes no difference whether or not a man has been circumcised. The important thing is to keep God's commandments.

[20]Yes, each of you should remain as you were when God called you. [21]Are you a slave? Don't let that worry you—but if you get a chance to be free, take it. [22]And remember, if you were a slave when the Lord called you, you are now free in the Lord. And if you were free when the Lord called you, you are now a slave of Christ. [23]God paid a high price for you, so don't be enslaved by the world.* [24]Each of you, dear brothers and sisters,* should remain as you were when God first called you.

[25]Now regarding your question about the young women who are not yet married. I do not have a command from the Lord for them. But the Lord in his mercy has given me wisdom that can be trusted, and I will share it with you. [26]Because of the present crisis,* I think it is best to remain as you are. [27]If you have a wife, do not seek to end the marriage. If you do not have a wife, do not seek to get married. [28]But if you do get married, it is not a sin. And if a young woman gets married, it is not a sin. However, those who get married at this time will have troubles, and I am trying to spare you those problems.

[29]But let me say this, dear brothers and sisters: The time that remains is very short. So from now on, those with wives should not focus only on their marriage. [30]Those who weep or who rejoice or who buy things should not be absorbed by their weeping or their joy or their possessions. [31]Those who use the things of the world should not become attached to them. For this world as we know it will soon pass away.

[32]I want you to be free from the concerns of this life. An unmarried man can spend his time doing the Lord's work and thinking how to

please him. ³³But a married man has to think about his earthly responsibilities and how to please his wife. ³⁴His interests are divided. In the same way, a woman who is no longer married or has never been married can be devoted to the Lord and holy in body and in spirit. But a married woman has to think about her earthly responsibilities and how to please her husband. ³⁵I am saying this for your benefit, not to place restrictions on you. I want you to do whatever will help you serve the Lord best, with as few distractions as possible.

³⁶But if a man thinks that he's treating his fiancée improperly and will inevitably give in to his passion, let him marry her as he wishes. It is not a sin. ³⁷But if he has decided firmly not to marry and there is no urgency and he can control his passion, he does well not to marry. ³⁸So the person who marries his fiancée does well, and the person who doesn't marry does even better.

³⁹A wife is bound to her husband as long as he lives. If her husband dies, she is free to marry anyone she wishes, but only if he loves the Lord.* ⁴⁰But in my opinion it would be better for her to stay single, and I think I am giving you counsel from God's Spirit when I say this.

Food Sacrificed to Idols

8 Now regarding your question about food that has been offered to idols. Yes, we know that "we all have knowledge" about this issue. But while knowledge makes us feel important, it is love that strengthens the church. ²Anyone who claims to know all the answers doesn't really know very much. ³But the person who loves God is the one whom God recognizes.*

⁴So, what about eating meat that has been offered to idols? Well, we all know that an idol is not really a god and that there is only one God. ⁵There may be so-called gods both in heaven and on earth, and some people actually worship many gods and many lords. ⁶But for us,

There is one God, the Father,
by whom all things were created,
and for whom we live.
And there is one Lord, Jesus Christ,
through whom all things were created,
and through whom we live.

⁷However, not all believers know this. Some are accustomed to thinking of idols as being real, so when they eat food that has been offered to idols, they think of it as the worship of real gods, and their weak consciences are violated. ⁸It's true that we can't win God's approval by what we eat. We don't lose anything if we don't eat it, and we don't gain anything if we do.

⁹But you must be careful so that your freedom does not cause others with a weaker conscience to stum-

7:39 Greek *but only in the Lord.* **8:3** Some manuscripts read *the person who loves has full knowledge.*

ble. [10]For if others see you—with your "superior knowledge"—eating in the temple of an idol, won't they be encouraged to violate their conscience by eating food that has been offered to an idol? [11]So because of your superior knowledge, a weak believer* for whom Christ died will be destroyed. [12]And when you sin against other believers* by encouraging them to do something they believe is wrong, you are sinning against Christ. [13]So if what I eat causes another believer to sin, I will never eat meat again as long as I live—for I don't want to cause another believer to stumble.

Paul Gives Up His Rights

9 Am I not as free as anyone else? Am I not an apostle? Haven't I seen Jesus our Lord with my own eyes? Isn't it because of my work that you belong to the Lord? [2]Even if others think I am not an apostle, I certainly am to you. You yourselves are proof that I am the Lord's apostle.

[3]This is my answer to those who question my authority.* [4]Don't we have the right to live in your homes and share your meals? [5]Don't we have the right to bring a believing wife* with us as the other apostles and the Lord's brothers do, and as Peter* does? [6]Or is it only Barnabas and I who have to work to support ourselves?

[7]What soldier has to pay his own expenses? What farmer plants a vineyard and doesn't have the right to eat some of its fruit? What shepherd cares for a flock of sheep and isn't allowed to drink some of the milk? [8]Am I expressing merely a human opinion, or does the law say the same thing? [9]For the law of Moses says, "You must not muzzle an ox to keep it from eating as it treads out the grain."* Was God thinking only about oxen when he said this? [10]Wasn't he actually speaking to us? Yes, it was written for us, so that the one who plows and the one who threshes the grain might both expect a share of the harvest.

[11]Since we have planted spiritual seed among you, aren't we entitled to a harvest of physical food and drink? [12]If you support others who preach to you, shouldn't we have an even greater right to be supported? But we have never used this right. We would rather put up with anything than be an obstacle to the Good News about Christ.

[13]Don't you realize that those who work in the temple get their meals from the offerings brought to the temple? And those who serve at the altar get a share of the sacrificial offerings. [14]In the same way, the Lord ordered that those who preach the Good News should be supported by those who benefit from it. [15]Yet I have never used any of these rights. And I am not writing this to suggest

8:11 Greek *brother*; also in 8:13.   8:12 Greek *brothers*.   9:3 Greek *those who examine me*.
9:5a Greek *a sister a wife*.   9:5b Greek *Cephas*.   9:9 Deut 25:4.

that I want to start now. In fact, I would rather die than lose my right to boast about preaching without charge. ¹⁶Yet preaching the Good News is not something I can boast about. I am compelled by God to do it. How terrible for me if I didn't preach the Good News!

¹⁷If I were doing this on my own initiative, I would deserve payment. But I have no choice, for God has given me this sacred trust. ¹⁸What then is my pay? It is the opportunity to preach the Good News without charging anyone. That's why I never demand my rights when I preach the Good News.

¹⁹Even though I am a free man with no master, I have become a slave to all people to bring many to Christ. ²⁰When I was with the Jews, I lived like a Jew to bring the Jews to Christ. When I was with those who follow the Jewish law, I too lived under that law. Even though I am not subject to the law, I did this so I could bring to Christ those who are under the law. ²¹When I am with the Gentiles who do not follow the Jewish law,* I too live apart from that law so I can bring them to Christ. But I do not ignore the law of God; I obey the law of Christ.

²²When I am with those who are weak, I share their weakness, for I want to bring the weak to Christ. Yes, I try to find common ground with everyone, doing everything I can to save some. ²³I do everything to spread the Good News and share in its blessings.

²⁴Don't you realize that in a race everyone runs, but only one person gets the prize? So run to win! ²⁵All athletes are disciplined in their training. They do it to win a prize that will fade away, but we do it for an eternal prize. ²⁶So I run with purpose in every step. I am not just shadowboxing. ²⁷I discipline my body like an athlete, training it to do what it should. Otherwise, I fear that after preaching to others I myself might be disqualified.

Lessons from Israel's Idolatry

10 I don't want you to forget, dear brothers and sisters,* about our ancestors in the wilderness long ago. All of them were guided by a cloud that moved ahead of them, and all of them walked through the sea on dry ground. ²In the cloud and in the sea, all of them were baptized as followers of Moses. ³All of them ate the same spiritual food, ⁴and all of them drank the same spiritual water. For they drank from the spiritual rock that traveled with them, and that rock was Christ. ⁵Yet God was not pleased with most of them, and their bodies were scattered in the wilderness.

⁶These things happened as a warning to us, so that we would not crave evil things as they did, ⁷or worship idols as some of them did. As the Scriptures say, "The people cele-

9:21 Greek *those without the law.* **10:1** Greek *brothers.*

brated with feasting and drinking, and they indulged in pagan revelry."* ⁸And we must not engage in sexual immorality as some of them did, causing 23,000 of them to die in one day.

⁹Nor should we put Christ* to the test, as some of them did and then died from snakebites. ¹⁰And don't grumble as some of them did, and then were destroyed by the angel of death. ¹¹These things happened to them as examples for us. They were written down to warn us who live at the end of the age.

¹²If you think you are standing strong, be careful not to fall. ¹³The temptations in your life are no different from what others experience. And God is faithful. He will not allow the temptation to be more than you can stand. When you are tempted, he will show you a way out so that you can endure.

¹⁴So, my dear friends, flee from the worship of idols. ¹⁵You are reasonable people. Decide for yourselves if what I am saying is true. ¹⁶When we bless the cup at the Lord's Table, aren't we sharing in the blood of Christ? And when we break the bread, aren't we sharing in the body of Christ? ¹⁷And though we are many, we all eat from one loaf of bread, showing that we are one body. ¹⁸Think about the people of Israel. Weren't they united by eating the sacrifices at the altar?

¹⁹What am I trying to say? Am I saying that food offered to idols has some significance, or that idols are real gods? ²⁰No, not at all. I am saying that these sacrifices are offered to demons, not to God. And I don't want you to participate with demons. ²¹You cannot drink from the cup of the Lord and from the cup of demons, too. You cannot eat at the Lord's Table and at the table of demons, too. ²²What? Do we dare to rouse the Lord's jealousy? Do you think we are stronger than he is?

²³You say, "I am allowed to do anything"*—but not everything is good for you. You say, "I am allowed to do anything"—but not everything is beneficial. ²⁴Don't be concerned for your own good but for the good of others.

²⁵So you may eat any meat that is sold in the marketplace without raising questions of conscience. ²⁶For "the earth is the LORD's, and everything in it."*

²⁷If someone who isn't a believer asks you home for dinner, accept the invitation if you want to. Eat whatever is offered to you without raising questions of conscience. ²⁸(But suppose someone tells you, "This meat was offered to an idol." Don't eat it, out of consideration for the conscience of the one who told you. ²⁹It might not be a matter of conscience for you, but it is for the other person.) For why should my

10:7 Exod 32:6. 10:9 Some manuscripts read *the Lord.* 10:23 Greek *All things are lawful;* also in 10:23b. 10:26 Ps 24:1.

freedom be limited by what some-one else thinks? ³⁰If I can thank God for the food and enjoy it, why should I be condemned for eating it?

³¹So whether you eat or drink, or whatever you do, do it all for the glory of God. ³²Don't give offense to Jews or Gentiles* or the church of God. ³³I, too, try to please everyone in everything I do. I don't just do what is best for me; I do what is best for others so that many may be saved. ¹¹:¹And you should imitate me, just as I imitate Christ.

Instructions for Public Worship

11 ²I am so glad that you always keep me in your thoughts, and that you are following the teachings I passed on to you. ³But there is one thing I want you to know: The head of every man is Christ, the head of woman is man, and the head of Christ is God.* ⁴A man dishonors his head* if he covers his head while praying or prophesying. ⁵But a woman dishonors her head* if she prays or prophesies without a cover-ing on her head, for this is the same as shaving her head. ⁶Yes, if she re-fuses to wear a head covering, she should cut off all her hair! But since it is shameful for a woman to have her hair cut or her head shaved, she should wear a covering.*

⁷A man should not wear anything on his head when worshiping, for man is made in God's image and re-flects God's glory. And woman re-flects man's glory. ⁸For the first man didn't come from woman, but the first woman came from man. ⁹And man was not made for woman, but woman was made for man. ¹⁰For this reason, and because the angels are watching, a woman should wear a covering on her head to show she is under authority.*

¹¹But among the Lord's people, women are not independent of men, and men are not independent of women. ¹²For although the first woman came from man, every other man was born from a woman, and everything comes from God.

¹³Judge for yourselves. Is it right for a woman to pray to God in public without covering her head? ¹⁴Isn't it obvious that it's disgraceful for a man to have long hair? ¹⁵And isn't long hair a woman's pride and joy? For it has been given to her as a cov-ering. ¹⁶But if anyone wants to argue about this, I simply say that we have no other custom than this, and nei-ther do God's other churches.

Order at the Lord's Supper

¹⁷But in the following instructions, I cannot praise you. For it sounds as if more harm than good is done when you meet together. ¹⁸First, I

10:32 Greek *or Greeks.* **11:3** Or *to know: The source of every man is Christ, the source of woman is man, and the source of Christ is God.* Or *to know: Every man is responsible to Christ, a woman is responsible to her husband, and Christ is responsible to God.* **11:4** Or *dishonors Christ.* **11:5** Or *dishonors her husband.* **11:6** Or *should have long hair.* **11:10** Greek *should have an authority on her head.*

hear that there are divisions among you when you meet as a church, and to some extent I believe it. ¹⁹But, of course, there must be divisions among you so that you who have God's approval will be recognized!

²⁰When you meet together, you are not really interested in the Lord's Supper. ²¹For some of you hurry to eat your own meal without sharing with others. As a result, some go hungry while others get drunk. ²²What? Don't you have your own homes for eating and drinking? Or do you really want to disgrace God's church and shame the poor? What am I supposed to say? Do you want me to praise you? Well, I certainly will not praise you for this!

²³For I pass on to you what I received from the Lord himself. On the night when he was betrayed, the Lord Jesus took some bread ²⁴and gave thanks to God for it. Then he broke it in pieces and said, "This is my body, which is given for you.* Do this in remembrance of me." ²⁵In the same way, he took the cup of wine after supper, saying, "This cup is the new covenant between God and his people—an agreement confirmed with my blood. Do this in remembrance of me as often as you drink it." ²⁶For every time you eat this bread and drink this cup, you are announcing the Lord's death until he comes again.

²⁷So anyone who eats this bread or drinks this cup of the Lord unworthily is guilty of sinning against* the body and blood of the Lord. ²⁸That is why you should examine yourself before eating the bread and drinking the cup. ²⁹For if you eat the bread or drink the cup without honoring the body of Christ,* you are eating and drinking God's judgment upon yourself. ³⁰That is why many of you are weak and sick and some have even died.

³¹But if we would examine ourselves, we would not be judged by God in this way. ³²Yet when we are judged by the Lord, we are being disciplined so that we will not be condemned along with the world.

³³So, my dear brothers and sisters,* when you gather for the Lord's Supper, wait for each other. ³⁴If you are really hungry, eat at home so you won't bring judgment upon yourselves when you meet together. I'll give you instructions about the other matters after I arrive.

Spiritual Gifts

12 Now, dear brothers and sisters,* regarding your question about the special abilities the Spirit gives us. I don't want you to misunderstand this. ²You know that when you were still pagans, you were led astray and swept along in worshiping speechless idols. ³So

---

11:24 Greek *which is for you;* other manuscripts read *which is broken for you.* **11:27** Or *is responsible for.* **11:29** Greek *the body;* other manuscripts read *the Lord's body.* **11:33** Greek *brothers.* **12:1** Greek *brothers.*

I want you to know that no one speaking by the Spirit of God will curse Jesus, and no one can say Jesus is Lord, except by the Holy Spirit.

[4]There are different kinds of spiritual gifts, but the same Spirit is the source of them all. [5]There are different kinds of service, but we serve the same Lord. [6]God works in different ways, but it is the same God who does the work in all of us.

[7]A spiritual gift is given to each of us so we can help each other. [8]To one person the Spirit gives the ability to give wise advice*; to another the same Spirit gives a message of special knowledge.* [9]The same Spirit gives great faith to another, and to someone else the one Spirit gives the gift of healing. [10]He gives one person the power to perform miracles, and another the ability to prophesy. He gives someone else the ability to discern whether a message is from the Spirit of God or from another spirit. Still another person is given the ability to speak in unknown languages,* while another is given the ability to interpret what is being said. [11]It is the one and only Spirit who distributes all these gifts. He alone decides which gift each person should have.

One Body with Many Parts

[12]The human body has many parts, but the many parts make up one whole body. So it is with the body of Christ. [13]Some of us are Jews, some are Gentiles,* some are slaves, and some are free. But we have all been baptized into one body by one Spirit, and we all share the same Spirit.*

[14]Yes, the body has many different parts, not just one part. [15]If the foot says, "I am not a part of the body because I am not a hand," that does not make it any less a part of the body. [16]And if the ear says, "I am not part of the body because I am not an eye," would that make it any less a part of the body? [17]If the whole body were an eye, how would you hear? Or if your whole body were an ear, how would you smell anything?

[18]But our bodies have many parts, and God has put each part just where he wants it. [19]How strange a body would be if it had only one part! [20]Yes, there are many parts, but only one body. [21]The eye can never say to the hand, "I don't need you." The head can't say to the feet, "I don't need you."

[22]In fact, some parts of the body that seem weakest and least important are actually the most necessary. [23]And the parts we regard as less honorable are those we clothe with the greatest care. So we carefully protect those parts that should not be seen, [24]while the more honorable

12:8a Or *gives a word of wisdom.* **12:8b** Or *gives a word of knowledge.* **12:10** Or *in various tongues; also in 12:28, 30.* **12:13a** Greek *some are Greeks.* **12:13b** Greek *we were all given one Spirit to drink.*

parts do not require this special care. So God has put the body together such that extra honor and care are given to those parts that have less dignity. ²⁵This makes for harmony among the members, so that all the members care for each other. ²⁶If one part suffers, all the parts suffer with it, and if one part is honored, all the parts are glad.

²⁷All of you together are Christ's body, and each of you is a part of it. ²⁸Here are some of the parts God has appointed for the church:

first are apostles,
second are prophets,
third are teachers,
then those who do miracles,
those who have the gift of
  healing,
those who can help others,
those who have the gift of
  leadership,
those who speak in unknown
  languages.

²⁹Are we all apostles? Are we all prophets? Are we all teachers? Do we all have the power to do miracles? ³⁰Do we all have the gift of healing? Do we all have the ability to speak in unknown languages? Do we all have the ability to interpret unknown languages? Of course not! ³¹So you should earnestly desire the most helpful gifts.

But now let me show you a way of life that is best of all.

Love Is the Greatest

13 If I could speak all the languages of earth and of angels, but didn't love others, I would only be a noisy gong or a clanging cymbal. ²If I had the gift of prophecy, and if I understood all of God's secret plans and possessed all knowledge, and if I had such faith that I could move mountains, but didn't love others, I would be nothing. ³If I gave everything I have to the poor and even sacrificed my body, I could boast about it;* but if I didn't love others, I would have gained nothing.

⁴Love is patient and kind. Love is not jealous or boastful or proud ⁵or rude. It does not demand its own way. It is not irritable, and it keeps no record of being wronged. ⁶It does not rejoice about injustice but rejoices whenever the truth wins out. ⁷Love never gives up, never loses faith, is always hopeful, and endures through every circumstance.

⁸Prophecy and speaking in unknown languages* and special knowledge will become useless. But love will last forever! ⁹Now our knowledge is partial and incomplete, and even the gift of prophecy reveals only part of the whole picture! ¹⁰But when the time of perfection comes, these partial things will become useless.

¹¹When I was a child, I spoke and thought and reasoned as a child. But when I grew up, I put away childish things. ¹²Now we see things

13:3 Some manuscripts read *sacrificed my body to be burned.*   **13:8** Or *in tongues.*

imperfectly, like puzzling reflections in a mirror, but then we will see everything with perfect clarity.* All that I know now is partial and incomplete, but then I will know everything completely, just as God now knows me completely.

¹³Three things will last forever—faith, hope, and love—and the greatest of these is love.

Tongues and Prophecy

14 Let love be your highest goal! But you should also desire the special abilities the Spirit gives—especially the ability to prophesy. ²For if you have the ability to speak in tongues,* you will be talking only to God, since people won't be able to understand you. You will be speaking by the power of the Spirit,* but it will all be mysterious. ³But one who prophesies strengthens others, encourages them, and comforts them. ⁴A person who speaks in tongues is strengthened personally, but one who speaks a word of prophecy strengthens the entire church.

⁵I wish you could all speak in tongues, but even more I wish you could all prophesy. For prophecy is greater than speaking in tongues, unless someone interprets what you are saying so that the whole church will be strengthened.

⁶Dear brothers and sisters,* if I should come to you speaking in an unknown language,* how would that help you? But if I bring you a revelation or some special knowledge or prophecy or teaching, that will be helpful. ⁷Even lifeless instruments like the flute or the harp must play the notes clearly, or no one will recognize the melody. ⁸And if the bugler doesn't sound a clear call, how will the soldiers know they are being called to battle?

⁹It's the same for you. If you speak to people in words they don't understand, how will they know what you are saying? You might as well be talking into empty space.

¹⁰There are many different languages in the world, and every language has meaning. ¹¹But if I don't understand a language, I will be a foreigner to someone who speaks it, and the one who speaks it will be a foreigner to me. ¹²And the same is true for you. Since you are so eager to have the special abilities the Spirit gives, seek those that will strengthen the whole church.

¹³So anyone who speaks in tongues should pray also for the ability to interpret what has been said. ¹⁴For if I pray in tongues, my spirit is praying, but I don't understand what I am saying.

¹⁵Well then, what shall I do? I will pray in the spirit,* and I will also pray in words I understand. I will sing in the spirit, and I will also sing

13:12 Greek *see face to face.* 14:2a Or *in unknown languages;* also in 14:4, 5, 13, 14, 18, 22, 26, 27, 28, 39. 14:2b Or *speaking in your spirit.* 14:6a Greek *brothers;* also in 14:20, 26, 39. 14:6b Or *in tongues;* also in 14:19, 23. 14:15 Or *in the Spirit;* also in 14:15b, 16.

in words I understand. [16]For if you praise God only in the spirit, how can those who don't understand you praise God along with you? How can they join you in giving thanks when they don't understand what you are saying? [17]You will be giving thanks very well, but it won't strengthen the people who hear you.

[18]I thank God that I speak in tongues more than any of you. [19]But in a church meeting I would rather speak five understandable words to help others than ten thousand words in an unknown language.

[20]Dear brothers and sisters, don't be childish in your understanding of these things. Be innocent as babies when it comes to evil, but be mature in understanding matters of this kind. [21]It is written in the Scriptures*:

> "I will speak to my own people
>   through strange languages
>   and through the lips of
>   foreigners.
> But even then, they will not
>   listen to me,"*
>   says the LORD.

[22]So you see that speaking in tongues is a sign, not for believers, but for unbelievers. Prophecy, however, is for the benefit of believers, not unbelievers. [23]Even so, if unbelievers or people who don't understand these things come into your church meeting and hear everyone speaking in an unknown language,

they will think you are crazy. [24]But if all of you are prophesying, and unbelievers or people who don't understand these things come into your meeting, they will be convicted of sin and judged by what you say. [25]As they listen, their secret thoughts will be exposed, and they will fall to their knees and worship God, declaring, "God is truly here among you."

A Call to Orderly Worship

[26]Well, my brothers and sisters, let's summarize. When you meet together, one will sing, another will teach, another will tell some special revelation God has given, one will speak in tongues, and another will interpret what is said. But everything that is done must strengthen all of you.

[27]No more than two or three should speak in tongues. They must speak one at a time, and someone must interpret what they say. [28]But if no one is present who can interpret, they must be silent in your church meeting and speak in tongues to God privately.

[29]Let two or three people prophesy, and let the others evaluate what is said. [30]But if someone is prophesying and another person receives a revelation from the Lord, the one who is speaking must stop. [31]In this way, all who prophesy will have a turn to speak, one after the other, so that everyone will learn and be

14:21a Greek *in the law.* 14:21b Isa 28:11-12.

encouraged. [32]Remember that people who prophesy are in control of their spirit and can take turns. [33]For God is not a God of disorder but of peace, as in all the meetings of God's holy people.*

[34]Women should be silent during the church meetings. It is not proper for them to speak. They should be submissive, just as the law says. [35]If they have any questions, they should ask their husbands at home, for it is improper for women to speak in church meetings.*

[36]Or do you think God's word originated with you Corinthians? Are you the only ones to whom it was given? [37]If you claim to be a prophet or think you are spiritual, you should recognize that what I am saying is a command from the Lord himself. [38]But if you do not recognize this, you yourself will not be recognized.*

[39]So, my dear brothers and sisters, be eager to prophesy, and don't forbid speaking in tongues. [40]But be sure that everything is done properly and in order.

The Resurrection of Christ

15 Let me now remind you, dear brothers and sisters,* of the Good News I preached to you before. You welcomed it then, and you still stand firm in it. [2]It is this Good News that saves you if you continue to believe the message I told you—

unless, of course, you believed something that was never true in the first place.*

[3]I passed on to you what was most important and what had also been passed on to me. Christ died for our sins, just as the Scriptures said. [4]He was buried, and he was raised from the dead on the third day, just as the Scriptures said. [5]He was seen by Peter* and then by the Twelve. [6]After that, he was seen by more than 500 of his followers* at one time, most of whom are still alive, though some have died. [7]Then he was seen by James and later by all the apostles. [8]Last of all, as though I had been born at the wrong time, I also saw him. [9]For I am the least of all the apostles. In fact, I'm not even worthy to be called an apostle after the way I persecuted God's church.

[10]But whatever I am now, it is all because God poured out his special favor on me—and not without results. For I have worked harder than any of the other apostles; yet it was not I but God who was working through me by his grace. [11]So it makes no difference whether I preach or they preach, for we all preach the same message you have already believed.

The Resurrection of the Dead

[12]But tell me this—since we preach that Christ rose from the dead, why

---

14:33 The phrase *as in all the meetings of God's holy people* could instead be joined to the beginning of 14:34.   **14:35** Some manuscripts place verses 34-35 after 14:40.   **14:38** Some manuscripts read *If you are ignorant of this, stay in your ignorance.*   **15:1** Greek *brothers;* also in 15:31, 50, 58.   **15:2** Or *unless you never believed it in the first place.*   **15:5** Greek *Cephas.*   **15:6** Greek *the brothers.*

are some of you saying there will be no resurrection of the dead? [13]For if there is no resurrection of the dead, then Christ has not been raised either. [14]And if Christ has not been raised, then all our preaching is useless, and your faith is useless. [15]And we apostles would all be lying about God—for we have said that God raised Christ from the grave. But that can't be true if there is no resurrection of the dead. [16]And if there is no resurrection of the dead, then Christ has not been raised. [17]And if Christ has not been raised, then your faith is useless and you are still guilty of your sins. [18]In that case, all who have died believing in Christ are lost! [19]And if our hope in Christ is only for this life, we are more to be pitied than anyone in the world.

[20]But in fact, Christ has been raised from the dead. He is the first of a great harvest of all who have died.

[21]So you see, just as death came into the world through a man, now the resurrection from the dead has begun through another man. [22]Just as everyone dies because we all belong to Adam, everyone who belongs to Christ will be given new life. [23]But there is an order to this resurrection: Christ was raised as the first of the harvest; then all who belong to Christ will be raised when he comes back.

[24]After that the end will come, when he will turn the Kingdom over to God the Father, having destroyed every ruler and authority and power. [25]For Christ must reign until he humbles all his enemies beneath his feet. [26]And the last enemy to be destroyed is death. [27]For the Scriptures say, "God has put all things under his authority."* (Of course, when it says "all things are under his authority," that does not include God himself, who gave Christ his authority.) [28]Then, when all things are under his authority, the Son will put himself under God's authority, so that God, who gave his Son authority over all things, will be utterly supreme over everything everywhere.

[29]If the dead will not be raised, what point is there in people being baptized for those who are dead? Why do it unless the dead will someday rise again?

[30]And why should we ourselves risk our lives hour by hour? [31]For I swear, dear brothers and sisters, that I face death daily. This is as certain as my pride in what Christ Jesus our Lord has done in you. [32]And what value was there in fighting wild beasts—those people of Ephesus*—if there will be no resurrection from the dead? And if there is no resurrection, "Let's feast and drink, for tomorrow we die!"* [33]Don't be fooled by those who say such things, for "bad company corrupts good character." [34]Think carefully about what is right, and

15:27 Ps 8:6. 15:32a Greek *fighting wild beasts in Ephesus.* 15:32b Isa 22:13.

stop sinning. For to your shame I say that some of you don't know God at all.

The Resurrection Body

[35]But someone may ask, "How will the dead be raised? What kind of bodies will they have?" [36]What a foolish question! When you put a seed into the ground, it doesn't grow into a plant unless it dies first. [37]And what you put in the ground is not the plant that will grow, but only a bare seed of wheat or whatever you are planting. [38]Then God gives it the new body he wants it to have. A different plant grows from each kind of seed. [39]Similarly there are different kinds of flesh—one kind for humans, another for animals, another for birds, and another for fish.

[40]There are also bodies in the heavens and bodies on the earth. The glory of the heavenly bodies is different from the glory of the earthly bodies. [41]The sun has one kind of glory, while the moon and stars each have another kind. And even the stars differ from each other in their glory.

[42]It is the same way with the resurrection of the dead. Our earthly bodies are planted in the ground when we die, but they will be raised to live forever. [43]Our bodies are buried in brokenness, but they will be raised in glory. They are buried in weakness, but they will be raised in strength. [44]They are buried as natural human bodies, but they will be raised as spiritual bodies. For just as there are natural bodies, there are also spiritual bodies.

[45]The Scriptures tell us, "The first man, Adam, became a living person."* But the last Adam—that is, Christ—is a life-giving Spirit. [46]What comes first is the natural body, then the spiritual body comes later. [47]Adam, the first man, was made from the dust of the earth, while Christ, the second man, came from heaven. [48]Earthly people are like the earthly man, and heavenly people are like the heavenly man. [49]Just as we are now like the earthly man, we will someday be like* the heavenly man.

[50]What I am saying, dear brothers and sisters, is that our physical bodies cannot inherit the Kingdom of God. These dying bodies cannot inherit what will last forever.

[51]But let me reveal to you a wonderful secret. We will not all die, but we will all be transformed! [52]It will happen in a moment, in the blink of an eye, when the last trumpet is blown. For when the trumpet sounds, those who have died will be raised to live forever. And we who are living will also be transformed. [53]For our dying bodies must be transformed into bodies that will never die; our mortal bodies must be transformed into immortal bodies. [54]Then, when our dying bodies

15:45 Gen 2:7. **15:49** Some manuscripts read *let us be like.*

have been transformed into bodies that will never die,* this Scripture will be fulfilled:

"Death is swallowed up in
    victory.*
55 O death, where is your victory?
    O death, where is your
        sting?*"

56For sin is the sting that results in death, and the law gives sin its power. 57But thank God! He gives us victory over sin and death through our Lord Jesus Christ.

58So, my dear brothers and sisters, be strong and immovable. Always work enthusiastically for the Lord, for you know that nothing you do for the Lord is ever useless.

The Collection for Jerusalem

16 Now regarding your question about the money being collected for God's people in Jerusalem. You should follow the same procedure I gave to the churches in Galatia. 2On the first day of each week, you should each put aside a portion of the money you have earned. Don't wait until I get there and then try to collect it all at once. 3When I come, I will write letters of recommendation for the messengers you choose to deliver your gift to Jerusalem. 4And if it seems appropriate for me to go along, they can travel with me.

Paul's Final Instructions

5I am coming to visit you after I have been to Macedonia,* for I am planning to travel through Macedonia. 6Perhaps I will stay awhile with you, possibly all winter, and then you can send me on my way to my next destination. 7This time I don't want to make just a short visit and then go right on. I want to come and stay awhile, if the Lord will let me. 8In the meantime, I will be staying here at Ephesus until the Festival of Pentecost. 9There is a wide-open door for a great work here, although many oppose me.

10When Timothy comes, don't intimidate him. He is doing the Lord's work, just as I am. 11Don't let anyone treat him with contempt. Send him on his way with your blessing when he returns to me. I expect him to come with the other believers.*

12Now about our brother Apollos—I urged him to visit you with the other believers, but he was not willing to go right now. He will see you later when he has the opportunity.

13Be on guard. Stand firm in the faith. Be courageous.* Be strong. 14And do everything with love.

15You know that Stephanas and his household were the first of the harvest of believers in Greece,* and they are spending their lives in service to God's people. I urge you, dear

---

15:54a Some manuscripts add *and our mortal bodies have been transformed into immortal bodies.* 15:54b Isa 25:8.   15:55 Hos 13:14 (Greek version).   16:5 *Macedonia* was in the northern region of Greece.   16:11 Greek *with the brothers;* also in 16:12.   16:13 Greek *Be men.*   16:15a Greek *in Achaia,* the southern region of the Greek peninsula.

brothers and sisters,* ¹⁶to submit to them and others like them who serve with such devotion. ¹⁷I am very glad that Stephanas, Fortunatus, and Achaicus have come here. They have been providing the help you weren't here to give me. ¹⁸They have been a wonderful encouragement to me, as they have been to you. You must show your appreciation to all who serve so well.

Paul's Final Greetings

¹⁹The churches here in the province of Asia* send greetings in the Lord, as do Aquila and Priscilla* and all the others who gather in their home for church meetings. ²⁰All the brothers and sisters here send greetings to you. Greet each other with a sacred kiss.

²¹HERE IS MY GREETING IN MY OWN HANDWRITING—PAUL.

²²If anyone does not love the Lord, that person is cursed. Our Lord, come!*

²³May the grace of the Lord Jesus be with you.

²⁴My love to all of you in Christ Jesus.*

16:15b Greek *brothers;* also in 16:20. 16:19a *Asia* was a Roman province in what is now western Turkey. 16:19b Greek *Prisca.* 16:22 From Aramaic, *Marana tha.* Some manuscripts read *Maran atha,* "Our Lord has come." 16:24 Some manuscripts add *Amen.*

2 Corinthians

Greetings from Paul

1 This letter is from Paul, chosen by the will of God to be an apostle of Christ Jesus, and from our brother Timothy.

I am writing to God's church in Corinth and to all of his holy people throughout Greece.*

²May God our Father and the Lord Jesus Christ give you grace and peace.

God Offers Comfort to All

³All praise to God, the Father of our Lord Jesus Christ. God is our merciful Father and the source of all comfort. ⁴He comforts us in all our troubles so that we can comfort others. When they are troubled, we will be able to give them the same comfort God has given us. ⁵For the more we suffer for Christ, the more God will shower us with his comfort through Christ. ⁶Even when we are weighed down with troubles, it is for your comfort and salvation! For when we ourselves are comforted, we will certainly comfort you. Then you can patiently endure the same things we suffer. ⁷We are confident that as you share in our sufferings, you will also share in the comfort God gives us.

⁸We think you ought to know, dear brothers and sisters,* about the trouble we went through in the province of Asia. We were crushed and overwhelmed beyond our ability to endure, and we thought we would never live through it. ⁹In fact, we expected to die. But as a result, we stopped relying on ourselves and learned to rely only on God, who raises the dead. ¹⁰And he did rescue us from mortal danger, and he will rescue us again. We have placed our confidence in him, and he will continue to rescue us. ¹¹And you are helping us by praying for us. Then many people will give thanks because God has graciously answered so many prayers for our safety.

Paul's Change of Plans

¹²We can say with confidence and a clear conscience that we have lived with a God-given holiness* and sincerity in all our dealings. We have depended on God's grace, not on our own human wisdom. That is how we have conducted ourselves before the world, and especially toward you.

1:1 Greek *Achaia,* the southern region of the Greek peninsula. 1:8 Greek *brothers*. 1:12 Some manuscripts read *honesty*.

305

¹³Our letters have been straightforward, and there is nothing written between the lines and nothing you can't understand. I hope someday you will fully understand us, ¹⁴even if you don't understand us now. Then on the day when the Lord Jesus* returns, you will be proud of us in the same way we are proud of you.

¹⁵Since I was so sure of your understanding and trust, I wanted to give you a double blessing by visiting you twice—¹⁶first on my way to Macedonia and again when I returned from Macedonia.* Then you could send me on my way to Judea.

¹⁷You may be asking why I changed my plan. Do you think I make my plans carelessly? Do you think I am like people of the world who say "Yes" when they really mean "No"? ¹⁸As surely as God is faithful, our word to you does not waver between "Yes" and "No." ¹⁹For Jesus Christ, the Son of God, does not waver between "Yes" and "No." He is the one whom Silas,* Timothy, and I preached to you, and as God's ultimate "Yes," he always does what he says. ²⁰For all of God's promises have been fulfilled in Christ with a resounding "Yes!" And through Christ, our "Amen" (which means "Yes") ascends to God for his glory.

²¹It is God who enables us, along with you, to stand firm for Christ. He has commissioned us, ²²and he has identified us as his own by placing the Holy Spirit in our hearts as the first installment that guarantees everything he has promised us.

²³Now I call upon God as my witness that I am telling the truth. The reason I didn't return to Corinth was to spare you from a severe rebuke. ²⁴But that does not mean we want to dominate you by telling you how to put your faith into practice. We want to work together with you so you will be full of joy, for it is by your own faith that you stand firm.

2 So I decided that I would not bring you grief with another painful visit. ²For if I cause you grief, who will make me glad? Certainly not someone I have grieved. ³That is why I wrote to you as I did, so that when I do come, I won't be grieved by the very ones who ought to give me the greatest joy. Surely you all know that my joy comes from your being joyful. ⁴I wrote that letter in great anguish, with a troubled heart and many tears. I didn't want to grieve you, but I wanted to let you know how much love I have for you.

Forgiveness for the Sinner

⁵I am not overstating it when I say that the man who caused all the trouble hurt all of you more than he hurt me. ⁶Most of you opposed him, and that was punishment enough. ⁷Now, however, it is time to forgive and comfort him. Otherwise he may be overcome by discourage-

1:14 Some manuscripts read *our Lord Jesus.*　1:16 *Macedonia* was in the northern region of Greece.
1:19 Greek *Silvanus.*

ment. [8]So I urge you now to reaffirm your love for him.

[9]I wrote to you as I did to test you and see if you would fully comply with my instructions. [10]When you forgive this man, I forgive him, too. And when I forgive whatever needs to be forgiven, I do so with Christ's authority for your benefit, [11]so that Satan will not outsmart us. For we are familiar with his evil schemes.

[12]When I came to the city of Troas to preach the Good News of Christ, the Lord opened a door of opportunity for me. [13]But I had no peace of mind because my dear brother Titus hadn't yet arrived with a report from you. So I said good-bye and went on to Macedonia to find him.

Ministers of the New Covenant

[14]But thank God! He has made us his captives and continues to lead us along in Christ's triumphal procession. Now he uses us to spread the knowledge of Christ everywhere, like a sweet perfume. [15]Our lives are a Christ-like fragrance rising up to God. But this fragrance is perceived differently by those who are being saved and by those who are perishing. [16]To those who are perishing, we are a dreadful smell of death and doom. But to those who are being saved, we are a life-giving perfume. And who is adequate for such a task as this?

[17]You see, we are not like the many hucksters* who preach for personal profit. We preach the word of God with sincerity and with Christ's authority, knowing that God is watching us.

3 Are we beginning to praise ourselves again? Are we like others, who need to bring you letters of recommendation, or who ask you to write such letters on their behalf? Surely not! [2]The only letter of recommendation we need is you yourselves. Your lives are a letter written in our* hearts; everyone can read it and recognize our good work among you. [3]Clearly, you are a letter from Christ showing the result of our ministry among you. This "letter" is written not with pen and ink, but with the Spirit of the living God. It is carved not on tablets of stone, but on human hearts.

[4]We are confident of all this because of our great trust in God through Christ. [5]It is not that we think we are qualified to do anything on our own. Our qualification comes from God. [6]He has enabled us to be ministers of his new covenant. This is a covenant not of written laws, but of the Spirit. The old written covenant ends in death; but under the new covenant, the Spirit gives life.

The Glory of the New Covenant

[7]The old way,* with laws etched in stone, led to death, though it began

2:17 Some manuscripts read *the rest of the hucksters.*　**3:2** Some manuscripts read *your.*　**3:7** Or *ministry;* also in 3:8, 9, 10, 11, 12.

with such glory that the people of Israel could not bear to look at Moses' face. For his face shone with the glory of God, even though the brightness was already fading away. ⁸Shouldn't we expect far greater glory under the new way, now that the Holy Spirit is giving life? ⁹If the old way, which brings condemnation, was glorious, how much more glorious is the new way, which makes us right with God! ¹⁰In fact, that first glory was not glorious at all compared with the overwhelming glory of the new way. ¹¹So if the old way, which has been replaced, was glorious, how much more glorious is the new, which remains forever!

¹²Since this new way gives us such confidence, we can be very bold. ¹³We are not like Moses, who put a veil over his face so the people of Israel would not see the glory, even though it was destined to fade away. ¹⁴But the people's minds were hardened, and to this day whenever the old covenant is being read, the same veil covers their minds so they cannot understand the truth. And this veil can be removed only by believing in Christ. ¹⁵Yes, even today when they read Moses' writings, their hearts are covered with that veil, and they do not understand.

¹⁶But whenever someone turns to the Lord, the veil is taken away. ¹⁷For the Lord is the Spirit, and wherever the Spirit of the Lord is, there is freedom. ¹⁸So all of us who have had

that veil removed can see and reflect the glory of the Lord. And the Lord—who is the Spirit—makes us more and more like him as we are changed into his glorious image.

Treasure in Fragile Clay Jars

4 Therefore, since God in his mercy has given us this new way,* we never give up. ²We reject all shameful deeds and underhanded methods. We don't try to trick anyone or distort the word of God. We tell the truth before God, and all who are honest know this.

³If the Good News we preach is hidden behind a veil, it is hidden only from people who are perishing. ⁴Satan, who is the god of this world, has blinded the minds of those who don't believe. They are unable to see the glorious light of the Good News. They don't understand this message about the glory of Christ, who is the exact likeness of God.

⁵You see, we don't go around preaching about ourselves. We preach that Jesus Christ is Lord, and we ourselves are your servants for Jesus' sake. ⁶For God, who said, "Let there be light in the darkness," has made this light shine in our hearts so we could know the glory of God that is seen in the face of Jesus Christ.

⁷We now have this light shining in our hearts, but we ourselves are like fragile clay jars containing this

4:1 Or *ministry*.

great treasure.* This makes it clear that our great power is from God, not from ourselves.

[8]We are pressed on every side by troubles, but we are not crushed. We are perplexed, but not driven to despair. [9]We are hunted down, but never abandoned by God. We get knocked down, but we are not destroyed. [10]Through suffering, our bodies continue to share in the death of Jesus so that the life of Jesus may also be seen in our bodies.

[11]Yes, we live under constant danger of death because we serve Jesus, so that the life of Jesus will be evident in our dying bodies. [12]So we live in the face of death, but this has resulted in eternal life for you.

[13]But we continue to preach because we have the same kind of faith the psalmist had when he said, "I believed in God, so I spoke."* [14]We know that God, who raised the Lord Jesus,* will also raise us with Jesus and present us to himself together with you. [15]All of this is for your benefit. And as God's grace reaches more and more people, there will be great thanksgiving, and God will receive more and more glory.

[16]That is why we never give up. Though our bodies are dying, our spirits are* being renewed every day. [17]For our present troubles are small and won't last very long. Yet they produce for us a glory that vastly outweighs them and will last

forever! [18]So we don't look at the troubles we can see now; rather, we fix our gaze on things that cannot be seen. For the things we see now will soon be gone, but the things we cannot see will last forever.

New Bodies

5 For we know that when this earthly tent we live in is taken down (that is, when we die and leave this earthly body), we will have a house in heaven, an eternal body made for us by God himself and not by human hands. [2]We grow weary in our present bodies, and we long to put on our heavenly bodies like new clothing. [3]For we will put on heavenly bodies; we will not be spirits without bodies.* [4]While we live in these earthly bodies, we groan and sigh, but it's not that we want to die and get rid of these bodies that clothe us. Rather, we want to put on our new bodies so that these dying bodies will be swallowed up by life. [5]God himself has prepared us for this, and as a guarantee he has given us his Holy Spirit.

[6]So we are always confident, even though we know that as long as we live in these bodies we are not at home with the Lord. [7]For we live by believing and not by seeing. [8]Yes, we are fully confident, and we would rather be away from these earthly bodies, for then we will be at home with the Lord. [9]So whether we are

---

4:7 Greek *We now have this treasure in clay jars.*   **4:13** Ps 116:10.   **4:14** Some manuscripts read *who raised Jesus.*   **4:16** Greek *our inner being is.*   **5:3** Greek *we will not be naked.*

here in this body or away from this body, our goal is to please him. ¹⁰For we must all stand before Christ to be judged. We will each receive whatever we deserve for the good or evil we have done in this earthly body.

We Are God's Ambassadors

¹¹Because we understand our fearful responsibility to the Lord, we work hard to persuade others. God knows we are sincere, and I hope you know this, too. ¹²Are we commending ourselves to you again? No, we are giving you a reason to be proud of us,* so you can answer those who brag about having a spectacular ministry rather than having a sincere heart. ¹³If it seems we are crazy, it is to bring glory to God. And if we are in our right minds, it is for your benefit. ¹⁴Either way, Christ's love controls us.* Since we believe that Christ died for all, we also believe that we have all died to our old life.* ¹⁵He died for everyone so that those who receive his new life will no longer live for themselves. Instead, they will live for Christ, who died and was raised for them.

¹⁶So we have stopped evaluating others from a human point of view. At one time we thought of Christ merely from a human point of view. How differently we know him now! ¹⁷This means that anyone who belongs to Christ has become a new person. The old life is gone; a new life has begun!

¹⁸And all of this is a gift from God, who brought us back to himself through Christ. And God has given us this task of reconciling people to him. ¹⁹For God was in Christ, reconciling the world to himself, no longer counting people's sins against them. And he gave us this wonderful message of reconciliation. ²⁰So we are Christ's ambassadors; God is making his appeal through us. We speak for Christ when we plead, "Come back to God!" ²¹For God made Christ, who never sinned, to be the offering for our sin,* so that we could be made right with God through Christ.

6 As God's partners,* we beg you not to accept this marvelous gift of God's kindness and then ignore it. ²For God says,

"At just the right time, I heard
   you.
   On the day of salvation,
      I helped you."*

Indeed, the "right time" is now. Today is the day of salvation.

Paul's Hardships

³We live in such a way that no one will stumble because of us, and no one will find fault with our ministry.

5:12 Some manuscripts read *proud of yourselves.* **5:14a** Or *urges us on.* **5:14b** Greek *Since one died for all, then all died.* **5:21** Or *to become sin itself.* **6:1** Or *As we work together.* **6:2** Isa 49:8 (Greek version).

[4]In everything we do, we show that we are true ministers of God. We patiently endure troubles and hardships and calamities of every kind. [5]We have been beaten, been put in prison, faced angry mobs, worked to exhaustion, endured sleepless nights, and gone without food. [6]We prove ourselves by our purity, our understanding, our patience, our kindness, by the Holy Spirit within us,* and by our sincere love. [7]We faithfully preach the truth. God's power is working in us. We use the weapons of righteousness in the right hand for attack and the left hand for defense. [8]We serve God whether people honor us or despise us, whether they slander us or praise us. We are honest, but they call us impostors. [9]We are ignored, even though we are well known. We live close to death, but we are still alive. We have been beaten, but we have not been killed. [10]Our hearts ache, but we always have joy. We are poor, but we give spiritual riches to others. We own nothing, and yet we have everything.

[11]Oh, dear Corinthian friends! We have spoken honestly with you, and our hearts are open to you. [12]There is no lack of love on our part, but you have withheld your love from us. [13]I am asking you to respond as if you were my own children. Open your hearts to us!

The Temple of the Living God

[14]Don't team up with those who are unbelievers. How can righteousness be a partner with wickedness? How can light live with darkness? [15]What harmony can there be between Christ and the devil*? How can a believer be a partner with an unbeliever? [16]And what union can there be between God's temple and idols? For we are the temple of the living God. As God said:

"I will live in them
    and walk among them.
I will be their God,
    and they will be my people.*
[17] Therefore, come out from among unbelievers,
    and separate yourselves from
       them, says the LORD.
Don't touch their filthy things,
    and I will welcome you.*
[18] And I will be your Father,
    and you will be my sons and
       daughters,
    says the LORD Almighty.*"

7 Because we have these promises, dear friends, let us cleanse ourselves from everything that can defile our body or spirit. And let us work toward complete holiness because we fear God.

[2]Please open your hearts to us. We have not done wrong to anyone, nor led anyone astray, nor taken advantage of anyone. [3]I'm not saying

6:6 Or *by our holiness of spirit*. 6:15 Greek *Beliar;* various other manuscripts render this proper name of the devil as *Belian, Beliab,* or *Belial*. 6:16 Lev 26:12; Ezek 37:27. 6:17 Isa 52:11; Ezek 20:34 (Greek version). 6:18 2 Sam 7:14.

this to condemn you. I said before that you are in our hearts, and we live or die together with you. [4]I have the highest confidence in you, and I take great pride in you. You have greatly encouraged me and made me happy despite all our troubles.

Paul's Joy at the Church's Repentance

[5]When we arrived in Macedonia, there was no rest for us. We faced conflict from every direction, with battles on the outside and fear on the inside. [6]But God, who encourages those who are discouraged, encouraged us by the arrival of Titus. [7]His presence was a joy, but so was the news he brought of the encouragement he received from you. When he told us how much you long to see me, and how sorry you are for what happened, and how loyal you are to me, I was filled with joy!

[8]I am not sorry that I sent that severe letter to you, though I was sorry at first, for I know it was painful to you for a little while. [9]Now I am glad I sent it, not because it hurt you, but because the pain caused you to repent and change your ways. It was the kind of sorrow God wants his people to have, so you were not harmed by us in any way. [10]For the kind of sorrow God wants us to experience leads us away from sin and results in salvation. There's no regret for that kind of sorrow. But worldly sorrow, which lacks repentance, results in spiritual death.

[11]Just see what this godly sorrow produced in you! Such earnestness, such concern to clear yourselves, such indignation, such alarm, such longing to see me, such zeal, and such a readiness to punish wrong. You showed that you have done everything necessary to make things right. [12]My purpose, then, was not to write about who did the wrong or who was wronged. I wrote to you so that in the sight of God you could see for yourselves how loyal you are to us. [13]We have been greatly encouraged by this.

In addition to our own encouragement, we were especially delighted to see how happy Titus was about the way all of you welcomed him and set his mind* at ease. [14]I had told him how proud I was of you—and you didn't disappoint me. I have always told you the truth, and now my boasting to Titus has also proved true! [15]Now he cares for you more than ever when he remembers the way all of you obeyed him and welcomed him with such fear and deep respect. [16]I am very happy now because I have complete confidence in you.

A Call to Generous Giving

8 Now I want you to know, dear brothers and sisters,* what God in his kindness has done through the churches in Macedonia. [2]They

7:13 Greek *his spirit.* **8:1** Greek *brothers.*

are being tested by many troubles, and they are very poor. But they are also filled with abundant joy, which has overflowed in rich generosity.

³For I can testify that they gave not only what they could afford, but far more. And they did it of their own free will. ⁴They begged us again and again for the privilege of sharing in the gift for the believers in Jerusalem.* ⁵They even did more than we had hoped, for their first action was to give themselves to the Lord and to us, just as God wanted them to do.

⁶So we have urged Titus, who encouraged your giving in the first place, to return to you and encourage you to finish this ministry of giving. ⁷Since you excel in so many ways—in your faith, your gifted speakers, your knowledge, your enthusiasm, and your love from us*—I want you to excel also in this gracious act of giving.

⁸I am not commanding you to do this. But I am testing how genuine your love is by comparing it with the eagerness of the other churches.

⁹You know the generous grace of our Lord Jesus Christ. Though he was rich, yet for your sakes he became poor, so that by his poverty he could make you rich.

¹⁰Here is my advice: It would be good for you to finish what you started a year ago. Last year you were the first who wanted to give, and you were the first to begin doing it. ¹¹Now you should finish what you started. Let the eagerness you showed in the beginning be matched now by your giving. Give in proportion to what you have. ¹²Whatever you give is acceptable if you give it eagerly. And give according to what you have, not what you don't have. ¹³Of course, I don't mean your giving should make life easy for others and hard for yourselves. I only mean that there should be some equality. ¹⁴Right now you have plenty and can help those who are in need. Later, they will have plenty and can share with you when you need it. In this way, things will be equal. ¹⁵As the Scriptures say,

"Those who gathered a lot had
nothing left over,
and those who gathered only
a little had enough."*

Titus and His Companions

¹⁶But thank God! He has given Titus the same enthusiasm for you that I have. ¹⁷Titus welcomed our request that he visit you again. In fact, he himself was very eager to go and see you. ¹⁸We are also sending another brother with Titus. All the churches praise him as a preacher of the Good News. ¹⁹He was appointed by the churches to accompany us as we take the offering to Jerusalem*— a service that glorifies the Lord and shows our eagerness to help.

8:4 Greek *for God's holy people.* 8:7 Some manuscripts read *your love for us.* 8:15 Exod 16:18.
8:19 See 1 Cor 16:3-4.

[20]We are traveling together to guard against any criticism for the way we are handling this generous gift. [21]We are careful to be honorable before the Lord, but we also want everyone else to see that we are honorable.

[22]We are also sending with them another of our brothers who has proven himself many times and has shown on many occasions how eager he is. He is now even more enthusiastic because of his great confidence in you. [23]If anyone asks about Titus, say that he is my partner who works with me to help you. And the brothers with him have been sent by the churches,* and they bring honor to Christ. [24]So show them your love, and prove to all the churches that our boasting about you is justified.

The Collection for Christians in Jerusalem

9 I really don't need to write to you about this ministry of giving for the believers in Jerusalem.* [2]For I know how eager you are to help, and I have been boasting to the churches in Macedonia that you in Greece* were ready to send an offering a year ago. In fact, it was your enthusiasm that stirred up many of the Macedonian believers to begin giving.

[3]But I am sending these brothers to be sure you really are ready, as I have been telling them, and that your money is all collected. I don't want to be wrong in my boasting about you. [4]We would be embarrassed—not to mention your own embarrassment—if some Macedonian believers came with me and found that you weren't ready after all I had told them! [5]So I thought I should send these brothers ahead of me to make sure the gift you promised is ready. But I want it to be a willing gift, not one given grudgingly.

[6]Remember this—a farmer who plants only a few seeds will get a small crop. But the one who plants generously will get a generous crop. [7]You must each decide in your heart how much to give. And don't give reluctantly or in response to pressure. "For God loves a person who gives cheerfully."* [8]And God will generously provide all you need. Then you will always have everything you need and plenty left over to share with others. [9]As the Scriptures say,

> "They share freely and give
> generously to the poor.
> Their good deeds will be
> remembered forever."*

[10]For God is the one who provides seed for the farmer and then bread to eat. In the same way, he will provide and increase your resources

8:23 Greek *are apostles of the churches.*   **9:1** Greek *about the offering for God's holy people.*
9:2 Greek *in Achaia,* the southern region of the Greek peninsula. *Macedonia* was in the northern region of Greece.   **9:7** See footnote on Prov 22:8.   **9:9** Ps 112:9.

and then produce a great harvest of generosity* in you.

¹¹Yes, you will be enriched in every way so that you can always be generous. And when we take your gifts to those who need them, they will thank God. ¹²So two good things will result from this ministry of giving—the needs of the believers in Jerusalem* will be met, and they will joyfully express their thanks to God.

¹³As a result of your ministry, they will give glory to God. For your generosity to them and to all believers will prove that you are obedient to the Good News of Christ. ¹⁴And they will pray for you with deep affection because of the overflowing grace God has given to you. ¹⁵Thank God for this gift* too wonderful for words!

Paul Defends His Authority

10 Now I, Paul, appeal to you with the gentleness and kindness of Christ—though I realize you think I am timid in person and bold only when I write from far away. ²Well, I am begging you now so that when I come I won't have to be bold with those who think we act from human motives.

³We are human, but we don't wage war as humans do. ⁴*We use God's mighty weapons, not worldly weapons, to knock down the strongholds of human reasoning and to destroy false arguments. ⁵We destroy every proud obstacle that keeps people from knowing God. We capture their rebellious thoughts and teach them to obey Christ. ⁶And after you have become fully obedient, we will punish everyone who remains disobedient.

⁷Look at the obvious facts.* Those who say they belong to Christ must recognize that we belong to Christ as much as they do. ⁸I may seem to be boasting too much about the authority given to us by the Lord. But our authority builds you up; it doesn't tear you down. So I will not be ashamed of using my authority.

⁹I'm not trying to frighten you by my letters. ¹⁰For some say, "Paul's letters are demanding and forceful, but in person he is weak, and his speeches are worthless!" ¹¹Those people should realize that our actions when we arrive in person will be as forceful as what we say in our letters from far away.

¹²Oh, don't worry; we wouldn't dare say that we are as wonderful as these other men who tell you how important they are! But they are only comparing themselves with each other, using themselves as the standard of measurement. How ignorant!

¹³We will not boast about things done outside our area of authority.

9:10 Greek *righteousness.* **9:12** Greek *of God's holy people.* **9:15** Greek *his gift.* **10:4** English translations divide verses 4 and 5 in various ways. **10:7** Or *You look at things only on the basis of appearance.*

We will boast only about what has happened within the boundaries of the work God has given us, which includes our working with you. ¹⁴We are not reaching beyond these boundaries when we claim authority over you, as if we had never visited you. For we were the first to travel all the way to Corinth with the Good News of Christ.

¹⁵Nor do we boast and claim credit for the work someone else has done. Instead, we hope that your faith will grow so that the boundaries of our work among you will be extended. ¹⁶Then we will be able to go and preach the Good News in other places far beyond you, where no one else is working. Then there will be no question of our boasting about work done in someone else's territory. ¹⁷As the Scriptures say, "If you want to boast, boast only about the LORD."*

¹⁸When people commend themselves, it doesn't count for much. The important thing is for the Lord to commend them.

Paul and the False Apostles

11 I hope you will put up with a little more of my foolishness. Please bear with me. ²For I am jealous for you with the jealousy of God himself. I promised you as a pure bride* to one husband—Christ. ³But I fear that somehow your pure and undivided devotion to Christ will be corrupted, just as Eve was deceived by the cunning ways of the serpent. ⁴You happily put up with whatever anyone tells you, even if they preach a different Jesus than the one we preach, or a different kind of Spirit than the one you received, or a different kind of gospel than the one you believed.

⁵But I don't consider myself inferior in any way to these "super apostles" who teach such things. ⁶I may be unskilled as a speaker, but I'm not lacking in knowledge. We have made this clear to you in every possible way.

⁷Was I wrong when I humbled myself and honored you by preaching God's Good News to you without expecting anything in return? ⁸I "robbed" other churches by accepting their contributions so I could serve you at no cost. ⁹And when I was with you and didn't have enough to live on, I did not become a financial burden to anyone. For the brothers who came from Macedonia brought me all that I needed. I have never been a burden to you, and I never will be. ¹⁰As surely as the truth of Christ is in me, no one in all of Greece* will ever stop me from boasting about this. ¹¹Why? Because I don't love you? God knows that I do.

¹²But I will continue doing what I have always done. This will undercut those who are looking for an opportunity to boast that their

10:17 Jer 9:24. **11:2** Greek *a virgin.* **11:10** Greek *Achaia,* the southern region of the Greek peninsula.

work is just like ours. [13]These people are false apostles. They are deceitful workers who disguise themselves as apostles of Christ. [14]But I am not surprised! Even Satan disguises himself as an angel of light. [15]So it is no wonder that his servants also disguise themselves as servants of righteousness. In the end they will get the punishment their wicked deeds deserve.

Paul's Many Trials

[16]Again I say, don't think that I am a fool to talk like this. But even if you do, listen to me, as you would to a foolish person, while I also boast a little. [17]Such boasting is not from the Lord, but I am acting like a fool. [18]And since others boast about their human achievements, I will, too. [19]After all, you think you are so wise, but you enjoy putting up with fools! [20]You put up with it when someone enslaves you, takes everything you have, takes advantage of you, takes control of everything, and slaps you in the face. [21]I'm ashamed to say that we've been too "weak" to do that!

But whatever they dare to boast about—I'm talking like a fool again—I dare to boast about it, too. [22]Are they Hebrews? So am I. Are they Israelites? So am I. Are they descendants of Abraham? So am I. [23]Are they servants of Christ? I know I sound like a madman, but I have served him far more! I have worked harder, been put in prison more often, been whipped times without number, and faced death again and again. [24]Five different times the Jewish leaders gave me thirty-nine lashes. [25]Three times I was beaten with rods. Once I was stoned. Three times I was shipwrecked. Once I spent a whole night and a day adrift at sea. [26]I have traveled on many long journeys. I have faced danger from rivers and from robbers. I have faced danger from my own people, the Jews, as well as from the Gentiles. I have faced danger in the cities, in the deserts, and on the seas. And I have faced danger from men who claim to be believers but are not.* [27]I have worked hard and long, enduring many sleepless nights. I have been hungry and thirsty and have often gone without food. I have shivered in the cold, without enough clothing to keep me warm.

[28]Then, besides all this, I have the daily burden of my concern for all the churches. [29]Who is weak without my feeling that weakness? Who is led astray, and I do not burn with anger?

[30]If I must boast, I would rather boast about the things that show how weak I am. [31]God, the Father of our Lord Jesus, who is worthy of eternal praise, knows I am not lying. [32]When I was in Damascus, the governor under King Aretas kept guards at the city gates to catch me.

11:26 Greek *from false brothers.*

[33]I had to be lowered in a basket through a window in the city wall to escape from him.

Paul's Vision and His Thorn in the Flesh

12 This boasting will do no good, but I must go on. I will reluctantly tell about visions and revelations from the Lord. [2]I* was caught up to the third heaven fourteen years ago. Whether I was in my body or out of my body, I don't know—only God knows. [3]Yes, only God knows whether I was in my body or outside my body. But I do know [4]that I was caught up* to paradise and heard things so astounding that they cannot be expressed in words, things no human is allowed to tell.

[5]That experience is worth boasting about, but I'm not going to do it. I will boast only about my weaknesses. [6]If I wanted to boast, I would be no fool in doing so, because I would be telling the truth. But I won't do it, because I don't want anyone to give me credit beyond what they can see in my life or hear in my message, [7]even though I have received such wonderful revelations from God. So to keep me from becoming proud, I was given a thorn in my flesh, a messenger from Satan to torment me and keep me from becoming proud.

[8]Three different times I begged the Lord to take it away. [9]Each time he said, "My grace is all you need. My power works best in weakness." So now I am glad to boast about my weaknesses, so that the power of Christ can work through me. [10]That's why I take pleasure in my weaknesses, and in the insults, hardships, persecutions, and troubles that I suffer for Christ. For when I am weak, then I am strong.

Paul's Concern for the Corinthians

[11]You have made me act like a fool. You ought to be writing commendations for me, for I am not at all inferior to these "super apostles," even though I am nothing at all. [12]When I was with you, I certainly gave you proof that I am an apostle. For I patiently did many signs and wonders and miracles among you. [13]The only thing I failed to do, which I do in the other churches, was to become a financial burden to you. Please forgive me for this wrong!

[14]Now I am coming to you for the third time, and I will not be a burden to you. I don't want what you have—I want you. After all, children don't provide for their parents. Rather, parents provide for their children. [15]I will gladly spend myself and all I have for you, even though it seems that the more I love you, the less you love me.

[16]Some of you admit I was not a

12:2 Greek *I know a man in Christ who.* **12:3-4** Greek *But I know such a man, [4]that he was caught up.*

burden to you. But others still think I was sneaky and took advantage of you by trickery. ¹⁷But how? Did any of the men I sent to you take advantage of you? ¹⁸When I urged Titus to visit you and sent our other brother with him, did Titus take advantage of you? No! For we have the same spirit and walk in each other's steps, doing things the same way.

¹⁹Perhaps you think we're saying these things just to defend ourselves. No, we tell you this as Christ's servants, and with God as our witness. Everything we do, dear friends, is to strengthen you. ²⁰For I am afraid that when I come I won't like what I find, and you won't like my response. I am afraid that I will find quarreling, jealousy, anger, selfishness, slander, gossip, arrogance, and disorderly behavior. ²¹Yes, I am afraid that when I come again, God will humble me in your presence. And I will be grieved because many of you have not given up your old sins. You have not repented of your impurity, sexual immorality, and eagerness for lustful pleasure.

Paul's Final Advice

13 This is the third time I am coming to visit you (and as the Scriptures say, "The facts of every case must be established by the testimony of two or three witnesses"*). ²I have already warned those who had been sinning when I was there on my second visit. Now I again warn them and all others, just as I did before, that next time I will not spare them.

³I will give you all the proof you want that Christ speaks through me. Christ is not weak when he deals with you; he is powerful among you. ⁴Although he was crucified in weakness, he now lives by the power of God. We, too, are weak, just as Christ was, but when we deal with you we will be alive with him and will have God's power.

⁵Examine yourselves to see if your faith is genuine. Test yourselves. Surely you know that Jesus Christ is among you*; if not, you have failed the test of genuine faith. ⁶As you test yourselves, I hope you will recognize that we have not failed the test of apostolic authority.

⁷We pray to God that you will not do what is wrong by refusing our correction. I hope we won't need to demonstrate our authority when we arrive. Do the right thing before we come—even if that makes it look like we have failed to demonstrate our authority. ⁸For we cannot oppose the truth, but must always stand for the truth. ⁹We are glad to seem weak if it helps show that you are actually strong. We pray that you will become mature.

¹⁰I am writing this to you before I come, hoping that I won't need to deal severely with you when I do come. For I want to use the

13:1 Deut 19:15.   **13:5** Or *in you.*

authority the Lord has given me to strengthen you, not to tear you down.

Paul's Final Greetings

[11]Dear brothers and sisters,* I close my letter with these last words: Be joyful. Grow to maturity. Encourage each other. Live in harmony and peace. Then the God of love and peace will be with you.

[12]Greet each other with a sacred kiss. [13]All of God's people here send you their greetings.

[14]*May the grace of the Lord Jesus Christ, the love of God, and the fellowship of the Holy Spirit be with you all.

13:11 Greek *Brothers.* **13:14** Some English translations include verse 13 as part of verse 12, and then verse 14 becomes verse 13.

Galatians

Greetings from Paul

1 This letter is from Paul, an apostle. I was not appointed by any group of people or any human authority, but by Jesus Christ himself and by God the Father, who raised Jesus from the dead.

²All the brothers and sisters* here join me in sending this letter to the churches of Galatia.

³May God the Father and our Lord Jesus Christ* give you grace and peace. ⁴Jesus gave his life for our sins, just as God our Father planned, in order to rescue us from this evil world in which we live. ⁵All glory to God forever and ever! Amen.

There Is Only One Good News

⁶I am shocked that you are turning away so soon from God, who called you to himself through the loving mercy of Christ.* You are following a different way that pretends to be the Good News ⁷but is not the Good News at all. You are being fooled by those who deliberately twist the truth concerning Christ.

⁸Let God's curse fall on anyone, including us or even an angel from heaven, who preaches a different kind of Good News than the one we preached to you. ⁹I say again what we have said before: If anyone preaches any other Good News than the one you welcomed, let that person be cursed.

¹⁰Obviously, I'm not trying to win the approval of people, but of God. If pleasing people were my goal, I would not be Christ's servant.

Paul's Message Comes from Christ

¹¹Dear brothers and sisters, I want you to understand that the gospel message I preach is not based on mere human reasoning. ¹²I received my message from no human source, and no one taught me. Instead, I received it by direct revelation from Jesus Christ.*

¹³You know what I was like when I followed the Jewish religion—how I violently persecuted God's church. I did my best to destroy it. ¹⁴I was far ahead of my fellow Jews in my zeal for the traditions of my ancestors.

¹⁵But even before I was born, God chose me and called me by his marvelous grace. Then it pleased him ¹⁶to reveal his Son to me* so that I

1:2 Greek *brothers*; also in 1:11. **1:3** Some manuscripts read *God our Father and the Lord Jesus Christ.* **1:6** Some manuscripts read *through loving mercy.* **1:12** Or *by the revelation of Jesus Christ.* **1:16a** Or *in me.*

would proclaim the Good News about Jesus to the Gentiles.

When this happened, I did not rush out to consult with any human being.* [17]Nor did I go up to Jerusalem to consult with those who were apostles before I was. Instead, I went away into Arabia, and later I returned to the city of Damascus.

[18]Then three years later I went to Jerusalem to get to know Peter,* and I stayed with him for fifteen days. [19]The only other apostle I met at that time was James, the Lord's brother. [20]I declare before God that what I am writing to you is not a lie.

[21]After that visit I went north into the provinces of Syria and Cilicia. [22]And still the churches in Christ that are in Judea didn't know me personally. [23]All they knew was that people were saying, "The one who used to persecute us is now preaching the very faith he tried to destroy!" [24]And they praised God because of me.

The Apostles Accept Paul

2 Then fourteen years later I went back to Jerusalem again, this time with Barnabas; and Titus came along, too. [2]I went there because God revealed to me that I should go. While I was there I met privately with those considered to be leaders of the church and shared with them the message I had been preaching to the Gentiles. I wanted to make sure that we were in agreement, for fear that all my efforts had been wasted and I was running the race for nothing. [3]And they supported me and did not even demand that my companion Titus be circumcised, though he was a Gentile.*

[4]Even that question came up only because of some so-called believers there—false ones, really*—who were secretly brought in. They sneaked in to spy on us and take away the freedom we have in Christ Jesus. They wanted to enslave us and force us to follow their Jewish regulations. [5]But we refused to give in to them for a single moment. We wanted to preserve the truth of the gospel message for you.

[6]And the leaders of the church had nothing to add to what I was preaching. (By the way, their reputation as great leaders made no difference to me, for God has no favorites.) [7]Instead, they saw that God had given me the responsibility of preaching the gospel to the Gentiles, just as he had given Peter the responsibility of preaching to the Jews. [8]For the same God who worked through Peter as the apostle to the Jews also worked through me as the apostle to the Gentiles.

[9]In fact, James, Peter,* and John, who were known as pillars of the church, recognized the gift God had given me, and they accepted Barnabas and me as their co-workers.

1:16b Greek *with flesh and blood.* 1:18 Greek *Cephas.* 2:3 Greek *a Greek.* 2:4 Greek *some false brothers.* 2:9 Greek *Cephas;* also in 2:11, 14.

They encouraged us to keep preaching to the Gentiles, while they continued their work with the Jews. [10]Their only suggestion was that we keep on helping the poor, which I have always been eager to do.

Paul Confronts Peter

[11]But when Peter came to Antioch, I had to oppose him to his face, for what he did was very wrong. [12]When he first arrived, he ate with the Gentile believers, who were not circumcised. But afterward, when some friends of James came, Peter wouldn't eat with the Gentiles anymore. He was afraid of criticism from these people who insisted on the necessity of circumcision. [13]As a result, other Jewish believers followed Peter's hypocrisy, and even Barnabas was led astray by their hypocrisy.

[14]When I saw that they were not following the truth of the gospel message, I said to Peter in front of all the others, "Since you, a Jew by birth, have discarded the Jewish laws and are living like a Gentile, why are you now trying to make these Gentiles follow the Jewish traditions?

[15]"You and I are Jews by birth, not 'sinners' like the Gentiles. [16]Yet we know that a person is made right with God by faith in Jesus Christ, not by obeying the law. And we have believed in Christ Jesus, so that we might be made right with God because of our faith in Christ, not because we have obeyed the law. For no one will ever be made right with God by obeying the law."*

[17]But suppose we seek to be made right with God through faith in Christ and then we are found guilty because we have abandoned the law. Would that mean Christ has led us into sin? Absolutely not! [18]Rather, I am a sinner if I rebuild the old system of law I already tore down. [19]For when I tried to keep the law, it condemned me. So I died to the law—I stopped trying to meet all its requirements—so that I might live for God. [20]My old self has been crucified with Christ.* It is no longer I who live, but Christ lives in me. So I live in this earthly body by trusting in the Son of God, who loved me and gave himself for me. [21]I do not treat the grace of God as meaningless. For if keeping the law could make us right with God, then there was no need for Christ to die.

The Law and Faith in Christ

3 Oh, foolish Galatians! Who has cast an evil spell on you? For the meaning of Jesus Christ's death was made as clear to you as if you had seen a picture of his death on the cross. [2]Let me ask you this one question: Did you receive the Holy Spirit by obeying the law of Moses? Of course not! You received the

---

2:16 Some translators hold that the quotation extends through verse 14; others through verse 16; and still others through verse 21.　**2:20** Some English translations put this sentence in verse 19.

Spirit because you believed the message you heard about Christ. ³How foolish can you be? After starting your new lives in the Spirit, why are you now trying to become perfect by your own human effort? ⁴Have you experienced* so much for nothing? Surely it was not in vain, was it?

⁵I ask you again, does God give you the Holy Spirit and work miracles among you because you obey the law? Of course not! It is because you believe the message you heard about Christ.

⁶In the same way, "Abraham believed God, and God counted him as righteous because of his faith."* ⁷The real children of Abraham, then, are those who put their faith in God.

⁸What's more, the Scriptures looked forward to this time when God would make the Gentiles right in his sight because of their faith. God proclaimed this good news to Abraham long ago when he said, "All nations will be blessed through you."* ⁹So all who put their faith in Christ share the same blessing Abraham received because of his faith.

¹⁰But those who depend on the law to make them right with God are under his curse, for the Scriptures say, "Cursed is everyone who does not observe and obey all the commands that are written in God's Book of the Law."* ¹¹So it is clear that no one can be made right with God by trying to keep the law. For the Scriptures say, "It is through faith that a righteous person has life."* ¹²This way of faith is very different from the way of law, which says, "It is through obeying the law that a person has life."*

¹³But Christ has rescued us from the curse pronounced by the law. When he was hung on the cross, he took upon himself the curse for our wrongdoing. For it is written in the Scriptures, "Cursed is everyone who is hung on a tree."* ¹⁴Through Christ Jesus, God has blessed the Gentiles with the same blessing he promised to Abraham, so that we who are believers might receive the promised* Holy Spirit through faith.

The Law and God's Promise

¹⁵Dear brothers and sisters,* here's an example from everyday life. Just as no one can set aside or amend an irrevocable agreement, so it is in this case. ¹⁶God gave the promises to Abraham and his child.* And notice that the Scripture doesn't say "to his children,*" as if it meant many descendants. Rather, it says "to his child"—and that, of course, means Christ. ¹⁷This is what I am trying to say: The agreement God made with Abraham could not be

3:4 Or *Have you suffered.* **3:6** Gen 15:6. **3:8** Gen 12:3; 18:18; 22:18. **3:10** Deut 27:26.
3:11 Hab 2:4. **3:12** Lev 18:5. **3:13** Deut 21:23 (Greek version). **3:14** Some manuscripts read *the blessing of the.* **3:15** Greek *Brothers.* **3:16a** Greek *seed;* also in 3:16c, 19. See notes on Gen 12:7 and 13:15. **3:16b** Greek *seeds.*

canceled 430 years later when God gave the law to Moses. God would be breaking his promise. ¹⁸For if the inheritance could be received by keeping the law, then it would not be the result of accepting God's promise. But God graciously gave it to Abraham as a promise.

¹⁹Why, then, was the law given? It was given alongside the promise to show people their sins. But the law was designed to last only until the coming of the child who was promised. God gave his law through angels to Moses, who was the mediator between God and the people. ²⁰Now a mediator is helpful if more than one party must reach an agreement. But God, who is one, did not use a mediator when he gave his promise to Abraham.

²¹Is there a conflict, then, between God's law and God's promises?* Absolutely not! If the law could give us new life, we could be made right with God by obeying it. ²²But the Scriptures declare that we are all prisoners of sin, so we receive God's promise of freedom only by believing in Jesus Christ.

God's Children through Faith

²³Before the way of faith in Christ was available to us, we were placed under guard by the law. We were kept in protective custody, so to speak, until the way of faith was revealed.

²⁴Let me put it another way. The law was our guardian until Christ came; it protected us until we could be made right with God through faith. ²⁵And now that the way of faith has come, we no longer need the law as our guardian.

²⁶For you are all children* of God through faith in Christ Jesus. ²⁷And all who have been united with Christ in baptism have put on Christ, like putting on new clothes.* ²⁸There is no longer Jew or Gentile,* slave or free, male and female. For you are all one in Christ Jesus. ²⁹And now that you belong to Christ, you are the true children* of Abraham. You are his heirs, and God's promise to Abraham belongs to you.

4 Think of it this way. If a father dies and leaves an inheritance for his young children, those children are not much better off than slaves until they grow up, even though they actually own everything their father had. ²They have to obey their guardians until they reach whatever age their father set. ³And that's the way it was with us before Christ came. We were like children; we were slaves to the basic spiritual principles* of this world.

⁴But when the right time came, God sent his Son, born of a woman, subject to the law. ⁵God sent him to buy freedom for us who were slaves to the law, so that he could adopt

3:21 Some manuscripts read *and the promises?* 3:26 Greek *sons.* 3:27 Greek *have put on Christ.* 3:28 Greek *Jew or Greek.* 3:29 Greek *seed.* 4:3 Or *powers;* also in 4:9.

us as his very own children.* [6]And because we* are his children, God has sent the Spirit of his Son into our hearts, prompting us to call out, "Abba, Father."* [7]Now you are no longer a slave but God's own child.* And since you are his child, God has made you his heir.

Paul's Concern for the Galatians

[8]Before you Gentiles knew God, you were slaves to so-called gods that do not even exist. [9]So now that you know God (or should I say, now that God knows you), why do you want to go back again and become slaves once more to the weak and useless spiritual principles of this world? [10]You are trying to earn favor with God by observing certain days or months or seasons or years. [11]I fear for you. Perhaps all my hard work with you was for nothing. [12]Dear brothers and sisters,* I plead with you to live as I do in freedom from these things, for I have become like you Gentiles—free from those laws.

You did not mistreat me when I first preached to you. [13]Surely you remember that I was sick when I first brought you the Good News. [14]But even though my condition tempted you to reject me, you did not despise me or turn me away. No, you took me in and cared for me as though I were an angel from God or even Christ Jesus himself. [15]Where is that joyful and grateful spirit you felt then? I am sure you would have taken out your own eyes and given them to me if it had been possible. [16]Have I now become your enemy because I am telling you the truth?

[17]Those false teachers are so eager to win your favor, but their intentions are not good. They are trying to shut you off from me so that you will pay attention only to them. [18]If someone is eager to do good things for you, that's all right; but let them do it all the time, not just when I'm with you.

[19]Oh, my dear children! I feel as if I'm going through labor pains for you again, and they will continue until Christ is fully developed in your lives. [20]I wish I were with you right now so I could change my tone. But at this distance I don't know how else to help you.

Abraham's Two Children

[21]Tell me, you who want to live under the law, do you know what the law actually says? [22]The Scriptures say that Abraham had two sons, one from his slave wife and one from his freeborn wife.* [23]The son of the slave wife was born in a human attempt to bring about the fulfillment of God's promise. But the son of the freeborn wife was born as God's own fulfillment of his promise.

[24]These two women serve as an illustration of God's two covenants.

4:5 Greek sons; also in 4:6.   4:6a Greek you.   4:6b Abba is an Aramaic term for "father."   4:7 Greek son; also in 4:7b.   4:12 Greek brothers; also in 4:28, 31.   4:22 See Gen 16:15; 21:2-3.

and then produce a great harvest of generosity* in you.

11Yes, you will be enriched in every way so that you can always be generous. And when we take your gifts to those who need them, they will thank God. 12So two good things will result from this ministry of giving—the needs of the believers in Jerusalem* will be met, and they will joyfully express their thanks to God.

13As a result of your ministry, they will give glory to God. For your generosity to them and to all believers will prove that you are obedient to the Good News of Christ. 14And they will pray for you with deep affection because of the overflowing grace God has given to you. 15Thank God for this gift* too wonderful for words!

Paul Defends His Authority

10 Now I, Paul, appeal to you with the gentleness and kindness of Christ—though I realize you think I am timid in person and bold only when I write from far away. 2Well, I am begging you now so that when I come I won't have to be bold with those who think we act from human motives.

3We are human, but we don't wage war as humans do. 4*We use God's mighty weapons, not worldly weapons, to knock down the strongholds of human reasoning and to destroy false arguments. 5We destroy every proud obstacle that keeps people from knowing God. We capture their rebellious thoughts and teach them to obey Christ. 6And after you have become fully obedient, we will punish everyone who remains disobedient.

7Look at the obvious facts.* Those who say they belong to Christ must recognize that we belong to Christ as much as they do. 8I may seem to be boasting too much about the authority given to us by the Lord. But our authority builds you up; it doesn't tear you down. So I will not be ashamed of using my authority.

9I'm not trying to frighten you by my letters. 10For some say, "Paul's letters are demanding and forceful, but in person he is weak, and his speeches are worthless!" 11Those people should realize that our actions when we arrive in person will be as forceful as what we say in our letters from far away.

12Oh, don't worry; we wouldn't dare say that we are as wonderful as these other men who tell you how important they are! But they are only comparing themselves with each other, using themselves as the standard of measurement. How ignorant!

13We will not boast about things done outside our area of authority.

9:10 Greek *righteousness*. **9:12** Greek *of God's holy people*. **9:15** Greek *his gift*. **10:4** English translations divide verses 4 and 5 in various ways. **10:7** Or *You look at things only on the basis of appearance*.

We will boast only about what has happened within the boundaries of the work God has given us, which includes our working with you. [14]We are not reaching beyond these boundaries when we claim authority over you, as if we had never visited you. For we were the first to travel all the way to Corinth with the Good News of Christ.

[15]Nor do we boast and claim credit for the work someone else has done. Instead, we hope that your faith will grow so that the boundaries of our work among you will be extended. [16]Then we will be able to go and preach the Good News in other places far beyond you, where no one else is working. Then there will be no question of our boasting about work done in someone else's territory. [17]As the Scriptures say, "If you want to boast, boast only about the LORD."*

[18]When people commend themselves, it doesn't count for much. The important thing is for the Lord to commend them.

Paul and the False Apostles

11 I hope you will put up with a little more of my foolishness. Please bear with me. [2]For I am jealous for you with the jealousy of God himself. I promised you as a pure bride* to one husband—Christ. [3]But I fear that somehow your pure and undivided devotion to Christ will be corrupted, just as Eve was deceived by the cunning ways of the serpent. [4]You happily put up with whatever anyone tells you, even if they preach a different Jesus than the one we preach, or a different kind of Spirit than the one you received, or a different kind of gospel than the one you believed.

[5]But I don't consider myself inferior in any way to these "super apostles" who teach such things. [6]I may be unskilled as a speaker, but I'm not lacking in knowledge. We have made this clear to you in every possible way.

[7]Was I wrong when I humbled myself and honored you by preaching God's Good News to you without expecting anything in return? [8]I "robbed" other churches by accepting their contributions so I could serve you at no cost. [9]And when I was with you and didn't have enough to live on, I did not become a financial burden to anyone. For the brothers who came from Macedonia brought me all that I needed. I have never been a burden to you, and I never will be. [10]As surely as the truth of Christ is in me, no one in all of Greece* will ever stop me from boasting about this. [11]Why? Because I don't love you? God knows that I do.

[12]But I will continue doing what I have always done. This will undercut those who are looking for an opportunity to boast that their

10:17 Jer 9:24. **11:2** Greek *a virgin.* **11:10** Greek *Achaia,* the southern region of the Greek peninsula.

one, you are only fooling yourself. You are not that important.

⁴Pay careful attention to your own work, for then you will get the satisfaction of a job well done, and you won't need to compare yourself to anyone else. ⁵For we are each responsible for our own conduct.

⁶Those who are taught the word of God should provide for their teachers, sharing all good things with them.

⁷Don't be misled—you cannot mock the justice of God. You will always harvest what you plant. ⁸Those who live only to satisfy their own sinful nature will harvest decay and death from that sinful nature. But those who live to please the Spirit will harvest everlasting life from the Spirit. ⁹So let's not get tired of doing what is good. At just the right time we will reap a harvest of blessing if we don't give up. ¹⁰Therefore, whenever we have the opportunity, we should do good to everyone—especially to those in the family of faith.

Paul's Final Advice

¹¹NOTICE WHAT LARGE LETTERS I USE AS I WRITE THESE CLOSING WORDS IN MY OWN HANDWRITING.

¹²Those who are trying to force you to be circumcised want to look good to others. They don't want to be persecuted for teaching that the cross of Christ alone can save. ¹³And even those who advocate circumcision don't keep the whole law themselves. They only want you to be circumcised so they can boast about it and claim you as their disciples.

¹⁴As for me, may I never boast about anything except the cross of our Lord Jesus Christ. Because of that cross,* my interest in this world has been crucified, and the world's interest in me has also died. ¹⁵It doesn't matter whether we have been circumcised or not. What counts is whether we have been transformed into a new creation. ¹⁶May God's peace and mercy be upon all who live by this principle; they are the new people of God.*

¹⁷From now on, don't let anyone trouble me with these things. For I bear on my body the scars that show I belong to Jesus.

¹⁸Dear brothers and sisters,* may the grace of our Lord Jesus Christ be with your spirit. Amen.

6:14 Or *Because of him.* 6:16 Greek *this principle, and upon the Israel of God.* 6:18 Greek *Brothers.*

Ephesians

Greetings from Paul

1 This letter is from Paul, chosen by the will of God to be an apostle of Christ Jesus.

I am writing to God's holy people in Ephesus,* who are faithful followers of Christ Jesus.

²May God our Father and the Lord Jesus Christ give you grace and peace.

Spiritual Blessings

³All praise to God, the Father of our Lord Jesus Christ, who has blessed us with every spiritual blessing in the heavenly realms because we are united with Christ. ⁴Even before he made the world, God loved us and chose us in Christ to be holy and without fault in his eyes. ⁵God decided in advance to adopt us into his own family by bringing us to himself through Jesus Christ. This is what he wanted to do, and it gave him great pleasure. ⁶So we praise God for the glorious grace he has poured out on us who belong to his dear Son.* ⁷He is so rich in kindness and grace that he purchased our freedom with the blood of his Son and forgave our sins. ⁸He has showered his kindness on us, along with all wisdom and understanding.

⁹God has now revealed to us his mysterious will regarding Christ—which is to fulfill his own good plan. ¹⁰And this is the plan: At the right time he will bring everything together under the authority of Christ—everything in heaven and on earth. ¹¹Furthermore, because we are united with Christ, we have received an inheritance from God,* for he chose us in advance, and he makes everything work out according to his plan.

¹²God's purpose was that we Jews who were the first to trust in Christ would bring praise and glory to God. ¹³And now you Gentiles have also heard the truth, the Good News that God saves you. And when you believed in Christ, he identified you as his own* by giving you the Holy Spirit, whom he promised long ago. ¹⁴The Spirit is God's guarantee that he will give us the inheritance he promised and that he has purchased us to be his own people. He did this so we would praise and glorify him.

Paul's Prayer for Spiritual Wisdom

¹⁵Ever since I first heard of your strong faith in the Lord Jesus and

---

1:1 The most ancient manuscripts do not include *in Ephesus*.   **1:6** Greek *to us in the beloved*.
1:11 Or *we have become God's inheritance*.   **1:13** Or *he put his seal on you*.

your love for God's people every-where,* ¹⁶I have not stopped thanking God for you. I pray for you constantly, ¹⁷asking God, the glorious Father of our Lord Jesus Christ, to give you spiritual wisdom* and insight so that you might grow in your knowledge of God. ¹⁸I pray that your hearts will be flooded with light so that you can understand the confident hope he has given to those he called—his holy people who are his rich and glorious inheritance.*

¹⁹I also pray that you will understand the incredible greatness of God's power for us who believe him. This is the same mighty power ²⁰that raised Christ from the dead and seated him in the place of honor at God's right hand in the heavenly realms. ²¹Now he is far above any ruler or authority or power or leader or anything else—not only in this world but also in the world to come. ²²God has put all things under the authority of Christ and has made him head over all things for the benefit of the church. ²³And the church is his body; it is made full and complete by Christ, who fills all things everywhere with himself.

Made Alive with Christ

2 Once you were dead because of your disobedience and your many sins. ²You used to live in sin, just like the rest of the world, obeying the devil—the commander of the powers in the unseen world.* He is the spirit at work in the hearts of those who refuse to obey God. ³All of us used to live that way, following the passionate desires and inclinations of our sinful nature. By our very nature we were subject to God's anger, just like everyone else.

⁴But God is so rich in mercy, and he loved us so much, ⁵that even though we were dead because of our sins, he gave us life when he raised Christ from the dead. (It is only by God's grace that you have been saved!) ⁶For he raised us from the dead along with Christ and seated us with him in the heavenly realms because we are united with Christ Jesus. ⁷So God can point to us in all future ages as examples of the incredible wealth of his grace and kindness toward us, as shown in all he has done for us who are united with Christ Jesus.

⁸God saved you by his grace when you believed. And you can't take credit for this; it is a gift from God. ⁹Salvation is not a reward for the good things we have done, so none of us can boast about it. ¹⁰For we are God's masterpiece. He has created us anew in Christ Jesus, so we can do the good things he planned for us long ago.

1:15 Some manuscripts read *your faithfulness to the Lord Jesus and to God's people everywhere.*
1:17 Or *to give you the Spirit of wisdom.* 1:18 Or *called, and the rich and glorious inheritance he has given to his holy people.* 2:2 Greek *obeying the commander of the power of the air.*

Oneness and Peace in Christ

[11]Don't forget that you Gentiles used to be outsiders. You were called "uncircumcised heathens" by the Jews, who were proud of their circumcision, even though it affected only their bodies and not their hearts. [12]In those days you were living apart from Christ. You were excluded from citizenship among the people of Israel, and you did not know the covenant promises God had made to them. You lived in this world without God and without hope. [13]But now you have been united with Christ Jesus. Once you were far away from God, but now you have been brought near to him through the blood of Christ.

[14]For Christ himself has brought peace to us. He united Jews and Gentiles into one people when, in his own body on the cross, he broke down the wall of hostility that separated us. [15]He did this by ending the system of law with its commandments and regulations. He made peace between Jews and Gentiles by creating in himself one new people from the two groups. [16]Together as one body, Christ reconciled both groups to God by means of his death on the cross, and our hostility toward each other was put to death.

[17]He brought this Good News of peace to you Gentiles who were far away from him, and peace to the Jews who were near. [18]Now all of us can come to the Father through the same Holy Spirit because of what Christ has done for us.

A Temple for the Lord

[19]So now you Gentiles are no longer strangers and foreigners. You are citizens along with all of God's holy people. You are members of God's family. [20]Together, we are his house, built on the foundation of the apostles and the prophets. And the cornerstone is Christ Jesus himself. [21]We are carefully joined together in him, becoming a holy temple for the Lord. [22]Through him you Gentiles are also being made part of this dwelling where God lives by his Spirit.

God's Mysterious Plan Revealed

3 When I think of all this, I, Paul, a prisoner of Christ Jesus for the benefit of you Gentiles* . . . [2]assuming, by the way, that you know God gave me the special responsibility of extending his grace to you Gentiles. [3]As I briefly wrote earlier, God himself revealed his mysterious plan to me. [4]As you read what I have written, you will understand my insight into this plan regarding Christ. [5]God did not reveal it to previous generations, but now by his Spirit he has revealed it to his holy apostles and prophets.

[6]And this is God's plan: Both Gentiles and Jews who believe the Good

3:1 Paul resumes this thought in verse 14: "When I think of all this, I fall to my knees and pray to the Father."

News share equally in the riches inherited by God's children. Both are part of the same body, and both enjoy the promise of blessings because they belong to Christ Jesus.* [7]By God's grace and mighty power, I have been given the privilege of serving him by spreading this Good News.

[8]Though I am the least deserving of all God's people, he graciously gave me the privilege of telling the Gentiles about the endless treasures available to them in Christ. [9]I was chosen to explain to everyone* this mysterious plan that God, the Creator of all things, had kept secret from the beginning.

[10]God's purpose in all this was to use the church to display his wisdom in its rich variety to all the unseen rulers and authorities in the heavenly places. [11]This was his eternal plan, which he carried out through Christ Jesus our Lord.

[12]Because of Christ and our faith in him,* we can now come boldly and confidently into God's presence. [13]So please don't lose heart because of my trials here. I am suffering for you, so you should feel honored.

Paul's Prayer for Spiritual Growth

[14]When I think of all this, I fall to my knees and pray to the Father,* [15]the Creator of everything in heaven and on earth.* [16]I pray that from his glorious, unlimited resources he will empower you with inner strength through his Spirit. [17]Then Christ will make his home in your hearts as you trust in him. Your roots will grow down into God's love and keep you strong. [18]And may you have the power to understand, as all God's people should, how wide, how long, how high, and how deep his love is. [19]May you experience the love of Christ, though it is too great to understand fully. Then you will be made complete with all the fullness of life and power that comes from God.

[20]Now all glory to God, who is able, through his mighty power at work within us, to accomplish infinitely more than we might ask or think. [21]Glory to him in the church and in Christ Jesus through all generations forever and ever! Amen.

Unity in the Body

4 Therefore I, a prisoner for serving the Lord, beg you to lead a life worthy of your calling, for you have been called by God. [2]Always be humble and gentle. Be patient with each other, making allowance for each other's faults because of your love. [3]Make every effort to keep yourselves united in the Spirit, binding yourselves together with peace. [4]For there is one body and one Spirit, just as you have been

3:6 Or *because they are united with Christ Jesus.* 3:9 Some manuscripts do not include *to everyone.*
3:12 Or *Because of Christ's faithfulness.* 3:14 Some manuscripts read *the Father of our Lord Jesus Christ.* 3:15 Or *from whom every family in heaven and on earth takes its name.*

called to one glorious hope for the future.

5 There is one Lord, one faith, one baptism,

6 one God and Father of all, who is over all, in all, and living through all.

7However, he has given each one of us a special gift* through the generosity of Christ. 8That is why the Scriptures say,

"When he ascended to the heights,
 he led a crowd of captives
 and gave gifts to his people."*

9Notice that it says "he ascended." This clearly means that Christ also descended to our lowly world.* 10And the same one who descended is the one who ascended higher than all the heavens, so that he might fill the entire universe with himself.

11Now these are the gifts Christ gave to the church: the apostles, the prophets, the evangelists, and the pastors and teachers. 12Their responsibility is to equip God's people to do his work and build up the church, the body of Christ. 13This will continue until we all come to such unity in our faith and knowledge of God's Son that we will be mature in the Lord, measuring up to the full and complete standard of Christ.

14Then we will no longer be immature like children. We won't be tossed and blown about by every wind of new teaching. We will not be influenced when people try to trick us with lies so clever they sound like the truth. 15Instead, we will speak the truth in love, growing in every way more and more like Christ, who is the head of his body, the church. 16He makes the whole body fit together perfectly. As each part does its own special work, it helps the other parts grow, so that the whole body is healthy and growing and full of love.

Living as Children of Light

17With the Lord's authority I say this: Live no longer as the Gentiles do, for they are hopelessly confused. 18Their minds are full of darkness; they wander far from the life God gives because they have closed their minds and hardened their hearts against him. 19They have no sense of shame. They live for lustful pleasure and eagerly practice every kind of impurity.

20But that isn't what you learned about Christ. 21Since you have heard about Jesus and have learned the truth that comes from him, 22throw off your old sinful nature and your former way of life, which is corrupted by lust and deception. 23Instead, let the Spirit renew your thoughts and attitudes. 24Put on your new nature, created to be like God—truly righteous and holy.

25So stop telling lies. Let us tell our neighbors the truth, for we are all parts of the same body. 26And "don't

4:7 Greek *a grace.* 4:8 Ps 68:18. 4:9 Some manuscripts read *to the lower parts of the earth.* 4:26 Ps 4:4.

sin by letting anger control you."* Don't let the sun go down while you are still angry, ²⁷for anger gives a foothold to the devil.

²⁸If you are a thief, quit stealing. Instead, use your hands for good hard work, and then give generously to others in need. ²⁹Don't use foul or abusive language. Let everything you say be good and helpful, so that your words will be an encouragement to those who hear them.

³⁰And do not bring sorrow to God's Holy Spirit by the way you live. Remember, he has identified you as his own,* guaranteeing that you will be saved on the day of redemption.

³¹Get rid of all bitterness, rage, anger, harsh words, and slander, as well as all types of evil behavior. ³²Instead, be kind to each other, tenderhearted, forgiving one another, just as God through Christ has forgiven you.

Living in the Light

5 Imitate God, therefore, in everything you do, because you are his dear children. ²Live a life filled with love, following the example of Christ. He loved us* and offered himself as a sacrifice for us, a pleasing aroma to God.

³Let there be no sexual immorality, impurity, or greed among you. Such sins have no place among God's people. ⁴Obscene stories, foolish talk, and coarse jokes— these are not for you. Instead, let there be thankfulness to God. ⁵You can be sure that no immoral, impure, or greedy person will inherit the Kingdom of Christ and of God. For a greedy person is an idolater, worshiping the things of this world.

⁶Don't be fooled by those who try to excuse these sins, for the anger of God will fall on all who disobey him. ⁷Don't participate in the things these people do. ⁸For once you were full of darkness, but now you have light from the Lord. So live as people of light! ⁹For this light within you produces only what is good and right and true.

¹⁰Carefully determine what pleases the Lord. ¹¹Take no part in the worthless deeds of evil and darkness; instead, expose them. ¹²It is shameful even to talk about the things that ungodly people do in secret. ¹³But their evil intentions will be exposed when the light shines on them, ¹⁴for the light makes everything visible. This is why it is said,

> "Awake, O sleeper,
> rise up from the dead,
> and Christ will give you light."

Living by the Spirit's Power

¹⁵So be careful how you live. Don't live like fools, but like those who are wise. ¹⁶Make the most of every opportunity in these evil days. ¹⁷Don't act thoughtlessly, but understand what the Lord wants you to do. ¹⁸Don't be drunk with wine, because

4:30 Or *has put his seal on you.* 5:2 Some manuscripts read *loved you.*

that will ruin your life. Instead, be filled with the Holy Spirit, [19]singing psalms and hymns and spiritual songs among yourselves, and making music to the Lord in your hearts. [20]And give thanks for everything to God the Father in the name of our Lord Jesus Christ.

Spirit-Guided Relationships: Wives and Husbands

[21]And further, submit to one another out of reverence for Christ.

[22]For wives, this means submit to your husbands as to the Lord. [23]For a husband is the head of his wife as Christ is the head of the church. He is the Savior of his body, the church. [24]As the church submits to Christ, so you wives should submit to your husbands in everything.

[25]For husbands, this means love your wives, just as Christ loved the church. He gave up his life for her [26]to make her holy and clean, washed by the cleansing of God's word.* [27]He did this to present her to himself as a glorious church without a spot or wrinkle or any other blemish. Instead, she will be holy and without fault. [28]In the same way, husbands ought to love their wives as they love their own bodies. For a man who loves his wife actually shows love for himself. [29]No one hates his own body but feeds and cares for it, just as Christ cares for the church. [30]And we are members of his body.

[31]As the Scriptures say, "A man leaves his father and mother and is joined to his wife, and the two are united into one."* [32]This is a great mystery, but it is an illustration of the way Christ and the church are one. [33]So again I say, each man must love his wife as he loves himself, and the wife must respect her husband.

Children and Parents

6 Children, obey your parents because you belong to the Lord,* for this is the right thing to do. [2]"Honor your father and mother." This is the first commandment with a promise: [3]If you honor your father and mother, "things will go well for you, and you will have a long life on the earth."*

[4]Fathers,* do not provoke your children to anger by the way you treat them. Rather, bring them up with the discipline and instruction that comes from the Lord.

Slaves and Masters

[5]Slaves, obey your earthly masters with deep respect and fear. Serve them sincerely as you would serve Christ. [6]Try to please them all the time, not just when they are watching you. As slaves of Christ, do the will of God with all your heart. [7]Work with enthusiasm, as though

5:26 Greek *washed by water with the word.* 5:31 Gen 2:24. 6:1 Or *Children, obey your parents who belong to the Lord;* some manuscripts read simply *Children, obey your parents.* 6:2-3 Exod 20:12; Deut 5:16. 6:4 Or *Parents.*

you were working for the Lord rather than for people. [8]Remember that the Lord will reward each one of us for the good we do, whether we are slaves or free.

[9]Masters, treat your slaves in the same way. Don't threaten them; remember, you both have the same Master in heaven, and he has no favorites.

The Whole Armor of God

[10]A final word: Be strong in the Lord and in his mighty power. [11]Put on all of God's armor so that you will be able to stand firm against all strategies of the devil. [12]For we* are not fighting against flesh-and-blood enemies, but against evil rulers and authorities of the unseen world, against mighty powers in this dark world, and against evil spirits in the heavenly places.

[13]Therefore, put on every piece of God's armor so you will be able to resist the enemy in the time of evil. Then after the battle you will still be standing firm. [14]Stand your ground, putting on the belt of truth and the body armor of God's righteousness. [15]For shoes, put on the peace that comes from the Good News so that you will be fully prepared.* [16]In addition to all of these, hold up the shield of faith to stop the fiery arrows of the devil.* [17]Put on salvation as your helmet, and take the sword of the Spirit, which is the word of God.

[18]Pray in the Spirit at all times and on every occasion. Stay alert and be persistent in your prayers for all believers everywhere.*

[19]And pray for me, too. Ask God to give me the right words so I can boldly explain God's mysterious plan that the Good News is for Jews and Gentiles alike.* [20]I am in chains now, still preaching this message as God's ambassador. So pray that I will keep on speaking boldly for him, as I should.

Final Greetings

[21]To bring you up to date, Tychicus will give you a full report about what I am doing and how I am getting along. He is a beloved brother and faithful helper in the Lord's work. [22]I have sent him to you for this very purpose—to let you know how we are doing and to encourage you.

[23]Peace be with you, dear brothers and sisters,* and may God the Father and the Lord Jesus Christ give you love with faithfulness. [24]May God's grace be eternally upon all who love our Lord Jesus Christ.

6:12 Some manuscripts read *you.*   6:15 Or *For shoes, put on the readiness to preach the Good News of peace with God.*   6:16 Greek *the evil one.*   6:18 Greek *all of God's holy people.*   6:19 Greek *explain the mystery of the Good News;* some manuscripts read simply *explain the mystery.* 6:23 Greek *brothers.*

Philippians

Greetings from Paul

1 This letter is from Paul and Timothy, slaves of Christ Jesus.

I am writing to all of God's holy people in Philippi who belong to Christ Jesus, including the church leaders* and deacons.

²May God our Father and the Lord Jesus Christ give you grace and peace.

Paul's Thanksgiving and Prayer

³Every time I think of you, I give thanks to my God. ⁴Whenever I pray, I make my requests for all of you with joy, ⁵for you have been my partners in spreading the Good News about Christ from the time you first heard it until now. ⁶And I am certain that God, who began the good work within you, will continue his work until it is finally finished on the day when Christ Jesus returns.

⁷So it is right that I should feel as I do about all of you, for you have a special place in my heart. You share with me the special favor of God, both in my imprisonment and in defending and confirming the truth of the Good News. ⁸God knows how much I love you and long for you with the tender compassion of Christ Jesus.

⁹I pray that your love will overflow more and more, and that you will keep on growing in knowledge and understanding. ¹⁰For I want you to understand what really matters, so that you may live pure and blameless lives until the day of Christ's return. ¹¹May you always be filled with the fruit of your salvation—the righteous character produced in your life by Jesus Christ*—for this will bring much glory and praise to God.

Paul's Joy That Christ Is Preached

¹²And I want you to know, my dear brothers and sisters,* that everything that has happened to me here has helped to spread the Good News. ¹³For everyone here, including the whole palace guard,* knows that I am in chains because of Christ. ¹⁴And because of my imprisonment, most of the believers* here have gained confidence and boldly speak God's message* without fear.

¹⁵It's true that some are preaching out of jealousy and rivalry. But others preach about Christ with

---

1:1 Or *overseers,* or *bishops.* **1:11** Greek *with the fruit of righteousness through Jesus Christ.*
1:12 Greek *brothers.* **1:13** Greek *including all the Praetorium.* **1:14a** Greek *brothers in the Lord.*
1:14b Some manuscripts read *speak the message.*

pure motives. [16]They preach because they love me, for they know I have been appointed to defend the Good News. [17]Those others do not have pure motives as they preach about Christ. They preach with selfish ambition, not sincerely, intending to make my chains more painful to me. [18]But that doesn't matter. Whether their motives are false or genuine, the message about Christ is being preached either way, so I rejoice. And I will continue to rejoice. [19]For I know that as you pray for me and the Spirit of Jesus Christ helps me, this will lead to my deliverance.

Paul's Life for Christ

[20]For I fully expect and hope that I will never be ashamed, but that I will continue to be bold for Christ, as I have been in the past. And I trust that my life will bring honor to Christ, whether I live or die. [21]For to me, living means living for Christ, and dying is even better. [22]But if I live, I can do more fruitful work for Christ. So I really don't know which is better. [23]I'm torn between two desires: I long to go and be with Christ, which would be far better for me. [24]But for your sakes, it is better that I continue to live.

[25]Knowing this, I am convinced that I will remain alive so I can continue to help all of you grow and experience the joy of your faith. [26]And when I come to you again, you will have even more reason to take pride in Christ Jesus because of what he is doing through me.

Live as Citizens of Heaven

[27]Above all, you must live as citizens of heaven, conducting yourselves in a manner worthy of the Good News about Christ. Then, whether I come and see you again or only hear about you, I will know that you are standing together with one spirit and one purpose, fighting together for the faith, which is the Good News. [28]Don't be intimidated in any way by your enemies. This will be a sign to them that they are going to be destroyed, but that you are going to be saved, even by God himself. [29]For you have been given not only the privilege of trusting in Christ but also the privilege of suffering for him. [30]We are in this struggle together. You have seen my struggle in the past, and you know that I am still in the midst of it.

Have the Attitude of Christ

2 Is there any encouragement from belonging to Christ? Any comfort from his love? Any fellowship together in the Spirit? Are your hearts tender and compassionate? [2]Then make me truly happy by agreeing wholeheartedly with each other, loving one another, and working together with one mind and purpose.

[3]Don't be selfish; don't try to impress others. Be humble, thinking of others as better than yourselves.

⁴Don't look out only for your own interests, but take an interest in others, too.

⁵You must have the same attitude that Christ Jesus had.

⁶ Though he was God,*
he did not think of equality with God
as something to cling to.
⁷ Instead, he gave up his divine privileges*;
he took the humble position of a slave*
and was born as a human being.
When he appeared in human form,*
⁸ he humbled himself in obedience to God
and died a criminal's death on a cross.

⁹ Therefore, God elevated him to the place of highest honor
and gave him the name above all other names,
¹⁰ that at the name of Jesus every knee should bow,
in heaven and on earth and under the earth,
¹¹ and every tongue declare that Jesus Christ is Lord,
to the glory of God the Father.

Shine Brightly for Christ

¹²Dear friends, you always followed my instructions when I was with you. And now that I am away, it is even more important. Work hard to show the results of your salvation, obeying God with deep reverence and fear. ¹³For God is working in you, giving you the desire and the power to do what pleases him.

¹⁴Do everything without complaining and arguing, ¹⁵so that no one can criticize you. Live clean, innocent lives as children of God, shining like bright lights in a world full of crooked and perverse people. ¹⁶Hold firmly to the word of life; then, on the day of Christ's return, I will be proud that I did not run the race in vain and that my work was not useless. ¹⁷But I will rejoice even if I lose my life, pouring it out like a liquid offering to God,* just like your faithful service is an offering to God. And I want all of you to share that joy. ¹⁸Yes, you should rejoice, and I will share your joy.

Paul Commends Timothy

¹⁹If the Lord Jesus is willing, I hope to send Timothy to you soon for a visit. Then he can cheer me up by telling me how you are getting along. ²⁰I have no one else like Timothy, who genuinely cares about your welfare. ²¹All the others care only for themselves and not for what matters to Jesus Christ. ²²But you know how Timothy has proved himself. Like a son with his father, he has served with me in preaching

---

2:6 Or *Being in the form of God.*   2:7a Greek *he emptied himself.*   2:7b Or *the form of a slave.*
2:7c Some English translations put this phrase in verse 8.   2:17 Greek *I will rejoice even if I am to be poured out as a liquid offering.*

the Good News. ²³I hope to send him to you just as soon as I find out what is going to happen to me here. ²⁴And I have confidence from the Lord that I myself will come to see you soon.

Paul Commends Epaphroditus

²⁵Meanwhile, I thought I should send Epaphroditus back to you. He is a true brother, co-worker, and fellow soldier. And he was your messenger to help me in my need. ²⁶I am sending him because he has been longing to see you, and he was very distressed that you heard he was ill. ²⁷And he certainly was ill; in fact, he almost died. But God had mercy on him—and also on me, so that I would not have one sorrow after another.

²⁸So I am all the more anxious to send him back to you, for I know you will be glad to see him, and then I will not be so worried about you. ²⁹Welcome him in the Lord's love* and with great joy, and give him the honor that people like him deserve. ³⁰For he risked his life for the work of Christ, and he was at the point of death while doing for me what you couldn't do from far away.

The Priceless Value of Knowing Christ

3 Whatever happens, my dear brothers and sisters,* rejoice in the Lord. I never get tired of telling you these things, and I do it to safeguard your faith.

²Watch out for those dogs, those people who do evil, those mutilators who say you must be circumcised to be saved. ³For we who worship by the Spirit of God* are the ones who are truly circumcised. We rely on what Christ Jesus has done for us. We put no confidence in human effort, ⁴though I could have confidence in my own effort if anyone could. Indeed, if others have reason for confidence in their own efforts, I have even more!

⁵I was circumcised when I was eight days old. I am a pure-blooded citizen of Israel and a member of the tribe of Benjamin—a real Hebrew if there ever was one! I was a member of the Pharisees, who demand the strictest obedience to the Jewish law. ⁶I was so zealous that I harshly persecuted the church. And as for righteousness, I obeyed the law without fault.

⁷I once thought these things were valuable, but now I consider them worthless because of what Christ has done. ⁸Yes, everything else is worthless when compared with the infinite value of knowing Christ Jesus my Lord. For his sake I have discarded everything else, counting it all as garbage, so that I could gain Christ ⁹and become one with him. I no longer count on my own righteousness through obeying the law;

2:29 Greek *in the Lord.* 3:1 Greek *brothers;* also in 3:13, 17. 3:3 Some manuscripts read *worship God in spirit;* one early manuscript reads *worship in spirit.*

rather, I become righteous through faith in Christ.* For God's way of making us right with himself depends on faith. ¹⁰I want to know Christ and experience the mighty power that raised him from the dead. I want to suffer with him, sharing in his death, ¹¹so that one way or another I will experience the resurrection from the dead!

Pressing toward the Goal

¹²I don't mean to say that I have already achieved these things or that I have already reached perfection. But I press on to possess that perfection for which Christ Jesus first possessed me. ¹³No, dear brothers and sisters, I have not achieved it,* but I focus on this one thing: Forgetting the past and looking forward to what lies ahead, ¹⁴I press on to reach the end of the race and receive the heavenly prize for which God, through Christ Jesus, is calling us.

¹⁵Let all who are spiritually mature agree on these things. If you disagree on some point, I believe God will make it plain to you. ¹⁶But we must hold on to the progress we have already made.

¹⁷Dear brothers and sisters, pattern your lives after mine, and learn from those who follow our example. ¹⁸For I have told you often before, and I say it again with tears in my eyes, that there are many whose conduct shows they are really enemies of the cross of Christ. ¹⁹They are headed for destruction. Their god is their appetite, they brag about shameful things, and they think only about this life here on earth. ²⁰But we are citizens of heaven, where the Lord Jesus Christ lives. And we are eagerly waiting for him to return as our Savior. ²¹He will take our weak mortal bodies and change them into glorious bodies like his own, using the same power with which he will bring everything under his control.

4 Therefore, my dear brothers and sisters,* stay true to the Lord. I love you and long to see you, dear friends, for you are my joy and the crown I receive for my work.

Words of Encouragement

²Now I appeal to Euodia and Syntyche. Please, because you belong to the Lord, settle your disagreement. ³And I ask you, my true partner,* to help these two women, for they worked hard with me in telling others the Good News. They worked along with Clement and the rest of my co-workers, whose names are written in the Book of Life.

⁴Always be full of joy in the Lord. I say it again—rejoice! ⁵Let everyone see that you are considerate in all you do. Remember, the Lord is coming soon.*

3:9 Or *through the faithfulness of Christ.* 3:13 Some manuscripts read *not yet achieved it.*
4:1 Greek *brothers;* also in 4:8. 4:3 Or *loyal Syzygus.* 4:5 Greek *the Lord is near.*

⁶Don't worry about anything; instead, pray about everything. Tell God what you need, and thank him for all he has done. ⁷Then you will experience God's peace, which exceeds anything we can understand. His peace will guard your hearts and minds as you live in Christ Jesus.

⁸And now, dear brothers and sisters, one final thing. Fix your thoughts on what is true, and honorable, and right, and pure, and lovely, and admirable. Think about things that are excellent and worthy of praise. ⁹Keep putting into practice all you learned and received from me—everything you heard from me and saw me doing. Then the God of peace will be with you.

Paul's Thanks for Their Gifts

¹⁰How I praise the Lord that you are concerned about me again. I know you have always been concerned for me, but you didn't have the chance to help me. ¹¹Not that I was ever in need, for I have learned how to be content with whatever I have. ¹²I know how to live on almost nothing or with everything. I have learned the secret of living in every situation, whether it is with a full stomach or empty, with plenty or little. ¹³For I can do everything through Christ,* who gives me strength. ¹⁴Even so, you have done well to share with me in my present difficulty.

¹⁵As you know, you Philippians were the only ones who gave me financial help when I first brought you the Good News and then traveled on from Macedonia. No other church did this. ¹⁶Even when I was in Thessalonica you sent help more than once. ¹⁷I don't say this because I want a gift from you. Rather, I want you to receive a reward for your kindness.

¹⁸At the moment I have all I need—and more! I am generously supplied with the gifts you sent me with Epaphroditus. They are a sweet-smelling sacrifice that is acceptable and pleasing to God. ¹⁹And this same God who takes care of me will supply all your needs from his glorious riches, which have been given to us in Christ Jesus.

²⁰Now all glory to God our Father forever and ever! Amen.

Paul's Final Greetings

²¹Give my greetings to each of God's holy people—all who belong to Christ Jesus. The brothers who are with me send you their greetings. ²²And all the rest of God's people send you greetings, too, especially those in Caesar's household.

²³May the grace of the Lord Jesus Christ be with your spirit.*

4:13 Greek *through the one.*   4:23 Some manuscripts add *Amen.*

Colossians

Greetings from Paul

1 This letter is from Paul, chosen by the will of God to be an apostle of Christ Jesus, and from our brother Timothy.

²We are writing to God's holy people in the city of Colosse, who are faithful brothers and sisters* in Christ.

May God our Father give you grace and peace.

Paul's Thanksgiving and Prayer

³We always pray for you, and we give thanks to God, the Father of our Lord Jesus Christ. ⁴For we have heard of your faith in Christ Jesus and your love for all of God's people, ⁵which come from your confident hope of what God has reserved for you in heaven. You have had this expectation ever since you first heard the truth of the Good News.

⁶This same Good News that came to you is going out all over the world. It is bearing fruit everywhere by changing lives, just as it changed your lives from the day you first heard and understood the truth about God's wonderful grace.

⁷You learned about the Good News from Epaphras, our beloved co-worker. He is Christ's faithful servant, and he is helping us on your behalf.* ⁸He has told us about the love for others that the Holy Spirit has given you.

⁹So we have not stopped praying for you since we first heard about you. We ask God to give you complete knowledge of his will and to give you spiritual wisdom and understanding. ¹⁰Then the way you live will always honor and please the Lord, and your lives will produce every kind of good fruit. All the while, you will grow as you learn to know God better and better.

¹¹We also pray that you will be strengthened with all his glorious power so you will have all the endurance and patience you need. May you be filled with joy,* ¹²always thanking the Father. He has enabled you to share in the inheritance that belongs to his people, who live in the light. ¹³For he has rescued us from the kingdom of darkness and transferred us into the Kingdom of his dear Son, ¹⁴who purchased our freedom* and forgave our sins.

1:2 Greek *faithful brothers.* **1:7** Or *he is ministering on your behalf;* some manuscripts read *he is ministering on our behalf.* **1:11** Or *all the patience and endurance you need with joy.* **1:14** Some manuscripts add *with his blood.*

Christ Is Supreme

15 Christ is the visible image of the
  invisible God.
  He existed before anything
    was created and is supreme
    over all creation,*
16 for through him God created
    everything
  in the heavenly realms and
    on earth.
  He made the things we can see
    and the things we can't see—
  such as thrones, kingdoms,
    rulers, and authorities in the
    unseen world.
  Everything was created
    through him and for him.
17 He existed before anything else,
    and he holds all creation
    together.
18 Christ is also the head of the
    church,
  which is his body.
  He is the beginning,
    supreme over all who rise
    from the dead.*
  So he is first in everything.
19 For God in all his fullness
    was pleased to live in Christ,
20 and through him God reconciled
    everything to himself.
  He made peace with everything
    in heaven and on earth
  by means of Christ's blood on
    the cross.

21 This includes you who were
once far away from God. You were
his enemies, separated from him by
your evil thoughts and actions. 22 Yet
now he has reconciled you to himself through the death of Christ in
his physical body. As a result, he has
brought you into his own presence,
and you are holy and blameless as
you stand before him without a
single fault.

23 But you must continue to believe this truth and stand firmly in
it. Don't drift away from the assurance you received when you heard
the Good News. The Good News has
been preached all over the world,
and I, Paul, have been appointed as
God's servant to proclaim it.

Paul's Work for the Church

24 I am glad when I suffer for you in
my body, for I am participating in
the sufferings of Christ that continue for his body, the church. 25 God
has given me the responsibility of
serving his church by proclaiming
his entire message to you. 26 This
message was kept secret for centu-
ries and generations past, but now it
has been revealed to God's people.
27 For God wanted them to know that
the riches and glory of Christ are for
you Gentiles, too. And this is the secret: Christ lives in you. This gives
you assurance of sharing his glory.

28 So we tell others about Christ,
warning everyone and teaching
everyone with all the wisdom
God has given us. We want to present them to God, perfect* in their
relationship to Christ. 29 That's why

1:15 Or *He is the firstborn of all creation.* 1:18 Or *the firstborn from the dead.* 1:28 Or *mature.*

I work and struggle so hard, depending on Christ's mighty power that works within me.

2 I want you to know how much I have agonized for you and for the church at Laodicea, and for many other believers who have never met me personally. ²I want them to be encouraged and knit together by strong ties of love. I want them to have complete confidence that they understand God's mysterious plan, which is Christ himself. ³In him lie hidden all the treasures of wisdom and knowledge.

⁴I am telling you this so no one will deceive you with well-crafted arguments. ⁵For though I am far away from you, my heart is with you. And I rejoice that you are living as you should and that your faith in Christ is strong.

Freedom from Rules and New Life in Christ

⁶And now, just as you accepted Christ Jesus as your Lord, you must continue to follow him. ⁷Let your roots grow down into him, and let your lives be built on him. Then your faith will grow strong in the truth you were taught, and you will overflow with thankfulness.

⁸Don't let anyone capture you with empty philosophies and high-sounding nonsense that come from human thinking and from the spiritual powers* of this world, rather than from Christ. ⁹For in Christ lives all the fullness of God in a human body.* ¹⁰So you also are complete through your union with Christ, who is the head over every ruler and authority.

¹¹When you came to Christ, you were "circumcised," but not by a physical procedure. Christ performed a spiritual circumcision—the cutting away of your sinful nature.* ¹²For you were buried with Christ when you were baptized. And with him you were raised to new life because you trusted the mighty power of God, who raised Christ from the dead.

¹³You were dead because of your sins and because your sinful nature was not yet cut away. Then God made you alive with Christ, for he forgave all our sins. ¹⁴He canceled the record of the charges against us and took it away by nailing it to the cross. ¹⁵In this way, he disarmed* the spiritual rulers and authorities. He shamed them publicly by his victory over them on the cross.

¹⁶So don't let anyone condemn you for what you eat or drink, or for not celebrating certain holy days or new moon ceremonies or Sabbaths. ¹⁷For these rules are only shadows of the reality yet to come. And Christ himself is that reality. ¹⁸Don't let anyone condemn you by insisting on pious self-denial or the wor-

2:8 Or *the spiritual principles;* also in 2:20. **2:9** Or *in him dwells all the completeness of the Godhead bodily.* **2:11** Greek *the cutting away of the body of the flesh.* **2:15** Or *he stripped off.*

ship of angels,* saying they have had visions about these things. Their sinful minds have made them proud, [19]and they are not connected to Christ, the head of the body. For he holds the whole body together with its joints and ligaments, and it grows as God nourishes it.

[20]You have died with Christ, and he has set you free from the spiritual powers of this world. So why do you keep on following the rules of the world, such as, [21]"Don't handle! Don't taste! Don't touch!"? [22]Such rules are mere human teachings about things that deteriorate as we use them. [23]These rules may seem wise because they require strong devotion, pious self-denial, and severe bodily discipline. But they provide no help in conquering a person's evil desires.

Living the New Life

3 Since you have been raised to new life with Christ, set your sights on the realities of heaven, where Christ sits in the place of honor at God's right hand. [2]Think about the things of heaven, not the things of earth. [3]For you died to this life, and your real life is hidden with Christ in God. [4]And when Christ, who is your* life, is revealed to the whole world, you will share in all his glory.

[5]So put to death the sinful, earthly things lurking within you. Have nothing to do with sexual immorality, impurity, lust, and evil desires. Don't be greedy, for a greedy person is an idolater, worshiping the things of this world. [6]Because of these sins, the anger of God is coming.* [7]You used to do these things when your life was still part of this world. [8]But now is the time to get rid of anger, rage, malicious behavior, slander, and dirty language. [9]Don't lie to each other, for you have stripped off your old sinful nature and all its wicked deeds. [10]Put on your new nature, and be renewed as you learn to know your Creator and become like him. [11]In this new life, it doesn't matter if you are a Jew or a Gentile,* circumcised or uncircumcised, barbaric, uncivilized,* slave, or free. Christ is all that matters, and he lives in all of us.

[12]Since God chose you to be the holy people he loves, you must clothe yourselves with tenderhearted mercy, kindness, humility, gentleness, and patience. [13]Make allowance for each other's faults, and forgive anyone who offends you. Remember, the Lord forgave you, so you must forgive others. [14]Above all, clothe yourselves with love, which binds us all together in perfect harmony. [15]And let the peace that comes from Christ rule in your hearts. For as members of one body you are called to live in peace. And always be thankful.

2:18 Or *or worshiping with angels.* **3:4** Some manuscripts read *our.* **3:6** Some manuscripts read *is coming on all who disobey him.* **3:11a** Greek *a Greek.* **3:11b** Greek *Barbarian, Scythian.*

¹⁶Let the message about Christ, in all its richness, fill your lives. Teach and counsel each other with all the wisdom he gives. Sing psalms and hymns and spiritual songs to God with thankful hearts. ¹⁷And whatever you do or say, do it as a representative of the Lord Jesus, giving thanks through him to God the Father.

Instructions for Christian Households

¹⁸Wives, submit to your husbands, as is fitting for those who belong to the Lord.

¹⁹Husbands, love your wives and never treat them harshly.

²⁰Children, always obey your parents, for this pleases the Lord. ²¹Fathers, do not aggravate your children, or they will become discouraged.

²²Slaves, obey your earthly masters in everything you do. Try to please them all the time, not just when they are watching you. Serve them sincerely because of your reverent fear of the Lord. ²³Work willingly at whatever you do, as though you were working for the Lord rather than for people. ²⁴Remember that the Lord will give you an inheritance as your reward, and that the Master you are serving is Christ.* ²⁵But if you do what is wrong, you will be paid back for the wrong you have done. For God has no favorites.

4 Masters, be just and fair to your slaves. Remember that you also have a Master—in heaven.

An Encouragement for Prayer

²Devote yourselves to prayer with an alert mind and a thankful heart. ³Pray for us, too, that God will give us many opportunities to speak about his mysterious plan concerning Christ. That is why I am here in chains. ⁴Pray that I will proclaim this message as clearly as I should.

⁵Live wisely among those who are not believers, and make the most of every opportunity. ⁶Let your conversation be gracious and attractive* so that you will have the right response for everyone.

Paul's Final Instructions and Greetings

⁷Tychicus will give you a full report about how I am getting along. He is a beloved brother and faithful helper who serves with me in the Lord's work. ⁸I have sent him to you for this very purpose—to let you know how we are doing and to encourage you. ⁹I am also sending Onesimus, a faithful and beloved brother, one of your own people. He and Tychicus will tell you everything that's happening here.

¹⁰Aristarchus, who is in prison with me, sends you his greetings, and so does Mark, Barnabas's cousin. As you were instructed be-

3:24 Or *and serve Christ as your Master.* 4:6 Greek *and seasoned with salt.*

fore, make Mark welcome if he comes your way. [11]Jesus (the one we call Justus) also sends his greetings. These are the only Jewish believers among my co-workers; they are working with me here for the Kingdom of God. And what a comfort they have been!

[12]Epaphras, a member of your own fellowship and a servant of Christ Jesus, sends you his greetings. He always prays earnestly for you, asking God to make you strong and perfect, fully confident that you are following the whole will of God. [13]I can assure you that he prays hard for you and also for the believers in Laodicea and Hierapolis.

[14]Luke, the beloved doctor, sends his greetings, and so does Demas. [15]Please give my greetings to our brothers and sisters* at Laodicea, and to Nympha and the church that meets in her house.

[16]After you have read this letter, pass it on to the church at Laodicea so they can read it, too. And you should read the letter I wrote to them.

[17]And say to Archippus, "Be sure to carry out the ministry the Lord gave you."

[18]HERE IS MY GREETING IN MY OWN HANDWRITING—PAUL.

Remember my chains.
May God's grace be with you.

4:15 Greek brothers.

1 Thessalonians

Greetings from Paul

1 This letter is from Paul, Silas,* and Timothy.

We are writing to the church in Thessalonica, to you who belong to God the Father and the Lord Jesus Christ.

May God give you grace and peace.

The Faith of the Thessalonian Believers

²We always thank God for all of you and pray for you constantly. ³As we pray to our God and Father about you, we think of your faithful work, your loving deeds, and the enduring hope you have because of our Lord Jesus Christ.

⁴We know, dear brothers and sisters,* that God loves you and has chosen you to be his own people. ⁵For when we brought you the Good News, it was not only with words but also with power, for the Holy Spirit gave you full assurance* that what we said was true. And you know of our concern for you from the way we lived when we were with you. ⁶So you received the message with joy from the Holy Spirit in spite of the severe suffering it brought you. In this way, you imitated both us and the Lord. ⁷As a result, you have become an example to all the believers in Greece—throughout both Macedonia and Achaia.*

⁸And now the word of the Lord is ringing out from you to people everywhere, even beyond Macedonia and Achaia, for wherever we go we find people telling us about your faith in God. We don't need to tell them about it, ⁹for they keep talking about the wonderful welcome you gave us and how you turned away from idols to serve the living and true God. ¹⁰And they speak of how you are looking forward to the coming of God's Son from heaven—Jesus, whom God raised from the dead. He is the one who has rescued us from the terrors of the coming judgment.

Paul Remembers His Visit

2 You yourselves know, dear brothers and sisters,* that our visit to you was not a failure. ²You know how badly we had been treated at Philippi just before we came to you and how much we suf-

---

1:1 Greek *Silvanus,* the Greek form of the name. 1:4 Greek *brothers.* 1:5 Or *with the power of the Holy Spirit, so you can have full assurance.* 1:7 *Macedonia* and *Achaia* were the northern and southern regions of Greece. 2:1 Greek *brothers;* also in 2:9, 14, 17.

fered there. Yet our God gave us the courage to declare his Good News to you boldly, in spite of great opposition. ³So you can see we were not preaching with any deceit or impure motives or trickery.

⁴For we speak as messengers approved by God to be entrusted with the Good News. Our purpose is to please God, not people. He alone examines the motives of our hearts. ⁵Never once did we try to win you with flattery, as you well know. And God is our witness that we were not pretending to be your friends just to get your money! ⁶As for human praise, we have never sought it from you or anyone else.

⁷As apostles of Christ we certainly had a right to make some demands of you, but instead we were like children* among you. Or we were like a mother feeding and caring for her own children. ⁸We loved you so much that we shared with you not only God's Good News but our own lives, too.

⁹Don't you remember, dear brothers and sisters, how hard we worked among you? Night and day we toiled to earn a living so that we would not be a burden to any of you as we preached God's Good News to you. ¹⁰You yourselves are our witnesses—and so is God—that we were devout and honest and faultless toward all of you believers. ¹¹And you know that we treated each of you as a father treats his own children. ¹²We

pleaded with you, encouraged you, and urged you to live your lives in a way that God would consider worthy. For he called you to share in his Kingdom and glory.

¹³Therefore, we never stop thanking God that when you received his message from us, you didn't think of our words as mere human ideas. You accepted what we said as the very word of God—which, of course, it is. And this word continues to work in you who believe.

¹⁴And then, dear brothers and sisters, you suffered persecution from your own countrymen. In this way, you imitated the believers in God's churches in Judea who, because of their belief in Christ Jesus, suffered from their own people, the Jews. ¹⁵For some of the Jews killed the prophets, and some even killed the Lord Jesus. Now they have persecuted us, too. They fail to please God and work against all humanity ¹⁶as they try to keep us from preaching the Good News of salvation to the Gentiles. By doing this, they continue to pile up their sins. But the anger of God has caught up with them at last.

Timothy's Good Report about the Church

¹⁷Dear brothers and sisters, after we were separated from you for a little while (though our hearts never left you), we tried very hard to come back because of our intense longing

---

2:7 Some manuscripts read *we were gentle.*

to see you again. [18]We wanted very much to come to you, and I, Paul, tried again and again, but Satan prevented us. [19]After all, what gives us hope and joy, and what will be our proud reward and crown as we stand before our Lord Jesus when he returns? It is you! [20]Yes, you are our pride and joy.

3 Finally, when we could stand it no longer, we decided to stay alone in Athens, [2]and we sent Timothy to visit you. He is our brother and God's co-worker* in proclaiming the Good News of Christ. We sent him to strengthen you, to encourage you in your faith, [3]and to keep you from being shaken by the troubles you were going through. But you know that we are destined for such troubles. [4]Even while we were with you, we warned you that troubles would soon come—and they did, as you well know. [5]That is why, when I could bear it no longer, I sent Timothy to find out whether your faith was still strong. I was afraid that the tempter had gotten the best of you and that our work had been useless.

[6]But now Timothy has just returned, bringing us good news about your faith and love. He reports that you always remember our visit with joy and that you want to see us as much as we want to see you. [7]So we have been greatly encouraged in the midst of our troubles and suffering, dear brothers and sisters,* because you have remained strong in your faith. [8]It gives us new life to know that you are standing firm in the Lord.

[9]How we thank God for you! Because of you we have great joy as we enter God's presence. [10]Night and day we pray earnestly for you, asking God to let us see you again to fill the gaps in your faith.

[11]May God our Father and our Lord Jesus bring us to you very soon. [12]And may the Lord make your love for one another and for all people grow and overflow, just as our love for you overflows. [13]May he, as a result, make your hearts strong, blameless, and holy as you stand before God our Father when our Lord Jesus comes again with all his holy people. Amen.

Live to Please God

4 Finally, dear brothers and sisters,* we urge you in the name of the Lord Jesus to live in a way that pleases God, as we have taught you. You live this way already, and we encourage you to do so even more. [2]For you remember what we taught you by the authority of the Lord Jesus.

[3]God's will is for you to be holy, so stay away from all sexual sin. [4]Then each of you will control his own

---

3:2 Other manuscripts read *and God's servant;* still others read *and a co-worker,* or *and a servant and co-worker for God,* or *and God's servant and our co-worker.* **3:7** Greek *brothers.* **4:1** Greek *brothers;* also in 4:10, 13.

body* and live in holiness and honor—⁵not in lustful passion like the pagans who do not know God and his ways. ⁶Never harm or cheat a fellow believer in this matter by violating his wife,* for the Lord avenges all such sins, as we have solemnly warned you before. ⁷God has called us to live holy lives, not impure lives. ⁸Therefore, anyone who refuses to live by these rules is not disobeying human teaching but is rejecting God, who gives his Holy Spirit to you.

⁹But we don't need to write to you about the importance of loving each other,* for God himself has taught you to love one another. ¹⁰Indeed, you already show your love for all the believers* throughout Macedonia. Even so, dear brothers and sisters, we urge you to love them even more.

¹¹Make it your goal to live a quiet life, minding your own business and working with your hands, just as we instructed you before. ¹²Then people who are not believers will respect the way you live, and you will not need to depend on others.

The Hope of the Resurrection

¹³And now, dear brothers and sisters, we want you to know what will happen to the believers who have died* so you will not grieve like people who have no hope. ¹⁴For since we believe that Jesus died and was raised to life again, we also believe that when Jesus returns, God will bring back with him the believers who have died.

¹⁵We tell you this directly from the Lord: We who are still living when the Lord returns will not meet him ahead of those who have died.* ¹⁶For the Lord himself will come down from heaven with a commanding shout, with the voice of the archangel, and with the trumpet call of God. First, the believers who have died* will rise from their graves. ¹⁷Then, together with them, we who are still alive and remain on the earth will be caught up in the clouds to meet the Lord in the air. Then we will be with the Lord forever. ¹⁸So encourage each other with these words.

5 Now concerning how and when all this will happen, dear brothers and sisters,* we don't really need to write you. ²For you know quite well that the day of the Lord's return will come unexpectedly, like a thief in the night. ³When people are saying, "Everything is peaceful and secure," then disaster will fall on them as suddenly as a pregnant woman's labor pains begin. And there will be no escape.

4:4 Or *will know how to take a wife for himself;* or *will learn to live with his own wife;* Greek reads *will know how to possess his own vessel.* 4:6 Greek *Never harm or cheat a brother in this matter.* 4:9 Greek *about brotherly love.* 4:10 Greek *the brothers.* 4:13 Greek *those who have fallen asleep;* also in 4:14. 4:15 Greek *those who have fallen asleep.* 4:16 Greek *the dead in Christ.* 5:1 Greek *brothers;* also in 5:4, 12, 14, 25, 26, 27.

[4] But you aren't in the dark about these things, dear brothers and sisters, and you won't be surprised when the day of the Lord comes like a thief.* [5] For you are all children of the light and of the day; we don't belong to darkness and night. [6] So be on your guard, not asleep like the others. Stay alert and be clearheaded. [7] Night is the time when people sleep and drinkers get drunk. [8] But let us who live in the light be clearheaded, protected by the armor of faith and love, and wearing as our helmet the confidence of our salvation.

[9] For God chose to save us through our Lord Jesus Christ, not to pour out his anger on us. [10] Christ died for us so that, whether we are dead or alive when he returns, we can live with him forever. [11] So encourage each other and build each other up, just as you are already doing.

Paul's Final Advice

[12] Dear brothers and sisters, honor those who are your leaders in the Lord's work. They work hard among you and give you spiritual guidance. [13] Show them great respect and wholehearted love because of their work. And live peacefully with each other.

[14] Brothers and sisters, we urge you to warn those who are lazy. Encourage those who are timid. Take tender care of those who are weak. Be patient with everyone.

[15] See that no one pays back evil for evil, but always try to do good to each other and to all people.

[16] Always be joyful. [17] Never stop praying. [18] Be thankful in all circumstances, for this is God's will for you who belong to Christ Jesus.

[19] Do not stifle the Holy Spirit. [20] Do not scoff at prophecies, [21] but test everything that is said. Hold on to what is good. [22] Stay away from every kind of evil.

Paul's Final Greetings

[23] Now may the God of peace make you holy in every way, and may your whole spirit and soul and body be kept blameless until our Lord Jesus Christ comes again. [24] God will make this happen, for he who calls you is faithful.

[25] Dear brothers and sisters, pray for us.

[26] Greet all the brothers and sisters with a sacred kiss.

[27] I command you in the name of the Lord to read this letter to all the brothers and sisters.

[28] May the grace of our Lord Jesus Christ be with you.

5:4 Some manuscripts read *comes upon you as if you were thieves.*

2 Thessalonians

Greetings from Paul

1 This letter is from Paul, Silas,* and Timothy.

We are writing to the church in Thessalonica, to you who belong to God our Father and the Lord Jesus Christ.

²May God our Father* and the Lord Jesus Christ give you grace and peace.

Encouragement during Persecution

³Dear brothers and sisters,* we can't help but thank God for you, because your faith is flourishing and your love for one another is growing. ⁴We proudly tell God's other churches about your endurance and faithfulness in all the persecutions and hardships you are suffering. ⁵And God will use this persecution to show his justice and to make you worthy of his Kingdom, for which you are suffering. ⁶In his justice he will pay back those who persecute you.

⁷And God will provide rest for you who are being persecuted and also for us when the Lord Jesus appears from heaven. He will come with his mighty angels, ⁸in flaming fire, bringing judgment on those who don't know God and on those who refuse to obey the Good News of our Lord Jesus. ⁹They will be punished with eternal destruction, forever separated from the Lord and from his glorious power. ¹⁰When he comes on that day, he will receive glory from his holy people—praise from all who believe. And this includes you, for you believed what we told you about him.

¹¹So we keep on praying for you, asking our God to enable you to live a life worthy of his call. May he give you the power to accomplish all the good things your faith prompts you to do. ¹²Then the name of our Lord Jesus will be honored because of the way you live, and you will be honored along with him. This is all made possible because of the grace of our God and Lord, Jesus Christ.*

Events prior to the Lord's Second Coming

2 Now, dear brothers and sisters,* let us clarify some things about the coming of our Lord Jesus Christ and how we will be gathered

---

1:1 Greek *Silvanus,* the Greek form of the name.   1:2 Some manuscripts read *God the Father.*
1:3 Greek *Brothers.*   1:12 Or *of our God and our Lord Jesus Christ.*   2:1 Greek *brothers;* also in 2:13, 15.

to meet him. ²Don't be so easily shaken or alarmed by those who say that the day of the Lord has already begun. Don't believe them, even if they claim to have had a spiritual vision, a revelation, or a letter supposedly from us. ³Don't be fooled by what they say. For that day will not come until there is a great rebellion against God and the man of lawlessness* is revealed—the one who brings destruction.* ⁴He will exalt himself and defy everything that people call god and every object of worship. He will even sit in the temple of God, claiming that he himself is God.

⁵Don't you remember that I told you about all this when I was with you? ⁶And you know what is holding him back, for he can be revealed only when his time comes. ⁷For this lawlessness is already at work secretly, and it will remain secret until the one who is holding it back steps out of the way. ⁸Then the man of lawlessness will be revealed, but the Lord Jesus will slay him with the breath of his mouth and destroy him by the splendor of his coming.

⁹This man will come to do the work of Satan with counterfeit power and signs and miracles. ¹⁰He will use every kind of evil deception to fool those on their way to destruction, because they refuse to love and accept the truth that would save them. ¹¹So God will cause them to be greatly deceived, and they will believe these lies. ¹²Then they will be condemned for enjoying evil rather than believing the truth.

Believers Should Stand Firm

¹³As for us, we can't help but thank God for you, dear brothers and sisters loved by the Lord. We are always thankful that God chose you to be among the first* to experience salvation—a salvation that came through the Spirit who makes you holy and through your belief in the truth. ¹⁴He called you to salvation when we told you the Good News; now you can share in the glory of our Lord Jesus Christ.

¹⁵With all these things in mind, dear brothers and sisters, stand firm and keep a strong grip on the teaching we passed on to you both in person and by letter.

¹⁶Now may our Lord Jesus Christ himself and God our Father, who loved us and by his grace gave us eternal comfort and a wonderful hope, ¹⁷comfort you and strengthen you in every good thing you do and say.

Paul's Request for Prayer

3 Finally, dear brothers and sisters,* we ask you to pray for us. Pray that the Lord's message will spread rapidly and be honored wherever it goes, just as when it

---

2:3a Some manuscripts read *the man of sin.* **2:3b** Greek *the son of destruction.* **2:13** Some manuscripts read *chose you from the very beginning.* **3:1** Greek *brothers;* also in 3:6, 13.

came to you. ²Pray, too, that we will be rescued from wicked and evil people, for not everyone is a believer. ³But the Lord is faithful; he will strengthen you and guard you from the evil one.* ⁴And we are confident in the Lord that you are doing and will continue to do the things we commanded you. ⁵May the Lord lead your hearts into a full understanding and expression of the love of God and the patient endurance that comes from Christ.

An Exhortation to Proper Living
⁶And now, dear brothers and sisters, we give you this command in the name of our Lord Jesus Christ: Stay away from all believers* who live idle lives and don't follow the tradition they received* from us. ⁷For you know that you ought to imitate us. We were not idle when we were with you. ⁸We never accepted food from anyone without paying for it. We worked hard day and night so we would not be a burden to any of you. ⁹We certainly had the right to ask you to feed us, but we wanted to give you an example to follow.

¹⁰Even while we were with you, we gave you this command: "Those unwilling to work will not get to eat." ¹¹Yet we hear that some of you are living idle lives, refusing to work and meddling in other people's business. ¹²We command such people and urge them in the name of the Lord Jesus Christ to settle down and work to earn their own living. ¹³As for the rest of you, dear brothers and sisters, never get tired of doing good.

¹⁴Take note of those who refuse to obey what we say in this letter. Stay away from them so they will be ashamed. ¹⁵Don't think of them as enemies, but warn them as you would a brother or sister.*

Paul's Final Greetings
¹⁶Now may the Lord of peace himself give you his peace at all times and in every situation. The Lord be with you all.

¹⁷HERE IS MY GREETING IN MY OWN HANDWRITING—PAUL. I DO THIS IN ALL MY LETTERS TO PROVE THEY ARE FROM ME.

¹⁸May the grace of our Lord Jesus Christ be with you all.

3:3 Or *from evil.*   **3:6a** Greek *from every brother.*   **3:6b** Some manuscripts read *you received.*
3:15 Greek *as a brother.*

1 Timothy

Greetings from Paul

1 This letter is from Paul, an apostle of Christ Jesus, appointed by the command of God our Savior and Christ Jesus, who gives us hope.

²I am writing to Timothy, my true son in the faith.

May God the Father and Christ Jesus our Lord give you grace, mercy, and peace.

Warnings against False Teachings

³When I left for Macedonia, I urged you to stay there in Ephesus and stop those whose teaching is contrary to the truth. ⁴Don't let them waste their time in endless discussion of myths and spiritual pedigrees. These things only lead to meaningless speculations,* which don't help people live a life of faith in God.*

⁵The purpose of my instruction is that all believers would be filled with love that comes from a pure heart, a clear conscience, and genuine faith. ⁶But some people have missed this whole point. They have turned away from these things and spend their time in meaningless discussions. ⁷They want to be known as teachers of the law of Moses, but they don't know what they are talking about, even though they speak so confidently.

⁸We know that the law is good when used correctly. ⁹For the law was not intended for people who do what is right. It is for people who are lawless and rebellious, who are ungodly and sinful, who consider nothing sacred and defile what is holy, who kill their father or mother or commit other murders. ¹⁰The law is for people who are sexually immoral, or who practice homosexuality, or are slave traders,* liars, promise breakers, or who do anything else that contradicts the wholesome teaching ¹¹that comes from the glorious Good News entrusted to me by our blessed God.

Paul's Gratitude for God's Mercy

¹²I thank Christ Jesus our Lord, who has given me strength to do his work. He considered me trustworthy and appointed me to serve him, ¹³even though I used to blaspheme the name of Christ. In my insolence, I persecuted his people. But God had mercy on me because I did it in ignorance and unbelief. ¹⁴Oh, how generous and gracious our Lord was! He filled me with the

1:4a Greek *in myths and endless genealogies, which cause speculation.* **1:4b** Greek *a stewardship of God in faith.* **1:10** Or *kidnappers.*

page 359 1 TIMOTHY 2

faith and love that come from Christ Jesus.

15This is a trustworthy saying, and everyone should accept it: "Christ Jesus came into the world to save sinners"—and I am the worst of them all. 16But God had mercy on me so that Christ Jesus could use me as a prime example of his great patience with even the worst sinners. Then others will realize that they, too, can believe in him and receive eternal life. 17All honor and glory to God forever and ever! He is the eternal King, the unseen one who never dies; he alone is God. Amen.

Timothy's Responsibility

18Timothy, my son, here are my instructions for you, based on the prophetic words spoken about you earlier. May they help you fight well in the Lord's battles. 19Cling to your faith in Christ, and keep your conscience clear. For some people have deliberately violated their consciences; as a result, their faith has been shipwrecked. 20Hymenaeus and Alexander are two examples. I threw them out and handed them over to Satan so they might learn not to blaspheme God.

Instructions about Worship

2 I urge you, first of all, to pray for all people. Ask God to help them; intercede on their behalf, and give thanks for them. 2Pray this way for kings and all who are in authority so that we can live peaceful and quiet lives marked by godliness and dignity. 3This is good and pleases God our Savior, 4who wants everyone to be saved and to understand the truth. 5For,

> There is one God and one Mediator who can reconcile God and humanity—the man Christ Jesus. 6He gave his life to purchase freedom for everyone.

This is the message God gave to the world at just the right time. 7And I have been chosen as a preacher and apostle to teach the Gentiles this message about faith and truth. I'm not exaggerating—just telling the truth.

8In every place of worship, I want men to pray with holy hands lifted up to God, free from anger and controversy.

9And I want women to be modest in their appearance.* They should wear decent and appropriate clothing and not draw attention to themselves by the way they fix their hair or by wearing gold or pearls or expensive clothes. 10For women who claim to be devoted to God should make themselves attractive by the good things they do.

11Women should learn quietly and submissively. 12I do not let women teach men or have authority over them.* Let them listen quietly. 13For God made Adam first, and afterward he made Eve. 14And it

2:9 Or *to pray in modest apparel.*   2:12 Or *teach men or usurp their authority.*

was not Adam who was deceived by Satan. The woman was deceived, and sin was the result. [15]But women will be saved through childbearing,* assuming they continue to live in faith, love, holiness, and modesty.

Leaders in the Church

3 This is a trustworthy saying: "If someone aspires to be a church leader,* he desires an honorable position." [2]So a church leader must be a man whose life is above reproach. He must be faithful to his wife.* He must exercise self-control, live wisely, and have a good reputation. He must enjoy having guests in his home, and he must be able to teach. [3]He must not be a heavy drinker* or be violent. He must be gentle, not quarrelsome, and not love money. [4]He must manage his own family well, having children who respect and obey him. [5]For if a man cannot manage his own household, how can he take care of God's church?

[6]A church leader must not be a new believer, because he might become proud, and the devil would cause him to fall.* [7]Also, people outside the church must speak well of him so that he will not be disgraced and fall into the devil's trap.

[8]In the same way, deacons must be well respected and have integrity. They must not be heavy drinkers or dishonest with money. [9]They must be committed to the mystery of the faith now revealed and must live with a clear conscience. [10]Before they are appointed as deacons, let them be closely examined. If they pass the test, then let them serve as deacons.

[11]In the same way, their wives* must be respected and must not slander others. They must exercise self-control and be faithful in everything they do.

[12]A deacon must be faithful to his wife, and he must manage his children and household well. [13]Those who do well as deacons will be rewarded with respect from others and will have increased confidence in their faith in Christ Jesus.

The Truths of Our Faith

[14]I am writing these things to you now, even though I hope to be with you soon, [15]so that if I am delayed, you will know how people must conduct themselves in the household of God. This is the church of the living God, which is the pillar and foundation of the truth.

[16]Without question, this is the great mystery of our faith*:

Christ* was revealed in a human body
and vindicated by the Spirit.*

2:15 Or *will be saved by accepting their role as mothers,* or *will be saved by the birth of the Child.* 3:1 Or *an overseer,* or *a bishop;* also in 3:2, 6. 3:2 Or *must have only one wife,* or *must be married only once;* Greek reads *must be the husband of one wife;* also in 3:12. 3:3 Greek *must not drink too much wine;* similarly in 3:8. 3:6 Or *he might fall into the same judgment as the devil.* 3:11 Or *the women deacons.* The Greek word can be translated *women* or *wives.* 3:16a Or *of godliness.* 3:16b Greek *He who;* other manuscripts read *God.* 3:16c Or *in his spirit.*

He was seen by angels
   and announced to the nations.
He was believed in throughout
   the world
   and taken to heaven in glory.

Warnings against False Teachers

4 Now the Holy Spirit tells us clearly that in the last times some will turn away from the true faith; they will follow deceptive spirits and teachings that come from demons. ²These people are hypocrites and liars, and their consciences are dead.*

³They will say it is wrong to be married and wrong to eat certain foods. But God created those foods to be eaten with thanks by faithful people who know the truth. ⁴Since everything God created is good, we should not reject any of it but receive it with thanks. ⁵For we know it is made acceptable* by the word of God and prayer.

A Good Servant of Christ Jesus

⁶If you explain these things to the brothers and sisters,* Timothy, you will be a worthy servant of Christ Jesus, one who is nourished by the message of faith and the good teaching you have followed. ⁷Do not waste time arguing over godless ideas and old wives' tales. Instead, train yourself to be godly. ⁸"Physical training is good, but training for godliness is much better, promising

benefits in this life and in the life to come." ⁹This is a trustworthy saying, and everyone should accept it. ¹⁰This is why we work hard and continue to struggle,* for our hope is in the living God, who is the Savior of all people and particularly of all believers.

¹¹Teach these things and insist that everyone learn them. ¹²Don't let anyone think less of you because you are young. Be an example to all believers in what you say, in the way you live, in your love, your faith, and your purity. ¹³Until I get there, focus on reading the Scriptures to the church, encouraging the believers, and teaching them.

¹⁴Do not neglect the spiritual gift you received through the prophecy spoken over you when the elders of the church laid their hands on you. ¹⁵Give your complete attention to these matters. Throw yourself into your tasks so that everyone will see your progress. ¹⁶Keep a close watch on how you live and on your teaching. Stay true to what is right for the sake of your own salvation and the salvation of those who hear you.

Advice about Widows, Elders, and Slaves

5 Never speak harshly to an older man,* but appeal to him respectfully as you would to your own father. Talk to younger men as you would to your own brothers. ²Treat

---

4:2 Greek *are seared.*   **4:5** Or *made holy.*   **4:6** Greek *brothers.*   **4:10** Some manuscripts read *continue to suffer.*   **5:1** Or *an elder.*

older women as you would your mother, and treat younger women with all purity as you would your own sisters.

³Take care of* any widow who has no one else to care for her. ⁴But if she has children or grandchildren, their first responsibility is to show godliness at home and repay their parents by taking care of them. This is something that pleases God.

⁵Now a true widow, a woman who is truly alone in this world, has placed her hope in God. She prays night and day, asking God for his help. ⁶But the widow who lives only for pleasure is spiritually dead even while she lives. ⁷Give these instructions to the church so that no one will be open to criticism.

⁸But those who won't care for their relatives, especially those in their own household, have denied the true faith. Such people are worse than unbelievers.

⁹A widow who is put on the list for support must be a woman who is at least sixty years old and was faithful to her husband.* ¹⁰She must be well respected by everyone because of the good she has done. Has she brought up her children well? Has she been kind to strangers and served other believers humbly?* Has she helped those who are in trouble? Has she always been ready to do good?

¹¹The younger widows should not be on the list, because their physical desires will overpower their devotion to Christ and they will want to remarry. ¹²Then they would be guilty of breaking their previous pledge. ¹³And if they are on the list, they will learn to be lazy and will spend their time gossiping from house to house, meddling in other people's business and talking about things they shouldn't. ¹⁴So I advise these younger widows to marry again, have children, and take care of their own homes. Then the enemy will not be able to say anything against them. ¹⁵For I am afraid that some of them have already gone astray and now follow Satan.

¹⁶If a woman who is a believer has relatives who are widows, she must take care of them and not put the responsibility on the church. Then the church can care for the widows who are truly alone.

¹⁷Elders who do their work well should be respected and paid well,* especially those who work hard at both preaching and teaching. ¹⁸For the Scripture says, "You must not muzzle an ox to keep it from eating as it treads out the grain." And in another place, "Those who work deserve their pay!"*

¹⁹Do not listen to an accusation against an elder unless it is confirmed by two or three witnesses. ²⁰Those who sin should be reprimanded in front of the whole

5:3 Or *Honor.* 5:9 Greek *was the wife of one husband.* 5:10 Greek *and washed the feet of God's holy people?* 5:17 Greek *should be worthy of double honor.* 5:18 Deut 25:4; Luke 10:7.

church; this will serve as a strong warning to others.

²¹I solemnly command you in the presence of God and Christ Jesus and the highest angels to obey these instructions without taking sides or showing favoritism to anyone.

²²Never be in a hurry about appointing a church leader.* Do not share in the sins of others. Keep yourself pure.

²³Don't drink only water. You ought to drink a little wine for the sake of your stomach because you are sick so often.

²⁴Remember, the sins of some people are obvious, leading them to certain judgment. But there are others whose sins will not be revealed until later. ²⁵In the same way, the good deeds of some people are obvious. And the good deeds done in secret will someday come to light.

6 All slaves should show full respect for their masters so they will not bring shame on the name of God and his teaching. ²If the masters are believers, that is no excuse for being disrespectful. Those slaves should work all the harder because their efforts are helping other believers* who are well loved.

False Teaching and True Riches

Teach these things, Timothy, and encourage everyone to obey them. ³Some people may contradict our teaching, but these are the whole-some teachings of the Lord Jesus Christ. These teachings promote a godly life. ⁴Anyone who teaches something different is arrogant and lacks understanding. Such a person has an unhealthy desire to quibble over the meaning of words. This stirs up arguments ending in jealousy, division, slander, and evil suspicions. ⁵These people always cause trouble. Their minds are corrupt, and they have turned their backs on the truth. To them, a show of godliness is just a way to become wealthy.

⁶Yet true godliness with contentment is itself great wealth. ⁷After all, we brought nothing with us when we came into the world, and we can't take anything with us when we leave it. ⁸So if we have enough food and clothing, let us be content.

⁹But people who long to be rich fall into temptation and are trapped by many foolish and harmful desires that plunge them into ruin and destruction. ¹⁰For the love of money is the root of all kinds of evil. And some people, craving money, have wandered from the true faith and pierced themselves with many sorrows.

Paul's Final Instructions

¹¹But you, Timothy, are a man of God; so run from all these evil things. Pursue righteousness and a godly life, along with faith, love, perseverance, and gentleness. ¹²Fight the good fight for the true faith. Hold tightly

5:22 Greek *about the laying on of hands.* **6:2** Greek *brothers.*

to the eternal life to which God has called you, which you have declared so well before many witnesses. [13]And I charge you before God, who gives life to all, and before Christ Jesus, who gave a good testimony before Pontius Pilate, [14]that you obey this command without wavering. Then no one can find fault with you from now until our Lord Jesus Christ comes again. [15]For,

At just the right time Christ will be revealed from heaven by the blessed and only almighty God, the King of all kings and Lord of all lords. [16]He alone can never die, and he lives in light so brilliant that no human can approach him. No human eye has ever seen him, nor ever will. All honor and power to him forever! Amen.

[17]Teach those who are rich in this world not to be proud and not to trust in their money, which is so unreliable. Their trust should be in God, who richly gives us all we need for our enjoyment. [18]Tell them to use their money to do good. They should be rich in good works and generous to those in need, always being ready to share with others. [19]By doing this they will be storing up their treasure as a good foundation for the future so that they may experience true life.

[20]Timothy, guard what God has entrusted to you. Avoid godless, foolish discussions with those who oppose you with their so-called knowledge. [21]Some people have wandered from the faith by following such foolishness.

May God's grace be with you all.

2 Timothy

Greetings from Paul

1 This letter is from Paul, chosen by the will of God to be an apostle of Christ Jesus. I have been sent out to tell others about the life he has promised through faith in Christ Jesus.

2I am writing to Timothy, my dear son.

May God the Father and Christ Jesus our Lord give you grace, mercy, and peace.

Encouragement to Be Faithful

3Timothy, I thank God for you—the God I serve with a clear conscience, just as my ancestors did. Night and day I constantly remember you in my prayers. 4I long to see you again, for I remember your tears as we parted. And I will be filled with joy when we are together again.

5I remember your genuine faith, for you share the faith that first filled your grandmother Lois and your mother, Eunice. And I know that same faith continues strong in you. 6This is why I remind you to fan into flames the spiritual gift God gave you when I laid my hands on you. 7For God has not given us a spirit of fear and timidity, but of power, love, and self-discipline.

8So never be ashamed to tell others about our Lord. And don't be ashamed of me, either, even though I'm in prison for him. With the strength God gives you, be ready to suffer with me for the sake of the Good News. 9For God saved us and called us to live a holy life. He did this, not because we deserved it, but because that was his plan from before the beginning of time—to show us his grace through Christ Jesus. 10And now he has made all of this plain to us by the appearing of Christ Jesus, our Savior. He broke the power of death and illuminated the way to life and immortality through the Good News. 11And God chose me to be a preacher, an apostle, and a teacher of this Good News.

12That is why I am suffering here in prison. But I am not ashamed of it, for I know the one in whom I trust, and I am sure that he is able to guard what I have entrusted to him* until the day of his return.

13Hold on to the pattern of wholesome teaching you learned from me—a pattern shaped by the faith and love that you have in Christ

1:12 Or *what has been entrusted to me*.

Jesus. [14]Through the power of the Holy Spirit who lives within us, carefully guard the precious truth that has been entrusted to you.

[15]As you know, everyone from the province of Asia has deserted me—even Phygelus and Hermogenes.

[16]May the Lord show special kindness to Onesiphorus and all his family because he often visited and encouraged me. He was never ashamed of me because I was in chains. [17]When he came to Rome, he searched everywhere until he found me. [18]May the Lord show him special kindness on the day of Christ's return. And you know very well how helpful he was in Ephesus.

A Good Soldier of Christ Jesus

2 Timothy, my dear son, be strong through the grace that God gives you in Christ Jesus. [2]You have heard me teach things that have been confirmed by many reliable witnesses. Now teach these truths to other trustworthy people who will be able to pass them on to others.

[3]Endure suffering along with me, as a good soldier of Christ Jesus. [4]Soldiers don't get tied up in the affairs of civilian life, for then they cannot please the officer who enlisted them. [5]And athletes cannot win the prize unless they follow the rules. [6]And hardworking farmers should be the first to enjoy the fruit of their labor. [7]Think about what I am saying. The Lord will help you understand all these things.

[8]Always remember that Jesus Christ, a descendant of King David, was raised from the dead. This is the Good News I preach. [9]And because I preach this Good News, I am suffering and have been chained like a criminal. But the word of God cannot be chained. [10]So I am willing to endure anything if it will bring salvation and eternal glory in Christ Jesus to those God has chosen.

[11]This is a trustworthy saying:

If we die with him,
we will also live with him.
[12] If we endure hardship,
we will reign with him.
If we deny him,
he will deny us.
[13] If we are unfaithful,
he remains faithful,
for he cannot deny who he is.

[14]Remind everyone about these things, and command them in God's presence to stop fighting over words. Such arguments are useless, and they can ruin those who hear them.

An Approved Worker

[15]Work hard so you can present yourself to God and receive his approval. Be a good worker, one who does not need to be ashamed and who correctly explains the word of truth. [16]Avoid worthless, foolish talk that only leads to more godless be-

havior. ¹⁷This kind of talk spreads like cancer,* as in the case of Hymenaeus and Philetus. ¹⁸They have left the path of truth, claiming that the resurrection of the dead has already occurred; in this way, they have turned some people away from the faith.

¹⁹But God's truth stands firm like a foundation stone with this inscription: "The LORD knows those who are his,"* and "All who belong to the LORD must turn away from evil."*

²⁰In a wealthy home some utensils are made of gold and silver, and some are made of wood and clay. The expensive utensils are used for special occasions, and the cheap ones are for everyday use. ²¹If you keep yourself pure, you will be a special utensil for honorable use. Your life will be clean, and you will be ready for the Master to use you for every good work.

²²Run from anything that stimulates youthful lusts. Instead, pursue righteous living, faithfulness, love, and peace. Enjoy the companionship of those who call on the Lord with pure hearts.

²³Again I say, don't get involved in foolish, ignorant arguments that only start fights. ²⁴A servant of the Lord must not quarrel but must be kind to everyone, be able to teach, and be patient with difficult people. ²⁵Gently instruct those who oppose the truth. Perhaps God will change those people's hearts, and they will learn the truth. ²⁶Then they will come to their senses and escape from the devil's trap. For they have been held captive by him to do whatever he wants.

The Dangers of the Last Days

3 You should know this, Timothy, that in the last days there will be very difficult times. ²For people will love only themselves and their money. They will be boastful and proud, scoffing at God, disobedient to their parents, and ungrateful. They will consider nothing sacred. ³They will be unloving and unforgiving; they will slander others and have no self-control. They will be cruel and hate what is good. ⁴They will betray their friends, be reckless, be puffed up with pride, and love pleasure rather than God. ⁵They will act religious, but they will reject the power that could make them godly. Stay away from people like that!

⁶They are the kind who work their way into people's homes and win the confidence of* vulnerable women who are burdened with the guilt of sin and controlled by various desires. ⁷(Such women are forever following new teachings, but they are never able to understand the truth.) ⁸These teachers oppose the truth just as Jannes and Jambres opposed Moses. They have depraved minds and a counterfeit faith. ⁹But they won't get away with this for long. Someday everyone

---

2:17 Greek *gangrene.*   **2:19a** Num 16:5.   **2:19b** See Isa 52:11.   **3:6** Greek *and take captive.*

will recognize what fools they are, just as with Jannes and Jambres.

Paul's Charge to Timothy

[10]But you, Timothy, certainly know what I teach, and how I live, and what my purpose in life is. You know my faith, my patience, my love, and my endurance. [11]You know how much persecution and suffering I have endured. You know all about how I was persecuted in Antioch, Iconium, and Lystra—but the Lord rescued me from all of it. [12]Yes, and everyone who wants to live a godly life in Christ Jesus will suffer persecution. [13]But evil people and impostors will flourish. They will deceive others and will themselves be deceived.

[14]But you must remain faithful to the things you have been taught. You know they are true, for you know you can trust those who taught you. [15]You have been taught the holy Scriptures from childhood, and they have given you the wisdom to receive the salvation that comes by trusting in Christ Jesus. [16]All Scripture is inspired by God and is useful to teach us what is true and to make us realize what is wrong in our lives. It corrects us when we are wrong and teaches us to do what is right. [17]God uses it to prepare and equip his people to do every good work.

4 I solemnly urge you in the presence of God and Christ Jesus, who will someday judge the living and the dead when he comes to set up his Kingdom: [2]Preach the word of God. Be prepared, whether the time is favorable or not. Patiently correct, rebuke, and encourage your people with good teaching.

[3]For a time is coming when people will no longer listen to sound and wholesome teaching. They will follow their own desires and will look for teachers who will tell them whatever their itching ears want to hear. [4]They will reject the truth and chase after myths.

[5]But you should keep a clear mind in every situation. Don't be afraid of suffering for the Lord. Work at telling others the Good News, and fully carry out the ministry God has given you.

[6]As for me, my life has already been poured out as an offering to God. The time of my death is near. [7]I have fought the good fight, I have finished the race, and I have remained faithful. [8]And now the prize awaits me—the crown of righteousness, which the Lord, the righteous Judge, will give me on the day of his return. And the prize is not just for me but for all who eagerly look forward to his appearing.

Paul's Final Words

[9]Timothy, please come as soon as you can. [10]Demas has deserted me because he loves the things of this life and has gone to Thessalonica. Crescens has gone to Galatia, and Titus has gone to Dalmatia. [11]Only

Luke is with me. Bring Mark with you when you come, for he will be helpful to me in my ministry. ¹²I sent Tychicus to Ephesus. ¹³When you come, be sure to bring the coat I left with Carpus at Troas. Also bring my books, and especially my papers.*

¹⁴Alexander the coppersmith did me much harm, but the Lord will judge him for what he has done. ¹⁵Be careful of him, for he fought against everything we said.

¹⁶The first time I was brought before the judge, no one came with me. Everyone abandoned me. May it not be counted against them. ¹⁷But the Lord stood with me and gave me strength so that I might preach the Good News in its entirety for all the Gentiles to hear.

And he rescued me from certain death.* ¹⁸Yes, and the Lord will deliver me from every evil attack and will bring me safely into his heavenly Kingdom. All glory to God forever and ever! Amen.

Paul's Final Greetings

¹⁹Give my greetings to Priscilla and Aquila and those living in the household of Onesiphorus. ²⁰Erastus stayed at Corinth, and I left Trophimus sick at Miletus.

²¹Do your best to get here before winter. Eubulus sends you greetings, and so do Pudens, Linus, Claudia, and all the brothers and sisters.*

²²May the Lord be with your spirit. And may his grace be with all of you.

4:13 Greek *especially the parchments.* 4:17 Greek *from the mouth of a lion.* 4:21 Greek *brothers.*

Titus

Greetings from Paul

1 This letter is from Paul, a slave of God and an apostle of Jesus Christ. I have been sent to proclaim faith to* those God has chosen and to teach them to know the truth that shows them how to live godly lives. ²This truth gives them confidence that they have eternal life, which God—who does not lie—promised them before the world began. ³And now at just the right time he has revealed this message, which we announce to everyone. It is by the command of God our Savior that I have been entrusted with this work for him.

⁴I am writing to Titus, my true son in the faith that we share.

May God the Father and Christ Jesus our Savior give you grace and peace.

Titus's Work in Crete

⁵I left you on the island of Crete so you could complete our work there and appoint elders in each town as I instructed you. ⁶An elder must live a blameless life. He must be faithful to his wife,* and his children must be believers who don't have a reputation for being wild or rebellious. ⁷A church leader* is a manager of God's household, so he must live a blameless life. He must not be arrogant or quick-tempered; he must not be a heavy drinker,* violent, or dishonest with money.

⁸Rather, he must enjoy having guests in his home, and he must love what is good. He must live wisely and be just. He must live a devout and disciplined life. ⁹He must have a strong belief in the trustworthy message he was taught; then he will be able to encourage others with wholesome teaching and show those who oppose it where they are wrong.

¹⁰For there are many rebellious people who engage in useless talk and deceive others. This is especially true of those who insist on circumcision for salvation. ¹¹They must be silenced, because they are turning whole families away from the truth by their false teaching. And they do it only for money. ¹²Even one of their own men, a prophet from Crete, has said about them, "The people of Crete are all liars, cruel animals, and lazy gluttons."* ¹³This is

---

1:1 Or *to strengthen the faith of.* **1:6** Or *must have only one wife,* or *must be married only once;* Greek reads *must be the husband of one wife.* **1:7a** Or *An overseer,* or *A bishop.* **1:7b** Greek *must not drink too much wine.* **1:12** This quotation is from Epimenides of Knossos.

true. So reprimand them sternly to make them strong in the faith. [14]They must stop listening to Jewish myths and the commands of people who have turned away from the truth.

[15]Everything is pure to those whose hearts are pure. But nothing is pure to those who are corrupt and unbelieving, because their minds and consciences are corrupted. [16]Such people claim they know God, but they deny him by the way they live. They are detestable and disobedient, worthless for doing anything good.

Promote Right Teaching

2 As for you, Titus, promote the kind of living that reflects wholesome teaching. [2]Teach the older men to exercise self-control, to be worthy of respect, and to live wisely. They must have sound faith and be filled with love and patience.

[3]Similarly, teach the older women to live in a way that honors God. They must not slander others or be heavy drinkers.* Instead, they should teach others what is good. [4]These older women must train the younger women to love their husbands and their children, [5]to live wisely and be pure, to work in their homes,* to do good, and to be submissive to their husbands. Then they will not bring shame on the word of God.

[6]In the same way, encourage the young men to live wisely. [7]And you yourself must be an example to them by doing good works of every kind. Let everything you do reflect the integrity and seriousness of your teaching. [8]Teach the truth so that your teaching can't be criticized. Then those who oppose us will be ashamed and have nothing bad to say about us.

[9]Slaves must always obey their masters and do their best to please them. They must not talk back [10]or steal, but must show themselves to be entirely trustworthy and good. Then they will make the teaching about God our Savior attractive in every way.

[11]For the grace of God has been revealed, bringing salvation to all people. [12]And we are instructed to turn from godless living and sinful pleasures. We should live in this evil world with wisdom, righteousness, and devotion to God, [13]while we look forward with hope to that wonderful day when the glory of our great God and Savior, Jesus Christ, will be revealed. [14]He gave his life to free us from every kind of sin, to cleanse us, and to make us his very own people, totally committed to doing good deeds.

[15]You must teach these things and encourage the believers to do them. You have the authority to correct them when necessary, so don't let anyone disregard what you say.

2:3 Greek *be enslaved to much wine.*   2:5 Some manuscripts read *to care for their homes.*

Do What Is Good

3 Remind the believers to submit to the government and its officers. They should be obedient, always ready to do what is good. ²They must not slander anyone and must avoid quarreling. Instead, they should be gentle and show true humility to everyone.

³Once we, too, were foolish and disobedient. We were misled and became slaves to many lusts and pleasures. Our lives were full of evil and envy, and we hated each other. ⁴But—

When God our Savior revealed his kindness and love, ⁵he saved us, not because of the righteous things we had done, but because of his mercy. He washed away our sins, giving us a new birth and new life through the Holy Spirit.* ⁶He generously poured out the Spirit upon us through Jesus Christ our Savior. ⁷Because of his grace he made us right in his sight and gave us confidence that we will inherit eternal life.

⁸This is a trustworthy saying, and I want you to insist on these teachings so that all who trust in God will devote themselves to doing good.

These teachings are good and beneficial for everyone. ⁹Do not get involved in foolish discussions about spiritual pedigrees* or in quarrels and fights about obedience to Jewish laws. These things are useless and a waste of time. ¹⁰If people are causing divisions among you, give a first and second warning. After that, have nothing more to do with them. ¹¹For people like that have turned away from the truth, and their own sins condemn them.

Paul's Final Remarks and Greetings

¹²I am planning to send either Artemas or Tychicus to you. As soon as one of them arrives, do your best to meet me at Nicopolis, for I have decided to stay there for the winter. ¹³Do everything you can to help Zenas the lawyer and Apollos with their trip. See that they are given everything they need. ¹⁴Our people must learn to do good by meeting the urgent needs of others; then they will not be unproductive.

¹⁵Everybody here sends greetings. Please give my greetings to the believers—all who love us.

May God's grace be with you all.

3:5 Greek *He saved us through the washing of regeneration and renewing of the Holy Spirit.*
3:9 Or *spiritual genealogies.*

Philemon

Greetings from Paul

This letter is from Paul, a prisoner for preaching the Good News about Christ Jesus, and from our brother Timothy.

I am writing to Philemon, our beloved co-worker, ²and to our sister Apphia, and to our fellow soldier Archippus, and to the church that meets in your* house.

³May God our Father and the Lord Jesus Christ give you grace and peace.

Paul's Thanksgiving and Prayer

⁴I always thank my God when I pray for you, Philemon, ⁵because I keep hearing about your faith in the Lord Jesus and your love for all of God's people. ⁶And I am praying that you will put into action the generosity that comes from your faith as you understand and experience all the good things we have in Christ. ⁷Your love has given me much joy and comfort, my brother, for your kindness has often refreshed the hearts of God's people.

Paul's Appeal for Onesimus

⁸That is why I am boldly asking a favor of you. I could demand it in the name of Christ because it is the right thing for you to do. ⁹But because of our love, I prefer simply to ask you. Consider this as a request from me—Paul, an old man and now also a prisoner for the sake of Christ Jesus.*

¹⁰I appeal to you to show kindness to my child, Onesimus. I became his father in the faith while here in prison. ¹¹Onesimus* hasn't been of much use to you in the past, but now he is very useful to both of us. ¹²I am sending him back to you, and with him comes my own heart.

¹³I wanted to keep him here with me while I am in these chains for preaching the Good News, and he would have helped me on your behalf. ¹⁴But I didn't want to do anything without your consent. I wanted you to help because you were willing, not because you were forced. ¹⁵It seems you lost Onesimus for a little while so that you could have him back forever. ¹⁶He is no longer like a slave to you. He is more than a slave, for he is a beloved brother, especially to me. Now he will mean much more to you, both as a man and as a brother in the Lord.

2 Throughout this letter, *you* and *your* are singular except in verses 3, 22, and 25. 9 Or *a prisoner of Christ Jesus.* 11 *Onesimus* means "useful."

¹⁷So if you consider me your partner, welcome him as you would welcome me. ¹⁸If he has wronged you in any way or owes you anything, charge it to me. ¹⁹I, PAUL, WRITE THIS WITH MY OWN HAND: I WILL REPAY IT. AND I WON'T MENTION THAT YOU OWE ME YOUR VERY SOUL!

²⁰Yes, my brother, please do me this favor* for the Lord's sake. Give me this encouragement in Christ.

²¹I am confident as I write this letter that you will do what I ask and even more! ²²One more thing—please prepare a guest room for me, for I am hoping that God will answer your prayers and let me return to you soon.

Paul's Final Greetings

²³Epaphras, my fellow prisoner in Christ Jesus, sends you his greetings. ²⁴So do Mark, Aristarchus, Demas, and Luke, my co-workers.

²⁵May the grace of the Lord Jesus Christ be with your spirit.

20 Greek *onaimen*, a play on the name Onesimus.

Hebrews

Jesus Christ Is God's Son

1 Long ago God spoke many times and in many ways to our ancestors through the prophets. ²And now in these final days, he has spoken to us through his Son. God promised everything to the Son as an inheritance, and through the Son he created the universe. ³The Son radiates God's own glory and expresses the very character of God, and he sustains everything by the mighty power of his command. When he had cleansed us from our sins, he sat down in the place of honor at the right hand of the majestic God in heaven. ⁴This shows that the Son is far greater than the angels, just as the name God gave him is greater than their names.

The Son Is Greater Than the Angels

⁵For God never said to any angel what he said to Jesus:

"You are my Son.
　Today I have become your
　　Father.*"

God also said,

"I will be his Father,
　and he will be my Son."*

⁶And when he brought his supreme* Son into the world, God said,*

"Let all of God's angels worship
　him."*

⁷Regarding the angels, he says,

"He sends his angels like the
　winds,
　his servants like flames
　　of fire."*

⁸But to the Son he says,

"Your throne, O God, endures
　forever and ever.
　You rule with a scepter
　　of justice.
⁹ You love justice and hate evil.
　Therefore, O God, your God
　　has anointed you,
　pouring out the oil of joy on
　　you more than on anyone
　　else."*

¹⁰He also says to the Son,

"In the beginning, Lord,
　you laid the foundation
　　of the earth
　and made the heavens with
　　your hands.
¹¹ They will perish, but you remain
　　forever.

1:5a Or *Today I reveal you as my Son.* Ps 2:7.　**1:5b** 2 Sam 7:14.　**1:6a** Or *firstborn.*　**1:6b** Or *when he again brings his supreme Son [or firstborn Son] into the world, God will say.*　**1:6c** Deut 32:43.
1:7 Ps 104:4 (Greek version).　**1:8-9** Ps 45:6-7.

375

They will wear out like old
clothing.
¹²You will fold them up like
a cloak
and discard them like old
clothing.
But you are always the same;
you will live forever."*

¹³And God never said to any of the
angels,

"Sit in the place of honor at my
right hand
until I humble your enemies,
making them a footstool
under your feet."*

¹⁴Therefore, angels are only servants—spirits sent to care for people who will inherit salvation.

A Warning against Drifting Away

2 So we must listen very carefully to the truth we have heard, or we may drift away from it. ²For the message God delivered through angels has always stood firm, and every violation of the law and every act of disobedience was punished. ³So what makes us think we can escape if we ignore this great salvation that was first announced by the Lord Jesus himself and then delivered to us by those who heard him speak? ⁴And God confirmed the message by giving signs and wonders and various miracles and gifts of the Holy Spirit whenever he chose.

Jesus, the Man

⁵And furthermore, it is not angels who will control the future world we are talking about. ⁶For in one place the Scriptures say,

"What are mere mortals
that you should think
about them,
or a son of man* that you
should care for him?
⁷Yet for a little while you made
them a little lower than the
angels
and crowned them with glory
and honor.*
⁸You gave them authority over
all things."*

Now when it says "all things," it means nothing is left out. But we have not yet seen all things put under their authority. ⁹What we do see is Jesus, who for a little while was given a position "a little lower than the angels"; and because he suffered death for us, he is now "crowned with glory and honor." Yes, by God's grace, Jesus tasted death for everyone. ¹⁰God, for whom and through whom everything was made, chose to bring many children into glory. And it was only right that he should make Jesus, through his suffering, a perfect leader, fit to bring them into their salvation.

¹¹So now Jesus and the ones he makes holy have the same Father. That is why Jesus is not ashamed to

call them his brothers and sisters.*
¹²For he said to God,

> "I will proclaim your name
>   to my brothers and
>   sisters.
>   I will praise you among your
>   assembled people."*

¹³He also said,

> "I will put my trust in him,"

that is, "I and the children God
has given me."*

¹⁴Because God's children are human beings—made of flesh and blood—the Son also became flesh and blood. For only as a human being could he die, and only by dying could he break the power of the devil, who had* the power of death. ¹⁵Only in this way could he set free all who have lived their lives as slaves to the fear of dying.

¹⁶We also know that the Son did not come to help angels; he came to help the descendants of Abraham. ¹⁷Therefore, it was necessary for him to be made in every respect like us, his brothers and sisters,* so that he could be our merciful and faithful High Priest before God. Then he could offer a sacrifice that would take away the sins of the people. ¹⁸Since he himself has gone through suffering and testing, he is able to help us when we are being tested.

Jesus Is Greater Than Moses

3 And so, dear brothers and sisters who belong to God and* are partners with those called to heaven, think carefully about this Jesus whom we declare to be God's messenger* and High Priest. ²For he was faithful to God, who appointed him, just as Moses served faithfully when he was entrusted with God's entire* house.

³But Jesus deserves far more glory than Moses, just as a person who builds a house deserves more praise than the house itself. ⁴For every house has a builder, but the one who built everything is God.

⁵Moses was certainly faithful in God's house as a servant. His work was an illustration of the truths God would reveal later. ⁶But Christ, as the Son, is in charge of God's entire house. And we are God's house, if we keep our courage and remain confident in our hope in Christ.*

⁷That is why the Holy Spirit says,

> "Today when you hear his voice,
> ⁸   don't harden your hearts
>   as Israel did when they rebelled,
>   when they tested me in the
>   wilderness.
> ⁹ There your ancestors tested and
>   tried my patience,
>   even though they saw my
>   miracles for forty years.
> ¹⁰ So I was angry with them, and
>   I said,

2:11 Greek *brothers;* also in 2:12. **2:12** Ps 22:22. **2:13** Isa 8:17-18. **2:14** Or *has.* **2:17** Greek *like the brothers.* **3:1a** Greek *And so, holy brothers who.* **3:1b** Greek *God's apostle.* **3:2** Some manuscripts do not include *entire.* **3:6** Some manuscripts add *faithful to the end.*

'Their hearts always turn away
    from me.
They refuse to do what I tell
    them.'

¹¹ So in my anger I took an oath:
    'They will never enter my
        place of rest.'"*

¹²Be careful then, dear brothers and sisters.* Make sure that your own hearts are not evil and unbelieving, turning you away from the living God. ¹³You must warn each other every day, while it is still "today," so that none of you will be deceived by sin and hardened against God. ¹⁴For if we are faithful to the end, trusting God just as firmly as when we first believed, we will share in all that belongs to Christ. ¹⁵Remember what it says:

"Today when you hear his
    voice,
  don't harden your hearts
  as Israel did when they
    rebelled."*

¹⁶And who was it who rebelled against God, even though they heard his voice? Wasn't it the people Moses led out of Egypt? ¹⁷And who made God angry for forty years? Wasn't it the people who sinned, whose corpses lay in the wilderness? ¹⁸And to whom was God speaking when he took an oath that they would never enter his rest? Wasn't it the people who disobeyed him? ¹⁹So we see that because of their unbelief they were not able to enter his rest.

Promised Rest for God's People

4 God's promise of entering his rest still stands, so we ought to tremble with fear that some of you might fail to experience it. ²For this good news—that God has prepared this rest—has been announced to us just as it was to them. But it did them no good because they didn't share the faith of those who listened to God.* ³For only we who believe can enter his rest. As for the others, God said,

"In my anger I took an oath:
  'They will never enter my place
    of rest,'"*

even though this rest has been ready since he made the world. ⁴We know it is ready because of the place in the Scriptures where it mentions the seventh day: "On the seventh day God rested from all his work."* ⁵But in the other passage God said, "They will never enter my place of rest."*

⁶So God's rest is there for people to enter, but those who first heard this good news failed to enter because they disobeyed God. ⁷So God set another time for entering his rest, and that time is today. God announced this through David much later in the words already quoted:

3:7-11 Ps 95:7-11.   3:12 Greek *brothers*.   3:15 Ps 95:7-8.   4:2 Some manuscripts read *they didn't combine what they heard with faith*.   4:3 Ps 95:11.   4:4 Gen 2:2.   4:5 Ps 95:11.

"Today when you hear his voice,
don't harden your hearts."*

[8] Now if Joshua had succeeded in giving them this rest, God would not have spoken about another day of rest still to come. [9] So there is a special rest* still waiting for the people of God. [10] For all who have entered into God's rest have rested from their labors, just as God did after creating the world. [11] So let us do our best to enter that rest. But if we disobey God, as the people of Israel did, we will fall.

[12] For the word of God is alive and powerful. It is sharper than the sharpest two-edged sword, cutting between soul and spirit, between joint and marrow. It exposes our innermost thoughts and desires. [13] Nothing in all creation is hidden from God. Everything is naked and exposed before his eyes, and he is the one to whom we are accountable.

Christ Is Our High Priest

[14] So then, since we have a great High Priest who has entered heaven, Jesus the Son of God, let us hold firmly to what we believe. [15] This High Priest of ours understands our weaknesses, for he faced all of the same testings we do, yet he did not sin. [16] So let us come boldly to the throne of our gracious God. There we will receive his mercy, and we will find grace to help us when we need it most.

5 Every high priest is a man chosen to represent other people in their dealings with God. He presents their gifts to God and offers sacrifices for their sins. [2] And he is able to deal gently with ignorant and wayward people because he himself is subject to the same weaknesses. [3] That is why he must offer sacrifices for his own sins as well as theirs.

[4] And no one can become a high priest simply because he wants such an honor. He must be called by God for this work, just as Aaron was. [5] That is why Christ did not honor himself by assuming he could become High Priest. No, he was chosen by God, who said to him,

"You are my Son.
Today I have become your
Father.*"

[6] And in another passage God said to him,

"You are a priest forever in the
order of Melchizedek."*

[7] While Jesus was here on earth, he offered prayers and pleadings, with a loud cry and tears, to the one who could rescue him from death. And God heard his prayers because of his deep reverence for God. [8] Even though Jesus was God's Son, he learned obedience from the things he suffered. [9] In this way, God qualified him as a perfect High Priest, and he became the source of eternal salvation for all those who obey

4:7 Ps 95:7-8. 4:9 Or *a Sabbath rest.* 5:5 Or *Today I reveal you as my Son.* Ps 2:7. 5:6 Ps 110:4.

him. ¹⁰And God designated him to be a High Priest in the order of Melchizedek.

A Call to Spiritual Growth

¹¹There is much more we would like to say about this, but it is difficult to explain, especially since you are spiritually dull and don't seem to listen. ¹²You have been believers so long now that you ought to be teaching others. Instead, you need someone to teach you again the basic things about God's word.* You are like babies who need milk and cannot eat solid food. ¹³For someone who lives on milk is still an infant and doesn't know how to do what is right. ¹⁴Solid food is for those who are mature, who through training have the skill to recognize the difference between right and wrong.

6 So let us stop going over the basic teachings about Christ again and again. Let us go on instead and become mature in our understanding. Surely we don't need to start again with the fundamental importance of repenting from evil deeds* and placing our faith in God. ²You don't need further instruction about baptisms, the laying on of hands, the resurrection of the dead, and eternal judgment. ³And so, God willing, we will move forward to further understanding.

⁴For it is impossible to bring back to repentance those who were once enlightened—those who have experienced the good things of heaven and shared in the Holy Spirit, ⁵who have tasted the goodness of the word of God and the power of the age to come—⁶and who then turn away from God. It is impossible to bring such people back to repentance; by rejecting the Son of God, they themselves are nailing him to the cross once again and holding him up to public shame.

⁷When the ground soaks up the falling rain and bears a good crop for the farmer, it has God's blessing. ⁸But if a field bears thorns and thistles, it is useless. The farmer will soon condemn that field and burn it.

⁹Dear friends, even though we are talking this way, we really don't believe it applies to you. We are confident that you are meant for better things, things that come with salvation. ¹⁰For God is not unjust. He will not forget how hard you have worked for him and how you have shown your love to him by caring for other believers,* as you still do. ¹¹Our great desire is that you will keep on loving others as long as life lasts, in order to make certain that what you hope for will come true. ¹²Then you will not become spiritually dull and indifferent. Instead, you will follow the example of those who are going to inherit God's promises because of their faith and endurance.

5:12 Or *about the oracles of God.* **6:1** Greek *from dead works.* **6:10** Greek *for God's holy people.*

God's Promises Bring Hope

¹³For example, there was God's promise to Abraham. Since there was no one greater to swear by, God took an oath in his own name, saying:

¹⁴ "I will certainly bless you,
   and I will multiply your descendants beyond number."*

¹⁵Then Abraham waited patiently, and he received what God had promised.

¹⁶Now when people take an oath, they call on someone greater than themselves to hold them to it. And without any question that oath is binding. ¹⁷God also bound himself with an oath, so that those who received the promise could be perfectly sure that he would never change his mind. ¹⁸So God has given both his promise and his oath. These two things are unchangeable because it is impossible for God to lie. Therefore, we who have fled to him for refuge can have great confidence as we hold to the hope that lies before us. ¹⁹This hope is a strong and trustworthy anchor for our souls. It leads us through the curtain into God's inner sanctuary. ²⁰Jesus has already gone in there for us. He has become our eternal High Priest in the order of Melchizedek.

Melchizedek Is Greater Than Abraham

7 This Melchizedek was king of the city of Salem and also a priest of God Most High. When Abraham was returning home after winning a great battle against the kings, Melchizedek met him and blessed him. ²Then Abraham took a tenth of all he had captured in battle and gave it to Melchizedek. The name Melchizedek means "king of justice," and king of Salem means "king of peace." ³There is no record of his father or mother or any of his ancestors—no beginning or end to his life. He remains a priest forever, resembling the Son of God.

⁴Consider then how great this Melchizedek was. Even Abraham, the great patriarch of Israel, recognized this by giving him a tenth of what he had taken in battle. ⁵Now the law of Moses required that the priests, who are descendants of Levi, must collect a tithe from the rest of the people of Israel,* who are also descendants of Abraham. ⁶But Melchizedek, who was not a descendant of Levi, collected a tenth from Abraham. And Melchizedek placed a blessing upon Abraham, the one who had already received the promises of God. ⁷And without question, the person who has the power to give a blessing is greater than the one who is blessed.

⁸The priests who collect tithes are men who die, so Melchizedek is greater than they are, because we are told that he lives on. ⁹In addition, we might even say that these Levites—the ones who collect the

6:14 Gen 22:17. **7:5** Greek *from their brothers.*

tithe—paid a tithe to Melchizedek when their ancestor Abraham paid a tithe to him. ¹⁰For although Levi wasn't born yet, the seed from which he came was in Abraham's body when Melchizedek collected the tithe from him.

¹¹So if the priesthood of Levi, on which the law was based, could have achieved the perfection God intended, why did God need to establish a different priesthood, with a priest in the order of Melchizedek instead of the order of Levi and Aaron?*

¹²And if the priesthood is changed, the law must also be changed to permit it. ¹³For the priest we are talking about belongs to a different tribe, whose members have never served at the altar as priests. ¹⁴What I mean is, our Lord came from the tribe of Judah, and Moses never mentioned priests coming from that tribe.

Jesus Is like Melchizedek

¹⁵This change has been made very clear since a different priest, who is like Melchizedek, has appeared. ¹⁶Jesus became a priest, not by meeting the physical requirement of belonging to the tribe of Levi, but by the power of a life that cannot be destroyed. ¹⁷And the psalmist pointed this out when he prophesied,

"You are a priest forever in the
order of Melchizedek."*

¹⁸Yes, the old requirement about the priesthood was set aside because it was weak and useless. ¹⁹For the law never made anything perfect. But now we have confidence in a better hope, through which we draw near to God.

²⁰This new system was established with a solemn oath. Aaron's descendants became priests without such an oath, ²¹but there was an oath regarding Jesus. For God said to him,

"The LORD has taken an oath and
will not break his vow:
'You are a priest forever.'"*

²²Because of this oath, Jesus is the one who guarantees this better covenant with God.

²³There were many priests under the old system, for death prevented them from remaining in office. ²⁴But because Jesus lives forever, his priesthood lasts forever. ²⁵Therefore he is able, once and forever, to save* those who come to God through him. He lives forever to intercede with God on their behalf.

²⁶He is the kind of high priest we need because he is holy and blameless, unstained by sin. He has been set apart from sinners and has been given the highest place of honor in heaven.* ²⁷Unlike those other high priests, he does not need to offer sacrifices every day. They did this for their own sins first and then for

7:11 Greek *the order of Aaron?* 7:17 Ps 110:4. 7:21 Ps 110:4. 7:25 Or *is able to save completely.*
7:26 Or *has been exalted higher than the heavens.*

the sins of the people. But Jesus did this once for all when he offered himself as the sacrifice for the people's sins. 28 The law appointed high priests who were limited by human weakness. But after the law was given, God appointed his Son with an oath, and his Son has been made the perfect High Priest forever.

Christ Is Our High Priest

8 Here is the main point: We have a High Priest who sat down in the place of honor beside the throne of the majestic God in heaven. 2There he ministers in the heavenly Tabernacle,* the true place of worship that was built by the Lord and not by human hands.

3And since every high priest is required to offer gifts and sacrifices, our High Priest must make an offering, too. 4If he were here on earth, he would not even be a priest, since there already are priests who offer the gifts required by the law. 5They serve in a system of worship that is only a copy, a shadow of the real one in heaven. For when Moses was getting ready to build the Tabernacle, God gave him this warning: "Be sure that you make everything according to the pattern I have shown you here on the mountain."*

6But now Jesus, our High Priest, has been given a ministry that is far superior to the old priesthood, for he is the one who mediates for us a far better covenant with God, based on better promises.

7If the first covenant had been faultless, there would have been no need for a second covenant to replace it. 8But when God found fault with the people, he said:

"The day is coming, says the Lord,
    when I will make a new covenant
    with the people of Israel and Judah.
9 This covenant will not be like the one
    I made with their ancestors
when I took them by the hand
    and led them out of the land of Egypt.
They did not remain faithful
    to my covenant,
    so I turned my back on them,
    says the Lord.
10 But this is the new covenant
    I will make
    with the people of Israel on that day,* says the Lord:
I will put my laws in their minds,
    and I will write them on their hearts.
I will be their God,
    and they will be my people.
11 And they will not need to teach their neighbors,
    nor will they need to teach their relatives,*
    saying, 'You should know the Lord.'

8:2 Or *tent;* also in 8:5. 8:5 Exod 25:40; 26:30. 8:10 Greek *after those days.* 8:11 Greek *their brother.*

For everyone, from the least
to the greatest,
will know me already.
[12] And I will forgive their
wickedness,
and I will never again
remember their sins."*

[13]When God speaks of a "new" covenant, it means he has made the first one obsolete. It is now out of date and will soon disappear.

Old Rules about Worship

9 That first covenant between God and Israel had regulations for worship and a place of worship here on earth. [2]There were two rooms in that Tabernacle.* In the first room were a lampstand, a table, and sacred loaves of bread on the table. This room was called the Holy Place. [3]Then there was a curtain, and behind the curtain was the second room* called the Most Holy Place. [4]In that room were a gold incense altar and a wooden chest called the Ark of the Covenant, which was covered with gold on all sides. Inside the Ark were a gold jar containing manna, Aaron's staff that sprouted leaves, and the stone tablets of the covenant. [5]Above the Ark were the cherubim of divine glory, whose wings stretched out over the Ark's cover, the place of atonement. But we cannot explain these things in detail now.

[6]When these things were all in place, the priests regularly entered the first room* as they performed their religious duties. [7]But only the high priest ever entered the Most Holy Place, and only once a year. And he always offered blood for his own sins and for the sins the people had committed in ignorance. [8]By these regulations the Holy Spirit revealed that the entrance to the Most Holy Place was not freely open as long as the Tabernacle* and the system it represented were still in use.

[9]This is an illustration pointing to the present time. For the gifts and sacrifices that the priests offer are not able to cleanse the consciences of the people who bring them. [10]For that old system deals only with food and drink and various cleansing ceremonies—physical regulations that were in effect only until a better system could be established.

Christ Is the Perfect Sacrifice

[11]So Christ has now become the High Priest over all the good things that have come.* He has entered that greater, more perfect Tabernacle in heaven, which was not made by human hands and is not part of this created world. [12]With his own blood—not the blood of goats and calves—he entered the Most Holy Place once for all time and secured our redemption forever.

[13]Under the old system, the blood

8:8-12 Jer 31:31-34.   **9:2** Or *tent;* also in 9:11, 21.   **9:3** Greek *second tent.*   **9:6** Greek *first tent.*   **9:8** Or *the first room;* Greek reads *the first tent.*   **9:11** Some manuscripts read *that are about to come.*

of goats and bulls and the ashes of a heifer could cleanse people's bodies from ceremonial impurity. [14]Just think how much more the blood of Christ will purify our consciences from sinful deeds* so that we can worship the living God. For by the power of the eternal Spirit, Christ offered himself to God as a perfect sacrifice for our sins. [15]That is why he is the one who mediates a new covenant between God and people, so that all who are called can receive the eternal inheritance God has promised them. For Christ died to set them free from the penalty of the sins they had committed under that first covenant.

[16]Now when someone leaves a will,* it is necessary to prove that the person who made it is dead.* [17]The will goes into effect only after the person's death. While the person who made it is still alive, the will cannot be put into effect.

[18]That is why even the first covenant was put into effect with the blood of an animal. [19]For after Moses had read each of God's commandments to all the people, he took the blood of calves and goats,* along with water, and sprinkled both the book of God's law and all the people, using hyssop branches and scarlet wool. [20]Then he said, "This blood confirms the covenant God has made with you."* [21]And in the same way, he sprinkled blood on the Tabernacle and on everything used for worship. [22]In fact, according to the law of Moses, nearly everything was purified with blood. For without the shedding of blood, there is no forgiveness.

[23]That is why the Tabernacle and everything in it, which were copies of things in heaven, had to be purified by the blood of animals. But the real things in heaven had to be purified with far better sacrifices than the blood of animals.

[24]For Christ did not enter into a holy place made with human hands, which was only a copy of the true one in heaven. He entered into heaven itself to appear now before God on our behalf. [25]And he did not enter heaven to offer himself again and again, like the high priest here on earth who enters the Most Holy Place year after year with the blood of an animal. [26]If that had been necessary, Christ would have had to die again and again, ever since the world began. But now, once for all time, he has appeared at the end of the age* to remove sin by his own death as a sacrifice.

[27]And just as each person is destined to die once and after that comes judgment, [28]so also Christ was offered once for all time as a sacrifice to take away the sins of many people. He will come again,

9:14 Greek *from dead works.* 9:16a Or *covenant;* also in 9:17. 9:16b Or *Now when someone makes a covenant, it is necessary to ratify it with the death of a sacrifice.* 9:19 Some manuscripts do not include *and goats.* 9:20 Exod 24:8. 9:26 Greek *the ages.*

not to deal with our sins, but to bring salvation to all who are eagerly waiting for him.

Christ's Sacrifice Once for All

10 The old system under the law of Moses was only a shadow, a dim preview of the good things to come, not the good things themselves. The sacrifices under that system were repeated again and again, year after year, but they were never able to provide perfect cleansing for those who came to worship. ²If they could have provided perfect cleansing, the sacrifices would have stopped, for the worshipers would have been purified once for all time, and their feelings of guilt would have disappeared.

³But instead, those sacrifices actually reminded them of their sins year after year. ⁴For it is not possible for the blood of bulls and goats to take away sins. ⁵That is why, when Christ* came into the world, he said to God,

> "You did not want animal
>   sacrifices or sin offerings.
> But you have given me a body
>   to offer.
> ⁶ You were not pleased with burnt
>   offerings
>   or other offerings for sin.
> ⁷ Then I said, 'Look, I have come
>   to do your will, O God—
>   as is written about me in the
>   Scriptures.'"*

⁸First, Christ said, "You did not want animal sacrifices or sin offerings or burnt offerings or other offerings for sin, nor were you pleased with them" (though they are required by the law of Moses). ⁹Then he said, "Look, I have come to do your will." He cancels the first covenant in order to put the second into effect. ¹⁰For God's will was for us to be made holy by the sacrifice of the body of Jesus Christ, once for all time.

¹¹Under the old covenant, the priest stands and ministers before the altar day after day, offering the same sacrifices again and again, which can never take away sins. ¹²But our High Priest offered himself to God as a single sacrifice for sins, good for all time. Then he sat down in the place of honor at God's right hand. ¹³There he waits until his enemies are humbled and made a footstool under his feet. ¹⁴For by that one offering he forever made perfect those who are being made holy.

¹⁵And the Holy Spirit also testifies that this is so. For he says,

> ¹⁶ "This is the new covenant I will
>   make
>   with my people on that day,*
>   says the LORD:
> I will put my laws in their
>   hearts,
>   and I will write them on their
>   minds."*

10:5 Greek *he;* also in 10:8. 10:5-7 Ps 40:6-8 (Greek version). 10:16a Greek *after those days.*
10:16b Jer 31:33a.

¹⁷Then he says,

> "I will never again remember
> their sins and lawless deeds."*

¹⁸And when sins have been forgiven, there is no need to offer any more sacrifices.

A Call to Persevere

¹⁹And so, dear brothers and sisters,* we can boldly enter heaven's Most Holy Place because of the blood of Jesus. ²⁰By his death,* Jesus opened a new and life-giving way through the curtain into the Most Holy Place. ²¹And since we have a great High Priest who rules over God's house, ²²let us go right into the presence of God with sincere hearts fully trusting him. For our guilty consciences have been sprinkled with Christ's blood to make us clean, and our bodies have been washed with pure water. ²³Let us hold tightly without wavering to the hope we affirm, for God can be trusted to keep his promise. ²⁴Let us think of ways to motivate one another to acts of love and good works. ²⁵And let us not neglect our meeting together, as some people do, but encourage one another, especially now that the day of his return is drawing near.

²⁶Dear friends, if we deliberately continue sinning after we have received knowledge of the truth, there is no longer any sacrifice that will cover these sins. ²⁷There is only the terrible expectation of God's judgment and the raging fire that will consume his enemies. ²⁸For anyone who refused to obey the law of Moses was put to death without mercy on the testimony of two or three witnesses. ²⁹Just think how much worse the punishment will be for those who have trampled on the Son of God, and have treated the blood of the covenant, which made us holy, as if it were common and unholy, and have insulted and disdained the Holy Spirit who brings God's mercy to us. ³⁰For we know the one who said,

> "I will take revenge.
> I will pay them back."*

He also said,

> "The LORD will judge his own
> people."*

³¹It is a terrible thing to fall into the hands of the living God.

³²Think back on those early days when you first learned about Christ.* Remember how you remained faithful even though it meant terrible suffering. ³³Sometimes you were exposed to public ridicule and were beaten, and sometimes you helped others who were suffering the same things. ³⁴You suffered along with those who were thrown into jail, and when all you owned was taken from

10:17 Jer 31:34b.   10:19 Greek *brothers*.   10:20 Greek *Through his flesh*.   10:30a Deut 32:35.
10:30b Deut 32:36.   10:32 Greek *when you were first enlightened*.

you, you accepted it with joy. You knew there were better things waiting for you that will last forever.

³⁵So do not throw away this confident trust in the Lord. Remember the great reward it brings you! ³⁶Patient endurance is what you need now, so that you will continue to do God's will. Then you will receive all that he has promised.

³⁷ "For in just a little while,
     the Coming One will come and
     not delay.
³⁸ And my righteous ones will live
     by faith.*
     But I will take no pleasure in
     anyone who turns away."*

³⁹But we are not like those who turn away from God to their own destruction. We are the faithful ones, whose souls will be saved.

Great Examples of Faith

11 Faith shows the reality of what we hope for; it is the evidence of things we cannot see. ²Through their faith, the people in days of old earned a good reputation.

³By faith we understand that the entire universe was formed at God's command, that what we now see did not come from anything that can be seen.

⁴It was by faith that Abel brought a more acceptable offering to God than Cain did. Abel's offering gave evidence that he was a righteous man, and God showed his approval of his gifts. Although Abel is long dead, he still speaks to us by his example of faith.

⁵It was by faith that Enoch was taken up to heaven without dying—"he disappeared, because God took him."* For before he was taken up, he was known as a person who pleased God. ⁶And it is impossible to please God without faith. Anyone who wants to come to him must believe that God exists and that he rewards those who sincerely seek him.

⁷It was by faith that Noah built a large boat to save his family from the flood. He obeyed God, who warned him about things that had never happened before. By his faith Noah condemned the rest of the world, and he received the righteousness that comes by faith.

⁸It was by faith that Abraham obeyed when God called him to leave home and go to another land that God would give him as his inheritance. He went without knowing where he was going. ⁹And even when he reached the land God promised him, he lived there by faith—for he was like a foreigner, living in tents. And so did Isaac and Jacob, who inherited the same promise. ¹⁰Abraham was confidently looking forward to a city with eternal foundations, a city designed and built by God.

10:38 Or *my righteous ones will live by their faithfulness;* Greek reads *my righteous one will live by faith.* **10:37-38** Hab 2:3-4. **11:5** Gen 5:24.

¹¹It was by faith that even Sarah was able to have a child, though she was barren and was too old. She believed* that God would keep his promise. ¹²And so a whole nation came from this one man who was as good as dead—a nation with so many people that, like the stars in the sky and the sand on the seashore, there is no way to count them.

¹³All these people died still believing what God had promised them. They did not receive what was promised, but they saw it all from a distance and welcomed it. They agreed that they were foreigners and nomads here on earth. ¹⁴Obviously people who say such things are looking forward to a country they can call their own. ¹⁵If they had longed for the country they came from, they could have gone back. ¹⁶But they were looking for a better place, a heavenly homeland. That is why God is not ashamed to be called their God, for he has prepared a city for them.

¹⁷It was by faith that Abraham offered Isaac as a sacrifice when God was testing him. Abraham, who had received God's promises, was ready to sacrifice his only son, Isaac, ¹⁸even though God had told him, "Isaac is the son through whom your descendants will be counted."* ¹⁹Abraham reasoned that if Isaac died, God was able to bring him back to life again. And in a sense, Abraham did receive his son back from the dead.

²⁰It was by faith that Isaac promised blessings for the future to his sons, Jacob and Esau.

²¹It was by faith that Jacob, when he was old and dying, blessed each of Joseph's sons and bowed in worship as he leaned on his staff.

²²It was by faith that Joseph, when he was about to die, said confidently that the people of Israel would leave Egypt. He even commanded them to take his bones with them when they left.

²³It was by faith that Moses' parents hid him for three months when he was born. They saw that God had given them an unusual child, and they were not afraid to disobey the king's command.

²⁴It was by faith that Moses, when he grew up, refused to be called the son of Pharaoh's daughter. ²⁵He chose to share the oppression of God's people instead of enjoying the fleeting pleasures of sin. ²⁶He thought it was better to suffer for the sake of Christ than to own the treasures of Egypt, for he was looking ahead to his great reward. ²⁷It was by faith that Moses left the land of Egypt, not fearing the king's anger. He kept right on going because he kept his eyes on the one who is invisible. ²⁸It was by faith that Moses commanded the people of Israel to keep the Passover and to

11:11 Or *It was by faith that he [Abraham] was able to have a child, even though Sarah was barren and he was too old. He believed.* **11:18** Gen 21:12.

sprinkle blood on the doorposts so that the angel of death would not kill their firstborn sons.

²⁹It was by faith that the people of Israel went right through the Red Sea as though they were on dry ground. But when the Egyptians tried to follow, they were all drowned.

³⁰It was by faith that the people of Israel marched around Jericho for seven days, and the walls came crashing down.

³¹It was by faith that Rahab the prostitute was not destroyed with the people in her city who refused to obey God. For she had given a friendly welcome to the spies.

³²How much more do I need to say? It would take too long to recount the stories of the faith of Gideon, Barak, Samson, Jephthah, David, Samuel, and all the prophets. ³³By faith these people overthrew kingdoms, ruled with justice, and received what God had promised them. They shut the mouths of lions, ³⁴quenched the flames of fire, and escaped death by the edge of the sword. Their weakness was turned to strength. They became strong in battle and put whole armies to flight. ³⁵Women received their loved ones back again from death.

But others were tortured, refusing to turn from God in order to be set free. They placed their hope in a better life after the resurrection. ³⁶Some were jeered at, and their backs were cut open with whips. Others were chained in prisons. ³⁷Some died by stoning, some were sawed in half,* and others were killed with the sword. Some went about wearing skins of sheep and goats, destitute and oppressed and mistreated. ³⁸They were too good for this world, wandering over deserts and mountains, hiding in caves and holes in the ground.

³⁹All these people earned a good reputation because of their faith, yet none of them received all that God had promised. ⁴⁰For God had something better in mind for us, so that they would not reach perfection without us.

God's Discipline Proves His Love

12 Therefore, since we are surrounded by such a huge crowd of witnesses to the life of faith, let us strip off every weight that slows us down, especially the sin that so easily trips us up. And let us run with endurance the race God has set before us. ²We do this by keeping our eyes on Jesus, the champion who initiates and perfects our faith.* Because of the joy* awaiting him, he endured the cross, disregarding its shame. Now he is seated in the place of honor beside God's throne. ³Think of all the hostility he endured from sinful

11:37 Some manuscripts add *some were tested.* **12:2a** Or *Jesus, the originator and perfecter of our faith.* **12:2b** Or *Instead of the joy.*

people;* then you won't become weary and give up. ⁴After all, you have not yet given your lives in your struggle against sin.

⁵And have you forgotten the encouraging words God spoke to you as his children?* He said,

> "My child,* don't make light of
>   the LORD's discipline,
> and don't give up when he
>   corrects you.
> ⁶ For the LORD disciplines those
>   he loves,
> and he punishes each one he
>   accepts as his child."*

⁷As you endure this divine discipline, remember that God is treating you as his own children. Who ever heard of a child who is never disciplined by its father? ⁸If God doesn't discipline you as he does all of his children, it means that you are illegitimate and are not really his children at all. ⁹Since we respected our earthly fathers who disciplined us, shouldn't we submit even more to the discipline of the Father of our spirits, and live forever?*

¹⁰For our earthly fathers disciplined us for a few years, doing the best they knew how. But God's discipline is always good for us, so that we might share in his holiness. ¹¹No discipline is enjoyable while it is happening—it's painful! But afterward there will be a peaceful harvest of right living for those who are trained in this way.

¹²So take a new grip with your tired hands and strengthen your weak knees. ¹³Mark out a straight path for your feet so that those who are weak and lame will not fall but become strong.

A Call to Listen to God

¹⁴Work at living in peace with everyone, and work at living a holy life, for those who are not holy will not see the Lord. ¹⁵Look after each other so that none of you fails to receive the grace of God. Watch out that no poisonous root of bitterness grows up to trouble you, corrupting many. ¹⁶Make sure that no one is immoral or godless like Esau, who traded his birthright as the firstborn son for a single meal. ¹⁷You know that afterward, when he wanted his father's blessing, he was rejected. It was too late for repentance, even though he begged with bitter tears.

¹⁸You have not come to a physical mountain,* to a place of flaming fire, darkness, gloom, and whirlwind, as the Israelites did at Mount Sinai. ¹⁹For they heard an awesome trumpet blast and a voice so terrible that they begged God to stop speaking. ²⁰They staggered back under God's command: "If even an animal touches the mountain, it must be

12:3 Some manuscripts read *Think of how people hurt themselves by opposing him.* **12:5a** Greek *sons;* also in 12:7, 8. **12:5b** Greek *son;* also in 12:6, 7. **12:5-6** Prov 3:11-12 (Greek version). **12:9** Or *and really live?* **12:18** Greek *to something that can be touched.*

stoned to death."* ²¹Moses himself was so frightened at the sight that he said, "I am terrified and trembling."*

²²No, you have come to Mount Zion, to the city of the living God, the heavenly Jerusalem, and to countless thousands of angels in a joyful gathering. ²³You have come to the assembly of God's firstborn children, whose names are written in heaven. You have come to God himself, who is the judge over all things. You have come to the spirits of the righteous ones in heaven who have now been made perfect. ²⁴You have come to Jesus, the one who mediates the new covenant between God and people, and to the sprinkled blood, which speaks of forgiveness instead of crying out for vengeance like the blood of Abel.

²⁵Be careful that you do not refuse to listen to the One who is speaking. For if the people of Israel did not escape when they refused to listen to Moses, the earthly messenger, we will certainly not escape if we reject the One who speaks to us from heaven! ²⁶When God spoke from Mount Sinai his voice shook the earth, but now he makes another promise: "Once again I will shake not only the earth but the heavens also."* ²⁷This means that all of creation will be shaken and removed, so that only unshakable things will remain.

²⁸Since we are receiving a Kingdom that is unshakable, let us be thankful and please God by worshiping him with holy fear and awe. ²⁹For our God is a devouring fire.

Concluding Words

13 Keep on loving each other as brothers and sisters.* ²Don't forget to show hospitality to strangers, for some who have done this have entertained angels without realizing it! ³Remember those in prison, as if you were there yourself. Remember also those being mistreated, as if you felt their pain in your own bodies.

⁴Give honor to marriage, and remain faithful to one another in marriage. God will surely judge people who are immoral and those who commit adultery.

⁵Don't love money; be satisfied with what you have. For God has said,

"I will never fail you.
   I will never abandon you."*

⁶So we can say with confidence,

"The LORD is my helper,
   so I will have no fear.
What can mere people
   do to me?"*

⁷Remember your leaders who taught you the word of God. Think of all the good that has come from their lives, and follow the example of their faith.

12:20 Exod 19:13.   **12:21** Deut 9:19.   **12:26** Hag 2:6.   **13:1** Greek *Continue in brotherly love.*
13:5 Deut 31:6, 8.   **13:6** Ps 118:6.

⁸Jesus Christ is the same yesterday, today, and forever. ⁹So do not be attracted by strange, new ideas. Your strength comes from God's grace, not from rules about food, which don't help those who follow them.

¹⁰We have an altar from which the priests in the Tabernacle* have no right to eat. ¹¹Under the old system, the high priest brought the blood of animals into the Holy Place as a sacrifice for sin, and the bodies of the animals were burned outside the camp. ¹²So also Jesus suffered and died outside the city gates to make his people holy by means of his own blood. ¹³So let us go out to him, outside the camp, and bear the disgrace he bore. ¹⁴For this world is not our permanent home; we are looking forward to a home yet to come.

¹⁵Therefore, let us offer through Jesus a continual sacrifice of praise to God, proclaiming our allegiance to his name. ¹⁶And don't forget to do good and to share with those in need. These are the sacrifices that please God.

¹⁷Obey your spiritual leaders, and do what they say. Their work is to watch over your souls, and they are accountable to God. Give them reason to do this with joy and not with sorrow. That would certainly not be for your benefit.

¹⁸Pray for us, for our conscience is clear and we want to live honorably in everything we do. ¹⁹And especially pray that I will be able to come back to you soon.

²⁰ Now may the God of peace—
who brought up from the dead
    our Lord Jesus,
the great Shepherd of the sheep,
and ratified an eternal
    covenant with his blood—
²¹ may he equip you with all you
    need
    for doing his will.
May he produce in you,*
    through the power of Jesus
    Christ,
every good thing that is pleasing
    to him.
    All glory to him forever and
    ever! Amen.

²²I urge you, dear brothers and sisters,* to pay attention to what I have written in this brief exhortation.

²³I want you to know that our brother Timothy has been released from jail. If he comes here soon, I will bring him with me to see you.

²⁴Greet all your leaders and all the believers there.* The believers from Italy send you their greetings.

²⁵May God's grace be with you all.

13:10 Or *tent.* 13:21 Some manuscripts read *in us.* 13:22 Greek *brothers.* 13:24 Greek *all of God's holy people.*

James

Greetings from James

1 This letter is from James, a slave of God and of the Lord Jesus Christ.

I am writing to the "twelve tribes" —Jewish believers scattered abroad.

Greetings!

Faith and Endurance

²Dear brothers and sisters,* when troubles of any kind come your way, consider it an opportunity for great joy. ³For you know that when your faith is tested, your endurance has a chance to grow. ⁴So let it grow, for when your endurance is fully developed, you will be perfect and complete, needing nothing.

⁵If you need wisdom, ask our generous God, and he will give it to you. He will not rebuke you for asking. ⁶But when you ask him, be sure that your faith is in God alone. Do not waver, for a person with divided loyalty is as unsettled as a wave of the sea that is blown and tossed by the wind. ⁷Such people should not expect to receive anything from the Lord. ⁸Their loyalty is divided between God and the world, and they are unstable in everything they do.

⁹Believers who are* poor have something to boast about, for God has honored them. ¹⁰And those who are rich should boast that God has humbled them. They will fade away like a little flower in the field. ¹¹The hot sun rises and the grass withers; the little flower droops and falls, and its beauty fades away. In the same way, the rich will fade away with all of their achievements.

¹²God blesses those who patiently endure testing and temptation. Afterward they will receive the crown of life that God has promised to those who love him. ¹³And remember, when you are being tempted, do not say, "God is tempting me." God is never tempted to do wrong,* and he never tempts anyone else. ¹⁴Temptation comes from our own desires, which entice us and drag us away. ¹⁵These desires give birth to sinful actions. And when sin is allowed to grow, it gives birth to death.

¹⁶So don't be misled, my dear brothers and sisters. ¹⁷Whatever is good and perfect is a gift coming down to us from God our Father, who created all the lights in the heavens.* He never changes or casts

---

1:2 Greek *brothers;* also in 1:16, 19.   **1:9** Greek *The brother who is.*   **1:13** Or *God should not be put to a test by evil people.*   **1:17a** Greek *from above, from the Father of lights.*

a shifting shadow.* ¹⁸He chose to give birth to us by giving us his true word. And we, out of all creation, became his prized possession.*

Listening and Doing

¹⁹Understand this, my dear brothers and sisters: You must all be quick to listen, slow to speak, and slow to get angry. ²⁰Human anger* does not produce the righteousness* God desires. ²¹So get rid of all the filth and evil in your lives, and humbly accept the word God has planted in your hearts, for it has the power to save your souls.

²²But don't just listen to God's word. You must do what it says. Otherwise, you are only fooling yourselves. ²³For if you listen to the word and don't obey, it is like glancing at your face in a mirror. ²⁴You see yourself, walk away, and forget what you look like. ²⁵But if you look carefully into the perfect law that sets you free, and if you do what it says and don't forget what you heard, then God will bless you for doing it.

²⁶If you claim to be religious but don't control your tongue, you are fooling yourself, and your religion is worthless. ²⁷Pure and genuine religion in the sight of God the Father means caring for orphans and widows in their distress and refusing to let the world corrupt you.

A Warning against Prejudice

2 My dear brothers and sisters,* how can you claim to have faith in our glorious Lord Jesus Christ if you favor some people over others? ²For example, suppose someone comes into your meeting* dressed in fancy clothes and expensive jewelry, and another comes in who is poor and dressed in dirty clothes. ³If you give special attention and a good seat to the rich person, but you say to the poor one, "You can stand over there, or else sit on the floor"—well, ⁴doesn't this discrimination show that your judgments are guided by evil motives?

⁵Listen to me, dear brothers and sisters. Hasn't God chosen the poor in this world to be rich in faith? Aren't they the ones who will inherit the Kingdom he promised to those who love him? ⁶But you dishonor the poor! Isn't it the rich who oppress you and drag you into court? ⁷Aren't they the ones who slander Jesus Christ, whose noble name* you bear?

⁸Yes indeed, it is good when you obey the royal law as found in the Scriptures: "Love your neighbor as yourself."* ⁹But if you favor some people over others, you are committing a sin. You are guilty of breaking the law.

¹⁰For the person who keeps all of

1:17b Some manuscripts read *He never changes, as a shifting shadow does.* **1:18** Greek *we became a kind of firstfruit of his creatures.* **1:20a** Greek *A man's anger.* **1:20b** Or *the justice.* **2:1** Greek *brothers;* also in 2:5, 14. **2:2** Greek *your synagogue.* **2:7** Greek *slander the noble name.* **2:8** Lev 19:18.

the laws except one is as guilty as a person who has broken all of God's laws. [11]For the same God who said, "You must not commit adultery," also said, "You must not murder."* So if you murder someone but do not commit adultery, you have still broken the law.

[12]So whatever you say or whatever you do, remember that you will be judged by the law that sets you free. [13]There will be no mercy for those who have not shown mercy to others. But if you have been merciful, God will be merciful when he judges you.

Faith without Good Deeds Is Dead

[14]What good is it, dear brothers and sisters, if you say you have faith but don't show it by your actions? Can that kind of faith save anyone? [15]Suppose you see a brother or sister who has no food or clothing, [16]and you say, "Good-bye and have a good day; stay warm and eat well"—but then you don't give that person any food or clothing. What good does that do?

[17]So you see, faith by itself isn't enough. Unless it produces good deeds, it is dead and useless.

[18]Now someone may argue, "Some people have faith; others have good deeds." But I say, "How can you show me your faith if you don't have good deeds? I will show you my faith by my good deeds."

[19]You say you have faith, for you believe that there is one God.* Good for you! Even the demons believe this, and they tremble in terror. [20]How foolish! Can't you see that faith without good deeds is useless?

[21]Don't you remember that our ancestor Abraham was shown to be right with God by his actions when he offered his son Isaac on the altar? [22]You see, his faith and his actions worked together. His actions made his faith complete. [23]And so it happened just as the Scriptures say: "Abraham believed God, and God counted him as righteous because of his faith."* He was even called the friend of God.* [24]So you see, we are shown to be right with God by what we do, not by faith alone.

[25]Rahab the prostitute is another example. She was shown to be right with God by her actions when she hid those messengers and sent them safely away by a different road. [26]Just as the body is dead without breath,* so also faith is dead without good works.

Controlling the Tongue

3 Dear brothers and sisters,* not many of you should become teachers in the church, for we who teach will be judged more strictly. [2]Indeed, we all make many mistakes. For if we could control our tongues, we would be perfect and could also control ourselves in every other way.

2:11 Exod 20:13-14; Deut 5:17-18. **2:19** Some manuscripts read *that God is one;* see Deut 6:4. **2:23a** Gen 15:6. **2:23b** See Isa 41:8. **2:26** Or *without spirit.* **3:1** Greek *brothers;* also in 3:10.

³We can make a large horse go wherever we want by means of a small bit in its mouth. ⁴And a small rudder makes a huge ship turn wherever the pilot chooses to go, even though the winds are strong. ⁵In the same way, the tongue is a small thing that makes grand speeches.

But a tiny spark can set a great forest on fire. ⁶And among all the parts of the body, the tongue is a flame of fire. It is a whole world of wickedness, corrupting your entire body. It can set your whole life on fire, for it is set on fire by hell itself.*

⁷People can tame all kinds of animals, birds, reptiles, and fish, ⁸but no one can tame the tongue. It is restless and evil, full of deadly poison. ⁹Sometimes it praises our Lord and Father, and sometimes it curses those who have been made in the image of God. ¹⁰And so blessing and cursing come pouring out of the same mouth. Surely, my brothers and sisters, this is not right! ¹¹Does a spring of water bubble out with both fresh water and bitter water? ¹²Does a fig tree produce olives, or a grapevine produce figs? No, and you can't draw fresh water from a salty spring.*

True Wisdom Comes from God

¹³If you are wise and understand God's ways, prove it by living an honorable life, doing good works with the humility that comes from wisdom. ¹⁴But if you are bitterly jealous and there is selfish ambition in your heart, don't cover up the truth with boasting and lying. ¹⁵For jealousy and selfishness are not God's kind of wisdom. Such things are earthly, unspiritual, and demonic. ¹⁶For wherever there is jealousy and selfish ambition, there you will find disorder and evil of every kind.

¹⁷But the wisdom from above is first of all pure. It is also peace loving, gentle at all times, and willing to yield to others. It is full of mercy and the fruit of good deeds. It shows no favoritism and is always sincere. ¹⁸And those who are peacemakers will plant seeds of peace and reap a harvest of righteousness.*

Drawing Close to God

4 What is causing the quarrels and fights among you? Don't they come from the evil desires at war within you? ²You want what you don't have, so you scheme and kill to get it. You are jealous of what others have, but you can't get it, so you fight and wage war to take it away from them. Yet you don't have what you want because you don't ask God for it. ³And even when you ask, you don't get it because your motives are all wrong—you want only what will give you pleasure.

⁴You adulterers!* Don't you realize that friendship with the world

3:6 Or *for it will burn in hell* (Greek *Gehenna*).   **3:12** Greek *from salt.*   **3:18** Or *of good things,* or *of justice.*   **4:4** Greek *You adulteresses!*

makes you an enemy of God? I say it again: If you want to be a friend of the world, you make yourself an enemy of God. [5]Do you think the Scriptures have no meaning? They say that God is passionate that the spirit he has placed within us should be faithful to him.* [6]And he gives grace generously. As the Scriptures say,

> "God opposes the proud
>   but gives grace to the humble."*

[7]So humble yourselves before God. Resist the devil, and he will flee from you. [8]Come close to God, and God will come close to you. Wash your hands, you sinners; purify your hearts, for your loyalty is divided between God and the world. [9]Let there be tears for what you have done. Let there be sorrow and deep grief. Let there be sadness instead of laughter, and gloom instead of joy. [10]Humble yourselves before the Lord, and he will lift you up in honor.

Warning against Judging Others

[11]Don't speak evil against each other, dear brothers and sisters.* If you criticize and judge each other, then you are criticizing and judging God's law. But your job is to obey the law, not to judge whether it applies to you. [12]God alone, who gave the law, is the Judge. He alone has the power to save or to destroy. So what right do you have to judge your neighbor?

Warning about Self-Confidence

[13]Look here, you who say, "Today or tomorrow we are going to a certain town and will stay there a year. We will do business there and make a profit." [14]How do you know what your life will be like tomorrow? Your life is like the morning fog—it's here a little while, then it's gone. [15]What you ought to say is, "If the Lord wants us to, we will live and do this or that." [16]Otherwise you are boasting about your own pretentious plans, and all such boasting is evil.

[17]Remember, it is sin to know what you ought to do and then not do it.

Warning to the Rich

5 Look here, you rich people: Weep and groan with anguish because of all the terrible troubles ahead of you. [2]Your wealth is rotting away, and your fine clothes are moth-eaten rags. [3]Your gold and silver are corroded. The very wealth you were counting on will eat away your flesh like fire. This corroded treasure you have hoarded will testify against you on the day of judgment. [4]For listen! Hear the cries of the field workers whom you have cheated of their pay. The cries of

---

4:5 Or *They say that the spirit God has placed within us is filled with envy;* or *They say that the Holy Spirit, whom God has placed within us, opposes our envy.* **4:6** Prov 3:34 (Greek version). **4:11** Greek *brothers.*

those who harvest your fields have reached the ears of the Lord of Heaven's Armies.

⁵You have spent your years on earth in luxury, satisfying your every desire. You have fattened yourselves for the day of slaughter. ⁶You have condemned and killed innocent people,* who do not resist you.*

Patience and Endurance

⁷Dear brothers and sisters,* be patient as you wait for the Lord's return. Consider the farmers who patiently wait for the rains in the fall and in the spring. They eagerly look for the valuable harvest to ripen. ⁸You, too, must be patient. Take courage, for the coming of the Lord is near.

⁹Don't grumble about each other, brothers and sisters, or you will be judged. For look—the Judge is standing at the door!

¹⁰For examples of patience in suffering, dear brothers and sisters, look at the prophets who spoke in the name of the Lord. ¹¹We give great honor to those who endure under suffering. For instance, you know about Job, a man of great endurance. You can see how the Lord was kind to him at the end, for the Lord is full of tenderness and mercy.

¹²But most of all, my brothers and sisters, never take an oath, by heaven or earth or anything else. Just say a simple yes or no, so that you will not sin and be condemned.

The Power of Prayer

¹³Are any of you suffering hardships? You should pray. Are any of you happy? You should sing praises. ¹⁴Are any of you sick? You should call for the elders of the church to come and pray over you, anointing you with oil in the name of the Lord. ¹⁵Such a prayer offered in faith will heal the sick, and the Lord will make you well. And if you have committed any sins, you will be forgiven.

¹⁶Confess your sins to each other and pray for each other so that you may be healed. The earnest prayer of a righteous person has great power and produces wonderful results. ¹⁷Elijah was as human as we are, and yet when he prayed earnestly that no rain would fall, none fell for three and a half years! ¹⁸Then, when he prayed again, the sky sent down rain and the earth began to yield its crops.

Restore Wandering Believers

¹⁹My dear brothers and sisters, if someone among you wanders away from the truth and is brought back, ²⁰you can be sure that whoever brings the sinner back from wandering will save that person from death and bring about the forgiveness of many sins.

5:6a Or *killed the Righteous One.* 5:6b Or *Don't they resist you?* or *Doesn't God oppose you?* or *Aren't they now accusing you before God?* 5:7 Greek *brothers;* also in 5:9, 10, 12, 19.

1 Peter

Greetings from Peter

1 This letter is from Peter, an apostle of Jesus Christ.

I am writing to God's chosen people who are living as foreigners in the provinces of Pontus, Galatia, Cappadocia, Asia, and Bithynia.* ²God the Father knew you and chose you long ago, and his Spirit has made you holy. As a result, you have obeyed him and have been cleansed by the blood of Jesus Christ.

May God give you more and more grace and peace.

The Hope of Eternal Life

³All praise to God, the Father of our Lord Jesus Christ. It is by his great mercy that we have been born again, because God raised Jesus Christ from the dead. Now we live with great expectation, ⁴and we have a priceless inheritance—an inheritance that is kept in heaven for you, pure and undefiled, beyond the reach of change and decay. ⁵And through your faith, God is protecting you by his power until you receive this salvation, which is ready to be revealed on the last day for all to see.

⁶So be truly glad.* There is won-derful joy ahead, even though you must endure many trials for a little while. ⁷These trials will show that your faith is genuine. It is being tested as fire tests and purifies gold—though your faith is far more precious than mere gold. So when your faith remains strong through many trials, it will bring you much praise and glory and honor on the day when Jesus Christ is revealed to the whole world.

⁸You love him even though you have never seen him. Though you do not see him now, you trust him; and you rejoice with a glorious, inex-pressible joy. ⁹The reward for trusting him will be the salvation of your souls.

¹⁰This salvation was something even the prophets wanted to know more about when they prophesied about this gracious salvation pre-pared for you. ¹¹They wondered what time or situation the Spirit of Christ within them was talking about when he told them in ad-vance about Christ's suffering and his great glory afterward.

¹²They were told that their mes-sages were not for themselves, but for you. And now this Good News

1:1 *Pontus, Galatia, Cappadocia, Asia,* and *Bithynia* were Roman provinces in what is now Turkey.
1:6 Or *So you are truly glad.*

has been announced to you by those who preached in the power of the Holy Spirit sent from heaven. It is all so wonderful that even the angels are eagerly watching these things happen.

A Call to Holy Living

[13]So prepare your minds for action and exercise self-control. Put all your hope in the gracious salvation that will come to you when Jesus Christ is revealed to the world. [14]So you must live as God's obedient children. Don't slip back into your old ways of living to satisfy your own desires. You didn't know any better then. [15]But now you must be holy in everything you do, just as God who chose you is holy. [16]For the Scriptures say, "You must be holy because I am holy."*

[17]And remember that the heavenly Father to whom you pray has no favorites. He will judge or reward you according to what you do. So you must live in reverent fear of him during your time here as "temporary residents." [18]For you know that God paid a ransom to save you from the empty life you inherited from your ancestors. And it was not paid with mere gold or silver, which lose their value. [19]It was the precious blood of Christ, the sinless, spotless Lamb of God. [20]God chose him as your ransom long before the world began, but now in these last days he has been revealed for your sake.

[21]Through Christ you have come to trust in God. And you have placed your faith and hope in God because he raised Christ from the dead and gave him great glory.

[22]You were cleansed from your sins when you obeyed the truth, so now you must show sincere love to each other as brothers and sisters.* Love each other deeply with all your heart.*

[23]For you have been born again, but not to a life that will quickly end. Your new life will last forever because it comes from the eternal, living word of God. [24]As the Scriptures say,

"People are like grass;
    their beauty is like a flower
        in the field.
The grass withers and the
        flower fades.
[25]   But the word of the Lord
        remains forever."*

And that word is the Good News that was preached to you.

2 So get rid of all evil behavior. Be done with all deceit, hypocrisy, jealousy, and all unkind speech. [2]Like newborn babies, you must crave pure spiritual milk so that you will grow into a full experience of salvation. Cry out for this nourishment, [3]now that you have had a taste of the Lord's kindness.

1:16 Lev 11:44-45; 19:2; 20:7.   **1:22a** Greek *must have brotherly love.*   **1:22b** Some manuscripts read *with a pure heart.*   **1:24-25** Isa 40:6-8.

Living Stones for God's House

[4]You are coming to Christ, who is the living cornerstone of God's temple. He was rejected by people, but he was chosen by God for great honor.

[5]And you are living stones that God is building into his spiritual temple. What's more, you are his holy priests.* Through the mediation of Jesus Christ, you offer spiritual sacrifices that please God. [6]As the Scriptures say,

"I am placing a cornerstone
    in Jerusalem,*
chosen for great honor,
and anyone who trusts in him
    will never be disgraced."*

[7]Yes, you who trust him recognize the honor God has given him.* But for those who reject him,

"The stone that the builders
    rejected
has now become the
    cornerstone."*

[8]And,

"He is the stone that makes
    people stumble,
the rock that makes them fall."*

They stumble because they do not obey God's word, and so they meet the fate that was planned for them. [9]But you are not like that, for you are a chosen people. You are royal priests,* a holy nation, God's very own possession. As a result, you can show others the goodness of God, for he called you out of the darkness into his wonderful light.

[10] "Once you had no identity as
        a people;
    now you are God's people.
Once you received no mercy;
    now you have received God's
        mercy."*

[11]Dear friends, I warn you as "temporary residents and foreigners" to keep away from worldly desires that wage war against your very souls. [12]Be careful to live properly among your unbelieving neighbors. Then even if they accuse you of doing wrong, they will see your honorable behavior, and they will give honor to God when he judges the world.*

Respecting People in Authority

[13]For the Lord's sake, submit to all human authority—whether the king as head of state, [14]or the officials he has appointed. For the king has sent them to punish those who do wrong and to honor those who do right. [15]It is God's will that your honorable lives should silence those ignorant people who make foolish accusations against you. [16]For you are free, yet you are God's slaves, so don't use your freedom as an excuse

2:5 Greek *holy priesthood.*   2:6a Greek *in Zion.*   2:6b Isa 28:16 (Greek version).   2:7a Or *Yes, for you who believe, there is honor.*   2:7b Ps 118:22.   2:8 Isa 8:14.   2:9 Greek *a royal priesthood.*
2:10 Hos 1:6, 9; 2:23.   2:12 Or *on the day of visitation.*

to do evil. [17]Respect everyone, and love the family of believers.* Fear God, and respect the king.

Slaves

[18]You who are slaves must submit to your masters with all respect.* Do what they tell you—not only if they are kind and reasonable, but even if they are cruel. [19]For God is pleased when, conscious of his will, you patiently endure unjust treatment. [20]Of course, you get no credit for being patient if you are beaten for doing wrong. But if you suffer for doing good and endure it patiently, God is pleased with you.

[21]For God called you to do good, even if it means suffering, just as Christ suffered* for you. He is your example, and you must follow in his steps.

[22] He never sinned,
    nor ever deceived anyone.*
[23] He did not retaliate when he
        was insulted,
    nor threaten revenge when
        he suffered.
    He left his case in the hands
        of God,
    who always judges fairly.
[24] He personally carried our sins
    in his body on the cross
    so that we can be dead to sin
    and live for what is right.
    By his wounds
    you are healed.

[25] Once you were like sheep
    who wandered away.
    But now you have turned to your
        Shepherd,
    the Guardian of your souls.

Wives

3 In the same way, you wives must accept the authority of your husbands. Then, even if some refuse to obey the Good News, your godly lives will speak to them without any words. They will be won over [2]by observing your pure and reverent lives.

[3]Don't be concerned about the outward beauty of fancy hairstyles, expensive jewelry, or beautiful clothes. [4]You should clothe yourselves instead with the beauty that comes from within, the unfading beauty of a gentle and quiet spirit, which is so precious to God. [5]This is how the holy women of old made themselves beautiful. They put their trust in God and accepted the authority of their husbands. [6]For instance, Sarah obeyed her husband, Abraham, and called him her master. You are her daughters when you do what is right without fear of what your husbands might do.

Husbands

[7]In the same way, you husbands must give honor to your wives. Treat your wife with understanding as you live together. She may be weaker than you are, but she is your

equal partner in God's gift of new life. Treat her as you should so your prayers will not be hindered.

All Christians

[8]Finally, all of you should be of one mind. Sympathize with each other. Love each other as brothers and sisters.* Be tenderhearted, and keep a humble attitude. [9]Don't repay evil for evil. Don't retaliate with insults when people insult you. Instead, pay them back with a blessing. That is what God has called you to do, and he will grant you his blessing. [10]For the Scriptures say,

"If you want to enjoy life
　　and see many happy days,
keep your tongue from speaking evil
　　and your lips from telling lies.
[11] Turn away from evil and do good.
　　Search for peace, and work
　　　to maintain it.
[12] The eyes of the LORD watch over
　　　those who do right,
　　and his ears are open to their
　　　prayers.
But the LORD turns his face
　　against those who do evil."*

Suffering for Doing Good

[13]Now, who will want to harm you if you are eager to do good? [14]But even if you suffer for doing what is right, God will reward you for it. So don't worry or be afraid of their threats.

[15]Instead, you must worship Christ as Lord of your life. And if someone asks about your hope as a believer, always be ready to explain it. [16]But do this in a gentle and respectful way.* Keep your conscience clear. Then if people speak against you, they will be ashamed when they see what a good life you live because you belong to Christ. [17]Remember, it is better to suffer for doing good, if that is what God wants, than to suffer for doing wrong!

[18]Christ suffered* for our sins once for all time. He never sinned, but he died for sinners to bring you safely home to God. He suffered physical death, but he was raised to life in the Spirit.*

[19]So he went and preached to the spirits in prison—[20]those who disobeyed God long ago when God waited patiently while Noah was building his boat. Only eight people were saved from drowning in that terrible flood.* [21]And that water is a picture of baptism, which now saves you, not by removing dirt from your body, but as a response to God from* a clean conscience. It is effective because of the resurrection of Jesus Christ.

[22]Now Christ has gone to heaven. He is seated in the place of honor next to God, and all the angels and authorities and powers accept his authority.

3:8 Greek *Show brotherly love.* **3:10-12** Ps 34:12-16. **3:16** Some English translations put this sentence in verse 15. **3:18a** Some manuscripts read *died.* **3:18b** Or *in spirit.* **3:20** Greek *saved through water.* **3:21** Or *as an appeal to God for.*

Living for God

4 So then, since Christ suffered physical pain, you must arm yourselves with the same attitude he had, and be ready to suffer, too. For if you have suffered physically for Christ, you have finished with sin.* ²You won't spend the rest of your lives chasing your own desires, but you will be anxious to do the will of God. ³You have had enough in the past of the evil things that godless people enjoy—their immorality and lust, their feasting and drunkenness and wild parties, and their terrible worship of idols.

⁴Of course, your former friends are surprised when you no longer plunge into the flood of wild and destructive things they do. So they slander you. ⁵But remember that they will have to face God, who stands ready to judge everyone, both the living and the dead. ⁶That is why the Good News was preached to those who are now dead*—so although they were destined to die like all people,* they now live forever with God in the Spirit.*

⁷The end of the world is coming soon. Therefore, be earnest and disciplined in your prayers. ⁸Most important of all, continue to show deep love for each other, for love covers a multitude of sins. ⁹Cheerfully share your home with those who need a meal or a place to stay.

¹⁰God has given each of you a gift from his great variety of spiritual gifts. Use them well to serve one another. ¹¹Do you have the gift of speaking? Then speak as though God himself were speaking through you. Do you have the gift of helping others? Do it with all the strength and energy that God supplies. Then everything you do will bring glory to God through Jesus Christ. All glory and power to him forever and ever! Amen.

Suffering for Being a Christian

¹²Dear friends, don't be surprised at the fiery trials you are going through, as if something strange were happening to you. ¹³Instead, be very glad—for these trials make you partners with Christ in his suffering, so that you will have the wonderful joy of seeing his glory when it is revealed to all the world.

¹⁴If you are insulted because you bear the name of Christ, you will be blessed, for the glorious Spirit of God* rests upon you.* ¹⁵If you suffer, however, it must not be for murder, stealing, making trouble, or prying into other people's affairs. ¹⁶But it is no shame to suffer for being a Christian. Praise God for the privilege of being called by his name! ¹⁷For the time has come for judgment, and it must begin with God's

---

4:1 Or *For the one* [or *One*] *who has suffered physically has finished with sin.* **4:6a** Greek *preached even to the dead.* **4:6b** Or *so although people had judged them worthy of death.* **4:6c** Or *in spirit.* **4:14a** Or *for the glory of God, which is his Spirit.* **4:14b** Some manuscripts add *On their part he is blasphemed, but on your part he is glorified.*

household. And if judgment begins with us, what terrible fate awaits those who have never obeyed God's Good News? [18]And also,

"If the righteous are barely saved,
    what will happen to godless
    sinners?"*

[19]So if you are suffering in a manner that pleases God, keep on doing what is right, and trust your lives to the God who created you, for he will never fail you.

Advice for Elders and Young Men

5 And now, a word to you who are elders in the churches. I, too, am an elder and a witness to the sufferings of Christ. And I, too, will share in his glory when he is revealed to the whole world. As a fellow elder, I appeal to you: [2]Care for the flock that God has entrusted to you. Watch over it willingly, not grudgingly—not for what you will get out of it, but because you are eager to serve God. [3]Don't lord it over the people assigned to your care, but lead them by your own good example. [4]And when the Great Shepherd appears, you will receive a crown of never-ending glory and honor.

[5]In the same way, you who are younger must accept the authority of the elders. And all of you, dress yourselves in humility as you relate to one another, for

"God opposes the proud
    but gives grace to the humble."*

[6]So humble yourselves under the mighty power of God, and at the right time he will lift you up in honor. [7]Give all your worries and cares to God, for he cares about you.

[8]Stay alert! Watch out for your great enemy, the devil. He prowls around like a roaring lion, looking for someone to devour. [9]Stand firm against him, and be strong in your faith. Remember that your family of believers* all over the world is going through the same kind of suffering you are.

[10]In his kindness God called you to share in his eternal glory by means of Christ Jesus. So after you have suffered a little while, he will restore, support, and strengthen you, and he will place you on a firm foundation. [11]All power to him forever! Amen.

Peter's Final Greetings

[12]I have written and sent this short letter to you with the help of Silas,* whom I commend to you as a faithful brother. My purpose in writing is to encourage you and assure you that what you are experiencing is truly part of God's grace for you. Stand firm in this grace.

[13]Your sister church here in Babylon* sends you greetings, and so does my son Mark. [14]Greet each other with a kiss of love.

Peace be with all of you who are in Christ.

4:18 Prov 11:31 (Greek version). 5:5 Prov 3:34 (Greek version). 5:9 Greek *your brotherhood.*
5:12 Greek *Silvanus.* 5:13 Greek *The elect one in Babylon.* Babylon was probably symbolic for Rome.

2 Peter

Greetings from Peter

1 This letter is from Simon* Peter, a slave and apostle of Jesus Christ.

I am writing to you who share the same precious faith we have. This faith was given to you because of the justice and fairness* of Jesus Christ, our God and Savior.

²May God give you more and more grace and peace as you grow in your knowledge of God and Jesus our Lord.

Growing in Faith

³By his divine power, God has given us everything we need for living a godly life. We have received all of this by coming to know him, the one who called us to himself by means of his marvelous glory and excellence. ⁴And because of his glory and excellence, he has given us great and precious promises. These are the promises that enable you to share his divine nature and escape the world's corruption caused by human desires.

⁵In view of all this, make every effort to respond to God's promises. Supplement your faith with a generous provision of moral excellence, and moral excellence with knowledge, ⁶and knowledge with self-control, and self-control with patient endurance, and patient endurance with godliness, ⁷and godliness with brotherly affection, and brotherly affection with love for everyone.

⁸The more you grow like this, the more productive and useful you will be in your knowledge of our Lord Jesus Christ. ⁹But those who fail to develop in this way are shortsighted or blind, forgetting that they have been cleansed from their old sins.

¹⁰So, dear brothers and sisters,* work hard to prove that you really are among those God has called and chosen. Do these things, and you will never fall away. ¹¹Then God will give you a grand entrance into the eternal Kingdom of our Lord and Savior Jesus Christ.

Paying Attention to Scripture

¹²Therefore, I will always remind you about these things—even though you already know them and are standing firm in the truth

1:1a Greek *Simeon.* 1:1b Or *to you in the righteousness.* 1:10 Greek *brothers.*

you have been taught. [13]And it is only right that I should keep on reminding you as long as I live.* [14]For our Lord Jesus Christ has shown me that I must soon leave this earthly life,* [15]so I will work hard to make sure you always remember these things after I am gone.

[16]For we were not making up clever stories when we told you about the powerful coming of our Lord Jesus Christ. We saw his majestic splendor with our own eyes [17]when he received honor and glory from God the Father. The voice from the majestic glory of God said to him, "This is my dearly loved Son, who brings me great joy."* [18]We ourselves heard that voice from heaven when we were with him on the holy mountain.

[19]Because of that experience, we have even greater confidence in the message proclaimed by the prophets. You must pay close attention to what they wrote, for their words are like a lamp shining in a dark place—until the Day dawns, and Christ the Morning Star shines* in your hearts. [20]Above all, you must realize that no prophecy in Scripture ever came from the prophet's own understanding,* [21]or from human initiative. No, those prophets were moved by the Holy Spirit, and they spoke from God.

The Danger of False Teachers

2 But there were also false prophets in Israel, just as there will be false teachers among you. They will cleverly teach destructive heresies and even deny the Master who bought them. In this way, they will bring sudden destruction on themselves. [2]Many will follow their evil teaching and shameful immorality. And because of these teachers, the way of truth will be slandered. [3]In their greed they will make up clever lies to get hold of your money. But God condemned them long ago, and their destruction will not be delayed.

[4]For God did not spare even the angels who sinned. He threw them into hell,* in gloomy pits of darkness,* where they are being held until the day of judgment. [5]And God did not spare the ancient world—except for Noah and the seven others in his family. Noah warned the world of God's righteous judgment. So God protected Noah when he destroyed the world of ungodly people with a vast flood. [6]Later, God condemned the cities of Sodom and Gomorrah and turned them into heaps of ashes. He made them an example of what will happen to ungodly people. [7]But God also rescued Lot out of Sodom because he was a righteous man who was sick of the shameful im-

---

1:13 Greek *as long as I am in this tent* [or *tabernacle*]. **1:14** Greek *I must soon put off my tent* [or *tabernacle*]. **1:17** Matt 17:5; Mark 9:7; Luke 9:35. **1:19** Or *rises.* **1:20** Or *is a matter of one's own interpretation.* **2:4a** Greek *Tartarus.* **2:4b** Some manuscripts read *in chains of gloom.*

morality of the wicked people around him. [8]Yes, Lot was a righteous man who was tormented in his soul by the wickedness he saw and heard day after day. [9]So you see, the Lord knows how to rescue godly people from their trials, even while keeping the wicked under punishment until the day of final judgment. [10]He is especially hard on those who follow their own twisted sexual desire, and who despise authority.

These people are proud and arrogant, daring even to scoff at supernatural beings* without so much as trembling. [11]But the angels, who are far greater in power and strength, do not dare to bring from the Lord* a charge of blasphemy against those supernatural beings.

[12]These false teachers are like unthinking animals, creatures of instinct, born to be caught and destroyed. They scoff at things they do not understand, and like animals, they will be destroyed. [13]Their destruction is their reward for the harm they have done. They love to indulge in evil pleasures in broad daylight. They are a disgrace and a stain among you. They delight in deception* even as they eat with you in your fellowship meals. [14]They commit adultery with their eyes, and their desire for sin is never satisfied. They lure unstable people into sin, and they are well trained in greed. They live under God's curse. [15]They have wandered off the right road and followed the footsteps of Balaam son of Beor,* who loved to earn money by doing wrong. [16]But Balaam was stopped from his mad course when his donkey rebuked him with a human voice.

[17]These people are as useless as dried-up springs or as mist blown away by the wind. They are doomed to blackest darkness. [18]They brag about themselves with empty, foolish boasting. With an appeal to twisted sexual desires, they lure back into sin those who have barely escaped from a lifestyle of deception. [19]They promise freedom, but they themselves are slaves of sin and corruption. For you are a slave to whatever controls you. [20]And when people escape from the wickedness of the world by knowing our Lord and Savior Jesus Christ and then get tangled up and enslaved by sin again, they are worse off than before. [21]It would be better if they had never known the way to righteousness than to know it and then reject the command they were given to live a holy life. [22]They prove the truth of this proverb: "A dog returns to its vomit."* And another says, "A washed pig returns to the mud."

2:10 Greek *at glorious ones,* which are probably evil angels. **2:11** Other manuscripts read *to the Lord;* still others do not include this phrase at all. **2:13** Some manuscripts read *in fellowship meals.* **2:15** Some manuscripts read *Bosor.* **2:22** Prov 26:11.

The Day of the Lord Is Coming

3 This is my second letter to you, dear friends, and in both of them I have tried to stimulate your wholesome thinking and refresh your memory. ²I want you to remember what the holy prophets said long ago and what our Lord and Savior commanded through your apostles.

³Most importantly, I want to remind you that in the last days scoffers will come, mocking the truth and following their own desires. ⁴They will say, "What happened to the promise that Jesus is coming again? From before the times of our ancestors, everything has remained the same since the world was first created."

⁵They deliberately forget that God made the heavens long ago by the word of his command, and he brought the earth out from the water and surrounded it with water. ⁶Then he used the water to destroy the ancient world with a mighty flood. ⁷And by the same word, the present heavens and earth have been stored up for fire. They are being kept for the day of judgment, when ungodly people will be destroyed.

⁸But you must not forget this one thing, dear friends: A day is like a thousand years to the Lord, and a thousand years is like a day. ⁹The Lord isn't really being slow about his promise, as some people think.

No, he is being patient for your sake. He does not want anyone to be destroyed, but wants everyone to repent. ¹⁰But the day of the Lord will come as unexpectedly as a thief. Then the heavens will pass away with a terrible noise, and the very elements themselves will disappear in fire, and the earth and everything on it will be found to deserve judgment.*

¹¹Since everything around us is going to be destroyed like this, what holy and godly lives you should live, ¹²looking forward to the day of God and hurrying it along. On that day, he will set the heavens on fire, and the elements will melt away in the flames. ¹³But we are looking forward to the new heavens and new earth he has promised, a world filled with God's righteousness.

¹⁴And so, dear friends, while you are waiting for these things to happen, make every effort to be found living peaceful lives that are pure and blameless in his sight.

¹⁵And remember, our Lord's patience gives people time to be saved. This is what our beloved brother Paul also wrote to you with the wisdom God gave him—¹⁶speaking of these things in all of his letters. Some of his comments are hard to understand, and those who are ignorant and unstable have twisted his letters to mean something quite different, just as they do with other

---

3:10 Other manuscripts read *will be burned up;* one early manuscript reads *will be found destroyed.*

parts of Scripture. And this will result in their destruction.

Peter's Final Words

[17] You already know these things, dear friends. So be on guard; then you will not be carried away by the errors of these wicked people and lose your own secure footing. [18] Rather, you must grow in the grace and knowledge of our Lord and Savior Jesus Christ.

All glory to him, both now and forever! Amen.

1 John

Introduction

1 We proclaim to you the one who existed from the beginning,* whom we have heard and seen. We saw him with our own eyes and touched him with our own hands. He is the Word of life. ²This one who is life itself was revealed to us, and we have seen him. And now we testify and proclaim to you that he is the one who is eternal life. He was with the Father, and then he was revealed to us. ³We proclaim to you what we ourselves have actually seen and heard so that you may have fellowship with us. And our fellowship is with the Father and with his Son, Jesus Christ. ⁴We are writing these things so that you may fully share our joy.*

Living in the Light

⁵This is the message we heard from Jesus* and now declare to you: God is light, and there is no darkness in him at all. ⁶So we are lying if we say we have fellowship with God but go on living in spiritual darkness; we are not practicing the truth. ⁷But if we are living in the light, as God is in the light, then we have fellowship with each other, and the blood of Jesus, his Son, cleanses us from all sin.

⁸If we claim we have no sin, we are only fooling ourselves and not living in the truth. ⁹But if we confess our sins to him, he is faithful and just to forgive us our sins and to cleanse us from all wickedness. ¹⁰If we claim we have not sinned, we are calling God a liar and showing that his word has no place in our hearts.

2 My dear children, I am writing this to you so that you will not sin. But if anyone does sin, we have an advocate who pleads our case before the Father. He is Jesus Christ, the one who is truly righteous. ²He himself is the sacrifice that atones for our sins—and not only our sins but the sins of all the world.

³And we can be sure that we know him if we obey his commandments. ⁴If someone claims, "I know God," but doesn't obey God's commandments, that person is a liar and is not living in the truth. ⁵But those who obey God's word truly show how completely they love him. That is how we know we are living in him. ⁶Those who say they live in God should live their lives as Jesus did.

1:1 Greek *What was from the beginning.* 1:4 Or *so that our joy may be complete;* some manuscripts read *your joy.* 1:5 Greek *from him.*

A New Commandment

7 Dear friends, I am not writing a new commandment for you; rather it is an old one you have had from the very beginning. This old commandment—to love one another—is the same message you heard before. 8 Yet it is also new. Jesus lived the truth of this commandment, and you also are living it. For the darkness is disappearing, and the true light is already shining.

9 If anyone claims, "I am living in the light," but hates a fellow believer,* that person is still living in darkness. 10 Anyone who loves a fellow believer* is living in the light and does not cause others to stumble. 11 But anyone who hates a fellow believer is still living and walking in darkness. Such a person does not know the way to go, having been blinded by the darkness.

12 I am writing to you who are
    God's children
  because your sins have
    been forgiven through
    Jesus.*
13 I am writing to you who are
    mature in the faith*
  because you know Christ,
    who existed from the
    beginning.
  I am writing to you who are
    young in the faith
  because you have won your
    battle with the evil one.

14 I have written to you who are
    God's children
  because you know the Father.
  I have written to you who are
    mature in the faith
  because you know Christ,
    who existed from the
    beginning.
  I have written to you who are
    young in the faith
  because you are strong.
  God's word lives in your
    hearts,
    and you have won your
    battle with the evil one.

Do Not Love This World

15 Do not love this world nor the things it offers you, for when you love the world, you do not have the love of the Father in you. 16 For the world offers only a craving for physical pleasure, a craving for everything we see, and pride in our achievements and possessions. These are not from the Father, but are from this world. 17 And this world is fading away, along with everything that people crave. But anyone who does what pleases God will live forever.

Warning about Antichrists

18 Dear children, the last hour is here. You have heard that the Antichrist is coming, and already many such antichrists have appeared. From this we know that the last

2:9 Greek hates his brother; also in 2:11.   2:10 Greek loves his brother.   2:12 Greek through his name.   2:13 Or to you fathers; also in 2:14.

hour has come. [19]These people left our churches, but they never really belonged with us; otherwise they would have stayed with us. When they left, it proved that they did not belong with us.

[20]But you are not like that, for the Holy One has given you his Spirit,* and all of you know the truth. [21]So I am writing to you not because you don't know the truth but because you know the difference between truth and lies. [22]And who is a liar? Anyone who says that Jesus is not the Christ.* Anyone who denies the Father and the Son is an antichrist.* [23]Anyone who denies the Son doesn't have the Father, either. But anyone who acknowledges the Son has the Father also.

[24]So you must remain faithful to what you have been taught from the beginning. If you do, you will remain in fellowship with the Son and with the Father. [25]And in this fellowship we enjoy the eternal life he promised us.

[26]I am writing these things to warn you about those who want to lead you astray. [27]But you have received the Holy Spirit,* and he lives within you, so you don't need anyone to teach you what is true. For the Spirit* teaches you everything you need to know, and what he teaches is true—it is not a lie. So just as he has taught you, remain in fellowship with Christ.

Living as Children of God

[28]And now, dear children, remain in fellowship with Christ so that when he returns, you will be full of courage and not shrink back from him in shame.

[29]Since we know that Christ is righteous, we also know that all who do what is right are God's children.

3 See how very much our Father loves us, for he calls us his children, and that is what we are! But the people who belong to this world don't recognize that we are God's children because they don't know him. [2]Dear friends, we are already God's children, but he has not yet shown us what we will be like when Christ appears. But we do know that we will be like him, for we will see him as he really is. [3]And all who have this eager expectation will keep themselves pure, just as he is pure.

[4]Everyone who sins is breaking God's law, for all sin is contrary to the law of God. [5]And you know that Jesus came to take away our sins, and there is no sin in him. [6]Anyone who continues to live in him will not sin. But anyone who keeps on sinning does not know him or understand who he is.

[7]Dear children, don't let anyone deceive you about this: When people do what is right, it shows that they are righteous, even as Christ is righteous. [8]But when people keep

---

2:20 Greek *But you have an anointing from the Holy One.*   **2:22a** Or *not the Messiah.*   **2:22b** Or *the antichrist.*   **2:27a** Greek *the anointing from him.*   **2:27b** Greek *the anointing.*

on sinning, it shows that they belong to the devil, who has been sinning since the beginning. But the Son of God came to destroy the works of the devil. [9]Those who have been born into God's family do not make a practice of sinning, because God's life* is in them. So they can't keep on sinning, because they are children of God. [10]So now we can tell who are children of God and who are children of the devil. Anyone who does not live righteously and does not love other believers* does not belong to God.

Love One Another

[11]This is the message you have heard from the beginning: We should love one another. [12]We must not be like Cain, who belonged to the evil one and killed his brother. And why did he kill him? Because Cain had been doing what was evil, and his brother had been doing what was righteous. [13]So don't be surprised, dear brothers and sisters,* if the world hates you.

[14]If we love our brothers and sisters who are believers,* it proves that we have passed from death to life. But a person who has no love is still dead. [15]Anyone who hates another brother or sister* is really a murderer at heart. And you know that murderers don't have eternal life within them.

[16]We know what real love is because Jesus gave up his life for us. So we also ought to give up our lives for our brothers and sisters. [17]If someone has enough money to live well and sees a brother or sister* in need but shows no compassion—how can God's love be in that person?

[18]Dear children, let's not merely say that we love each other; let us show the truth by our actions. [19]Our actions will show that we belong to the truth, so we will be confident when we stand before God. [20]Even if we feel guilty, God is greater than our feelings, and he knows everything.

[21]Dear friends, if we don't feel guilty, we can come to God with bold confidence. [22]And we will receive from him whatever we ask because we obey him and do the things that please him.

[23]And this is his commandment: We must believe in the name of his Son, Jesus Christ, and love one another, just as he commanded us. [24]Those who obey God's commandments remain in fellowship with him, and he with them. And we know he lives in us because the Spirit he gave us lives in us.

Discerning False Prophets

4 Dear friends, do not believe everyone who claims to speak by the Spirit. You must test them to see if the spirit they have comes from God. For there are many false prophets in the world. [2]This is how

3:9 Greek *because his seed.* 3:10 Greek *does not love his brother.* 3:13 Greek *brothers.* 3:14 Greek *the brothers;* similarly in 3:16. 3:15 Greek *hates his brother.* 3:17 Greek *sees his brother.*

we know if they have the Spirit of God: If a person claiming to be a prophet* acknowledges that Jesus Christ came in a real body, that person has the Spirit of God. [3]But if someone claims to be a prophet and does not acknowledge the truth about Jesus, that person is not from God. Such a person has the spirit of the Antichrist, which you heard is coming into the world and indeed is already here.

[4]But you belong to God, my dear children. You have already won a victory over those people, because the Spirit who lives in you is greater than the spirit who lives in the world. [5]Those people belong to this world, so they speak from the world's viewpoint, and the world listens to them. [6]But we belong to God, and those who know God listen to us. If they do not belong to God, they do not listen to us. That is how we know if someone has the Spirit of truth or the spirit of deception.

Loving One Another

[7]Dear friends, let us continue to love one another, for love comes from God. Anyone who loves is a child of God and knows God. [8]But anyone who does not love does not know God, for God is love.

[9]God showed how much he loved us by sending his one and only Son into the world so that we might have eternal life through him. [10]This is real love—not that we loved God, but that he loved us and sent his Son as a sacrifice to take away our sins.

[11]Dear friends, since God loved us that much, we surely ought to love each other. [12]No one has ever seen God. But if we love each other, God lives in us, and his love is brought to full expression in us.

[13]And God has given us his Spirit as proof that we live in him and he in us. [14]Furthermore, we have seen with our own eyes and now testify that the Father sent his Son to be the Savior of the world. [15]All who declare that Jesus is the Son of God have God living in them, and they live in God. [16]We know how much God loves us, and we have put our trust in his love.

God is love, and all who live in love live in God, and God lives in them. [17]And as we live in God, our love grows more perfect. So we will not be afraid on the day of judgment, but we can face him with confidence because we live like Jesus here in this world.

[18]Such love has no fear, because perfect love expels all fear. If we are afraid, it is for fear of punishment, and this shows that we have not fully experienced his perfect love. [19]We love each other* because he loved us first.

[20]If someone says, "I love God,"

4:2 Greek *If a spirit;* similarly in 4:3.   **4:19** Greek *We love.* Other manuscripts read *We love God;* still others read *We love him.*

but hates a fellow believer,* that person is a liar; for if we don't love people we can see, how can we love God, whom we cannot see? ²¹And he has given us this command: Those who love God must also love their fellow believers.*

Faith in the Son of God

5 Everyone who believes that Jesus is the Christ* has become a child of God. And everyone who loves the Father loves his children, too. ²We know we love God's children if we love God and obey his commandments. ³Loving God means keeping his commandments, and his commandments are not burdensome. ⁴For every child of God defeats this evil world, and we achieve this victory through our faith. ⁵And who can win this battle against the world? Only those who believe that Jesus is the Son of God.

⁶And Jesus Christ was revealed as God's Son by his baptism in water and by shedding his blood on the cross*—not by water only, but by water and blood. And the Spirit, who is truth, confirms it with his testimony. ⁷So we have these three witnesses*—⁸the Spirit, the water, and the blood—and all three agree. ⁹Since we believe human testimony, surely we can believe the greater testimony that comes from God. And God has testified about his Son. ¹⁰All who believe in the Son of God know in their hearts that this testimony is true. Those who don't believe this are actually calling God a liar because they don't believe what God has testified about his Son.

¹¹And this is what God has testified: He has given us eternal life, and this life is in his Son. ¹²Whoever has the Son has life; whoever does not have God's Son does not have life.

Conclusion

¹³I have written this to you who believe in the name of the Son of God, so that you may know you have eternal life. ¹⁴And we are confident that he hears us whenever we ask for anything that pleases him. ¹⁵And since we know he hears us when we make our requests, we also know that he will give us what we ask for.

¹⁶If you see a fellow beliver* sinning in a way that does not lead to death, you should pray, and God will give that person life. But there is a sin that leads to death, and I am not saying you should pray for those who commit it. ¹⁷All wicked actions are sin, but not every sin leads to death.

¹⁸We know that God's children do not make a practice of sinning, for God's Son holds them securely, and the evil one cannot touch them.

4:20 Greek *hates his brother.* 4:21 Greek *The one who loves God must also love his brother.* 5:1 Or *the Messiah.* 5:6 Greek *This is he who came by water and blood.* 5:7 A few very late manuscripts add *in heaven—the Father, the Word, and the Holy Spirit, and these three are one. And we have three witnesses on earth.* 5:16 Greek *a brother.*

[19]We know that we are children of God and that the world around us is under the control of the evil one.

[20]And we know that the Son of God has come, and he has given us understanding so that we can know the true God.* And now we live in fellowship with the true God because we live in fellowship with his Son, Jesus Christ. He is the only true God, and he is eternal life.

[21]Dear children, keep away from anything that might take God's place in your hearts.*

5:20 Greek *the one who is true.* **5:21** Greek *keep yourselves from idols.*

2 John

Greetings

This letter is from John, the elder.*

I am writing to the chosen lady and to her children,* whom I love in the truth—as does everyone else who knows the truth—²because the truth lives in us and will be with us forever.

³Grace, mercy, and peace, which come from God the Father and from Jesus Christ—the Son of the Father—will continue to be with us who live in truth and love.

Live in the Truth

⁴How happy I was to meet some of your children and find them living according to the truth, just as the Father commanded.

⁵I am writing to remind you, dear friends,* that we should love one another. This is not a new commandment, but one we have had from the beginning. ⁶Love means doing what God has commanded us, and he has commanded us to love one another, just as you heard from the beginning.

⁷I say this because many deceivers have gone out into the world. They deny that Jesus Christ came* in a real body. Such a person is a deceiver and an antichrist. ⁸Watch out that you do not lose what we* have worked so hard to achieve. Be diligent so that you receive your full reward. ⁹Anyone who wanders away from this teaching has no relationship with God. But anyone who remains in the teaching of Christ has a relationship with both the Father and the Son.

¹⁰If anyone comes to your meeting and does not teach the truth about Christ, don't invite that person into your home or give any kind of encouragement. ¹¹Anyone who encourages such people becomes a partner in their evil work.

Conclusion

¹²I have much more to say to you, but I don't want to do it with paper and ink. For I hope to visit you soon and talk with you face to face. Then our joy will be complete.

¹³Greetings from the children of your sister,* chosen by God.

1a Greek *From the elder.* 1b Or *the church God has chosen and its members.* 5 Greek *I urge you, lady.* 7 Or *will come.* 8 Some manuscripts read *you.* 13 Or *from the members of your sister church.*

3 John

Greetings

This letter is from John, the elder.*

I am writing to Gaius, my dear friend, whom I love in the truth.

[2]Dear friend, I hope all is well with you and that you are as healthy in body as you are strong in spirit. [3]Some of the traveling teachers* recently returned and made me very happy by telling me about your faithfulness and that you are living according to the truth. [4]I could have no greater joy than to hear that my children are following the truth.

Caring for the Lord's Workers

[5]Dear friend, you are being faithful to God when you care for the traveling teachers who pass through, even though they are strangers to you. [6]They have told the church here of your loving friendship. Please continue providing for such teachers in a manner that pleases God. [7]For they are traveling for the Lord,* and they accept nothing from people who are not believers.* [8]So we ourselves should support them so that we can be their partners as they teach the truth.

[9]I wrote to the church about this, but Diotrephes, who loves to be the leader, refuses to have anything to do with us. [10]When I come, I will report some of the things he is doing and the evil accusations he is making against us. Not only does he refuse to welcome the traveling teachers, he also tells others not to help them. And when they do help, he puts them out of the church.

[11]Dear friend, don't let this bad example influence you. Follow only what is good. Remember that those who do good prove that they are God's children, and those who do evil prove that they do not know God.*

[12]Everyone speaks highly of Demetrius, as does the truth itself. We ourselves can say the same for him, and you know we speak the truth.

Conclusion

[13]I have much more to say to you, but I don't want to write it with pen and ink. [14]For I hope to see you soon, and then we will talk face to face.

[15]*Peace be with you.

Your friends here send you their greetings. Please give my personal greetings to each of our friends there.

---

1 Greek *From the elder.* **3** Greek *the brothers;* also in verses 5 and 10. **7a** Greek *They went out on behalf of the Name.* **7b** Greek *from Gentiles.* **11** Greek *they have not seen God.* **15** Some English translations combine verses 14 and 15 into verse 14.

Jude

Greetings from Jude

This letter is from Jude, a slave of Jesus Christ and a brother of James.

I am writing to all who have been called by God the Father, who loves you and keeps you safe in the care of Jesus Christ.*

²May God give you more and more mercy, peace, and love.

The Danger of False Teachers

³Dear friends, I had been eagerly planning to write to you about the salvation we all share. But now I find that I must write about something else, urging you to defend the faith that God has entrusted once for all time to his holy people. ⁴I say this because some ungodly people have wormed their way into your churches, saying that God's marvelous grace allows us to live immoral lives. The condemnation of such people was recorded long ago, for they have denied our only Master and Lord, Jesus Christ.

⁵So I want to remind you, though you already know these things, that Jesus* first rescued the nation of Israel from Egypt, but later he destroyed those who did not remain faithful. ⁶And I remind you of the angels who did not stay within the limits of authority God gave them but left the place where they belonged. God has kept them securely chained in prisons of darkness, waiting for the great day of judgment. ⁷And don't forget Sodom and Gomorrah and their neighboring towns, which were filled with immorality and every kind of sexual perversion. Those cities were destroyed by fire and serve as a warning of the eternal fire of God's judgment.

⁸In the same way, these people—who claim authority from their dreams—live immoral lives, defy authority, and scoff at supernatural beings.* ⁹But even Michael, one of the mightiest of the angels,* did not dare accuse the devil of blasphemy, but simply said, "The Lord rebuke you!" (This took place when Michael was arguing with the devil about Moses' body.) ¹⁰But these people scoff at things they do not understand. Like unthinking animals, they do whatever their instincts tell

---

1 Or *keeps you for Jesus Christ.* **5** Other manuscripts read *[the] Lord,* or *God,* or *God Christ.* **8** Greek *at glorious ones,* which are probably evil angels. **9** Greek *Michael, the archangel.*

them, and so they bring about their own destruction. [11]What sorrow awaits them! For they follow in the footsteps of Cain, who killed his brother. Like Balaam, they deceive people for money. And like Korah, they perish in their rebellion.

[12]When these people eat with you in your fellowship meals commemorating the Lord's love, they are like dangerous reefs that can shipwreck you.* They are like shameless shepherds who care only for themselves. They are like clouds blowing over the land without giving any rain. They are like trees in autumn that are doubly dead, for they bear no fruit and have been pulled up by the roots. [13]They are like wild waves of the sea, churning up the foam of their shameful deeds. They are like wandering stars, doomed forever to blackest darkness.

[14]Enoch, who lived in the seventh generation after Adam, prophesied about these people. He said, "Listen! The Lord is coming with countless thousands of his holy ones [15]to execute judgment on the people of the world. He will convict every person of all the ungodly things they have done and for all the insults that ungodly sinners have spoken against him."*

[16]These people are grumblers and complainers, living only to satisfy their desires. They brag loudly about themselves, and they flatter others to get what they want.

A Call to Remain Faithful

[17]But you, my dear friends, must remember what the apostles of our Lord Jesus Christ predicted. [18]They told you that in the last times there would be scoffers whose purpose in life is to satisfy their ungodly desires. [19]These people are the ones who are creating divisions among you. They follow their natural instincts because they do not have God's Spirit in them.

[20]But you, dear friends, must build each other up in your most holy faith, pray in the power of the Holy Spirit,* [21]and await the mercy of our Lord Jesus Christ, who will bring you eternal life. In this way, you will keep yourselves safe in God's love.

[22]And you must show mercy to* those whose faith is wavering. [23]Rescue others by snatching them from the flames of judgment. Show mercy to still others,* but do so with great caution, hating the sins that contaminate their lives.*

12 Or *they are contaminants among you;* or *they are stains.* **14-15** The quotation comes from intertestamental literature: 1 Enoch 1:9. **20** Greek *pray in the Holy Spirit.* **22** Some manuscripts read *must reprove.* **22-23a** Some manuscripts have only two categories of people: (1) those whose faith is wavering and therefore need to be snatched from the flames of judgment, and (2) those who need to be shown mercy. **23b** Greek *with fear, hating even the clothing stained by the flesh.*

A Prayer of Praise

24 Now all glory to God, who is able to keep you from falling away and will bring you with great joy into his glorious presence without a single fault. 25 All glory to him who alone is God, our Savior through Jesus Christ our Lord. All glory, majesty, power, and authority are his before all time, and in the present, and beyond all time! Amen.

Revelation

Prologue

1 This is a revelation from* Jesus Christ, which God gave him to show his servants the events that must soon* take place. He sent an angel to present this revelation to his servant John, [2]who faithfully reported everything he saw. This is his report of the word of God and the testimony of Jesus Christ.

[3]God blesses the one who reads the words of this prophecy to the church, and he blesses all who listen to its message and obey what it says, for the time is near.

John's Greeting to the Seven Churches

[4]This letter is from John to the seven churches in the province of Asia.*

Grace and peace to you from the one who is, who always was, and who is still to come; from the sevenfold Spirit* before his throne; [5]and from Jesus Christ. He is the faithful witness to these things, the first to rise from the dead, and the ruler of all the kings of the world.

All glory to him who loves us and has freed us from our sins by shedding his blood for us. [6]He has made us a Kingdom of priests for God his Father. All glory and power to him forever and ever! Amen.

[7] Look! He comes with the clouds
of heaven.
And everyone will see him—
even those who pierced him.
And all the nations of the world
will mourn for him.
Yes! Amen!

[8]"I am the Alpha and the Omega—the beginning and the end,"* says the Lord God. "I am the one who is, who always was, and who is still to come—the Almighty One."

Vision of the Son of Man

[9]I, John, am your brother and your partner in suffering and in God's Kingdom and in the patient endurance to which Jesus calls us. I was exiled to the island of Patmos for preaching the word of God and for my testimony about Jesus. [10]It was the Lord's Day, and I was worshiping in the Spirit.* Suddenly, I heard behind me a loud voice like a trumpet blast. [11]It said, "Write in a book* everything you see, and send it to the seven churches in the cities of Ephe-

---

1:1a Or *of.* **1:1b** Or *suddenly,* or *quickly.* **1:4a** *Asia* was a Roman province in what is now western Turkey. **1:4b** Greek *the seven spirits.* **1:8** Greek *I am the Alpha and the Omega,* referring to the first and last letters of the Greek alphabet. **1:10** Or *in spirit.* **1:11** Or *on a scroll.*

sus, Smyrna, Pergamum, Thyatira, Sardis, Philadelphia, and Laodicea."

¹²When I turned to see who was speaking to me, I saw seven gold lampstands. ¹³And standing in the middle of the lampstands was someone like the Son of Man.* He was wearing a long robe with a gold sash across his chest. ¹⁴His head and his hair were white like wool, as white as snow. And his eyes were like flames of fire. ¹⁵His feet were like polished bronze refined in a furnace, and his voice thundered like mighty ocean waves. ¹⁶He held seven stars in his right hand, and a sharp two-edged sword came from his mouth. And his face was like the sun in all its brilliance.

¹⁷When I saw him, I fell at his feet as if I were dead. But he laid his right hand on me and said, "Don't be afraid! I am the First and the Last. ¹⁸I am the living one. I died, but look—I am alive forever and ever! And I hold the keys of death and the grave.*

¹⁹"Write down what you have seen—both the things that are now happening and the things that will happen.* ²⁰This is the meaning of the mystery of the seven stars you saw in my right hand and the seven gold lampstands: The seven stars are the angels* of the seven churches, and the seven lampstands are the seven churches.

The Message to the Church in Ephesus

2 "Write this letter to the angel* of the church in Ephesus. This is the message from the one who holds the seven stars in his right hand, the one who walks among the seven gold lampstands:

²"I know all the things you do. I have seen your hard work and your patient endurance. I know you don't tolerate evil people. You have examined the claims of those who say they are apostles but are not. You have discovered they are liars. ³You have patiently suffered for me without quitting.

⁴"But I have this complaint against you. You don't love me or each other as you did at first!* ⁵Look how far you have fallen! Turn back to me and do the works you did at first. If you don't repent, I will come and remove your lampstand from its place among the churches. ⁶But this is in your favor: You hate the evil deeds of the Nicolaitans, just as I do.

⁷"Anyone with ears to hear must listen to the Spirit and understand what he is saying to the churches. To everyone who is victorious I will give fruit from the tree of life in the paradise of God.

1:13 Or *like a son of man.* See Dan 7:13. "Son of Man" is a title Jesus used for himself.   **1:18** Greek *and Hades.*   **1:19** Or *what you have seen and what they mean—the things that have already begun to happen.*   **1:20** Or *the messengers.*   **2:1** Or *the messenger;* also in 2:8, 12, 18.   **2:4** Greek *You have lost your first love.*

The Message to the Church in Smyrna

8"Write this letter to the angel of the church in Smyrna. This is the message from the one who is the First and the Last, who was dead but is now alive:

9"I know about your suffering and your poverty—but you are rich! I know the blasphemy of those opposing you. They say they are Jews, but they are not, because their synagogue belongs to Satan. 10Don't be afraid of what you are about to suffer. The devil will throw some of you into prison to test you. You will suffer for ten days. But if you remain faithful even when facing death, I will give you the crown of life.

11"Anyone with ears to hear must listen to the Spirit and understand what he is saying to the churches. Whoever is victorious will not be harmed by the second death.

The Message to the Church in Pergamum

12"Write this letter to the angel of the church in Pergamum. This is the message from the one with the sharp two-edged sword:

13"I know that you live in the city where Satan has his throne, yet you have remained loyal to me. You refused to deny me even when Antipas, my faithful

witness, was martyred among you there in Satan's city.

14"But I have a few complaints against you. You tolerate some among you whose teaching is like that of Balaam, who showed Balak how to trip up the people of Israel. He taught them to sin by eating food offered to idols and by committing sexual sin. 15In a similar way, you have some Nicolaitans among you who follow the same teaching. 16Repent of your sin, or I will come to you suddenly and fight against them with the sword of my mouth.

17"Anyone with ears to hear must listen to the Spirit and understand what he is saying to the churches. To everyone who is victorious I will give some of the manna that has been hidden away in heaven. And I will give to each one a white stone, and on the stone will be engraved a new name that no one understands except the one who receives it.

The Message to the Church in Thyatira

18"Write this letter to the angel of the church in Thyatira. This is the message from the Son of God, whose eyes are like flames of fire, whose feet are like polished bronze:

19"I know all the things you do. I have seen your love, your faith, your service, and your patient endurance. And I can see your constant improvement in all these things.

20"But I have this complaint against you. You are permitting that woman—that Jezebel who calls herself a prophet—to lead my servants astray. She teaches them to commit sexual sin and to eat food offered to idols. 21I gave her time to repent, but she does not want to turn away from her immorality.

22"Therefore, I will throw her on a bed of suffering,* and those who commit adultery with her will suffer greatly unless they repent and turn away from her evil deeds. 23I will strike her children dead. Then all the churches will know that I am the one who searches out the thoughts and intentions of every person. And I will give to each of you whatever you deserve.

24"But I also have a message for the rest of you in Thyatira who have not followed this false teaching ('deeper truths,' as they call them—depths of Satan, actually). I will ask nothing more of you 25except that you hold tightly to what you have until I come. 26To all who are victorious, who obey me to the very end,

To them I will give authority
over all the nations.

27 They will rule the nations
with an iron rod
and smash them like
clay pots.*

28They will have the same authority I received from my Father, and I will also give them the morning star!

29"Anyone with ears to hear must listen to the Spirit and understand what he is saying to the churches.

The Message to the Church in Sardis

3 "Write this letter to the angel* of the church in Sardis. This is the message from the one who has the sevenfold Spirit* of God and the seven stars:

"I know all the things you do, and that you have a reputation for being alive—but you are dead. 2Wake up! Strengthen what little remains, for even what is left is almost dead. I find that your actions do not meet the requirements of my God. 3Go back to what you heard and believed at first; hold to it firmly. Repent and turn to me again. If you don't wake up, I will come to you suddenly, as unexpected as a thief.

4"Yet there are some in the church in Sardis who have not soiled their clothes with evil.

2:22 Greek *a bed.* 2:26-27 Ps 2:8-9 (Greek version). 3:1a Or *the messenger;* also in 3:7, 14.
3:1b Greek *the seven spirits.*

They will walk with me in white, for they are worthy. [5]All who are victorious will be clothed in white. I will never erase their names from the Book of Life, but I will announce before my Father and his angels that they are mine.

[6]"Anyone with ears to hear must listen to the Spirit and understand what he is saying to the churches.

The Message to the Church in Philadelphia

[7]"Write this letter to the angel of the church in Philadelphia.

This is the message from the one who is holy and true, the one who has the key of David.
What he opens, no one can close;
and what he closes, no one can open:*

[8]"I know all the things you do, and I have opened a door for you that no one can close. You have little strength, yet you obeyed my word and did not deny me. [9]Look, I will force those who belong to Satan's synagogue—those liars who say they are Jews but are not—to come and bow down at your feet. They will acknowledge that you are the ones I love.

[10]"Because you have obeyed my command to persevere, I will protect you from the great time of testing that will come upon the whole world to test those who belong to this world. [11]I am coming soon.* Hold on to what you have, so that no one will take away your crown. [12]All who are victorious will become pillars in the Temple of my God, and they will never have to leave it. And I will write on them the name of my God, and they will be citizens in the city of my God—the new Jerusalem that comes down from heaven from my God. And I will also write on them my new name.

[13]"Anyone with ears to hear must listen to the Spirit and understand what he is saying to the churches.

The Message to the Church in Laodicea

[14]"Write this letter to the angel of the church in Laodicea. This is the message from the one who is the Amen—the faithful and true witness, the beginning* of God's new creation:

[15]"I know all the things you do, that you are neither hot nor cold. I wish that you were one or the other! [16]But since you are like lukewarm water, neither hot nor cold, I will spit you out of my mouth! [17]You say, 'I am rich. I have everything I want. I don't need a thing!' And you don't

realize that you are wretched and miserable and poor and blind and naked. ¹⁸So I advise you to buy gold from me—gold that has been purified by fire. Then you will be rich. Also buy white garments from me so you will not be shamed by your nakedness, and ointment for your eyes so you will be able to see. ¹⁹I correct and discipline everyone I love. So be diligent and turn from your indifference.

²⁰"Look! I stand at the door and knock. If you hear my voice and open the door, I will come in, and we will share a meal together as friends. ²¹Those who are victorious will sit with me on my throne, just as I was victorious and sat with my Father on his throne.

²²"Anyone with ears to hear must listen to the Spirit and understand what he is saying to the churches."

Worship in Heaven

4 Then as I looked, I saw a door standing open in heaven, and the same voice I had heard before spoke to me like a trumpet blast. The voice said, "Come up here, and I will show you what must happen after this." ²And instantly I was in the Spirit,* and I saw a throne in heaven and someone sitting on it. ³The one sitting on the throne was as brilliant as gemstones—like jasper and car-

nelian. And the glow of an emerald circled his throne like a rainbow. ⁴Twenty-four thrones surrounded him, and twenty-four elders sat on them. They were all clothed in white and had gold crowns on their heads. ⁵From the throne came flashes of lightning and the rumble of thunder. And in front of the throne were seven torches with burning flames. This is the sevenfold Spirit* of God. ⁶In front of the throne was a shiny sea of glass, sparkling like crystal.

In the center and around the throne were four living beings, each covered with eyes, front and back. ⁷The first of these living beings was like a lion; the second was like an ox; the third had a human face; and the fourth was like an eagle in flight. ⁸Each of these living beings had six wings, and their wings were covered all over with eyes, inside and out. Day after day and night after night they keep on saying,

"Holy, holy, holy is the Lord God,
      the Almighty—
the one who always was, who
      is, and who is still to come."

⁹Whenever the living beings give glory and honor and thanks to the one sitting on the throne (the one who lives forever and ever), ¹⁰the twenty-four elders fall down and worship the one sitting on the throne (the one who lives forever and ever). And they lay their crowns before the throne and say,

4:2 Or *in spirit*.   4:5 Greek *They are the seven spirits*.

11 "You are worthy, O Lord our God,
  to receive glory and honor and
    power.
For you created all things,
  and they exist because you
    created what you pleased."

The Lamb Opens the Scroll

5 Then I saw a scroll* in the right hand of the one who was sitting on the throne. There was writing on the inside and the outside of the scroll, and it was sealed with seven seals. 2And I saw a strong angel, who shouted with a loud voice: "Who is worthy to break the seals on this scroll and open it?" 3But no one in heaven or on earth or under the earth was able to open the scroll and read it.

4Then I began to weep bitterly because no one was found worthy to open the scroll and read it. 5But one of the twenty-four elders said to me, "Stop weeping! Look, the Lion of the tribe of Judah, the heir to David's throne,* has won the victory. He is worthy to open the scroll and its seven seals."

6Then I saw a Lamb that looked as if it had been slaughtered, but it was now standing between the throne and the four living beings and among the twenty-four elders. He had seven horns and seven eyes, which represent the sevenfold Spirit* of God that is sent out into every part of the earth. 7He stepped forward and took the scroll from the right hand of the one sitting on the throne. 8And when he took the scroll, the four living beings and the twenty-four elders fell down before the Lamb. Each one had a harp, and they held gold bowls filled with incense, which are the prayers of God's people. 9And they sang a new song with these words:

"You are worthy to take the scroll
  and break its seals and
    open it.
For you were slaughtered, and
  your blood has ransomed
    people for God
  from every tribe and language
    and people and nation.
10 And you have caused them
    to become
  a Kingdom of priests for
    our God.
  And they will reign* on
    the earth."

11Then I looked again, and I heard the voices of thousands and millions of angels around the throne and of the living beings and the elders. 12And they sang in a mighty chorus:

"Worthy is the Lamb who was
    slaughtered—
  to receive power and riches
    and wisdom and strength
    and honor and glory and
      blessing."

5:1 Or book; also in 5:2, 3, 4, 5, 7, 8, 9.   5:5 Greek the root of David. See Isa 11:10.   5:6 Greek which are the seven spirits.   5:10 Some manuscripts read they are reigning.

¹³And then I heard every creature in heaven and on earth and under the earth and in the sea. They sang:

"Blessing and honor and glory
    and power
  belong to the one sitting
    on the throne
  and to the Lamb forever
    and ever."

¹⁴And the four living beings said, "Amen!" And the twenty-four elders fell down and worshiped the Lamb.

The Lamb Breaks the First Six Seals

6 As I watched, the Lamb broke the first of the seven seals on the scroll.* Then I heard one of the four living beings say with a voice like thunder, "Come!" ²I looked up and saw a white horse standing there. Its rider carried a bow, and a crown was placed on his head. He rode out to win many battles and gain the victory.

³When the Lamb broke the second seal, I heard the second living being say, "Come!" ⁴Then another horse appeared, a red one. Its rider was given a mighty sword and the authority to take peace from the earth. And there was war and slaughter everywhere.

⁵When the Lamb broke the third seal, I heard the third living being say, "Come!" I looked up and saw a black horse, and its rider was hold-ing a pair of scales in his hand. ⁶And I heard a voice from among the four living beings say, "A loaf of wheat bread or three loaves of barley will cost a day's pay.* And don't waste* the olive oil and wine."

⁷When the Lamb broke the fourth seal, I heard the fourth living being say, "Come!" ⁸I looked up and saw a horse whose color was pale green. Its rider was named Death, and his companion was the Grave.* These two were given authority over one-fourth of the earth, to kill with the sword and famine and disease* and wild animals.

⁹When the Lamb broke the fifth seal, I saw under the altar the souls of all who had been martyred for the word of God and for being faithful in their testimony. ¹⁰They shouted to the Lord and said, "O Sovereign Lord, holy and true, how long before you judge the people who belong to this world and avenge our blood for what they have done to us?" ¹¹Then a white robe was given to each of them. And they were told to rest a little longer until the full number of their brothers and sisters*—their fellow servants of Jesus who were to be martyred—had joined them.

¹²I watched as the Lamb broke the sixth seal, and there was a great earthquake. The sun became as dark as black cloth, and the moon

6:1 Or *book.* 6:6a Greek *A choinix* [1 quart or 1 liter] *of wheat for a denarius, and 3 choinix of barley for a denarius.* A denarius was equivalent to a laborer's full day's wage. 6:6b Or *harm.* 6:8a Greek *was Hades.* 6:8b Greek *death.* 6:11 Greek *their brothers.*

became as red as blood. [13]Then the stars of the sky fell to the earth like green figs falling from a tree shaken by a strong wind. [14]The sky was rolled up like a scroll, and all of the mountains and islands were moved from their places.

[15]Then everyone—the kings of the earth, the rulers, the generals, the wealthy, the powerful, and every slave and free person—all hid themselves in the caves and among the rocks of the mountains. [16]And they cried to the mountains and the rocks, "Fall on us and hide us from the face of the one who sits on the throne and from the wrath of the Lamb. [17]For the great day of their wrath has come, and who is able to survive?"

God's People Will Be Preserved

7 Then I saw four angels standing at the four corners of the earth, holding back the four winds so they did not blow on the earth or the sea, or even on any tree. [2]And I saw another angel coming up from the east, carrying the seal of the living God. And he shouted to those four angels, who had been given power to harm land and sea, [3]"Wait! Don't harm the land or the sea or the trees until we have placed the seal of God on the foreheads of his servants."

[4]And I heard how many were marked with the seal of God— 144,000 were sealed from all the tribes of Israel:

[5] from Judah	12,000
from Reuben	12,000
from Gad	12,000
[6] from Asher	12,000
from Naphtali	12,000
from Manasseh	12,000
[7] from Simeon	12,000
from Levi	12,000
from Issachar	12,000
[8] from Zebulun	12,000
from Joseph	12,000
from Benjamin	12,000

Praise from the Great Crowd

[9]After this I saw a vast crowd, too great to count, from every nation and tribe and people and language, standing in front of the throne and before the Lamb. They were clothed in white robes and held palm branches in their hands. [10]And they were shouting with a great roar,

"Salvation comes from our God
who sits on the throne
and from the Lamb!"

[11]And all the angels were standing around the throne and around the elders and the four living beings. And they fell before the throne with their faces to the ground and worshiped God. [12]They sang,

"Amen! Blessing and glory and wisdom
and thanksgiving and honor
and power and strength belong to our God
forever and ever! Amen."

¹³Then one of the twenty-four elders asked me, "Who are these who are clothed in white? Where did they come from?"

¹⁴And I said to him, "Sir, you are the one who knows."

Then he said to me, "These are the ones who died in* the great tribulation.* They have washed their robes in the blood of the Lamb and made them white.

¹⁵ "That is why they stand in front
      of God's throne
   and serve him day and night
      in his Temple.
   And he who sits on the throne
      will give them shelter.
¹⁶ They will never again be hungry
      or thirsty;
   they will never be scorched
      by the heat of the sun.
¹⁷ For the Lamb on the throne*
      will be their Shepherd.
   He will lead them to springs of
      life-giving water.
   And God will wipe every tear
      from their eyes."

The Lamb Breaks the Seventh Seal

8 When the Lamb broke the seventh seal on the scroll,* there was silence throughout heaven for about half an hour. ²I saw the seven angels who stand before God, and they were given seven trumpets.

³Then another angel with a gold incense burner came and stood at the altar. And a great amount of incense was given to him to mix with the prayers of God's people as an offering on the gold altar before the throne. ⁴The smoke of the incense, mixed with the prayers of God's holy people, ascended up to God from the altar where the angel had poured them out. ⁵Then the angel filled the incense burner with fire from the altar and threw it down upon the earth; and thunder crashed, lightning flashed, and there was a terrible earthquake.

The First Four Trumpets

⁶Then the seven angels with the seven trumpets prepared to blow their mighty blasts.

⁷The first angel blew his trumpet, and hail and fire mixed with blood were thrown down on the earth. One-third of the earth was set on fire, one-third of the trees were burned, and all the green grass was burned.

⁸Then the second angel blew his trumpet, and a great mountain of fire was thrown into the sea. One-third of the water in the sea became blood, ⁹one-third of all things living in the sea died, and one-third of all the ships on the sea were destroyed.

¹⁰Then the third angel blew his trumpet, and a great star fell from the sky, burning like a torch. It fell on one-third of the rivers and on the springs of water. ¹¹The name of

7:14a Greek *who came out of.* 7:14b Or *the great suffering.* 7:17 Greek *on the center of the throne.* 8:1 Or *book.*

the star was Bitterness.* It made one-third of the water bitter, and many people died from drinking the bitter water.

¹²Then the fourth angel blew his trumpet, and one-third of the sun was struck, and one-third of the moon, and one-third of the stars, and they became dark. And one-third of the day was dark, and also one-third of the night.

¹³Then I looked, and I heard a single eagle crying loudly as it flew through the air, "Terror, terror, terror to all who belong to this world because of what will happen when the last three angels blow their trumpets."

The Fifth Trumpet Brings the First Terror

9 Then the fifth angel blew his trumpet, and I saw a star that had fallen to earth from the sky, and he was given the key to the shaft of the bottomless pit.* ²When he opened it, smoke poured out as though from a huge furnace, and the sunlight and air turned dark from the smoke.

³Then locusts came from the smoke and descended on the earth, and they were given power to sting like scorpions. ⁴They were told not to harm the grass or plants or trees, but only the people who did not have the seal of God on their foreheads. ⁵They were told not to kill them but to torture them for five months with pain like the pain of a scorpion sting. ⁶In those days people will seek death but will not find it. They will long to die, but death will flee from them!

⁷The locusts looked like horses prepared for battle. They had what looked like gold crowns on their heads, and their faces looked like human faces. ⁸They had hair like women's hair and teeth like the teeth of a lion. ⁹They wore armor made of iron, and their wings roared like an army of chariots rushing into battle. ¹⁰They had tails that stung like scorpions, and for five months they had the power to torment people. ¹¹Their king is the angel from the bottomless pit; his name in Hebrew is *Abaddon,* and in Greek, *Apollyon*—the Destroyer.

¹²The first terror is past, but look, two more terrors are coming!

The Sixth Trumpet Brings the Second Terror

¹³Then the sixth angel blew his trumpet, and I heard a voice speaking from the four horns of the gold altar that stands in the presence of God. ¹⁴And the voice said to the sixth angel who held the trumpet, "Release the four angels who are bound at the great Euphrates River." ¹⁵Then the four angels who had been prepared for this hour and day and month and year were turned loose to kill one-third of all the people on earth. ¹⁶I heard the

8:11 Greek *Wormwood.* 9:1 Or *the abyss,* or *the underworld;* also in 9:11.

size of their army, which was 200 million mounted troops.

¹⁷And in my vision, I saw the horses and the riders sitting on them. The riders wore armor that was fiery red and dark blue and yellow. The horses had heads like lions, and fire and smoke and burning sulfur billowed from their mouths. ¹⁸One-third of all the people on earth were killed by these three plagues—by the fire and smoke and burning sulfur that came from the mouths of the horses. ¹⁹Their power was in their mouths and in their tails. For their tails had heads like snakes, with the power to injure people.

²⁰But the people who did not die in these plagues still refused to repent of their evil deeds and turn to God. They continued to worship demons and idols made of gold, silver, bronze, stone, and wood—idols that can neither see nor hear nor walk! ²¹And they did not repent of their murders or their witchcraft or their sexual immorality or their thefts.

The Angel and the Small Scroll

10 Then I saw another mighty angel coming down from heaven, surrounded by a cloud, with a rainbow over his head. His face shone like the sun, and his feet were like pillars of fire. ²And in his hand was a small scroll* that had been opened. He stood with his right foot on the sea and his left foot on the land. ³And he gave a great shout like the roar of a lion. And when he shouted, the seven thunders answered.

⁴When the seven thunders spoke, I was about to write. But I heard a voice from heaven saying, "Keep secret* what the seven thunders said, and do not write it down."

⁵Then the angel I saw standing on the sea and on the land raised his right hand toward heaven. ⁶He swore an oath in the name of the one who lives forever and ever, who created the heavens and everything in them, the earth and everything in it, and the sea and everything in it. He said, "There will be no more delay. ⁷When the seventh angel blows his trumpet, God's mysterious plan will be fulfilled. It will happen just as he announced it to his servants the prophets."

⁸Then the voice from heaven spoke to me again: "Go and take the open scroll from the hand of the angel who is standing on the sea and on the land."

⁹So I went to the angel and told him to give me the small scroll. "Yes, take it and eat it," he said. "It will be sweet as honey in your mouth, but it will turn sour in your stomach!" ¹⁰So I took the small scroll from the hand of the angel, and I ate it! It was sweet in my mouth, but when I swallowed it, it turned sour in my stomach.

10:2 Or *book;* also in 10:8, 9, 10.   **10:4** Greek *Seal up.*

¹¹Then I was told, "You must prophesy again about many peoples, nations, languages, and kings."

The Two Witnesses

11 Then I was given a measuring stick, and I was told, "Go and measure the Temple of God and the altar, and count the number of worshipers. ²But do not measure the outer courtyard, for it has been turned over to the nations. They will trample the holy city for 42 months. ³And I will give power to my two witnesses, and they will be clothed in burlap and will prophesy during those 1,260 days."

⁴These two prophets are the two olive trees and the two lampstands that stand before the Lord of all the earth. ⁵If anyone tries to harm them, fire flashes from their mouths and consumes their enemies. This is how anyone who tries to harm them must die. ⁶They have power to shut the sky so that no rain will fall for as long as they prophesy. And they have the power to turn the rivers and oceans into blood, and to strike the earth with every kind of plague as often as they wish.

⁷When they complete their testimony, the beast that comes up out of the bottomless pit* will declare war against them, and he will conquer them and kill them. ⁸And their bodies will lie in the main street of Jerusalem,* the city that is figuratively called "Sodom" and "Egypt," the city where their Lord was crucified. ⁹And for three and a half days, all peoples, tribes, languages, and nations will stare at their bodies. No one will be allowed to bury them. ¹⁰All the people who belong to this world will gloat over them and give presents to each other to celebrate the death of the two prophets who had tormented them.

¹¹But after three and a half days, God breathed life into them, and they stood up! Terror struck all who were staring at them. ¹²Then a loud voice from heaven called to the two prophets, "Come up here!" And they rose to heaven in a cloud as their enemies watched.

¹³At the same time there was a terrible earthquake that destroyed a tenth of the city. Seven thousand people died in that earthquake, and everyone else was terrified and gave glory to the God of heaven.

¹⁴The second terror is past, but look, the third terror is coming quickly.

The Seventh Trumpet Brings the Third Terror

¹⁵Then the seventh angel blew his trumpet, and there were loud voices shouting in heaven:

> "The world has now become the
>   Kingdom of our Lord and
>   of his Christ,*
>   and he will reign forever
>   and ever."

11:7 Or *the abyss,* or *the underworld.*   **11:8** Greek *the great city.*   **11:15** Or *his Messiah.*

¹⁶The twenty-four elders sitting on their thrones before God fell with their faces to the ground and worshiped him. ¹⁷And they said,

"We give thanks to you, Lord
    God, the Almighty,
the one who is and who
    always was,
for now you have assumed your
    great power
and have begun to reign.
¹⁸ The nations were filled with
    wrath,
    but now the time of your
        wrath has come.
It is time to judge the dead
    and reward your servants
        the prophets,
    as well as your holy people,
and all who fear your name,
    from the least to the greatest.
It is time to destroy
    all who have caused
        destruction on the earth."

¹⁹Then, in heaven, the Temple of God was opened and the Ark of his covenant could be seen inside the Temple. Lightning flashed, thunder crashed and roared, and there was an earthquake and a terrible hailstorm.

The Woman and the Dragon

12 Then I witnessed in heaven an event of great significance. I saw a woman clothed with the sun, with the moon beneath her feet, and a crown of twelve stars on her head.

²She was pregnant, and she cried out because of her labor pains and the agony of giving birth.

³Then I witnessed in heaven another significant event. I saw a large red dragon with seven heads and ten horns, with seven crowns on his heads. ⁴His tail swept away one-third of the stars in the sky, and he threw them to the earth. He stood in front of the woman as she was about to give birth, ready to devour her baby as soon as it was born.

⁵She gave birth to a son who was to rule all nations with an iron rod. And her child was snatched away from the dragon and was caught up to God and to his throne. ⁶And the woman fled into the wilderness, where God had prepared a place to care for her for 1,260 days.

⁷Then there was war in heaven. Michael and his angels fought against the dragon and his angels. ⁸And the dragon lost the battle, and he and his angels were forced out of heaven. ⁹This great dragon—the ancient serpent called the devil, or Satan, the one deceiving the whole world—was thrown down to the earth with all his angels.

¹⁰Then I heard a loud voice shouting across the heavens,

"It has come at last—
    salvation and power
and the Kingdom of our God,
    and the authority of his
        Christ.*

12:10a Or *his Messiah.*

For the accuser of our brothers
   and sisters*
   has been thrown down
      to earth—
   the one who accuses them
      before our God day and night.
[11] And they have defeated him by
   the blood of the Lamb
   and by their testimony.
   And they did not love their lives
      so much
   that they were afraid to die.
[12] Therefore, rejoice, O heavens!
   And you who live in the
      heavens, rejoice!
   But terror will come on the earth
      and the sea,
   for the devil has come down
      to you in great anger,
   knowing that he has little
      time."

[13]When the dragon realized that he had been thrown down to the earth, he pursued the woman who had given birth to the male child. [14]But she was given two wings like those of a great eagle so she could fly to the place prepared for her in the wilderness. There she would be cared for and protected from the dragon* for a time, times, and half a time. [15]Then the dragon tried to drown the woman with a flood of water that flowed from his mouth. [16]But the earth helped her by opening its mouth and swallowing the river that gushed out from the mouth of the dragon. [17]And the dragon was angry at the woman and declared war against the rest of her children—all who keep God's commandments and maintain their testimony for Jesus.

[18]Then the dragon took his stand* on the shore beside the sea.

The Beast out of the Sea

13 Then I saw a beast rising up out of the sea. It had seven heads and ten horns, with ten crowns on its horns. And written on each head were names that blasphemed God. [2]This beast looked like a leopard, but it had the feet of a bear and the mouth of a lion! And the dragon gave the beast his own power and throne and great authority.

[3]I saw that one of the heads of the beast seemed wounded beyond recovery—but the fatal wound was healed! The whole world marveled at this miracle and gave allegiance to the beast. [4]They worshiped the dragon for giving the beast such power, and they also worshiped the beast. "Who is as great as the beast?" they exclaimed. "Who is able to fight against him?"

[5]Then the beast was allowed to speak great blasphemies against God. And he was given authority to do whatever he wanted for forty-

12:10b Greek *brothers*.   **12:14** Greek *the serpent;* also in 12:15. See 12:9.   **12:18** Greek *Then he took his stand;* some manuscripts read *Then I took my stand*. Some translations put this entire sentence into 13:1.

two months. [6]And he spoke terrible words of blasphemy against God, slandering his name and his dwelling—that is, those who dwell in heaven.* [7]And the beast was allowed to wage war against God's holy people and to conquer them. And he was given authority to rule over every tribe and people and language and nation. [8]And all the people who belong to this world worshiped the beast. They are the ones whose names were not written in the Book of Life that belongs to the Lamb who was slaughtered before the world was made.*

[9] Anyone with ears to hear
    should listen and understand.
[10] Anyone who is destined for
      prison
    will be taken to prison.
    Anyone destined to die by the
      sword
    will die by the sword.

This means that God's holy people must endure persecution patiently and remain faithful.

The Beast out of the Earth
[11]Then I saw another beast come up out of the earth. He had two horns like those of a lamb, but he spoke with the voice of a dragon. [12]He exercised all the authority of the first beast. And he required all the earth and its people to worship the first

beast, whose fatal wound had been healed. [13]He did astounding miracles, even making fire flash down to earth from the sky while everyone was watching. [14]And with all the miracles he was allowed to perform on behalf of the first beast, he deceived all the people who belong to this world. He ordered the people to make a great statue of the first beast, who was fatally wounded and then came back to life. [15]He was then permitted to give life to this statue so that it could speak. Then the statue of the beast commanded that anyone refusing to worship it must die.

[16]He required everyone—small and great, rich and poor, free and slave—to be given a mark on the right hand or on the forehead. [17]And no one could buy or sell anything without that mark, which was either the name of the beast or the number representing his name. [18]Wisdom is needed here. Let the one with understanding solve the meaning of the number of the beast, for it is the number of a man.* His number is 666.*

The Lamb and the 144,000
14 Then I saw the Lamb standing on Mount Zion, and with him were 144,000 who had his name and his Father's name written on their foreheads. [2]And I heard a

13:6 Some manuscripts read *and his dwelling and all who dwell in heaven.*   **13:8** Or *not written in the Book of Life before the world was made—the Book that belongs to the Lamb who was slaughtered.*
13:18a Or *of humanity.*   **13:18b** Some manuscripts read *616.*

sound from heaven like the roar of mighty ocean waves or the rolling of loud thunder. It was like the sound of many harpists playing together.

³This great choir sang a wonderful new song in front of the throne of God and before the four living beings and the twenty-four elders. No one could learn this song except the 144,000 who had been redeemed from the earth. ⁴They have kept themselves as pure as virgins,* following the Lamb wherever he goes. They have been purchased from among the people on the earth as a special offering* to God and to the Lamb. ⁵They have told no lies; they are without blame.

The Three Angels
⁶And I saw another angel flying through the sky, carrying the eternal Good News to proclaim to the people who belong to this world—to every nation, tribe, language, and people. ⁷"Fear God," he shouted. "Give glory to him. For the time has come when he will sit as judge. Worship him who made the heavens, the earth, the sea, and all the springs of water."

⁸Then another angel followed him through the sky, shouting, "Babylon is fallen—that great city is fallen—because she made all the nations of the world drink the wine of her passionate immorality."

⁹Then a third angel followed them, shouting, "Anyone who worships the beast and his statue or who accepts his mark on the forehead or on the hand ¹⁰must drink the wine of God's anger. It has been poured full strength into God's cup of wrath. And they will be tormented with fire and burning sulfur in the presence of the holy angels and the Lamb. ¹¹The smoke of their torment will rise forever and ever, and they will have no relief day or night, for they have worshiped the beast and his statue and have accepted the mark of his name."

¹²This means that God's holy people must endure persecution patiently, obeying his commands and maintaining their faith in Jesus.

¹³And I heard a voice from heaven saying, "Write this down: Blessed are those who die in the Lord from now on. Yes, says the Spirit, they are blessed indeed, for they will rest from their hard work; for their good deeds follow them!"

The Harvest of the Earth
¹⁴Then I saw a white cloud, and seated on the cloud was someone like the Son of Man.* He had a gold crown on his head and a sharp sickle in his hand.

¹⁵Then another angel came from the Temple and shouted to the one sitting on the cloud, "Swing the sickle, for the time of harvest has come; the crop on earth is ripe."

14:4a Greek *They are virgins who have not defiled themselves with women.* 14:4b Greek *as firstfruits.* 14:14 Or *like a son of man.* See Dan 7:13. "Son of Man" is a title Jesus used for himself.

[16]So the one sitting on the cloud swung his sickle over the earth, and the whole earth was harvested.

[17]After that, another angel came from the Temple in heaven, and he also had a sharp sickle. [18]Then another angel, who had power to destroy with fire, came from the altar. He shouted to the angel with the sharp sickle, "Swing your sickle now to gather the clusters of grapes from the vines of the earth, for they are ripe for judgment." [19]So the angel swung his sickle over the earth and loaded the grapes into the great winepress of God's wrath. [20]The grapes were trampled in the winepress outside the city, and blood flowed from the winepress in a stream about 180 miles* long and as high as a horse's bridle.

The Song of Moses and of the Lamb

15 Then I saw in heaven another marvelous event of great significance. Seven angels were holding the seven last plagues, which would bring God's wrath to completion. [2]I saw before me what seemed to be a glass sea mixed with fire. And on it stood all the people who had been victorious over the beast and his statue and the number representing his name. They were all holding harps that God had given them. [3]And they were singing the song of Moses, the servant of God, and the song of the Lamb:

"Great and marvelous are your works,
     O Lord God, the Almighty.
Just and true are your ways,
     O King of the nations.*
[4]Who will not fear you, Lord,
     and glorify your name?
For you alone are holy.
All nations will come and
     worship before you,
     for your righteous deeds have
          been revealed."

The Seven Bowls of the Seven Plagues

[5]Then I looked and saw that the Temple in heaven, God's Tabernacle, was thrown wide open. [6]The seven angels who were holding the seven plagues came out of the Temple. They were clothed in spotless white linen* with gold sashes across their chests. [7]Then one of the four living beings handed each of the seven angels a gold bowl filled with the wrath of God, who lives forever and ever. [8]The Temple was filled with smoke from God's glory and power. No one could enter the Temple until the seven angels had completed pouring out the seven plagues.

16 Then I heard a mighty voice from the Temple say to the seven angels, "Go your ways and pour out on the earth the seven bowls containing God's wrath." [2]So the first angel left the Temple

14:20 Greek *1,600 stadia* [300 kilometers]. **15:3** Some manuscripts read *King of the ages.* **15:6** Other manuscripts read *white stone;* still others read *white [garments] made of linen.*

and poured out his bowl on the earth, and horrible, malignant sores broke out on everyone who had the mark of the beast and who worshiped his statue.

³Then the second angel poured out his bowl on the sea, and it became like the blood of a corpse. And everything in the sea died.

⁴Then the third angel poured out his bowl on the rivers and springs, and they became blood. ⁵And I heard the angel who had authority over all water saying,

"You are just, O Holy One, who is and who always was,
　　because you have sent these judgments.
⁶ Since they shed the blood
　　of your holy people and your prophets,
you have given them blood to drink.
　　It is their just reward."

⁷And I heard a voice from the altar,* saying,

"Yes, O Lord God, the Almighty,
　　your judgments are true and just."

⁸Then the fourth angel poured out his bowl on the sun, causing it to scorch everyone with its fire. ⁹Everyone was burned by this blast of heat, and they cursed the name of God, who had control over all these plagues. They did not repent of their sins and turn to God and give him glory.

¹⁰Then the fifth angel poured out his bowl on the throne of the beast, and his kingdom was plunged into darkness. His subjects ground their teeth* in anguish, ¹¹and they cursed the God of heaven for their pains and sores. But they did not repent of their evil deeds and turn to God.

¹²Then the sixth angel poured out his bowl on the great Euphrates River, and it dried up so that the kings from the east could march their armies toward the west without hindrance. ¹³And I saw three evil* spirits that looked like frogs leap from the mouths of the dragon, the beast, and the false prophet. ¹⁴They are demonic spirits who work miracles and go out to all the rulers of the world to gather them for battle against the Lord on that great judgment day of God the Almighty.

¹⁵"Look, I will come as unexpectedly as a thief! Blessed are all who are watching for me, who keep their clothing ready so they will not have to walk around naked and ashamed."

¹⁶And the demonic spirits gathered all the rulers and their armies to a place with the Hebrew name *Armageddon*.*

¹⁷Then the seventh angel poured out his bowl into the air. And a mighty shout came from the throne

16:7 Greek *I heard the altar.* **16:10** Greek *gnawed their tongues.* **16:13** Greek *unclean.* **16:16** Or *Harmagedon.*

in the Temple, saying, "It is finished!" [18]Then the thunder crashed and rolled, and lightning flashed. And a great earthquake struck—the worst since people were placed on the earth. [19]The great city of Babylon split into three sections, and the cities of many nations fell into heaps of rubble. So God remembered all of Babylon's sins, and he made her drink the cup that was filled with the wine of his fierce wrath. [20]And every island disappeared, and all the mountains were leveled. [21]There was a terrible hailstorm, and hailstones weighing as much as seventy-five pounds* fell from the sky onto the people below. They cursed God because of the terrible plague of the hailstorm.

The Great Prostitute

17 One of the seven angels who had poured out the seven bowls came over and spoke to me. "Come with me," he said, "and I will show you the judgment that is going to come on the great prostitute, who rules over many waters. [2]The kings of the world have committed adultery with her, and the people who belong to this world have been made drunk by the wine of her immorality."

[3]So the angel took me in the Spirit* into the wilderness. There I saw a woman sitting on a scarlet beast that had seven heads and ten horns, and blasphemies against

God were written all over it. [4]The woman wore purple and scarlet clothing and beautiful jewelry made of gold and precious gems and pearls. In her hand she held a gold goblet full of obscenities and the impurities of her immorality. [5]A mysterious name was written on her forehead: "Babylon the Great, Mother of All Prostitutes and Obscenities in the World." [6]I could see that she was drunk—drunk with the blood of God's holy people who were witnesses for Jesus. I stared at her in complete amazement.

[7]"Why are you so amazed?" the angel asked. "I will tell you the mystery of this woman and of the beast with seven heads and ten horns on which she sits. [8]The beast you saw was once alive but isn't now. And yet he will soon come up out of the bottomless pit* and go to eternal destruction. And the people who belong to this world, whose names were not written in the Book of Life before the world was made, will be amazed at the reappearance of this beast who had died.

[9]"This calls for a mind with understanding: The seven heads of the beast represent the seven hills where the woman rules. They also represent seven kings. [10]Five kings have already fallen, the sixth now reigns, and the seventh is yet to come, but his reign will be brief.

[11]"The scarlet beast that was, but is no longer, is the eighth king. He is

16:21 Greek *1 talent* [34 kilograms].   **17:3** Or *in spirit.*   **17:8** Or *the abyss,* or *the underworld.*

like the other seven, and he, too, is headed for destruction. ¹²The ten horns of the beast are ten kings who have not yet risen to power. They will be appointed to their kingdoms for one brief moment to reign with the beast. ¹³They will all agree to give him their power and authority. ¹⁴Together they will go to war against the Lamb, but the Lamb will defeat them because he is Lord of all lords and King of all kings. And his called and chosen and faithful ones will be with him."

¹⁵Then the angel said to me, "The waters where the prostitute is ruling represent masses of people of every nation and language. ¹⁶The scarlet beast and his ten horns all hate the prostitute. They will strip her naked, eat her flesh, and burn her remains with fire. ¹⁷For God has put a plan into their minds, a plan that will carry out his purposes. They will agree to give their authority to the scarlet beast, and so the words of God will be fulfilled. ¹⁸And this woman you saw in your vision represents the great city that rules over the kings of the world."

The Fall of Babylon

18 After all this I saw another angel come down from heaven with great authority, and the earth grew bright with his splendor. ²He gave a mighty shout:

"Babylon is fallen—that great city is fallen!
She has become a home for demons.
She is a hideout for every foul* spirit,
a hideout for every foul vulture and every foul and dreadful animal.*
³ For all the nations have fallen* because of the wine of her passionate immorality.
The kings of the world have committed adultery with her.
Because of her desires for extravagant luxury,
the merchants of the world have grown rich."

⁴Then I heard another voice calling from heaven,

"Come away from her, my people.
Do not take part in her sins,
or you will be punished with her.
⁵ For her sins are piled as high as heaven,
and God remembers her evil deeds.
⁶ Do to her as she has done to others.
Double her penalty* for all her evil deeds.
She brewed a cup of terror for others,
so brew twice as much* for her.

18:2a Greek *unclean;* also in each of the two following phrases.   18:2b Some manuscripts condense the last two lines to read *a hideout for every foul [unclean] and dreadful vulture.*   18:3 Some manuscripts read *have drunk.*   18:6a Or *Give her an equal penalty.*   18:6b Or *brew just as much.*

7 She glorified herself and lived in
luxury,
  so match it now with torment
  and sorrow.
She boasted in her heart,
  'I am queen on my throne.
I am no helpless widow,
  and I have no reason to
  mourn.'
8 Therefore, these plagues will
  overtake her in a single
  day—
  death and mourning and
  famine.
She will be completely
  consumed by fire,
  for the Lord God who judges
  her is mighty."

9 And the kings of the world who committed adultery with her and enjoyed her great luxury will mourn for her as they see the smoke rising from her charred remains. 10 They will stand at a distance, terrified by her great torment. They will cry out,

"How terrible, how terrible
  for you,
O Babylon, you great city!
In a single moment
  God's judgment came
  on you."

11 The merchants of the world will weep and mourn for her, for there is no one left to buy their goods. 12 She bought great quantities of gold, silver, jewels, and pearls; fine linen, purple, silk, and scarlet cloth; things made of fragrant thyine wood, ivory goods, and objects made of expensive wood; and bronze, iron, and marble. 13 She also bought cinnamon, spice, incense, myrrh, frankincense, wine, olive oil, fine flour, wheat, cattle, sheep, horses, wagons, and bodies—that is, human slaves.

14 "The fancy things you loved
  so much
  are gone," they cry.
"All your luxuries and splendor
  are gone forever,
  never to be yours again."

15 The merchants who became wealthy by selling her these things will stand at a distance, terrified by her great torment. They will weep and cry out,

16 "How terrible, how terrible for
  that great city!
She was clothed in finest
  purple and scarlet linens,
  decked out with gold and
  precious stones and pearls!
17 In a single moment
  all the wealth of the city
  is gone!"

And all the captains of the merchant ships and their passengers and sailors and crews will stand at a distance. 18 They will cry out as they watch the smoke ascend, and they will say, "Where is there another city as great as this?" 19 And they will weep and throw dust on their heads to show their grief. And they will cry out,

"How terrible, how terrible for
  that great city!
The shipowners became
  wealthy
  by transporting her great
  wealth on the seas.
In a single moment it is all
  gone."

20 Rejoice over her fate, O heaven
  and people of God and
  apostles and prophets!
For at last God has judged her
  for your sakes.

21 Then a mighty angel picked up
a boulder the size of a huge millstone. He threw it into the ocean
and shouted,

"Just like this, the great city
  Babylon
will be thrown down with
  violence
and will never be found again.
22 The sound of harps, singers,
  flutes, and trumpets
will never be heard in you
  again.
No craftsmen and no trades
  will ever be found in you
  again.
The sound of the mill
will never be heard in
  you again.
23 The light of a lamp
will never shine in you again.
The happy voices of brides and
  grooms

will never be heard in you
  again.
For your merchants were the
  greatest in the world,
  and you deceived the nations
  with your sorceries.
24 In your* streets flowed the blood
  of the prophets and of God's
  holy people
and the blood of people
  slaughtered all over the
  world."

Songs of Victory in Heaven

19 After this, I heard what sounded like a vast crowd in heaven
shouting,

"Praise the LORD!*
Salvation and glory and power
  belong to our God.
2 His judgments are true and just.
He has punished the great
  prostitute
who corrupted the earth with
  her immorality.
He has avenged the murder
  of his servants."

3 And again their voices rang out:

"Praise the LORD!
The smoke from that city
  ascends forever and ever!"

4 Then the twenty-four elders and
the four living beings fell down and
worshiped God, who was sitting on
the throne. They cried out, "Amen!
Praise the LORD!"

18:24 Greek *her.* 19:1 Greek *Hallelujah;* also in 19:3, 4, 6. *Hallelujah* is the transliteration of a
Hebrew term that means "Praise the LORD."

[5]And from the throne came a voice that said,

> "Praise our God,
>> all his servants,
>> all who fear him,
>>> from the least to the greatest."

[6]Then I heard again what sounded like the shout of a vast crowd or the roar of mighty ocean waves or the crash of loud thunder:

> "Praise the LORD!
>> For the Lord our God,* the Almighty, reigns.
> [7] Let us be glad and rejoice,
>> and let us give honor to him.
>> For the time has come for the wedding feast of the Lamb,
>>> and his bride has prepared herself.
> [8] She has been given the finest of pure white linen to wear."
>> For the fine linen represents the good deeds of God's holy people.

[9]And the angel said to me, "Write this: Blessed are those who are invited to the wedding feast of the Lamb." And he added, "These are true words that come from God."

[10]Then I fell down at his feet to worship him, but he said, "No, don't worship me. I am a servant of God, just like you and your brothers and sisters* who testify about their faith in Jesus. Worship only God. For the essence of prophecy is to give a clear witness for Jesus.*"

The Rider on the White Horse

[11]Then I saw heaven opened, and a white horse was standing there. Its rider was named Faithful and True, for he judges fairly and wages a righteous war. [12]His eyes were like flames of fire, and on his head were many crowns. A name was written on him that no one understood except himself. [13]He wore a robe dipped in blood, and his title was the Word of God. [14]The armies of heaven, dressed in the finest of pure white linen, followed him on white horses. [15]From his mouth came a sharp sword to strike down the nations. He will rule them with an iron rod. He will release the fierce wrath of God, the Almighty, like juice flowing from a winepress. [16]On his robe at his thigh* was written this title: King of all kings and Lord of all lords.

[17]Then I saw an angel standing in the sun, shouting to the vultures flying high in the sky: "Come! Gather together for the great banquet God has prepared. [18]Come and eat the flesh of kings, generals, and strong warriors; of horses and their riders; and of all humanity, both free and slave, small and great."

[19]Then I saw the beast and the kings of the world and their armies gathered together to fight against

---

19:6 Some manuscripts read *the Lord God.*   **19:10a** Greek *brothers.*   **19:10b** Or *is the message confirmed by Jesus.*   **19:16** Or *On his robe and thigh.*

the one sitting on the horse and his army. [20]And the beast was captured, and with him the false prophet who did mighty miracles on behalf of the beast—miracles that deceived all who had accepted the mark of the beast and who worshiped his statue. Both the beast and his false prophet were thrown alive into the fiery lake of burning sulfur. [21]Their entire army was killed by the sharp sword that came from the mouth of the one riding the white horse. And the vultures all gorged themselves on the dead bodies.

The Thousand Years

20 Then I saw an angel coming down from heaven with the key to the bottomless pit* and a heavy chain in his hand. [2]He seized the dragon—that old serpent, who is the devil, Satan—and bound him in chains for a thousand years. [3]The angel threw him into the bottomless pit, which he then shut and locked so Satan could not deceive the nations anymore until the thousand years were finished. Afterward he must be released for a little while.

[4]Then I saw thrones, and the people sitting on them had been given the authority to judge. And I saw the souls of those who had been beheaded for their testimony about Jesus and for proclaiming the word of God. They had not worshiped the beast or his statue, nor accepted his mark on their foreheads or their hands. They all came to life again, and they reigned with Christ for a thousand years.

[5]This is the first resurrection. (The rest of the dead did not come back to life until the thousand years had ended.) [6]Blessed and holy are those who share in the first resurrection. For them the second death holds no power, but they will be priests of God and of Christ and will reign with him a thousand years.

The Defeat of Satan

[7]When the thousand years come to an end, Satan will be let out of his prison. [8]He will go out to deceive the nations—called Gog and Magog—in every corner of the earth. He will gather them together for battle—a mighty army, as numberless as sand along the seashore. [9]And I saw them as they went up on the broad plain of the earth and surrounded God's people and the beloved city. But fire from heaven came down on the attacking armies and consumed them.

[10]Then the devil, who had deceived them, was thrown into the fiery lake of burning sulfur, joining the beast and the false prophet. There they will be tormented day and night forever and ever.

The Final Judgment

[11]And I saw a great white throne and the one sitting on it. The earth and

20:1 Or *the abyss,* or *the underworld;* also in 20:3.

sky fled from his presence, but they found no place to hide. [12]I saw the dead, both great and small, standing before God's throne. And the books were opened, including the Book of Life. And the dead were judged according to what they had done, as recorded in the books. [13]The sea gave up its dead, and death and the grave* gave up their dead. And all were judged according to their deeds. [14]Then death and the grave were thrown into the lake of fire. This lake of fire is the second death. [15]And anyone whose name was not found recorded in the Book of Life was thrown into the lake of fire.

The New Jerusalem

21 Then I saw a new heaven and a new earth, for the old heaven and the old earth had disappeared. And the sea was also gone. [2]And I saw the holy city, the new Jerusalem, coming down from God out of heaven like a bride beautifully dressed for her husband.

[3]I heard a loud shout from the throne, saying, "Look, God's home is now among his people! He will live with them, and they will be his people. God himself will be with them.* [4]He will wipe every tear from their eyes, and there will be no more death or sorrow or crying or pain. All these things are gone forever."

[5]And the one sitting on the throne said, "Look, I am making everything new!" And then he said to me, "Write this down, for what I tell you is trustworthy and true." [6]And he also said, "It is finished! I am the Alpha and the Omega—the Beginning and the End. To all who are thirsty I will give freely from the springs of the water of life. [7]All who are victorious will inherit all these blessings, and I will be their God, and they will be my children.

[8]"But cowards, unbelievers, the corrupt, murderers, the immoral, those who practice witchcraft, idol worshipers, and all liars—their fate is in the fiery lake of burning sulfur. This is the second death."

[9]Then one of the seven angels who held the seven bowls containing the seven last plagues came and said to me, "Come with me! I will show you the bride, the wife of the Lamb."

[10]So he took me in the Spirit* to a great, high mountain, and he showed me the holy city, Jerusalem, descending out of heaven from God. [11]It shone with the glory of God and sparkled like a precious stone—like jasper as clear as crystal. [12]The city wall was broad and high, with twelve gates guarded by twelve angels. And the names of the twelve tribes of Israel were written on the gates. [13]There were three gates on each side—east, north, south, and west. [14]The wall of the city had twelve foundation stones, and on

20:13 Greek *and Hades;* also in 20:14.   **21:3** Some manuscripts read *God himself will be with them, their God.*   **21:10** Or *in spirit.*

them were written the names of the twelve apostles of the Lamb.

¹⁵The angel who talked to me held in his hand a gold measuring stick to measure the city, its gates, and its wall. ¹⁶When he measured it, he found it was a square, as wide as it was long. In fact, its length and width and height were each 1,400 miles.* ¹⁷Then he measured the walls and found them to be 216 feet thick* (according to the human standard used by the angel).

¹⁸The wall was made of jasper, and the city was pure gold, as clear as glass. ¹⁹The wall of the city was built on foundation stones inlaid with twelve precious stones:* the first was jasper, the second sapphire, the third agate, the fourth emerald, ²⁰the fifth onyx, the sixth carnelian, the seventh chrysolite, the eighth beryl, the ninth topaz, the tenth chrysoprase, the eleventh jacinth, the twelfth amethyst.

²¹The twelve gates were made of pearls—each gate from a single pearl! And the main street was pure gold, as clear as glass.

²²I saw no temple in the city, for the Lord God Almighty and the Lamb are its temple. ²³And the city has no need of sun or moon, for the glory of God illuminates the city, and the Lamb is its light. ²⁴The nations will walk in its light, and the kings of the world will enter the city in all their glory. ²⁵Its gates will never be closed at the end of day because there is no night there. ²⁶And all the nations will bring their glory and honor into the city. ²⁷Nothing evil* will be allowed to enter, nor anyone who practices shameful idolatry and dishonesty—but only those whose names are written in the Lamb's Book of Life.

22 Then the angel showed me a river with the water of life, clear as crystal, flowing from the throne of God and of the Lamb. ²It flowed down the center of the main street. On each side of the river grew a tree of life, bearing twelve crops of fruit,* with a fresh crop each month. The leaves were used for medicine to heal the nations.

³No longer will there be a curse upon anything. For the throne of God and of the Lamb will be there, and his servants will worship him. ⁴And they will see his face, and his name will be written on their foreheads. ⁵And there will be no night there—no need for lamps or sun— for the Lord God will shine on them. And they will reign forever and ever.

⁶Then the angel said to me, "Everything you have heard and seen is trustworthy and true. The Lord God, who inspires his prophets,* has sent his angel to tell his servants what will happen soon.*"

21:16 Greek *12,000 stadia* [2,220 kilometers]. **21:17** Greek *144 cubits* [65 meters]. **21:19** The identification of some of these gemstones is uncertain. **21:27** Or *ceremonially unclean.* **22:2** Or *twelve kinds of fruit.* **22:6a** Or *The Lord, the God of the spirits of the prophets.* **22:6b** Or *suddenly,* or *quickly;* also in 22:7, 12, 20.

Jesus Is Coming

7"Look, I am coming soon! Blessed are those who obey the words of prophecy written in this book.*"

8I, John, am the one who heard and saw all these things. And when I heard and saw them, I fell down to worship at the feet of the angel who showed them to me. 9But he said, "No, don't worship me. I am a servant of God, just like you and your brothers the prophets, as well as all who obey what is written in this book. Worship only God!"

10Then he instructed me, "Do not seal up the prophetic words in this book, for the time is near. 11Let the one who is doing harm continue to do harm; let the one who is vile continue to be vile; let the one who is righteous continue to live righteously; let the one who is holy continue to be holy."

12"Look, I am coming soon, bringing my reward with me to repay all people according to their deeds. 13I am the Alpha and the Omega, the First and the Last, the Beginning and the End."

14Blessed are those who wash their robes. They will be permitted to enter through the gates of the city and eat the fruit from the tree of life. 15Outside the city are the dogs—the sorcerers, the sexually immoral, the murderers, the idol worshipers, and all who love to live a lie.

16"I, Jesus, have sent my angel to give you this message for the churches. I am both the source of David and the heir to his throne.* I am the bright morning star."

17The Spirit and the bride say, "Come." Let anyone who hears this say, "Come." Let anyone who is thirsty come. Let anyone who desires drink freely from the water of life. 18And I solemnly declare to everyone who hears the words of prophecy written in this book: If anyone adds anything to what is written here, God will add to that person the plagues described in this book. 19And if anyone removes any of the words from this book of prophecy, God will remove that person's share in the tree of life and in the holy city that are described in this book.

20He who is the faithful witness to all these things says, "Yes, I am coming soon!"

Amen! Come, Lord Jesus!

21May the grace of the Lord Jesus be with God's holy people.*

22:7 Or scroll; also in 22:9, 10, 18, 19. 22:16 Greek I am the root and offspring of David. 22:21 Other manuscripts read be with all; still others read be with all of God's holy people. Some manuscripts add Amen.

PSALMS

Psalms

BOOK ONE (Psalms 1–41)

1 ¹ Oh, the joys of those who do not
follow the advice of the wicked,
or stand around with sinners,
or join in with mockers.
² But they delight in the law of the LORD,
meditating on it day and night.
³ They are like trees planted along the riverbank,
bearing fruit each season.
Their leaves never wither,
and they prosper in all they do.

⁴ But not the wicked!
They are like worthless chaff,
scattered by the wind.
⁵ They will be condemned at the time of judgment.
Sinners will have no place among the godly.
⁶ For the LORD watches over the path of the godly,
but the path of the wicked leads to destruction.

2 ¹ Why are the nations so angry?
Why do they waste their time with futile plans?
² The kings of the earth prepare for battle;
the rulers plot together
against the LORD
and against his anointed one.
³ "Let us break their chains," they cry,
"and free ourselves from slavery to God."

⁴ But the one who rules in heaven laughs.
The Lord scoffs at them.
⁵ Then in anger he rebukes them,
terrifying them with his fierce fury.
⁶ For the Lord declares, "I have placed my chosen king on the throne
in Jerusalem,* on my holy mountain."

⁷ The king proclaims the LORD's decree:
"The LORD said to me, 'You are my son.*
Today I have become your Father.*
⁸ Only ask, and I will give you the nations as your inheritance,
the whole earth as your possession.
⁹ You will break* them with an iron rod
and smash them like clay pots.'"

2:6 Hebrew *on Zion.* **2:7a** Or *Son;* also in 2:12. **2:7b** Or *Today I reveal you as my son.*
2:9 Greek version reads *rule.* Compare Rev 2:27.

¹⁰ Now then, you kings, act wisely!
  Be warned, you rulers of the
    earth!
¹¹ Serve the LORD with reverent
    fear,
  and rejoice with trembling.
¹² Submit to God's royal son,* or
    he will become angry,
  and you will be destroyed in
    the midst of all your
    activities—
for his anger flares up in an
    instant.
  But what joy for all who take
    refuge in him!

3 *A psalm of David, regarding the
time David fled from his son
Absalom.*

¹ O LORD, I have so many
    enemies;
  so many are against me.
² So many are saying,
  "God will never rescue him!"
                              *Interlude**

³ But you, O LORD, are a shield
    around me;
  you are my glory, the one who
    holds my head high.
⁴ I cried out to the LORD,
  and he answered me from his
    holy mountain.   *Interlude*

⁵ I lay down and slept,
  yet I woke up in safety,
  for the LORD was watching
    over me.

⁶ I am not afraid of ten thousand
    enemies
  who surround me on every side.
⁷ Arise, O LORD!
  Rescue me, my God!
Slap all my enemies in the face!
  Shatter the teeth of the wicked!
⁸ Victory comes from you, O LORD.
  May you bless your people.
                              Interlude

4 *For the choir director: A psalm
of David, to be accompanied
by stringed instruments.*

¹ Answer me when I call to you,
  O God who declares me
    innocent.
Free me from my troubles.
  Have mercy on me and hear
    my prayer.

² How long will you people ruin
    my reputation?
  How long will you make
    groundless accusations?
  How long will you continue
    your lies?   *Interlude*
³ You can be sure of this:
  The LORD set apart the godly
    for himself.
  The LORD will answer when
    I call to him.

⁴ Don't sin by letting anger control
    you.
  Think about it overnight and
    remain silent.   *Interlude*

2:12 The meaning of the Hebrew is uncertain. 3:2 Hebrew *Selah.* The meaning of this word is uncertain, though it is probably a musical or literary term. It is rendered *Interlude* throughout the Psalms.

⁵ Offer sacrifices in the right spirit,
  and trust the LORD.

⁶ Many people say, "Who will
    show us better times?"
  Let your face smile on us,
    LORD.
⁷ You have given me greater joy
    than those who have abundant
    harvests of grain and new
    wine.
⁸ In peace I will lie down and
    sleep,
  for you alone, O LORD, will
    keep me safe.

5 *For the choir director: A psalm
    of David, to be accompanied
by the flute.*

¹ O LORD, hear me as I pray;
  pay attention to my groaning.
² Listen to my cry for help, my
    King and my God,
  for I pray to no one but you.
³ Listen to my voice in the
    morning, LORD.
  Each morning I bring my
    requests to you and wait
    expectantly.

⁴ O God, you take no pleasure in
    wickedness;
  you cannot tolerate the sins
    of the wicked.
⁵ Therefore, the proud may not
    stand in your presence,
  for you hate all who do evil.
⁶ You will destroy those who
    tell lies.

The LORD detests murderers
    and deceivers.

⁷ Because of your unfailing love,
  I can enter your house;
  I will worship at your Temple
    with deepest awe.
⁸ Lead me in the right path,
    O LORD,
  or my enemies will conquer me.
  Make your way plain for me to
    follow.

⁹ My enemies cannot speak
    a truthful word.
  Their deepest desire is to
    destroy others.
  Their talk is foul, like the stench
    from an open grave.
  Their tongues are filled with
    flattery.*
¹⁰ O God, declare them guilty.
  Let them be caught in their
    own traps.
  Drive them away because of
    their many sins,
  for they have rebelled against
    you.

¹¹ But let all who take refuge in you
    rejoice;
  let them sing joyful praises
    forever.
  Spread your protection over
    them,
  that all who love your name
    may be filled with joy.
¹² For you bless the godly, O LORD;
  you surround them with your
    shield of love.

5:9 Greek version reads *with lies*. Compare Rom 3:13.

6

For the choir director: A psalm of David, to be accompanied by an eight-stringed instrument.*

1 O LORD, don't rebuke me in your anger
   or discipline me in your rage.
2 Have compassion on me, LORD, for I am weak.
   Heal me, LORD, for my bones are in agony.
3 I am sick at heart.
   How long, O LORD, until you restore me?

4 Return, O LORD, and rescue me.
   Save me because of your unfailing love.
5 For the dead do not remember you.
   Who can praise you from the grave?*

6 I am worn out from sobbing.
   All night I flood my bed with weeping,
   drenching it with my tears.
7 My vision is blurred by grief;
   my eyes are worn out because of all my enemies.

8 Go away, all you who do evil,
   for the LORD has heard my weeping.
9 The LORD has heard my plea;
   the LORD will answer my prayer.
10 May all my enemies be disgraced and terrified.
   May they suddenly turn back in shame.

7

A psalm* of David, which he sang to the LORD concerning Cush of the tribe of Benjamin.

1 I come to you for protection,
   O LORD my God.
   Save me from my persecutors—rescue me!
2 If you don't, they will maul me like a lion,
   tearing me to pieces with no one to rescue me.

3 O LORD my God, if I have done wrong
   or am guilty of injustice,
4 if I have betrayed a friend
   or plundered my enemy without cause,
5 then let my enemies capture me.
   Let them trample me into the ground
   and drag my honor in the dust.   *Interlude*

6 Arise, O LORD, in anger!
   Stand up against the fury of my enemies!
   Wake up, my God, and bring justice!
7 Gather the nations before you.
   Rule over them from on high.
8   The LORD judges the nations.
   Declare me righteous, O LORD,
   for I am innocent, O Most High!
9 End the evil of those who are wicked,
   and defend the righteous.

6:TITLE Hebrew *with stringed instruments; according to the sheminith.*   6:5 Hebrew *from Sheol?*
7:TITLE Hebrew *a shiggaion*, probably indicating a musical setting for the psalm.

For you look deep within the
   mind and heart,
   O righteous God.

10 God is my shield,
   saving those whose hearts are
   true and right.
11 God is an honest judge.
   He is angry with the wicked
   every day.

12 If a person does not repent,
   God* will sharpen his sword;
   he will bend and string his
   bow.
13 He will prepare his deadly
   weapons
   and shoot his flaming arrows.

14 The wicked conceive evil;
   they are pregnant with trouble
   and give birth to lies.
15 They dig a deep pit to trap
   others,
   then fall into it themselves.
16 The trouble they make for others
   backfires on them.
   The violence they plan falls on
   their own heads.

17 I will thank the LORD because he
   is just;
   I will sing praise to the name
   of the LORD Most High.

8 *For the choir director: A psalm
   of David, to be accompanied by
   a stringed instrument.**

1 O LORD, our Lord, your majestic
   name fills the earth!
   Your glory is higher than the
   heavens.
2 You have taught children and
   infants
   to tell of your strength,*
   silencing your enemies
   and all who oppose you.

3 When I look at the night sky
   and see the work of your
   fingers—
   the moon and the stars you set
   in place—
4 what are mere mortals that you
   should think about them,
   human beings that you should
   care for them?*
5 Yet you made them only a little
   lower than God*
   and crowned them* with glory
   and honor.
6 You gave them charge of
   everything you made,
   putting all things under their
   authority—
7 the flocks and the herds
   and all the wild animals,
8 the birds in the sky, the fish in
   the sea,
   and everything that swims the
   ocean currents.

9 O LORD, our Lord, your majestic
   name fills the earth!

7:12 Hebrew *he.* **8:TITLE** Hebrew *according to the gittith.* **8:2** Greek version reads *to give you
praise.* Compare Matt 21:16. **8:4** Hebrew *what is man that you should think of him, / the son of
man that you should care for him?* **8:5a** Or *Yet you made them only a little lower than the angels;*
Hebrew reads *Yet you made him* [i.e., man] *a little lower than Elohim.* **8:5b** Hebrew *him* [i.e., man];
similarly in 8:6.

9 *For the choir director: A psalm of David, to be sung to the tune "Death of the Son."*

1 I will praise you, LORD, with all
     my heart;
   I will tell of all the marvelous
     things you have done.
2 I will be filled with joy because
     of you.
   I will sing praises to your
     name, O Most High.

3 My enemies retreated;
   they staggered and died when
     you appeared.
4 For you have judged in my favor;
   from your throne you have
     judged with fairness.
5 You have rebuked the nations
   and destroyed the wicked;
   you have erased their names
     forever.
6 The enemy is finished, in
     endless ruins;
   the cities you uprooted are
     now forgotten.

7 But the LORD reigns forever,
   executing judgment from his
     throne.
8 He will judge the world with
     justice
   and rule the nations with
     fairness.
9 The LORD is a shelter for the
     oppressed,
   a refuge in times of trouble.
10 Those who know your name
     trust in you,
   for you, O LORD, do not
     abandon those who search
     for you.

11 Sing praises to the LORD who
     reigns in Jerusalem.*
   Tell the world about his
     unforgettable deeds.
12 For he who avenges murder
     cares for the helpless.
   He does not ignore the cries
     of those who suffer.

13 LORD, have mercy on me.
   See how my enemies torment
     me.
   Snatch me back from the jaws
     of death.
14 Save me so I can praise you
     publicly at Jerusalem's gates,
   so I can rejoice that you have
     rescued me.

15 The nations have fallen into the
     pit they dug for others.
   Their own feet have been
     caught in the trap they set.
16 The LORD is known for his justice.
   The wicked are trapped by
     their own deeds.
                    *Quiet Interlude**

17 The wicked will go down to the
     grave.*
   This is the fate of all the
     nations who ignore God.
18 But the needy will not be ignored
     forever;
   the hopes of the poor will not
     always be crushed.

9:11 Hebrew *Zion*; also in 9:14.   9:16 Hebrew *Higgaion Selah*. The meaning of this phrase is
uncertain.   9:17 Hebrew *to Sheol*.

¹⁹ Arise, O Lord!
  Do not let mere mortals defy
    you!
  Judge the nations!
²⁰ Make them tremble in fear,
    O Lord.
  Let the nations know they are
    merely human.   *Interlude*

10 ¹ O Lord, why do you stand
           so far away?
  Why do you hide when I am
    in trouble?
² The wicked arrogantly hunt
    down the poor.
  Let them be caught in the evil
    they plan for others.
³ For they brag about their evil
    desires;
  they praise the greedy and
    curse the Lord.

⁴ The wicked are too proud to
    seek God.
  They seem to think that God
    is dead.
⁵ Yet they succeed in everything
    they do.
  They do not see your
    punishment awaiting
    them.
  They sneer at all their
    enemies.
⁶ They think, "Nothing bad will
    ever happen to us!
  We will be free of trouble
    forever!"

⁷ Their mouths are full of cursing,
    lies, and threats.*

Trouble and evil are on the tips
    of their tongues.
⁸ They lurk in ambush in the
    villages,
  waiting to murder innocent
    people.
  They are always searching for
    helpless victims.
⁹ Like lions crouched in hiding,
  they wait to pounce on the
    helpless.
  Like hunters they capture the
    helpless
  and drag them away in nets.
¹⁰ Their helpless victims are
    crushed;
  they fall beneath the strength
    of the wicked.
¹¹ The wicked think, "God isn't
    watching us!
  He has closed his eyes and
    won't even see what we do!"

¹² Arise, O Lord!
  Punish the wicked, O God!
  Do not ignore the helpless!
¹³ Why do the wicked get away
    with despising God?
  They think, "God will never
    call us to account."
¹⁴ But you see the trouble and grief
    they cause.
  You take note of it and punish
    them.
  The helpless put their trust in
    you.
  You defend the orphans.

¹⁵ Break the arms of these wicked,
    evil people!

10:7 Greek version reads *cursing and bitterness.* Compare Rom 3:14.

Go after them until the last
one is destroyed.
16 The LORD is king forever and ever!
The godless nations will
vanish from the land.
17 LORD, you know the hopes of the
helpless.
Surely you will hear their cries
and comfort them.
18 You will bring justice to the
orphans and the oppressed,
so mere people can no longer
terrify them.

11

*For the choir director:
A psalm of David.*

1 I trust in the LORD for protection.
So why do you say to me,
"Fly like a bird to the
mountains for safety!
2 The wicked are stringing their
bows
and fitting their arrows on the
bowstrings.
They shoot from the shadows
at those whose hearts are right.
3 The foundations of law and
order have collapsed.
What can the righteous do?"

4 But the LORD is in his holy
Temple;
the LORD still rules from
heaven.
He watches everyone closely,
examining every person on
earth.
5 The LORD examines both the
righteous and the wicked.

He hates those who love
violence.
6 He will rain down blazing coals
and burning sulfur on the
wicked,
punishing them with
scorching winds.
7 For the righteous LORD loves
justice.
The virtuous will see his face.

12

*For the choir director: A psalm
of David, to be accompanied
by an eight-stringed instrument.**

1 Help, O LORD, for the godly are
fast disappearing!
The faithful have vanished
from the earth!
2 Neighbors lie to each other,
speaking with flattering lips
and deceitful hearts.
3 May the LORD cut off their
flattering lips
and silence their boastful
tongues.
4 They say, "We will lie to our
hearts' content.
Our lips are our own—who can
stop us?"

5 The LORD replies, "I have seen
violence done to the helpless,
and I have heard the groans of
the poor.
Now I will rise up to rescue
them,
as they have longed for me
to do."
6 The LORD's promises are pure,

12:TITLE Hebrew *according to the sheminith.*

like silver refined in a furnace,
   purified seven times over.
⁷ Therefore, Lᴏʀᴅ, we know you
      will protect the oppressed,
   preserving them forever from
      this lying generation,
⁸ even though the wicked strut
      about,
   and evil is praised throughout
      the land.

13 For the choir director:
A psalm of David.

¹ O Lᴏʀᴅ, how long will you forget
      me? Forever?
   How long will you look the
      other way?
² How long must I struggle with
      anguish in my soul,
   with sorrow in my heart every
      day?
   How long will my enemy have
      the upper hand?

³ Turn and answer me, O Lᴏʀᴅ
      my God!
   Restore the sparkle to my eyes,
      or I will die.
⁴ Don't let my enemies gloat,
      saying, "We have defeated
      him!"
   Don't let them rejoice at my
      downfall.

⁵ But I trust in your unfailing love.
   I will rejoice because you have
      rescued me.
⁶ I will sing to the Lᴏʀᴅ
   because he is good to me.

14 For the choir director:
A psalm of David.

¹ Only fools say in their hearts,
   "There is no God."
They are corrupt, and their
      actions are evil;
   not one of them does good!

² The Lᴏʀᴅ looks down from
      heaven
   on the entire human race;
he looks to see if anyone is truly
      wise,
   if anyone seeks God.
³ But no, all have turned away;
   all have become corrupt.*
No one does good,
   not a single one!

⁴ Will those who do evil never
      learn?
   They eat up my people like
      bread
   and wouldn't think of praying
      to the Lᴏʀᴅ.
⁵ Terror will grip them,
   for God is with those who obey
      him.
⁶ The wicked frustrate the plans
      of the oppressed,
   but the Lᴏʀᴅ will protect his
      people.
⁷ Who will come from Mount Zion
      to rescue Israel?
   When the Lᴏʀᴅ restores his
      people,
   Jacob will shout with joy, and
      Israel will rejoice.

14:3 Greek version reads *have become useless.* Compare Rom 3:12.

15 *A psalm of David.*

¹ Who may worship in your
   sanctuary, LORD?
   Who may enter your presence
   on your holy hill?
² Those who lead blameless lives
   and do what is right,
   speaking the truth from
   sincere hearts.
³ Those who refuse to gossip
   or harm their neighbors
   or speak evil of their friends.
⁴ Those who despise flagrant
   sinners,
   and honor the faithful
   followers of the LORD,
   and keep their promises even
   when it hurts.
⁵ Those who lend money without
   charging interest,
   and who cannot be bribed to
   lie about the innocent.
   Such people will stand firm
   forever.

16 *A psalm* of David.*

¹ Keep me safe, O God,
   for I have come to you for
   refuge.
² I said to the LORD, "You are my
   Master!
   Every good thing I have comes
   from you."
³ The godly people in the land

are my true heroes!
   I take pleasure in them!
⁴ Troubles multiply for those who
   chase after other gods.
   I will not take part in their
   sacrifices of blood
   or even speak the names of
   their gods.
⁵ LORD, you alone are my
   inheritance, my cup of
   blessing.
   You guard all that is mine.
⁶ The land you have given me is
   a pleasant land.
   What a wonderful inheritance!
⁷ I will bless the LORD who
   guides me;
   even at night my heart
   instructs me.
⁸ I know the LORD is always
   with me.
   I will not be shaken, for he
   is right beside me.
⁹ No wonder my heart is glad,
   and I rejoice.*
   My body rests in safety.
¹⁰ For you will not leave my soul
   among the dead*
   or allow your holy one* to rot
   in the grave.
¹¹ You will show me the way of life,
   granting me the joy of your
   presence
   and the pleasures of living
   with you forever.*

17 *A prayer of David.*

1 O Lord, hear my plea for justice.
  Listen to my cry for help.
  Pay attention to my prayer,
    for it comes from honest lips.
2 Declare me innocent,
    for you see those who do right.

3 You have tested my thoughts and
    examined my heart in the
    night.
  You have scrutinized me and
    found nothing wrong.
  I am determined not to sin
    in what I say.
4 I have followed your commands,
    which keep me from following
    cruel and evil people.
5 My steps have stayed on your path;
  I have not wavered from
    following you.

6 I am praying to you because
    I know you will answer,
    O God.
  Bend down and listen as I pray.
7 Show me your unfailing love in
    wonderful ways.
  By your mighty power you
    rescue
  those who seek refuge from
    their enemies.
8 Guard me as you would guard
    your own eyes.*
  Hide me in the shadow of your
    wings.
9 Protect me from wicked people
    who attack me,

from murderous enemies who
    surround me.
10 They are without pity.
  Listen to their boasting!
11 They track me down and
    surround me,
  watching for the chance to
    throw me to the ground.
12 They are like hungry lions, eager
    to tear me apart—
  like young lions hiding in
    ambush.

13 Arise, O Lord!
  Stand against them, and bring
    them to their knees!
  Rescue me from the wicked
    with your sword!
14 By the power of your hand,
    O Lord,
  destroy those who look to this
    world for their reward.
  But satisfy the hunger of your
    treasured ones.
  May their children have plenty,
    leaving an inheritance for their
    descendants.
15 Because I am righteous, I will see
    you.
  When I awake, I will see you
    face to face and be satisfied.

18 *For the choir director: A psalm of David, the servant of the Lord. He sang this song to the Lord on the day the Lord rescued him from all his enemies and from Saul. He sang:*

1 I love you, Lord;
  you are my strength.

17:8 Hebrew *as the pupil of your eye.*

2 The LORD is my rock, my fortress,
   and my savior;
   my God is my rock, in whom
   I find protection.
   He is my shield, the power that
   saves me,
   and my place of safety.
3 I called on the LORD, who is
   worthy of praise,
   and he saved me from my
   enemies.

4 The ropes of death entangled
   me;
   floods of destruction swept
   over me.
5 The grave* wrapped its ropes
   around me;
   death laid a trap in my path.
6 But in my distress I cried out
   to the LORD;
   yes, I prayed to my God for
   help.
   He heard me from his sanctuary;
   my cry to him reached his
   ears.

7 Then the earth quaked and
   trembled.
   The foundations of the
   mountains shook;
   they quaked because of his
   anger.
8 Smoke poured from his nostrils;
   fierce flames leaped from his
   mouth.
   Glowing coals blazed forth
   from him.
9 He opened the heavens and
   came down;

dark storm clouds were
   beneath his feet.
10 Mounted on a mighty angelic
   being,* he flew,
   soaring on the wings of the
   wind.
11 He shrouded himself in
   darkness,
   veiling his approach with dark
   rain clouds.
12 Thick clouds shielded the
   brightness around him
   and rained down hail and
   burning coals.*
13 The LORD thundered from
   heaven;
   the voice of the Most High
   resounded
   amid the hail and burning
   coals.
14 He shot his arrows and scattered
   his enemies;
   great bolts of lightning flashed,
   and they were confused.
15 Then at your command, O LORD,
   at the blast of your breath,
   the bottom of the sea could be
   seen,
   and the foundations of the
   earth were laid bare.

16 He reached down from heaven
   and rescued me;
   he drew me out of deep
   waters.
17 He rescued me from my
   powerful enemies,
   from those who hated me and
   were too strong for me.

18:5 Hebrew Sheol.   18:10 Hebrew a cherub.   18:12 Or and lightning bolts; also in 18:13.

18 They attacked me at a moment
  when I was in distress,
  but the LORD supported me.
19 He led me to a place of safety;
  he rescued me because he
  delights in me.
20 The LORD rewarded me for doing
  right;
  he restored me because of my
  innocence.
21 For I have kept the ways of the
  LORD;
  I have not turned from my God
  to follow evil.
22 I have followed all his regulations;
  I have never abandoned his
  decrees.
23 I am blameless before God;
  I have kept myself from sin.
24 The LORD rewarded me for doing
  right.
  He has seen my innocence.

25 To the faithful you show yourself
  faithful;
  to those with integrity you
  show integrity.
26 To the pure you show yourself
  pure,
  but to the crooked you show
  yourself shrewd.
27 You rescue the humble,
  but you humiliate the proud.
28 You light a lamp for me.
  The LORD, my God, lights up
  my darkness.
29 In your strength I can crush an
  army;
  with my God I can scale any wall.

30 God's way is perfect.
  All the LORD's promises prove
  true.
  He is a shield for all who look
  to him for protection.
31 For who is God except the LORD?
  Who but our God is a solid
  rock?
32 God arms me with strength,
  and he makes my way perfect.
33 He makes me as surefooted as a
  deer,
  enabling me to stand on
  mountain heights.
34 He trains my hands for battle;
  he strengthens my arm to
  draw a bronze bow.
35 You have given me your shield
  of victory.
  Your right hand supports me;
  your help* has made me great.
36 You have made a wide path for
  my feet
  to keep them from slipping.

37 I chased my enemies and caught
  them;
  I did not stop until they were
  conquered.
38 I struck them down so they
  could not get up;
  they fell beneath my feet.
39 You have armed me with
  strength for the battle;
  you have subdued my enemies
  under my feet.
40 You placed my foot on their necks.
  I have destroyed all who
  hated me.

18:35 Hebrew *your humility*; compare 2 Sam 22:36.

41 They called for help, but no one
   came to their rescue.
   They even cried to the Lord,
   but he refused to answer.
42 I ground them as fine as dust in
   the wind.
   I swept them into the gutter
   like dirt.
43 You gave me victory over my
   accusers.
   You appointed me ruler over
   nations;
   people I don't even know now
   serve me.
44 As soon as they hear of me, they
   submit;
   foreign nations cringe
   before me.
45 They all lose their courage
   and come trembling from
   their strongholds.

46 The Lord lives! Praise to my Rock!
   May the God of my salvation
   be exalted!
47 He is the God who pays back
   those who harm me;
   he subdues the nations
   under me
48   and rescues me from my
   enemies.
   You hold me safe beyond the
   reach of my enemies;
   you save me from violent
   opponents.
49 For this, O Lord, I will praise you
   among the nations;
   I will sing praises to your
   name.

50 You give great victories to your
   king;
   you show unfailing love to
   your anointed,
   to David and all his
   descendants forever.

19 *For the choir director:
   A psalm of David.*

1 The heavens proclaim the glory
   of God.
   The skies display his
   craftsmanship.
2 Day after day they continue
   to speak;
   night after night they make
   him known.
3 They speak without a sound
   or word;
   their voice is never heard.*
4 Yet their message has gone
   throughout the earth,
   and their words to all the
   world.

   God has made a home in the
   heavens for the sun.
5 It bursts forth like a radiant
   bridegroom after his
   wedding.
   It rejoices like a great athlete
   eager to run the race.
6 The sun rises at one end of the
   heavens
   and follows its course to the
   other end.
   Nothing can hide from its
   heat.

19:3 Or *There is no speech or language where their voice is not heard.*

7 The instructions of the LORD are
  perfect,
    reviving the soul.
  The decrees of the LORD are
  trustworthy,
    making wise the simple.
8 The commandments of the LORD
  are right,
    bringing joy to the heart.
  The commands of the LORD are
  clear,
    giving insight for living.
9 Reverence for the LORD is pure,
    lasting forever.
  The laws of the LORD are true;
    each one is fair.
10 They are more desirable than
   gold,
     even the finest gold.
  They are sweeter than honey,
    even honey dripping from the
    comb.
11 They are a warning to your
   servant,
     a great reward for those who
     obey them.

12 How can I know all the sins
   lurking in my heart?
     Cleanse me from these hidden
     faults.
13 Keep your servant from
   deliberate sins!
     Don't let them control me.
  Then I will be free of guilt
    and innocent of great sin.

14 May the words of my mouth
     and the meditation of my heart
  be pleasing to you,

20:2 Hebrew *Zion.*

O LORD, my rock and my
  redeemer.

20 *For the choir director:*
A psalm of David.

1 In times of trouble, may the
  LORD answer your cry.
  May the name of the God of
    Jacob keep you safe from all
    harm.
2 May he send you help from his
    sanctuary
  and strengthen you from
    Jerusalem.*
3 May he remember all your gifts
    and look favorably on your
      burnt offerings.   *Interlude*

4 May he grant your heart's desires
    and make all your plans
    succeed.
5 May we shout for joy when we
    hear of your victory
  and raise a victory banner in
    the name of our God.
  May the LORD answer all your
    prayers.

6 Now I know that the LORD
    rescues his anointed
    king.
  He will answer him from his
    holy heaven
  and rescue him by his great
    power.
7 Some nations boast of their
    chariots and horses,
  but we boast in the name
    of the LORD our God.

8 Those nations will fall down and
    collapse,
  but we will rise up and stand
    firm.
9 Give victory to our king,
    O LORD!
  Answer our cry for help.

21
*For the choir director:
A psalm of David.*

1 How the king rejoices in your
    strength, O LORD!
  He shouts with joy because
    you give him victory.
2 For you have given him his
    heart's desire;
  you have withheld nothing he
    requested.   *Interlude*

3 You welcomed him back with
    success and prosperity.
  You placed a crown of finest
    gold on his head.
4 He asked you to preserve his life,
    and you granted his request.
  The days of his life stretch on
    forever.
5 Your victory brings him great
    honor,
  and you have clothed him with
    splendor and majesty.
6 You have endowed him with
    eternal blessings
  and given him the joy of your
    presence.
7 For the king trusts in the LORD.
  The unfailing love of the Most
    High will keep him from
    stumbling.

8 You will capture all your
    enemies.
  Your strong right hand will
    seize all who hate you.
9 You will throw them in a flaming
    furnace
    when you appear.
  The LORD will consume them in
    his anger;
  fire will devour them.
10 You will wipe their children from
    the face of the earth;
  they will never have
    descendants.
11 Although they plot against you,
    their evil schemes will never
    succeed.
12 For they will turn and run
  when they see your arrows
    aimed at them.
13 Rise up, O LORD, in all your
    power.
  With music and singing we
    celebrate your mighty acts.

22
*For the choir director: A psalm
of David, to be sung to the
tune "Doe of the Dawn."*

1 My God, my God, why have you
    abandoned me?
  Why are you so far away when
    I groan for help?
2 Every day I call to you, my God,
    but you do not answer.
  Every night I lift my voice, but
    I find no relief.
3 Yet you are holy,
  enthroned on the praises of
    Israel.

4 Our ancestors trusted in you,
　　and you rescued them.
5 They cried out to you and were
　　saved.
　They trusted in you and were
　　never disgraced.

6 But I am a worm and not a man.
　　I am scorned and despised
　　by all!
7 Everyone who sees me
　　mocks me.
　They sneer and shake their
　　heads, saying,
8 "Is this the one who relies on
　　the Lord?
　Then let the Lord save him!
　If the Lord loves him so much,
　　let the Lord rescue him!"

9 Yet you brought me safely from
　　my mother's womb
　and led me to trust you at my
　　mother's breast.
10 I was thrust into your arms at
　　my birth.
　You have been my God from
　　the moment I was born.

11 Do not stay so far from me,
　　for trouble is near,
　and no one else can help me.
12 My enemies surround me like
　　a herd of bulls;
　fierce bulls of Bashan have
　　hemmed me in!
13 Like lions they open their jaws
　　against me,
　roaring and tearing into their
　　prey.

14 My life is poured out like
　　water,
　and all my bones are out of
　　joint.
　My heart is like wax,
　　melting within me.
15 My strength has dried up like
　　sunbaked clay.
　My tongue sticks to the roof
　　of my mouth.
　You have laid me in the dust
　　and left me for dead.
16 My enemies surround me like
　　a pack of dogs;
　an evil gang closes in on me.
　They have pierced* my hands
　　and feet.
17 I can count all my bones.
　My enemies stare at me and
　　gloat.
18 They divide my garments among
　　themselves
　and throw dice* for my
　　clothing.

19 O Lord, do not stay far away!
　You are my strength; come
　　quickly to my aid!
20 Save me from the sword;
　spare my precious life from
　　these dogs.
21 Snatch me from the lion's jaws
　　and from the horns of these
　　wild oxen.
22 I will proclaim your name to my
　　brothers and sisters.*
　I will praise you among your
　　assembled people.

22:16 As in some Hebrew manuscripts and Greek and Syriac versions; most Hebrew manuscripts read *They are like a lion at.* 22:18 Hebrew *cast lots.* 22:22 Hebrew *my brothers.*

23 Praise the LORD, all you who fear him!
 Honor him, all you descendants of Jacob!
 Show him reverence, all you descendants of Israel!
24 For he has not ignored or belittled the suffering of the needy.
 He has not turned his back on them,
 but has listened to their cries for help.

25 I will praise you in the great assembly.
 I will fulfill my vows in the presence of those who worship you.
26 The poor will eat and be satisfied.
 All who seek the LORD will praise him.
 Their hearts will rejoice with everlasting joy.
27 The whole earth will acknowledge the LORD and return to him.
 All the families of the nations will bow down before him.
28 For royal power belongs to the LORD.
 He rules all the nations.

29 Let the rich of the earth feast and worship.
 Bow before him, all who are mortal,
 all whose lives will end as dust.
30 Our children will also serve him.

 Future generations will hear about the wonders of the Lord.
31 His righteous acts will be told to those not yet born.
 They will hear about everything he has done.

23 *A psalm of David.*

1 The LORD is my shepherd;
 I have all that I need.
2 He lets me rest in green meadows;
 he leads me beside peaceful streams.
3   He renews my strength.
 He guides me along right paths,
 bringing honor to his name.
4 Even when I walk through the darkest valley,*
 I will not be afraid,
 for you are close beside me.
 Your rod and your staff protect and comfort me.
5 You prepare a feast for me in the presence of my enemies.
 You honor me by anointing my head with oil.
 My cup overflows with blessings.
6 Surely your goodness and unfailing love will pursue me all the days of my life,
 and I will live in the house of the LORD forever.

23:4 Or *the dark valley of death.*

24
A psalm of David.

¹ The earth is the LORD's, and
   everything in it.
   The world and all its people
   belong to him.
² For he laid the earth's
   foundation on the seas
   and built it on the ocean
   depths.

³ Who may climb the mountain
   of the LORD?
   Who may stand in his holy
   place?
⁴ Only those whose hands and
   hearts are pure,
   who do not worship idols
   and never tell lies.
⁵ They will receive the LORD's
   blessing
   and have a right relationship
   with God their savior.
⁶ Such people may seek you
   and worship in your presence,
   O God of Jacob.*   *Interlude*

⁷ Open up, ancient gates!
   Open up, ancient doors,
   and let the King of glory
   enter.
⁸ Who is the King of glory?
   The LORD, strong and mighty;
   the LORD, invincible in battle.
⁹ Open up, ancient gates!
   Open up, ancient doors,
   and let the King of glory
   enter.

¹⁰ Who is the King of glory?
   The LORD of Heaven's
   Armies—
   he is the King of glory.
                    Interlude

25*
A psalm of David.

¹ O LORD, I give my life to you.
² I trust in you, my God!
   Do not let me be disgraced,
   or let my enemies rejoice in
   my defeat.
³ No one who trusts in you will
   ever be disgraced,
   but disgrace comes to those
   who try to deceive others.

⁴ Show me the right path,
   O LORD;
   point out the road for me
   to follow.
⁵ Lead me by your truth and
   teach me,
   for you are the God who
   saves me.
   All day long I put my hope in
   you.
⁶ Remember, O LORD, your
   compassion and unfailing
   love,
   which you have shown from
   long ages past.
⁷ Do not remember the rebellious
   sins of my youth.
   Remember me in the light of
   your unfailing love,
   for you are merciful, O LORD.

24:6 As in two Hebrew manuscripts and Greek and Syriac versions; most Hebrew manuscripts read *O Jacob.*   25 This psalm is a Hebrew acrostic poem; each verse begins with a successive letter of the Hebrew alphabet.

⁸ The LORD is good and does what
   is right;
      he shows the proper path to
      those who go astray.
⁹ He leads the humble in doing
   right,
      teaching them his way.
¹⁰ The LORD leads with unfailing
    love and faithfulness
      all who keep his covenant and
      obey his demands.

¹¹ For the honor of your name,
      O LORD,
      forgive my many, many sins.
¹² Who are those who fear the
      LORD?
      He will show them the path
      they should choose.
¹³ They will live in prosperity,
      and their children will inherit
      the land.
¹⁴ The LORD is a friend to those
      who fear him.
      He teaches them his covenant.
¹⁵ My eyes are always on the LORD,
      for he rescues me from the
      traps of my enemies.

¹⁶ Turn to me and have mercy,
      for I am alone and in deep
      distress.
¹⁷ My problems go from bad to
      worse.
      Oh, save me from them all!
¹⁸ Feel my pain and see my trouble.
      Forgive all my sins.
¹⁹ See how many enemies I have
      and how viciously they hate me!
²⁰ Protect me! Rescue my life from
      them!

Do not let me be disgraced, for
      in you I take refuge.
²¹ May integrity and honesty
      protect me,
      for I put my hope in you.

²² O God, ransom Israel
      from all its troubles.

26 *A psalm of David.*

¹ Declare me innocent, O LORD,
      for I have acted with integrity;
      I have trusted in the LORD
      without wavering.
² Put me on trial, LORD, and cross-
      examine me.
      Test my motives and my heart.
³ For I am always aware of your
      unfailing love,
      and I have lived according to
      your truth.
⁴ I do not spend time with liars
      or go along with hypocrites.
⁵ I hate the gatherings of those
      who do evil,
      and I refuse to join in with the
      wicked.
⁶ I wash my hands to declare my
      innocence.
      I come to your altar, O LORD,
⁷ singing a song of thanksgiving
      and telling of all your
      wonders.
⁸ I love your sanctuary, LORD,
      the place where your glorious
      presence dwells.
⁹ Don't let me suffer the fate of
      sinners.

Don't condemn me along with
    murderers.
10 Their hands are dirty with evil
    schemes,
    and they constantly take bribes.
11 But I am not like that; I live with
    integrity.
    So redeem me and show me
    mercy.
12 Now I stand on solid ground,
    and I will publicly praise the
    LORD.

27 *A psalm of David.*

1 The LORD is my light and my
    salvation—
    so why should I be afraid?
    The LORD is my fortress,
    protecting me from danger,
    so why should I tremble?
2 When evil people come to
    devour me,
    when my enemies and foes
    attack me,
    they will stumble and fall.
3 Though a mighty army
    surrounds me,
    my heart will not be afraid.
    Even if I am attacked,
    I will remain confident.
4 The one thing I ask of the
    LORD—
    the thing I seek most—
    is to live in the house of the
    LORD all the days of my life,
    delighting in the LORD's
    perfections
    and meditating in his Temple.

5 For he will conceal me there
    when troubles come;
    he will hide me in his sanctuary.
    He will place me out of reach
    on a high rock.
6 Then I will hold my head high
    above my enemies who
    surround me.
    At his sanctuary I will offer
    sacrifices with shouts of joy,
    singing and praising the LORD
    with music.

7 Hear me as I pray, O LORD.
    Be merciful and answer me!
8 My heart has heard you say,
    "Come and talk with me."
    And my heart responds, "LORD,
    I am coming."
9 Do not turn your back on me.
    Do not reject your servant in
    anger.
    You have always been my
    helper.
    Don't leave me now; don't
    abandon me,
    O God of my salvation!
10 Even if my father and mother
    abandon me,
    the LORD will hold me close.

11 Teach me how to live, O LORD.
    Lead me along the right path,
    for my enemies are waiting
    for me.
12 Do not let me fall into their
    hands.
    For they accuse me of things
    I've never done;
    with every breath they
    threaten me with violence.

¹³ Yet I am confident I will see the
  Lord's goodness
    while I am here in the land of
    the living.

¹⁴ Wait patiently for the Lord.
    Be brave and courageous.
    Yes, wait patiently for the Lord.

28 *A psalm of David.*

¹ I pray to you, O Lord, my rock.
    Do not turn a deaf ear to me.
  For if you are silent,
    I might as well give up and die.
² Listen to my prayer for mercy
    as I cry out to you for help,
    as I lift my hands toward your
    holy sanctuary.

³ Do not drag me away with the
  wicked—
    with those who do evil—
  those who speak friendly words
    to their neighbors
  while planning evil in their
    hearts.
⁴ Give them the punishment they
    so richly deserve!
  Measure it out in proportion
    to their wickedness.
  Pay them back for all their evil
    deeds!
  Give them a taste of what they
    have done to others.
⁵ They care nothing for what the
    Lord has done
  or for what his hands have
    made.

So he will tear them down,
    and they will never be rebuilt!

⁶ Praise the Lord!
    For he has heard my cry for
    mercy.
⁷ The Lord is my strength and
    shield.
  I trust him with all my heart.
  He helps me, and my heart is
    filled with joy.
  I burst out in songs of
    thanksgiving.

⁸ The Lord gives his people
    strength.
  He is a safe fortress for his
    anointed king.
⁹ Save your people!
  Bless Israel, your special
    possession.*
  Lead them like a shepherd,
    and carry them in your arms
    forever.

29 *A psalm of David.*

¹ Honor the Lord, you heavenly
    beings*;
  honor the Lord for his glory
    and strength.
² Honor the Lord for the glory
    of his name.
  Worship the Lord in the
    splendor of his holiness.
³ The voice of the Lord echoes
    above the sea.
  The God of glory thunders.

28:9 Hebrew *Bless your inheritance.* **29:1** Hebrew *you sons of God.*

The Lord thunders over the
    mighty sea.
4 The voice of the Lord is powerful;
    the voice of the Lord is
    majestic.
5 The voice of the Lord splits the
    mighty cedars;
    the Lord shatters the cedars
    of Lebanon.
6 He makes Lebanon's mountains
    skip like a calf;
    he makes Mount Hermon*
    leap like a young wild ox.
7 The voice of the Lord strikes
    with bolts of lightning.
8 The voice of the Lord makes the
    barren wilderness quake;
    the Lord shakes the
    wilderness of Kadesh.
9 The voice of the Lord twists
    mighty oaks*
    and strips the forests bare.
    In his Temple everyone shouts,
    "Glory!"
10 The Lord rules over the
    floodwaters.
    The Lord reigns as king
    forever.
11 The Lord gives his people
    strength.
    The Lord blesses them with
    peace.

30 *A psalm of David. A song for
the dedication of the Temple.*

1 I will exalt you, Lord, for you
    rescued me.

You refused to let my enemies
    triumph over me.
2 O Lord my God, I cried to you
    for help,
    and you restored my health.
3 You brought me up from the
    grave,* O Lord.
    You kept me from falling into
    the pit of death.

4 Sing to the Lord, all you godly
    ones!
    Praise his holy name.
5 For his anger lasts only a
    moment,
    but his favor lasts a lifetime!
    Weeping may last through the
    night,
    but joy comes with the
    morning.

6 When I was prosperous, I said,
    "Nothing can stop me now!"
7 Your favor, O Lord, made me as
    secure as a mountain.
    Then you turned away from
    me, and I was shattered.

8 I cried out to you, O Lord.
    I begged the Lord for mercy,
    saying,
9 "What will you gain if I die,
    if I sink into the grave?
    Can my dust praise you?
    Can it tell of your
    faithfulness?
10 Hear me, Lord, and have mercy
    on me.
    Help me, O Lord."

29:6 Hebrew *Sirion,* another name for Mount Hermon.   **29:9** Or *causes the deer to writhe in labor.*
30:3 Hebrew *from Sheol.*

11 You have turned my mourning
      into joyful dancing.
   You have taken away my
      clothes of mourning and
      clothed me with joy,
12 that I might sing praises to you
      and not be silent.
   O Lord my God, I will give you
      thanks forever!

31 *For the choir director:
      A psalm of David.*

1 O Lord, I have come to you for
      protection;
   don't let me be disgraced.
   Save me, for you do what is
      right.
2 Turn your ear to listen to me;
      rescue me quickly.
   Be my rock of protection,
      a fortress where I will be safe.
3 You are my rock and my fortress.
   For the honor of your name,
      lead me out of this danger.
4 Pull me from the trap my
      enemies set for me,
   for I find protection in you
      alone.
5 I entrust my spirit into your hand.
   Rescue me, Lord, for you are a
      faithful God.

6 I hate those who worship
      worthless idols.
   I trust in the Lord.
7 I will be glad and rejoice in your
      unfailing love,
   for you have seen my troubles,
   and you care about the
      anguish of my soul.

8 You have not handed me over to
      my enemies
   but have set me in a safe place.
9 Have mercy on me, Lord, for
      I am in distress.
   Tears blur my eyes.
   My body and soul are
      withering away.
10 I am dying from grief;
      my years are shortened by
      sadness.
   Sin has drained my strength;
      I am wasting away from within.
11 I am scorned by all my enemies
      and despised by my
      neighbors—
   even my friends are afraid to
      come near me.
   When they see me on the street,
      they run the other way.
12 I am ignored as if I were dead,
      as if I were a broken pot.
13 I have heard the many rumors
      about me,
   and I am surrounded by terror.
   My enemies conspire against me,
      plotting to take my life.

14 But I am trusting you, O Lord,
      saying, "You are my God!"
15 My future is in your hands.
   Rescue me from those who
      hunt me down relentlessly.
16 Let your favor shine on your
      servant.
   In your unfailing love, rescue
      me.
17 Don't let me be disgraced,
      O Lord,
   for I call out to you for help.

Let the wicked be disgraced;
  let them lie silent in the grave.*
18 Silence their lying lips—
  those proud and arrogant lips
    that accuse the godly.

19 How great is the goodness
  you have stored up for those
    who fear you.
  You lavish it on those who come
    to you for protection,
  blessing them before the
    watching world.
20 You hide them in the shelter of
    your presence,
  safe from those who conspire
    against them.
  You shelter them in your
    presence,
  far from accusing tongues.

21 Praise the Lord,
  for he has shown me the
    wonders of his unfailing
    love.
  He kept me safe when my city
    was under attack.
22 In panic I cried out,
  "I am cut off from the Lord!"
  But you heard my cry for mercy
    and answered my call for help.

23 Love the Lord, all you godly ones!
  For the Lord protects those
    who are loyal to him,
  but he harshly punishes the
    arrogant.
24 So be strong and courageous,
  all you who put your hope in
    the Lord!

32 A psalm* of David.

1 Oh, what joy for those
  whose disobedience is forgiven,
  whose sin is put out of sight!
2 Yes, what joy for those
  whose record the Lord has
    cleared of guilt,*
  whose lives are lived in
    complete honesty!
3 When I refused to confess my
    sin,
  my body wasted away,
  and I groaned all day long.
4 Day and night your hand of
    discipline was heavy on me.
  My strength evaporated like
    water in the summer heat.
                          Interlude

5 Finally, I confessed all my sins
    to you
  and stopped trying to hide
    my guilt.
  I said to myself, "I will confess
    my rebellion to the Lord."
  And you forgave me! All my
    guilt is gone.   *Interlude*

6 Therefore, let all the godly pray
    to you while there is still
    time,
  that they may not drown in the
    floodwaters of judgment.
7 For you are my hiding place;
  you protect me from trouble.
  You surround me with songs
    of victory.   *Interlude*

31:17 Hebrew *in Sheol.*   32:TITLE Hebrew *maskil.* This may be a literary or musical term.
32:2 Greek version reads *of sin.* Compare Rom 4:7.

8 The LORD says, "I will guide you
    along the best pathway for
    your life.
  I will advise you and watch
    over you.
9 Do not be like a senseless horse
    or mule
  that needs a bit and bridle to
    keep it under control."

10 Many sorrows come to the
    wicked,
  but unfailing love surrounds
    those who trust the LORD.
11 So rejoice in the LORD and be
    glad, all you who obey him!
  Shout for joy, all you whose
    hearts are pure!

33 ¹Let the godly sing for joy to
      the LORD;
  it is fitting for the pure to
    praise him.
2 Praise the LORD with melodies
    on the lyre;
  make music for him on the
    ten-stringed harp.
3 Sing a new song of praise to him;
  play skillfully on the harp, and
    sing with joy.
4 For the word of the LORD holds
    true,
  and we can trust everything he
    does.
5 He loves whatever is just and
    good;
  the unfailing love of the LORD
    fills the earth.
6 The LORD merely spoke,
  and the heavens were created.

He breathed the word,
  and all the stars were born.
7 He assigned the sea its
    boundaries
  and locked the oceans in vast
    reservoirs.
8 Let the whole world fear the
    LORD,
  and let everyone stand in awe
    of him.
9 For when he spoke, the world
    began!
  It appeared at his command.

10 The LORD frustrates the plans of
    the nations
  and thwarts all their
    schemes.
11 But the LORD's plans stand firm
    forever;
  his intentions can never be
    shaken.

12 What joy for the nation whose
    God is the LORD,
  whose people he has chosen
    as his inheritance.

13 The LORD looks down from
    heaven
  and sees the whole human
    race.
14 From his throne he observes
  all who live on the earth.
15 He made their hearts,
  so he understands everything
    they do.
16 The best-equipped army cannot
    save a king,
  nor is great strength enough to
    save a warrior.

¹⁷ Don't count on your warhorse to
  give you victory—
    for all its strength, it cannot
    save you.

¹⁸ But the LORD watches over those
  who fear him,
    those who rely on his unfailing
    love.

¹⁹ He rescues them from death
  and keeps them alive in times
    of famine.

²⁰ We put our hope in the LORD.
  He is our help and our shield.

²¹ In him our hearts rejoice,
  for we trust in his holy name.

²² Let your unfailing love surround
  us, LORD,
    for our hope is in you alone.

34 * A psalm of David, regarding the time he pretended to be insane in front of Abimelech, who sent him away.

¹ I will praise the LORD at all times.
  I will constantly speak his
    praises.

² I will boast only in the LORD;
  let all who are helpless take
    heart.

³ Come, let us tell of the LORD's
    greatness;
  let us exalt his name together.

⁴ I prayed to the LORD, and he
    answered me.
  He freed me from all my fears.

⁵ Those who look to him for help
  will be radiant with joy;
    no shadow of shame will
    darken their faces.

⁶ In my desperation I prayed, and
    the LORD listened;
  he saved me from all my
    troubles.

⁷ For the angel of the LORD is a
    guard;
  he surrounds and defends all
    who fear him.

⁸ Taste and see that the LORD is
    good.
  Oh, the joys of those who take
    refuge in him!

⁹ Fear the LORD, you his godly
    people,
  for those who fear him will
    have all they need.

¹⁰ Even strong young lions
    sometimes go hungry,
  but those who trust in the
    LORD will lack no good thing.

¹¹ Come, my children, and listen
    to me,
  and I will teach you to fear the
    LORD.

¹² Does anyone want to live a life
    that is long and prosperous?

¹³ Then keep your tongue from
    speaking evil
  and your lips from telling lies!

¹⁴ Turn away from evil and do
    good.
  Search for peace, and work to
    maintain it.

34 This psalm is a Hebrew acrostic poem; each verse begins with a successive letter of the Hebrew alphabet.

15 The eyes of the LORD watch over
   those who do right;
   his ears are open to their cries
   for help.
16 But the LORD turns his face
   against those who do evil;
   he will erase their memory
   from the earth.
17 The LORD hears his people when
   they call to him for help.
   He rescues them from all their
   troubles.
18 The LORD is close to the
   brokenhearted;
   he rescues those whose spirits
   are crushed.

19 The righteous person faces
   many troubles,
   but the LORD comes to the
   rescue each time.
20 For the LORD protects the bones
   of the righteous;
   not one of them is broken!
21 Calamity will surely destroy the
   wicked,
   and those who hate the
   righteous will be punished.
22 But the LORD will redeem those
   who serve him.
   No one who takes refuge in
   him will be condemned.

35 *A psalm of David.*

1 O LORD, oppose those who
   oppose me.
   Fight those who fight
   against me.

2 Put on your armor, and take up
   your shield.
   Prepare for battle, and come to
   my aid.
3 Lift up your spear and javelin
   against those who pursue me.
   Let me hear you say,
   "I will give you victory!"
4 Bring shame and disgrace on
   those trying to kill me;
   turn them back and humiliate
   those who want to harm me.
5 Blow them away like chaff in
   the wind—
   a wind sent by the angel of
   the LORD.
6 Make their path dark and
   slippery,
   with the angel of the LORD
   pursuing them.
7 I did them no wrong, but they
   laid a trap for me.
   I did them no wrong, but they
   dug a pit to catch me.
8 So let sudden ruin come upon
   them!
   Let them be caught in the trap
   they set for me!
   Let them be destroyed in the
   pit they dug for me.

9 Then I will rejoice in the LORD.
   I will be glad because he
   rescues me.
10 With every bone in my body
   I will praise him:
   "LORD, who can compare
   with you?
   Who else rescues the helpless
   from the strong?

Who else protects the helpless
   and poor from those who
   rob them?"

11 Malicious witnesses testify
      against me.
   They accuse me of crimes
      I know nothing about.
12 They repay me evil for good.
   I am sick with despair.
13 Yet when they were ill, I grieved
      for them.
   I denied myself by fasting for
      them,
   but my prayers returned
      unanswered.
14 I was sad, as though they were
      my friends or family,
   as if I were grieving for my
      own mother.
15 But they are glad now that I am
      in trouble;
   they gleefully join together
      against me.
   I am attacked by people I don't
      even know;
   they slander me constantly.
16 They mock me and call me
      names;
   they snarl at me.

17 How long, O Lord, will you look
      on and do nothing?
   Rescue me from their fierce
      attacks.
   Protect my life from these
      lions!
18 Then I will thank you in front of
      the great assembly.
   I will praise you before all the
      people.

19 Don't let my treacherous
      enemies rejoice over my
      defeat.
   Don't let those who hate me
      without cause gloat over my
      sorrow.
20 They don't talk of peace;
   they plot against innocent
      people who mind their own
      business.
21 They shout, "Aha! Aha!
   With our own eyes we saw him
      do it!"

22 O Lord, you know all about this.
   Do not stay silent.
   Do not abandon me now,
      O Lord.
23 Wake up! Rise to my defense!
   Take up my case, my God and
      my Lord.
24 Declare me not guilty, O Lord
      my God, for you give justice.
   Don't let my enemies laugh
      about me in my troubles.
25 Don't let them say, "Look, we got
      what we wanted!
   Now we will eat him alive!"

26 May those who rejoice at my
      troubles
   be humiliated and disgraced.
   May those who triumph over me
      be covered with shame and
      dishonor.
27 But give great joy to those who
      came to my defense.
   Let them continually say,
   "Great is the Lord,
   who delights in blessing his
      servant with peace!"

²⁸ Then I will proclaim your justice,
  and I will praise you all day
  long.

36 *For the choir director: A psalm
of David, the servant
of the LORD.*

¹ Sin whispers to the wicked, deep
  within their hearts.*
  They have no fear of God at all.
² In their blind conceit,
  they cannot see how wicked
  they really are.
³ Everything they say is crooked
  and deceitful.
  They refuse to act wisely or do
  good.
⁴ They lie awake at night, hatching
  sinful plots.
  Their actions are never good.
  They make no attempt to turn
  from evil.

⁵ Your unfailing love, O LORD, is as
  vast as the heavens;
  your faithfulness reaches
  beyond the clouds.
⁶ Your righteousness is like the
  mighty mountains,
  your justice like the ocean
  depths.
  You care for people and animals
  alike, O LORD.
⁷   How precious is your unfailing
  love, O God!
  All humanity finds shelter
  in the shadow of your wings.
⁸ You feed them from the
abundance of your own
  house,
  letting them drink from your
  river of delights.
⁹ For you are the fountain of life,
  the light by which we see.

¹⁰ Pour out your unfailing love on
  those who love you;
  give justice to those with
  honest hearts.
¹¹ Don't let the proud trample me
  or the wicked push me
  around.
¹² Look! Those who do evil have
  fallen!
  They are thrown down, never
  to rise again.

37 *A psalm of David.*

¹ Don't worry about the wicked
  or envy those who do wrong.
² For like grass, they soon fade
  away.
  Like spring flowers, they soon
  wither.
³ Trust in the LORD and do good.
  Then you will live safely in the
  land and prosper.
⁴ Take delight in the LORD,
  and he will give you your
  heart's desires.
⁵ Commit everything you do to
  the LORD.
  Trust him, and he will help
  you.

36:1 As in some Hebrew manuscripts and Syriac version, which read *in his heart*. Masoretic Text reads
in my heart.   **37** This psalm is a Hebrew acrostic poem; each stanza begins with a successive letter of
the Hebrew alphabet.

6 He will make your innocence
    radiate like the dawn,
  and the justice of your cause
    will shine like the noonday
    sun.

7 Be still in the presence of the
    Lord,
  and wait patiently for him to
    act.
  Don't worry about evil people
    who prosper
  or fret about their wicked
    schemes.

8 Stop being angry!
    Turn from your rage!
  Do not lose your temper—
    it only leads to harm.

9 For the wicked will be destroyed,
    but those who trust in the
    Lord will possess the land.

10 Soon the wicked will disappear.
    Though you look for them,
      they will be gone.

11 The lowly will possess the land
    and will live in peace and
      prosperity.

12 The wicked plot against the godly;
    they snarl at them in defiance.

13 But the Lord just laughs,
    for he sees their day of
      judgment coming.

14 The wicked draw their swords
    and string their bows
  to kill the poor and the
    oppressed,
  to slaughter those who do
    right.

15 But their swords will stab their
    own hearts,
  and their bows will be broken.

16 It is better to be godly and have
    little
  than to be evil and rich.

17 For the strength of the wicked
    will be shattered,
  but the Lord takes care of the
    godly.

18 Day by day the Lord takes care
    of the innocent,
  and they will receive an
    inheritance that lasts forever.

19 They will not be disgraced in
    hard times;
  even in famine they will have
    more than enough.

20 But the wicked will die.
    The Lord's enemies are like
      flowers in a field—
  they will disappear like smoke.

21 The wicked borrow and never
    repay,
  but the godly are generous
    givers.

22 Those the Lord blesses will
    possess the land,
  but those he curses will die.

23 The Lord directs the steps of the
    godly.
  He delights in every detail of
    their lives.

24 Though they stumble, they will
    never fall,
  for the Lord holds them by
    the hand.

25 Once I was young, and now I am old.
   Yet I have never seen the godly abandoned
   or their children begging for bread.
26 The godly always give generous loans to others,
   and their children are a blessing.

27 Turn from evil and do good,
   and you will live in the land forever.
28 For the Lord loves justice,
   and he will never abandon the godly.

   He will keep them safe forever,
   but the children of the wicked will die.
29 The godly will possess the land
   and will live there forever.

30 The godly offer good counsel;
   they teach right from wrong.
31 They have made God's law their own,
   so they will never slip from his path.

32 The wicked wait in ambush for the godly,
   looking for an excuse to kill them.
33 But the Lord will not let the wicked succeed
   or let the godly be condemned when they are put on trial.

34 Put your hope in the Lord.
   Travel steadily along his path.
   He will honor you by giving you the land.
   You will see the wicked destroyed.

35 I have seen wicked and ruthless people
   flourishing like a tree in its native soil.
36 But when I looked again, they were gone!
   Though I searched for them,
   I could not find them!

37 Look at those who are honest and good,
   for a wonderful future awaits those who love peace.
38 But the rebellious will be destroyed;
   they have no future.

39 The Lord rescues the godly;
   he is their fortress in times of trouble.
40 The Lord helps them,
   rescuing them from the wicked.
   He saves them,
   and they find shelter in him.

38 *A psalm of David, asking God to remember him.*

1 O Lord, don't rebuke me in your anger
   or discipline me in your rage!
2 Your arrows have struck deep,
   and your blows are crushing me.
3 Because of your anger, my whole body is sick;

my health is broken because
of my sins.
⁴ My guilt overwhelms me—
it is a burden too heavy to
bear.
⁵ My wounds fester and stink
because of my foolish sins.
⁶ I am bent over and racked with
pain.
All day long I walk around
filled with grief.
⁷ A raging fever burns within me,
and my health is broken.
⁸ I am exhausted and completely
crushed.
My groans come from an
anguished heart.

⁹ You know what I long for, Lord;
you hear my every sigh.
¹⁰ My heart beats wildly, my
strength fails,
and I am going blind.
¹¹ My loved ones and friends stay
away, fearing my disease.
Even my own family stands
at a distance.
¹² Meanwhile, my enemies lay traps
to kill me.
Those who wish me harm
make plans to ruin me.
All day long they plan their
treachery.
¹³ But I am deaf to all their threats.
I am silent before them as one
who cannot speak.
¹⁴ I choose to hear nothing,
and I make no reply.
¹⁵ For I am waiting for you, O LORD.

You must answer for me,
O Lord my God.
¹⁶ I prayed, "Don't let my enemies
gloat over me
or rejoice at my downfall."
¹⁷ I am on the verge of collapse,
facing constant pain.
¹⁸ But I confess my sins;
I am deeply sorry for what
I have done.
¹⁹ I have many aggressive
enemies;
they hate me without reason.
²⁰ They repay me evil for good
and oppose me for pursuing
good.
²¹ Do not abandon me, O LORD.
Do not stand at a distance,
my God.
²² Come quickly to help me,
O Lord my savior.

39 *For Jeduthun, the choir
director: A psalm of David.*

¹ I said to myself, "I will watch
what I do
and not sin in what I say.
I will hold my tongue
when the ungodly are around
me."
² But as I stood there in silence—
not even speaking of good
things—
the turmoil within me grew
worse.
³ The more I thought about it,
the hotter I got,
igniting a fire of words:

⁴ "LORD, remind me how brief my
     time on earth will be.
Remind me that my days are
     numbered—
how fleeting my life is.
⁵ You have made my life no longer
     than the width of my hand.
My entire lifetime is just a
     moment to you;
at best, each of us is but a
     breath."   *Interlude*

⁶ We are merely moving shadows,
     and all our busy rushing ends
     in nothing.
We heap up wealth,
     not knowing who will spend it.
⁷ And so, Lord, where do I put my
     hope?
My only hope is in you.
⁸ Rescue me from my rebellion.
     Do not let fools mock me.
⁹ I am silent before you; I won't say
     a word,
for my punishment is from you.
¹⁰ But please stop striking me!
     I am exhausted by the blows
     from your hand.
¹¹ When you discipline us for our
     sins,
you consume like a moth what
     is precious to us.
Each of us is but a breath.
                                   Interlude

¹² Hear my prayer, O LORD!
     Listen to my cries for help!
     Don't ignore my tears.
For I am your guest—
     a traveler passing through,
     as my ancestors were before me.

¹³ Leave me alone so I can smile
     again
before I am gone and exist no
     more.

40

*For the choir director:
A psalm of David.*

¹ I waited patiently for the LORD
     to help me,
and he turned to me and
     heard my cry.
² He lifted me out of the pit of
     despair,
     out of the mud and the mire.
He set my feet on solid ground
     and steadied me as I walked
     along.
³ He has given me a new song to
     sing,
     a hymn of praise to our God.
Many will see what he has done
     and be amazed.
They will put their trust in the
     LORD.

⁴ Oh, the joys of those who trust
     the LORD,
who have no confidence in the
     proud
or in those who worship idols.
⁵ O LORD my God, you have
     performed many wonders
     for us.
Your plans for us are too
     numerous to list.
You have no equal.
If I tried to recite all your
     wonderful deeds,
I would never come to the end
     of them.

6 You take no delight in sacrifices
or offerings.
Now that you have made
me listen, I finally
understand*—
you don't require burnt
offerings or sin offerings.
7 Then I said, "Look, I have come.
As is written about me in the
Scriptures:
8 I take joy in doing your will, my
God,
for your instructions are
written on my heart."

9 I have told all your people about
your justice.
I have not been afraid to speak
out,
as you, O LORD, well know.
10 I have not kept the good news of
your justice hidden in my
heart;
I have talked about your
faithfulness and saving
power.
I have told everyone in the great
assembly
of your unfailing love and
faithfulness.

11 LORD, don't hold back your
tender mercies from me.
Let your unfailing love and
faithfulness always
protect me.
12 For troubles surround me—
too many to count!
My sins pile up so high
I can't see my way out.

They outnumber the hairs on
my head.
I have lost all courage.

13 Please, LORD, rescue me!
Come quickly, LORD, and
help me.
14 May those who try to destroy me
be humiliated and put to
shame.
May those who take delight in
my trouble
be turned back in disgrace.
15 Let them be horrified by their
shame,
for they said, "Aha! We've got
him now!"
16 But may all who search for you
be filled with joy and gladness
in you.
May those who love your
salvation
repeatedly shout, "The LORD
is great!"
17 As for me, since I am poor and
needy,
let the Lord keep me in his
thoughts.
You are my helper and my
savior.
O my God, do not delay.

41 *For the choir director:
A psalm of David.*

1 Oh, the joys of those who are
kind to the poor!
The LORD rescues them when
they are in trouble.

40:6 Greek version reads *You have given me a body.* Compare Heb 10:5.

2 The LORD protects them
    and keeps them alive.
  He gives them prosperity in the
    land
    and rescues them from their
    enemies.
3 The LORD nurses them when
    they are sick
    and restores them to health.

4 "O LORD," I prayed, "have mercy
    on me.
  Heal me, for I have sinned
    against you."
5 But my enemies say nothing but
    evil about me.
  "How soon will he die and be
    forgotten?" they ask.
6 They visit me as if they were my
    friends,
    but all the while they gather
    gossip,
    and when they leave, they
    spread it everywhere.
7 All who hate me whisper about
    me,
    imagining the worst.
8 "He has some fatal disease,"
    they say.
  "He will never get out of that
    bed!"
9 Even my best friend, the one
    I trusted completely,
    the one who shared my food,
    has turned against me.

10 LORD, have mercy on me.
    Make me well again, so I can
    pay them back!
11 I know you are pleased with me,

for you have not let my
    enemies triumph over me.
12 You have preserved my life
    because I am innocent;
    you have brought me into your
    presence forever.

13 Praise the LORD, the God of
    Israel,
    who lives from everlasting to
    everlasting.
  Amen and amen!

BOOK TWO (Psalms 42–72)

42 *For the choir director:
A psalm* of the descendants
of Korah.*

1 As the deer longs for streams of
    water,
    so I long for you, O God.
2 I thirst for God, the living God.
    When can I go and stand
    before him?
3 Day and night I have only tears
    for food,
    while my enemies continually
    taunt me, saying,
    "Where is this God of yours?"

4 My heart is breaking
    as I remember how it used
    to be:
  I walked among the crowds of
    worshipers,
    leading a great procession to
    the house of God,
  singing for joy and giving thanks
    amid the sound of a great
    celebration!

42:TITLE Hebrew *maskil.* This may be a literary or musical term.

⁵ Why am I discouraged?
     Why is my heart so sad?
I will put my hope in God!
     I will praise him again—
     my Savior and ⁶my God!

Now I am deeply discouraged,
     but I will remember you—
even from distant Mount
         Hermon, the source of the
         Jordan,
     from the land of Mount Mizar.
⁷ I hear the tumult of the raging
         seas
     as your waves and surging
         tides sweep over me.
⁸ But each day the LORD pours his
         unfailing love upon me,
     and through each night I sing
         his songs,
     praying to God who gives me
         life.

⁹ "O God my rock," I cry,
     "Why have you forgotten me?
Why must I wander around in
         grief,
     oppressed by my enemies?"
¹⁰ Their taunts break my bones.
     They scoff, "Where is this God
         of yours?"

¹¹ Why am I discouraged?
     Why is my heart so sad?
I will put my hope in God!
     I will praise him again—
     my Savior and my God!

43

¹Declare me innocent,
         O God!

Defend me against these
         ungodly people.
Rescue me from these unjust
         liars.
² For you are God, my only safe
         haven.
Why have you tossed me
         aside?
Why must I wander around
         in grief,
     oppressed by my enemies?
³ Send out your light and your
         truth;
     let them guide me.
Let them lead me to your holy
         mountain,
     to the place where you live.
⁴ There I will go to the altar
         of God,
     to God—the source of all
         my joy.
I will praise you with my harp,
     O God, my God!

⁵ Why am I discouraged?
     Why is my heart so sad?
I will put my hope in God!
     I will praise him again—
     my Savior and my God!

44

*For the choir director:
A psalm* of the descendants
of Korah.*

¹ O God, we have heard it with our
         own ears—
     our ancestors have told us
of all you did in their day,
     in days long ago:

44:TITLE Hebrew *maskil*. This may be a literary or musical term.

2 You drove out the pagan nations
  by your power
and gave all the land to our
  ancestors.
You crushed their enemies
  and set our ancestors free.
3 They did not conquer the land
  with their swords;
it was not their own strong
  arm that gave them victory.
It was your right hand and
  strong arm
and the blinding light from
  your face that helped them,
for you loved them.

4 You are my King and my God.
  You command victories for
  Israel.*
5 Only by your power can we push
  back our enemies;
only in your name can we
  trample our foes.
6 I do not trust in my bow;
  I do not count on my sword
  to save me.
7 You are the one who gives us
  victory over our enemies;
you disgrace those who
  hate us.
8 O God, we give glory to you all
  day long
and constantly praise your
  name.   *Interlude*

9 But now you have tossed us aside
  in dishonor.
You no longer lead our armies
  to battle.

10 You make us retreat from our
  enemies
and allow those who hate us to
  plunder our land.
11 You have butchered us like sheep
  and scattered us among the
  nations.
12 You sold your precious people
  for a pittance,
making nothing on the sale.
13 You let our neighbors mock us.
  We are an object of scorn and
  derision to those around us.
14 You have made us the butt of
  their jokes;
they shake their heads at us
  in scorn.
15 We can't escape the constant
  humiliation;
shame is written across our
  faces.
16 All we hear are the taunts of our
  mockers.
All we see are our vengeful
  enemies.

17 All this has happened though
  we have not forgotten you.
We have not violated your
  covenant.
18 Our hearts have not deserted
  you.
We have not strayed from
  your path.
19 Yet you have crushed us in the
  jackal's desert home.
You have covered us with
  darkness and death.

44:4 Hebrew *for Jacob.* The names "Jacob" and "Israel" are often interchanged throughout the Old
Testament, referring sometimes to the individual patriarch and sometimes to the nation.

20 If we had forgotten the name of
     our God
        or spread our hands in prayer
        to foreign gods,
21 God would surely have known it,
        for he knows the secrets of
        every heart.
22 But for your sake we are killed
     every day;
        we are being slaughtered like
        sheep.

23 Wake up, O Lord! Why do you
     sleep?
        Get up! Do not reject us forever.
24 Why do you look the other way?
        Why do you ignore our
        suffering and oppression?
25 We collapse in the dust,
        lying face down in the dirt.
26 Rise up! Help us!
        Ransom us because of your
        unfailing love.

45

*For the choir director: A love
song to be sung to the tune
"Lilies." A psalm* of the descendants
of Korah.*

1 Beautiful words stir my heart.
     I will recite a lovely poem
        about the king,
        for my tongue is like the pen
        of a skillful poet.

2 You are the most handsome of all.
     Gracious words stream from
        your lips.
        God himself has blessed you
        forever.

3 Put on your sword, O mighty
     warrior!
        You are so glorious, so
        majestic!
4 In your majesty, ride out to
     victory,
        defending truth, humility,
        and justice.
        Go forth to perform awe-
        inspiring deeds!
5 Your arrows are sharp, piercing
     your enemies' hearts.
        The nations fall beneath your
        feet.
6 Your throne, O God,* endures
     forever and ever.
        You rule with a scepter of
        justice.
7 You love justice and hate evil.
     Therefore God, your God, has
        anointed you,
        pouring out the oil of joy on
        you more than on anyone
        else.
8 Myrrh, aloes, and cassia perfume
     your robes.
        In ivory palaces the music of
        strings entertains you.
9 Kings' daughters are among your
     noble women.
        At your right side stands the
        queen,
        wearing jewelry of finest gold
        from Ophir!

10 Listen to me, O royal daughter;
        take to heart what I say.
        Forget your people and your
        family far away.

45:TITLE Hebrew *maskil.* This may be a literary or musical term.   **45:6** Or *Your divine throne.*

11 For your royal husband delights
      in your beauty;
   honor him, for he is your lord.
12 The princess of Tyre* will
      shower you with gifts.
   The wealthy will beg your
      favor.
13 The bride, a princess, looks
      glorious
   in her golden gown.
14 In her beautiful robes, she is led
      to the king,
   accompanied by her
      bridesmaids.
15 What a joyful and enthusiastic
      procession
   as they enter the king's palace!

16 Your sons will become kings like
      their father.
   You will make them rulers
      over many lands.
17 I will bring honor to your name
      in every generation.
   Therefore, the nations will
      praise you forever and ever.

46 *For the choir director: A song
of the descendants of Korah,
to be sung by soprano voices.**

1 God is our refuge and strength,
   always ready to help in times
      of trouble.
2 So we will not fear when
      earthquakes come
   and the mountains crumble
      into the sea.
3 Let the oceans roar and foam.

Let the mountains tremble as
      the waters surge! *Interlude*

4 A river brings joy to the city of
      our God,
   the sacred home of the Most
      High.
5 God dwells in that city; it cannot
      be destroyed.
   From the very break of day,
      God will protect it.
6 The nations are in chaos,
   and their kingdoms crumble!
God's voice thunders,
   and the earth melts!
7 The LORD of Heaven's Armies is
      here among us;
   the God of Israel* is our
      fortress. *Interlude*

8 Come, see the glorious works of
      the LORD:
   See how he brings destruction
      upon the world.
9 He causes wars to end
      throughout the earth.
   He breaks the bow and snaps
      the spear;
   he burns the shields with fire.

10 "Be still, and know that I am God!
   I will be honored by every
      nation.
   I will be honored throughout
      the world."

11 The LORD of Heaven's Armies is
      here among us;
   the God of Israel is our
      fortress. *Interlude*

45:12 Hebrew *The daughter of Tyre.* 46:TITLE Hebrew *according to alamoth.* 46:7 Hebrew *of
Jacob;* also in 46:11. See note on 44:4.

47
For the choir director: A psalm of the descendants of Korah.

¹ Come, everyone! Clap your hands!
  Shout to God with joyful
    praise!
² For the Lᴏʀᴅ Most High is
    awesome.
  He is the great King of all the
    earth.
³ He subdues the nations before us,
    putting our enemies beneath
    our feet.
⁴ He chose the Promised Land as
    our inheritance,
  the proud possession of
    Jacob's descendants, whom
    he loves.   *Interlude*

⁵ God has ascended with a mighty
    shout.
  The Lᴏʀᴅ has ascended with
    trumpets blaring.
⁶ Sing praises to God, sing praises;
    sing praises to our King, sing
    praises!
⁷ For God is the King over all the
    earth.
  Praise him with a psalm.*
⁸ God reigns above the nations,
    sitting on his holy throne.
⁹ The rulers of the world have
    gathered together
  with the people of the God
    of Abraham.
  For all the kings of the earth
    belong to God.
  He is highly honored
    everywhere.

48
A song. A psalm of the descendants of Korah.

¹ How great is the Lᴏʀᴅ,
    how deserving of praise,
  in the city of our God,
    which sits on his holy
    mountain!
² It is high and magnificent;
    the whole earth rejoices to see it!
  Mount Zion, the holy mountain,*
    is the city of the great King!
³ God himself is in Jerusalem's
    towers,
  revealing himself as its
    defender.

⁴ The kings of the earth joined
    forces
  and advanced against the city.
⁵ But when they saw it, they were
    stunned;
  they were terrified and ran away.
⁶ They were gripped with terror
    and writhed in pain like a
    woman in labor.
⁷ You destroyed them like the
    mighty ships of Tarshish
  shattered by a powerful east
    wind.

⁸ We had heard of the city's glory,
    but now we have seen it
    ourselves—
  the city of the Lᴏʀᴅ of
    Heaven's Armies.
  It is the city of our God;
    he will make it safe forever.
                              Interlude

47:7 Hebrew *maskil*. This may be a literary or musical term. **48:2** Or *Mount Zion, in the far north;*
Hebrew reads *Mount Zion, the heights of Zaphon.*

9 O God, we meditate on your
    unfailing love
    as we worship in your Temple.
10 As your name deserves, O God,
    you will be praised to the ends
      of the earth.
    Your strong right hand is filled
      with victory.
11 Let the people on Mount Zion
    rejoice.
    Let all the towns of Judah be
      glad
    because of your justice.

12 Go, inspect the city of Jerusalem.*
    Walk around and count the
      many towers.
13 Take note of the fortified walls,
    and tour all the citadels,
    that you may describe them
      to future generations.
14 For that is what God is like.
    He is our God forever and
      ever,
    and he will guide us until
      we die.

49

*For the choir director: A psalm
of the descendants of Korah.*

1 Listen to this, all you people!
    Pay attention, everyone in the
      world!
2 High and low,
    rich and poor—listen!
3 For my words are wise,
    and my thoughts are filled
      with insight.

4 I listen carefully to many proverbs
    and solve riddles with
      inspiration from a harp.

5 Why should I fear when trouble
      comes,
    when enemies surround me?
6 They trust in their wealth
    and boast of great riches.
7 Yet they cannot redeem
      themselves from death*
    by paying a ransom to God.
8 Redemption does not come so
      easily,
    for no one can ever pay enough
9 to live forever
    and never see the grave.

10 Those who are wise must finally
      die,
    just like the foolish and
      senseless,
    leaving all their wealth behind.
11 The grave* is their eternal home,
    where they will stay forever.
    They may name their estates
      after themselves,
12   but their fame will not last.
    They will die, just like animals.
13 This is the fate of fools,
    though they are remembered
      as being wise.*   *Interlude*

14 Like sheep, they are led to the
      grave,*
    where death will be their
      shepherd.
In the morning the godly will
      rule over them.

48:12 Hebrew *Zion.* 49:7 Some Hebrew manuscripts read *no one can redeem the life of another.*
49:11 As in Greek and Syriac versions; Hebrew reads *Their inward [thought].* 49:13 The meaning
of the Hebrew is uncertain. 49:14 Hebrew *Sheol;* also in 49:14b, 15.

Their bodies will rot in the
　　grave,
　　far from their grand estates.
15 But as for me, God will redeem
　　my life.
　　He will snatch me from the
　　power of the grave.　　*Interlude*

16 So don't be dismayed when the
　　wicked grow rich
　　and their homes become ever
　　more splendid.
17 For when they die, they take
　　nothing with them.
　　Their wealth will not follow
　　them into the grave.
18 In this life they consider
　　themselves fortunate
　　and are applauded for their
　　success.
19 But they will die like all before
　　them
　　and never again see the light
　　of day.
20 People who boast of their wealth
　　don't understand;
　　they will die, just like animals.

50 *A psalm of Asaph.*

1 The LORD, the Mighty One, is
　　God,
　　and he has spoken;
　　he has summoned all humanity
　　from where the sun rises to
　　where it sets.
2 From Mount Zion, the perfection
　　of beauty,
　　God shines in glorious radiance.

3 Our God approaches,
　　and he is not silent.
　　Fire devours everything in
　　his way,
　　and a great storm rages
　　around him.
4 He calls on the heavens above
　　and earth below
　　to witness the judgment of his
　　people.
5 "Bring my faithful people to me—
　　those who made a covenant
　　with me by giving
　　sacrifices."
6 Then let the heavens proclaim
　　his justice,
　　for God himself will be the
　　judge.　　*Interlude*

7 "O my people, listen as I speak.
　　Here are my charges against
　　you, O Israel:
　　I am God, your God!
8 I have no complaint about your
　　sacrifices
　　or the burnt offerings you
　　constantly offer.
9 But I do not need the bulls from
　　your barns
　　or the goats from your pens.
10 For all the animals of the forest
　　are mine,
　　and I own the cattle on a
　　thousand hills.
11 I know every bird on the
　　mountains,
　　and all the animals of the field
　　are mine.
12 If I were hungry, I would not
　　tell you,

for all the world is mine and everything in it.

¹³ Do I eat the meat of bulls?
Do I drink the blood of goats?

¹⁴ Make thankfulness your sacrifice to God,
and keep the vows you made to the Most High.

¹⁵ Then call on me when you are in trouble,
and I will rescue you,
and you will give me glory."

¹⁶ But God says to the wicked:
"Why bother reciting my decrees and pretending to obey my covenant?

¹⁷ For you refuse my discipline and treat my words like trash.

¹⁸ When you see thieves, you approve of them,
and you spend your time with adulterers.

¹⁹ Your mouth is filled with wickedness,
and your tongue is full of lies.

²⁰ You sit around and slander your brother—
your own mother's son.

²¹ While you did all this,
I remained silent,
and you thought I didn't care.
But now I will rebuke you,
listing all my charges against you.

²² Repent, all of you who forget me,
or I will tear you apart,
and no one will help you.

²³ But giving thanks is a sacrifice that truly honors me.
If you keep to my path,
I will reveal to you the salvation of God."

51 *For the choir director: A psalm of David, regarding the time Nathan the prophet came to him after David had committed adultery with Bathsheba.*

¹ Have mercy on me, O God,
because of your unfailing love.
Because of your great compassion,
blot out the stain of my sins.

² Wash me clean from my guilt.
Purify me from my sin.

³ For I recognize my rebellion;
it haunts me day and night.

⁴ Against you, and you alone, have I sinned;
I have done what is evil in your sight.
You will be proved right in what you say,
and your judgment against me is just.*

⁵ For I was born a sinner—
yes, from the moment my mother conceived me.

⁶ But you desire honesty from the womb,*
teaching me wisdom even there.

⁷ Purify me from my sins,* and I will be clean;

51:4 Greek version reads *and you will win your case in court.* Compare Rom 3:4.   51:6 Or *from the heart;* Hebrew reads *in the inward parts.*   51:7 Hebrew *Purify me with the hyssop branch.*

wash me, and I will be whiter
than snow.

⁸ Oh, give me back my joy again;
you have broken me—
now let me rejoice.

⁹ Don't keep looking at my sins.
Remove the stain of my guilt.

¹⁰ Create in me a clean heart,
O God.
Renew a loyal spirit within me.

¹¹ Do not banish me from your
presence,
and don't take your Holy
Spirit* from me.

¹² Restore to me the joy of your
salvation,
and make me willing to obey
you.

¹³ Then I will teach your ways to
rebels,
and they will return to you.

¹⁴ Forgive me for shedding blood,
O God who saves;
then I will joyfully sing of your
forgiveness.

¹⁵ Unseal my lips, O Lord,
that my mouth may praise you.

¹⁶ You do not desire a sacrifice, or I
would offer one.
You do not want a burnt
offering.

¹⁷ The sacrifice you desire is a
broken spirit.
You will not reject a broken
and repentant heart, O God.

¹⁸ Look with favor on Zion and help
her;
rebuild the walls of Jerusalem.

¹⁹ Then you will be pleased with
sacrifices offered in the
right spirit—
with burnt offerings and
whole burnt offerings.
Then bulls will again be
sacrificed on your altar.

52

For the choir director: A psalm
of David, regarding the time
Doeg the Edomite said to Saul, "David
has gone to see Ahimelech."*

¹ Why do you boast about your
crimes, great warrior?
Don't you realize God's justice
continues forever?

² All day long you plot destruction.
Your tongue cuts like a sharp
razor;
you're an expert at telling lies.

³ You love evil more than good
and lies more than truth.

Interlude

⁴ You love to destroy others with
your words,
you liar!

⁵ But God will strike you down
once and for all.
He will pull you from your home
and uproot you from the land
of the living.   *Interlude*

⁶ The righteous will see it and be
amazed.
They will laugh and say,

⁷ "Look what happens to mighty
warriors
who do not trust in God.

51:11 Or *your spirit of holiness.*   **52:TITLE** Hebrew *maskil.* This may be a literary or musical term.

They trust their wealth instead
and grow more and more bold
in their wickedness."

8 But I am like an olive tree,
thriving in the house of God.
I will always trust in God's
unfailing love.
9 I will praise you forever, O God,
for what you have done.
I will trust in your good name
in the presence of your
faithful people.

53 For the choir director:
A meditation; a psalm* of David.

1 Only fools say in their hearts,
"There is no God."
They are corrupt, and their
actions are evil;
not one of them does good!

2 God looks down from heaven
on the entire human race;
he looks to see if anyone is truly
wise,
if anyone seeks God.
3 But no, all have turned away;
all have become corrupt.*
No one does good,
not a single one!

4 Will those who do evil never
learn?
They eat up my people like
bread
and wouldn't think of praying
to God.

5 Terror will grip them,
terror like they have never
known before.
God will scatter the bones of
your enemies.
You will put them to shame,
for God has rejected them.

6 Who will come from Mount Zion
to rescue Israel?
When God restores his people,
Jacob will shout with joy, and
Israel will rejoice.

54 For the choir director:
A psalm* of David, regarding the time the Ziphites came and said to Saul, "We know where David is hiding." To be accompanied by stringed instruments.

1 Come with great power, O God,
and rescue me!
Defend me with your might.
2 Listen to my prayer, O God.
Pay attention to my plea.
3 For strangers are attacking me;
violent people are trying to
kill me.
They care nothing for God.
                              Interlude

4 But God is my helper.
The Lord keeps me alive!
5 May the evil plans of my
enemies be turned against
them.
Do as you promised and put
an end to them.

53:TITLE Hebrew *According to mahalath; a maskil.* These may be literary or musical terms.
53:3 Greek version reads *have become useless.* Compare Rom 3:12. **54:TITLE** Hebrew *maskil.* This may be a literary or musical term.

⁶ I will sacrifice a voluntary
    offering to you;
  I will praise your name,
    O Lᴏʀᴅ,
    for it is good.
⁷ For you have rescued me from
    my troubles
  and helped me to triumph
    over my enemies.

55 *For the choir director: A psalm* of David, to be accompanied by stringed instruments.*

¹ Listen to my prayer, O God.
  Do not ignore my cry for
    help!
² Please listen and answer me,
  for I am overwhelmed by my
    troubles.
³ My enemies shout at me,
  making loud and wicked
    threats.
  They bring trouble on me
  and angrily hunt me down.

⁴ My heart pounds in my chest.
  The terror of death assaults me.
⁵ Fear and trembling overwhelm
    me,
  and I can't stop shaking.
⁶ Oh, that I had wings like a dove;
  then I would fly away and
    rest!
⁷ I would fly far away
  to the quiet of the wilderness.
                 Interlude
⁸ How quickly I would escape—
  far from this wild storm of
    hatred.

⁹ Confuse them, Lord, and
  frustrate their plans,
  for I see violence and conflict
    in the city.
¹⁰ Its walls are patrolled day and
    night against invaders,
  but the real danger is
    wickedness within the city.
¹¹ Everything is falling apart;
  threats and cheating are
    rampant in the streets.

¹² It is not an enemy who taunts
    me—
  I could bear that.
  It is not my foes who so
    arrogantly insult me—
  I could have hidden from
    them.
¹³ Instead, it is you—my equal,
  my companion and close
    friend.
¹⁴ What good fellowship we once
    enjoyed
  as we walked together to the
    house of God.

¹⁵ Let death stalk my enemies;
  let the grave* swallow them
    alive,
  for evil makes its home within
    them.

¹⁶ But I will call on God,
  and the Lᴏʀᴅ will rescue me.
¹⁷ Morning, noon, and night
  I cry out in my distress,
  and the Lᴏʀᴅ hears my voice.
¹⁸ He ransoms me and keeps me
    safe

55:ᴛɪᴛʟᴇ Hebrew *maskil.* This may be a literary or musical term.   **55:15** Hebrew *let Sheol.*

from the battle waged against
   me,
though many still oppose me.
¹⁹ God, who has ruled forever,
   will hear me and humble
      them.   *Interlude*
For my enemies refuse to change
      their ways;
   they do not fear God.

²⁰ As for my companion, he
      betrayed his friends;
   he broke his promises.
²¹ His words are as smooth as
      butter,
   but in his heart is war.
His words are as soothing as
      lotion,
   but underneath are daggers!

²² Give your burdens to the Lord,
   and he will take care of you.
He will not permit the godly
   to slip and fall.

²³ But you, O God, will send the
      wicked
   down to the pit of destruction.
Murderers and liars will die
      young,
   but I am trusting you to save me.

56 *For the choir director: A psalm*
of David, regarding the time
the Philistines seized him in Gath. To
be sung to the tune "Dove on Distant
Oaks."*

¹ O God, have mercy on me,
   for people are hounding me.
   My foes attack me all day long.

² I am constantly hounded by
      those who slander me,
   and many are boldly
      attacking me.
³ But when I am afraid,
   I will put my trust in you.
⁴ I praise God for what he has
      promised.
   I trust in God, so why should
      I be afraid?
   What can mere mortals do
      to me?

⁵ They are always twisting what
      I say;
   they spend their days plotting
      to harm me.
⁶ They come together to spy
      on me—
   watching my every step, eager
      to kill me.
⁷ Don't let them get away with
      their wickedness;
   in your anger, O God, bring
      them down.

⁸ You keep track of all my
      sorrows.*
   You have collected all my tears
      in your bottle.
   You have recorded each one in
      your book.
⁹ My enemies will retreat when
      I call to you for help.
   This I know: God is on my side!
¹⁰ I praise God for what he has
      promised;
   yes, I praise the Lord for what
      he has promised.

56:TITLE Hebrew *miktam*. This may be a literary or musical term.   56:8 Or *my wanderings*.

11 I trust in God, so why should I
   be afraid?
   What can mere mortals do
   to me?

12 I will fulfill my vows to you,
   O God,
   and will offer a sacrifice of
   thanks for your help.
13 For you have rescued me from
   death;
   you have kept my feet from
   slipping.
   So now I can walk in your
   presence, O God,
   in your life-giving light.

57

For the choir director: A psalm*
of David, regarding the time he
fled from Saul and went into the cave.
To be sung to the tune "Do Not
Destroy!"

1 Have mercy on me, O God, have
   mercy!
   I look to you for protection.
   I will hide beneath the shadow
   of your wings
   until the danger passes by.
2 I cry out to God Most High,*
   to God who will fulfill his
   purpose for me.
3 He will send help from heaven to
   rescue me,
   disgracing those who hound
   me.   *Interlude*
   My God will send forth his
   unfailing love and
   faithfulness.

4 I am surrounded by fierce lions
   who greedily devour human
   prey—
   whose teeth pierce like spears
   and arrows,
   and whose tongues cut like
   swords.
5 Be exalted, O God, above the
   highest heavens!
   May your glory shine over all
   the earth.

6 My enemies have set a trap for
   me.
   I am weary from distress.
   They have dug a deep pit in my
   path,
   but they themselves have
   fallen into it.   *Interlude*

7 My heart is confident in you,
   O God;
   my heart is confident.
   No wonder I can sing your
   praises!
8 Wake up, my heart!
   Wake up, O lyre and harp!
   I will wake the dawn with my
   song.
9 I will thank you, Lord, among all
   the people.
   I will sing your praises among
   the nations.
10 For your unfailing love is as high
   as the heavens.
   Your faithfulness reaches to
   the clouds.
11 Be exalted, O God, above the
   highest heavens.

57:TITLE Hebrew *miktam*. This may be a literary or musical term. 57:2 Hebrew *Elohim-Elyon*.

May your glory shine over all
the earth.

58

For the choir director: A psalm*
of David, to be sung to the tune
"Do Not Destroy!"

1 Justice—do you rulers* know the
meaning of the word?
Do you judge the people fairly?
2 No! You plot injustice in your
hearts.
You spread violence
throughout the land.
3 These wicked people are born
sinners;
even from birth they have lied
and gone their own way.
4 They spit venom like deadly
snakes;
they are like cobras that refuse
to listen,
5 ignoring the tunes of the snake
charmers,
no matter how skillfully they
play.
6 Break off their fangs, O God!
Smash the jaws of these lions,
O LORD!
7 May they disappear like water
into thirsty ground.
Make their weapons useless in
their hands.*
8 May they be like snails that
dissolve into slime,
like a stillborn child who will
never see the sun.

9 God will sweep them away, both
young and old,
faster than a pot heats over
burning thorns.
10 The godly will rejoice when they
see injustice avenged.
They will wash their feet in the
blood of the wicked.
11 Then at last everyone will say,
"There truly is a reward for
those who live for God;
surely there is a God who
judges justly here on earth."

59

For the choir director: A psalm*
of David, regarding the time
Saul sent soldiers to watch David's
house in order to kill him. To be sung
to the tune "Do Not Destroy!"

1 Rescue me from my enemies,
O God.
Protect me from those who
have come to destroy me.
2 Rescue me from these criminals;
save me from these murderers.
3 They have set an ambush for me.
Fierce enemies are out there
waiting, LORD,
though I have not sinned or
offended them.
4 I have done nothing wrong,
yet they prepare to attack me.
Wake up! See what is
happening and help me!
5 O LORD God of Heaven's Armies,
the God of Israel,

58:TITLE Hebrew *miktam*. This may be a literary or musical term. **58:1** Or *you gods*. **58:7** Or *Let*
them be trodden down and wither like grass. The meaning of the Hebrew is uncertain.
59:TITLE Hebrew *miktam*. This may be a literary or musical term.

wake up and punish those
	hostile nations.
Show no mercy to wicked
	traitors. *Interlude*

⁶ They come out at night,
	snarling like vicious dogs
	as they prowl the streets.
⁷ Listen to the filth that comes
	from their mouths;
	their words cut like swords.
	"After all, who can hear us?"
	they sneer.
⁸ But LORD, you laugh at them.
	You scoff at all the hostile
	nations.
⁹ You are my strength; I wait for
	you to rescue me,
	for you, O God, are my fortress.
¹⁰ In his unfailing love, my God will
	stand with me.
	He will let me look down in
	triumph on all my enemies.

¹¹ Don't kill them, for my people
	soon forget such lessons;
	stagger them with your power,
	and bring them to their
	knees,
	O Lord our shield.
¹² Because of the sinful things they
	say,
	because of the evil that is on
	their lips,
	let them be captured by their
	pride,
	their curses, and their lies.
¹³ Destroy them in your anger!
	Wipe them out completely!

Then the whole world will know
	that God reigns in Israel.*
	                    Interlude
¹⁴ My enemies come out at night,
	snarling like vicious dogs
	as they prowl the streets.
¹⁵ They scavenge for food
	but go to sleep unsatisfied.*

¹⁶ But as for me, I will sing about
	your power.
	Each morning I will sing with
	joy about your unfailing
	love.
For you have been my refuge,
	a place of safety when I am in
	distress.
¹⁷ O my Strength, to you I sing
	praises,
	for you, O God, are my refuge,
	the God who shows me
	unfailing love.

60 *For the choir director: A psalm* of David useful for teaching, regarding the time David fought Aram-naharaim and Aram-zobah, and Joab returned and killed 12,000 Edomites in the Valley of Salt. To be sung to the tune "Lily of the Testimony."*

¹ You have rejected us, O God, and
	broken our defenses.
	You have been angry with us;
	now restore us to your favor.
² You have shaken our land and
	split it open.

59:13 Hebrew *in Jacob.* See note on 44:4.   **59:15** Or *and growl if they don't get enough.*
60:TITLE Hebrew *miktam.* This may be a literary or musical term.

Seal the cracks, for the land
trembles.
3 You have been very hard on us,
making us drink wine that
sent us reeling.
4 But you have raised a banner for
those who fear you—
a rallying point in the face of
attack.   *Interlude*

5 Now rescue your beloved people.
Answer and save us by your
power.
6 God has promised this by his
holiness*:
"I will divide up Shechem with
joy.
I will measure out the valley
of Succoth.
7 Gilead is mine,
and Manasseh, too.
Ephraim, my helmet, will
produce my warriors,
and Judah, my scepter, will
produce my kings.
8 But Moab, my washbasin, will
become my servant,
and I will wipe my feet on Edom
and shout in triumph over
Philistia."

9 Who will bring me into the
fortified city?
Who will bring me victory
over Edom?
10 Have you rejected us, O God?
Will you no longer march with
our armies?
11 Oh, please help us against our
enemies,

for all human help is useless.
12 With God's help we will do
mighty things,
for he will trample down our
foes.

61 *For the choir director: A psalm
of David, to be accompanied
by stringed instruments.*

1 O God, listen to my cry!
Hear my prayer!
2 From the ends of the earth,
I cry to you for help
when my heart is
overwhelmed.
Lead me to the towering rock
of safety,
3 for you are my safe refuge,
a fortress where my enemies
cannot reach me.
4 Let me live forever in your
sanctuary,
safe beneath the shelter of
your wings!   *Interlude*

5 For you have heard my vows,
O God.
You have given me an
inheritance reserved for
those who fear your
name.
6 Add many years to the life of the
king!
May his years span the
generations!
7 May he reign under God's
protection forever.
May your unfailing love and
faithfulness watch over him.

60:6 Or *in his sanctuary.*

8 Then I will sing praises to your
    name forever
    as I fulfill my vows each day.

62 For Jeduthun, the choir director: A psalm of David.

1 I wait quietly before God,
    for my victory comes from him.
2 He alone is my rock and my
    salvation,
    my fortress where I will never
    be shaken.

3 So many enemies against one
    man—
    all of them trying to kill me.
To them I'm just a broken-down
    wall
    or a tottering fence.
4 They plan to topple me from my
    high position.
    They delight in telling lies
    about me.
They praise me to my face
    but curse me in their hearts.
                                Interlude

5 Let all that I am wait quietly
    before God,
    for my hope is in him.
6 He alone is my rock and my
    salvation,
    my fortress where I will not be
    shaken.
7 My victory and honor come from
    God alone.
    He is my refuge, a rock where
    no enemy can reach me.
8 O my people, trust in him at all
    times.

Pour out your heart to him,
    for God is our refuge.
                                Interlude

9 Common people are as worthless
    as a puff of wind,
    and the powerful are not what
    they appear to be.
If you weigh them on the scales,
    together they are lighter than
    a breath of air.

10 Don't make your living by
    extortion
    or put your hope in stealing.
And if your wealth increases,
    don't make it the center of
    your life.

11 God has spoken plainly,
    and I have heard it many
    times:
Power, O God, belongs to you;
12   unfailing love, O Lord,
    is yours.
Surely you repay all people
    according to what they have
    done.

63 A psalm of David, regarding a time when David was in the wilderness of Judah.

1 O God, you are my God;
    I earnestly search for you.
My soul thirsts for you;
    my whole body longs for you
in this parched and weary land
    where there is no water.
2 I have seen you in your sanctuary
    and gazed upon your power
    and glory.

³ Your unfailing love is better than
  life itself;
    how I praise you!
⁴ I will praise you as long as I live,
  lifting up my hands to you in
    prayer.
⁵ You satisfy me more than the
  richest feast.
    I will praise you with songs
    of joy.

⁶ I lie awake thinking of you,
  meditating on you through
    the night.
⁷ Because you are my helper,
  I sing for joy in the shadow
    of your wings.
⁸ I cling to you;
  your strong right hand holds
    me securely.

⁹ But those plotting to destroy me
  will come to ruin.
    They will go down into the
    depths of the earth.
¹⁰ They will die by the sword
  and become the food of
    jackals.
¹¹ But the king will rejoice in God.
  All who swear to tell the truth
    will praise him,
    while liars will be silenced.

64 *For the choir director:*
A psalm of David.

¹ O God, listen to my complaint.
  Protect my life from my
    enemies' threats.
² Hide me from the plots of this
    evil mob,

from this gang of wrongdoers.
³ They sharpen their tongues like
    swords
    and aim their bitter words like
    arrows.
⁴ They shoot from ambush at the
    innocent,
    attacking suddenly and
    fearlessly.
⁵ They encourage each other to
    do evil
    and plan how to set their traps
    in secret.
    "Who will ever notice?" they
    ask.
⁶ As they plot their crimes, they
    say,
    "We have devised the perfect
    plan!"
    Yes, the human heart and
    mind are cunning.

⁷ But God himself will shoot them
    with his arrows,
    suddenly striking them
    down.
⁸ Their own tongues will ruin
    them,
    and all who see them will
    shake their heads in scorn.
⁹ Then everyone will be afraid;
    they will proclaim the mighty
    acts of God
    and realize all the amazing
    things he does.
¹⁰ The godly will rejoice in the
    LORD
    and find shelter in him.
  And those who do what is right
    will praise him.

65

*For the choir director:
A song. A psalm of David.*

¹ What mighty praise, O God,
 belongs to you in Zion.
 We will fulfill our vows to you,
² for you answer our prayers.
 All of us must come to you.
³ Though we are overwhelmed
 by our sins,
 you forgive them all.
⁴ What joy for those you choose
 to bring near,
 those who live in your holy
 courts.
 What festivities await us
 inside your holy Temple.

⁵ You faithfully answer our
 prayers with awesome
 deeds,
 O God our savior.
 You are the hope of everyone on
 earth,
 even those who sail on distant
 seas.
⁶ You formed the mountains by
 your power
 and armed yourself with
 mighty strength.
⁷ You quieted the raging oceans
 with their pounding waves
 and silenced the shouting of
 the nations.
⁸ Those who live at the ends of the
 earth
 stand in awe of your
 wonders.
 From where the sun rises to
 where it sets,
 you inspire shouts of joy.

⁹ You take care of the earth and
 water it,
 making it rich and fertile.
 The river of God has plenty of
 water;
 it provides a bountiful harvest
 of grain,
 for you have ordered it so.
¹⁰ You drench the plowed ground
 with rain,
 melting the clods and leveling
 the ridges.
 You soften the earth with
 showers
 and bless its abundant crops.
¹¹ You crown the year with a
 bountiful harvest;
 even the hard pathways
 overflow with abundance.
¹² The grasslands of the wilderness
 become a lush pasture,
 and the hillsides blossom with
 joy.
¹³ The meadows are clothed with
 flocks of sheep,
 and the valleys are carpeted
 with grain.
 They all shout and sing for joy!

66

*For the choir director:
A song. A psalm.*

¹ Shout joyful praises to God, all
 the earth!
² Sing about the glory of his
 name!
 Tell the world how glorious
 he is.
³ Say to God, "How awesome are
 your deeds!

Your enemies cringe before
  your mighty power.
4 Everything on earth will worship
    you;
  they will sing your praises,
  shouting your name in
    glorious songs."   *Interlude*

5 Come and see what our God has
    done,
  what awesome miracles he
    performs for people!
6 He made a dry path through the
    Red Sea,*
  and his people went across
    on foot.
  There we rejoiced in him.
7 For by his great power he rules
    forever.
  He watches every movement
    of the nations;
  let no rebel rise in defiance.
                      Interlude

8 Let the whole world bless our
    God
  and loudly sing his praises.
9 Our lives are in his hands,
  and he keeps our feet from
    stumbling.
10 You have tested us, O God;
  you have purified us like silver.
11 You captured us in your net
  and laid the burden of slavery
    on our backs.
12 Then you put a leader over us.*
  We went through fire and
    flood,
  but you brought us to a place
    of great abundance.

13 Now I come to your Temple with
    burnt offerings
  to fulfill the vows I made to
    you—
14 yes, the sacred vows that
    I made
  when I was in deep trouble.
15 That is why I am sacrificing
    burnt offerings to you—
  the best of my rams as a
    pleasing aroma,
  and a sacrifice of bulls and
    male goats.   *Interlude*

16 Come and listen, all you who fear
    God,
  and I will tell you what he did
    for me.
17 For I cried out to him for help,
  praising him as I spoke.
18 If I had not confessed the sin in
    my heart,
  the Lord would not have
    listened.
19 But God did listen!
  He paid attention to my
    prayer.
20 Praise God, who did not ignore
    my prayer
  or withdraw his unfailing love
    from me.

67 *For the choir director: A song.
A psalm, to be accompanied
by stringed instruments.*

1 May God be merciful and
    bless us.
  May his face smile with favor
    on us.   *Interlude*

66:6 Hebrew *the sea.* **66:12** Or *You made people ride over our heads.*

² May your ways be known
    throughout the earth,
    your saving power among
    people everywhere.
³ May the nations praise you,
    O God.
    Yes, may all the nations praise
    you.
⁴ Let the whole world sing
    for joy,
    because you govern the
    nations with justice
    and guide the people of the
    whole world.   *Interlude*

⁵ May the nations praise you,
    O God.
    Yes, may all the nations praise
    you.
⁶ Then the earth will yield its
    harvests,
    and God, our God, will richly
    bless us.
⁷ Yes, God will bless us,
    and people all over the world
    will fear him.

68 *For the choir director: A song. A psalm of David.*

¹ Rise up, O God, and scatter your
    enemies.
    Let those who hate God run
    for their lives.
² Blow them away like smoke.
    Melt them like wax in a fire.
    Let the wicked perish in the
    presence of God.
³ But let the godly rejoice.

Let them be glad in God's
    presence.
    Let them be filled with joy.
⁴ Sing praises to God and to his
    name!
    Sing loud praises to him who
    rides the clouds.*
His name is the LORD—
    rejoice in his presence!
⁵ Father to the fatherless, defender
    of widows—
    this is God, whose dwelling is
    holy.
⁶ God places the lonely in families;
    he sets the prisoners free and
    gives them joy.
But he makes the rebellious live
    in a sun-scorched land.

⁷ O God, when you led your people
    out from Egypt,
    when you marched through
    the dry wasteland, *Interlude*
⁸ the earth trembled, and the
    heavens poured down rain
    before you, the God of Sinai,
    before God, the God of Israel.
⁹ You sent abundant rain, O God,
    to refresh the weary land.
¹⁰ There your people finally
    settled,
    and with a bountiful harvest,
    O God,
    you provided for your needy
    people.

¹¹ The Lord gives the word,
    and a great army* brings the
    good news.

68:4 Or *rides through the deserts.* 68:11 Or *a host of women.*

12 Enemy kings and their armies flee,
   while the women of Israel
      divide the plunder.
13 Even those who lived among the
      sheepfolds found
      treasures—
   doves with wings of silver
      and feathers of gold.
14 The Almighty scattered the
      enemy kings
   like a blowing snowstorm on
      Mount Zalmon.

15 The mountains of Bashan are
      majestic,
   with many peaks stretching
      high into the sky.
16 Why do you look with envy,
      O rugged mountains,
   at Mount Zion, where God has
      chosen to live,
   where the LORD himself will
      live forever?

17 Surrounded by unnumbered
      thousands of chariots,
   the Lord came from Mount
      Sinai into his sanctuary.
18 When you ascended to the
      heights,
   you led a crowd of captives.
   You received gifts from the
      people,
   even from those who rebelled
      against you.
   Now the LORD God will live
      among us there.

19 Praise the Lord; praise God our
      savior!

For each day he carries us in
   his arms.   *Interlude*
20 Our God is a God who saves!
   The Sovereign LORD rescues
      us from death.

21 But God will smash the heads
      of his enemies,
   crushing the skulls of those
      who love their guilty ways.
22 The Lord says, "I will bring my
      enemies down from
      Bashan;
   I will bring them up from the
      depths of the sea.
23 You, my people, will wash* your
      feet in their blood,
   and even your dogs will get
      their share!"

24 Your procession has come into
      view, O God—
   the procession of my God and
      King as he goes into the
      sanctuary.
25 Singers are in front, musicians
      behind;
   between them are young
      women playing
      tambourines.
26 Praise God, all you people of
      Israel;
   praise the LORD, the source of
      Israel's life.
27 Look, the little tribe of Benjamin
      leads the way.
   Then comes a great throng of
      rulers from Judah
   and all the rulers of Zebulun
      and Naphtali.

68:23 As in Greek and Syriac versions; Hebrew reads *shatter.*

28 Summon your might, O God.*
Display your power, O God, as
you have in the past.
29 The kings of the earth are
bringing tribute
to your Temple in Jerusalem.
30 Rebuke these enemy nations—
these wild animals lurking in
the reeds,
this herd of bulls among the
weaker calves.
Make them bring bars of silver in
humble tribute.
Scatter the nations that delight
in war.
31 Let Egypt come with gifts of
precious metals*;
let Ethiopia* bring tribute
to God.
32 Sing to God, you kingdoms of
the earth.
Sing praises to the Lord. *Interlude*
33 Sing to the one who rides across
the ancient heavens,
his mighty voice thundering
from the sky.
34 Tell everyone about God's power.
His majesty shines down on
Israel;
his strength is mighty in the
heavens.
35 God is awesome in his
sanctuary.
The God of Israel gives power
and strength to his people.

Praise be to God!

69 *For the choir director: A psalm of David, to be sung to the tune "Lilies."*

1 Save me, O God,
for the floodwaters are up to
my neck.
2 Deeper and deeper I sink into
the mire;
I can't find a foothold.
I am in deep water,
and the floods overwhelm me.
3 I am exhausted from crying for
help;
my throat is parched.
My eyes are swollen with
weeping,
waiting for my God to help me.
4 Those who hate me without
cause
outnumber the hairs on my
head.
Many enemies try to destroy me
with lies,
demanding that I give back
what I didn't steal.

5 O God, you know how foolish
I am;
my sins cannot be hidden
from you.
6 Don't let those who trust in you
be ashamed because of me,
O Sovereign LORD of Heaven's
Armies.
Don't let me cause them to be
humiliated,
O God of Israel.
7 For I endure insults for your sake;

68:28 As in some Hebrew manuscripts and Greek and Syriac versions; most Hebrew manuscripts read *Your God has commanded your strength.* **68:31a** Or *of rich cloth.* **68:31b** Hebrew *Cush.*

humiliation is written all over
    my face.
⁸ Even my own brothers pretend
    they don't know me;
    they treat me like a stranger.

⁹ Passion for your house has
    consumed me,
    and the insults of those who
    insult you have fallen on me.
¹⁰ When I weep and fast,
    they scoff at me.
¹¹ When I dress in burlap to show
    sorrow,
    they make fun of me.
¹² I am the favorite topic of town
    gossip,
    and all the drunks sing about
    me.

¹³ But I keep praying to you, LORD,
    hoping this time you will show
    me favor.
In your unfailing love, O God,
    answer my prayer with your
    sure salvation.
¹⁴ Rescue me from the mud;
    don't let me sink any deeper!
Save me from those who hate
    me,
    and pull me from these deep
    waters.
¹⁵ Don't let the floods overwhelm
    me,
    or the deep waters swallow me,
    or the pit of death devour me.

¹⁶ Answer my prayers, O LORD,

for your unfailing love is
    wonderful.
Take care of me,
    for your mercy is so plentiful.
¹⁷ Don't hide from your servant;
    answer me quickly, for I am in
    deep trouble!
¹⁸ Come and redeem me;
    free me from my enemies.

¹⁹ You know of my shame, scorn,
    and disgrace.
You see all that my enemies
    are doing.
²⁰ Their insults have broken my
    heart,
    and I am in despair.
If only one person would show
    some pity;
    if only one would turn and
    comfort me.
²¹ But instead, they give me
    poison* for food;
    they offer me sour wine for my
    thirst.

²² Let the bountiful table set before
    them become a snare
and their prosperity become a
    trap.*
²³ Let their eyes go blind so they
    cannot see,
    and make their bodies shake
    continually.*
²⁴ Pour out your fury on them;
    consume them with your
    burning anger.

69:21 Or *gall.*   **69:22** Greek version reads *Let their bountiful table set before them become a snare,
/ a trap that makes them think all is well. / Let their blessings cause them to stumble, / and let them
get what they deserve.* Compare Rom 11:9.   **69:23** Greek version reads *and let their backs be bent
forever.* Compare Rom 11:10.

25 Let their homes become
       desolate
    and their tents be deserted.
26 To the one you have punished,
       they add insult to injury;
    they add to the pain of those
       you have hurt.
27 Pile their sins up high,
    and don't let them go free.
28 Erase their names from the Book
       of Life;
    don't let them be counted
       among the righteous.

29 I am suffering and in pain.
    Rescue me, O God, by your
       saving power.
30 Then I will praise God's name
       with singing,
    and I will honor him with
       thanksgiving.
31 For this will please the Lord
       more than sacrificing cattle,
    more than presenting a bull
       with its horns and hooves.
32 The humble will see their God
       at work and be glad.
    Let all who seek God's help be
       encouraged.
33 For the Lord hears the cries of
       the needy;
    he does not despise his
       imprisoned people.

34 Praise him, O heaven and earth,
    the seas and all that move in
       them.
35 For God will save Jerusalem*
    and rebuild the towns of Judah.

His people will live there
    and settle in their own
       land.
36 The descendants of those who
       obey him will inherit the
       land,
    and those who love him will
       live there in safety.

70 *For the choir director: A psalm
       of David, asking God to
remember him.*

1 Please, God, rescue me!
    Come quickly, Lord, and help
       me.
2 May those who try to kill me
       be humiliated and put to
       shame.
    May those who take delight in
       my trouble
    be turned back in disgrace.
3 Let them be horrified by their
       shame,
    for they said, "Aha! We've got
       him now!"
4 But may all who search for you
       be filled with joy and gladness
       in you.
    May those who love your
       salvation
    repeatedly shout, "God is
       great!"
5 But as for me, I am poor and
       needy;
    please hurry to my aid, O God.
    You are my helper and my
       savior;
    O Lord, do not delay.

69:35 Hebrew *Zion.*

71

¹ O Lord, I have come to
     you for protection;
     don't let me be disgraced.
² Save me and rescue me,
     for you do what is right.
Turn your ear to listen to me,
     and set me free.
³ Be my rock of safety
     where I can always hide.
Give the order to save me,
     for you are my rock and my
     fortress.
⁴ My God, rescue me from the
     power of the wicked,
     from the clutches of cruel
     oppressors.
⁵ O Lord, you alone are my hope.
     I've trusted you, O Lord, from
     childhood.
⁶ Yes, you have been with me from
     birth;
     from my mother's womb you
     have cared for me.
No wonder I am always
     praising you!
⁷ My life is an example to many,
     because you have been my
     strength and protection.
⁸ That is why I can never stop
     praising you;
     I declare your glory all day long.
⁹ And now, in my old age, don't set
     me aside.
Don't abandon me when my
     strength is failing.
¹⁰ For my enemies are whispering
     against me.
They are plotting together to
     kill me.

¹¹ They say, "God has abandoned
     him.
Let's go and get him,
     for no one will help him now."
¹² O God, don't stay away.
     My God, please hurry to help
     me.
¹³ Bring disgrace and destruction
     on my accusers.
Humiliate and shame those
     who want to harm me.
¹⁴ But I will keep on hoping for
     your help;
     I will praise you more and more.
¹⁵ I will tell everyone about your
     righteousness.
All day long I will proclaim
     your saving power,
     though I am not skilled with
     words.*
¹⁶ I will praise your mighty deeds,
     O Sovereign Lord.
I will tell everyone that you
     alone are just.
¹⁷ O God, you have taught me from
     my earliest childhood,
and I constantly tell others
     about the wonderful things
     you do.
¹⁸ Now that I am old and gray,
     do not abandon me, O God.
Let me proclaim your power to
     this new generation,
     your mighty miracles to all
     who come after me.
¹⁹ Your righteousness, O God,
     reaches to the highest
     heavens.

71:15 Or *though I cannot count it.*

You have done such wonderful things.
Who can compare with you, O God?

20 You have allowed me to suffer much hardship,
but you will restore me to life again
and lift me up from the depths of the earth.

21 You will restore me to even greater honor
and comfort me once again.

22 Then I will praise you with music on the harp,
because you are faithful to your promises, O my God.
I will sing praises to you with a lyre,
O Holy One of Israel.

23 I will shout for joy and sing your praises,
for you have ransomed me.

24 I will tell about your righteous deeds
all day long,
for everyone who tried to hurt me
has been shamed and humiliated.

72 *A psalm of Solomon.*

1 Give your love of justice to the king, O God,
and righteousness to the king's son.

2 Help him judge your people in the right way;
let the poor always be treated fairly.

3 May the mountains yield prosperity for all,
and may the hills be fruitful.

4 Help him to defend the poor,
to rescue the children of the needy,
and to crush their oppressors.

5 May they fear you* as long as the sun shines,
as long as the moon remains in the sky.
Yes, forever!

6 May the king's rule be refreshing like spring rain on freshly cut grass,
like the showers that water the earth.

7 May all the godly flourish during his reign.
May there be abundant prosperity until the moon is no more.

8 May he reign from sea to sea,
and from the Euphrates River* to the ends of the earth.

9 Desert nomads will bow before him;
his enemies will fall before him in the dust.

10 The western kings of Tarshish and other distant lands
will bring him tribute.
The eastern kings of Sheba and Seba

72:5 Greek version reads *May they endure.* 72:8 Hebrew *the river.*

will bring him gifts.

11 All kings will bow before him,
    and all nations will serve him.

12 He will rescue the poor when
       they cry to him;
    he will help the oppressed,
       who have no one to defend
          them.

13 He feels pity for the weak and
       the needy,
    and he will rescue them.

14 He will redeem them from
       oppression and violence,
    for their lives are precious
       to him.

15 Long live the king!
    May the gold of Sheba be
       given to him.
    May the people always pray for
       him
    and bless him all day long.

16 May there be abundant grain
       throughout the land,
    flourishing even on the
       hilltops.
    May the fruit trees flourish like
       the trees of Lebanon,
    and may the people thrive like
       grass in a field.

17 May the king's name endure
       forever;
    may it continue as long as the
       sun shines.
    May all nations be blessed
       through him
    and bring him praise.

18 Praise the Lord God, the God
       of Israel,

who alone does such
    wonderful things.

19 Praise his glorious name forever!
    Let the whole earth be filled
       with his glory.
    Amen and amen!

20 (This ends the prayers of David
       son of Jesse.)

BOOK THREE (Psalms 73–89)

73 *A psalm of Asaph.*

1 Truly God is good to Israel,
    to those whose hearts are pure.

2 But as for me, I almost lost my
       footing.
    My feet were slipping, and
       I was almost gone.

3 For I envied the proud
    when I saw them prosper
       despite their wickedness.

4 They seem to live such painless
       lives;
    their bodies are so healthy and
       strong.

5 They don't have troubles like
       other people;
    they're not plagued with
       problems like everyone else.

6 They wear pride like a jeweled
       necklace
    and clothe themselves with
       cruelty.

7 These fat cats have everything
    their hearts could ever wish for!

8 They scoff and speak only evil;
    in their pride they seek to
       crush others.

⁹ They boast against the very
heavens,
and their words strut
throughout the earth.
¹⁰ And so the people are dismayed
and confused,
drinking in all their words.
¹¹ "What does God know?" they ask.
"Does the Most High even
know what's happening?"
¹² Look at these wicked people—
enjoying a life of ease while
their riches multiply.

¹³ Did I keep my heart pure for
nothing?
Did I keep myself innocent for
no reason?
¹⁴ I get nothing but trouble all day
long;
every morning brings me pain.

¹⁵ If I had really spoken this way
to others,
I would have been a traitor to
your people.
¹⁶ So I tried to understand why the
wicked prosper.
But what a difficult task it is!
¹⁷ Then I went into your sanctuary,
O God,
and I finally understood the
destiny of the wicked.
¹⁸ Truly, you put them on a slippery
path
and send them sliding over the
cliff to destruction.
¹⁹ In an instant they are destroyed,
completely swept away by
terrors.

²⁰ When you arise, O Lord,
you will laugh at their silly ideas
as a person laughs at dreams
in the morning.
²¹ Then I realized that my heart
was bitter,
and I was all torn up inside.
²² I was so foolish and ignorant—
I must have seemed like a
senseless animal to you.
²³ Yet I still belong to you;
you hold my right hand.
²⁴ You guide me with your counsel,
leading me to a glorious destiny.
²⁵ Whom have I in heaven but you?
I desire you more than
anything on earth.
²⁶ My health may fail, and my spirit
may grow weak,
but God remains the strength
of my heart;
he is mine forever.

²⁷ Those who desert him will
perish,
for you destroy those who
abandon you.
²⁸ But as for me, how good it is to
be near God!
I have made the Sovereign
LORD my shelter,
and I will tell everyone about
the wonderful things you do.

74 A psalm* of Asaph.

¹ O God, why have you rejected us
so long?

74:TITLE Hebrew *maskil*. This may be a literary or musical term.

Why is your anger so intense
against the sheep of your
own pasture?
² Remember that we are the
people you chose long ago,
the tribe you redeemed
as your own special
possession!
And remember Jerusalem,*
your home here on earth.
³ Walk through the awful ruins of
the city;
see how the enemy has
destroyed your sanctuary.

⁴ There your enemies shouted
their victorious battle cries;
there they set up their battle
standards.
⁵ They swung their axes
like woodcutters in a forest.
⁶ With axes and picks,
they smashed the carved
paneling.
⁷ They burned your sanctuary
to the ground.
They defiled the place that
bears your name.
⁸ Then they thought, "Let's destroy
everything!"
So they burned down all the
places where God was
worshiped.

⁹ We no longer see your
miraculous signs.
All the prophets are gone,
and no one can tell us when it
will end.

¹⁰ How long, O God, will you allow
our enemies to insult you?
Will you let them dishonor
your name forever?
¹¹ Why do you hold back your
strong right hand?
Unleash your powerful fist
and destroy them.

¹² You, O God, are my king from
ages past,
bringing salvation to the earth.
¹³ You split the sea by your strength
and smashed the heads of the
sea monsters.
¹⁴ You crushed the heads of
Leviathan*
and let the desert animals eat
him.
¹⁵ You caused the springs and
streams to gush forth,
and you dried up rivers that
never run dry.
¹⁶ Both day and night belong to you;
you made the starlight* and
the sun.
¹⁷ You set the boundaries of the
earth,
and you made both summer
and winter.

¹⁸ See how these enemies insult
you, Lord.
A foolish nation has
dishonored your name.
¹⁹ Don't let these wild beasts
destroy your turtledoves.
Don't forget your suffering
people forever.

74:2 Hebrew *Mount Zion.* 74:14 The identification of Leviathan is disputed, ranging from an earthly creature to a mythical sea monster in ancient literature. 74:16 Or *moon;* Hebrew reads *light.*

20 Remember your covenant
      promises,
   for the land is full of darkness
      and violence!
21 Don't let the downtrodden be
      humiliated again.
   Instead, let the poor and needy
      praise your name.

22 Arise, O God, and defend your
      cause.
   Remember how these fools
      insult you all day long.
23 Don't overlook what your
      enemies have said
   or their growing uproar.

75

*For the choir director:
A psalm of Asaph. A song to
be sung to the tune "Do Not Destroy!"*

1 We thank you, O God!
   We give thanks because you
      are near.
   People everywhere tell of your
      wonderful deeds.

2 God says, "At the time I have
      planned,
   I will bring justice against the
      wicked.
3 When the earth quakes and its
      people live in turmoil,
   I am the one who keeps its
      foundations firm. *Interlude*

4 "I warned the proud, 'Stop your
      boasting!'
   I told the wicked, 'Don't raise
      your fists!

5 Don't raise your fists in defiance
      at the heavens
   or speak with such
      arrogance.'"
6 For no one on earth—from east
      or west,
   or even from the wilderness—
      should raise a defiant fist.*
7 It is God alone who judges;
   he decides who will rise and
      who will fall.
8 For the LORD holds a cup in his
      hand
   that is full of foaming wine
      mixed with spices.
   He pours out the wine in
      judgment,
   and all the wicked must
      drink it,
   draining it to the dregs.
9 But as for me, I will always
      proclaim what God has
      done;
   I will sing praises to the God
      of Jacob.
10 For God says, "I will break the
      strength of the wicked,
   but I will increase the power
      of the godly."

76

*For the choir director:
A psalm of Asaph. A song
to be accompanied by stringed
instruments.*

1 God is honored in Judah;
   his name is great in Israel.
2 Jerusalem* is where he lives;
   Mount Zion is his home.

75:6 Hebrew *should lift.* 76:2 Hebrew *Salem,* another name for Jerusalem.

3 There he has broken the fiery
     arrows of the enemy,
  the shields and swords and
     weapons of war.   *Interlude*

4 You are glorious and more
     majestic
  than the everlasting
     mountains.*
5 Our boldest enemies have been
     plundered.
  They lie before us in the sleep
     of death.
  No warrior could lift a hand
     against us.
6 At the blast of your breath,
     O God of Jacob,
  their horses and chariots
     lay still.

7 No wonder you are greatly feared!
  Who can stand before you
     when your anger explodes?
8 From heaven you sentenced your
     enemies;
  the earth trembled and stood
     silent before you.
9 You stand up to judge those who
     do evil, O God,
  and to rescue the oppressed of
     the earth.   *Interlude*
10 Human defiance only enhances
     your glory,
  for you use it as a weapon.*

11 Make vows to the LORD your
     God, and keep them.
  Let everyone bring tribute to
     the Awesome One.

12 For he breaks the pride of princes,
  and the kings of the earth
     fear him.

77 *For Jeduthun, the choir
       director: A psalm of Asaph.*

1 I cry out to God; yes, I shout.
  Oh, that God would listen to
     me!
2 When I was in deep trouble,
  I searched for the Lord.
  All night long I prayed, with
     hands lifted toward heaven,
  but my soul was not
     comforted.
3 I think of God, and I moan,
  overwhelmed with longing for
     his help.   *Interlude*

4 You don't let me sleep.
  I am too distressed even to
     pray!
5 I think of the good old days,
     long since ended,
6 when my nights were filled with
     joyful songs.
  I search my soul and ponder
     the difference now.
7 Has the Lord rejected me
     forever?
  Will he never again be kind to
     me?
8 Is his unfailing love gone
     forever?
  Have his promises
     permanently failed?
9 Has God forgotten to be
     gracious?

76:4 As in Greek version; Hebrew reads *than mountains filled with beasts of prey.* 76:10 The meaning of the Hebrew is uncertain.

Has he slammed the door on
    his compassion?   *Interlude*

[10] And I said, "This is my fate;
    the Most High has turned his
    hand against me."

[11] But then I recall all you have
    done, O Lord;
    I remember your wonderful
    deeds of long ago.

[12] They are constantly in my
    thoughts.
    I cannot stop thinking about
    your mighty works.

[13] O God, your ways are holy.
    Is there any god as mighty
    as you?

[14] You are the God of great wonders!
    You demonstrate your
    awesome power among the
    nations.

[15] By your strong arm, you
    redeemed your people,
    the descendants of Jacob and
    Joseph.   *Interlude*

[16] When the Red Sea* saw you,
    O God,
    its waters looked and trembled!
    The sea quaked to its very
    depths.

[17] The clouds poured down rain;
    the thunder rumbled in the
    sky.
    Your arrows of lightning
    flashed.

[18] Your thunder roared from the
    whirlwind;
    the lightning lit up the world!

The earth trembled and shook.

[19] Your road led through the sea,
    your pathway through the
    mighty waters—
    a pathway no one knew was
    there!

[20] You led your people along that
    road like a flock of sheep,
    with Moses and Aaron as their
    shepherds.

78 *A psalm* of Asaph.

[1] O my people, listen to my
    instructions.
    Open your ears to what I am
    saying,
[2]   for I will speak to you in
    a parable.
    I will teach you hidden lessons
    from our past—
[3]   stories we have heard and
    known,
    stories our ancestors handed
    down to us.
[4] We will not hide these truths
    from our children;
    we will tell the next generation
    about the glorious deeds of the
    Lord,
    about his power and his
    mighty wonders.
[5] For he issued his laws to Jacob;
    he gave his instructions to
    Israel.
    He commanded our ancestors
    to teach them to their
    children,

77:16 Hebrew *the waters.*   78:title Hebrew *maskil.* This may be a literary or musical term.

6 so the next generation might
    know them—
    even the children not yet
    born—
  and they in turn will teach
    their own children.
7 So each generation should set
    its hope anew on God,
  not forgetting his glorious
    miracles
  and obeying his commands.
8 Then they will not be like their
    ancestors—
  stubborn, rebellious, and
    unfaithful,
  refusing to give their hearts
    to God.

9 The warriors of Ephraim, though
    armed with bows,
  turned their backs and fled
    on the day of battle.
10 They did not keep God's
    covenant
  and refused to live by his
    instructions.
11 They forgot what he had done—
    the great wonders he had
    shown them,
12 the miracles he did for their
    ancestors
  on the plain of Zoan in the
    land of Egypt.
13 For he divided the sea and led
    them through,
  making the water stand up like
    walls!
14 In the daytime he led them by a
    cloud,
  and all night by a pillar of fire.

15 He split open the rocks in the
    wilderness
  to give them water, as from
    a gushing spring.
16 He made streams pour from the
    rock,
  making the waters flow down
    like a river!

17 Yet they kept on sinning against
    him,
  rebelling against the Most
    High in the desert.
18 They stubbornly tested God in
    their hearts,
  demanding the foods they
    craved.
19 They even spoke against God
    himself, saying,
  "God can't give us food in the
    wilderness.
20 Yes, he can strike a rock so water
    gushes out,
  but he can't give his people
    bread and meat."
21 When the Lord heard them, he
    was furious.
  The fire of his wrath burned
    against Jacob.
  Yes, his anger rose against
    Israel,
22 for they did not believe God
  or trust him to care for them.
23 But he commanded the skies to
    open;
  he opened the doors of heaven.
24 He rained down manna for them
    to eat;
  he gave them bread from
    heaven.

25 They ate the food of angels!
   God gave them all they could
      hold.
26 He released the east wind in the
      heavens
   and guided the south wind by
      his mighty power.
27 He rained down meat as thick
      as dust—
   birds as plentiful as the sand
      on the seashore!
28 He caused the birds to fall within
      their camp
   and all around their tents.
29 The people ate their fill.
   He gave them what they
      craved.
30 But before they satisfied their
      craving,
   while the meat was yet in their
      mouths,
31 the anger of God rose against
      them,
   and he killed their strongest
      men.
   He struck down the finest of
      Israel's young men.
32 But in spite of this, the people
      kept sinning.
   Despite his wonders, they
      refused to trust him.
33 So he ended their lives in
      failure,
   their years in terror.
34 When God began killing them,
      they finally sought him.
   They repented and took God
      seriously.

35 Then they remembered that God
      was their rock,
   that God Most High* was their
      redeemer.
36 But all they gave him was lip
      service;
   they lied to him with their
      tongues.
37 Their hearts were not loyal to him.
   They did not keep his
      covenant.
38 Yet he was merciful and forgave
      their sins
   and did not destroy them all.
   Many times he held back his
      anger
   and did not unleash his fury!
39 For he remembered that they
      were merely mortal,
   gone like a breath of wind that
      never returns.

40 Oh, how often they rebelled
      against him in the
      wilderness
   and grieved his heart in that
      dry wasteland.
41 Again and again they tested
      God's patience
   and provoked the Holy One
      of Israel.
42 They did not remember his
      power
   and how he rescued them
      from their enemies.
43 They did not remember his
      miraculous signs in Egypt,
   his wonders on the plain
      of Zoan.

78:35 Hebrew *El-Elyon.*

⁴⁴ For he turned their rivers into
   blood,
   so no one could drink from
   the streams.
⁴⁵ He sent vast swarms of flies to
   consume them
   and hordes of frogs to ruin
   them.
⁴⁶ He gave their crops to
   caterpillars;
   their harvest was consumed
   by locusts.
⁴⁷ He destroyed their grapevines
   with hail
   and shattered their sycamore-
   figs with sleet.
⁴⁸ He abandoned their cattle to
   the hail,
   their livestock to bolts of
   lightning.
⁴⁹ He loosed on them his fierce
   anger—
   all his fury, rage, and
   hostility.
   He dispatched against them
   a band of destroying angels.
⁵⁰ He turned his anger against
   them;
   he did not spare the Egyptians'
   lives
   but ravaged them with the
   plague.
⁵¹ He killed the oldest son in each
   Egyptian family,
   the flower of youth
   throughout the land of
   Egypt.*
⁵² But he led his own people like
   a flock of sheep,

guiding them safely through
   the wilderness.
⁵³ He kept them safe so they were
   not afraid;
   but the sea covered their
   enemies.
⁵⁴ He brought them to the border
   of his holy land,
   to this land of hills he had won
   for them.
⁵⁵ He drove out the nations before
   them;
   he gave them their inheritance
   by lot.
   He settled the tribes of Israel
   into their homes.

⁵⁶ But they kept testing and
   rebelling against God Most
   High.
   They did not obey his laws.
⁵⁷ They turned back and were as
   faithless as their parents.
   They were as undependable
   as a crooked bow.
⁵⁸ They angered God by building
   shrines to other gods;
   they made him jealous with
   their idols.
⁵⁹ When God heard them, he was
   very angry,
   and he completely rejected
   Israel.
⁶⁰ Then he abandoned his dwelling
   at Shiloh,
   the Tabernacle where he had
   lived among the people.
⁶¹ He allowed the Ark of his might
   to be captured;

78:51 Hebrew *in the tents of Ham.*

he surrendered his glory into
   enemy hands.
⁶² He gave his people over to be
      butchered by the sword,
   because he was so angry with
      his own people—his special
      possession.
⁶³ Their young men were killed
      by fire;
   their young women died
      before singing their
      wedding songs.
⁶⁴ Their priests were slaughtered,
   and their widows could not
      mourn their deaths.

⁶⁵ Then the Lord rose up as though
      waking from sleep,
   like a warrior aroused from
      a drunken stupor.
⁶⁶ He routed his enemies
   and sent them to eternal
      shame.
⁶⁷ But he rejected Joseph's
      descendants;
   he did not choose the tribe
      of Ephraim.
⁶⁸ He chose instead the tribe of
      Judah,
   and Mount Zion, which he
      loved.
⁶⁹ There he built his sanctuary as
      high as the heavens,
   as solid and enduring as the
      earth.
⁷⁰ He chose his servant David,
   calling him from the sheep
      pens.
⁷¹ He took David from tending the
      ewes and lambs

and made him the shepherd
   of Jacob's descendants—
   God's own people, Israel.
⁷² He cared for them with a true
      heart
   and led them with skillful
      hands.

79 *A psalm of Asaph.*

¹ O God, pagan nations have
      conquered your land,
   your special possession.
   They have defiled your holy
      Temple
   and made Jerusalem a heap
      of ruins.
² They have left the bodies of your
      servants
   as food for the birds of heaven.
   The flesh of your godly ones
      has become food for the wild
      animals.
³ Blood has flowed like water all
      around Jerusalem;
   no one is left to bury the dead.
⁴ We are mocked by our
      neighbors,
   an object of scorn and
      derision to those around us.

⁵ O LORD, how long will you be
      angry with us? Forever?
   How long will your jealousy
      burn like fire?
⁶ Pour out your wrath on the
      nations that refuse to
      acknowledge you—
   on kingdoms that do not call
      upon your name.

7 For they have devoured your
     people Israel,*
  making the land a desolate
     wilderness.
8 Do not hold us guilty for the sins
     of our ancestors!
  Let your compassion quickly
     meet our needs,
  for we are on the brink of
     despair.

9 Help us, O God of our salvation!
     Help us for the glory of your
     name.
  Save us and forgive our sins
     for the honor of your name.
10 Why should pagan nations be
     allowed to scoff,
  asking, "Where is their God?"
  Show us your vengeance against
     the nations,
  for they have spilled the blood
     of your servants.
11 Listen to the moaning of the
     prisoners.
  Demonstrate your great power
     by saving those condemned
     to die.

12 O Lord, pay back our neighbors
     seven times
  for the scorn they have hurled
     at you.
13 Then we your people, the sheep
     of your pasture,
  will thank you forever and
     ever,
  praising your greatness from
     generation to generation.

80

*For the choir director: A psalm
of Asaph, to be sung to the
tune "Lilies of the Covenant."*

1 Please listen, O Shepherd of
     Israel,
  you who lead Joseph's
     descendants like a flock.
  O God, enthroned above the
     cherubim,
  display your radiant glory
2   to Ephraim, Benjamin, and
     Manasseh.
  Show us your mighty power.
  Come to rescue us!

3 Turn us again to yourself, O God.
  Make your face shine down
     upon us.
  Only then will we be saved.
4 O LORD God of Heaven's Armies,
  how long will you be angry
     with our prayers?
5 You have fed us with sorrow
  and made us drink tears by
     the bucketful.
6 You have made us the scorn*
  of neighboring nations.
  Our enemies treat us as a joke.

7 Turn us again to yourself, O God
     of Heaven's Armies.
  Make your face shine down
     upon us.
  Only then will we be saved.
8 You brought us from Egypt like
     a grapevine;
  you drove away the pagan
     nations and transplanted
     us into your land.

79:7 Hebrew *devoured Jacob.* See note on 44:4.   **80:6** As in Syriac version; Hebrew reads *the strife.*

9 You cleared the ground for us,
　　and we took root and filled the
　　land.
10 Our shade covered the mountains;
　　our branches covered the
　　mighty cedars.
11 We spread our branches west to
　　the Mediterranean Sea;
　　our shoots spread east to the
　　Euphrates River.*
12 But now, why have you broken
　　down our walls
　　so that all who pass by may
　　steal our fruit?
13 The wild boar from the forest
　　devours it,
　　and the wild animals feed on it.

14 Come back, we beg you, O God
　　of Heaven's Armies.
　　Look down from heaven and
　　see our plight.
　　Take care of this grapevine
15 　　that you yourself have planted,
　　this son you have raised for
　　yourself.
16 For we are chopped up and
　　burned by our enemies.
　　May they perish at the sight
　　of your frown.
17 Strengthen the man you love,
　　the son of your choice.
18 Then we will never abandon you
　　again.
　　Revive us so we can call on
　　your name once more.

19 Turn us again to yourself, O LORD
　　God of Heaven's Armies.

Make your face shine down
　　upon us.
　　Only then will we be saved.

81

*For the choir director: A psalm
of Asaph, to be accompanied
by a stringed instrument.*

1 Sing praises to God, our strength.
　　Sing to the God of Jacob.
2 Sing! Beat the tambourine.
　　Play the sweet lyre and the
　　harp.
3 Blow the ram's horn at new moon,
　　and again at full moon to call
　　a festival!
4 For this is required by the
　　decrees of Israel;
　　it is a regulation of the God
　　of Jacob.
5 He made it a law for Israel*
　　when he attacked Egypt to set
　　us free.

I heard an unknown voice say,
6 "Now I will take the load from
　　your shoulders;
　　I will free your hands from
　　their heavy tasks.
7 You cried to me in trouble, and
　　I saved you;
　　I answered out of the
　　thundercloud
　　and tested your faith when
　　there was no water at
　　Meribah.　　　　　*Interlude*

8 "Listen to me, O my people, while
　　I give you stern warnings.

80:11 Hebrew *west to the sea, . . . east to the river.* 81:TITLE Hebrew *according to the gittith.*
81:5 Hebrew *for Joseph.*

O Israel, if you would only
  listen to me!
⁹ You must never have a foreign
  god;
  you must not bow down
    before a false god.
¹⁰ For it was I, the LORD your God,
  who rescued you from the
    land of Egypt.
  Open your mouth wide, and I
    will fill it with good things.
¹¹ "But no, my people wouldn't
    listen.
  Israel did not want me around.
¹² So I let them follow their own
    stubborn desires,
  living according to their own
    ideas.
¹³ Oh, that my people would listen
    to me!
  Oh, that Israel would follow
    me, walking in my paths!
¹⁴ How quickly I would then
    subdue their enemies!
  How soon my hands would be
    upon their foes!
¹⁵ Those who hate the LORD would
    cringe before him;
  they would be doomed forever.
¹⁶ But I would feed you with the
    finest wheat.
  I would satisfy you with wild
    honey from the rock."

82

A psalm of Asaph.

¹ God presides over heaven's court;
  he pronounces judgment on
    the heavenly beings:

² "How long will you hand down
    unjust decisions
  by favoring the wicked?

Interlude

³ "Give justice to the poor and the
    orphan;
  uphold the rights of the
    oppressed and the destitute.
⁴ Rescue the poor and helpless;
  deliver them from the grasp of
    evil people.
⁵ But these oppressors know
    nothing;
  they are so ignorant!
  They wander about in darkness,
    while the whole world is
    shaken to the core.
⁶ I say, 'You are gods;
  you are all children of the Most
    High.
⁷ But you will die like mere mortals
  and fall like every other ruler.'"

⁸ Rise up, O God, and judge the
    earth,
  for all the nations belong to you.

83

A song. A psalm of Asaph.

¹ O God, do not be silent!
  Do not be deaf.
  Do not be quiet, O God.
² Don't you hear the uproar of
    your enemies?
  Don't you see that your
    arrogant enemies are
    rising up?
³ They devise crafty schemes
    against your people;

they conspire against your
precious ones.
4 "Come," they say, "let us wipe out
Israel as a nation.
We will destroy the very
memory of its existence."
5 Yes, this was their unanimous
decision.
They signed a treaty as allies
against you—
6 these Edomites and Ishmaelites;
Moabites and Hagrites;
7 Gebalites, Ammonites, and
Amalekites;
and people from Philistia and
Tyre.
8 Assyria has joined them, too,
and is allied with the
descendants of Lot.
Interlude

9 Do to them as you did to the
Midianites
and as you did to Sisera and
Jabin at the Kishon River.
10 They were destroyed at Endor,
and their decaying corpses
fertilized the soil.
11 Let their mighty nobles die as
Oreb and Zeeb did.
Let all their princes die like
Zebah and Zalmunna,
12 for they said, "Let us seize for
our own use
these pasturelands of God!"
13 O my God, scatter them like
tumbleweed,
like chaff before the wind!
14 As a fire burns a forest

and as a flame sets mountains
ablaze,
15 chase them with your fierce
storm;
terrify them with your
tempest.
16 Utterly disgrace them
until they submit to your
name, O Lord.
17 Let them be ashamed and
terrified forever.
Let them die in disgrace.
18 Then they will learn that you
alone are called the Lord,
that you alone are the Most
High,
supreme over all the earth.

84 *For the choir director: A psalm
of the descendants of Korah,
to be accompanied by a stringed
instrument.**

1 How lovely is your dwelling
place,
O Lord of Heaven's Armies.
2 I long, yes, I faint with longing
to enter the courts of the
Lord.
With my whole being, body
and soul,
I will shout joyfully to the
living God.
3 Even the sparrow finds a home,
and the swallow builds her
nest and raises her young
at a place near your altar,
O Lord of Heaven's Armies,
my King and my God!

84:TITLE Hebrew *according to the gittith.*

⁴ What joy for those who can live
    in your house,
    always singing your praises.
                                Interlude

⁵ What joy for those whose
    strength comes from the
    LORD,
    who have set their minds on
    a pilgrimage to Jerusalem.
⁶ When they walk through the
    Valley of Weeping,*
    it will become a place of
    refreshing springs.
    The autumn rains will clothe
    it with blessings.
⁷ They will continue to grow
    stronger,
    and each of them will appear
    before God in Jerusalem.*

⁸ O LORD God of Heaven's Armies,
    hear my prayer.
    Listen, O God of Jacob.
                                Interlude

⁹ O God, look with favor upon the
    king, our shield!
    Show favor to the one you have
    anointed.

¹⁰ A single day in your courts
    is better than a thousand
    anywhere else!
    I would rather be a gatekeeper
    in the house of my God
    than live the good life in the
    homes of the wicked.
¹¹ For the LORD God is our sun and
    our shield.

He gives us grace and glory.
    The LORD will withhold no good
    thing
    from those who do what is
    right.
¹² O LORD of Heaven's Armies,
    what joy for those who trust
    in you.

85 *For the choir director:
      A psalm of the descendants
of Korah.*

¹ LORD, you poured out blessings
    on your land!
    You restored the fortunes of
    Israel.*
² You forgave the guilt of your
    people—
    yes, you covered all their sins.
                                Interlude
³ You held back your fury.
    You kept back your blazing
    anger.

⁴ Now restore us again, O God of
    our salvation.
    Put aside your anger against us
    once more.
⁵ Will you be angry with us
    always?
    Will you prolong your wrath to
    all generations?
⁶ Won't you revive us again,
    so your people can rejoice in
    you?
⁷ Show us your unfailing love,
    O LORD,
    and grant us your salvation.

84:6 Or *Valley of Poplars;* Hebrew reads *valley of Baca.* **84:7** Hebrew *Zion.* **85:1** Hebrew *of Jacob.*
See note on 44:4.

⁸ I listen carefully to what God the
    Lᴏʀᴅ is saying,
    for he speaks peace to his
        faithful people.
    But let them not return to their
        foolish ways.
⁹ Surely his salvation is near to
    those who fear him,
    so our land will be filled with
        his glory.

¹⁰ Unfailing love and truth have
    met together.
    Righteousness and peace have
        kissed!
¹¹ Truth springs up from the earth,
    and righteousness smiles
        down from heaven.
¹² Yes, the Lᴏʀᴅ pours down his
    blessings.
    Our land will yield its
        bountiful harvest.
¹³ Righteousness goes as a herald
    before him,
    preparing the way for his
        steps.

86 *A prayer of David.*

¹ Bend down, O Lᴏʀᴅ, and hear
    my prayer;
    answer me, for I need your
        help.
² Protect me, for I am devoted
    to you.
    Save me, for I serve you and
        trust you.
    You are my God.
³ Be merciful to me, O Lord,

for I am calling on you
    constantly.
⁴ Give me happiness, O Lord,
    for I give myself to you.
⁵ O Lord, you are so good, so ready
    to forgive,
    so full of unfailing love for all
        who ask for your help.
⁶ Listen closely to my prayer,
    O Lᴏʀᴅ;
    hear my urgent cry.
⁷ I will call to you whenever I'm
    in trouble,
    and you will answer me.

⁸ No pagan god is like you, O Lord.
    None can do what you do!
⁹ All the nations you made
    will come and bow before you,
        Lord;
    they will praise your holy name.
¹⁰ For you are great and perform
    wonderful deeds.
    You alone are God.

¹¹ Teach me your ways, O Lᴏʀᴅ,
    that I may live according to
        your truth!
    Grant me purity of heart,
        so that I may honor you.
¹² With all my heart I will praise
    you, O Lord my God.
    I will give glory to your name
        forever,
¹³ for your love for me is very great.
    You have rescued me from the
        depths of death.*

¹⁴ O God, insolent people rise up
    against me;

86:13 Hebrew *of Sheol.*

a violent gang is trying to
  kill me.
You mean nothing to them.
[15] But you, O Lord,
  are a God of compassion and
    mercy,
slow to get angry
  and filled with unfailing love
    and faithfulness.
[16] Look down and have mercy
    on me.
  Give your strength to your
    servant;
  save me, the son of your
    servant.
[17] Send me a sign of your favor.
  Then those who hate me will
    be put to shame,
  for you, O Lord, help and
    comfort me.

87

*A song. A psalm of the
descendants of Korah.*

[1] On the holy mountain
  stands the city founded by
    the Lord.
[2] He loves the city of Jerusalem
  more than any other city in
    Israel.*
[3] O city of God,
  what glorious things are said
    of you!   *Interlude*

[4] I will count Egypt* and Babylon
  among those who know me—

also Philistia and Tyre, and
  even distant Ethiopia.*
They have all become citizens
  of Jerusalem!
[5] Regarding Jerusalem* it will be
    said,
  "Everyone enjoys the rights
    of citizenship there."
And the Most High will
  personally bless this city.
[6] When the Lord registers the
    nations, he will say,
  "They have all become citizens
    of Jerusalem."   *Interlude*

[7] The people will play flutes* and
    sing,
  "The source of my life springs
    from Jerusalem!"

88

*For the choir director: A psalm
of the descendants of Korah.
A song to be sung to the tune "The
Suffering of Affliction." A psalm*
of Heman the Ezrahite.*

[1] O Lord, God of my salvation,
  I cry out to you by day.
  I come to you at night.
[2] Now hear my prayer;
  listen to my cry.
[3] For my life is full of troubles,
  and death* draws near.
[4] I am as good as dead,
  like a strong man with no
    strength left.

87:2 Hebrew *He loves the gates of Zion more than all the dwellings of Jacob.* See note on 44:4.
87:4a Hebrew *Rahab,* the name of a mythical sea monster that represents chaos in ancient literature.
The name is used here as a poetic name for Egypt. **87:4b** Hebrew *Cush.* **87:5** Hebrew *Zion.*
87:7 Or *will dance.* **88:title** Hebrew *maskil.* This may be a literary or musical term.
88:3 Hebrew *Sheol.*

⁵ They have left me among the
    dead,
  and I lie like a corpse in a grave.
  I am forgotten,
    cut off from your care.
⁶ You have thrown me into the
    lowest pit,
  into the darkest depths.
⁷ Your anger weighs me down;
  with wave after wave you have
    engulfed me.   *Interlude*

⁸ You have driven my friends away
    by making me repulsive to
    them.
  I am in a trap with no way of
    escape.
⁹   My eyes are blinded by my
    tears.
  Each day I beg for your help,
    O LORD;
  I lift my hands to you for mercy.
¹⁰ Are your wonderful deeds of any
    use to the dead?
  Do the dead rise up and praise
    you?   *Interlude*

¹¹ Can those in the grave declare
    your unfailing love?
  Can they proclaim your
    faithfulness in the place of
    destruction?*
¹² Can the darkness speak of your
    wonderful deeds?
  Can anyone in the land of
    forgetfulness talk about
    your righteousness?
¹³ O LORD, I cry out to you.
  I will keep on pleading day
    by day.

¹⁴ O LORD, why do you reject me?
  Why do you turn your face
    from me?
¹⁵ I have been sick and close to
    death since my youth.
  I stand helpless and desperate
    before your terrors.
¹⁶ Your fierce anger has
    overwhelmed me.
  Your terrors have paralyzed me.
¹⁷ They swirl around me like
    floodwaters all day long.
  They have engulfed me
    completely.
¹⁸ You have taken away my
    companions and loved ones.
  Darkness is my closest friend.

89 A psalm* of Ethan the Ezrahite.

¹ I will sing of the LORD's unfailing
    love forever!
  Young and old will hear of
    your faithfulness.
² Your unfailing love will last
    forever.
  Your faithfulness is as
    enduring as the heavens.

³ The LORD said, "I have made a
    covenant with David, my
    chosen servant.
  I have sworn this oath to him:
⁴ 'I will establish your descendants
    as kings forever;
  they will sit on your throne
    from now until eternity.'"
                        Interlude

88:11 Hebrew *in Abaddon?* 89:TITLE Hebrew *maskil.* This may be a literary or musical term.

⁵ All heaven will praise your great
    wonders, Lord;
    myriads of angels will praise
    you for your faithfulness.
⁶ For who in all of heaven can
    compare with the Lord?
    What mightiest angel is
    anything like the Lord?
⁷ The highest angelic powers
    stand in awe of God.
    He is far more awesome than
    all who surround his throne.
⁸ O Lord God of Heaven's Armies!
    Where is there anyone as
    mighty as you, O Lord?
    You are entirely faithful.
⁹ You rule the oceans.
    You subdue their storm-tossed
    waves.
¹⁰ You crushed the great sea
    monster.*
    You scattered your enemies
    with your mighty arm.
¹¹ The heavens are yours, and the
    earth is yours;
    everything in the world is
    yours—you created it all.
¹² You created north and south.
    Mount Tabor and Mount
    Hermon praise your name.
¹³ Powerful is your arm!
    Strong is your hand!
    Your right hand is lifted high
    in glorious strength.
¹⁴ Righteousness and justice are the
    foundation of your throne.
    Unfailing love and truth walk
    before you as attendants.

¹⁵ Happy are those who hear the
    joyful call to worship,
    for they will walk in the light
    of your presence, Lord.
¹⁶ They rejoice all day long in your
    wonderful reputation.
    They exult in your
    righteousness.
¹⁷ You are their glorious strength.
    It pleases you to make us
    strong.
¹⁸ Yes, our protection comes from
    the Lord,
    and he, the Holy One of Israel,
    has given us our king.

¹⁹ Long ago you spoke in a vision
    to your faithful people.
    You said, "I have raised up a
    warrior.
    I have selected him from the
    common people to be king.
²⁰ I have found my servant David.
    I have anointed him with my
    holy oil.
²¹ I will steady him with my hand;
    with my powerful arm I will
    make him strong.
²² His enemies will not defeat him,
    nor will the wicked overpower
    him.
²³ I will beat down his adversaries
    before him
    and destroy those who hate
    him.
²⁴ My faithfulness and unfailing
    love will be with him,
    and by my authority he will
    grow in power.

89:10 Hebrew *Rahab,* the name of a mythical sea monster that represents chaos in ancient literature.

25 I will extend his rule over the
        sea,
    his dominion over the rivers.
26 And he will call out to me, 'You
        are my Father,
    my God, and the Rock of my
        salvation.'
27 I will make him my firstborn
        son,
    the mightiest king on earth.
28 I will love him and be kind to
        him forever;
    my covenant with him will
        never end.
29 I will preserve an heir for him;
    his throne will be as endless as
        the days of heaven.
30 But if his descendants forsake
        my instructions
    and fail to obey my
        regulations,
31 if they do not obey my decrees
    and fail to keep my
        commands,
32 then I will punish their sin with
        the rod,
    and their disobedience with
        beating.
33 But I will never stop loving him
    nor fail to keep my promise
        to him.
34 No, I will not break my covenant;
    I will not take back a single
        word I said.
35 I have sworn an oath to David,
    and in my holiness I cannot
        lie:
36 His dynasty will go on forever;
    his kingdom will endure as
        the sun.

37 It will be as eternal as the moon,
    my faithful witness in the sky!"
                                    Interlude

38 But now you have rejected him
        and cast him off.
    You are angry with your
        anointed king.
39 You have renounced your
        covenant with him;
    you have thrown his crown
        in the dust.
40 You have broken down the walls
        protecting him
    and ruined every fort
        defending him.
41 Everyone who comes along has
        robbed him,
    and he has become a joke to
        his neighbors.
42 You have strengthened his
        enemies
    and made them all rejoice.
43 You have made his sword
        useless
    and refused to help him in
        battle.
44 You have ended his splendor
    and overturned his throne.
45 You have made him old before
        his time
    and publicly disgraced him.
                                    Interlude

46 O LORD, how long will this go on?
    Will you hide yourself forever?
    How long will your anger burn
        like fire?
47 Remember how short my life is,
    how empty and futile this
        human existence!

⁴⁸ No one can live forever; all will die.
  No one can escape the power
      of the grave.*   *Interlude*

⁴⁹ Lord, where is your unfailing
      love?
  You promised it to David with
      a faithful pledge.
⁵⁰ Consider, Lord, how your
      servants are disgraced!
  I carry in my heart the insults
      of so many people.
⁵¹ Your enemies have mocked me,
      O LORD;
  they mock your anointed king
      wherever he goes.

⁵² Praise the LORD forever!
  Amen and amen!

BOOK FOUR (Psalms 90–106)

90 *A prayer of Moses, the man of God.*

¹ Lord, through all the generations
      you have been our home!
² Before the mountains were born,
      before you gave birth to the
      earth and the world,
  from beginning to end, you are
      God.

³ You turn people back to dust,
      saying,
  "Return to dust, you mortals!"
⁴ For you, a thousand years are as a
      passing day,
  as brief as a few night hours.
⁵ You sweep people away like
      dreams that disappear.

They are like grass that springs
      up in the morning.
⁶ In the morning it blooms and
      flourishes,
  but by evening it is dry and
      withered.
⁷ We wither beneath your anger;
  we are overwhelmed by your
      fury.
⁸ You spread out our sins before
      you—
  our secret sins—and you see
      them all.
⁹ We live our lives beneath your
      wrath,
  ending our years with a groan.

¹⁰ Seventy years are given to us!
  Some even live to eighty.
  But even the best years are filled
      with pain and trouble;
  soon they disappear, and we
      fly away.
¹¹ Who can comprehend the power
      of your anger?
  Your wrath is as awesome as
      the fear you deserve.
¹² Teach us to realize the brevity
      of life,
  so that we may grow in
      wisdom.

¹³ O LORD, come back to us!
  How long will you delay?
  Take pity on your servants!
¹⁴ Satisfy us each morning with
      your unfailing love,
  so we may sing for joy to the
      end of our lives.

89:48 Hebrew *of Sheol.*

15 Give us gladness in proportion
to our former misery!
Replace the evil years with
good.
16 Let us, your servants, see you
work again;
let our children see your
glory.
17 And may the Lord our God show
us his approval
and make our efforts
successful.
Yes, make our efforts
successful!

91

1 Those who live in the
shelter of the Most High
will find rest in the shadow of
the Almighty.
2 This I declare about the LORD:
He alone is my refuge, my place
of safety;
he is my God, and I trust him.
3 For he will rescue you from
every trap
and protect you from deadly
disease.
4 He will cover you with his
feathers.
He will shelter you with his
wings.
His faithful promises are your
armor and protection.
5 Do not be afraid of the terrors of
the night,
nor the arrow that flies in the
day.
6 Do not dread the disease that
stalks in darkness,

nor the disaster that strikes at
midday.
7 Though a thousand fall at your
side,
though ten thousand are dying
around you,
these evils will not touch you.
8 Just open your eyes,
and see how the wicked are
punished.

9 If you make the LORD your
refuge,
if you make the Most High
your shelter,
10 no evil will conquer you;
no plague will come near your
home.
11 For he will order his angels
to protect you wherever you
go.
12 They will hold you up with their
hands
so you won't even hurt your
foot on a stone.
13 You will trample upon lions and
cobras;
you will crush fierce lions and
serpents under your feet!
14 The LORD says, "I will rescue
those who love me.
I will protect those who trust
in my name.
15 When they call on me, I will
answer;
I will be with them in trouble.
I will rescue and honor them.
16 I will reward them with a long
life
and give them my salvation."

92
A psalm. A song to be sung on the Sabbath Day.

1 It is good to give thanks to the
Lord,
  to sing praises to the Most
  High.
2 It is good to proclaim your
  unfailing love in the
  morning,
  your faithfulness in the
  evening,
3 accompanied by a ten-stringed
  instrument, a harp,
  and the melody of a lyre.

4 You thrill me, Lord, with all you
  have done for me!
  I sing for joy because of what
  you have done.
5 O Lord, what great works you do!
  And how deep are your
  thoughts.
6 Only a simpleton would not
  know,
  and only a fool would not
  understand this:
7 Though the wicked sprout like
  weeds
  and evildoers flourish,
  they will be destroyed forever.

8 But you, O Lord, will be exalted
  forever.
9 Your enemies, Lord, will surely
  perish;
  all evildoers will be scattered.
10 But you have made me as strong
  as a wild ox.
  You have anointed me with the
  finest oil.

11 My eyes have seen the downfall
  of my enemies;
  my ears have heard the
  defeat of my wicked
  opponents.
12 But the godly will flourish like
  palm trees
  and grow strong like the
  cedars of Lebanon.
13 For they are transplanted to the
  Lord's own house.
  They flourish in the courts of
  our God.
14 Even in old age they will still
  produce fruit;
  they will remain vital and
  green.
15 They will declare, "The Lord
  is just!
  He is my rock!
  There is no evil in him!"

93
1 The Lord is king! He is
  robed in majesty.
  Indeed, the Lord is robed in
  majesty and armed with
  strength.
  The world stands firm
  and cannot be shaken.

2 Your throne, O Lord, has stood
  from time immemorial.
  You yourself are from the
  everlasting past.
3 The floods have risen up,
  O Lord.
  The floods have roared like
  thunder;
  the floods have lifted their
  pounding waves.

4 But mightier than the violent
  raging of the seas,
  mightier than the breakers
  on the shore—
  the Lord above is mightier
  than these!
5 Your royal laws cannot be
  changed.
  Your reign, O Lord, is holy
  forever and ever.

94

¹ O Lord, the God of
  vengeance,
  O God of vengeance, let your
  glorious justice shine forth!
² Arise, O Judge of the earth.
  Give the proud what they
  deserve.
³ How long, O Lord?
  How long will the wicked be
  allowed to gloat?
⁴ How long will they speak with
  arrogance?
  How long will these evil people
  boast?
⁵ They crush your people, Lord,
  hurting those you claim as
  your own.
⁶ They kill widows and foreigners
  and murder orphans.
⁷ "The Lord isn't looking," they
  say,
  "and besides, the God of
  Israel* doesn't care."
⁸ Think again, you fools!
  When will you finally catch on?
⁹ Is he deaf—the one who made
  your ears?

Is he blind—the one who
  formed your eyes?
¹⁰ He punishes the nations—won't
  he also punish you?
  He knows everything—doesn't
  he also know what you are
  doing?
¹¹ The Lord knows people's
  thoughts;
  he knows they are worthless!

¹² Joyful are those you discipline,
  Lord,
  those you teach with your
  instructions.
¹³ You give them relief from
  troubled times
  until a pit is dug to capture
  the wicked.
¹⁴ The Lord will not reject his
  people;
  he will not abandon his special
  possession.
¹⁵ Judgment will again be founded
  on justice,
  and those with virtuous hearts
  will pursue it.

¹⁶ Who will protect me from the
  wicked?
  Who will stand up for me
  against evildoers?
¹⁷ Unless the Lord had
  helped me,
  I would soon have settled in
  the silence of the grave.
¹⁸ I cried out, "I am slipping!"
  but your unfailing love,
  O Lord, supported me.
¹⁹ When doubts filled my mind,

94:7 Hebrew *of Jacob*. See note on 44:4.

your comfort gave me renewed
hope and cheer.

20 Can unjust leaders claim that
God is on their side—
leaders whose decrees permit
injustice?
21 They gang up against the
righteous
and condemn the innocent to
death.
22 But the LORD is my fortress;
my God is the mighty rock
where I hide.
23 God will turn the sins of evil
people back on them.
He will destroy them for their
sins.
The LORD our God will destroy
them.

95

1 Come, let us sing to the
LORD!
Let us shout joyfully to the
Rock of our salvation.
2 Let us come to him with
thanksgiving.
Let us sing psalms of praise
to him.
3 For the LORD is a great God,
a great King above all gods.
4 He holds in his hands the depths
of the earth
and the mightiest mountains.
5 The sea belongs to him, for he
made it.
His hands formed the dry land,
too.

6 Come, let us worship and bow
down.

Let us kneel before the LORD
our maker,
7 for he is our God.
We are the people he watches
over,
the flock under his care.

If only you would listen to his
voice today!
8 The LORD says, "Don't harden
your hearts as Israel did at
Meribah,
as they did at Massah in the
wilderness.
9 For there your ancestors tested
and tried my patience,
even though they saw
everything I did.
10 For forty years I was angry with
them, and I said,
'They are a people whose hearts
turn away from me.
They refuse to do what I tell
them.'
11 So in my anger I took an oath:
'They will never enter my place
of rest.'"

96

1 Sing a new song to the
LORD!
Let the whole earth sing to the
LORD!
2 Sing to the LORD; praise his
name.
Each day proclaim the good
news that he saves.
3 Publish his glorious deeds
among the nations.
Tell everyone about the
amazing things he does.

⁴ Great is the Lᴏʀᴅ! He is most
    worthy of praise!
  He is to be feared above all
    gods.
⁵ The gods of other nations are
    mere idols,
  but the Lᴏʀᴅ made the
    heavens!
⁶ Honor and majesty surround
    him;
  strength and beauty fill his
    sanctuary.

⁷ O nations of the world, recognize
    the Lᴏʀᴅ;
  recognize that the Lᴏʀᴅ is
    glorious and strong.
⁸ Give to the Lᴏʀᴅ the glory he
    deserves!
  Bring your offering and come
    into his courts.
⁹ Worship the Lᴏʀᴅ in all his holy
    splendor.
  Let all the earth tremble before
    him.
¹⁰ Tell all the nations, "The Lᴏʀᴅ
    reigns!"
  The world stands firm and
    cannot be shaken.
  He will judge all peoples fairly.

¹¹ Let the heavens be glad, and the
    earth rejoice!
  Let the sea and everything in
    it shout his praise!
¹² Let the fields and their crops
    burst out with joy!
  Let the trees of the forest sing
    for joy
¹³ before the Lᴏʀᴅ, for he is coming!

97:8 Hebrew *Zion.*

He is coming to judge the earth.
  He will judge the world with
    justice,
  and the nations with his truth.

97 ¹ The Lᴏʀᴅ is king!
        Let the earth rejoice!
  Let the farthest coastlands
    be glad.
² Dark clouds surround him.
  Righteousness and justice are
    the foundation of his throne.
³ Fire spreads ahead of him
  and burns up all his foes.
⁴ His lightning flashes out across
    the world.
  The earth sees and trembles.
⁵ The mountains melt like wax
    before the Lᴏʀᴅ,
  before the Lord of all the
    earth.
⁶ The heavens proclaim his
    righteousness;
  every nation sees his glory.
⁷ Those who worship idols are
    disgraced—
  all who brag about their
    worthless gods—
  for every god must bow to him.
⁸ Jerusalem* has heard and
    rejoiced,
  and all the towns of Judah are
    glad
  because of your justice, O Lᴏʀᴅ!
⁹ For you, O Lᴏʀᴅ, are supreme
    over all the earth;
  you are exalted far above all
    gods.

10 You who love the LORD, hate evil!
  He protects the lives of his
    godly people
  and rescues them from the
    power of the wicked.
11 Light shines on the godly,
  and joy on those whose hearts
    are right.
12 May all who are godly rejoice in
    the LORD
  and praise his holy name!

98 *A psalm.*

1 Sing a new song to the LORD,
  for he has done wonderful
    deeds.
  His right hand has won a mighty
    victory;
  his holy arm has shown his
    saving power!
2 The LORD has announced his
    victory
  and has revealed his
    righteousness to every
    nation!
3 He has remembered his promise
    to love and be faithful to
    Israel.
  The ends of the earth have
    seen the victory of our God.

4 Shout to the LORD, all the earth;
  break out in praise and sing
    for joy!
5 Sing your praise to the LORD with
    the harp,
  with the harp and melodious
    song,

6 with trumpets and the sound of
    the ram's horn.
  Make a joyful symphony
    before the LORD, the King!

7 Let the sea and everything in it
    shout his praise!
  Let the earth and all living
    things join in.
8 Let the rivers clap their hands in
    glee!
  Let the hills sing out their
    songs of joy
9 before the LORD,
  for he is coming to judge the
    earth.
  He will judge the world with
    justice,
  and the nations with fairness.

99 1 The LORD is king!
  Let the nations tremble!
  He sits on his throne between
    the cherubim.
  Let the whole earth quake!
2 The LORD sits in majesty in
    Jerusalem,*
  exalted above all the nations.
3 Let them praise your great and
    awesome name.
  Your name is holy!
4 Mighty King, lover of justice,
  you have established fairness.
  You have acted with justice
  and righteousness throughout
    Israel.*
5 Exalt the LORD our God!
  Bow low before his feet, for he
    is holy!

99:2 Hebrew *Zion.*   99:4 Hebrew *Jacob.* See note on 44:4.

6 Moses and Aaron were among
    his priests;
  Samuel also called on his name.
  They cried to the LORD for help,
    and he answered them.
7 He spoke to Israel from the pillar
    of cloud,
  and they followed the laws and
    decrees he gave them.
8 O LORD our God, you answered
    them.
  You were a forgiving God to
    them,
  but you punished them when
    they went wrong.

9 Exalt the LORD our God,
  and worship at his holy
    mountain in Jerusalem,
  for the LORD our God is holy!

100 A psalm of thanksgiving.

1 Shout with joy to the LORD, all
    the earth!
2   Worship the LORD with
      gladness.
  Come before him, singing
    with joy.
3 Acknowledge that the LORD is
    God!
  He made us, and we are his.*
  We are his people, the sheep
    of his pasture.
4 Enter his gates with thanksgiving;
  go into his courts with praise.
  Give thanks to him and praise
    his name.

5 For the LORD is good.
  His unfailing love continues
    forever,
  and his faithfulness continues
    to each generation.

101 A psalm of David.

1 I will sing of your love and
    justice, LORD.
  I will praise you with songs.
2 I will be careful to live a
    blameless life—
  when will you come to
    help me?
  I will lead a life of integrity
    in my own home.
3 I will refuse to look at
    anything vile and vulgar.
  I hate all who deal crookedly;
    I will have nothing to do with
      them.
4 I will reject perverse ideas
    and stay away from every evil.
5 I will not tolerate people who
    slander their neighbors.
  I will not endure conceit and
    pride.

6 I will search for faithful people
    to be my companions.
  Only those who are above
    reproach
  will be allowed to serve me.
7 I will not allow deceivers to serve
    in my house,
  and liars will not stay in my
    presence.

100:3 As in an alternate reading in the Masoretic Text; the other alternate and some ancient versions
read *and not we ourselves.*

8 My daily task will be to ferret out
the wicked
and free the city of the LORD
from their grip.

102 *A prayer of one overwhelmed with trouble,
pouring out problems before the LORD.*

1 LORD, hear my prayer!
Listen to my plea!
2 Don't turn away from me
in my time of distress.
Bend down to listen,
and answer me quickly when
I call to you.
3 For my days disappear like smoke,
and my bones burn like red-
hot coals.
4 My heart is sick, withered like
grass,
and I have lost my appetite.
5 Because of my groaning,
I am reduced to skin and bones.
6 I am like an owl in the desert,
like a little owl in a far-off
wilderness.
7 I lie awake,
lonely as a solitary bird on the
roof.
8 My enemies taunt me day after
day.
They mock and curse me.
9 I eat ashes for food.
My tears run down into my
drink
10 because of your anger and wrath.
For you have picked me up
and thrown me out.

11 My life passes as swiftly as the
evening shadows.
I am withering away like grass.
12 But you, O LORD, will sit on your
throne forever.
Your fame will endure to every
generation.
13 You will arise and have mercy on
Jerusalem*—
and now is the time to pity her,
now is the time you promised
to help.
14 For your people love every stone
in her walls
and cherish even the dust in
her streets.
15 Then the nations will tremble
before the LORD.
The kings of the earth will
tremble before his glory.
16 For the LORD will rebuild
Jerusalem.
He will appear in his glory.
17 He will listen to the prayers of
the destitute.
He will not reject their pleas.
18 Let this be recorded for future
generations,
so that a people not yet born
will praise the LORD.
19 Tell them the LORD looked down
from his heavenly sanctuary.
He looked down to earth from
heaven
20 to hear the groans of the
prisoners,
to release those condemned
to die.

102:13 Hebrew *Zion;* also in 102:16.

21 And so the LORD's fame will be
    celebrated in Zion,
        his praises in Jerusalem,
22 when multitudes gather together
    and kingdoms come to
        worship the LORD.

23 He broke my strength in midlife,
    cutting short my days.
24 But I cried to him, "O my God,
    who lives forever,
        don't take my life while I am so
            young!
25 Long ago you laid the foundation
    of the earth
        and made the heavens with
            your hands.
26 They will perish, but you remain
    forever;
        they will wear out like old
            clothing.
    You will change them like a
        garment
            and discard them.
27 But you are always the same;
    you will live forever.
28 The children of your people
    will live in security.
        Their children's children
            will thrive in your presence."

103 *A psalm of David.*

1 Let all that I am praise the LORD;
    with my whole heart, I will
        praise his holy name.
2 Let all that I am praise the LORD;
    may I never forget the good
        things he does for me.
3 He forgives all my sins

and heals all my diseases.
4 He redeems me from death
    and crowns me with love and
        tender mercies.
5 He fills my life with good things.
    My youth is renewed like the
        eagle's!

6 The LORD gives righteousness
    and justice to all who are
        treated unfairly.
7 He revealed his character to Moses
    and his deeds to the people
        of Israel.
8 The LORD is compassionate and
    merciful,
        slow to get angry and filled
            with unfailing love.
9 He will not constantly accuse us,
    nor remain angry forever.
10 He does not punish us for all our
    sins;
        he does not deal harshly with
            us, as we deserve.
11 For his unfailing love toward
    those who fear him
        is as great as the height of the
            heavens above the earth.
12 He has removed our sins as far
    from us
        as the east is from the west.
13 The LORD is like a father to his
    children,
        tender and compassionate
            to those who fear him.
14 For he knows how weak we are;
    he remembers we are only dust.
15 Our days on earth are like grass;
    like wildflowers, we bloom
        and die.

¹⁶ The wind blows, and we are
  gone—
    as though we had never been
    here.
¹⁷ But the love of the LORD remains
  forever
    with those who fear him.
  His salvation extends to the
    children's children
¹⁸   of those who are faithful to
    his covenant,
    of those who obey his
    commandments!

¹⁹ The LORD has made the heavens
  his throne;
    from there he rules over
    everything.

²⁰ Praise the LORD, you angels,
    you mighty ones who carry out
    his plans,
    listening for each of his
    commands.
²¹ Yes, praise the LORD, you armies
  of angels
    who serve him and do his will!
²² Praise the LORD, everything he
  has created,
    everything in all his kingdom.

Let all that I am praise the LORD.

104 ¹Let all that I am praise
  the LORD.

O LORD my God, how great you
  are!
    You are robed with honor and
    majesty.

²   You are dressed in a robe of
    light.
  You stretch out the starry curtain
    of the heavens;
³   you lay out the rafters of your
    home in the rain clouds.
  You make the clouds your
    chariot;
    you ride upon the wings of the
    wind.
⁴ The winds are your messengers;
    flames of fire are your
    servants.*

⁵ You placed the world on its
    foundation
    so it would never be moved.
⁶ You clothed the earth with
    floods of water,
    water that covered even the
    mountains.
⁷ At your command, the water fled;
    at the sound of your thunder,
    it hurried away.
⁸ Mountains rose and valleys sank
    to the levels you decreed.
⁹ Then you set a firm boundary for
    the seas,
    so they would never again
    cover the earth.

¹⁰ You make springs pour water
    into the ravines,
    so streams gush down from
    the mountains.
¹¹ They provide water for all the
    animals,
    and the wild donkeys quench
    their thirst.

104:4 Greek version reads *He sends his angels like the winds, / his servants like flames of fire.*
Compare Heb 1:7.

12 The birds nest beside the streams
    and sing among the branches
        of the trees.
13 You send rain on the mountains
        from your heavenly home,
    and you fill the earth with the
        fruit of your labor.
14 You cause grass to grow for the
        livestock
    and plants for people to use.
    You allow them to produce food
        from the earth—
15   wine to make them glad,
    olive oil to soothe their skin,
        and bread to give them
        strength.
16 The trees of the LORD are well
        cared for—
    the cedars of Lebanon that he
        planted.
17 There the birds make their
        nests,
    and the storks make their
        homes in the cypresses.
18 High in the mountains live the
        wild goats,
    and the rocks form a refuge
        for the hyraxes.*
19 You made the moon to mark the
        seasons,
    and the sun knows when to set.
20 You send the darkness, and it
        becomes night,
    when all the forest animals
        prowl about.
21 Then the young lions roar for
        their prey,

stalking the food provided by
    God.
22 At dawn they slink back
    into their dens to rest.
23 Then people go off to their work,
    where they labor until evening.
24 O LORD, what a variety of things
        you have made!
    In wisdom you have made
        them all.
    The earth is full of your
        creatures.
25 Here is the ocean, vast and wide,
    teeming with life of every
        kind,
    both large and small.
26 See the ships sailing along,
    and Leviathan,* which you
        made to play in the sea.
27 They all depend on you
    to give them food as they
        need it.
28 When you supply it, they
        gather it.
    You open your hand to feed
        them,
    and they are richly satisfied.
29 But if you turn away from them,
        they panic.
    When you take away their
        breath,
    they die and turn again to dust.
30 When you give them your
        breath,* life is created,
    and you renew the face of the
        earth.

104:18 Or coneys, or rock badgers. 104:26 The identification of Leviathan is disputed, ranging from an earthly creature to a mythical sea monster in ancient literature. 104:30 Or When you send your Spirit.

31 May the glory of the LORD
    continue forever!
  The LORD takes pleasure in all
    he has made!
32 The earth trembles at his
    glance;
  the mountains smoke at his
    touch.
33 I will sing to the LORD as long
    as I live.
  I will praise my God to my last
    breath!
34 May all my thoughts be pleasing
    to him,
  for I rejoice in the LORD.
35 Let all sinners vanish from the
    face of the earth;
  let the wicked disappear
    forever.

Let all that I am praise the LORD.

Praise the LORD!

105 1 Give thanks to the LORD
        and proclaim his
        greatness.
  Let the whole world know
    what he has done.
2 Sing to him; yes, sing his praises.
  Tell everyone about his
    wonderful deeds.
3 Exult in his holy name;
  rejoice, you who worship the
    LORD.
4 Search for the LORD and for his
    strength;
  continually seek him.
5 Remember the wonders he has
    performed,

his miracles, and the rulings
    he has given,
6 you children of his servant
    Abraham,
  you descendants of Jacob, his
    chosen ones.

7 He is the LORD our God.
  His justice is seen throughout
    the land.
8 He always stands by his
    covenant—
  the commitment he made to
    a thousand generations.
9 This is the covenant he made
    with Abraham
  and the oath he swore to Isaac.
10 He confirmed it to Jacob as a
    decree,
  and to the people of Israel as
    a never-ending covenant:
11 "I will give you the land of Canaan
    as your special possession."

12 He said this when they were few
    in number,
  a tiny group of strangers in
    Canaan.
13 They wandered from nation to
    nation,
  from one kingdom to another.
14 Yet he did not let anyone oppress
    them.
  He warned kings on their
    behalf:
15 "Do not touch my chosen people,
    and do not hurt my prophets."

16 He called for a famine on the
    land of Canaan,
  cutting off its food supply.

¹⁷ Then he sent someone to Egypt
ahead of them—
Joseph, who was sold as a
slave.
¹⁸ They bruised his feet with fetters
and placed his neck in an iron
collar.
¹⁹ Until the time came to fulfill his
dreams,*
the LORD tested Joseph's
character.
²⁰ Then Pharaoh sent for him and
set him free;
the ruler of the nation opened
his prison door.
²¹ Joseph was put in charge of all
the king's household;
he became ruler over all the
king's possessions.
²² He could instruct* the king's
aides as he pleased
and teach the king's advisers.

²³ Then Israel arrived in Egypt;
Jacob lived as a foreigner in
the land of Ham.
²⁴ And the LORD multiplied the
people of Israel
until they became too mighty
for their enemies.
²⁵ Then he turned the Egyptians
against the Israelites,
and they plotted against the
LORD's servants.

²⁶ But the LORD sent his servant
Moses,
along with Aaron, whom he
had chosen.

²⁷ They performed miraculous
signs among the Egyptians,
and wonders in the land of
Ham.
²⁸ The LORD blanketed Egypt in
darkness,
for they had defied* his
commands to let his
people go.
²⁹ He turned their water into blood,
poisoning all the fish.
³⁰ Then frogs overran the land
and even invaded the king's
bedrooms.
³¹ When the LORD spoke, flies
descended on the Egyptians,
and gnats swarmed across
Egypt.
³² He sent them hail instead of rain,
and lightning flashed over the
land.
³³ He ruined their grapevines and
fig trees
and shattered all the trees.
³⁴ He spoke, and hordes of locusts
came—
young locusts beyond number.
³⁵ They ate up everything green in
the land,
destroying all the crops in
their fields.
³⁶ Then he killed the oldest son
in each Egyptian home,
the pride and joy of each family.

³⁷ The LORD brought his people out
of Egypt, loaded with silver
and gold;

105:19 Hebrew *his word.* **105:22** As in Greek and Syriac versions; Hebrew reads *bind* or *imprison.*
105:28 As in Greek and Syriac versions; Hebrew reads *had not defied.*

and not one among the tribes
of Israel even stumbled.

³⁸ Egypt was glad when they were
gone,
for they feared them greatly.

³⁹ The Lord spread a cloud above
them as a covering
and gave them a great fire to
light the darkness.

⁴⁰ They asked for meat, and he sent
them quail;
he satisfied their hunger with
manna—bread from heaven.

⁴¹ He split open a rock, and water
gushed out
to form a river through the dry
wasteland.

⁴² For he remembered his sacred
promise
to his servant Abraham.

⁴³ So he brought his people out of
Egypt with joy,
his chosen ones with rejoicing.

⁴⁴ He gave his people the lands of
pagan nations,
and they harvested crops that
others had planted.

⁴⁵ All this happened so they would
follow his decrees
and obey his instructions.

Praise the Lord!

106

¹ Praise the Lord!

Give thanks to the Lord,
for he is good!
His faithful love endures forever.

² Who can list the glorious
miracles of the Lord?

Who can ever praise him
enough?

³ There is joy for those who deal
justly with others
and always do what is right.

⁴ Remember me, Lord, when you
show favor to your people;
come near and rescue me.

⁵ Let me share in the prosperity of
your chosen ones.
Let me rejoice in the joy of
your people;
let me praise you with those
who are your heritage.

⁶ Like our ancestors, we have
sinned.
We have done wrong! We have
acted wickedly!

⁷ Our ancestors in Egypt
were not impressed by the
Lord's miraculous deeds.
They soon forgot his many acts
of kindness to them.
Instead, they rebelled against
him at the Red Sea.*

⁸ Even so, he saved them—
to defend the honor of his
name
and to demonstrate his mighty
power.

⁹ He commanded the Red Sea* to
dry up.
He led Israel across the sea as
if it were a desert.

¹⁰ So he rescued them from their
enemies
and redeemed them from
their foes.

106:7 Hebrew *at the sea, the sea of reeds.* **106:9** Hebrew *sea of reeds;* also in 106:22.

¹¹ Then the water returned and
    covered their enemies;
  not one of them survived.
¹² Then his people believed his
    promises.
  Then they sang his praise.

¹³ Yet how quickly they forgot what
    he had done!
  They wouldn't wait for his
    counsel!
¹⁴ In the wilderness their desires
    ran wild,
  testing God's patience in that
    dry wasteland.
¹⁵ So he gave them what they asked
    for,
  but he sent a plague along
    with it.
¹⁶ The people in the camp were
    jealous of Moses
  and envious of Aaron, the
    Lord's holy priest.
¹⁷ Because of this, the earth
    opened up;
  it swallowed Dathan
  and buried Abiram and the
    other rebels.
¹⁸ Fire fell upon their followers;
  a flame consumed the wicked.

¹⁹ The people made a calf at Mount
    Sinai*;
  they bowed before an image
    made of gold.
²⁰ They traded their glorious God
  for a statue of a grass-eating
    bull.
²¹ They forgot God, their savior,

who had done such great
    things in Egypt—
²² such wonderful things in the
    land of Ham,
  such awesome deeds at the
    Red Sea.
²³ So he declared he would destroy
    them.
  But Moses, his chosen one,
    stepped between the Lord
    and the people.
  He begged him to turn from
    his anger and not destroy
    them.
²⁴ The people refused to enter the
    pleasant land,
  for they wouldn't believe his
    promise to care for them.
²⁵ Instead, they grumbled in their
    tents
  and refused to obey the
    Lord.
²⁶ Therefore, he solemnly swore
  that he would kill them in the
    wilderness,
²⁷ that he would scatter their
    descendants* among the
    nations,
  exiling them to distant lands.

²⁸ Then our ancestors joined in the
    worship of Baal at Peor;
  they even ate sacrifices
    offered to the dead!
²⁹ They angered the Lord with all
    these things,
  so a plague broke out among
    them.

106:19 Hebrew *at Horeb,* another name for Sinai. **106:27** As in Syriac version; Hebrew reads *he would cause their descendants to fall.*

30 But Phinehas had the courage
to intervene,
and the plague was stopped.
31 So he has been regarded as a
righteous man
ever since that time.
32 At Meribah, too, they angered the
Lord,
causing Moses serious trouble.
33 They made Moses angry,*
and he spoke foolishly.
34 Israel failed to destroy the
nations in the land,
as the Lord had commanded
them.
35 Instead, they mingled among
the pagans
and adopted their evil customs.
36 They worshiped their idols,
which led to their downfall.
37 They even sacrificed their sons
and their daughters to the
demons.
38 They shed innocent blood,
the blood of their sons and
daughters.
By sacrificing them to the idols
of Canaan,
they polluted the land with
murder.
39 They defiled themselves by their
evil deeds,
and their love of idols was
adultery in the Lord's sight.
40 That is why the Lord's anger
burned against his people,
and he abhorred his own
special possession.

41 He handed them over to pagan
nations,
and they were ruled by those
who hated them.
42 Their enemies crushed them
and brought them under their
cruel power.
43 Again and again he rescued them,
but they chose to rebel against
him,
and they were finally
destroyed by their sin.
44 Even so, he pitied them in their
distress
and listened to their cries.
45 He remembered his covenant
with them
and relented because of his
unfailing love.
46 He even caused their captors
to treat them with kindness.

47 Save us, O Lord our God!
Gather us back from among
the nations,
so we can thank your holy name
and rejoice and praise you.

48 Praise the Lord, the God of Israel,
who lives from everlasting to
everlasting!
Let all the people say, "Amen!"

Praise the Lord!

BOOK FIVE (Psalms 107–150)

107 1 Give thanks to the Lord,
for he is good!
His faithful love endures
forever.

106:33 Hebrew *They embittered his spirit.*

2 Has the Lord redeemed you?
    Then speak out!
    Tell others he has redeemed
    you from your enemies.
3 For he has gathered the exiles
    from many lands,
    from east and west,
    from north and south.*

4 Some wandered in the
    wilderness,
    lost and homeless.
5 Hungry and thirsty,
    they nearly died.
6 "Lord, help!" they cried in their
    trouble,
    and he rescued them from
    their distress.
7 He led them straight to safety,
    to a city where they could live.
8 Let them praise the Lord for his
    great love
    and for the wonderful things
    he has done for them.
9 For he satisfies the thirsty
    and fills the hungry with good
    things.

10 Some sat in darkness and
    deepest gloom,
    imprisoned in iron chains of
    misery.
11 They rebelled against the words
    of God,
    scorning the counsel of the
    Most High.
12 That is why he broke them with
    hard labor;
    they fell, and no one was there
    to help them.

13 "Lord, help!" they cried in their
    trouble,
    and he saved them from their
    distress.
14 He led them from the darkness
    and deepest gloom;
    he snapped their chains.
15 Let them praise the Lord for his
    great love
    and for the wonderful things
    he has done for them.
16 For he broke down their prison
    gates of bronze;
    he cut apart their bars
    of iron.

17 Some were fools; they rebelled
    and suffered for their sins.
18 They couldn't stand the thought
    of food,
    and they were knocking on
    death's door.
19 "Lord, help!" they cried in their
    trouble,
    and he saved them from their
    distress.
20 He sent out his word and healed
    them,
    snatching them from the door
    of death.
21 Let them praise the Lord for his
    great love
    and for the wonderful things
    he has done for them.
22 Let them offer sacrifices of
    thanksgiving
    and sing joyfully about his
    glorious acts.

23 Some went off to sea in ships,

107:3 Hebrew *and sea.*

plying the trade routes of the world.

24 They, too, observed the LORD's power in action,
his impressive works on the deepest seas.

25 He spoke, and the winds rose,
stirring up the waves.

26 Their ships were tossed to the heavens
and plunged again to the depths;
the sailors cringed in terror.

27 They reeled and staggered like drunkards
and were at their wits' end.

28 "LORD, help!" they cried in their trouble,
and he saved them from their distress.

29 He calmed the storm to a whisper
and stilled the waves.

30 What a blessing was that stillness
as he brought them safely into harbor!

31 Let them praise the LORD for his great love
and for the wonderful things he has done for them.

32 Let them exalt him publicly
before the congregation
and before the leaders of the nation.

33 He changes rivers into deserts,
and springs of water into dry, thirsty land.

34 He turns the fruitful land into salty wastelands,
because of the wickedness of those who live there.

35 But he also turns deserts into pools of water,
the dry land into springs of water.

36 He brings the hungry to settle there
and to build their cities.

37 They sow their fields, plant their vineyards,
and harvest their bumper crops.

38 How he blesses them!
They raise large families there,
and their herds of livestock increase.

39 When they decrease in number
and become impoverished
through oppression, trouble, and sorrow,

40 the LORD pours contempt on their princes,
causing them to wander in trackless wastelands.

41 But he rescues the poor from trouble
and increases their families like flocks of sheep.

42 The godly will see these things and be glad,
while the wicked are struck silent.

43 Those who are wise will take all this to heart;
they will see in our history the faithful love of the LORD.

108 *A song. A psalm of David.*

1 My heart is confident in you,
O God;

no wonder I can sing your
    praises with all my heart!
2 Wake up, lyre and harp!
    I will wake the dawn with my
      song.
3 I will thank you, LORD, among all
    the people.
    I will sing your praises among
      the nations.
4 For your unfailing love is higher
    than the heavens.
    Your faithfulness reaches to
      the clouds.
5 Be exalted, O God, above the
    highest heavens.
    May your glory shine over all
      the earth.

6 Now rescue your beloved people.
    Answer and save us by your
      power.
7 God has promised this by his
    holiness*:
    "I will divide up Shechem with joy.
    I will measure out the valley of
      Succoth.
8 Gilead is mine,
    and Manasseh, too.
    Ephraim, my helmet, will
      produce my warriors,
    and Judah, my scepter, will
      produce my kings.
9 But Moab, my washbasin, will
    become my servant,
    and I will wipe my feet on Edom
    and shout in triumph over
      Philistia."
10 Who will bring me into the
    fortified city?

Who will bring me victory
    over Edom?
11 Have you rejected us, O God?
    Will you no longer march with
      our armies?
12 Oh, please help us against our
    enemies,
    for all human help is useless.
13 With God's help we will do
    mighty things,
    for he will trample down our foes.

109 *For the choir director:
A psalm of David.*

1 O God, whom I praise,
    don't stand silent and aloof
2 while the wicked slander me
    and tell lies about me.
3 They surround me with hateful
    words
    and fight against me for no
      reason.
4 I love them, but they try to
    destroy me with accusations
    even as I am praying for them!
5 They repay evil for good,
    and hatred for my love.

6 They say,* "Get an evil person
    to turn against him.
    Send an accuser to bring him
      to trial.
7 When his case comes up for
    judgment,
    let him be pronounced guilty.
    Count his prayers as sins.
8 Let his years be few;
    let someone else take his
      position.

108:7 Or *in his sanctuary.*   **109:6** Hebrew lacks *They say.*

⁹ May his children become
fatherless,
and his wife a widow.
¹⁰ May his children wander as
beggars
and be driven from* their
ruined homes.
¹¹ May creditors seize his entire
estate,
and strangers take all he has
earned.
¹² Let no one be kind to him;
let no one pity his fatherless
children.
¹³ May all his offspring die.
May his family name be
blotted out in the next
generation.
¹⁴ May the LORD never forget the
sins of his fathers;
may his mother's sins never
be erased from the record.
¹⁵ May the LORD always remember
these sins,
and may his name disappear
from human memory.
¹⁶ For he refused all kindness to
others;
he persecuted the poor and
needy,
and he hounded the
brokenhearted to death.
¹⁷ He loved to curse others;
now you curse him.
He never blessed others;
now don't you bless him.
¹⁸ Cursing is as natural to him as
his clothing,
or the water he drinks,

or the rich food he eats.
¹⁹ Now may his curses return and
cling to him like clothing;
may they be tied around him
like a belt."

²⁰ May those curses become the
LORD's punishment
for my accusers who speak
evil of me.
²¹ But deal well with me,
O Sovereign LORD,
for the sake of your own
reputation!
Rescue me
because you are so faithful
and good.
²² For I am poor and needy,
and my heart is full of pain.
²³ I am fading like a shadow at
dusk;
I am brushed off like a locust.
²⁴ My knees are weak from fasting,
and I am skin and bones.
²⁵ I am a joke to people everywhere;
when they see me, they shake
their heads in scorn.

²⁶ Help me, O LORD my God!
Save me because of your
unfailing love.
²⁷ Let them see that this is your
doing,
that you yourself have done it,
LORD.
²⁸ Then let them curse me if they
like,
but you will bless me!
When they attack me, they will
be disgraced!

109:10 As in Greek version; Hebrew reads *and seek*.

But I, your servant, will go
    right on rejoicing!
²⁹ May my accusers be clothed
    with disgrace;
    may their humiliation cover
    them like a cloak.
³⁰ But I will give repeated thanks
    to the LORD,
    praising him to everyone.
³¹ For he stands beside the needy,
    ready to save them from those
    who condemn them.

110 *A psalm of David.*

¹ The LORD said to my Lord,*
    "Sit in the place of honor at
    my right hand
until I humble your enemies,
    making them a footstool
    under your feet."

² The LORD will extend your
    powerful kingdom from
    Jerusalem*;
    you will rule over your enemies.
³ When you go to war,
    your people will serve you
    willingly.
You are arrayed in holy garments,
    and your strength will be
    renewed each day like the
    morning dew.

⁴ The LORD has taken an oath and
    will not break his vow:
    "You are a priest forever in the
    order of Melchizedek."

⁵ The Lord stands at your right
    hand to protect you.
He will strike down many
    kings when his anger erupts.
⁶ He will punish the nations
    and fill their lands with corpses;
    he will shatter heads over the
    whole earth.
⁷ But he himself will be refreshed
    from brooks along the way.
He will be victorious.

111 * ¹ Praise the LORD!

I will thank the LORD
    with all my heart
as I meet with his godly
    people.
² How amazing are the deeds of
    the LORD!
All who delight in him should
    ponder them.
³ Everything he does reveals his
    glory and majesty.
His righteousness never fails.
⁴ He causes us to remember his
    wonderful works.
How gracious and merciful
    is our LORD!
⁵ He gives food to those who fear
    him;
    he always remembers his
    covenant.
⁶ He has shown his great power
    to his people
    by giving them the lands of
    other nations.
⁷ All he does is just and good,

110:1 Or *my lord.* 110:2 Hebrew *Zion.* 111 This psalm is a Hebrew acrostic poem; after the
introductory note of praise, each line begins with a successive letter of the Hebrew alphabet.

and all his commandments
  are trustworthy.
8 They are forever true,
  to be obeyed faithfully and
    with integrity.
9 He has paid a full ransom for
  his people.
  He has guaranteed his
    covenant with them forever.
  What a holy, awe-inspiring
    name he has!
10 Fear of the LORD is the
  foundation of true wisdom.
  All who obey his
    commandments will grow in
    wisdom.

Praise him forever!

112 * 1 Praise the LORD!

  How joyful are those
    who fear the LORD
  and delight in obeying his
    commands.
2 Their children will be successful
  everywhere;
  an entire generation of godly
    people will be blessed.
3 They themselves will be wealthy,
  and their good deeds will last
    forever.
4 Light shines in the darkness for
  the godly.
  They are generous,
    compassionate, and
    righteous.
5 Good comes to those who lend
  money generously

and conduct their business
  fairly.
6 Such people will not be
  overcome by evil.
  Those who are righteous will
    be long remembered.
7 They do not fear bad news;
  they confidently trust the
    LORD to care for them.
8 They are confident and fearless
  and can face their foes
    triumphantly.
9 They share freely and give
  generously to those in need.
  Their good deeds will be
    remembered forever.
  They will have influence and
    honor.
10 The wicked will see this and be
  infuriated.
  They will grind their teeth in
    anger;
  they will slink away, their
    hopes thwarted.

113 1 Praise the LORD!
  Yes, give praise,
    O servants of the
    LORD.
  Praise the name of the LORD!
2 Blessed be the name of the LORD
  now and forever.
3 Everywhere—from east to west—
  praise the name of the LORD.
4 For the LORD is high above the
  nations;
  his glory is higher than the
    heavens.

112 This psalm is a Hebrew acrostic poem; after the introductory note of praise, each line begins with
a successive letter of the Hebrew alphabet.

⁵ Who can be compared with the
        Lord our God,
    who is enthroned on high?
⁶ He stoops to look down
    on heaven and on earth.
⁷ He lifts the poor from the dust
    and the needy from the
        garbage dump.
⁸ He sets them among princes,
    even the princes of his own
        people!
⁹ He gives the childless woman a
        family,
    making her a happy mother.

Praise the Lord!

114

¹ When the Israelites
        escaped from Egypt—
    when the family of Jacob left
        that foreign land—
² the land of Judah became God's
        sanctuary,
    and Israel became his kingdom.

³ The Red Sea* saw them coming
        and hurried out of their way!
    The water of the Jordan River
        turned away.
⁴ The mountains skipped like
        rams,
    the hills like lambs!
⁵ What's wrong, Red Sea, that
        made you hurry out of their
        way?
    What happened, Jordan River,
        that you turned away?
⁶ Why, mountains, did you skip
        like rams?
    Why, hills, like lambs?

⁷ Tremble, O earth, at the presence
        of the Lord,
    at the presence of the God of
        Jacob.
⁸ He turned the rock into a pool of
        water;
    yes, a spring of water flowed
        from solid rock.

115

¹ Not to us, O Lord, not
        to us,
    but to your name goes all the
        glory
    for your unfailing love and
        faithfulness.
² Why let the nations say,
    "Where is their God?"
³ Our God is in the heavens,
    and he does as he wishes.
⁴ Their idols are merely things of
        silver and gold,
    shaped by human hands.
⁵ They have mouths but cannot
        speak,
    and eyes but cannot see.
⁶ They have ears but cannot hear,
    and noses but cannot smell.
⁷ They have hands but cannot
        feel,
    and feet but cannot walk,
    and throats but cannot make
        a sound.
⁸ And those who make idols are
        just like them,
    as are all who trust in them.

⁹ O Israel, trust the Lord!
    He is your helper and your
        shield.

114:3 Hebrew *the sea;* also in 114:5.

10 O priests, descendants of Aaron,
    trust the LORD!
  He is your helper and your
    shield.
11 All you who fear the LORD, trust
    the LORD!
  He is your helper and your
    shield.
12 The LORD remembers us and will
    bless us.
  He will bless the people of
    Israel
  and bless the priests, the
    descendants of Aaron.
13 He will bless those who fear the
    LORD,
    both great and lowly.
14 May the LORD richly bless
    both you and your children.
15 May you be blessed by the LORD,
    who made heaven and earth.
16 The heavens belong to the LORD,
    but he has given the earth to
    all humanity.
17 The dead cannot sing praises to
    the LORD,
  for they have gone into the
    silence of the grave.
18 But we can praise the LORD
    both now and forever!

  Praise the LORD!

116

1 I love the LORD because
    he hears my voice
  and my prayer for mercy.
2 Because he bends down to listen,
    I will pray as long as I have
    breath!

3 Death wrapped its ropes
    around me;
  the terrors of the grave*
    overtook me.
  I saw only trouble and sorrow.
4 Then I called on the name of the
    LORD:
  "Please, LORD, save me!"
5 How kind the LORD is! How good
    he is!
  So merciful, this God of ours!
6 The LORD protects those of
    childlike faith;
  I was facing death, and he
    saved me.
7 Let my soul be at rest again,
  for the LORD has been good
    to me.
8 He has saved me from death,
    my eyes from tears,
    my feet from stumbling.
9 And so I walk in the LORD's
    presence
  as I live here on earth!
10 I believed in you, so I said,
  "I am deeply troubled, LORD."
11 In my anxiety I cried out to you,
  "These people are all liars!"
12 What can I offer the LORD
  for all he has done for me?
13 I will lift up the cup of salvation
  and praise the LORD's name for
    saving me.
14 I will keep my promises to the
    LORD
  in the presence of all his people.
15 The LORD cares deeply
    when his loved ones die.

116:3 Hebrew *of Sheol.*

¹⁶ O LORD, I am your servant;
   yes, I am your servant, born
      into your household;
   you have freed me from my
      chains.
¹⁷ I will offer you a sacrifice of
      thanksgiving
   and call on the name of the
      LORD.
¹⁸ I will fulfill my vows to the
      LORD
   in the presence of all his
      people—
¹⁹ in the house of the LORD
   in the heart of Jerusalem.

Praise the LORD!

117

¹ Praise the LORD, all you
      nations.
   Praise him, all you people of
      the earth.
² For his unfailing love for us is
      powerful;
   the LORD's faithfulness
      endures forever.

Praise the LORD!

118

¹ Give thanks to the LORD,
      for he is good!
   His faithful love endures
      forever.

² Let all Israel repeat:
   "His faithful love endures
      forever."
³ Let Aaron's descendants, the
      priests, repeat:
   "His faithful love endures
      forever."

⁴ Let all who fear the LORD repeat:
   "His faithful love endures
      forever."

⁵ In my distress I prayed to the
      LORD,
   and the LORD answered me
      and set me free.
⁶ The LORD is for me, so I will have
      no fear.
   What can mere people do
      to me?
⁷ Yes, the LORD is for me; he will
      help me.
   I will look in triumph at those
      who hate me.
⁸ It is better to take refuge in the
      LORD
   than to trust in people.
⁹ It is better to take refuge in the
      LORD
   than to trust in princes.

¹⁰ Though hostile nations
      surrounded me,
   I destroyed them all with the
      authority of the LORD.
¹¹ Yes, they surrounded and
      attacked me,
   but I destroyed them all with
      the authority of the LORD.
¹² They swarmed around me like
      bees;
   they blazed against me like
      a crackling fire.
   But I destroyed them all with
      the authority of the LORD.
¹³ My enemies did their best to
      kill me,
   but the LORD rescued me.

14 The LORD is my strength and my
   song;
      he has given me victory.
15 Songs of joy and victory are sung
   in the camp of the godly.
      The strong right arm of the
      LORD has done glorious
      things!
16 The strong right arm of the LORD
   is raised in triumph.
      The strong right arm of the
      LORD has done glorious
      things!
17 I will not die; instead, I will live
      to tell what the LORD has done.
18 The LORD has punished me
   severely,
      but he did not let me die.
19 Open for me the gates where the
   righteous enter,
      and I will go in and thank the
      LORD.
20 These gates lead to the presence
   of the LORD,
      and the godly enter there.
21 I thank you for answering my
   prayer
      and giving me victory!
22 The stone that the builders
   rejected
      has now become the
      cornerstone.
23 This is the LORD's doing,
      and it is wonderful to see.
24 This is the day the LORD has
   made.

We will rejoice and be glad in it.
25 Please, LORD, please save us.
      Please, LORD, please give us
      success.
26 Bless the one who comes in the
   name of the LORD.
      We bless you from the house
      of the LORD.
27 The LORD is God, shining upon us.
      Take the sacrifice and bind it
      with cords on the altar.
28 You are my God, and I will praise
   you!
      You are my God, and I will
      exalt you!

29 Give thanks to the LORD, for he is
   good!
      His faithful love endures
      forever.

119*

Aleph

1 Joyful are people of integrity,
      who follow the instructions of
      the LORD.
2 Joyful are those who obey his laws
      and search for him with all
      their hearts.
3 They do not compromise with
   evil,
      and they walk only in his paths.
4 You have charged us
      to keep your commandments
      carefully.
5 Oh, that my actions would
   consistently
      reflect your decrees!

119 This psalm is a Hebrew acrostic poem; there are twenty-two stanzas, one for each successive
letter of the Hebrew alphabet. Each of the eight verses within each stanza begins with the Hebrew
letter named in its heading.

⁶ Then I will not be ashamed
when I compare my life with
your commands.
⁷ As I learn your righteous
regulations,
I will thank you by living as
I should!
⁸ I will obey your decrees.
Please don't give up on me!

Beth

⁹ How can a young person stay
pure?
By obeying your word.
¹⁰ I have tried hard to find you—
don't let me wander from your
commands.
¹¹ I have hidden your word in my
heart,
that I might not sin against you.
¹² I praise you, O Lord;
teach me your decrees.
¹³ I have recited aloud
all the regulations you have
given us.
¹⁴ I have rejoiced in your laws
as much as in riches.
¹⁵ I will study your commandments
and reflect on your ways.
¹⁶ I will delight in your decrees
and not forget your word.

Gimel

¹⁷ Be good to your servant,
that I may live and obey your
word.
¹⁸ Open my eyes to see
the wonderful truths in your
instructions.
¹⁹ I am only a foreigner in the land.

Don't hide your commands
from me!
²⁰ I am always overwhelmed
with a desire for your
regulations.
²¹ You rebuke the arrogant;
those who wander from your
commands are cursed.
²² Don't let them scorn and
insult me,
for I have obeyed your laws.
²³ Even princes sit and speak
against me,
but I will meditate on your
decrees.
²⁴ Your laws please me;
they give me wise advice.

Daleth

²⁵ I lie in the dust;
revive me by your word.
²⁶ I told you my plans, and you
answered.
Now teach me your decrees.
²⁷ Help me understand the
meaning of your
commandments,
and I will meditate on your
wonderful deeds.
²⁸ I weep with sorrow;
encourage me by your word.
²⁹ Keep me from lying to myself;
give me the privilege of
knowing your instructions.
³⁰ I have chosen to be faithful;
I have determined to live by
your regulations.
³¹ I cling to your laws.
Lord, don't let me be put to
shame!

32 I will pursue your commands,
　　for you expand my
　　understanding.

He

33 Teach me your decrees, O LORD;
　　I will keep them to the end.
34 Give me understanding and I will
　　obey your instructions;
　　I will put them into practice
　　with all my heart.
35 Make me walk along the path of
　　your commands,
　　for that is where my happiness
　　is found.
36 Give me an eagerness for your
　　laws
　　rather than a love for money!
37 Turn my eyes from worthless
　　things,
　　and give me life through your
　　word.*
38 Reassure me of your promise,
　　made to those who fear you.
39 Help me abandon my shameful
　　ways;
　　for your regulations are good.
40 I long to obey your
　　commandments!
　　Renew my life with your
　　goodness.

Waw

41 LORD, give me your unfailing
　　love,
　　the salvation that you
　　promised me.
42 Then I can answer those who
　　taunt me,
　　for I trust in your word.

43 Do not snatch your word of truth
　　from me,
　　for your regulations are my
　　only hope.
44 I will keep on obeying your
　　instructions
　　forever and ever.
45 I will walk in freedom,
　　for I have devoted myself to
　　your commandments.
46 I will speak to kings about your
　　laws,
　　and I will not be ashamed.
47 How I delight in your
　　commands!
　　How I love them!
48 I honor and love your commands.
　　I meditate on your decrees.

Zayin

49 Remember your promise to me;
　　it is my only hope.
50 Your promise revives me;
　　it comforts me in all my
　　troubles.
51 The proud hold me in utter
　　contempt,
　　but I do not turn away from
　　your instructions.
52 I meditate on your age-old
　　regulations;
　　O LORD, they comfort me.
53 I become furious with the
　　wicked,
　　because they reject your
　　instructions.
54 Your decrees have been the
　　theme of my songs
　　wherever I have lived.

119:37 Some manuscripts read *in your ways.*

⁵⁵ I reflect at night on who you are,
    O Lord;
    therefore, I obey your
        instructions.
⁵⁶ This is how I spend my life:
    obeying your commandments.

Heth

⁵⁷ Lord, you are mine!
    I promise to obey your words!
⁵⁸ With all my heart I want your
        blessings.
    Be merciful as you promised.
⁵⁹ I pondered the direction of
        my life,
    and I turned to follow your
        laws.
⁶⁰ I will hurry, without delay,
    to obey your commands.
⁶¹ Evil people try to drag me into
        sin,
    but I am firmly anchored to
        your instructions.
⁶² I rise at midnight to thank you
    for your just regulations.
⁶³ I am a friend to anyone who
        fears you—
    anyone who obeys your
        commandments.
⁶⁴ O Lord, your unfailing love fills
        the earth;
    teach me your decrees.

Teth

⁶⁵ You have done many good things
        for me, Lord,
    just as you promised.
⁶⁶ I believe in your commands;
    now teach me good judgment
        and knowledge.

⁶⁷ I used to wander off until you
        disciplined me;
    but now I closely follow your
        word.
⁶⁸ You are good and do only good;
    teach me your decrees.
⁶⁹ Arrogant people smear me with
        lies,
    but in truth I obey your
        commandments with all
        my heart.
⁷⁰ Their hearts are dull and stupid,
    but I delight in your
        instructions.
⁷¹ My suffering was good for me,
    for it taught me to pay
        attention to your decrees.
⁷² Your instructions are more
        valuable to me
    than millions in gold and
        silver.

Yodh

⁷³ You made me; you created me.
    Now give me the sense to
        follow your commands.
⁷⁴ May all who fear you find in me
        a cause for joy,
    for I have put my hope in your
        word.
⁷⁵ I know, O Lord, that your
        regulations are fair;
    you disciplined me because
        I needed it.
⁷⁶ Now let your unfailing love
        comfort me,
    just as you promised me, your
        servant.
⁷⁷ Surround me with your tender
        mercies so I may live,

for your instructions are my
delight.

78 Bring disgrace upon the arrogant
people who lied about me;
meanwhile, I will concentrate
on your commandments.

79 Let me be united with all who
fear you,
with those who know your
laws.

80 May I be blameless in keeping
your decrees;
then I will never be ashamed.

Kaph

81 I am worn out waiting for your
rescue,
but I have put my hope in your
word.

82 My eyes are straining to see your
promises come true.
When will you comfort me?

83 I am shriveled like a wineskin in
the smoke,
but I have not forgotten to
obey your decrees.

84 How long must I wait?
When will you punish those
who persecute me?

85 These arrogant people who hate
your instructions
have dug deep pits to trap me.

86 All your commands are
trustworthy.
Protect me from those who
hunt me down without
cause.

87 They almost finished me off,
but I refused to abandon your
commandments.

88 In your unfailing love, spare my
life;
then I can continue to obey
your laws.

Lamedh

89 Your eternal word, O LORD,
stands firm in heaven.

90 Your faithfulness extends to
every generation,
as enduring as the earth you
created.

91 Your regulations remain true to
this day,
for everything serves your
plans.

92 If your instructions hadn't
sustained me with joy,
I would have died in my misery.

93 I will never forget your
commandments,
for by them you give me life.

94 I am yours; rescue me!
For I have worked hard at
obeying your
commandments.

95 Though the wicked hide along
the way to kill me,
I will quietly keep my mind
on your laws.

96 Even perfection has its limits,
but your commands have no
limit.

Mem

97 Oh, how I love your instructions!
I think about them all day
long.

98 Your commands make me wiser
than my enemies,
for they are my constant guide.

99 Yes, I have more insight than my
       teachers,
   for I am always thinking of
       your laws.
100 I am even wiser than my
       elders,
   for I have kept your
       commandments.
101 I have refused to walk on any
       evil path,
   so that I may remain obedient
       to your word.
102 I haven't turned away from your
       regulations,
   for you have taught me well.
103 How sweet your words taste
       to me;
   they are sweeter than honey.
104 Your commandments give me
       understanding;
   no wonder I hate every false
       way of life.

Nun

105 Your word is a lamp to guide
       my feet
   and a light for my path.
106 I've promised it once, and I'll
       promise it again:
   I will obey your righteous
       regulations.
107 I have suffered much, O LORD;
   restore my life again as you
       promised.
108 LORD, accept my offering of
       praise,
   and teach me your
       regulations.
109 My life constantly hangs in the
       balance,

but I will not stop obeying
       your instructions.
110 The wicked have set their traps
       for me,
   but I will not turn from your
       commandments.
111 Your laws are my treasure;
   they are my heart's delight.
112 I am determined to keep your
       decrees
   to the very end.

Samekh

113 I hate those with divided
       loyalties,
   but I love your instructions.
114 You are my refuge and my
       shield;
   your word is my source of
       hope.
115 Get out of my life, you evil-
       minded people,
   for I intend to obey the
       commands of my God.
116 LORD, sustain me as you
       promised, that I may live!
   Do not let my hope be crushed.
117 Sustain me, and I will be
       rescued;
   then I will meditate
       continually on your
       decrees.
118 But you have rejected all who
       stray from your decrees.
   They are only fooling
       themselves.
119 You skim off the wicked of the
       earth like scum;
   no wonder I love to obey your
       laws!

120 I tremble in fear of you;
    I stand in awe of your
    regulations.

Ayin

121 Don't leave me to the mercy of
    my enemies,
    for I have done what is just
    and right.
122 Please guarantee a blessing
    for me.
    Don't let the arrogant
    oppress me!
123 My eyes strain to see your rescue,
    to see the truth of your
    promise fulfilled.
124 I am your servant; deal with me
    in unfailing love,
    and teach me your decrees.
125 Give discernment to me, your
    servant;
    then I will understand your
    laws.
126 LORD, it is time for you to act,
    for these evil people have
    violated your instructions.
127 Truly, I love your commands
    more than gold, even the
    finest gold.
128 Each of your commandments
    is right.
    That is why I hate every false
    way.

Pe

129 Your laws are wonderful.
    No wonder I obey them!
130 The teaching of your word gives
    light,
    so even the simple can
    understand.

131 I pant with expectation,
    longing for your commands.
132 Come and show me your mercy,
    as you do for all who love
    your name.
133 Guide my steps by your word,
    so I will not be overcome by
    evil.
134 Ransom me from the
    oppression of evil people;
    then I can obey your
    commandments.
135 Look upon me with love;
    teach me your decrees.
136 Rivers of tears gush from my
    eyes
    because people disobey your
    instructions.

Tsadhe

137 O LORD, you are righteous,
    and your regulations are fair.
138 Your laws are perfect
    and completely trustworthy.
139 I am overwhelmed with
    indignation,
    for my enemies have
    disregarded your words.
140 Your promises have been
    thoroughly tested;
    that is why I love them so
    much.
141 I am insignificant and despised,
    but I don't forget your
    commandments.
142 Your justice is eternal,
    and your instructions are
    perfectly true.
143 As pressure and stress bear
    down on me,

I find joy in your commands.

¹⁴⁴ Your laws are always right;
help me to understand them
so I may live.

Qoph

¹⁴⁵ I pray with all my heart; answer
me, Lᴏʀᴅ!
I will obey your decrees.

¹⁴⁶ I cry out to you; rescue me,
that I may obey your laws.

¹⁴⁷ I rise early, before the sun
is up;
I cry out for help and put my
hope in your words.

¹⁴⁸ I stay awake through the night,
thinking about your promise.

¹⁴⁹ In your faithful love, O Lᴏʀᴅ,
hear my cry;
let me be revived by following
your regulations.

¹⁵⁰ Lawless people are coming to
attack me;
they live far from your
instructions.

¹⁵¹ But you are near, O Lᴏʀᴅ,
and all your commands are
true.

¹⁵² I have known from my earliest
days
that your laws will last
forever.

Resh

¹⁵³ Look upon my suffering and
rescue me,
for I have not forgotten your
instructions.

¹⁵⁴ Argue my case; take my side!
Protect my life as you
promised.

¹⁵⁵ The wicked are far from rescue,
for they do not bother with
your decrees.

¹⁵⁶ Lᴏʀᴅ, how great is your mercy;
let me be revived by following
your regulations.

¹⁵⁷ Many persecute and
trouble me,
yet I have not swerved from
your laws.

¹⁵⁸ Seeing these traitors makes me
sick at heart,
because they care nothing for
your word.

¹⁵⁹ See how I love your
commandments, Lᴏʀᴅ.
Give back my life because of
your unfailing love.

¹⁶⁰ The very essence of your words
is truth;
all your just regulations will
stand forever.

Shin

¹⁶¹ Powerful people harass me
without cause,
but my heart trembles only
at your word.

¹⁶² I rejoice in your word
like one who discovers a great
treasure.

¹⁶³ I hate and abhor all falsehood,
but I love your instructions.

¹⁶⁴ I will praise you seven times
a day
because all your regulations
are just.

¹⁶⁵ Those who love your
instructions have great
peace

and do not stumble.

166 I long for your rescue, LORD,
 so I have obeyed your
  commands.
167 I have obeyed your laws,
 for I love them very much.
168 Yes, I obey your commandments
 and laws
 because you know everything
  I do.

Taw

169 O LORD, listen to my cry;
 give me the discerning mind
  you promised.
170 Listen to my prayer;
 rescue me as you
  promised.
171 Let praise flow from my lips,
 for you have taught me your
  decrees.
172 Let my tongue sing about your
  word,
 for all your commands are
  right.
173 Give me a helping hand,
 for I have chosen to follow
  your commandments.
174 O LORD, I have longed for your
  rescue,
 and your instructions are my
  delight.
175 Let me live so I can praise you,
 and may your regulations
  help me.
176 I have wandered away like a lost
  sheep;
 come and find me,
 for I have not forgotten your
  commands.

120 *A song for pilgrims ascending to Jerusalem.*

1 I took my troubles to the LORD;
 I cried out to him, and he
  answered my prayer.
2 Rescue me, O LORD, from liars
 and from all deceitful people.

3 O deceptive tongue, what will
  God do to you?
 How will he increase your
  punishment?
4 You will be pierced with sharp
  arrows
 and burned with glowing coals.

5 How I suffer in far-off Meshech.
 It pains me to live in distant
  Kedar.
6 I am tired of living
 among people who hate peace.
7 I search for peace;
 but when I speak of peace,
  they want war!

121 *A song for pilgrims ascending to Jerusalem.*

1 I look up to the mountains—
 does my help come from there?
2 My help comes from the LORD,
 who made heaven and earth!

3 He will not let you stumble;
 the one who watches over you
  will not slumber.
4 Indeed, he who watches over
  Israel
 never slumbers or sleeps.

5 The LORD himself watches over
  you!

The LORD stands beside you as
your protective shade.
6 The sun will not harm you by day,
nor the moon at night.

7 The LORD keeps you from all
harm
and watches over your life.
8 The LORD keeps watch over you
as you come and go,
both now and forever.

122 *A song for pilgrims
ascending to Jerusalem.*
A psalm of David.

1 I was glad when they said to me,
"Let us go to the house of the
LORD."
2 And now here we are,
standing inside your gates,
O Jerusalem.
3 Jerusalem is a well-built city;
its seamless walls cannot be
breached.
4 All the tribes of Israel—the
LORD's people—
make their pilgrimage here.
They come to give thanks to the
name of the LORD,
as the law requires of Israel.
5 Here stand the thrones where
judgment is given,
the thrones of the dynasty
of David.

6 Pray for peace in Jerusalem.
May all who love this city
prosper.
7 O Jerusalem, may there be peace
within your walls

and prosperity in your palaces.
8 For the sake of my family and
friends, I will say,
"May you have peace."
9 For the sake of the house of the
LORD our God,
I will seek what is best for you,
O Jerusalem.

123 *A song for pilgrims
ascending to Jerusalem.*

1 I lift my eyes to you,
O God, enthroned in heaven.
2 We keep looking to the LORD our
God for his mercy,
just as servants keep their eyes
on their master,
as a slave girl watches her
mistress for the slightest
signal.
3 Have mercy on us, LORD, have
mercy,
for we have had our fill of
contempt.
4 We have had more than our fill
of the scoffing of the proud
and the contempt of the
arrogant.

124 *A song for pilgrims
ascending to Jerusalem.*
A psalm of David.

1 What if the LORD had not been
on our side?
Let all Israel repeat:
2 What if the LORD had not been
on our side
when people attacked us?

³ They would have swallowed
    us alive
    in their burning anger.
⁴ The waters would have
    engulfed us;
    a torrent would have
    overwhelmed us.
⁵ Yes, the raging waters of their fury
    would have overwhelmed our
    very lives.

⁶ Praise the LORD,
    who did not let their teeth tear
    us apart!
⁷ We escaped like a bird from a
    hunter's trap.
    The trap is broken, and we are
    free!
⁸ Our help is from the LORD,
    who made heaven and earth.

125 *A song for pilgrims ascending to Jerusalem.*

¹ Those who trust in the LORD are
    as secure as Mount Zion;
    they will not be defeated but
    will endure forever.
² Just as the mountains surround
    Jerusalem,
    so the LORD surrounds his
    people, both now and forever.
³ The wicked will not rule the land
    of the godly,
    for then the godly might be
    tempted to do wrong.
⁴ O LORD, do good to those who
    are good,
    whose hearts are in tune with
    you.

⁵ But banish those who turn to
    crooked ways, O LORD.
    Take them away with those
    who do evil.

May Israel have peace!

126 *A song for pilgrims ascending to Jerusalem.*

¹ When the LORD brought back his
    exiles to Jerusalem,*
    it was like a dream!
² We were filled with laughter,
    and we sang for joy.
    And the other nations said,
    "What amazing things the
    LORD has done for them."
³ Yes, the LORD has done amazing
    things for us!
    What joy!

⁴ Restore our fortunes, LORD,
    as streams renew the desert.
⁵ Those who plant in tears
    will harvest with shouts of joy.
⁶ They weep as they go to plant
    their seed,
    but they sing as they return
    with the harvest.

127 *A song for pilgrims ascending to Jerusalem. A psalm of Solomon.*

¹ Unless the LORD builds a house,
    the work of the builders is
    wasted.
    Unless the LORD protects a city,
    guarding it with sentries will
    do no good.

126:1 Hebrew *Zion.*

2 It is useless for you to work so
hard
from early morning until late
at night,
anxiously working for food to eat;
for God gives rest to his loved
ones.

3 Children are a gift from the LORD;
they are a reward from him.
4 Children born to a young man
are like arrows in a warrior's
hands.
5 How joyful is the man whose
quiver is full of them!
He will not be put to shame
when he confronts his
accusers at the city gates.

128 *A song for pilgrims ascending to Jerusalem.*

1 How joyful are those who fear
the LORD—
all who follow his ways!
2 You will enjoy the fruit of your
labor.
How joyful and prosperous
you will be!
3 Your wife will be like a fruitful
grapevine,
flourishing within your home.
Your children will be like
vigorous young olive trees
as they sit around your table.
4 That is the LORD's blessing
for those who fear him.

5 May the LORD continually bless
you from Zion.

May you see Jerusalem prosper
as long as you live.
6 May you live to enjoy your
grandchildren.
May Israel have peace!

129 *A song for pilgrims ascending to Jerusalem.*

1 From my earliest youth my
enemies have persecuted
me.
Let all Israel repeat this:
2 From my earliest youth my
enemies have persecuted
me,
but they have never defeated
me.
3 My back is covered with cuts,
as if a farmer had plowed long
furrows.
4 But the LORD is good;
he has cut me free from the
ropes of the ungodly.

5 May all who hate Jerusalem*
be turned back in shameful
defeat.
6 May they be as useless as grass
on a rooftop,
turning yellow when only
half grown,
7 ignored by the harvester,
despised by the binder.
8 And may those who pass by
refuse to give them this
blessing:
"The LORD bless you;
we bless you in the LORD's
name."

129:5 Hebrew *Zion.*

130

*A song for pilgrims
ascending to Jerusalem.*

¹ From the depths of despair,
      O Lord,
   I call for your help.
² Hear my cry, O Lord.
   Pay attention to my prayer.

³ Lord, if you kept a record of our
      sins,
   who, O Lord, could ever
      survive?
⁴ But you offer forgiveness,
   that we might learn to fear you.

⁵ I am counting on the Lord;
   yes, I am counting on him.
   I have put my hope in his
      word.
⁶ I long for the Lord
   more than sentries long for the
      dawn,
   yes, more than sentries long
      for the dawn.

⁷ O Israel, hope in the Lord;
   for with the Lord there is
      unfailing love.
   His redemption overflows.
⁸ He himself will redeem Israel
   from every kind of sin.

131

*A song for pilgrims
ascending to Jerusalem.
A psalm of David.*

¹ Lord, my heart is not proud;
   my eyes are not haughty.
   I don't concern myself with
      matters too great

or too awesome for me to grasp.
² Instead, I have calmed and
      quieted myself,
   like a weaned child who no
      longer cries for its mother's
      milk.
   Yes, like a weaned child is my
      soul within me.

³ O Israel, put your hope in the
      Lord—
   now and always.

132

*A song for pilgrims
ascending to Jerusalem.*

¹ Lord, remember David
   and all that he suffered.
² He made a solemn promise to
      the Lord.
   He vowed to the Mighty One
      of Israel,*
³ "I will not go home;
   I will not let myself rest.
⁴ I will not let my eyes sleep
   nor close my eyelids in
      slumber
⁵ until I find a place to build a
      house for the Lord,
   a sanctuary for the Mighty One
      of Israel."

⁶ We heard that the Ark was in
      Ephrathah;
   then we found it in the distant
      countryside of Jaar.
⁷ Let us go to the sanctuary of the
      Lord;
   let us worship at the footstool
      of his throne.

132:2 Hebrew *of Jacob;* also in 132:5. See note on 44:4.

8 Arise, O LORD, and enter your
    resting place,
    along with the Ark, the symbol
    of your power.
9 May your priests be clothed in
    godliness;
    may your loyal servants sing
    for joy.
10 For the sake of your servant
    David,
    do not reject the king you have
    anointed.
11 The LORD swore an oath to David
    with a promise he will never
    take back:
    "I will place one of your
    descendants
    on your throne.
12 If your descendants obey the
    terms of my covenant
    and the laws that I teach them,
    then your royal line
    will continue forever and
    ever."
13 For the LORD has chosen
    Jerusalem*;
    he has desired it for his home.
14 "This is my resting place
    forever," he said.
    "I will live here, for this is the
    home I desired.
15 I will bless this city and make it
    prosperous;
    I will satisfy its poor with food.
16 I will clothe its priests with
    godliness;
    its faithful servants will sing
    for joy.

17 Here I will increase the power of
    David;
    my anointed one will be a light
    for my people.
18 I will clothe his enemies with
    shame,
    but he will be a glorious king."

133 *A song for pilgrims ascending to Jerusalem.*
A psalm of David.

1 How wonderful and pleasant it is
    when brothers live together in
    harmony!
2 For harmony is as precious as
    the anointing oil
    that was poured over Aaron's
    head,
    that ran down his beard
    and onto the border of his robe.
3 Harmony is as refreshing as the
    dew from Mount Hermon
    that falls on the mountains
    of Zion.
    And there the LORD has
    pronounced his blessing,
    even life everlasting.

134 *A song for pilgrims ascending to Jerusalem.*

1 Oh, praise the LORD, all you
    servants of the LORD,
    you who serve at night in the
    house of the LORD.
2 Lift your hands toward the
    sanctuary,
    and praise the LORD.

132:13 Hebrew *Zion.*

3 May the LORD, who made heaven
    and earth,
   bless you from Jerusalem.*

135 1 Praise the LORD!

Praise the name of the
    LORD!
Praise him, you who serve the
    LORD,
2 you who serve in the house of
    the LORD,
   in the courts of the house of
    our God.

3 Praise the LORD, for the LORD is
    good;
   celebrate his lovely name with
    music.
4 For the LORD has chosen Jacob
    for himself,
   Israel for his own special
    treasure.

5 I know the greatness of the LORD—
   that our Lord is greater than
    any other god.
6 The LORD does whatever pleases
    him
   throughout all heaven and earth,
   and on the seas and in their
    depths.
7 He causes the clouds to rise over
    the whole earth.
   He sends the lightning with
    the rain
   and releases the wind from his
    storehouses.

8 He destroyed the firstborn in
    each Egyptian home,

both people and animals.
9 He performed miraculous signs
    and wonders in Egypt
   against Pharaoh and all his
    people.
10 He struck down great nations
    and slaughtered mighty kings—
11 Sihon king of the Amorites,
    Og king of Bashan,
   and all the kings of Canaan.
12 He gave their land as an
    inheritance,
   a special possession to his
    people Israel.

13 Your name, O LORD, endures
    forever;
   your fame, O LORD, is known
    to every generation.
14 For the LORD will give justice
    to his people
   and have compassion on his
    servants.

15 The idols of the nations are
    merely things of silver and
    gold,
   shaped by human hands.
16 They have mouths but cannot
    speak,
   and eyes but cannot see.
17 They have ears but cannot hear,
   and mouths but cannot breathe.
18 And those who make idols are
    just like them,
   as are all who trust in them.

19 O Israel, praise the LORD!
   O priests—descendants of
    Aaron—praise the LORD!

134:3 Hebrew *Zion*.

20 O Levites, praise the LORD!
  All you who fear the LORD,
    praise the LORD!
21 The LORD be praised from
    Zion,
  for he lives here in Jerusalem.

Praise the LORD!

136
¹ Give thanks to the LORD,
    for he is good!
  His faithful love endures forever.
² Give thanks to the God of gods.
  His faithful love endures forever.
³ Give thanks to the Lord of lords.
  His faithful love endures forever.

⁴ Give thanks to him who alone
    does mighty miracles.
  His faithful love endures forever.
⁵ Give thanks to him who made
    the heavens so skillfully.
  His faithful love endures forever.
⁶ Give thanks to him who placed
    the earth among the waters.
  His faithful love endures forever.
⁷ Give thanks to him who made
    the heavenly lights—
  His faithful love endures forever.
⁸ the sun to rule the day,
  His faithful love endures forever.
⁹ and the moon and stars to rule
    the night.
  His faithful love endures forever.

¹⁰ Give thanks to him who killed
    the firstborn of Egypt.
  His faithful love endures forever.
¹¹ He brought Israel out of Egypt.
  His faithful love endures forever.

¹² He acted with a strong hand and
    powerful arm.
  His faithful love endures forever.
¹³ Give thanks to him who parted
    the Red Sea.*
  His faithful love endures forever.
¹⁴ He led Israel safely through,
  His faithful love endures forever.
¹⁵ but he hurled Pharaoh and his
    army into the Red Sea.
  His faithful love endures forever.
¹⁶ Give thanks to him who led his
    people through the
    wilderness.
  His faithful love endures forever.

¹⁷ Give thanks to him who struck
    down mighty kings.
  His faithful love endures forever.
¹⁸ He killed powerful kings—
  His faithful love endures forever.
¹⁹ Sihon king of the Amorites,
  His faithful love endures forever.
²⁰ and Og king of Bashan.
  His faithful love endures forever.
²¹ God gave the land of these kings
    as an inheritance—
  His faithful love endures forever.
²² a special possession to his
    servant Israel.
  His faithful love endures forever.

²³ He remembered us in our
    weakness.
  His faithful love endures forever.
²⁴ He saved us from our enemies.
  His faithful love endures forever.
²⁵ He gives food to every living
    thing.
  His faithful love endures forever.

136:13 Hebrew *sea of reeds;* also in 136:15.

²⁶ Give thanks to the God of
heaven.
His faithful love endures forever.

137 ¹ Beside the rivers of
Babylon, we sat and
wept
as we thought of Jerusalem.*
² We put away our harps,
hanging them on the branches
of poplar trees.
³ For our captors demanded
a song from us.
Our tormentors insisted on
a joyful hymn:
"Sing us one of those songs
of Jerusalem!"
⁴ But how can we sing the songs
of the Lord
while in a pagan land?

⁵ If I forget you, O Jerusalem,
let my right hand forget how
to play the harp.
⁶ May my tongue stick to the roof
of my mouth
if I fail to remember you,
if I don't make Jerusalem my
greatest joy.

⁷ O Lord, remember what the
Edomites did
on the day the armies of
Babylon captured
Jerusalem.
"Destroy it!" they yelled.
"Level it to the ground!"
⁸ O Babylon, you will be destroyed.
Happy is the one who pays you
back

for what you have done to us.
⁹ Happy is the one who takes your
babies
and smashes them against the
rocks!

138 *A psalm of David.*

¹ I give you thanks, O Lord, with
all my heart;
I will sing your praises before
the gods.
² I bow before your holy Temple as
I worship.
I praise your name for your
unfailing love and
faithfulness;
for your promises are backed
by all the honor of your
name.
³ As soon as I pray, you answer me;
you encourage me by giving
me strength.
⁴ Every king in all the earth will
thank you, Lord,
for all of them will hear your
words.
⁵ Yes, they will sing about the
Lord's ways,
for the glory of the Lord is
very great.
⁶ Though the Lord is great, he
cares for the humble,
but he keeps his distance from
the proud.
⁷ Though I am surrounded by
troubles,

137:1 Hebrew *Zion;* also in 137:3.

you will protect me from the
   anger of my enemies.
You reach out your hand,
   and the power of your right
   hand saves me.
⁸ The Lord will work out his plans
   for my life—
   for your faithful love, O Lord,
   endures forever.
   Don't abandon me, for you
   made me.

139 *For the choir director:
A psalm of David.*

¹ O Lord, you have examined my
   heart
   and know everything about me.
² You know when I sit down or
   stand up.
   You know my thoughts even
   when I'm far away.
³ You see me when I travel
   and when I rest at home.
   You know everything I do.
⁴ You know what I am going to say
   even before I say it, Lord.
⁵ You go before me and follow me.
   You place your hand of
   blessing on my head.
⁶ Such knowledge is too
   wonderful for me,
   too great for me to
   understand!

⁷ I can never escape from your
   Spirit!
   I can never get away from your
   presence!
⁸ If I go up to heaven, you are there;

if I go down to the grave,* you
   are there.
⁹ If I ride the wings of the
   morning,
   if I dwell by the farthest oceans,
¹⁰ even there your hand will
   guide me,
   and your strength will
   support me.
¹¹ I could ask the darkness to
   hide me
   and the light around me to
   become night—
¹²   but even in darkness I cannot
   hide from you.
   To you the night shines as bright
   as day.
   Darkness and light are the
   same to you.

¹³ You made all the delicate, inner
   parts of my body
   and knit me together in my
   mother's womb.
¹⁴ Thank you for making me so
   wonderfully complex!
   Your workmanship is
   marvelous—how well I
   know it.
¹⁵ You watched me as I was
   being formed in utter
   seclusion,
   as I was woven together in the
   dark of the womb.
¹⁶ You saw me before I was born.
   Every day of my life was
   recorded in your book.
   Every moment was laid out
   before a single day had passed.

139:8 Hebrew *to Sheol.*

¹⁷ How precious are your thoughts
    about me,* O God.
  They cannot be numbered!
¹⁸ I can't even count them;
    they outnumber the grains of
        sand!
  And when I wake up,
    you are still with me!

¹⁹ O God, if only you would destroy
    the wicked!
  Get out of my life, you
    murderers!
²⁰ They blaspheme you;
    your enemies misuse your
        name.
²¹ O Lord, shouldn't I hate those
    who hate you?
  Shouldn't I despise those who
    oppose you?
²² Yes, I hate them with total hatred,
    for your enemies are my
        enemies.

²³ Search me, O God, and know my
    heart;
  test me and know my anxious
    thoughts.
²⁴ Point out anything in me that
    offends you,
  and lead me along the path of
    everlasting life.

140 *For the choir director: A psalm of David.*

¹ O Lord, rescue me from evil
    people.
  Protect me from those who are
    violent,

² those who plot evil in their hearts
    and stir up trouble all day long.
³ Their tongues sting like a snake;
    the venom of a viper drips
        from their lips.   *Interlude*

⁴ O Lord, keep me out of the
    hands of the wicked.
  Protect me from those who are
    violent,
  for they are plotting against me.
⁵ The proud have set a trap to
    catch me;
  they have stretched out a net;
  they have placed traps all
    along the way.   *Interlude*

⁶ I said to the Lord, "You are my
    God!"
  Listen, O Lord, to my cries for
    mercy!
⁷ O Sovereign Lord, the strong one
    who rescued me,
  you protected me on the day
    of battle.
⁸ Lord, do not let evil people have
    their way.
  Do not let their evil schemes
    succeed,
  or they will become proud.
                              Interlude

⁹ Let my enemies be destroyed
    by the very evil they have
        planned for me.
¹⁰ Let burning coals fall down on
    their heads.
  Let them be thrown into the fire
  or into watery pits from which
    they can't escape.

139:17 Or *How precious to me are your thoughts.*

11 Don't let liars prosper here in our
     land.
     Cause great disasters to fall on
         the violent.
12 But I know the Lord will help
     those they persecute;
     he will give justice to the
         poor.
13 Surely righteous people are
     praising your name;
     the godly will live in your
         presence.

141 *A psalm of David.*

1 O Lord, I am calling to you.
     Please hurry!
     Listen when I cry to you for
         help!
2 Accept my prayer as incense
     offered to you,
     and my upraised hands as an
         evening offering.

3 Take control of what I say, O Lord,
     and guard my lips.
4 Don't let me drift toward evil
     or take part in acts of
         wickedness.
     Don't let me share in the
         delicacies
     of those who do wrong.

5 Let the godly strike me!
     It will be a kindness!
     If they correct me, it is soothing
         medicine.
     Don't let me refuse it.

But I pray constantly
     against the wicked and their
         deeds.
6 When their leaders are thrown
     down from a cliff,
     the wicked will listen to my
         words and find them true.
7 Like rocks brought up by a plow,
     the bones of the wicked
         will lie scattered without
             burial.*

8 I look to you for help,
     O Sovereign Lord.
     You are my refuge; don't let
         them kill me.
9 Keep me from the traps they
     have set for me,
     from the snares of those who
         do wrong.
10 Let the wicked fall into their
     own nets,
     but let me escape.

142 *A psalm* of David,*
regarding his experience
in the cave. A prayer.

1 I cry out to the Lord;
     I plead for the Lord's mercy.
2 I pour out my complaints before
     him
     and tell him all my troubles.
3 When I am overwhelmed,
     you alone know the way
         I should turn.
     Wherever I go,
     my enemies have set traps
         for me.

141:7 Hebrew *our bones will be scattered at the mouth of Sheol.*   142:title Hebrew *maskil.* This
may be a literary or musical term.

⁴ I look for someone to come and
   help me,
      but no one gives me a passing
         thought!
   No one will help me;
      no one cares a bit what
         happens to me.
⁵ Then I pray to you, O LORD.
   I say, "You are my place of
      refuge.
   You are all I really want in life.
⁶ Hear my cry,
   for I am very low.
   Rescue me from my persecutors,
      for they are too strong for me.
⁷ Bring me out of prison
   so I can thank you.
   The godly will crowd around me,
      for you are good to me."

143 *A psalm of David.*

¹ Hear my prayer, O LORD;
   listen to my plea!
      Answer me because you are
         faithful and righteous.
² Don't put your servant on trial,
   for no one is innocent before
      you.
³ My enemy has chased me.
   He has knocked me to the
      ground
   and forces me to live in
      darkness like those in the
         grave.
⁴ I am losing all hope;
   I am paralyzed with fear.
⁵ I remember the days of old.
   I ponder all your great works

and think about what you have
   done.
⁶ I lift my hands to you in prayer.
   I thirst for you as parched land
      thirsts for rain.   *Interlude*
⁷ Come quickly, LORD, and answer
      me,
   for my depression deepens.
   Don't turn away from me,
      or I will die.
⁸ Let me hear of your unfailing
      love each morning,
   for I am trusting you.
   Show me where to walk,
      for I give myself to you.
⁹ Rescue me from my enemies,
      LORD;
   I run to you to hide me.
¹⁰ Teach me to do your will,
   for you are my God.
   May your gracious Spirit lead me
      forward
   on a firm footing.
¹¹ For the glory of your name,
      O LORD, preserve my life.
   Because of your faithfulness,
      bring me out of this
         distress.
¹² In your unfailing love, silence
      all my enemies
   and destroy all my foes,
      for I am your servant.

144 *A psalm of David.*

¹ Praise the LORD, who is my rock.
   He trains my hands for war
   and gives my fingers skill for
      battle.

2 He is my loving ally and my
    fortress,
  my tower of safety, my rescuer.
He is my shield, and I take refuge
    in him.
  He makes the nations* submit
    to me.

3 O LORD, what are human beings
    that you should notice
    them,
  mere mortals that you should
    think about them?
4 For they are like a breath of air;
  their days are like a passing
    shadow.

5 Open the heavens, LORD, and
    come down.
  Touch the mountains so they
    billow smoke.
6 Hurl your lightning bolts and
    scatter your enemies!
  Shoot your arrows and
    confuse them!
7 Reach down from heaven and
    rescue me;
  rescue me from deep waters,
    from the power of my
    enemies.
8 Their mouths are full of lies;
  they swear to tell the truth,
    but they lie instead.

9 I will sing a new song to you,
    O God!
  I will sing your praises with
    a ten-stringed harp.
10 For you grant victory to kings!

You rescued your servant
    David from the fatal sword.
11 Save me!
  Rescue me from the power of
    my enemies.
Their mouths are full of lies;
  they swear to tell the truth, but
    they lie instead.

12 May our sons flourish in their
    youth
  like well-nurtured plants.
May our daughters be like
    graceful pillars,
  carved to beautify a palace.
13 May our barns be filled
  with crops of every kind.
May the flocks in our fields
    multiply by the thousands,
  even tens of thousands,
14   and may our oxen be loaded
    down with produce.
May there be no enemy breaking
    through our walls,
  no going into captivity,
  no cries of alarm in our town
    squares.
15 Yes, joyful are those who live like
    this!
  Joyful indeed are those whose
    God is the LORD.

145* *A psalm of praise of David.*

1 I will exalt you, my God and King,
  and praise your name forever
    and ever.
2 I will praise you every day;

144:2 Some manuscripts read *my people*. 145 This psalm is a Hebrew acrostic poem; each verse
(including 13b) begins with a successive letter of the Hebrew alphabet.

yes, I will praise you forever.
3 Great is the LORD! He is most
worthy of praise!
No one can measure his
greatness.

4 Let each generation tell its
children of your mighty acts;
let them proclaim your power.
5 I will meditate on your majestic,
glorious splendor
and your wonderful miracles.
6 Your awe-inspiring deeds will be
on every tongue;
I will proclaim your greatness.
7 Everyone will share the story of
your wonderful goodness;
they will sing with joy about
your righteousness.

8 The LORD is merciful and
compassionate,
slow to get angry and filled
with unfailing love.
9 The LORD is good to everyone.
He showers compassion on all
his creation.
10 All of your works will thank you,
LORD,
and your faithful followers will
praise you.
11 They will speak of the glory of
your kingdom;
they will give examples of your
power.
12 They will tell about your mighty
deeds
and about the majesty and
glory of your reign.

13 For your kingdom is an
everlasting kingdom.
You rule throughout all
generations.

The LORD always keeps his
promises;
he is gracious in all he
does.*
14 The LORD helps the fallen
and lifts those bent beneath
their loads.
15 The eyes of all look to you in
hope;
you give them their food as
they need it.
16 When you open your hand,
you satisfy the hunger and
thirst of every living
thing.
17 The LORD is righteous in
everything he does;
he is filled with kindness.
18 The LORD is close to all who call
on him,
yes, to all who call on him in
truth.
19 He grants the desires of those
who fear him;
he hears their cries for help
and rescues them.
20 The LORD protects all those who
love him,
but he destroys the wicked.

21 I will praise the LORD,
and may everyone on earth
bless his holy name
forever and ever.

145:13 As in Dead Sea Scrolls and Greek and Syriac versions; the Masoretic Text lacks the final two
lines of this verse.

146

¹ Praise the LORD!

Let all that I am praise the LORD.
² I will praise the LORD as long as I live.
I will sing praises to my God with my dying breath.

³ Don't put your confidence in powerful people;
there is no help for you there.
⁴ When they breathe their last, they return to the earth,
and all their plans die with them.

⁵ But joyful are those who have the God of Israel* as their helper,
whose hope is in the LORD their God.
⁶ He made heaven and earth, the sea, and everything in them.
He keeps every promise forever.
⁷ He gives justice to the oppressed and food to the hungry.
The LORD frees the prisoners.
⁸ The LORD opens the eyes of the blind.
The LORD lifts up those who are weighed down.
The LORD loves the godly.
⁹ The LORD protects the foreigners among us.
He cares for the orphans and widows,
but he frustrates the plans of the wicked.

¹⁰ The LORD will reign forever.
He will be your God,
O Jerusalem,* throughout the generations.

Praise the LORD!

147

¹ Praise the LORD!

How good to sing praises to our God!
How delightful and how fitting!
² The LORD is rebuilding Jerusalem
and bringing the exiles back to Israel.
³ He heals the brokenhearted and bandages their wounds.
⁴ He counts the stars and calls them all by name.
⁵ How great is our Lord! His power is absolute!
His understanding is beyond comprehension!
⁶ The LORD supports the humble,
but he brings the wicked down into the dust.

⁷ Sing out your thanks to the LORD;
sing praises to our God with a harp.
⁸ He covers the heavens with clouds,
provides rain for the earth,
and makes the grass grow in mountain pastures.
⁹ He gives food to the wild animals
and feeds the young ravens when they cry.

¹⁰ He takes no pleasure in the
    strength of a horse
    or in human might.
¹¹ No, the LORD's delight is in those
    who fear him,
    those who put their hope in
    his unfailing love.

¹² Glorify the LORD, O Jerusalem!
    Praise your God, O Zion!
¹³ For he has strengthened the bars
    of your gates
    and blessed your children
    within your walls.
¹⁴ He sends peace across your
    nation
    and satisfies your hunger with
    the finest wheat.

¹⁵ He sends his orders to the world—
    how swiftly his word flies!
¹⁶ He sends the snow like white
    wool;
    he scatters frost upon the
    ground like ashes.
¹⁷ He hurls the hail like stones.*
    Who can stand against his
    freezing cold?
¹⁸ Then, at his command, it all melts.
    He sends his winds, and the
    ice thaws.
¹⁹ He has revealed his words to
    Jacob,
    his decrees and regulations
    to Israel.
²⁰ He has not done this for any
    other nation;
    they do not know his
    regulations.

    Praise the LORD!

148 ¹Praise the LORD!
    Praise the LORD from
    the heavens!
    Praise him from the skies!
² Praise him, all his angels!
    Praise him, all the armies of
    heaven!
³ Praise him, sun and moon!
    Praise him, all you twinkling
    stars!
⁴ Praise him, skies above!
    Praise him, vapors high above
    the clouds!
⁵ Let every created thing give
    praise to the LORD,
    for he issued his command,
    and they came into being.
⁶ He set them in place forever and
    ever.
    His decree will never be
    revoked.

⁷ Praise the LORD from the earth,
    you creatures of the ocean
    depths,
⁸ fire and hail, snow and clouds,*
    wind and weather that obey
    him,
⁹ mountains and all hills,
    fruit trees and all cedars,
¹⁰ wild animals and all livestock,
    small scurrying animals and
    birds,
¹¹ kings of the earth and all
    people,
    rulers and judges of the
    earth,
¹² young men and young women,
    old men and children.

147:17 Hebrew *like bread crumbs.* **148:8** Or *mist,* or *smoke.*

13 Let them all praise the name of
      the LORD.
    For his name is very great;
    his glory towers over the earth
      and heaven!
14 He has made his people strong,
    honoring his faithful ones—
    the people of Israel who are
      close to him.

Praise the LORD!

149 1 Praise the LORD!

      Sing to the LORD a new
        song.
    Sing his praises in the
      assembly of the faithful.

2 O Israel, rejoice in your Maker.
    O people of Jerusalem,* exult
      in your King.
3 Praise his name with dancing,
    accompanied by tambourine
      and harp.
4 For the LORD delights in his
      people;
    he crowns the humble with
      victory.
5 Let the faithful rejoice that he
      honors them.
    Let them sing for joy as they
      lie on their beds.

6 Let the praises of God be in their
      mouths,
    and a sharp sword in their
      hands—

149:2 Hebrew *Zion.*

7 to execute vengeance on the
      nations
    and punishment on the
      peoples,
8 to bind their kings with shackles
    and their leaders with iron
      chains,
9 to execute the judgment written
      against them.
    This is the glorious privilege
      of his faithful ones.

Praise the LORD!

150 1 Praise the LORD!

      Praise God in his
        sanctuary;
    praise him in his mighty heaven!
2 Praise him for his mighty works;
    praise his unequaled
      greatness!
3 Praise him with a blast of the
      ram's horn;
    praise him with the lyre and
      harp!
4 Praise him with the tambourine
      and dancing;
    praise him with strings and
      flutes!
5 Praise him with a clash of
      cymbals;
    praise him with loud clanging
      cymbals.
6 Let everything that breathes sing
      praises to the LORD!

Praise the LORD!